Supply Chains and Total Pro

Supply Chains and Total Product Systems
A Reader

Editors
Ed Rhodes, James P. Warren
and Ruth Carter

in association with

The Open
University

Blackwell
Publishing

BLACKWELL PUBLISHING

350 Main Street, Malden, MA 02148-5020, USA
9600 Garsington Road, Oxford OX4 2DQ, UK
550 Swanston Street, Carlton, Victoria 3053, Australia

First published 2006 by The Open University and Blackwell Publishing

1   2006

Library of Congress Cataloging-in-Publication Data

Supply chains and total product systems : a reader / editors Ed Rhodes,
James P. Warren and Ruth Carter.
p. cm.
Includes bibliographical references and index.
ISBN-13: 978-1-4051-2410-2 (hardcover)
ISBN-10: 1-4051-2410-5 (hardcover)
ISBN-13: 978-1-4051-2409-6 (pbk.)
ISBN-10: 1-4051-2409-1 (pbk.)
1. Business logistics.   I. Rhodes, Ed.   II. Warren, James P.   III. Carter, Ruth.

HD38.5.S8953 2006
658.7—dc22
2005025648

A catalogue record for this title is available from the British Library.

Set in 10/12.5pt Galliard
by Graphicraft Limited, Hong Kong
Printed and bound in Great Britain
by TJ International, Padstow, Cornwall

For further information on
Blackwell Publishing, visit our website:
www.blackwellpublishing.com

Contents

List of Figures

List of Tables

Editors' Note

This reader has been produced in conjunction with an Open University course *T882 Supply Chain Innovation, Strategy and Management*, part of a Masters programme in Technology Management. The course is primarily intended for students and practitioners in the field of supply chains and total product systems. However, in common with this book, it is also of interest to a much wider audience (see www.open.ac.uk/courses).

The reader includes material drawn from an extensive range of sources and disciplines. The case studies in the chapters illustrate practice in four continents and many countries. We believe that its breadth is distinctive, both in scope and in focus.

Our focus is on the complete 'cradle-to-grave' life cycle of total product systems and not, as the casual browser might assume, on purchasing and supply. This is reflected in the selections we present.

Acknowledgements

We wish to thank all those who contributed to the preparation of this reader, in particular colleagues at the Open University: Giles Clark for supporting our project and finding a publisher; Katie Meade for copyright clearances; Roger Harris for his thorough approach in linking the reader to course materials; Clive Walter, Senior Research Fellow in the Centre for the Analysis of Supply Chain Innovation and Dynamics (CASCAID), for comments and suggestions; and Deirdre Bethune in Milton Keynes and Simon Betts in Cambridge for their solid secretarial and clerical assistance, taking on those tedious tasks without which the reader could not have been produced. We are also indebted to Rosemary Nixon, Joanna Pyke, Brian Goodale and Linda Auld of the Blackwell team for transforming the papers into a readable book.

Any omissions are unintentional.

Grateful acknowledgement is made to the following sources for permission to reproduce material within this book:

1.1 With permission from Ed Rhodes.

1.2 Harland, C. M. 'Supply Chain Management: Relationships, Chains and Networks', *British Journal of Management*, vol. 7, Special Issue, March 1996. Blackwell Publishing Ltd.

1.3 Kaplinsky, R. 'Globalisation and Unequalisation: What Can Be Learned from Value Chain Analysis?', *Journal of Development Studies*, Special Issue. Frank Cass & Co. Ltd 2000.

1.4 Hampson, I. 'Lean Production and the Toyota Production System – Or, the Case of the Forgotten Production Concepts', *Economic and Industrial Democracy*, vol. 20, no. 3. © Sage Publications Ltd 2000.

The research and fieldwork for this article were supported by a grant from the Faculty of Commerce and Economics of the University of New South Wales.

1.5 Katayama, H. and Bennett, D. 'Lean Production in a Changing Competitive World: A Japanese Perspective', *International Journal of Operations & Production Management*, vol. 16, no. 2, 1996. MCB University Press Ltd.

1.6 Lund, J. and Wright, C. 'Integrating the Supply Chain: Industrial Relations Implications in US Grocery Distribution', *New Technology, Work and Employment*, vol. 18, no. 2, 2003. Blackwell Publishing Ltd.

1.7 Den Hertog, P., Bilderbeek, R. and Maltha, S. 'Intangibles: The Soft Side of Innovation', *Futures*, vol. 29, no. 1. Copyright 1997, reprinted with permission from Elsevier.

1.8 Leiper, Q. J., Riley, P. and Uren, S. 'The Environmental Challenge for Supply-Chain Management', *Proceedings of The Institution of Civil Engineers: Civil Engineering Special Issue*, vol. 238, no. 2, 2000. The Institution of Civil Engineers, with permission from Professor Q. J. Leiper.

2.1 Cooray, S. and Ratnatunga, J. 'Buyer–Supplier Relationships: A Case Study of Japanese and Western Alliance', *Long Range Planning*, vol. 34. © 2001, reprinted with permission from Elsevier.

2.2 Handfield, R., Krause, D. R., Scannell, T. V. and Monczka, R. M. 'Avoid the Pitfalls in Supplier Development', *Sloan Management Review*, Winter 2000. Tribune Media Services International.

2.3 Liker, J. and Wu, Y.-C. 'Japanese Automakers, US Suppliers and Supply-Chain Superiority', *Sloan Management Review*, Fall 2000. Tribune Media Services International.

2.4 Harvey, M. 'Innovation and Competition in UK Supermarkets', *Supply Chain Management*, vol. 5, no. 1, 2000. MCB University Press Ltd.

2.5 den Hond, F. 'The "Similarity" and "Heterogeneity" Theses in Studying Innovation: Evidence from the End-of Life Vehicle Case', *Technology Analysis & Strategic Management*, vol. 10, no. 4, 1998. Taylor & Francis Ltd, 4 Park Square, Milton Park, Abingdon, OX14 4RN.

The end-of-life vehicle case study was financially supported by the EC DGXII Monitor/SAST and HuCaMo programmes.

2.6 Berry, A. J., Cullen, J. and Seal, W. *Supply Chains and Management Accounting*, Open University Seminar, 24 February 1999. CIMA with the support of ISCAN in Sheffield.

The research project on supply chains and management accounting was financed by the Chartered Institute of Management Accountant (CIMA) with the support of Innovative Supply Chains and Networks (ISCAN).

2.7 Winstanley, D., Clark, J. and Leeson, H. 'Approaches to Child Labour in the Supply Chain', *Business Ethics: A European Review*, vol. 11, no. 3, 2002. Blackwell Publishing Ltd.

3.1 Pilkington, A. 'Manufacturing Strategy Regained: Evidence for the Demise of Best-Practice', *California Management Review*, vol. 41, no. 1. Copyright © 1998 by the Regents of the University of California. Reprinted by permission of The Regents.

3.2 Fucini, J. I. and Fucini, S. *Working for the Japanese: Inside Mazda's American Auto Plant*. Copyright © 1990 by Joseph J. Fucini and Suzy Fucini. Reprinted with permission of The Free Press, a Division of Simon & Schuster Adult Publishing Group.

3.3 Bamber, L. and Dale, B. G. 'Lean Production: A Study of Application in a Traditional Manufacturing Environment', *Production Planning & Control*, vol. 11, no. 3, 2000. Taylor & Francis Ltd, 4 Park Square, Milton Park, Abingdon, OX14 4RN.

3.4 Lewis, M. A. 'Lean Production and Sustainable Competitive Advantage', *International Journal of Operations & Production Management*, vol. 20, no. 8, 2000. MCB University Press Ltd.

3.5 Emiliani, M. L. 'Supporting Small Businesses in Their Transition to Lean Production', *Supply Chain Management: An International Journal*, vol. 5, no. 2, 2000. MCB University Press Ltd.

3.6 Åhlström, P. and Karlsson, C. 'Change Processes towards Lean Production: The Role of the Management Accounting System', *International Journal of Operations & Production Management*, vol. 16, no. 11, 1996. MCB University Press Ltd.

3.7 Shank, J. K. and Fisher, J. 'Target Costing as a Strategic Tool', *Sloan Management Review*, Fall 1999. Tribune Media Services International.

3.8 Guide, V. D. R. Jr, Jayaraman, V., Srivastava, S. and Benton, W. C. 'Supply-Chain Management for Recoverable Manufacturing Systems', *Interfaces*, vol. 30, no. 3, May–June 2000. Copyright © 2000 the Institute for Operations Research and the Management Sciences (INFORMS), 901 Elkridge Landing Road, Suite 400, Linthicum, Maryland 21090-2909 USA. Reprinted by permission.

4.1 Bryson, J. R. and Daniels, P. W. 'The Secrets of Industry Are in the Air or "on the Jungle Drums in the Village": Traded and Untraded Knowledge and Expertise Interdependencies between SMEs', *21st ISBA National Small Firms Conference: Celebrating the Small Business*, 1998. With permission of Dr John Bryson.

The research on which this article is based was supported by a research grant from the Economic and Social Science Research Council (ESRC) (R000236366) and by the NatWest Group Charitable Trust. Any views expressed do not necessarily reflect those of the sponsoring organizations.

4.2 Palpacuer, F. and Parisotto, A. 'Global Production and Local Jobs', *Global Networks*, vol. 3, no. 2. Copyright © 2003 Blackwell Publishing Ltd & Global Networks Partnership.

4.3 Cave, F., West, C. and Matthews, A. 'The Role of an Integrator Organisation in a Virtual Supply Chain', *Proceedings of the 32nd EISB International Conference*, September 2003.

4.4 Amesse, F., Dragoste, L., Nollet, J. and Ponce, S. 'Issues on Partnering: Evidences from Subcontracting in Aeronautics', *Technovation*, vol. 21. © 2001, reprinted with permission from Elsevier.

4.5 Gupta, S. M. and Brennan, L. 'Implementation of Just-in-Time Methodology in a Small Company', *Production Planning & Control*, vol. 6, no. 4. Taylor & Francis Ltd, 4 Park Square, Milton Park, Abingdon, OX14 4RN.

4.6   Cano, M., Drummond, S., Miller, C. and Barclay, S. 'Learning from Others: Benchmarking in Diverse Tourism Enterprises', *Total Quality Management*, vol. 12, no. 7/8, 2001. Taylor & Francis Ltd, 4 Park Square, Milton Park, Abingdon, OX14 4RN.

4.7   Wagner, B. A., Fillis, I. and Johansson, U. 'E-Business and E-Supply Strategy in Small and Medium Sized Businesses (SMEs)', *Supply Chain Management: An International Journal*, vol. 8, no. 4, 2003. Emerald Group Publishing Ltd. Copyright © MCB University Press Ltd.

Every effort has been made to contact copyright owners. If any have been inadvertently overlooked, the publishers will be pleased to make the necessary arrangements.

Introduction to the Reader

In the development of this reader we had four main, and interrelated, considerations in mind. First, the term 'supply chain' presents a number of analytical difficulties. It is widely used among managers and by some academic observers as a generic shorthand. But it is applied to widely differing types of approach. In relation to supply chain management (SCM), Harland (Chapter 1.2) observes that 'there is little consistency in the use of the term and little evidence of clarity of meaning', a point that is illustrated by four main categories of use. These range from management of the intra-firm supply chain through to management of networks of inter-connected businesses. Furthermore, supply chain practice is evolving dynamically, adding to the lack of clarity. An additional difficulty is that, across the wider literature, 'supply chain' jostles with a range of other conceptualizations which broadly focus on much the same phenomena but with different emphases. Alternative conceptualizations include 'value chains' (used by a variety of authors developing from Porter, 1985 – and subsequently among practitioners who appreciated its disciplined focus), 'supply networks or inter-business networks' (e.g. Harland, Chapter 1.2; Harland et al., 2004), 'global production networks' (e.g. Palpacuer and Parisotto, Chapter 4.2), 'commodity chains' (e.g. Hopkins and Wallerstein, 1986; 1994; Gereffi and Korzeniewicz, 1994), 'global commodity chains' (e.g. Gereffi and Korzeniewicz, 1994; Raikes et al., 2000), 'product systems' (e.g. Lauret, 1983) and 'total product systems' (Rhodes, Chapter 1.1).

These various concepts reflect differences in the purpose of analysis and in academic traditions which, in turn, are reflected in contrasting emphases in analysis and diversity in interpretation. The variety of approaches emphasizes that cross-disciplinary perspectives are important for the development of a comprehensive understanding of these phenomena and their implications, both for practitioners and for the wider society. Thus we have sought to reflect some of the diversity in analysis.

The second consideration was that this appears to be a field that is already well provided for. Although this is of fairly recent origin as a subject area, the body of non-journal supply chain literature has become voluminous. This is illustrated by the

108,837 publications that were listed in a search for 'supply chain' at Amazon.com (August 2004). This may indicate a particular American preoccupation with the subject area (a search at Amazon.co.uk produced a mere 337 results). This volume of publication may also relate to perceived shortcomings among US companies in this respect, particularly in comparison with leading Japanese companies, such as in the automotive sector (Dyer, 1996). Alternatively – or as well – it may reflect the subject's location within the cockpit of management fashion or, more simply, it may represent recognition of the critical nature of this area of management for competitive performance.

Whatever the reasons, the scale of existing publication presents a challenge in terms of establishing market distinctiveness. We take the view that the combination of readings in this volume, which are drawn from diverse research and practitioner sources, and which provide a range of contrasting perspectives and concerns, do provide a collection that is differentiated from the bulk of existing material. While we have only been able to review a small proportion of the 108,837 publications referred to above, they mostly appear to range from prescriptive manuals concerned with, say, the implementation of a particular supply chain software package through to more comprehensive volumes advancing, and seeking to develop, concepts of best practice in areas such as purchasing and supply, logistics or supply chain management and strategy. The latter are concerned with fundamental areas, but we suggest (in Chapter 1.1) that practice is moving on. In particular, combinations of the strategies of lead companies and external regulation such as on environmental and labour issues are pushing *de facto* practice towards what we term 'total product systems'. Management in this context require management approaches that are even more holistic that those of integrated SCM.

Third, we have been concerned to emphasize the relevance of 'supply chain' issues to a broader group of practitioners and academics than has generally been concerned with them. Lund and Wright (Chapter 1.6) suggest that much of the discussion about SCM is undertaken from engineering and logistics perspectives. They point to the absence of consideration – and limited awareness among practitioners – of the implications of changing supply chain practice for industrial relations, their own area of concern. This is only one of several areas of analysis that receive limited attention in both the standard supply chain texts and the wider supply chain literature. One such is accountancy which, as Berry et al. (Chapter 2.6) observe, tends to ignore value created outside the firm – a surprising gap when it is common for well over 50 per cent of an organization's costs to derive from external purchasing. But they also found that management accounting practice is being modified by 'the supply chain impact'. Such gaps lead Harland et al. to observe that the 'existing literature on supply networks tends to focus on the integration of logistic activities and resources; little attention has been paid to more behavioural aspects, such as how individual actors in supply networks resolve conflicts or make decisions' (2004, p. 18).

The issues extend beyond the particular problems of adjustment within particular management functional areas. Much of the evolution of supply chain strategy and practice has been driven under the umbrella of SCM, and this has been a major factor in reshaping practice and strategy in organizations of all types. But changes in approach to product supply are, in growing numbers of cases, linked to major reorganizations of activities that are global in their reach. SCM strategies are primarily shaped by large organizations that are dominant in particular products, brands or categories. In the main, the lead organizations are based in the industrialized countries but operate on a transnational or a global scale. Their corporate structures have evolved from the predominant model of the past of 'a portfolio of national businesses' and towards forms that are unified on a transnational or a global scale (Murray and Trudeau, 2004). The process has been well summarized by Gereffi (1994) in terms of 'the emergence of a global manufacturing system in which production capacity is dispersed to an unprecedented number of developing as well as industrialized countries . . . The revolution in transportation and communications technologies has permitted manufacturers and retailers alike to establish international production and distribution networks that cover vast geographical distances.' Thus the management and functioning of supply chains – and total product systems – and their impacts need to be considered on this scale, as is reflected in several of the chapters in this volume.

Fourth, our selection was shaped by the intention to use this reader within an Open University postgraduate course on supply chain innovation, strategy and management that forms part of a Masters in Technology Management. The students taking this course were expected to be (and are) mostly experienced managers, and so the combination of academic criteria and relevance to those able to draw on a substantial reservoir of experience has also contributed to the process of selection. Thus, while much of the material is academic, and includes a range of research studies drawn from many sectors, there is also an emphasis on experience in practice. Consequently, we hope that it will be relevant to two other groups: first, students from a variety of academic backgrounds with concerns within, or impinging on, the broad supply chain and product system area; and second, senior and middle managers who wish to extend their knowledge, awareness and capabilities in this rapidly developing context. It is pertinent to the service, manufacturing and process sectors, including the public sector as the significance of supply chain issues is given greater recognition there, and to many, if not most, management functions, including finance, design, production, environmental management, information systems and marketing – as well as logistics and purchasing.

This reader has four major parts concentrating on the following themes:

- theoretical and conceptual issues within the supply context;
- inter-organizational relationships within product systems;
- accomplishing change within organizations (i.e. intra-organizational development and practice);
- issues and challenges for small and medium enterprises (SMEs) presented by large-firm-driven supply chain integration, and potential responses for these enterprises.

REFERENCES

Dyer, J H: Does governance matter? *Keiretsu* alliances and asset specificity as sources of Japanese competitive advantage, *Organization Science*, vol. 7, no. 6, 1996

Gereffi, G: The organization of buyer-driven global commodity chains: how US retailers shape overseas production networks, in Gereffi, G & Korzeniewicz, M: *Commodity Chains and Global Capitalism*, Greenwood, Westport, CT, 1994

Gereffi, G & Korzeniewicz, M: *Commodity Chains and Global Capitalism*, Greenwood, Westport, CT, 1994

Harland, C, Zheng, J, Johnsen, T & Lamming, R: A conceptual model for researching the creation and operation of supply networks, *British Journal of Management*, vol. 15, no. 1, 2004

Hopkins, T K & Wallerstein, I: Commodity chains in the world economy prior to 1800, *Review*, vol. 10, no. 1, 1986

Hopkins, T K & Wallerstein, I: Conclusions about commodity chains, in Gereffi & Korzeniewicz, 1994

Lauret, F: Sur les études de filières agro-alimentaires, *Économies et Sociétés*, vol. 17, no. 5, 1983, quoted in Raikes et al., 2000

Murray, G & Trudeau, G: Towards a social regulation of the global firm?, *Relations Industrielles/Industrial Relations*, vol. 59, no. 1, 2004

Porter, M: *Competitive Advantage: Creating and Sustaining Superior Performance*, Free, New York, 1985

Raikes, P, Jensen, M F & Ponte, S: Global commodity chain analysis and the French *filière* approach, *Economy and Society*, vol. 29, no. 3, 2000

Part 1

Theoretical and Conceptual Issues

In this part we address some of the fundamental issues in supply chain innovation, strategy and management.

Ed Rhodes (Chapter 1.1) sets out the approach which underpins the emphasis in this book on holistic treatments of analysis and practice in the supply chain context. The chapter provides an introduction to supply chain practice and to some key ways in which it is analysed. It develops the case for moving from a fairly narrow focus on supply chain problems and performance to more systemic views that reflect emerging practice in lead companies, and which take account of the effects of evolving regulatory regimes related to environmental and other issues. These are reshaping approaches to product design and process organization across a supply chain, contributing to changes in supply in the aftermarket, and bringing the processing of end-of-life products into a central role. These changes are conceptualized as 'total product systems'. They encompass the conventionally defined areas of supply chain activity together with the aftermarket and end-of-life phases. Among other issues, this emphasizes the importance of integrated management of the various component and materials feedback loops within product and aftermarket processes. The materials inputs and waste emissions associated with all stages of production are also integral to systemic management of supply chains and product systems.

Harland (Chapter 1.2) traces the development and application of the term 'supply chain management' (SCM) since its appearance in the early 1980s. The review identifies four different, distinct uses of SCM and the literature associated with each of them. It builds a systemic framework – for SCM research and practice – linking these approaches and emphasizes the network character of strategic, inter-business SCM.

Kaplinsky (Chapter 1.3), writing from the perspective of a scholar in development studies, discusses the impact of globalized value chains (essentially synonymous with supply chains), teasing out some critical lessons from the way in which they operate. He emphasizes growing inequalities, both between countries and within industrialized and developing countries, and suggests that the critical issue for participation in the global economy is identifying approaches that are likely to yield both sustainable and equitable growth in incomes for the participants. Analysis of value chains is critical to the processes of identification, and Kaplinsky suggests three critical elements of this analysis: dynamic rents, governance and systemic gains in efficiency. Governance is a particularly important issue for understanding the functioning of supply chains and value chains, and Kaplinsky suggests a typology of three forms of intra-chain and external governance: *legislative*, which sets the conditions for participating in the chain; *judicial*, which audits performance and compliance with the conditions; and *executive*, that is proactive governance which helps participants within the chain to operate to meet the conditions set. He emphasizes that governance is the responsibility not only of lead companies, but of all organizations within the chain. His chapter provides some insights into the importance of corporate and governmental policy formulation and implementation with respect to globalized product systems.

The next two chapters, Hampson (Chapter 1.4) and Katayama and Bennett (Chapter 1.5), describe, analyse and, taken together, develop a powerful critique of lean production. They demonstrate that, despite their many proponents in manufacturing sectors, lean approaches, with their inevitable rigidities, are not always appropriate for tackling production issues. If they are abstracted from their original context and applied elsewhere, the benefits claimed for them, such as high skill levels and a job for life, often turn out to be illusory. Out of context, they bring stress, have variable benefit and may not be sufficiently supply chain specific.

Hampson focuses on the political environment and industrial relations aspects of lean manufacturing such as quality of work and working conditions – in particular, how to counter 'management by stress'. (Shockingly, he refers to studies of *karoshi* – death from overwork – in Japanese lean production plants.) His conclusions concern the potential for industrial relations systems to shape the outcomes of work reorganization. Katayama and Bennett are concerned with issues of technical organization and draw on case studies, undertaken in the mid 1990s, in four different Japanese manufacturing plants (autos, PCBs, refrigerators and air conditioners). They find lean production lacking in robustness in a climate of variable demand, which leads them to develop the notion of 'adaptable production' – the more versatile design of production systems to allow for changing circumstances.

Supply chain practice is primarily shaped by large, lead companies such as brand manufacturers and retailers. These are able to use their large market shares and buying power to shape practice within the firms involved in the various production stages. This tends to include an emphasis on cost reduction throughout a chain, which is achieved through one combination or another of improvements in organization and practice applied by most firms in a chain, the use of advanced logistics methods and a continuous, global search for low cost sources. Among other issues, these approaches put pressure on wage costs and working conditions, particularly in high wage industrialized countries (ICs). A critical issue is then: how can workers and unions in the ICs respond to these challenges? In Chapter 1.6, Lund and Wright review aspects of supply chain practice and consider the impact of supply chain integration on industrial relations. They draw on experience in the US grocery sector to examine the issues. They suggest that management–union relationships can be changed in some powerful ways but that these are not all one sided. Integrated supply chain practice can create both challenges and opportunities for all the parties involved. For example, inter-organizational collaboration can bring advantages to the organizations involved but also involves dependencies and vulnerabilities. Unions and their members can derive bargaining and other advantages from these changes. But this requires new approaches, such as action that is more inclusive in relation to the wider community – for example, developing awareness among consumers to the point where they are prepared to give support through boycotts and other action.

On a more specific issue that links knowledge management (KM) to change processes, den Hertog et al. (Chapter 1.7) draw our attention to the way that 'intangible investments are still a widely underestimated area of the knowledge-based economy'. They discuss 'de-materialization' – in which a steadily increasing share of value in a product can now be attributed to intangibles, for example training, licensing, distribution and servicing. Such intangibles represent the soft components of innovativeness and competitiveness. They explore definitions of intangible investments and examine their role in five sectors: fashion, flowers, brewing, publishing and financial services. Their conclusions point to the increasing role of service activity in innovation and the development of greater numbers of linkages and mutual dependencies between industrial and service organizations. The authors emphasize the importance of knowledge management within organizations and suggest that future industrial and technology policy must take account of the higher profile of intangible investments in innovation processes. This underlines the growing importance of a systemic view of supply activity which values and seeks to understand rich inter-organizational connectivity.

Leiper et al. (Chapter 1.8) illustrate one aspect of the total product system concept through a case study of an environmental supply chain management (ESCM) initiative in a leading construction company. They report a substantive shift in the sector's environmental agenda from such concerns as waste minimization and environmental project management to considering 'the more complex issues of sustainability and the life-cycle impacts of products and services used and consumed in the creation, maintenance and operation of the built environment'. In their case study they evaluate the extent to which four key 'best practice activities' have been applied by the company. They find that the commitment and performance of the many suppliers involved in a construction project are paramount for the main contractor and describe an array of tools and techniques that were applied. These include a risk-based approach to ESCM and introducing SME suppliers to a sustainability philosophy through a programme of training and accreditation. They conclude by identifying a major sectoral challenge: to convince as yet unconverted clients and suppliers of 'the benefits of a business philosophy centred on environmental awareness and the concept of sustainability'.

From Supply Chains to Total Product Systems

Ed Rhodes

Introduction

The evolution of supply chain management and practice has had an integral and expanding role in contemporary global economic and socio-political change over the past 25 years or so. This role is moving closer to centre stage with the emergence of business models equating to 'total product systems'. The impacts of advanced supply chain practice include driving fundamental changes in approach to product design, the concept of 'product', production methods, distribution, marketing, aftermarket support and end-of-life (EOL) reprocessing. Viewed in their full context, methods of supply chain management (SCM) have major influences on societal functioning and on economic development at global, national and local levels. Even the supply chains for simple products can involve several different industries and link many companies, large and small. Those for complex products may span several techno-logical domains and economic sectors, linking hundreds or sometimes thousands of companies.

Complexity is evident, for instance, in the scale and scope of supply chain opera-tion in capital and consumer goods sectors (such as aircraft, cars and apparel) and in services (such as hotel chains, fast-food franchises and financial services). In such cases, elements of the design, production and distribution processes associated with an end-product, together with the associated management and support services, may be carried out in large numbers of organizations in many countries in all continents. This provides the context in which 'a very small firm in one country may be directly linked into a global production network' (Dicken, 2004, p. 253). 'Geographic dispersion has occurred on a massive scale' (Ernst, 2002, p. 504). Supply chain organization has provided the channels through which much of this has occurred. Consumer and other products, together with the methods of production and market-ing that underpin them, are projected from the countries of the industrial core into those of the semi-periphery and periphery, reshaping economies and societies. But this is not one-way traffic. There is also substantial movement in the opposite direction as patterns of specialization and integration are fostered on a global scale. Also, transnational companies have developed in newly industrialized countries (NICs) and in some developing countries (DCs), and become engaged in similar management of supply chains on an international or global scale. At the individual level, developing supply chain practice is directly or indirectly reshaping people's lives, whether as workers (in all categories), subsistence farmers, consumers or owners of small retail and other businesses. Those not affected must now be a dwindling minority of the world's population.

An extensive academic literature is concerned with aspects of these phenomena. Much of it is located in management accountancy, business management, organizational behaviour, and various branches of economics, as well as the supply chain 'mainstream'. Not surprisingly, the mainstream literature is primarily concerned with overall supply chain strategy, with practice in areas such as purchasing and logistics, and with analysing issues of 'lean supply' and other perceived problems. The emphasis of this literature is primarily technicist, presenting supposedly 'neutral' solutions to current managerial preoccupations. There is a focus on what are thought to be the most efficient methods for achieving high standards of performance in target areas that include cost reduction, managing outsourcing, shortening replenishment cycles, minimizing inventory, achieving consistent high standards of product quality, reducing time to market and 'getting close to the customer'.

These are highly significant competitive objectives, although the difficulties confronting those who seek to achieve them are not always adequately explored or are underestimated. Supply chains are highly complex phenomena, and the long term challenges of co-ordinating and developing their functioning are ill matched with managerial cultures where rapid career moves are combined with the influence of successive management fads and fashions (Pascale, 1990; Scarborough and Swan, 2001; MacDonald, 2004). A further problem is that supply chain practice tends to be abstracted from its broader contexts and effects. For example, the pursuit of cost reduction on a global scale takes several routes. Increased outsourcing has been one of the vehicles of change, and the search for suppliers offering ever lower costs can lead to suppliers who exploit lax regulation of labour conditions, environmental protection, and so on. The product flow in such cases has been traced to large retailers and brand owners with highly damaging consequences – a factor that is reshaping approaches to SCM.

It might be expected that these broader socio-economic issues are central to the supply chain literature. Instead (with some exceptions) they are the concern of different bodies of literature including development studies, geography, industrial relations and some branches of economics. For instance, development studies specialists seek to understand the relationships between commodity chain functioning and economic development and associated extreme disparities in the global distribution of economic activity and wealth. Approaches from these fields potentially contribute towards more holistic perspectives of contemporary supply chain functioning and management. However, as Harland points out (Chapter 1.2), the various bodies of knowledge 'have remained largely unconnected' – although she and colleagues have subsequently taken steps towards establishing such connections (Harland et al., 2004). If there is a shift towards management of total product systems as is suggested here, multi-disciplinary research and analysis are ever more urgent.

Different academic traditions apply a varied terminology to what, broadly, are the same phenomena. Usage includes supply networks, value chains, global commodity chains and product systems. The chain metaphor is probably the most widely used, particularly among practitioners. But it conveys images of rigidities, whereas the multiple connections, the dynamic changes in patterns of sourcing and the varied roles of the actors that are found in practice, are more adequately captured by the metaphors of networks and systems. A further step is needed – I suggest the concept of total product systems – to capture the full implications of current advances in practice. Combinations of factors, including the lead actors' competitive strategies, activism among consumer, union and other groups, and the effects of environmental regulation are reshaping the SCM agenda. This is reflected in evolving approaches to production and product design and organization, and in shifts towards integrated management of the four phases of the 'cradle-to-grave' (C2G) product life cycle:

1   production phase – all stages from raw material generation through intermediate processing stages to completion of end-products;
2   distribution and sale of end-products;
3   product use and support in the aftermarket;
4   end-of-life (EOL) stages.

The rest of this chapter is divided into two main sections. The first establishes some of the main contours and issues evident in supply chain development. The second reviews the concept of total product systems as an extension of SCM.

Mapping the Issues

Supply chain evolution

Major differences in approach, methodologies and patterns of contemporary evolution in supply chains are evident within, across and between industrial sectors, and at the national level. They demonstrate contrasting strategies and varying patterns of practice – differences that, in substantial part, are attributable to the lead companies in chains, also referred to as: key actors (Kaplinsky, Chapter 1.3); focal firms (Harland et al., 2004); original equipment makers (OEMs) or 'primes' (Amesse et al., Chapter 4.4). In general terms, supply chains have been perceived primarily in terms of materials flows through the various stages from processing primary materials to intermediate processing and end-manufacture and on to the delivery of finished products to end-users – as in the example in Figure 1. But service products also have supply chains and, for some types of product, data generation and processing constitute the counterpart of materials flows, for instance in handling applications, cases

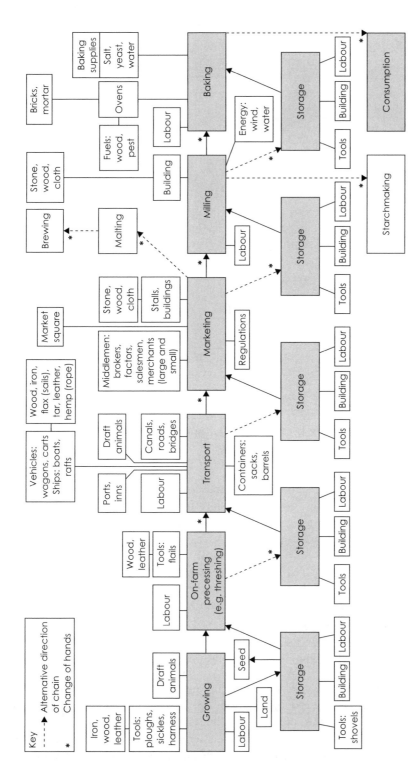

Figure 1 Grain flour supply chain: material flows from primary processing to delivery (Pelizzon, 1994, p. 35)

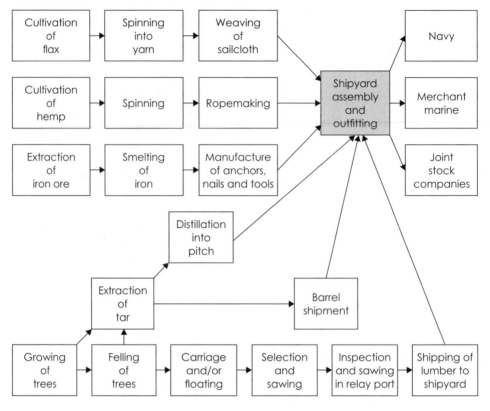

Figure 2   Shipbuilding supply chain: convergence of intermediate products
(Özveren, 1994, p. 22)

and claims in public services and in the financial sector. Figure 2 illustrates a further general characteristic in the downstream flow towards the final assembly of end-products. There is a progressive convergence of intermediate products (components, subsystems etc.) that derive from different sectors with distinct materials technologies and process technologies. Such convergence from different technological domains adds to the challenges that face attempts to co-ordinate on a chain-wide basis.[1]

The seventeenth- and eighteenth-century 'commodity chains' in Figures 1 and 2 establish the long standing antecedents of some of the issues encountered in contemporary practice. They are summarized by Hopkins and Wallerstein (1994) as chains that 'were geographically extensive, complex, and in constant recomposition' with, in the grain flour example, a 'constant geographical reshuffling of the links in the chain'. Concern with 'flows and stocks' of materials, components and so on reflects the influence of logistics and procurement as core functions within SCM. The 'management of physical distribution' appears to have provided initial steps towards SCM in the 1960s and early 1970s (Gattorna and Walters, 1996), while Harland (Chapter 1.2) suggests that the actual term SCM dates from 1982. This shift in terminology and associated changes in practice relate to a number of developments.

Purposive SCM Hopkins and Wallerstein suggest that, in the above examples, 'it would be imprudent to assume that production decisions were made by anyone without some awareness of the existence of such chains, at least to the degree of appreciating that there were alternative possible sources of inputs and alternative possible outlets for outputs' (1994, pp. 48–9). In contemporary practice, 'awareness' has developed into highly purposive approaches to SCM in which the lead actors aim to intervene across all the stages of a chain, determining their spatial distribution by co-ordinating production, marketing and distribution on a global scale. For consumer products in particular, co-ordination aims at progressive integration across the total production flow from raw material processing through to the sale of end-products. Most recently, integration has moved towards product support in the aftermarket and, tentatively, to processing EOL products. This represents a clear movement towards management of 'product systems'.

Service inputs At each supply chain stage, inputs from outside the core processing flow are essential to chain functioning. Many of these are service activities, including energy supplies, logistics services, the design and operation of information and communications systems, hardware and software supply, maintenance services, 'consumables', and product design and development. Thus Palpacuer and Parisotto (Chapter 4.2) refer to views of 'the new role of services, or intangible activities, as superior sources of value creation'. Their significance is indicated by estimates by Quinn (1988) and Quinn et al. (1990) that 'within manufacturing, 75 to 85% of all value added, and a similar percentage of costs, are due to service activities' (quoted in den Hertog et al., Chapter 1.7: see further discussion in that chapter). The role of service inputs in overall chain activity is also related to the changing character of intermediate products and end-products, many of which are marketed as 'product offers' that include a variety of support and other value-adding services.

SCM as organizational capability Organizational competencies have become 'primary sources of competitive advantage' (Palpacuer and Parisotto, Chapter 4.2). SCM capabilities are among these, particularly when focused both outwards and inwards – on the internal supply chain. For lead actors, the external focus is most likely to include chain-wide co-ordination. In other organizations, the proximal supply chain – immediate buyers and suppliers – is likely to be the main concern, although there may be some positioning by proactive upstream firms in relation to specific lead companies and chains. Either way, the focus has tended to intensify under the umbrella of SCM, drawing disparate functional areas such as purchasing, production management, quality and logistics into closer co-ordination – in the more successful cases. Lund and Wright (Chapter 1.6) suggest that the concept of SCM 'has grown rapidly in popularity in North American industry over the last five years'. Increased popularity, in the US as elsewhere, has been reflected in supply chain strategies of varying coherence – among which lean concepts have been influential (but see various chapters in this volume).

Internationalization   Supply chain co-ordination and strategic focus have increasingly been applied on an international, if not a global, scale to the point where 'final products, almost without exception, involve substantial inputs across the value chain that are produced in diverse locations across the globe . . . For instance, the supply chain of a computer company typically spans different time zones and continents, and integrates a multitude of transactions and local clusters' (Ernst, 2002, p. 504). Ernst terms such examples 'global production networks', but many of them are part of more extensive global distribution and retailing networks which may be co-ordinated by the same key actors on both the production and the distribution sides. In many cases, these key actors are either long standing transnational companies or large companies that have moved to transnational operation through outsourcing. This makes efficient SCM mandatory for survival, emphasizing the co-ordination of activities 'through a diverse array of intra-firm and inter-firm arrangements' (Palpacuer and Parisotto, Chapter 4.2).

Deepening inter-organizational relationships (IORs)   Efficient organization of the process flows emphasized by Figures 1 and 2 is only one of several categories of activity that, in contemporary economic conditions, potentially strengthen links between supply chain participants and the overall competitiveness of a chain. Several types of inter-organizational link may develop, extending an organization's critical resources beyond its boundaries (Dyer and Singh, 1998). Potentially, these links draw on a comprehensive cross-section of an organization's intangible resources involving a wide range of occupational groups, and may involve working across organizational boundaries. However, this range of connections: (1) does not invariably develop, but follows from shifts towards collaborative relationships between actors; and (2) is generally confined to a limited number of key players in a chain.

As is illustrated at the dyadic level in Figure 3, these links include:

1   Emphasis on upgrading existing products and on designing and developing new ones as collaborative ventures, often as part of outsourcing. In sectors as diverse as aerospace, automotive, textiles and food products, product development has become a collaborative, supply-chain-based process that is critical to competitive performance (Bidault et al., 1998; Fraser et al., 2003).
2   Collaborative innovation driven by pressures for process and/or product improvements. Both radical and incremental innovation have the potential to reshape activities of all types in all stages in a chain, including production processes, logistics and information systems design. The role of supply chain relationships in this respect is emphasized by Dyer and Singh who summarize earlier studies as suggesting 'that a firm's alliance partners are, in many cases, the most important source of new ideas and information that result in performance-enhancing technology and innovation' (1998, p. 665).
3   The development of new capabilities, knowledge and ideas in significant parts of a chain which may be fostered by lead companies. This places distinct demands on the actors, although 'knowledge sharing routines can create inter-organizational competitive advantage' (Dyer and Singh, 1998).

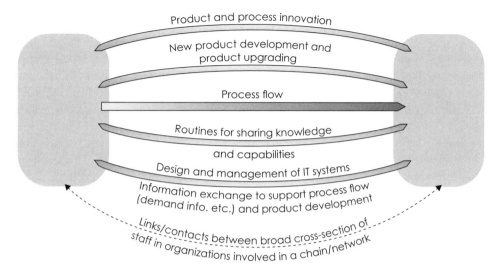

Figure 3   Inter-organizational relationships

4   The design and management of intra-chain systems using advanced information and communication technologies (ICTs) has become central to the development and co-ordination of other types of activity, including linking operations across the total chain to demand conditions at the point of sale and in the aftermarket. There is a 'potential for "real-time" information transfer . . . across enterprises and industries'; this supposedly offers 'unparalleled opportunities for customer responsiveness, and cost and productivity improvement' (Lund and Wright, Chapter 1.6), but can go seriously wrong (see below).

5   The application of standardized – and long established – methods of production analysis and organization to improve inter-company or chain-wide process performance, much of which has aimed at achieving demand-driven production. For instance, this emphasizes the use of 'lean' methods and techniques derived from the Toyota production system, such as JIT and continuous improvement (see Pilkington, Chapter 3.1). The overall objective is to identify, improve and co-ordinate value-adding processes 'across functional and company boundaries in both the design and delivery of the appropriate product–service bundle . . . [in which the] focus of attention should not be on the company or functional department but instead on the complete value stream' (Hines et al., 2000, p. 5).

The advantages of IORs such as these are compelling, as is reflected in the well publicized experience of companies such as Toyota, Rolls-Royce, Dell Computers and Tesco. For all of them, supply chain strategies have been a central (but far from the sole) element in sustained growth and expansion and in competitive success against seemingly dominant rivals. Performance in this respect reflects the transition from a focus on 'point efficiency' towards a sustained focus on systemic efficiency

(Kaplinsky, Chapter 1.3), The potential gains from effective long term systemic efficiency are indicated by the proportions of organizational activity – 60 to 70 per cent or more – now commonly accounted for by purchased inputs. The targets extend beyond reductions in total costs across a chain to consistent high standards of quality, high levels of product availability, speed of response to short and longer term market changes, and rapid introduction of innovative new products. Hence, competition has come to be viewed as 'not company against company but rather supply chain against supply chain' (Christopher, 1992). Dyer similarly identifies the need for a shift of emphasis in analysis 'from the competitive advantage of firms to the competitive advantage of value chains/networks' (1996, p. 663). This involves the development of sophisticated supply chain strategies and their consistent, long term application to all areas of a chain.

In aggregate, the developments in practice outlined above fit an ideal-type model that is reflected in much of the management literature. But substantial constraints stand in the path of the model's realization, and make intra-chain integration hard to achieve and slow. Many constraints are evident in the highly diverse national, cultural, legal, economic and social conditions across which most supply chains operate. Others are inter-organizational, and are evident in contrasting organizational objectives, cultures and systems. Organizations linked in a supply chain tend to have different priorities and ways of doing things. These reflect intra-organizational factors such as rivalries between functional groups, differences in occupational and learning cultures, organizational inertia and so on. Further constraints relate to the emphasis on ICT applications in many supply chain programmes. There are many striking examples of technical achievements in B2B (business-to-business) e-commerce, including the real-time use of point-of-sale data by retailers' head offices and suppliers, and simultaneous use of design data between buyers and suppliers. But technical possibilities need to be set beside failures in supply chain applications as part of the more widely observed 'discrepancy between IT investment and IT performance' (Macdonald, 2004). Allowing for achievements in some lead companies, it seems doubtful that SCM in general has been significantly more immune from the 'IT productivity paradox' than other areas of management – as is indicated by UK examples of costly, IT-centred supply chain failures such as Mothercare (Politi, 2002) and Sainsbury (Macalister, 2005).

Networks – routes and roles

A growing preference in the literature for the looser concept of networks and a corresponding emphasis on network management may partly reflect the challenges of co-ordination and integration across a supply chain. As a metaphor, 'network' captures variations in conditions more effectively – such as those associated with differing supplier roles, resources, capabilities and depth of involvement. Links between buyers and suppliers change for many reasons, including the introduction of upgraded or new products that require different materials, processes, components, support services, and so on. In fashion apparel, designs, fibre types, colouring methods, fabric types, garment construction and accessories change continually – as do the suppliers. In other cases, new knowledge and/or skills are sought for innovatory or modified products. Changes also follow from buyers' pursuit of lower cost materials or components. Similarly, suppliers such as design consultancies, equipment manufacturers and software houses may have only intermittent involvements but nonetheless provide powerful contributions to the competitive and innovatory capabilities of a product network.

Network concepts have become fashionable through visions of the ICT-centred 'new economy' – including the flamboyant version of Evans and Wurster who predict the defenestration of older organizational forms, including supply chains, by new, Internet-based methods of organizing collective activity that 'allow buyers who want the best product to find suppliers who offer the best product – worldwide' (2000, p. 189). Perhaps in response to this style of approach, Dicken et al. (2001) describe networks as 'a much abused concept, "more of a chaotic conception" than a rational abstraction'. It has been co-opted by the management fashion industry: 'the business and management literature now bulges with books and articles that eulogize the new network paradigm as the prescription for business success' (ibid.). Their view of networks is as 'neither purely organizational forms nor structures . . . [they] are essentially relational processes'.

Emphasis on the dynamics of network relationships and processes captures the constant shifts in the cast of actors that are usually associated with product supply, and their varied roles, shifting with continuous evolution in product ranges and the behind the scenes effort to sustain, for consumer products, what retailers sometimes refer to as 'the theatre of shopping'. It also reflects more closely the realities of management roles that involve juggling and sustaining buyer–supplier relationships, in contrast to the static, linear imagery of chains. The network metaphor accommodates the typically wide variations in buyer–supplier relationships within a product flow, for instance in levels of participation and dependency among the actors. It allows for the overlaps in patterns of supply where firms sell in competing networks. But the looser framework implied by the network concept is misleading if it is taken to imply a rough equality among the participants. In network governance and in the distribution of rewards among the participants, the lead actors' roles are central.

Lead actors

The lead actors are generally large organizations that, in supply chain terms, are located close to, or at, the interface with end-customers, whether these are other organizations or consumers. In both service and industrial sectors, 'competition between supply chains' is primarily defined by the lead companies in particular sectors and product categories. Competitive success is shaped by their strategies, their objectives, their selection of key partners, their approaches to the management of relationships with these partners and other actors further upstream or downstream, and their success or failure in shaping performance across the chain.

Gereffi (1994) distinguishes between lead companies in two commodity chain categories: 'producer-driven' chains in which large transnational industrial organizations are dominant, and 'buyer-driven' chains dominated by 'large retailers, brand-named merchandisers and trading companies' (see also Kaplinsky, Chapter 1.3). The most critical distinction he makes between the two categories is greater centralized power over production organization in supplier-driven chains compared with buyer-driven chains. But, in this and other respects, the contrasts emphasized by Gereffi have been eroded. The divisions between supplying and buying at the retailer–producer juncture have become highly blurred, not least by changes in relative size where retailers have grown to become larger than most of their suppliers, and have developed large-scale international retail operations. Some retail franchise operations in the food sector and in apparel exert a tight hold on production organization and supply to their franchisees whose operations are also kept under control, as is illustrated in the fast-food sector (Schlosser, 2001) and by Benetton (Camuffo et al., 2001). The point is reinforced by the significance of retailers' 'own brands' or 'private labels' in Western Europe, particularly in the UK. Where own brands are used aggressively, retailers are drawn into proactive roles in marketing and in product development. Retailers' brands often compete directly with those of manufacturers, and can be highly innovative – as in the example of cook-chill meals. In such cases, retailers enter the direct organization of supplier activities by developing product designs and/or specifications and by monitoring suppliers' production methods, standards and performance. In other cases, retailers collaborate with suppliers in product development. Thus, reviewing survey evidence at much the same time as Gereffi's work, Fernie concluded that 'the initiative for forging relationships has come from the retailers as they have become more responsive to their domestic markets, and take responsibility for elements of the value-added chain which were once the sole prerogative of the manufacturer' (1995, p. 143). Since that time, the proactive roles of retailers have been reinforced by increasingly intensive application of ICTs – in some cases, with high levels of success.

Two other categories of key actors need to be considered in the UK context. First, changing government policies have pushed public sector organizations towards more co-ordinated approaches to product supply. These have necessarily evolved in a distinctive way. For example, purchasing agencies act on behalf of large numbers of end-users in the defence and healthcare sectors. The challenges include keeping within the constraints on public sector tendering and other sourcing processes set by national and transnational regulatory bodies. These inhibit the development of collaborative buyer–supplier relationships comparable to those common in the private sector. Second, many private sector service organizations, including large financial companies, energy suppliers, engineering and other consultancies, and software and computing businesses, have developed significant supply chain roles. Many of these organizations now operate transnationally. To a significant extent, they rely on outsourcing and franchising within their product networks, such as in the design and operation of IT services, in accounts processing and other back office functions, and in processing customer enquiries in call centres. In both public and service sector categories, distinct patterns of operation, product supply and business development are evolving.

However, the roles of lead companies are limited in several respects. One constraint is the influence of 'external governance' (see below) on the policies and practices fostered by lead firms. Another is the sheer difficulty of exerting consistent influence across networks of disparate, far flung suppliers with divergent interests. The roles and position of network participants vary widely in their criticality to the final 'product package'. Suppliers producing commodity components or services are vulnerable to price pressure and short term decisions from buyers. Those supplying products that embody specialized intangible assets such as hard-to-replicate skills and knowledge are in stronger positions. Others are large companies which control strong consumer brands that the large retailers have to stock or which produce major subsystems or components for which there are few alternatives. Examples include some types of microprocessors, electrical and electronic subsystems. Products like these give their producers significant power and autonomy in relation to lead actors, and signify a further type of constraint. In such cases, the distribution of knowledge and competencies among buyers and suppliers, together with rising levels of investment and risk associated with major process innovation and new products, can present a compelling case for inter-firm partnerships. These may extend to multi-firm collaboration: 'in some cases, strategy will be formulated at the network level by a group of firms that explicitly take into account the resources and capabilities that reside within the network in formulating strategy. Individual firm strategy will be constrained and shaped by the network – meaning the strategies and resources of other firms in the network' (Dyer and Singh, 1999, p. 185).

Governance

If the overall direction of a chain or network is shaped by lead actors, one critical question is how this is accomplished. Significant sections of the literature focus on issues of supply chain governance but, broadly, deal with these issues in two very different ways. One set of approaches, primarily linked to the development literature, focuses on the macro level – the chain or the network. They include concerns with the influences that shape the behaviour of the various actors, the distribution of activities among them, and their comparative rewards. The second (considered in the following section) focuses on the cost-effective organization of production at the micro level, primarily in terms of dyadic make or buy decisions.

The means by which lead companies exert their influence across diverse sectors and organizations linked within a product network are captured by Gereffi's description of governance structures as 'authority and power relationships that determine how financial, material and human resources are allocated and flow within a chain' (1994, p. 97). Kaplinsky (Chapter 1.3) distinguishes between intra-chain ('internal') governance and external governance. External governance primarily derives from national and international state entities, shaping supply chain practice through regulatory controls and other forms of influence. As an example of the latter, Solis

(2001) refers to US government pressure on US-based Japanese automakers to weaken ties with their *keiretsu* suppliers (i.e. Japanese suppliers with which the automakers had close ties, including cross-shareholdings) with the aim of increasing opportunities for US suppliers. This contributed to changes in buyer–supplier relationships among formerly closely linked companies.[2] External governance also derives from the influence of some types of NGO, including trade unions and environmental and consumer groups.

The influence of external governance is mostly sectoral, or wider, in its effects. The distinct identities and coherence of specific product networks are primarily shaped by internal governance, particularly by large lead companies. But there are widely divergent approaches. Some largely rely on market power, others on more formalized assertion of influence across a chain to establish comprehensive governance regimes that combine a strategic overview with operational rules. Strategic level action takes two main paths.

First, many large companies have outsourced substantial elements of their supply chain management to trusted core suppliers, often as an extension of outsourcing production and other activities. Tactics vary, but they tend to involve fostering long term relationships with the core suppliers, some of whom are pressed to take responsibility – as lead or 'tier 1' suppliers – for the lines of supply associated with main components, sub-assemblies, complete product modules or specific product lines, such as lettuce suppliers to a grocery chain. This includes dealing with, and managing on guidelines established by the lead company, suppliers in the lower tiers (2, 3, 4 etc.) who are involved in that line of supply. Examples are found in sectors as diverse as apparel manufacture, retailing, automotive manufacture and aerospace. A lead company may thus deal directly with far fewer suppliers while retaining a strong indirect influence over other actors in the supply chain.

Overall, such supplier hierarchies reflect practice in some Japanese companies, providing lead companies with a 'clustered control structure' (Solis, 2001). But there are important and potentially critical differences when western supplier hierarchies are compared with the pioneering Toyota production system (TPS) on which western interpretations have tended to be based (see various chapters in this volume). The TPS developed organically over many years in participation with main suppliers (Ohno, 1988; Shingo, 1989), and is still evolving through continuous innovation, learning and adaptation. This approach also involved cross-shareholdings between Toyota and key suppliers. In contrast, shifts by some western companies towards aspects of the TPS model appear to have been largely formulaic, 'top down' (in a rather different way to Toyota) and attempted within short timescales that are not best suited to the operational changes, learning and acculturation required of internal workforces, suppliers and customers. Such approaches are also vulnerable to changes in key personnel and to shifting management fashions.

Second, again reflecting the TPS model, some lead companies have outsourced other areas of responsibility to main suppliers along the lines identified in Figure 3. This potentially involves the design and development of key subsystems, components etc., ICT applications, knowledge sharing and so on. These forms of outsourcing – or collaboration – further extend the governmental reach of lead companies across a chain or network, partly by shaping what core suppliers require from their own suppliers.

These strategic relationships are underpinned by actions that, in the main, are operational in character. In 'ideal-type' cases, these include the following.

1 Lead companies continually seek new sources of advantage across a chain. These are found across a spectrum that, at one end, extends to large, primary materials suppliers. The objectives may be innovatory (e.g. developing new or improved materials) and/or may focus on economies of scale by requiring intermediate suppliers to source from core primary suppliers. Examples include steel and specialist metals producers (vehicles and aerospace) and textiles (apparel retailers, brand owners). The other end of the spectrum encompasses core subsystem suppliers, equipment and software producers and others close to a chain's main technological domains – such as university departments. Lead companies thus stay close to emerging developments and their innovative and organizational possibilities.

2 Lead companies and tier 1 suppliers set terms of supply that extend beyond price to a range of performance standards. These typically include: tight quality requirements; supply on a just-in-time (JIT) basis, sometimes linked to insistence on a supplier's adoption of 'lean' practices; and conformance to the lead company's ICT standards. Standards are also set for product specifications, product cost profiles (schedules for cost reduction that allow for the learning curve), delivery methods and schedules. Uniform application of these standards aims to maximize competitive advantages across the whole network – although there are substantial obstacles in the path of such standardization.

3 Operational standards are sometimes supplemented by codes of conduct for suppliers which extend to standards of environmental, ethical and employment practice.

4 Large companies continually monitor supplier performance, reflected in emphasis on using metrics that provide clear data on operational performance in areas such as quality and delivery (see Åhlström and Karlsson, Chapter 3.6). Ideally, these standards extend through all lines of supply.

5 Performance monitoring may be supplemented by periodic assessment of suppliers by lead companies or their agents. These range from production methods and procedures through to training standards and capabilities relevant to design and innovation. Processes of measurement and review build up a continually evolving picture of suppliers' strengths and weaknesses, and their contributions to overall chain competitiveness.

6 'Best practice' as defined by lead actors and main suppliers is cascaded to upstream and downstream companies in a network. Some lead companies (reflecting the TPS model) establish supplier associations to support supplier development and to encourage knowledge sharing. Support may include the secondment of staff between buyers and suppliers for joint problem solving, and may facilitate training to standardize process methods and techniques or product development methods between companies. Similarly, the use of *kaizen* (continuous improvement) approaches may be encouraged.

These examples emphasize the scope and sophistication of internal governance extending across parts, at least, of the more developed networks. In such cases, governance permeates a wide range of practice and thinking within the organizations involved. These 'regimes of practice', and the associated intra-chain culture that may develop, extend across national boundaries. However, reiterating an earlier point, there are substantial differences in approach, by lead companies and others, to managing buyer–supplier relationships.

Buyer–supplier relationships

Divergences in approaches to SCM can, up to a point, be compressed within the three-part typology associated with the transaction cost (TC) model. Briefly, the model emphasizes firms' capacities for separating or integrating process activities at their boundaries. 'Technologically separable interfaces' (TSIs) provide critical locations in a process flow, hinge points at which firms have 'make or buy' choices. These choices are mapped onto three categories of supply relationship. One is 'hierarchical governance' (i.e. production within a vertically integrated organization) in which, to a degree, the instruments of managerial control such as fiat, monitoring and sanctions integrate and control operations across adjacent TSIs. Until the 1980s, shifts towards high levels of vertical integration appeared to be 'the dominant trend in the west' (Dore, 1983 p. 463). This was overtaken by a progressive shift towards the international relocation of production, increased use of outsourcing and related changes in modes of governance. For instance, 'older hierarchical forms' are seen as giving way 'to the flatter network architectures of global production systems . . . [which are] characterized by a multiplicity of inter-firm relationships and a blurring of organizational boundaries' (Murray and Trudeau, 2004, p. 17). A wide range of factors has contributed to this shift, including improvements in international transport systems, ICT applications, and the influence of management fashions such as lean production.

In the TC model, sourcing from external suppliers ('market governance') is the direct alternative to vertically integrated production. Choices between markets and hierarchies are viewed in terms of trade-offs, principally between production costs and transaction costs. Attention has focused on transaction costs, partly because of assumptions about their role but also because they are a significant business cost. North (1990) and Butler et al. (1997) suggest that transaction costs may account for a third or more of the costs associated with economic activity (quoted by Dyer and Chu, 2003, p. 59). These estimates may reflect the prevailing, low trust US business culture which emphasizes a continuous search for lower cost suppliers. Large numbers of staff in purchasing, sales and legal departments and areas such as inbound inspection are required to negotiate and draft contracts, and to monitor and enforce them. By contrast, management controls where there is hierarchical governance are held, generally, to keep comparable costs down.

The model predicts that where search processes are efficient, production costs are likely to be lower in market relationships, but to be outweighed by high transaction costs. This becomes more probable where buyers have highly specific needs and suppliers need specialized assets such as skills and equipment to meet them. In such cases of high asset specificity, each party is regarded as vulnerable to 'opportunistic' behaviour by the other. For example, a buyer may seek to force a supplier's prices downwards where assets are too specialized to be used to supply other customers. Equally, customers who are dependent on specialized suppliers may encounter upward pressure on prices if those suppliers exploit the difficulties the customer faces in finding alternative sources. The need to guard against such behaviour incurs high transaction costs.

These issues are reflected in the wider supply chain literature, and in practice. For example, 'market governance' equates to what are characterized as 'traditional' buyer relationships with suppliers. Purchasing staff are given incentives to search continually for lower price sources, and relationships with suppliers are generally arm's-length, adversarial, short term and, in the US at least, heavily dependent on lengthy, very detailed contract documents.[3] Kaplan and Cooper mention how 'the major US automobile companies would not enter into long term relationships with their suppliers. Every six months, they would put their steel demand out for bid and all the steel companies would compete to win the business by offering the lowest price for the next six months' (1998, p. 203). They relate this to confusion between prices and costs. The seeming gains for buyers from lower supplier prices can be negated by high transaction costs (such as from inspection and other supplier monitoring) and by costs such as transport from distant 'low price' locations which contribute to high 'total costs of ownership'. These additional costs may be hidden within multiple budget heads, a consequence of poorly designed management accounting systems (for example, see Åhlström and Karlsson, Chapter 3.6). Traditional approaches may also be reinforced by employment practice. The UK Competition Commission's (2000) enquiry into grocery retailing refers to the periodic rotation of retail multiples' purchasing staff as a part of career development, sometimes every 12 months. This practice contrasted with the Commission's observation that 'Continuity is an important element in maintaining a good multiple/supplier relationship' (§11.46). As one of the suppliers' organizations pointed out, routine changes at short notice make 'it extremely difficult to maintain stability within the industry' (§11.26).

Both parties incur cost and other penalties because of corresponding 'traditional' supplier behaviour. For example, total transaction costs are increased where traditional buying practices necessitate a continuous search by suppliers for new customers. There are potential long term adverse effects on suppliers' technological capabilities where they 'have little incentive to invest their own capital in product innovations' (Dertouzos et al., 1989, p. 100). This seems particularly likely in relation to investment in specialized human and other assets, as in the example of suppliers to the US automotive industry who 'rationally refused to make relation-specific investments with a payback period longer than the length of the contract' (Dyer, 1997, p. 550).

The TC model's third category – 'hybrid forms of organization' – encompasses joint ventures, partnerships and other collaborative arrangements between buyers and suppliers. These combine elements of market governance (since they include contractual components and are open to market comparison and termination, at least in the medium to longer term) with elements of hierarchical governance (see earlier). As with market governance, reliance on highly specialized assets, or co-specialized assets (i.e. where the parties share site, physical or human assets, such as at Smartville[4]), the TC model predicts high transaction costs for the same reasons – i.e. to guard against opportunistic behaviour by the other party.

Several issues stand out in relation to this category. Much of the retreat from vertical integration discussed above has been towards various forms of partnership, both within the context of general supply chain practice, and with more specific objectives such as innovation-centred collaboration. But the three types of approach in the TC model are complementary rather than alternative. Firms generally have to source from substantial numbers of suppliers to meet different types of needs. Large firms, at least, are likely to use a mix of approaches to governance, retaining vertical integration in core areas, relying on market focused sourcing for relatively standardized commodity products for which there are many suppliers, and entering into partnerships with organizations that can provide specialized inputs. These include technological expertise, organizational capabilities and occupation of critical points in the total supply flow – for example, manufacturers of critical proprietary subsystems. Rather than the partnership model, such mixed approaches to supply may reflect practice in Japan where 'enterprises developed complex supply mechanisms that combined vertical integration, arm's-length purchases and commissioned production' (Solis, 2001).

The opportunism attributed to individual and organizational motivation in the TC model is criticized as founded in narrow, 'atomistic' interpretations of behaviour that do not take account of the 'embeddedness' of economic behaviour in social structure and interaction (Dore, 1983; Granovetter, 1985; Uzzi, 1997). Factors in the social structure can impose constraints on opportunistic behaviour by firms and emphasize gains from collaborative behaviour. For example, firms may prefer to do business with customers or suppliers who have a proven track record of reliability and avoid those known to be over-opportunistic (Rooks et al., 2000). The TC model is thus said to underestimate the potential for trust between the parties and 'for leveraging the human ability to take initiative, co-operate and to learn' (Ghosal and Moran, 1996, p. 42). In practice, long standing, seemingly high trust, collaborative relationships between buyers and supplier are not unknown – confounding the 'traditional' model's nomenclature. Examples include Marks and Spencer's relationship with its manufacturing suppliers from the 1920s to the 1990s (Tse, 1985; Bevan 2001),[5] the Swedish printing industry between 1880 and 1990 (Ottosson and Lundgren, 1996), weaving mills in Blackburn (Dore, 1983) and manufacturers in Wisconsin (Macaulay, 1963).

Overall, collaboration depends on high levels of trust, particularly when buyer–supplier relationships develop beyond the limited process flow relationships that the TC model focuses on, and extend into product development and other elements of inter-organizational co-operation. Dyer and Chu (2003) suggest that high levels of trust can be an effective governance mechanism, such as where trust contributes to low transaction costs through supplier self-monitoring and self-enforcement which uphold the agreed terms of supply to a customer. They found evidence of this in relationships between Japanese automotive OEMs and their suppliers, whereas the lower trust relationships of their US counterparts were reflected in substantially higher transaction costs. But costs are only part of the equation. Dyer and Chu argue that the focus of the TC model 'is almost entirely on *cost minimizing* rather than on *value-creation*' (2003, emphasis in the original). This limited focus lags well behind changes in supply chain relationships. For example, Dicken (2004) observes that moves to subcontracting on an international scale were initially driven by cost minimization, but suggests that this may have changed with the spread of JIT production. The competitive effectiveness of JIT systems depends on commitment across a supply chain to uniform high standards of product quality within tight delivery schedules, and collaboration on aspects of product development. However, customer expectations increasingly go beyond the performance demands associated with JIT. Large firms evaluate their suppliers' performance across multiple indicators. Dyer and Singh (1998, p. 864) also emphasize the importance of innovative capabilities, drawing from von Hippel's (1988) conclusion 'that a production network with superior knowledge-transfer mechanisms among users, suppliers and manufacturers will be able to "out-innovate" production networks with less effective knowledge sharing routines'.

Innovative capabilities are particularly critical with the emergence of two interlinked developments: (1) the growing scope and mounting influence of external governance on activities within product networks; and (2) increasingly systematic management of performance across the full C2G life cycle. Both extend beyond the direct product flows associated with production and distribution since they place other types of input and output firmly on the management agenda, and they raise the issue of the management of materials and other flows that move in the reverse, upstream, direction. This agenda is being vigorously pursued by some trailblazing companies where it draws other groups of managers into the 'supply chain arena'. In aggregate, these developments are best viewed as shifts towards management of total product systems.

Towards Total Product Systems

Supply chains span the total production process and, in many cases, are closely linked – if not integrated – with product distribution and retailing. Co-ordination is underpinned by varied, often sophisticated, systems of governance. Recent developments reach far outside the traditional preoccupations of SCM to the point where activities such as supplier selection are shaped by criteria that extend well beyond concerns with, say, cost, quality and delivery. For instance, sourcing decisions may have to weigh the social and economic implications of different choices. The adverse consequences of ignoring these issues can far outweigh apparent short term gains. Similarly, product design and development can be shaped by product supply considerations – for instance, to take account of the environmental impacts and resource consequences of different options. This emphasis on intra-chain interdependencies reinforces pressures for inter-functional co-ordination and shifts attention towards the total product system.

The potential adverse effects emanate from a variety of external factors, including the growing body of environmental, consumer and other regulation that is reshaping external governance and forcing changes in practice across all four phases of the C2G life cycle. These pressures are reinforced by action from consumer, union, environmental and other groups. These external forces, in combination with competitive pressures, are reflected in actions by lead actors that move them, in effect, towards management of their total product systems – a development that can offer competitive advantages. This is evident in more systematic and vigorous aftermarket activity and in involvement in the EOL phase of the C2G life cycle, both of which strengthen feedback loops to the prior life cycle stages.

Aftermarket integration

The aftermarket has long been an important source of revenue for OEMs such as manufacturers of civil aircraft engines and cars. In the latter case, poor profits from car manufacture associated with excess production capacity in the industry contrast with aftermarket activity 'which generates significant profits for vehicle manufacturers and their retail network' (Seitz and Peattie, 2004). Aftermarket involvement is significant in many other sectors, including office equipment (e.g. desktop printing and copying), transport equipment, buildings infrastructure (lifts, escalators, climate control and so on), and various types of household equipment and services. Partly as a consequence of regulatory pressures, aftermarket support has high priority in the financial services sector where it is associated with the development of extensive SCM roles by lead companies, such as where customer support services are outsourced. The overall significance of aftermarket activity is indicated by Gallagher et al.'s (2005) estimate of aftermarket sales of parts in the USA at more than $400 billion. They also suggest that aftermarket revenues account for some 40 per cent of profits for a wide range of companies.

Integration of aftermarket activity with the earlier life cycle stages reflects the influence of several factors. Some firms have recognized that gains from improved efficiency in the main production flows are also applicable to aftermarket supply: for instance in the systematic organization of 'reverse logistics' to handle product returns from retailers or individual purchasers requiring warranty or other servicing. Generally, however, management of aftermarket supply appears to have been poorly co-ordinated with main product flows, and is often 'a mere afterthought', the operational and financial ramifications of which are poorly understood by managers, with consequences that can include 'value destroying behaviour' (Gallagher et al., 2005). The same authors suggest that while some manufacturers accept low margins on an initial product sale in order to secure future income streams, others sacrifice the latter by:

- the offer of future discounts on parts sales as incentives to secure initial product sales;

- poor co-ordination of manufacture of new products with production for the aftermarket;
- poor organization of the transition to aftermarket support alone when a product is discontinued;
- neglect of the overall dynamics of aftermarket supply.

The revenue potential and the opportunities for more cost-efficient, customer-oriented aftermarket services emphasize the importance of integrating aftermarket strategy within the overall organization of all the phases of the supply or product system. A further factor is regulatory intervention, for instance where consumer protection rules place continuing aftermarket responsibilities on end-manufacturers and on service providers such as the financial services sector. These responsibilities necessarily extend upstream in such respects as the reliability and traceability of product components and materials, and of selling methods for services. Another factor is evolving competitive and marketing practice in which, particularly in relation to consumer durables, firms seek to strengthen and lengthen relationships with end-users through expanded 'product packages' and extended product warranties.

Development of the aftermarket is also linked to high – and rising – standards of product reliability which, in some cases, have changed patterns of aftermarket revenues and activity, confronting producers with some critical dilemmas. The significance of aftermarket profits for car manufacturers has been referred to, but these revenues have been eroded by increased product reliability and extended warranty periods, both of which have become essential components of competitive product packages. Similarly, a competitive focus on the performance of civil aircraft engines has increased 'time on the wing' between major engine servicing and reduced demand for replacement parts. In both cases, the responses of lead actors have included reducing costs by improving efficiency in the 'aftermarket supply chain', a challenge that presents different problems to those encountered in the organization of the main supply chain. For instance, demand for replacement parts is very difficult to predict, so that 'lean solutions' are not a realistic option; high levels of inventory are needed to bridge potential gaps between the supply of units for reprocessing and the demand for reprocessed parts (Seitz and Peattie, 2004; Guide and Pentico, 2003). Within the organization, supply to the aftermarket has to be fitted within – and compete with – mainstream production resources and activities. In effect, aftermarket supply has to be sustained as a separate venture, particularly once sale of a main product has been discontinued and the associated production chain has been closed down. Yet aftermarket support may be needed for long afterwards – for instance, 15 years or more in the case of cars and some financial products, and over 30 years for aircraft, aircraft engines, generating and transport equipment.

Lead companies have responded by pursuing new aftermarket opportunities. For example, by 2003, 44 per cent of Rolls-Royce's turnover derived from its aftermarket activities (Done, 2003). To sustain and develop this revenue, the company has extended its range of aftermarket services to provide customers with data from real-time monitoring of the performance of individual engines, contributing to reduced aircraft maintenance costs. It has set up joint ventures with airline customers and maintenance specialists to build a new network of maintenance facilities for the current generation of large engines such as its Trent series. This ties in with a drive by airlines to outsource non-core activities which, in the case of engine maintenance, received impetus from the need for facilities able to handle the new generation of very large engines. Similarly, some car manufacturers have sought to develop new revenue streams from in-car information systems. Some have expanded their presence in the markets for 'premium' second-hand cars and for car parts. In such cases, adaptation of product supply to accommodate the aftermarket is essential to viability.

The end-of-life phase

The importance of aftermarket integration is increased by emerging responsibilities for, and management of, the EOL phase. This is evident in the EU countries through Directives which regulate EOL processing of electrical and electronic products and cars.[6] Two central provisions in the EU regulation are: (1) the requirement for what Seitz and Peattie (2004) term 'extended producer responsibility' in which producers have to take responsibility for recovering and reprocessing EOL products; and (2) setting targets for the volume of materials, components and substances that must be recovered for reuse. For instance, there are targets of 90 per cent by weight for large electrical and electronic appliances and 85 per cent by weight for cars. But it is the top of the recycling hierarchy – the remanufacture of products or parts – that is the most significant in terms of resource conservation and in economic terms, primarily in relation to aftermarket supply. The potential is indicated in the automotive aftermarket where, in the EU, some 30 per cent of sales of steering racks and air-conditioning compressors were of remanufactured products in 2003. This share is forecast to increase to 80 per cent by 2008 as the EU moves towards the American pattern of greater use of remanufactured products (Seitz and Peattie, 2004, p. 77).

Reprocessing to extend the life of products or parts is viewed as movement towards 'closed-loop industrial systems' (Guide et al., Chapter 3.8). However, progress in this direction presents some formidable challenges. These include matching demand for components or parts from EOL sources to supply, and the organization of reprocessing. Seitz and Peattie (2004) demonstrate that, for car engines, the challenges of an unpredictable supply of engines suitable for refurbishment contrast with the much higher predictability of manufacturing new engines. The challenges multiply with the proliferation of product variants associated with product customization. Meeting these challenges requires dedicated organizational facilities and management. Similarly, separate logistic networks are needed to recover EOL products, to distribute them to reprocessing centres,[7] and to route remanufactured products to purchasers.

Logistic and reprocessing arrangements are organizationally distinct from mainstream product supply and distribution, but they are part of wider and increasing interdependencies that extend across the product life cycle. This is reflected in pressures on product designers to reduce the scale and costs of product variation and, more generally, to reduce materials and energy use by improving product manufacturability. Product designers also have to take account of issues in the aftermarket and EOL phases. For example, Seitz and Peattie (2004) suggest that design engineers need to include aftermarket considerations within design briefs – for instance through more disciplined product customization that reduces the 'inventory bloat' that can blight remanufacturing. Similarly, in materials selection, designers need to avoid compound materials that cannot be recovered cost-effectively in EOL reprocessing. Likewise, 'design for disassembly' aims to maximize recovery levels and to contain recovery costs. Nevertheless, in current management thinking and practice, the aftermarket and EOL phases seem, at best, to be only loosely connected to mainstream production, the distribution of new products, and other elements of supply chain organization – which is why the integrated management of total product systems is needed and can offer competitive advantages to those who pursue the opportunities at an early stage.

Interaction between external and intra-chain factors

The case for extending the management of supply chains or product networks towards the total product system is reinforced by the impacts of external factors that are linked to growing concerns about the environmental impacts and damage associated with global economic activity and lifestyles. Where these concerns are reflected in regulation, they interact with functioning at the process and other levels within a system by modifying the cost and dynamics of product system functioning. Their significance is illustrated by the emphasis on identifying and eradicating all cost bearing forms of waste in the TPS[8] and in comparable emphasis on lean-type intra-chain approaches. The potential rigour and cost advantages are underlined by Shingo: 'The Toyota production system is said to be so powerful that it could squeeze water from a dry towel . . . at Toyota, we search for the waste that usually escapes notice because it has become accepted as a natural part of everyday work' (1989, p. 76).

The changing context of supply chain organization relates to the issues that have developed around other forms of waste from production processes and other activity – specifically, to the liquid, solid and gaseous wastes that result from energy use and materials processing in *every* stage and activity across the C2G life cycle. These externalized wastes (*muda*) have hardly figured in the cost-conscious equations and concerns with efficiency in lean production and other methods of production organization.[9] The various natural environmental systems (atmospheric, hydrological etc.) could be relied on for their disposal because they were, in effect, 'free goods', largely free of charge to the disposer – or polluter – with few constraints on their use. This is changing rapidly as a growing body of regulation attaches direct costs to the polluting effects of production, distribution and product use.[10] For instance, regulation now prohibits or limits the use of certain types of materials; levies taxes on or prohibits the use of landfill; controls gaseous and liquid emissions; promotes the recycling of packaging and other materials; and, as mentioned above, requires the EOL reprocessing of some durable products.[11]

Such intervention impinges directly on individual firms but particularly on lead actors and on inter-chain competitiveness. Once costs are attached to environmental impacts, Shingo's 'dry towel' becomes both larger and distinctly damp. The compelling logic of competitive advantage that favours those who are the most successful in eliminating internal wastes, then applies to reducing the costs attributable to environmental regulation – and seeking compliance across a whole network. Where environmental regulation is extended, these costs rise further, contributing to an ever more compelling case for comprehensive intra-chain action to reduce costs by:

- standardizing methods for reducing the total product system costs that are attributable to emissions and other externalized wastes;
- improving intra-firm recycling and reprocessing across all stages in a process flow;
- responsible management of processing unavoidable wastes and their safe, non-polluting disposal;
- achieving high standards of efficiency in all other energy consuming and emission generating aspects of supply chain activity. Katayama and Bennett (Chapter 1.5) provide the example of controversies over JIT deliveries in a number of Japanese cities; Leiper et al. (Chapter 1.8) refer to management of the built environment.

In some cases, the cost pressures linked to environmental impacts on OEMs and their product networks are reinforced by action such as consumer boycotts, as in the case of highly publicized environmental failures like the *Exxon Valdez* oil spill. A wide array of impacts on product networks is attributable to campaigning action by activist groups and other NGOs. Leiper et al. (Chapter 1.8) relate Carillion's development of environmentally sensitive sourcing practices to the 'trigger event' of an activist group invading the company's AGM. The cost pressures in such cases extend to intangible costs such as damage to a firm's or a brand's reputation. In combination, the costs associated with environmental accidents, environmental regulation and activism by environmentalist groups are contributing to a reshaping of supply chain policy and practice – as in moves by some lead companies towards 'sustainable sourcing'.

Social and labour conditions

The economic and social consequences associated with global supply chain activities are subject to highly divergent interpretations. Concerns about the general impacts of global product systems, combined with action directed at specific instances of exploitative or damaging behaviour, have contributed to pressures that are moving lead companies towards total product system approaches. These concerns are diverse, extending from the use of child labour, dire working conditions and lack of protection of worker health and safety through to the effects of sourcing practices and the scale of product distribution on society and economy, particularly in developing countries, They also extend to conditions in the industrialized countries. Hampson (Chapter 1.4) relates 'stress-driven production' in intensive lean approaches to longer term damage to workers' health which has wider social effects: 'such problems may be paid for by the host country's health system'.

Issues like these contribute to what Murray and Trudeau refer to as 'alarmist scenarios', in which lack of global regulation is viewed as likely 'to precipitate a downward spiral in terms and conditions of employment' (2004, p. 18). Other perspectives view the potential outcomes less pessimistically. *Laissez-faire* perspectives anticipate resolution of the issues by long term market functioning whereas social regulation perspectives emphasize the scope for state and non-state actors to influence the behaviour of global firms. But Murray and Trudeau point out that social regulation is highly fragmented in the global context. Globally organized firms and product systems are able to exploit differences in national fiscal, regulatory and other regimes. They suggest that the way forward in this perspective lies in diversified approaches, including working 'through supply chains to ensure that these new standards are widely diffused to sub-contracting firms' (2004, p. 24).

This begs the question of how powerful lead companies might be induced to apply such standards, particularly since employment conditions contrast with environmental standards which are advanced by the external regulation that, in some cases, is applied internationally. One possible answer that might be viewed as a form of 'social regulation' lies in the vulnerability of many lead companies in terms of their images, market positions and brands. They are at risk to consumer, union and other pressure groups that are able to generate adverse publicity, initiate boycotts or take industrial action. This is illustrated by Lund and Wright's example (Chapter 1.6) of the Teamsters Union's carefully co-ordinated – and ultimately successful – combination of industrial action, media advertising and mass leafleting that initiated a consumer boycott. Lund and Wright observe that, in the area of industrial relations, 'Supply chain integration poses a distinct set of challenges and opportunities for employers and unions alike.' Different types of example are provided by Winstanley et al. (Chapter 2.7), including that of a prolonged student campaign against Nike's association with their suppliers' use of child labour and poor labour practices. This led to what is said to be 'the biggest student protest in the US since the opposition to the Vietnam War'. The effectiveness of this campaign may be indicated by changes in Nike's approach. These include terminating the outsourcing of monitoring the company's supplier code of conduct in order to establish more active supervision and, most recently, public disclosure of the names and addresses of all their suppliers. The most significant development in the wider context may be the company's active campaigning for common standards for the global apparel, footwear and sports equipment industries (nikebiz.com, 2005).

As in these examples, action by consumer and other pressure groups appears to be primarily targeted at lead companies. Their strength in relation to their suppliers and the other actors in a product system can also be a potential source of vulnerability. Large-scale market presence raises the profile of their sourcing and marketing policies, exposing them to the risks of continuing adverse publicity and mass action. They are vulnerable to the practices of distant suppliers, such as the use of child labour and other forms of labour exploitation, even where they claim to be unaware of it. One response for lead companies has been to develop extensive supplier codes of practice covering issues of employment practice, the prohibition of child labour and environmental standards. The practical significance of such codes depends on the flow of information combined with active monitoring and policing. Where this takes place, *and* where activism by consumer, union and other groups is effective, there appears to be a substantial enlargement of the scope of governance regimes that fits the social regulation perspective. It is an approach that national governments and inter-governmental bodies should examine for its potential to advance standards in environmental and employment practice, and to support more balanced global economic development.

For companies, the interdependencies and responsibilities that span the full cradle-to-grave product cycle point to the need to co-ordinate design, production, accounting and other functions across the full product cycle, and among the full range of actors within the broad network or system that is linked to the C2G life cycle. Needs for co-ordination on this scale are compounded at the macro product system level by the increasing globalization of supply chain functioning. These developments underline the need for co-ordinated management of the 'total product system' which, very gradually, is being fulfilled. Thus, beyond the view of contemporary competition as being between supply chains or value chains, factors such as those explored in the final two sections suggest that there is a transition towards competition between total product systems. Competitive success in this context becomes heavily dependent on the ability of key players, both large and small, to relate to the total product system and to derive the maximum advantages from tackling 'external *muda*', the various issues associated with product EOL and the other challenges that have been discussed here. However, these are challenges that large, lead companies are most attuned to. For most small and medium enterprises, these same challenges indicate the evolving context in which they have to seek to survive and to grow.

NOTES

This chapter derives from research in retail, apparel, aerospace, healthcare and automotive product systems. It develops from a paper first presented to EIASM's 2nd European Forum on Market Driven Supply Chains: From Supply Chains to Demand Chains, Milan, Italy, 5–6 April 2005. Support and suggestions from my colleague and co-researcher, Ruth Carter, have made important contributions to this chapter. Thanks also to Stuart MacDonald for some very constructive comments on the initial draft.

1   Technological domain is used here to refer to the different types of knowledge that are required to produce and support end-products. It also includes economic and operational factors that contribute to differences in priorities, time horizons, cost constraints and so on.

2   Solis also points out that changes in ownership, as western companies gained controlling interests in all the Japanese auto manufacturers except Toyota and Honda, also led to changes in supply chain organization. For instance, Renault's control of Nissan led to a 40 per cent reduction in supplier numbers, disinvestment in suppliers and increased reliance on global sourcing.

3   The examples tend to be drawn from the US literature and from practice influenced by US transnational companies. But different patterns may prevail in other countries and legal systems. For example, the UK's Competition Commission (2000) found that, in the grocery industry, 'full written agreements between the main parties and their suppliers

were unusual' (vol. 2, §11.56). Yet multiple retailers and their suppliers 'gave very different views on their interdependence' (§11.11). While descriptions of relationships were often couched in terms of partnership – at least by retailer representatives – many suppliers described relationships that were, in many respects, 'traditional' in character (e.g. see §11.26).

4 'Smartville' is the purpose-built site shared by MCC (a Daimler–Chrysler subsidiary, assemblers of the Smart Car) with the company's system partners (main suppliers) in a series of closely linked, dedicated, facilities – i.e. co-specialized assets.

5 Bevan links M&S's decline to, among other things, the jettisoning by senior management of the company's long standing collaborative relationships with suppliers.

6 Guide and Pentico (2003) emphasize alternative approaches to this issue, contrasting the EU's 'waste stream approach' with the 'market-driven approach' favoured in the USA.

7 Seitz and Peattie (2004) contrast those run by the OEMs with those of specialist independent remanufacturers, highlighting contrasts in knowledge and experience between these two groups, and the potential conflicts between them.

8 For example, Ohno (1988) refers to the TPS's emphasis on the seven wastes of overproduction; waiting; transporting; overprocessing; inventories; moving; making defective parts and products. But this concept of 'waste' is grounded in the manufacturing shopfloor and concepts of 'direct labour costs'. Subsequent approaches have encompassed service activities, in the manufacturing and service sectors, applying broader definitions of waste.

9 Lean-type approaches may contribute to reduced use of energy and materials and decreased environmental impacts – but note Katayama and Bennett's example (Chapter 1.5) of adverse reactions in Japanese cities to the pollution and other impacts associated with JIT delivery.

10 The list of such interventions is a long one but, to illustrate, range from action to remove lead additives in petrol – essentially national initiatives, so that coverage is far from universal; to European Union action to regulate waste streams such as through the End-of-Life Vehicle Directive; to, at the international level, the Montreal Protocol concerned with compounds that deplete the ozone layer.

11 Use of other types of resources, particularly non-renewables, forms part of the overall picture. But these are generally left to solution by the market through supply–demand relationships and the competitive advantages associated with efficient resource use.

REFERENCES

Bevan, J: *The Rise and Fall of Marks and Spencer*, Profile, 2001

Bidault, F, Despres, C & Butler, C: *Leveraged Innovation – Unlocking the Innovation Potential of Strategic Supply*, Macmillan, 1998

Butler, P T W, Hanna, A M, Mendoca, B, Augustus, J & Manyika, A S: A revolution in interaction, *McKinsey Quarterly*, no. 1, 1997

Camuffo, A, Romano, P & Vinelli, A: Back to the future: Benetton transforms its network, *MIT Sloan Management Review*, fall, 2001

Christopher, M: *Logistics and Supply Chain Management: Strategies for Reducing Costs and Improving Services*, Financial Times, Pitman, London, 1992

Competition Commission: *Supermarkets: A Report on the Supply of Groceries from Multiple Stores in the United Kingdom* (3 vols), Cm 4842, Stationery Office, Norwich, 2000

Dertouzos, M L, Lester, R K & Solow, R M: *Made in America – Regaining the Productive Edge*, MIT Press, 1989

Dicken, P: *Global Shift – Reshaping the Global Economic Map in the 21st Century*, Sage, London, 4th edn, 2004

Dicken, P, Kelley, P F, Olds, K & Wai-Chung Yeung, H: Chains and networks, territories and scales: towards a relationship framework for analysing the global economy, *Global Networks*, vol. 1, no. 2, 2001

Done, K: Rolls-Royce again dips into reserves, *Financial Times*, 5 March 2003, p. 24

Dore, R: Goodwill and the spirit of market capitalism, *British Journal of Sociology*, vol. XXXIV, no. 4, 1983

Dyer, J H: Does governance matter? *Keiretsu* alliances and asset specificity as sources of Japanese competitive advantage, *Organization Science*, vol. 7, no. 6, 1996

Dyer, J H: Effective interfirm collaboration: how firms minimize transaction costs and maximize transaction value, *Strategic Management Journal*, vol. 8, no. 7, 1997

Dyer, J H & Chu, W: The role of trustworthiness in reducing transaction costs and improving performance: empirical evidence from the United States, Japan, and Korea, *Organization Science*, vol. 14, no. 1, 2003

Dyer, J H & Singh, H: The relational view: cooperative strategy and sources of inter-organizational competitive advantage, *Academy of Management Review*, vol. 23, no. 4, 1998

Dyer, J H & Singh, H: Dialogue: response to relational view commentary, *Academy of Management Review*, vol. 24, no. 2, 1999

Ernst, D: Global production networks and the changing geography of innovation systems: implications for developing countries, *Economics of Innovation & New Technology*, vol. 11, no. 6, 2002

Evans, P & Wurster, T S: *Blown to Bits: How the New Economics of Information Transforms Strategy*, Harvard Business School Press, 2000

Fernie, J: International comparisons of supply chain management in grocery retailing, *Service Industries Journal*, vol. 15, no. 4, 1995

Fraser, P, Farrukh, C & Gregory, M: Managing product development collaborations – a process maturity approach, *Proceedings of the Institute of Mechanical Engineers*, vol. 217, part B, *Engineering Manufacture*, 2003

Gallagher, T, Mitchke, M D & Rogers, M C: Profiting from spare parts, *The McKinsey Quarterly*, February 2005

Gattorna, J L & Walters, D W: *Managing the Supply Chain: A Strategic Perspective*, Macmillan, London, 1996

Gereffi, G: The organization of buyer-driven global commodity chains: how US retailers shape overseas production networks, in Gereffi & Korzeniewicz, 1994

Gereffi, G & Korzeniewicz, M (eds): *Commodity Chains and Global Capitalism*, Praeger, Westport, CT, 1994

Ghosal, S & Moran, P: Bad for practice: a critique of the transaction cost theory, *Academy of Management Review*, vol. 21, no. 1, 1996

Granovetter, M: Economic action and social structure: the problem of embeddedness, *American Journal of Sociology*, vol. 91, no. 3, 1985

Guide, V D R Jr & Pentico, D W: A hierarchical decision model for re-manufacturing and re-use, *International Journal of Logistics: Research and Applications*, vol. 6, no. 1–2, 2003

Harland, C M, Zheng, J, Johnsen, T & Lamming, R C: A conceptual model for researching the creation and operation of supply networks, *British Journal of Management*, vol. 15, pp. 1–21, 2004

Hines, P, Lamming, R, Jones, D, Cousins, P & Rich, N: *Value Stream Management – Strategy and Excellence in the Supply Chain*, Financial Times, Prentice Hall, Harlow, 2000

Hopkins, T K & Wallerstein, I: Conclusions about commodity chains, in Gereffi & Korzeniewicz, 1994

Kaplan, R S & Cooper, R: *Cost and Effect: Using Integrated Cost Systems to Drive Profitability and Performance*, Harvard Business School Press, 1998

Macalister, T: Sainsbury IT chief denies poor performance, *The Guardian*, 20/01/05

Macaulay, S: Non-contractual relations in business, *American Sociological Review*, vol. 28, no. 1, pp. 55–66, 1963

Macdonald, S: Collusion and technological determinism: the manager, his consultant's method and information technology, *Journal of International Business and Entrepreneurship Development*, vol. 2, no. 2, 2004

Murray, G & Trudeau, G: Towards a social regulation of the global firm?, *Relations Industrielles/Industrial Relations*, vol. 59, no. 1, 2004

nikebiz.com: *Evolution: shifting our approach to labour compliance*, www.nike.com/nikebiz, accessed May 2005

North, D C: *Institutions, Institutional Change and Economic Performance*, Cambridge University Press, 1990

Ohno, Taichi: *Toyota Production System – Beyond Large Scale Production*, Productivity Press, Portland, OR, 1988

Ottosson, J & Lundgren, A: AB Gust Carlsson, 1880–1990: networks and survival in the Swedish printing industry, *Business History*, vol. 38, no. 3, 1996

Özveren, E: The shipbuilding commodity chain, 1590–1790, in Gereffi & Korzeniewicz, 1994

Pascale, R T: *Managing on the Edge*, Viking, London, 1990

Pelizzon, S: The grain flour commodity chain, 1590–1790, in Gereffi & Korzeniewicz, 1994

Politi, J: Supply chain headache for Mothercare's new broom, *Financial Times*, 23 November 2002

Quinn, J B: Technology in services: past myths and future challenges, *Technological Forecasting and Social Change*, vol. 34, no. 4, 1988

Quinn, J B, Doorley, T L & Paquette, P C: Beyond products: services-based strategy, *Harvard Business Review*, March 1990

Rooks, G, Raub, W, Selten, R & Tazelaar, F: How inter-firm co-operation depends on social embeddedness: a vignette study, *Acta Sociologica*, vol. 43, 2000

Scarborough, H & Swan, J: Explaining the diffusion of knowledge management: the role of fashion, *British Journal of Management*, vol. 12, pp. 3–12, 2001

Schlosser, E: *Fast Food Nation: What the All-American Meal is Doing to the World*, Penguin, 2001

Seitz, M A & Peattie, K: Meeting the closed-loop challenge: the case of remanufacturing, *California Management Review*, vol. 16, no. 2, winter 2004

Shingo, Shigeo: *A Study of the Toyota Production System*, Productivity Press, Portland, OR, 1989

Solis, M: On the myth of the *keiretsu* network: Japanese electronics in North America, *Business and Politics*, vol. 5, no. 3, 2001

Tse, K K: *Marks & Spencer – Anatomy of Britain's Most Efficiently Managed Company*, Pergamon, 1985

Uzzi, B: Social structure and competition in interfirm networks: the paradox of embeddedness, *Administrative Science Quarterly*, vol. 42, 1997

Von Hippel, E: *The Sources of Innovation*, Oxford University Press, 1988

Supply Chain Management: Relationships, Chains and Networks

C. M. Harland

Introduction

The phrase 'supply chain management' appears to have originated in the early 1980s: Oliver and Webber (1982) discussed the potential benefits of integrating the internal business functions of purchasing, manufacturing, sales and distribution. Today it is a phrase that appears in many company strategies and reports, practitioner and academic journals and texts. However, there is little consistency in the use of the term and little evidence of clarity of meaning (Harland, 1995a). Rather it appears to be a term used in several emerging bodies of knowledge which, to date, have remained largely unconnected.

This research had the following objectives:

- to provide some coordination and clarification of existing disparate work in supply chain management;
- to provide an integrating framework to help locate supply chain research;
- to build on existing behavioural work in the areas of service operations management and consumer behaviour;
- to test whether existing, proven principles of supply chains apply to soft features as well as to hard logistics features of chains;
- to identify if network differences appear to impact on performance in relationships, chains and networks.

The initial data collection was carried out in the European automotive aftermarket. Subsequent quantitative analysis of these data has revealed new insights into supply chain management. The differing uses of the term will be examined.

Supply Chain Management

There are four main uses of the term 'supply chain management':

- first, the internal supply chain that integrates business functions involved in the flow of materials and information from inbound to outbound ends of the business;
- secondly, the management of dyadic or two-party relationships with immediate suppliers;
- thirdly, the management of a chain of businesses including a supplier, a supplier's suppliers, a customer and a customer's customer, and so on;
- fourthly, the management of a network of interconnected businesses involved in the ultimate provision of product and service packages required by end customers.

The first of these definitions – the internal supply chain – is adopted by Oliver and Webber (1982), Houlihan (1984), Stevens (1989), Saunders (1994), Jones and Riley (1985). It relates closely to the pre-existing concepts of materials management (Ammer, 1968; Lee and Dobler, 1965) and the value chain (Porter, 1985; Johnston and Lawrence, 1988; Kogut, 1985). However, this paper is concerned with inter-business, not intra-business integration. Therefore, the last three of these definitions will be examined here. The first body of work to be discussed, therefore, is that which defines supply chain management as the management of supply relationships.

Supply Chain Management as the Management of Supply Relationships

A body of research is evolving that defines and discusses supply chain management as an intermediate type of relationship within a spectrum ranging from integrated hierarchy (vertical integration) to pure market. Christopher (1992) defined supply chain management as an alternative to vertical integration. Ellram (1991a) positioned supply chain management as shown in Figure 1. This perspective of supply chain management has as its foundations an industrial organization and contract view of the firm as a nexus of contracts (Aoki, Gustafsson and Williamson, 1990). Marshall (1923) and Coase (1937) originally identified the existence of alternative forms of organization to either vertical integration or market. The types of alternative form were defined later by Richardson (1972) and Blois (1972).

Business trends and the management of supply relationships

Authors and practitioners from many different disciplines and functions are highlighting an increasing dependence on relationships with suppliers (see, for example, Sabel et al., 1987; Christopher, 1992; Slack, 1991; Schonberger, 1986). Closer,

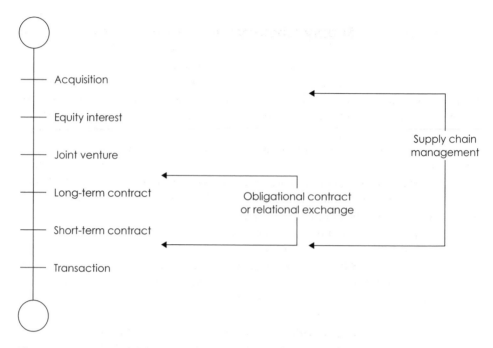

Figure 1   Supply chain management as a type of relationship

longer-term relationships are evident in some industries, reported notably in the Japanese automotive industry (Lamming, 1993; Womack et al., 1990), the Japanese textile industry (Dore, 1983), craft-based Italian industries (Lorenzoni and Ornati, 1988) and various Swedish manufacturing industries (Hakansson, 1987).

Supply chain relationships are discussed here in the context of different business trends. These trends include (1) a reported increasing incidence of vertical disintegration, (2) implementation of supplier base reduction programmes, (3) focusing of operations, (4) outsourcing, (5) just-in-time and (6) the increasing popularity of partnerships and partnership sourcing.

Vertical disintegration   A trend towards vertical disintegration has been reported in a range of industries (Thackray, 1986; Porter, 1987). One of the given reasons for vertical disintegration is that integrated businesses face a risk of becoming locked into inappropriate technologies (Abernathy, 1978; Harrigan, 1983; Miles and Snow, 1987). Once committed to these technologies, they may lose flexibility. However, companies that form relationships with other businesses may be able to switch to another supplier with a better technological fit to changing market conditions. Switching relationships may not be easy, but it is likely to be easier than divesting vertically integrated parts of a business.

Supplier base reduction   A second business trend that increases the importance of supply relationships is the reported movement away from multi-sourced adversarial trading towards single or dual sourcing. For example, Rank Xerox had almost 5,000 suppliers in 1981 but reduced this number to 300 by 1987 (Morgan, 1987). Lamming (1989) reported that Japanese lean producers involved fewer than 300 suppliers in new product development projects compared to typical Western manufacturers who dealt with 1,000–2,500. Hakansson (1987) discussed increasing concentration in most industries studied in Sweden. As supply bases are reduced, more intense supplier development may be performed with the remaining suppliers.

Focusing of operations   Focused operations concentrate on a limited, manageable set of tasks (Skinner, 1969) that meet the order-winning criteria of customer groups (Hill, 1985; Christopher, 1992). Focus can be applied at different levels – plant level, plant-within-plant and cell. Plant-within-plant and the formation of cells may not affect inter-business relationships. However, focus at the level of the plant concentrates each plant on a different set of products/markets, processes, volumes or order-winning criteria. Harland (1995b) stretched the concept of focus beyond the boundary of the firm to consider the impact on supply chain relationships. This is clearly related to vertical disintegration; however, there is little discussion apparent in the existing literatures on focus and vertical disintegration to connect the two.

Outsourcing   Outsourcing is a term that has been used to describe the 'putting out' of non-core internal processes such as catering, site security, estate management, legal services, recruitment, logistics and information systems. One issue of concern is what is considered to be core and non-core (Fitzgerald, 1995). Conceptually there are common features of outsourcing and focus. Both rationalize the business to concentrate on a core set of manageable tasks and both are likely to result in greater dependence on relationships. Focus tends to have been limited to consideration of production operations and outsourcing to service operations.

Just-in-time   Just-in-time (JIT) requires elimination of waste – JIT supply requires delivery of perfect parts and services at exactly the time they are required. Frazier et al. (1988) and Lascelles and Dale (1989) identified that traditional adversarial relationships were not conducive to generating good quality. A movement towards JIT therefore necessarily involves supplier development, usually with a reduced supplier base.

Partnership and partnership sourcing   Macbeth and Ferguson (1994) use the phrase 'partnership' to refer to the intermediate types of relationship shown in Figure 2.

The phrase appears to be used to describe non-equity cooperative relationships. Recently there has been increasing attention paid to partnerships – phrases such as 'win–win' are enticing businesses to favour partnerships over other types of relationship. However, not all relationships should be partnerships – rather it is more a case of 'horses for courses' with an appropriate type of relationship being selected for a particular set of circumstances (Cox, 1995).

All the above business trends provide the context for increasing interest in the management of supply relationships or, as some of this set of researchers may term

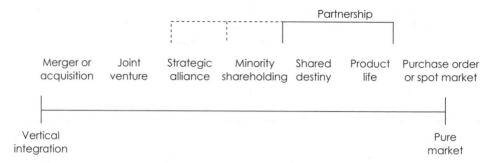

Figure 2   Partnership as a type of relationship

it (Ellram, 1991a; Macbeth and Ferguson, 1994), 'supply chain management'. How-ever, the relationship work concentrates at the level of the dyad, i.e. a two-party relationship. Whilst relationships are the building blocks of chains and networks, two links don't make a chain. The next level of system to be considered here is the inter-business chain.

Supply Chain Management as the Management of Inter-Business Chains

In the operations strategy area Hayes and Wheelwright (1984) described a commercial chain with the elements shown in Figure 3. Other authors have described the supply chain as a pipeline (see, for example, Farmer and Ploos von Amstel, 1991).

Hayes and Wheelwright discussed the direction, extent and balance of vertical integration in the chain. They also identified that a firm's physical position in the chain would affect demand volatility, asset intensity, profitability, technological change and scale and balance.

To date there is little evidence of empirical work supporting these effects other than in the industrial dynamics literature (Forrester, 1961; Burbidge, 1961; Towill, 1991). Studies of industrial dynamics in supply chains have supported the conclusion that upstream businesses suffer greater volatility and 'noise' than do downstream businesses. This Forrester effect has to date been shown to impact on logistical information such as orders, forecasts, volumes and timing. However, there is little evidence of investigation into softer aspects of chains.

The fourth systems level is the level of the inter-business network.

Figure 3   An inter-business supply chain

Supply Chain Management as Strategic Management of Inter-Business Networks

A network has been defined as a specific type of relation linking a defined set of persons, objects or events. The set of persons, objects or events of which the network is composed can be called *actors* or *nodes* (Mitchell, 1969).

Christopher (1992) defined supply chain management as the management of:

> the network of organisations that are involved, through upstream and downstream linkages, in the different processes and activities that produce value in the form of products and services in the hands of the ultimate consumer. Thus, for example, a shirt manufacturer is a part of a supply chain that extends upstream through the weavers of fabrics to the manufacturers of fibres, and downstream through distributors and retailers to the final consumer.

Different aspects of networks have been considered in the literature to date. These include:

- competitive position in networks;
- definitions of components of networks;
- network structures;
- network performance.

Network performance is considered later, but a brief summary of research in the first three areas is provided here.

Competitive position in networks

Competitive advantage may be gained by harnessing the resource potential of the network in a more effective manner than competing firms (Cunningham, 1990). Taking a network perspective can influence competitive behaviour and identifies the following issues as important:

- selection of collaborative partners in the network;
- establishing a competitive position in the network;
- monitoring your own and your competitors' positions in the network;
- how the network relationships are handled.

Quoted examples of firms that appear to have strategically managed their networks to improve competitive position include Toyota (Womack et al., 1990), Benetton (Christopher, 1992) and Nissan (Nishiguchi, 1994). However, there is a group of academics in the Swedish networks school who believe that industrial networks cannot be managed and that actors within them merely cope (Hakansson and Snehota,

1995). This school has been instrumental in the development of a language to describe business networks and their components.

Definitions of components of networks

The components of networks of actors, resources and activities are dependent on each other. Actors are defined by the activities they perform and the resources they control; they are connected to other actors via resources and activities. Each actor's unique combination of resources and activities constitutes its identity. Actors develop and organize their activities partly in response to how their customers and suppliers perform and organize theirs (Dubois, 1994). Actors undertake transformation activities, such as production. Activities undertaken between actors are called exchange or transaction activities.

Relationships between actors represent valuable bridges as they give one actor access to the resources of another. The network model shown in Figure 4 is based on resource dependency theory; through relationships it is possible for individual actors to mobilize resources.

The network model indicates some of the complexity of the study of networks. Some researchers may use the term to describe a network of actors, others to discuss a network of processes or activities. Networking activities such as guest engineering

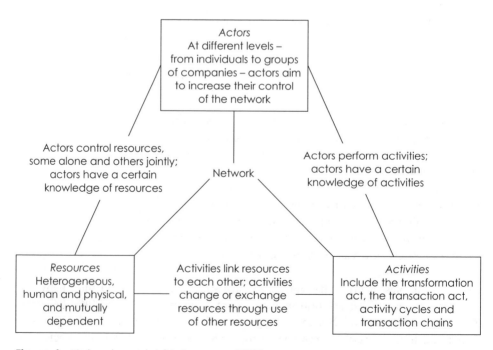

Figure 4   Network model (Hakansson, 1987)

relate to sharing of resources in networks. Therefore, care should be taken when describing a firm's network; it should be made clear which of these networks are being considered.

Network structures

Nishiguchi (1994) reported how Toyota and other Japanese companies organized their suppliers into hierarchies; first-tier or primary suppliers provided systems rather than components. This had the effect of significantly reducing the number of suppliers dealt with on a direct-supply basis, though not necessarily reducing the number of supply sources in the network in total. It did impose more levels in the network. It also made the buying company more dependent on each supplier, whereas the traditional broader network attempted to reduce dependency to suppress prices and maintain competition.

Therefore, it can be seen that the study of networks may be related to networks of actors (firms or individuals), activities (or processes) and resources. Examination of all these types of network is valid; what is important is that the appropriate network is chosen for the type of study. Network performance will be considered in the next section.

Supply Chain Management and Performance

Different researchers have attempted to assess performance in different ways, depending on whether they were researching at the level of the network, the external chain or the relationship.

Network performance

Easton and Quayle (1990) investigated performance differences between single-sourcing and multiple-sourcing networks. They proposed that single-sourcing networks would be more rigid and stronger as there would be dense flows of exchanges within them. It would also be easier to retain confidentiality in single sourcing. However, the advantages of multi-source or broad networks included an ability to adapt to changes in the environment through switching and a larger base to generate innovation from. Puto et al. (1985) advocated multiple sourcing as an important strategy for firms who needed to reduce uncertainty in purchasing.

Therefore, it can be seen that, whilst there is general agreement on the reduction of multi-sourcing in networks, there is a range of views on the relative merits of single and multi-sourcing. Some of these views of the relative merits are summarized in Table 1.

Most of the work to date on inter-business network performance has tended to concentrate on varying performance given different structures. The aspects of

Table 1   Relative merits of broad versus narrow networks

Advantages of broad networks	Advantages of narrow networks
Adaptable to change	Collaborative innovation
More switching opportunities	Rigid and strong
Wider access to knowledge	Dense flows of information
Hedge against uncertainty	Higher confidentiality
Cost competitive	Shared destiny

performance that have been considered are more oriented towards economic performance than to other aspects of performance such as customer satisfaction.

Chain performance

Most of the existing work on chain performance has been contributed by the industrial dynamics and logistics literatures. Industrial dynamics research (see Forrester, 1961; Towill 1991; Burbidge, 1961) has identified that demand information about timing and volume of requirements becomes increasingly distorted further upstream in supply chains. This distortion is caused by time delays in ordering, batching of information and of requirements, safety stock provision, problems in communication and inaccurate forecasting. The resulting Forrester effect, shown in Figure 5, is an increasing amplitude of perceived demand which causes lumpy and irregular schedules in upstream businesses.

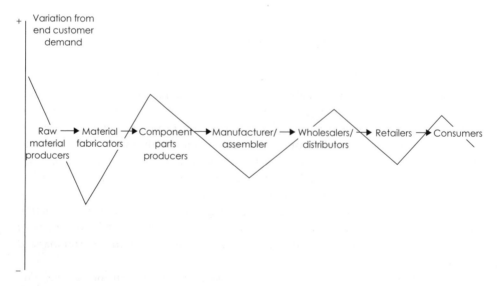

Figure 5   Forrester effect on supply chain performance

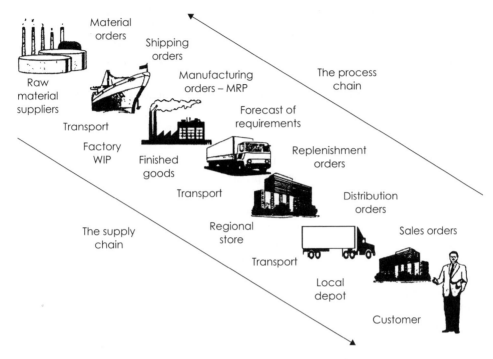

Figure 6 Logistics chains (derived from Braithwaite, 1992)

Logistics research into chain performance has focused primarily on improving speed and cost performance (see Stalk and Hout, 1990; Bowersox et al., 1992; Christopher, 1992). Improvements in speed and cost may relate to:

- the physical supply chain, through which materials are converted and goods flow to end customers;
- the process chain of orders and demand transmission.

The logistics literature considers the physical distribution and information distribution connections between nodes in the chain, as shown in Figure 6. The work on chain performance has considered customer satisfaction but related to delivery reliability, cost/price and time to market aspects of performance. Other aspects of customer satisfaction have not been considered in as much depth.

Relationship performance

As far back as 1963, industrial purchasing authors have written about performance dimensions to evaluate suppliers. At the time the term 'relationship' was not used to describe dealings with suppliers as the Western commercial climate of the time was one of price competition and adversarial transactions. However, assessment of relationship performance was evident at that time. The National Association for Purchasing Agents (NAPA) in the USA published the results of a research study by Smith et al. (1963), identifying the value of assessing supplier performance in terms of quality, delivery and price. Post-purchase performance evaluation of suppliers along these dimensions was supported by Lee and Dobler (1965) as providing the buyer with 'objective information to use in subsequent negotiations and in making future sourcing decisions'.

A growing body of work in the study of relationships emphasizes that there are opportunities for mutual advantage if information is shared between the parties (Christopher, 1992; Ellram, 1990; 1991b; Macbeth and Ferguson, 1994; Hines, 1994). Recent purchasing literature emphasizes the increasing importance of measuring and monitoring performance within relationships because of the increased dependency between the parties (Ellram and Carr, 1994).

A performance measurement system implemented by the purchasing party can enhance the buy–sell relationship (Monczka and Trencha, 1988). However, most performance measurement systems in use fail to do this for three main reasons. First, they incorporate mostly hard, objective measures which may not be appropriate for measuring softer features of capability and performance (Ellram, 1990; Macbeth and Ferguson, 1994). Secondly, the measurement systems are usually designed by the purchasing organization for the purchasing organization, rather than for the relationship as a quasi-organization (Lamming, 1993). Thirdly, the measurement system is imposed on suppliers using power leverage (Gregory, 1986). These three failings are in direct conflict with the shared destiny principles of partnership and long-term relationships.

Therefore, if newer, more appropriate forms of performance measurement are required to support longer-term relationships, this requires identification of what these newer performance measurements should be. Marketing and service-management-based views particularly emphasize that the customer's perception is critical in a relationship (Zeithaml et al., 1990; Christopher, 1992). The connection between expectations, perceptions of performance and satisfaction/dissatisfaction are well proven; Berry and Parasuraman (1991), Brogowicz et al. (1990), Gronroos (1990), Davidow and Uttal (1989) and Haywood-Farmer and Nollet (1991) all claim that customer satisfaction arises as a result of the customer comparing their expectations to their perception of performance. These service-based issues are of far greater importance in measuring long-term relationship performance than in measuring short-term transactions between parties, with no long-term commitment.

However, parties to a relationship may misperceive each other's actions (Borys and Jemison, 1989). This misperception may result in the customer perceiving its requirements as being A while the supplier perceives them as being B. Similarly, the customer may perceive the supplier's performance as being C whereas the supplier perceives it as D.

Therefore, it seems reasonable to hypothesize that if parties wish to develop closer relationships, they should identify and close these perception gaps at the outset, then jointly work on an agreed and understood programme to improve performance within the relationship.

. . .

REFERENCES

Abernathy, W. (1978). *The Productivity Dilemma*. Johns Hopkins University Press, Baltimore, USA.

Ammer, D. S. (1968). *Materials Management*. Irwin, Homewood, IL, USA.

Aoki, M., B. Gustafsson and O. E. Williamson (1990). *The Firm as a Nexus of Treaties*. Sage, London, UK.

Berry, L. L. and A. Parasuraman (1991). *Marketing Services: Competing Through Quality*. Free Press, New York, USA.

Blois, K. (1972). 'Vertical Quasi-Integration', *Journal of Industrial Economics*, 20 (3), pp. 33–41.

Borys, B. and D. B. Jemison (1989). 'Hybrid Organisations as Strategic Alliances: Theoretical Issues in Organisational Combinations', *Academy of Management Review*, 14 (2), pp. 234–249.

Bowersox, D. J., P. J. Daugherty, C. L. Droge, R. N. Germain and D. S. Rogers (1992). *Logistical Excellence: It's Not Just Business as Usual*. Digital Press, Burlington, MA, USA.

Braithwaite, A. (1992). 'A Pragmatic Route to Effective Benchmarking', *Proceedings of BPICS 27th Annual Conference*, Birmingham, pp. 197–209.

Brogowicz, A. A., L. M. Delene and D. M. Lyth (1990). 'A Synthesised Service Model with Managerial Implications'. *International Journal of Service Industry Management*, 1 (1), pp. 27–46.

Burbidge, J. L. (1961). 'The New Approach to Production', *Production Engineer*, December. 40 (12), pp. 769–784.

Christopher, M. G. (1992). *Logistics and Supply Chain Management*. Pitman Publishing, London, UK.

Coase, R. H. (1937). 'The Nature of the Firm', *Economica*, Vol. V.

Cox, A. (1995). 'Pro-Activity, Value Engineering and Strategic Procurement Management: An Entrepreneurial Contractual Model for the Firm', *Proceedings of First Worldwide Research Symposium on Purchasing and Supply Chain Management*, pp. 72–89.

Cunningham, M. T. (1990). 'Survival and Growth Strategies in New Technology Markets', *Proceedings of the 6th IMP Conference*, Milan, pp. 346–372.

Davidow, W. H. and B. Uttal (1989). 'Service Companies: Focus or Falter', *Harvard Business Review*, July/August.

Dore R. (1983). 'Goodwill and the Spirit of Market Capitalism', *British Journal of Sociology*, 34 (4), December, pp. 459–482.

Dubois, A. (1994). *Organising Industrial Activities. An Analytical Framework*. Department of Industrial Marketing, Chalmers University of Technology, Sweden.

Easton, G. and M. Quayle (1990). 'Single and Multiple Network Sourcing – Network Implications', *Proceedings of 6th IMP Conference*, pp. 474–488, Milan.

Ellram, L. M. (1990). 'The Supplier Selection Decision in Strategic Partnerships', *Journal of Purchasing and Materials and Management*, Fall, pp. 8–14.

Ellram, L. M. (1991a). 'Supply Chain Management: The Industrial Organisation Perspective', *International Journal of Physical Distribution and Logistics Management*, 21 (1), pp. 13–22.

Ellram, L. M. (1991b). 'A Managerial Guideline for the Development and Implementation of Purchasing Partnerships', *International Journal of Purchasing and Materials Management*, Summer, pp. 2–8.

Ellram, L. M. and A. Carr (1994). 'Strategic Purchasing: A History and Review of the Literature', *International Journal of Purchasing and Materials Management*, Spring, pp. 10–18.

Farmer, D. H. and R. Ploos von Amstel (1991). *Effective Pipeline Management*. Gower, UK.

Fitzgerald, G. (1995). 'The Outsourcing of Information Technology: Revenge of the Business Manager or Legitimate Strategic Option?', Unpublished paper, Birkbeck College, University of London, UK.

Forrester, J. W. (1961). *Industrial Dynamics*. MIT Press, Boston, MA, USA.

Frazier, G. L., R. E. Spekman and C. R. O'Neal (1988). 'Just-in-Time Exchange Relationships in Industrial Markets', *Journal of Marketing*, 52 (October), pp. 52–67.

Gregory, R. E. (1986). 'Source Selection: A Matrix Approach', *Journal of Purchasing and Materials Management*, Summer.

Gronroos, C. (1990). *Service Management and Marketing*. Lexington Books, MA, USA.

Hakansson, H. (ed.) (1987). *Industrial Technological Development: A Network Approach*. Croom Helm, London, UK.

Hakansson, H. and I. Snehota (1995). *Developing Relationships in Business Networks*. Routledge, London, UK.

Harland, C. M. (1995a). 'The Dynamics of Customer Dissatisfaction in Supply Chains', *Production Planning and Control, Special Issue on Supply Chain Management*, 6 (3), May–June, pp. 209–217.

Harland, C. M. (1995b). 'Focus in Supply Chains', *Proceedings of 2nd International Symposium on Logistics*, Nottingham, July.

Harrigan, K. R. (1983). *Strategies for Vertical Integration*. Lexington, MA, USA.

Hayes, R. and S. C. Wheelwright (1984). *Restoring our Competitive Edge: Competing Through Manufacturing*. John Wiley, New York, USA.

Haywood-Farmer, J. and J. Nollet (1991). *Services Plus: Effective Service Management*. Morin, Boucherville, Quebec, Canada.

Hill, T. (1985). *Manufacturing Strategy*. Macmillan, London, UK.

Hines, P. (1994). *Creating World Class Suppliers: Unlocking Mutual and Competitive Advantage*. Pitman, London, UK.

Houlihan, J. (1984). 'Supply Chain Management', *Proceedings of 19th International Technical Conference*, BPICS, pp. 101–110.

Johnston, R., and P. R. Lawrence (1988). 'Beyond Vertical Integration: the Rise of Value Adding Partnerships', *Harvard Business Review*, July–August, pp. 94–101.

Jones, T. C. and D. W. Riley (1985). 'Using Inventory for Competitive Advantage Through Supply Chain Management', *International Journal of Physical Distribution and Materials Management*, 15 (5), pp. 16–26.

Kogut, B. (1985). 'Designing Global Strategies: Comparative and Competitive Value Added Chains', *Sloan Management Review*, Summer, pp. 15–28.

Lamming, R. (1989). 'The Causes and Effects of Structural Change in the European Automotive Components Industry', Working paper of the International Motor Vehicle Program. MIT, Cambridge, MA, USA.

Lamming, R. (1993). *Beyond Partnership: Strategies for Innovation and Lean Supply*. Prentice-Hall, Hemel Hempstead, UK.

Lascelles, D. M. and B. G. Dale (1989). 'The Buyer–Supplier Relationship in Total Quality Management', *Journal of Purchasing and Materials Management*, Summer, pp. 10–19.

Lee, L. and D. Dobler (1965). *Purchasing and Materials Management*. McGraw-Hill, New York, USA.

Lorenzoni, G. and O. Ornati (1988). 'Constellations of Firms and New Ventures', *Journal of Business Venturing*, 3, pp. 41–57.

Macbeth, D. K. and N. Ferguson (1994). *Partnership Sourcing: an Integrated Supply Chain Approach*. Pitman, London.

Marshall, A. (1923). *Industry and Trade*. Macmillan, London.

Miles, R. and C. Snow (1987). 'Network Organisations: New Concepts for New Forms', *California Management Review*, 28 (3), pp. 62–73.

Mitchell, J. C. (1969). 'The Concept and Use of Social Networks'. In: J. C. Mitchell (ed.), *Social Networks in Urban Situations*, pp. 1–50. Manchester University Press, Manchester.

Monczka, R. M. and S. J. Trencha (1988). 'Cost Based Supplier Performance Evaluation', *Journal of Purchasing and Materials Management*, Spring.

Morgan, I. (1987). 'The Purchasing Revolution', *McKinsey Quarterly*, Spring, pp. 49–55.

Nishiguchi, T. (1994). *Strategic Industrial Sourcing*, Oxford University Press, Oxford.

Oliver, R. K. and M. D. Webber (1982). 'Supply Chain Management: Logistics Catches Up With Strategy'. In: M. Christopher (1992). *Logistics: The Strategic Issues*, pp. 63–75. Chapman and Hall, London, UK.

Porter, M. E. (1985). *Competitive Advantage: Creating and Sustaining Superior Performance*. Free Press, New York, USA.

Porter, M. E. (1987). 'Managing Value – From Competitive Advantage to Corporate Strategy', *Harvard Business Review*, May–June.

Puto, C., W. Patton and R. King (1985). 'Risk Handling Strategies in Industrial Vendor Selection Decisions', *Journal of Marketing*, 49, Winter, pp. 89–98.

Richardson, G. B. (1972). 'The Organisation of Industry', *Economic Journal*, No. 82.

Sabel, C., G. Herrigel, R. Kazis and R. Deeg (1987). 'How to Keep Mature Industries Innovative', *Technology Review*, 90 (3), pp. 26–35.

Saunders, M. (1994). *Strategic Purchasing and Supply Chain Management*. Pitman, London, UK.

Schonberger, R. J. (1986). *World Class Manufacturing: The Lessons of Simplicity Applied*. Free Press, New York, USA.

Skinner, W. (1969). 'Manufacturing – Missing Link in Corporate Strategy', *Harvard Business Review*, May–June, pp. 136–145.

Slack, N. (1991). *The Manufacturing Advantage*. Mercury Business Books, London.

Smith, D. V., B. G. Lowe, D. H. Lyons and W. H. Old (1963). *The Development Project Committee on Standards for Vendor Evaluation*, National Association of Purchasing Agents, New York, USA.

Stalk, G. H. and T. M. Hout (1990). *Competing Against Time: How Time Based Competition is Reshaping Global Markets*. Free Press, New York, USA.

Stevens, G. C. (1989). 'Integrating the Supply Chain', *International Journal of Physical Distribution and Materials Management*, 19 (8), pp. 3–8.

Thackray, J. (1986). 'America's Vertical Cutback', *Management Today*, June.

Towill, D. (1991). 'Supply Chain Dynamics', *Computer Integrated Manufacturing*, 4 (4), pp. 197–208.

Womack, J. P., D. T. Jones and D. Roos (1990). *The Machine that Changed the World*. Macmillan International, New York, USA.

Zeithaml, V. A., A. Parasuraman and L. L. Berry (1990). *Delivering Quality Service: Balancing Customer Perceptions and Expectations*. Free Press, New York, USA.

Globalisation and Unequalisation: What Can Be Learned from Value Chain Analysis?

Raphael Kaplinsky

Introduction

For many of the world's population, the growing integration of the global economy has provided the opportunity for substantial income growth. This is reflected not only in higher incomes, but also in the improved availability of better quality and increasingly differentiated final products. However, at the same time, globalisation has had its dark side. There has been an increasing tendency towards growing unequalisation within and between countries and a stubborn incidence in the absolute levels of poverty, not just in poor countries. These positive and negative attributes of globalisation have been experienced at a number of different levels – the individual, the household, the firm, the town, the region, the sector and the nation. The distributional pattern emerging in recent decades of globalisation is thus simultaneously heterogeneous and complex.

If those who had lost from globalisation had been confined to the non-participants, the policy implications would be clear – take every step to be an active participant in global production and trade. However, the challenge is much more daunting than this, since the losers include many of those who have participated actively in the process of global integration. Hence, there is a need to manage the mode of insertion into the global economy, to ensure that incomes are not reduced or further polarised.

Three central questions arise from these observations. First, why has there been so little correspondence between the geographical spread of economic activity and the spreading of the gains from participating in global product markets?

Secondly, to what extent is it possible to identify a causal link between globalisation and inequality? And, thirdly, what can be done to arrest the unequalising tendencies of globalisation? These three related questions have important methodological implications – what is the best way to generate the information required to document these developments in production and appropriation, and how can we identify policy instruments which might halt and perhaps partially reverse these developments?

It is the central contention of this study that value chain analysis provides an important framework for addressing these crucial questions. In developing this argument, in the second section we will posit a causal relationship between increasing inequality and the global integration of production and trade. In the third section we outline the central elements of value chain analysis, show how it differs from conventional industry analysis, and suggest ways in which it augments the analysis of economics and other social sciences.

. . .

The study concludes by drawing conclusions for both future research and policy design and implementation.

Globalisation and Unequalisation

Globalisation is not a new phenomenon; it has ebbed and flowed over the past century. There are many measures of 'globalisation', none of which is free from imperfections. However, one indication of growing integration is the proportion of production which is traded; this has grown significantly in most parts of the global economy. At the same time, many indicators of inequality, within and between countries, have increased, and the absolute numbers of those living below $1 per day in 1985 purchasing parity prices have remained stubbornly large (at around 1.2 billion).[1]

One possible explanation for these rising levels of inequality is that globalisation has bypassed much of the world's population, particularly those living in poor countries. Perhaps, but more and more economic activity in virtually all countries is affected by the global interchange of goods and services (in addition to other components of globalisation). Moreover, many of those countries that have suffered in distributional terms have seen a substantial increase in their trade/GDP ratios. For example, the trade/GDP ratio for sub-Saharan Africa (SSA) rose from 51 to 56.1 per cent between 1985 and 1995, whilst its share of global output fell markedly (Kaplinsky, 2000a). So, the explanation for increased inequality will have to also explain how it is that countries and regions can increase their participation in global exchange and at the same time see a decline in their relative income shares (and also sometimes even in their absolute standards of living). For this reason, the focus of attention must also lie with the mode in which firms, countries and regions participate in the process of global production and exchange.

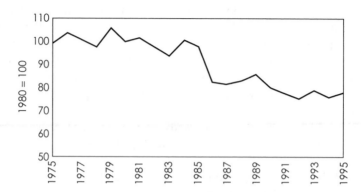

Figure 1 Price of developing country manufactured exports relative to developed country manufactured exports of machinery, transport equipment and services

An explanation for these declining country shares in global income in the context of growing participation in global markets can be found in the concentration of developing countries in commodity sectors. These have experienced declining terms of trade over a sustained period (Singer, 1950; Prebisch, 1950). This is indeed a problem still encountered in many developing countries, particularly in SSA. As a consequence, it has long been held that structural change should aim wherever possible to encompass the transition from the growing and extraction of primary commodities to the manufacture of industrial products. But, here, since the mid 1980s we have seen an emerging trend for the terms of trade of a range of manufac-tured commodities – particularly those produced by developing countries – to decline (Figure 1).[2] It is significant that this decline in the terms of trade of developing country manufacturing exports coincides with China's entry into global markets.[3]

The problem of falling returns confronts not only economies, but also individual firms. When firms confine their competences to the simple assembly of imported materials, they become subject to increasing competition and hence to falling returns. For example, in the Dominican Republic in the early 1990s, the assembly of jeans in export processing zones occurred in the context of intense regional competition (often surfacing in competitive devaluations), resulting in sustained falls in unit prices (Table 1).[4]

The consequence of the failure of individual firms, groups of firms and national economies to insert themselves appropriately into global markets is that the spectre is raised of *immiserising growth*. This describes a situation where there is increasing economic activity (more output and more employment) but falling economic returns. For example, over the past two decades Brazilian shoe producers have commanded more than 12 per cent of global leather shoe exports. At the same time, between 1970 and 1980 average real wages in the sector were stagnant, and during the following decade they fell by approximately 40 per cent in real terms (Schmitz, 1995). In the Dominican Republic, real wages (as measured in international purchasing

Table 1   Increasing competition and declining unit prices: the case of jeans manufacturing in the Dominican Republic

	Volume (per week)	Unit price ($)
January 1990	9,000	2.18
October 1990	5,000	2.05
December 1990	3,000	1.87
February 1991	Arrangement terminated and assembly transferred to Honduras	
Total investment in equipment by Dominican Republic firm was US$150,000		

Source: Kaplinsky, 1993

power) fell by 45 per cent during the second half of the 1990s, largely as a consequence of competitive devaluations in the region (Kaplinsky, 1993).[5]

Is it possible to determine those factors which drive the distribution of the gains from global production and exchange, explaining both why some parties have gained and others have lost from globalisation? Moreover, can we then use this analysis to identify policy levers – relevant at the level of individuals, households, firms, regions and countries – which may lead to a different and more favourable distributional outcome? The objective of this study is to show that value chain analysis has an important role to play in meeting these objectives.

The Contribution of Value Chain Analysis

Many factors associated with globalisation will affect the distribution of returns. For example, macro economic disturbances associated with capital mobility (and particularly capital volatility) can have major consequences for the living standards of many millions of people, as was the case following the Asian crisis of 1997 (Griffith-Jones and Cailloux, 1999). But, in so far as distribution is an outcome of the globalisation of production and exchange, value chain analysis provides a valuable methodological tool for explaining these developments.

What is a value chain?

The value chain describes the full range of activities which are required to bring a product or service from conception, through the intermediary phases of production (involving a combination of physical transformation and the input of various producer services), delivery to final consumers, and final disposal after use. Considered in its most elementary form, it takes the shape as described in Figure 2, although in reality value chains are considerably more extended than this. As can be seen from

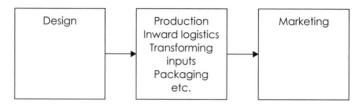

Figure 2   A simple value chain

this, production *per se* is only one of a number of value added links. Moreover, there is a range of activities within each link of the chain (only those for production are detailed in the figure).

The concept of the value chain was used in the 1960s and the 1970s by analysts charting a path of development for mineral-exporting economies (Girvan, 1987). It was also adopted in recent French planning literature in the form of the *filière*.[6] But during the 1990s, value chain analysis has become widely used, particularly as a consequence of the writings of Michael Porter (1985; 1990) and in an influential book by Womack and Jones (1996) (who refer to it as the 'value stream'). A further source of the recent prominence of the concept of the value chain, particularly in relation to developing countries, arises from the work of Gereffi, building on world system analysis. We shall consider this literature in more detail below.

Considered in this way, the value chain is merely a descriptive construct, at most providing a heuristic framework for the generation of data. However, recent developments of the value chain framework have begun to provide an analytical structure which, as we shall see below, provides important insights into our twin concerns with the determinants of global income distribution and the identification of effective policy levers to ameliorate trends towards unequalisation.[7] There are three important components of value chains which need to be recognised and which transform a heuristic device into an analytical tool:

- Value chains are repositories for rent, and these rents are dynamic.
- Effectively functioning value chains involve some degree of 'governance'.
- Effective value chains arise from systemic, as opposed to point, efficiency.

Three key elements of value chain analysis

Barriers to entry and rent   The theory of economic rent was first formulated by Ricardo, who distinguished between rent as a factor income – 'In popular language, the term is applied to whatever is annually paid by a farmer to his landlord' – and economic rent – 'Rent is that portion of the produce of the earth which is paid to the landlord for the use of the original and indestructible powers of the soil' (1817: 33). Here Ricardo was highlighting the significant role played by scarcity, since economic rent does not arise from the differential fertility of land itself (which was central to Ricardo's analysis), but from unequal access to this resource.[8]

But as Schumpeter showed, scarcity can be constructed. That is, it can arise from purposive actions rather than as a consequence of the bounty of nature. For Schumpeter, the entrepreneur played a unique role in 'the carrying out of new combinations' (1961: 107). Entrepreneurial surplus is the return to the innovation of a 'new combination' and arises when the price of the product following the introduction of the 'new combination' provides greater returns than are required to meet the cost of the innovation. These returns to innovation are a form of super-profit and act as an inducement to replication by other entrepreneurs:

Thus, in summary:

- Economic rent arises in the case of differential productivity of factors (including entrepreneurship) *and* barriers to entry (that is, scarcity).
- Economic rent may arise not just from natural bounty, but also as producer surpluses that are created by purposive action.[9] These augmented rents have become increasingly important since the rise of technological intensity in the mid nineteenth century (Freeman, 1976) and the growth of differentiated products after the 1970s (Piore and Sabel, 1984).
- Most economic rent is dynamic in nature, eroded by the forces of competition. Producer rent is then transferred into consumer surplus through the process of competition.
- The process of competition – the search for 'new combinations' to allow entrepreneurs to escape the tyranny of the normal rate of profit, and the subsequent bidding away of this economic rent by competitors – fuels the innovation process which drives capitalism forward.

As more and more countries have developed their capabilities in industrial activities, so barriers to entry in production have fallen and the competitive pressures have heightened (Figure 3). This has become particularly apparent since China, with its abundant supplies of educated labour, entered the world market in the mid 1980s.[10] It is this, too, which underlies the falling terms of trade in manufactures of developing countries (see above). Consequently, the primary economic rents in the chain of production are increasingly to be found in areas outside of production.

Governance   A second consideration which helps to transform the value chain from a heuristic to an analytical concept is that the various activities in the chain – within firms and in the division of labour between firms – are subject to what Gereffi (1994) has usefully termed 'governance'. That is, there are key actors in the chain who take responsibility for the inter-firm division of labour, and for the capacities of particular participants to upgrade their activities.

Why is this important? It is because of the nature rather than the extent of trade in the recent era of globalisation. For many countries the trade/GDP shares in the late nineteenth/early twentieth century and the late twentieth century were not dissimilar. The key difference is that in the earlier period this trade was largely in arm's-length relationships, with final products being largely manufactured in a particular country and then exported. By contrast, in the latter period, trade was

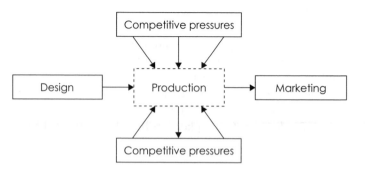

Figure 3 Competitive pressures in the value chain

increasingly in sub-components and services and was consequently considerably more complex (Feenstra, 1998; Hummels et al., 1999). (This contrast allows us to make the useful distinction between what might be called 'internationalisation' in the late nineteenth century and 'globalisation' in the late twentieth century.) The intricacy and complexity of trade in the globalisation era require sophisticated forms of co-ordination, not merely with respect to logistics (who ships what, where and when), but also in relation to the integration of components into the design of the final products and the quality standards with which this integration is achieved. It is this role of coordination, and the complementary role of identifying dynamic rent oppor-tunities and apportioning roles to key players, which reflect the act of governance.

This concept of governance – and the distinction between different types of chains – is a major contribution to our understanding of the workings of value chains. What it does is to throw light on those factors determining the nature of the insertion of different producers into the global division of labour. For, as we observed above, it is not just a matter of whether producers participate in the global economy which determines their returns to production, but how and on what terms they do so.

Extending Gereffi's (1994) concept, it is possible to distinguish three forms of governance, based on principles of civic governance. The basic rules which define the conditions for participation in the chain need to be set. This can be termed *legislative governance*. It is also necessary to audit performance and to check compli-ance with these rules – this can be seen as *judicial governance*. However in order to meet these rules of participation, there needs to be some form of proactive govern-ance (which might be termed *executive governance*) which provides assistance to value chain participants in meeting these operating rules. Much of the existing discussion of governance fails to recognise this threefold distinction, which is one of the reasons why there is often confusion about which party actually governs a particular value chain and a reluctance to recognise that different parties may engage in different forms of governance in the same chain. As Table 2 shows, these governance roles may be provided from within, or from without, the chain.

Building on this concept of governance, Gereffi (1994) has made the very useful distinction between two types of value chains. The first describes those chains where

Table 2 Examples of legislative, judicial and executive value chain governance

	Exercised by parties internal to chain	Exercised by parties external to chain
Legislative governance	Setting standards for suppliers in relation to on-time deliveries, frequency of deliveries and quality	Environmental standards Child labour standards
Judicial governance	Monitoring the performance of suppliers in meeting these standards	Monitoring of labour standards by NGOs Specialised firms monitoring conformance to ISO standards
Executive governance	Supply chain management assisting suppliers to meet these standards Producer associations assisting members to meet these standards	Specialised service providers Government industrial policy support

the critical governing role is played by a buyer. *Buyer-driven chains* are characteristic of labour-intensive industries (and therefore highly relevant to developing countries) such as footwear, clothing, furniture and toys. The second describes a world where key producers in the chain, generally commanding vital technologies, play the role of coordinating the various links – *producer-driven chains*. Here producers take responsibility for assisting the efficiency of both their suppliers and their customers. In more recent work, Gereffi (1999a) has pointed out that producer-driven chains are more likely to be characterised by FDI (foreign direct investment) than are buyer-driven chains. Governance in individual chains often arises from multiple sources and is frequently contested; moreover, as the sources of rent change, so does the focus of governance activities.

Systemic efficiency A third analytical element of value chain analysis is that it moves the focus of attention from 'point' to 'systemic' (that is, value chain) efficiency. Why might this be important? A useful example can be drawn from the strategic restructuring of one of Europe's major retailers. Tesco has achieved a significant growth in its market share and profitability from its ability to slim down its own inventories, ensuring a process of just-in-time deliveries from its own warehouses and those of key suppliers to its retail stores. But it has increasingly come to realise that these activities account for only a thin share of the product's total value added and, unless it 'governs' its chain to achieve broader levels of systemic integration, little more could be done to achieve competitive advantage. For example, in an exercise designed to identify areas of wasted activity in the value chain of a particular product, an analysis of the value added activities involved in the production and cooling of a tin of cola was undertaken. This revealed that in an optimum situation it would take a total minimum time of three hours to produce the complete product. Yet in reality, the actual elapsed time in this process was 319 days, leading to a significant cost in working capital throughout the chain (Womack and Jones, 1996). Tesco has thus begun to put significant resources into trying to improve efficiency throughout the chain, since it has come to realise that the activities which it is directly responsible for in its internal operations account for only a small share of total product costs.

As value chains become increasingly disarticulated and subject to a finer and finer division of labour – an inevitable process given the increasing knowledge content of production – so the ability to make an impact on competitiveness by improving the efficiency of individual links in the chain has become increasingly limited. Systemic integration involves closer cooperation between links in the chain, and this often involves enhanced responsibilities for governors, as well as the growth of greater levels of trust between different links in the chain. Perhaps most importantly from our perspective, value chains increasingly span national boundaries, and governors therefore are also forced to learn how to upgrade producers in low income countries.

How do these three analytical characteristics of value chains relate to our concerns with spreading the gains from globalisation?

These three analytical elements – dynamic rents, governorship and systemic efficiency gains – are closely linked. The central driver is the prevalence of competition which forces down profits by lowering barriers to entry, and which increases as producers in more and more countries enter global trade.[11] This induces participants through-out the chain to search for new forms of rent. In achieving this, the more powerful actors in the chain are increasingly required to induce (and assist) their suppliers and customers to change their own operating procedures. At the same time they continually search for new suppliers (systematically striving to lower barriers to entry in other links in the chain) and customers. These objectives require them to act as value chain governors, although to varying degrees. The resulting growth in the social division of labour requires that these governors act over an increasingly large geographical and institutional terrain to search for systemic efficiency.

We observed earlier that as this global spread of activities has increased, so the inter-country distribution of income has become more complex and generally has worsened. How are these phenomena linked? First, barriers to entry are the determinants of the distribution of rents. That is, they determine who gains and who loses in the chain of production. Those who command rents, and have the ability to create new domains of rent when barriers to entry fall, are the beneficiaries. By contrast, those who are stuck in activities with low barriers to entry lose, and in a world of increasing competition, the extent of these losses will increase over time. Secondly, the growing areas of rent are increasingly found in the intangible parts of the value chain. A distinct development over the past decade has seen the barriers to entry in manufacturing – formerly a key scarce capability lodged predominantly in the industrially advanced countries – begin to fall. More and more countries, with lower and lower wage costs (especially China and India), have developed the capacity to reliably transform physical inputs into high quality physical outputs at a low cost. It is this which explains the diminishing terms of trade of developing countries' exports of manufactures observed above. At the same time, copyright and brand names have a very long life (more than 70 years for the former and in perpetuity for the latter), and these represent 'absolute and immutable' forms of economic rent. It is not surprising, therefore, that the high income countries in general (and the US in particular) have placed so much emphasis on intellectual property rights in recent years. Similarly, as value chains become increasingly complex and subject to coordination, the rent accruing from governorship itself – a particular form of relational rent (Kaplinsky, 1998) – has grown.

All of this affects the inter-country distribution of income. But participation in global value chains also affects the intra-country distribution of income. This is because the requirements of final product markets in high income markets invariably require capabilities which are outside of the reach of poor people and poor farms and enterprises (often SMEs (small to medium enterprises)). These demands tend to be more exacting in 'governed value chains' than in arm's-length trade. Consequently, small farms and firms and those people reliant for their incomes from smallholdings and small enterprises may suffer, and those locked into large farm production may gain.

How does value chain analysis differ from conventional industry studies and from what social scientists (and especially economists) normally do?[12]

Traditionally, the focus on productive activities and the insertion of local producers into global markets has been on the economic branch and the economic sector. Developing countries have been seen to have a potential comparative advantage in the primary branch, and the industrial countries in secondary economic activities and value added traded services. Within the industrial branch, the focus has most often been on individual sectors (based on ISIC (International Standard Industrial Classification) or SITC/HS classifications) such as clothing, shoes, chemicals, electronics and food processing, and in a national context. Hence, the analysis has tended to focus on the size and growth of the sector in terms of employees and gross output (rather than net value added), trade performance and the size distribution of firms.

Value chain analysis throws more light on the determinants of income distribution, both within and between countries, and especially over time than this traditional industry analysis. For example:

- Because it focuses on the dynamics of rent, a value chain perspective forces the analysis to transcend economic branches and sectors. For example, in the forestry and furniture chain, the rent-rich activities are increasingly found in the genetics of seed design and in the design and branding of the furniture, rather than in the individual agricultural, industrial or service sub-sectors (which tend to be the

domain of traditional branch and sectoral analyses). It is only through a comprehensive view of the whole chain *that the links in the chain or segments in
product markets which are characterised by high or growing rent* can be identified.

- Related to this, value chain analysis makes it possible to trace through a particular thread of *rent-rich activities* which are not easily captured by branch and
  industry analysis. For example, we have observed that intangible knowledge is
  increasingly characterised by high barriers to entry, and that the owners of this
  knowledge gain most from the globalisation of production and exchange.
  Similarly, in addition to imposing barriers to entry, governance may itself often
  be subject to significant barriers to entry and hence provide high returns. This
  being the case, the ability to identify rent-rich activities along the whole chain of
  added value provides the key to understanding the global appropriation of the
  returns to production.

- The *data* which are characteristically generated in most branch and sectoral
  analyses make it difficult to interpret the significance of key indicators such as
  'output', 'sales' and 'costs'. Consequently the determinants of income distribution
  are difficult to unravel. Trade statistics are especially problematic here, since they
  provide little capacity to unpick value added. For example, in the late 1980s, the
  Dominican Republic saw a significant increase in the gross value of shoe output
  and exports. But 'shoe production' occurred in EPZs utilising imported inputs –
  the unit value of a shoe export was a mere $0.23. By contrast unit shoe exports
  from Italy may more fully reflect value added. In what senses, then, may the
  shoe sectors in these two countries be compared unless a value chain analysis
  – incorporating a more sophisticated mapping of input–output relationships –
  is utilised?

- The dynamic nature of rents generated in the global activities of a value chain
  are *obscured by a focus on national industries*. For example, when production
  occurs in the context of falling global product prices, national accounting
  systems may reflect a growth in activity and value which does not correspond
  with the international purchasing power of this sectoral activity. The problem is particularly acute when decisions about *national* resource allocation –
  affecting income streams over time – are made without reference to the *global*
  dynamics of returns to different activities in the chain. Thus it is the global focus
  of value chain analysis that more accurately identifies suitable opportunities to
  augment incomes in a national context than the national focus of industry
  studies.

- Studies of market structure which fail to locate the analysis within a value
  chain perspective are not able to adequately explain the *determinants of firm-size
  distribution*. For example, the high concentration of ownership in the South
  African furniture industry does not arise from market conduct within the furniture
  sector. Instead, it is explained by high levels of concentration in the retail sector,
  which in turn is linked to concentration in financial intermediation (Kaplinsky
  and Manning, 1998). Similar observations have been made with respect to the
  footwear industry, but in this case the inter-sectoral linkages which are involved
  span national boundaries (Schmitz and Knorringa, 2000).[13]

So much for the content of research enquiry. But what of the implications for disciplinary focus?

- Because value chain enquiry spans different economic branches and sectors, effective analysis requires the participation of different disciplines. This is most clearly the case in relation to the focus on agricultural and manufacturing production systems, but the focus on the dynamics of rent also requires inputs from management studies and engineering. Moreover, since power is a key component of governance, and trust is critical to enhanced inter-firm cooperation and new forms of work organisation, there is a simultaneous need to draw on the insights of political science and sociology. It is for this reason that Wood reflects that value chain analysis provides 'a *meeting ground* for economics, business administration and industrial sociology in the study of one important aspect of globalisation, namely the simultaneous economic integration of countries, and disintegration of production processes' (1999: 24, emphasis added).

- A number of challenges are posed to much of traditional *economic analysis*. The Heckscher–Ohlin factor-price equalisation theorem predicts that in an open economy, factor returns such as wages will tend to converge across (and within some) national boundaries. Yet, this is often not the case, in part due to the falling costs of mobility as highly skilled workers, operating within coordinated value chains, interact with skilled and unskilled workers in different economies (Wood, 1999). The ability to identify and capture the role played by these mobile skills is significantly enhanced when analysis occurs through the lens of the value chain. Much economic analysis of income distribution also tends to focus on the individual as the unit of account, and it is certainly the case that incomes do accrue to individual people as holders of assets (for example, skills and equity). Yet, while individuals may receive incomes, these returns are defined by their participation in institutions (that is, firms) which systematically pursue policies designed to enhance these incomes by constructing barriers to entry against competition. Understanding the processes whereby barriers to entry are constructed takes the analysis beyond the domain of much of economic analysis which treats technological progress as exogenous, and fails to recognise the ability of firms to construct the competitive environment in which they operate (rather than acting as price-takers). Moreover, an understanding of the nature and importance of trust in inter-firm relationships within the value chain requires economists to also engage with the contingency and sociology of the determinants of social capital.

- In a similar way, other disciplines are also forced to rethink their analytical frameworks by a focus on value chains. Wood (1999) argues that economics not only provides an accounting framework in which value chains can be mapped, but also forces the enquiry to focus on the economic determinants of location, notably on cost structures. Thus, a (complementary) division of labour can be characterised as one in which economists determine the basis of *comparative advantage* (that is, the potential which different environments provide for reaping economic rents), and other disciplines identify the determinants of *competitive advantage* (the factors which explain why some firms are able to appropriate these economic rents).

Do these attributes of value chain analysis improve the policy relevance of research? Our primary conclusion is that this analytic framework provides the potential for identifying those policy actions – by both private and public actors – which may influence distributional outcomes. We will return to this in the concluding discussion below, but four observations can be made at this stage:

- As we have seen, value chain analysis covers a range of interconnected economic activities, spanning branches and sectors, and thus provides the potential for coordinating what might be termed '*joined-up policies*' between different arms of government.
- By focusing on the institutional determinants of rent, value chain analysis points policy towards instruments which influence the behaviour *of individuals grouped within firms and other organisations* which shape the distribution of returns from production and exchange. Thus, the key to sustaining the growth and spread of incomes lies in the ability to influence the behaviour of groups of people acting in concert, rather than that of individuals who benefit from these joint activities.
- By focusing on the dynamics of rent, value chain analysis points policy towards the *development of those capabilities and institutional trajectories* that can sustain incomes over time.
- Realising systemic value chain efficiency requires inputs from a range of institutions that are not direct participants in the chain themselves, for example producer service providers, scientific institutions and the education sector. This directs the focus of policy attention to the strengthening of the national system of innovation (Lundvall, 1992).

These are strong assertions which make powerful claims for the primacy of value chain analysis. But can these assertions be borne out in practice? The findings of our research into a series of selected value chains provide support for these claims.

. . .

Conclusions

The objective of this study is to illustrate how value chain analysis can contribute to a better understanding of the determinants of inter- and intra-country income distribution, and consequently also to the identification of policies which might improve the distributional outcome of countries' insertion into the global economy. We have argued that a focus on three elements of value chains – the dynamics of rents within the chain, the governance of the chains and their transnational systemic character – is necessary to turn a heuristic construct into an analytical tool.

Our work illustrates the way in which value chains – understood in their analytical sense – can explain why some parties gain and some lose from the globalisation of production and exchange. They consequently contribute to an explanation, rooted in production and exchange (rather than in finance or other spheres of globalisation), of why the growing global spread of economic activity has not been associated with an equivalent spreading of the gains from this economic activity.

But can value chain analysis tell us about the policies which are required to reverse these malign outcomes? Here, two key insights are provided by value chain analysis. First, global production networks are becoming increasingly complex and arm's-length trade is increasingly being confined to commodities with low returns. Access to high income yielding activities therefore requires participating in global value chains. The key challenges are thus to identify ways in which poor countries and poor producers can both enter these chains, and participate in ways which lead to sustainable income growth. Secondly, the analysis of governance relations which permeate value chains leads to the identification of the major institutional actors. This provides insights into policy levers which might influence the behaviour of key stakeholders in the value chain.

Value chains are not homogeneous, and the opportunities for rent appropriation by different parties will vary. Essentially, however, when threatened by competition, there are four directions in which *economic actors* can move, and these paths are not mutually exclusive:

- increasing the efficiency of internal operations such that these are significantly better than those of rivals;
- enhancing inter-firm linkages to a greater degree than that achieved by competitors;
- introducing new products or improving old products faster than rivals;
- changing the mix of activities conducted within the firm or moving the locus of activities to different links in the chain, for example from manufacturing to design.

Our analysis of fruit and automotive value chains suggests that on their own, the first two steps are unlikely to realise a greater share of value chain returns. This is because these capabilities are increasingly widely diffused through the global economy (underlying the falling terms of trade of developing countries' trade in manufactures observed earlier) and concentration in these areas (particularly in intra-firm efficiency) may well lead to immiserising growth. In other words, they are generally only the necessary conditions for an enhanced spreading of the gains from participating in global markets. It is the third and fourth steps that are likely to provide the greatest results. But here, poor producers and producers in poor countries run up against relations of power, embedded in value chain governance (Table 3). These are highly protected domains, precisely because they are repositories of economic rent. As Schmitz and Knorringa (2000) observe with regard to the footwear value chain, the global buyers who dominate this chain are happy to assist developing country producers in the first three of these policy alternatives, but zealously exclude them from the fourth.

The fact that the move into other links in the chain is difficult does not reduce the necessity for action, since in almost all value chains this is clearly the optimal route.

Table 3 Scope for actions to promote the spreading of gains to low income producers

	Upgrade within link	Upgrade relationship between firms	Redefining activities undertaken within links	Move to new links in the chain
Canned deciduous fruit	Special assistance needed for small growers	Need to improve vertical and horizontal cooperation, especially in relation to participation by SMEs	Little scope for additional action	May be possible to build global or regional brand names
Automobile components	Special assistance needed for SMEs	Supply chain efficiency and learning are critical, especially in relation to participation by SMEs	Possible for first-tier suppliers mainly, but few in low income countries	Difficult as buyers block move into design

It also does not mean that firms should always pursue this path at the expense of upgrading their internal operations, improving their links with other parts of the domestic chain or increasing the range of activities or repositioning themselves within the link in which they already operate. In each of the four cases, there is scope for pursuing multiple objectives.

It is likely that the same conclusion will apply to many other value chains in which poor countries operate. In some cases, the judgement may be that barriers to entry are so low throughout the chain that it will never support acceptable levels of income. This, for example, may be the case in CDF (Children's Defense Fund), where producer surpluses are systematically channelled into consumer surpluses through the competitive process and where, over time, the returns to production are whittled away in 'a race to the bottom'.

So much for the policy response from the corporate sector. But, *what can governments do?* Governments have a number of key roles to play. First, they can proactively assist the private sector, workers' organisations and other stakeholders to recognise the opportunities and threats posed by participating in global value chains. Secondly, measures can be taken to assist producers to enter these chains. Thirdly, various policy instruments can be used to support the repositioning of the corporate sector within value chains so that they can derive a greater share of the gains. (This occurred in the UK through the Enterprise Initiative Programme during the 1980s, for example.) Support can be provided for the enhancement of design skills, as the Spanish government showed with regard to the clothing and footwear industries in the same decade, and as local government does in Brazil for footwear (Schmitz, 1999).

But, fourthly, producer rents are not the only form of economic rent which may bolster the returns accruing to poor countries and poor producers (Kaplinsky, 1998). Producers require relatively good access to a range of complementary assets. For example, as Wood and Jordan (2000) show for Uganda, physical infrastructure is an important determinant of participating in global product markets, particularly in the manufacturing sector. In the past this meant relatively good roads, railways and ports but increasingly it also applies to telecommunications. Other forms of rent where government has a role to play include financial intermediation (relatively smooth access by producers to adequate levels of productive capital, which may or may not be provided by 'efficiently functioning financial markets') and human resource rents (access to relatively skilled workers at relatively low wages). Critically, it also includes trade policy rents, where the government either negotiates trade policy privileges, or acts to erode the privileges open to other producers. It is also important that governments help their producers – especially poor producers – to take advantage of trade policy rents, since in many cases low income countries do not fill their quotas or benefit from preferential tariffs in high income markets.

Value chain analysis is crucial to this joined-up policy support because it enables governments to focus on the dynamics of rent, on the pervasive and complex nature of support which is required to build institutions, and on managing the integration of individual sectors (and of the whole economy) into the global economy in a manner which provides for sustainable and equitable income growth.

. . .

Increasing inequalities are not just being experienced at the inter-country level, but also with regard to intranational distribution, affecting different regions, different sized firms, different households and different genders. But here, too, value chain analysis has a role to play, particularly in regard to those production structures which involve international exchange. What it does do is illustrate how critical success factors in external markets, allied to governance structures within individual chains, circumscribe the role played by domestic actors. Our studies show the implications which this has for SMEs in the South African furniture industry (and for small farms in fresh fruit and vegetables: Dolan and Humphrey, 2000), but this is an underexplored issue, particularly with regard to gender and household distributional factors.

In summary, it is not so much that value chain analysis tells us anything new, for most of these policy responses have found their way into corporate and government decision-making in many chains and in many sectors. But what it does do is to provide a comprehensive framework for a 'joined-up' series of responses by a range of stakeholders which forces us into a wider, dynamic and more strategic consideration of these issues. Partial analysis and partial responses are likely to be severely suboptimal in meeting the challenges which are posed, particularly in relation to medium and long run positioning of poor producers and poor countries. To return to the beginning of this paper, positioning and path dependency are critical since participation in the global economy in itself may not provide a path to sustainable income growth or to an equitable distribution of returns.

NOTES

1 For data on the simultaneous advance of global integration of production and exchange, as well as various indicators of inequality, see Kaplinsky (2000a).

2 The falling manufacturing terms of trade of developing countries were hypothesised in the early 1970s by Hans Singer (1971). A recent study of the barter terms of trade in manufactures between developing countries and the European Union estimates an annual rate of depreciation of 2.2 per cent between 1979 and 1994 (Maizels et al., 1998). A further study, on the terms of trade in manufactures between the US and developing countries for the period 1981–97, concludes that 'Over the whole period, the relative terms of trade trend of developing countries, compared with that of developed countries, has significantly worsened' (Maizels et al., 1999: 23). It is significant that neither of these recent studies reflects the fall in developing country manufactured export prices following the East Asian crisis of 1997–98.

3 For data on China's rapidly growing share of global markets in labour-intensive products, see Kaplinsky (2000b).

4 The ability of Dominican Republic firms to upgrade was constrained by the terms of the Caribbean Trade Initiative which limited their capacity to utilise local textile inputs (Kaplinsky, 1993).

5 An extended discussion of immiserising growth needs to take account of the purchasing power parity of incomes, whether falling barter terms of trade are associated with falling income terms of trade, and of the opportunity costs of exporting activities in the context of falling barter terms of trade. Some of these issues are discussed further in Kaplinsky and Readman (2000).

6 Literally, the word *filière* means 'thread'. It was first used in the 1960s in the analysis of agricultural policy in the French colonies, and then in the late 1970s and early 1980s to describe the perceived need for French industrial capability to span the complete thread of a value chain (Kydd et al., 1996, cited in Raikes et al., 2000).

7 Unfortunately, the phrase 'value chain' covers both the heuristic and analytical categories. This has led some to search for a different nomenclature. For example, Gereffi (1994) coined the phrase 'global commodity chain' (GCC) and in a recent contribution argues that the GCC is distinct in that it incorporates an international dimension, that it focuses on power of lead firms and the coordination of global activities, and that it explicitly recognises the importance of organisational learning (Gereffi, 1999b). These are proximate to the three characteristics addressed in this paper. But, although representing a major contribution to our thinking on global production networks, the *phrase* 'global commodity chain' suffers because the word 'commodity' implies the production of undifferentiated products in processes with low barriers to entry. The problem with this is that the search for sustainable income growth requires producers to position themselves precisely in non-commodity, high barriers to entry activities in the value chain. For these reasons, and in the absence of an agreed phraseology, we will continue to use the words 'value chain', but to do so in an analytical context.

8 For a longer discussion of economic rent see Kaplinsky (1998).

9 Although monopoly rent (as defined by the rent-seeking literature) also arises as a result of purposive action, it is usefully distinguished from various forms of innovation rents that reflect the search for new combinations in the pursuit of entrepreneurial surplus.

10 The share of manufacturing in Chinese exports rose from 49.4 per cent in 1985 to 85.6 per cent in 1995 (Khan, 1999).

11 I am grateful to Hubert Schmitz for pointing out this quote: 'The GCC approach explains the distribution of wealth within a chain as an outcome of the relative intensity of competition within different nodes' (Gereffi et al., 1994: 4).

12 This discussion has been helpfully informed by memos prepared for the Spreading the Gains from Globalisation research network by Gereffi et al. (2000) and Wood (1999).

13 As a consequence, the growing concentration in the Italian, Spanish and Greek retail sectors is likely to undermine the historic strength of the SME sectors in these countries.

REFERENCES

Dolan, C. and J. Humphrey, 2000, 'Governance and Trade in Fresh Vegetables: The Impact of UK Supermarkets on the African Horticulture Industry', *Journal of Development Studies*, Vol. 27, No. 2.

Feenstra, R.C., 1998, 'Integration of Trade and Disintegration of Production in the Global Economy', *Journal of Economic Perspectives*, Vol. 12, No. 4, pp. 31–50.

Freeman, C., 1976, *The Economics of Industrial Innovation*, London: Penguin Books.

Gereffi, G., 1994, 'The Organization of Buyer-Driven Global Commodity Chains: How U.S. Retailers Shape Overseas Production Networks', in Gereffi and Korzeniewicz (eds.) (1994).

Gereffi, G., 1999a, 'International Trade and Industrial Upgrading in the Apparel Commodity Chain', *Journal of International Economics*, Vol. 48, No. 1, pp. 37–70.

Gereffi, G., 1999b, 'A Commodity Chains Framework for Analysing Global Industries', in Institute of Development Studies (1999).

Gereffi, G. and M. Korzeniewicz (eds.), 1994, *Commodity Chains and Global Capitalism*, London: Praeger.

Gereffi, G., Korzeniewicz, M. and R.P. Korzeniewicz, 1994, 'Introduction', in Gereffi and Korzeniewicz (eds.) (1994).

Gereffi, G., Humphrey, J. and T. Sturgeon, 2000, 'Proposal for Value Chain Meeting', mimeo, Institute of Development Studies, University of Sussex, Brighton.

Girvan, N., 1987, 'Transnational Corporations and Non-Fuel Primary Commodities in Developing Countries', *World Development*, Vol. 15, No. 3, pp. 713–40.

Griffith-Jones, S. and J. Cailloux, 1999, 'Global Capital Flows to East Asia, Surges and Reversals', *Paper Presented to Workshop on Global Capital Flows*, Institute of Development Studies, Brighton.

Hummels, D., Jun Ishii and Kei-Mu Yi, 1999, 'The Nature and Growth of Vertical Specialization in World Trade', *Staff Reports Number 72*, New York: Federal Reserve Bank of New York.

Institute of Development Studies, 1999, 'Background Notes for Workshop on Spreading the Gains from Globalisation', www.ids.ac.uk/ids/global/conf/wkscf.html.

Kaplinsky, R., 1993, 'Export Processing Zones in the Dominican Republic: Transforming Manufactures into Commodities', *World Development*, Vol. 22, No. 3, pp. 1851–65.

Kaplinsky, R., 1998, 'Globalisation, Industrialisation and Sustainable Growth: The Pursuit of the Nth Rent', *Discussion Paper 365*, Brighton: Institute of Development Studies, University of Sussex.

Kaplinsky, R., 2000a, 'Spreading the Gains from Globalisation: What Can Be Learned from Value Chain Analysis?', *Working Paper No. 110*, Brighton: Institute of Development Studies, University of Sussex.

Kaplinsky, R., 2000b, 'Is Globalisation All It Is Really Cracked Up to Be?', *Journal of International Political Economy*, forthcoming.

Kaplinsky, R. and C. Manning, 1998, 'Concentration, Competition Policy and the Role of Small and Medium Sized Enterprises in South Africa's Industrial Development', *The Journal of Development Studies*, Vol. 35, No. 1, pp. 139–61.

Kaplinsky, R. and J. Readman, 2000, 'Globalisation and Upgrading: What Can (and Cannot) Be Learnt from International Trade Statistics in the Wood Furniture Sector?', mimeo, Brighton, Centre for Research in Innovation Management, University of Brighton and Institute of Development Studies, University of Sussex.

Khan, A.R., 1999, 'Poverty in China in the Period of Globalization: New Evidence on Trend and Pattern', *Issues in Development Discussion Paper 22*, Geneva: ILO.

Lundvall, B.A., 1992, *National Systems of Innovation*, London: Frances Pinter.

Maizels, A., Berge, K., Crowe, T. and T.B. Palaskas, 1998, 'Trends in the Manufactures Terms of Trade of Developing Countries', mimeo, Oxford: Finance and Trade Policy Centre, Queen Elizabeth House.

Maizels, A., Berge, K., Crowe, T. and T.B. Palaskas, 1999, 'The Manufactures Terms of Trade of Developing Countries with the United States, 1981–97', mimeo, Oxford: Finance and Trade Policy Centre, Queen Elizabeth House.

Piore, M.J. and C. Sabel, 1984, *The Second Industrial Divide: Possibilities for Prosperity*, New York: Basic Books.

Porter, M.E., 1985, *Competitive Advantage: Creating and Sustaining Superior Performance*, New York: The Free Press.

Porter, M.E., 1990, *The Competitive Advantage of Nations*, London: Macmillan.

Prebisch, R., 1950, *The Economic Development of Latin America and Its Principal Problems*, New York: ECLA, UN Department of Economic Affairs.

Raikes, P., Friis-Jensen, M. and S. Ponte, 2000, 'Global Commodity Chain Analysis and the French Filière Approach', *Economy and Society*, forthcoming.

Ricardo, D., 1817, *The Principles of Political Economy and Taxation*, London: Dent (reprinted 1973).

Schmitz, H., 1995, 'Small Shoemakers and Fordist Giants: Tales of a Supercluster', *World Development*, Vol. 23, No. 1, pp. 9–28.

Schmitz, H., 1999, 'From Ascribed to Earned Trust in Exporting Clusters', *Journal of International Economics*, Vol. 48, No. 1, pp. 139–50.

Schmitz, H. and P. Knorringa, 2000, 'Learning from Global Buyers', *Journal of Development Studies*, Vol. 37, No. 2.

Schumpeter, J., 1961, *The Theory of Economic Development*, Oxford: Oxford University Press.

Singer, H., 1950, 'The Distribution of Gains Between Borrowing and Investing Countries', *American Economic Review*, Vol. 40, pp. 473–85.

Singer, H., 1971, 'The Distribution of Gains Revisited', reprinted in A. Cairncross and M. Puri (eds.), *The Strategy of International Development*, London: Macmillan (1975).

Womack, J.P. and D.T. Jones, 1996, *Lean Thinking: Banish Waste and Create Wealth in Your Corporation*, New York: Simon & Schuster.

Wood, A., 1997, 'Openness and Wage Inequality in Developing Countries: The Latin American Challenge to East Asian Conventional Wisdom', *World Bank Economic Review*, Vol. 11, No. 1, pp. 33–57.

Wood, A., 1999, 'Value Chains: An Economist's Perspective', in Institute of Development Studies [1999].

Wood, A. and K. Jordan, 2000, 'Why Does Zimbabwe Export Manufactures and Uganda Not? Econometrics Meets History', *Journal of Development Studies*, Vol. 37, No. 2.

Lean Production and the Toyota Production System – Or, the Case of the Forgotten Production Concepts

Ian Hampson

Introduction

From the late 1980s, debate around work organization converged on the concept of 'lean production' which was, according to its advocates, a 'post-Fordist' system of work that is at once supremely efficient and yet 'humane', even democratic (Kenney and Florida, 1988: 122; Adler, 1993; Mathews, 1991: 9, 21; 1988: 20, 23). However, critical research found that, rather than being liberating, lean production can actually intensify work to the point where worker stress becomes a serious problem, because it generates constant improvements (*kaizen*) by applying stress and fixing the breakdowns that result. It thus attracted such descriptions as 'management by stress', 'management by blame', 'management by fear' (Parker and Slaughter, 1988; Sewell and Wilkinson, 1992; Dohse et al., 1985).

Ironically, at the same time as lean production was becoming the latest fad in the West, there was an urgent debate in Japan about the quality of work (Berggren, 1995; Benders, 1996). The phenomenon of *karoshi* – death from overwork – was seen as evidence of the way the pursuit of 'leanness' stressed workers, causing highly deleterious social consequences (NDCVK, 1991; Kato, 1994; Nishiyama and Johnson, 1997). The normally pliant Japan Auto Workers' Union produced a report critical of working conditions in the national vehicle assembly industry (Sandberg, 1995: 23). As a result of this and other factors, some key Japanese auto producers retreated from 'leanness', and set up exemplary models of work that were interesting hybrids of the Toyota production system and 'humanized' work principles (Benders, 1996; Shimizu, 1995; Berggren, 1995). Critical researchers have also suggested that the way forward for the organization of work might be to combine elements of lean production with principles of 'humanized work' (Berggren, 1992: 16, 232, Ch. 13; Sandberg, 1995: 2). Such combinations are conceivable, and the Japanese experiments question the assumed identity between 'lean production' and the Toyota production system.

This article argues that the focus on 'leanness' by critics and advocates alike has distracted the gaze of researchers from certain 'anti-lean' concepts contained within Toyota production system theory and practice. The article also suggests that the degree of 'leanness' in particular plants is shaped by surrounding institutional frameworks. Management strategy will seek to move down the lean path ('doing more with less'), while conditions in the labour market, industrial relations and the resources of affected unions may limit leanness. The first section surveys the dominant 'lean' image of the Toyota production system. The second section explicates the Toyota production system's 'forgotten production concepts'. The third section explores the mechanisms by which a particular plant's degree of 'leanness' comes to express the balance of forces in the industrial relations system and its political-institutional surrounds. The section also notes how shifts in this balance have driven a certain 'humanizing' of the Toyota production system in Japan, and canvasses the interesting case of Australia, where characteristics of the industrial relations system deflected the test case Toyota Altona plant from paradigmatic 'leanness'.

The Toyota Production System: 'Lean Production' or 'Management by Stress'?

The report of the MIT project into the world car industry attributed Japanese economic success to 'lean production' (Womack et al., 1990). This term quickly shaped images of the Toyota production system, for advocates and critics alike. Resonating with athletic imagery, later purveyors of the concept would emphasize 'agile' production, while critics would emphasize the deleterious effects of 'management by stress' and the dangers of corporate anorexia.

The Toyota production system was developed in the postwar period, and owes much to the production engineer Taiichi Ohno, himself a formidable advocate of 'leanness' (see Ohno, 1988: 44–5). By the late 1980s, owing in part to some deft marketing efforts, 'lean production' became the focal point of the debate about work organization, and was portrayed as nothing less than the future of work.

> Lean production is a superior way for humans to make things. It provides better products in wider variety at lower cost. Equally important, it provides more challenging and fulfilling work for employees at every level . . . It follows that the whole world should adopt lean production, as quickly as possible. (Womack et al., 1990: 225)

Lean production is lean, its advocates argue, because it uses 'less of everything', even as little as half (1990: 13). While this is certainly an exaggeration (Williams et al., 1992; Unterweger, 1992: 3), the claim that lean production could combine efficiency with quality of work life quickly became widely accepted. 'Lean production' became seen as 'best practice' (e.g. PCEK/T, 1990: Ch. 4; Dertouzos et al., 1989). The principles were transferred to other countries, as Japanese auto and other producers shifted production facilities overseas, where they met a mixed reception.

Many accounts of the Toyota production system accord centrality to the concept of *kaizen* or 'constant improvement' (Womack et al., 1990: 56; Oliver and Wilkinson, 1992: 35; Fucini and Fucini, 1990: 36, Ch. 3). Improvement means the removal of all activities that do not add value, which are defined as waste or (in Japanese) *muda*. The concept of *muda* can refer to excessive set-up time, excessive inventory and work in progress, defective materials/products that require rework or repairs, cluttered work areas, overproduction, unnecessary motions, too much quality (overspecification), double handling in conveyance of materials and, above all, idle time (Oliver and Wilkinson, 1992: 26; Monden, 1994: 199–200). Monden (1994: Ch. 13) also refers to such *muda* as *seiri* or 'dirt', and the removal of *muda* is thus a kind of cleansing (*seiso*). An important catalyst to *kaizen* is 'just-in-time' (JIT) production. Contrasting with allegedly traditional western approaches which accumulate stocks of components, JIT means producing only what is needed, as nearly as possible to when it is needed, and delivering it 'just in time' to be used (Monden, 1994: Ch. 2; Oliver and Wilkinson, 1992: 28).[1] *Kaizen*, 'leanness' and JIT converge on the mythological 'zero-buffer' principle. Buffers permit linked production processes to work at speeds somewhat independent of each other, and therefore enable workers to take short breaks, or to accommodate production irregularities without affecting adjacent production processes. Removing buffers makes visible production imbalances and other problems, prompting operators to fix them (Dohse et al., 1985: 129–30). Thus, the necessary counterpart of JIT production is *heijunka* or 'levelled production' – a condition in which all parts of the overall production process are synchronized with each other. We presently return to the concept of *heijunka*, which, neglected in the literature, is a focal point of this article.

Kaizen not only seeks to eliminate errors in production, but also to locate their sources (Womack et al., 1990: 56; Ohno, 1988: 17). Workers' 'participation' is crucial, through monitoring and detecting any variations in process or product. Workers also contribute ideas about reorganizing and improving production, and this delivers productivity improvements through incremental innovation (Rosenberg, 1982: 60–6; Sayer, 1986: 53). This provides some basis for the claims that 'lean production' is 'participatory', post-Taylorist and post-Fordist (e.g. Kenney and Florida, 1988: 122; 1989: 137; Womack et al., 1990: 102). But work procedures are closely analysed and written down on standard operating procedure charts, which are displayed in the workplace, and which workers are required to follow closely (Ohno, 1988: 21). Changes to work procedures must be given assent by team leaders and/or higher management. Standardized work provides the baseline for further improvement, and the charts, which record innovations to the work process, are a mechanism for 'organizational learning' (Adler and Cole, 1993).

The organization 'learns' by appropriating the innovations, sometimes driven by stress, which become standard practice. But the consequence is that workers cannot use their knowledge of the production process to protect themselves against pacing, since the system appropriates such knowledge. The Toyota production system can thus plausibly be portrayed as a solution to the classic problem of management – how to persuade employees to put their knowledge of the production process at the service of management, even where this means increasing their own workload (Dohse et al., 1985: 128). However, critics and advocates alike agree the system has the potential to cause stress.

> Most people . . . will find their jobs more challenging as lean production spreads. And they will certainly be more productive. At the same time they may find their work more stressful, because a key objective of lean production is to push responsibility far down the organizational ladder. Responsibility means freedom to control one's work – a big plus – but also raises anxiety about costly mistakes. (Womack et al., 1990: 14)

Taiichi Ohno, the architect of the Toyota production system, celebrates the role of stress. He once candidly described the thinking at the heart of his system in an interview.[2]

> If I found a job being done efficiently, I'd say try doing it with half the number of men [*sic*], and after a time, when they had done that, I'd say OK, half the number again.

Ohno described his 'philosophy' in these colourful words:

> There is an old Japanese saying 'the last fart of the ferret'. When a ferret is cornered and about to die, it will let out a terrible smell to repel its attacker. Now that's real nous, and it's the same with human beings. When they're under so much pressure that they feel it's a matter of life or death, they will come up with all kinds of ingenuity.

Critics too seek to capture the workings of the Toyota production system in the concept of 'management by stress'. As Slaughter puts it, 'the management by stress system stretches the whole production system – workers, the supplier network, managers – like a rubber band to the point of breaking' (1990: 10). Applying stress causes the system to break down, identifying sites where the production process can be redesigned, and improvements won (also see Dohse et al., 1985: 127–30). Reducing inventories keeps up the pressure for innovation, by denying the buffers that can provide some shelter from the pace of the line.

> *Kaizen* strips away layer after layer of redundant manpower, material and motions until a plant is left with the barest minimum of resources needed to satisfy its production requirements. The system tolerates no waste. It leaves virtually no room for errors. (Fucini and Fucini, 1990: 36)

The more resources are removed from the production system, the more fragile it becomes, making worker cooperation essential. Workers comply because of what

Monden calls 'social conventions and institutions [that] can be called the social production system' (1994: 336). These permit powerful management techniques. Total quality management (TQM) quickly traces problems to their source, be it mechanical or human. Dohse et al. (1985: 130–1) describe how workers having problems keeping up indicate that by pressing a button that illuminates a display. Management aggregates this information to indicate potential for staffing reductions. Sewell and Wilkinson (1992) note how the systems of quality control actually function as systems of *surveillance* and *discipline* (in a Foucauldian sense), promoting competition, humiliation and peer pressure. Workers are organized into teams, collectively responsible for a production area, and able to cover for one another in times of stress. This presupposes broad job descriptions, multi-skilling and cross-training, which effectively make workers *interchangeable*. Peer group pressure is mobilized against workers who 'let the team down' (Barker, 1993). For instance, when absent workers are not replaced, their colleagues have to pick up the slack, and they therefore police their workmates' sick leave.

In Japan, a complex system of payment and reward, subject to considerable managerial discretion, provides a powerful management control system. Firm-wide pay increases do not filter down to individual workers equally. Workers receive a component related to seniority, and another composed of bonuses related to the team's performance. Another component is allocated according to workers' 'merit'. Thus a wage rise could be from 85 percent to 115 percent of the amount allocated after cross-firm, seniority and team components have been allocated (Dohse et al., 1985: 139; Berggren, 1992: 132). The key figure allocating the 'merit' component is the frontline supervisor, who may also be the workers' union representative, taking a stint on the shopfloor before moving on to a career in management (Moore, 1987: 144).

Historians of the Japanese labour movement note that the Japanese unions were defeated in the postwar period, and structured into pliant enterprise unions, less able to defend their members against work intensification, and allowing the functions of union representation and managerial supervision to blur (Moore, 1987). The renowned practice of 'lifetime employment' and firm-specific training and career paths make for a lack of inter-firm mobility, in turn reinforced by the strong 'core/periphery' division in the labour market. Thus an employee leaving a long-term career in a core firm risks falling into the periphery of insecure and less well paid employment (Dohse et al., 1985: 133–41; Kumazawa and Yamada, 1989). All in all, 'lean production' contains considerable potential for the degradation of work, precisely because it *is* lean.

The Toyota Production System's Forgotten Production Concepts

As argued earlier, popular renditions of the Toyota production system emphasize the elimination of 'waste', with a tendency to focus on 'idle time'. But at least some forms of waste may be eliminated through more efficient production management, as opposed to work intensification (Monden, 1994: 177). Identification of 'waste' in a broader sense may even aid work 'humanization'. Three Japanese words capture a wider range of 'waste', or its sources, than is usual. Fucini and Fucini (1990: 75–6) make reference to the 'three Evil Ms' – *muda, muri and mura* – although no attempt is made to tease out the crucial interrelations between them. *Muri* translates as 'overburden – when workers or machines are pushed beyond their capacity' (Oliver and Wilkinson, 1992: 26), or 'the placing of excessive demands on workers or production equipment' (Fucini and Fucini, 1990: 75–6). This may reduce the production life of both human beings and machines. *Mura* is 'the irregular or inconsistent use of a person or machine' (1990: 75), which might result from line imbalance or fluctuations in production pace, and which automatically results in some varieties of *muda*. This is because at least some workers and machines will be working below capacity for some of the time, perhaps while some others at bottlenecks are subjected to excessive stress, while yet others may overproduce. If one part of the production process is working at a low level of capacity utilization, while another is overworked, there is waste from both *mura* and *muri*.

The concept of *heijunka* means 'levelled', 'smoothed' or 'balanced' production, and one of its functions is to counter the kind of imbalance described earlier. Monden (1994: 8) refers to *heijunka* as 'the cornerstone of the Toyota production system'. This article suggests that the concept has been underexplored in the academic literature on the Toyota production system (also see Coleman and Vaghefi, 1994: 31). *Heijunka* is a strategy to meet the demands of the market including fluctuations – while carrying as little work in progress stock as possible. Elimination of work in progress inventory offers savings to the firm in terms of the capital that would have been invested in it, in the space needed to house it, in the workers necessary to count it, in losses due to rust, depreciation and so on (Monden, 1994: 2). The emphasis that Toyota production system literature places on *heijunka* suggests that it may be a more fertile source of productivity gains than simply seeking to eliminate 'idle time'.

Achieving *heijunka* is a difficult task of production management, which poses the problem of balancing losses from down-time against losses from carrying inventory in a situation where multiple products are made on the same line. Systems producing complex manufactures are not infinitely and instantly 'flexible' – that is, able to adjust to changes in demand, or accommodate variations between different models. (The Toyota Corona, for instance, came in S, CS, CSX and Avante models, each with different features, in addition to a choice of sedans or station wagons, with manual or automatic gearboxes.) Production has to be planned in advance – and the difficult task here is to aggregate the atomistic components of demand into a production schedule within the 'flexibility' capacities of existing production technology (especially the ability to quickly change press dies and jigs) while containing work in progress inventory. For instance, a month with high demand at its end but a slack period at the beginning, across a variety of models, could be 'levelled' by allocating an 'averaged' (and projected) demand to each day. The alternative would be to dedicate the line first to one model, then to another. But this would require stockpiling components and finished products of one model or another. Toyota's production engineers developed the 'mixed production system' (also called 'linear' or 'synchronous' production), where various models are produced on the same line on the same day, with quick changeovers. This ensures that all components of the production process are working at a 'synchronized' pace, minimizing buildup of work in progress inventory and other forms of 'waste', and achieving 'uniform plant loading' (Coleman and Vaghefi, 1994: 31; Park, 1993; Monden, 1994: Ch. 4; Shingo, 1989). Production plans are thus the outcome of complex and exacting calculations, that balance losses and economies from a variety of sources, and allow the reduction of work in progress inventory, productive capacity and lead times to the consumer (Coleman and Vaghefi, 1994: 32).

Heijunka also seeks to 'balance' the workload to be performed to the capacity or capability of the process (machines and operators) to complete that work (Shingo, 1989; cited in Coleman and Vaghefi, 1994: 31). It also seeks to balance workload between adjacent components of the production system, including between workers. As indicated above, imbalanced production procedures give rise to waste (*mura*, and possibly *muri*). Thus, and crucially for this article's argument, a strong tension exists between *kaizen* and *heijunka*, which intensifies as the buffers and work in progress inventory is lowered in quest of productivity increases. First, since *heijunka* presupposes 'balancing' the workload to the capacity of the operators and machines, increasing that workload to drive *kaizen* is antithetical to *heijunka*. Second, an important source of waste (*mura*) is unscheduled fluctuations in daily work volume (Monden, 1994: 64), and these often result from *kaizen* activities driven by 'management by stress'. Levelling is a counter-principle to this disruption. There is, therefore, a trade-off between economies attained through *heijunka* (levelled production) and those gained by removing buffers to drive innovation (*kaizen*). Since real interlinked production processes will never attain perfect balance, a certain amount of buffer stock is necessary to attain continuity of production. Reducing this can induce instability, and the need to rebalance adjacent production processes. Thus the notions of 'balanced', 'levelled' and 'stabilized' production and *continuous* production are intertwined.

Toyota production systems, in a context of considerable product variation, reach a balance between *kaizen* activities and *heijunka* – a balance which weighs losses caused by carrying 'excessive' resources against down-time resulting from attempts to remove those resources. The balance is shaped by who is to bear the costs and benefits, and their relative power resources. First, the costs of disruption to the smooth flow of production (*mura*), in particular down-time, caused by pursuing *kaizen*, might be externalized through short-notice and/or unpaid overtime. Monden argues that an essential support for the Toyota production system is *shojinka*, or 'the adjustment and rescheduling of human resources', and makes special reference to 'early attendance and overtime' (Monden, 1994: 159, 66). Such practices are in effect a large 'buffer' outside normal working time (Berggren, 1992: 52; 1995: 78). This 'buffer' *externalizes* to workers and communities the costs of excessively enthusiastic *kaizen*, with its attendant disruption of production and *mura*. On the other hand, if communities and unions reject short-notice and/or unpaid overtime, the company would be forced to place a higher value on careful production management to achieve quotas, therefore emphasizing *heijunka* over *kaizen* and the quest for leanness.

Second, in compliant industrial relations systems, the costs of *kaizen*- and stress-driven production strategies may be borne directly by workers. The effects of 'speedup'-induced stress on workers (*muri*) may not show up until after work hours, in the form of fatigue, sleep disturbance, digestive malfunction, headaches, injuries and so on. More immediate problems like occupational overuse syndrome may be 'externalized' by dismissal, and hiring another worker. Many such problems may be paid for by the host country's health system, or by the worker in later life. Such strategies depend on a plentiful supply of willing workers to take such jobs, and 'flexible' industrial relations systems. They also depend on a lax occupational health and safety regime, that either lacks legislation mandating safe work practices, or lacks the means of enforcement. To the extent that particular national social settlements and industrial relations systems permit such strategies, companies can be expected to pursue them.

The Political Shaping of the Toyota Production System

This section argues that the choice of management strategy that emphasizes *heijunka* and production continuity, or leanness and *kaizen*, is shaped by the nature of the surrounding social settlement and industrial relations system. If the latter permits (as the preceding section argued), the costs of pursuing *kaizen* and leanness can be externalized. On the other hand, some industrial relations systems reject extremes of 'leanness'. As Turner (1991: passim, 223–5) has argued, unions' and workers' fortunes in the 'new era' are crucially dependent on their ability to shape the course of industrial restructuring and work reorganization. This ability depends, first, on having an accurate analysis of contending images of work organization and industrial policy and their possible implications for unions and workers, and second, on having the 'power resources' to act out of such an analysis. Such power resources consist of legislation that mandates worker participation in decision-making, and/or 'corporatist' arrangements that enable union influence on public policy – in short, on a favour-able position within the industrial relations and political/institutional framework which shapes industrial adjustment. Where both exist, excessively 'lean' versions of the Toyota production system will be rejected, and the converse is true – the absence of these conditions may enable truly 'lean' production. In Japan, through most of the postwar period the balance of social and economic forces has clearly been in favour of the 'lean' version of the Toyota production system. 'Lean' plants are also to be found in the USA and UK, where labour is denied influence. On the other hand, in Japan, the early 1990s saw a certain trend away from 'leanness' and 'management by stress' because of a tightening of the labour market (Benders, 1996; Berggren, 1995). Tight labour markets also drove early experi-ments with work humanization in Sweden, but lately with rising unemployment and an economic liberal ideological offensive, 'lean' images of work have enjoyed increasing acceptance.

No better example of the systematic externalization of the costs of management by stress exists than the homeland of 'lean production'. Through the mid to late 1980s, the phenomenon of *karoshi* emerged into Japanese public life. The term was invented in 1982 to refer to the increasing number of deaths, typically from strokes or heart attacks, that were attributed to overwork. The National Defence Council for the Victims of Karoshi (NDCVK), a public advocacy group mainly comprising lawyers seeking redress and compensation for the families of victims, estimated there were 10,000 victims of this condition a year (NDCVK, 1991; see also Nishiyama and Johnson, 1997: 2). While the Japanese government officially denied that *karoshi* existed, even objecting to the use of the term by the ILO, by 1993 nearly half of the Japanese population feared they or an immediate family member might become a victim (Kato, 1994: 2).

The origins of *karoshi* lie in the oil crisis and the 'Nixon shocks' in 1973, which imposed a heavy load on Japanese companies, and caused them to demand greater efforts from their workforces (1994: 2). To deal with the oil shocks, Japanese companies emphasized 'stripped down management' (NDCVK, 1991: 98), later to be celebrated in the West as 'lean production'. This contributed to an increasing incidence of *karoshi*, the causes of which 'range from long working hours, a sudden increase in work load and the added mental pressures of expanded responsibilities and production quotas' (1991: 99). These are precisely the working conditions to be found in excessively 'lean' workplaces which, as we have seen, run on low levels of staffing, with problems that arise during the day fixed by a seemingly endless overtime buffer at the day's end. International comparative statistics put the hours worked by Japanese far in excess of other countries (except Korea), at least until the 1990 recession cut them back (NDCVK, 1991; Ross et al., 1998: 347). Furthermore, the widespread practice of unpaid overtime and the aggregation of hours across part-time workers systematically understated hours worked by many Japanese. Of the number of cases reported in a Tokyo hotline, the majority had been working in excess of 70 hours per week in stressful conditions (NDCVK, 1991: 99). To compound the situation, Japanese workers are allocated far fewer vacation days than their international counterparts, and do not take all of the days owing to them (1991: v).

The Japanese employer body Keidanren reported in a major survey that 88 percent of employers regularly use overtime (Kato, 1994: 2). This is because of the low overtime premium rates in Japan – 25 percent of the base wage, which itself is only a portion of the total wage (as the account in the second section of this article demonstrated), making the cost of hiring new employees greater than working existing employees on overtime (NDCVK, 1991: 87). Furthermore, the number of hours worked by employees is only weakly regulated in Japan, as state regulations are interpreted flexibly, and the onus for overtime regulation is placed on the company union or a 'collective representative'. Thus, most collective agreements contain a clause effectively giving management the right to demand short-notice overtime in a wide range of circumstances. In 1991 a long-running court battle over the celebrated case of Mr Tanaka – a Hitachi worker sacked for refusing overtime in 1967 – ended with a determination by the Supreme Court that effectively reinforced managerial prerogatives in this area (see Joint Committee of Trade Unions Supporting

Mr Tanaka's Trial, 1989).[3] The bursting of the bubble boom in 1990 caused Japanese companies to cut back on excessive overtime, thus somewhat defusing the issue (Berggren, 1995: 64). However, the case of *karoshi* underscores vividly how a 'flexible' industrial relations system permits the use of overtime to externalize the costs of 'leanness' on to the surrounding society.

The literature on the transplantation of Japanese production techniques contains many examples of pliant industrial relations systems allowing degrees of leanness that impose costs on workers and the surrounding community. As one example, the study by Fucini and Fucini (1990) of the Mazda plant at Flat Rock, Michigan, is replete with instances of leanness run riot. The company chose 3,500 applicants from a pool of 96,500, and maintained a steady supply of 'flexible' labour (1990: 1). As the plant got under way, and production volumes rose, production strategies increasingly emphasized 'leanness' through understaffing (1990: 147). Overtime was compulsory and workers were notified late, and this became a major point of contention (1990: 114, 145). Taking vacations was discouraged (1990: 155). There was a high and increasing incidence of repetitive strain injury due to the persistent and high production demands. There were few less demanding jobs for older workers or for workers on 'light duties' due to injury. Supervisors pressured workers to return to work before they were ready, in some cases aggravating the original injury, and in others prompting the worker to refuse, leading to dismissal (1990: 175–91). Unlike most transplants in the USA, the Mazda Flat Rock plant was unionized (as the result of it being a joint venture with Ford, the domestic operations of which had to accommodate the United Auto Workers), but the union adopted a compliant stance, perhaps showing particular 'flexibility' on the issue of overtime. (The outcome for the union was increasing worker discontent, and, ultimately, the development of a breakaway faction.) The extremes of leanness were permitted by the way the industrial relations system did not support workers' meaningful participation in decisions of work design. Such 'participation' was limited to *kaizen* activities, on terms controlled by management. The union's lack of power resources, and its accommodating stance with management, left workers with no institutional support to resist work intensification and excessive stress-driven *kaizen*.

On the other hand, well-known work organization experiments and traditions in Europe and Scandinavia embodied somewhat opposite calculations and conditions. Jurgens (1991) has identified a 'European model' of work, which contrasts with central principles of the Toyota production system. First, work organization should favour long-cycle jobs with higher degrees of skill, autonomy and discretion over short-cycle assembly line work. Second, notions of professionalism and skill are underpinned by public, not firm-level, skill formation and recognition infrastructure. And third, the 'European model' of work rejects Japanese-style 'team work' in favour of 'group work', where teams have more autonomy. The position of the team leader is more accountable to team members, by rotation or election. Fourth, adequate levels of buffer stocks protect against pacing (Jurgens, 1991: 245; Turner, 1991). While the success in terms of implementation is limited, the struggle over work reorganization in Europe can plausibly be portrayed as a clash between this model and the principles that underlie 'lean production'.

The well-known Swedish experiments in work organization reflected certain aspects of the Swedish social settlement of the 1970s and 1980s – tight labour markets, social democratic incumbency, influential unions and solidaristic wages which prevented employers compensating poor working conditions with extra pay. Although the initial experiments on work humanization were employer initiatives (Cole, 1989) the unions were able to influence them towards a more congenial form in certain areas. The 1970s saw unions' influence via 'corporatist' arrangements bear fruit in the form of 'codetermination' legislation that strengthened the ability of unions to influence work reorganization at shopfloor level (Turner, 1991).

Although the balance of forces in the Swedish social settlement that permitted such experiments is by now a fact of history, their ingredients are worth mentioning as counter-poles to 'lean production'. First, there is the oft-mentioned 'Scandinavian' emphasis on quality of work life, which favours 'buffers'.

> Scandinavian respect for the workers' quality of life requires that the worker have the ability to work quickly for a few minutes in order to take a small personal break without stopping the line. (Klein, 1989: 65)

Attempts to make work life more 'humanized' reached their apotheosis at the Volvo Uddevalla factory, which eschewed the assembly line in favour of dock assembly, in which teams of workers assembled whole cars in very long work cycles (Sandberg, 1995). But as is also well known, those union power resources were considerably wound back in the 1990s. Also, it seems, analysis of the implications of 'lean production' was lacking to the point where 'lean production' would acquire considerable legitimacy, complete with a shift to individualized payment systems, albeit under the guise of 'solidaristic work' (Kjellberg, 1992; Mahon, 1994).

This thesis of how the prominence given to 'leanness' or *heijunka* depends on the balance of forces in the industrial relations/political arena is also supported by relatively recent developments in Japan's automobile assembly industry. From the late 1980s, the Japan Auto Workers' Federation of Unions ran a public campaign against the conditions of work in the auto industry, which it characterized as demanding, dirty and dangerous (Joint Committee of Trade Unions, 1989). It issued a public report criticizing the industry in 1992 (JAW, 1992; Berggren, 1995: 75), and suggested that the working conditions might be improved if managers in the industry gave more attention to the concept of *muri*, and less to the more narrow concept of *muda* (Sandberg, 1995: 23). During the 'bubble boom' period, from 1986 to 1988, tightness in the labour market opened more job opportunities for workers outside the auto industry, leading to labour shortages (Benders, 1996: 14). Part of the employers' response was to undertake work humanization. In one of the ironies of history, this rejection of leanness proceeded just as the West's fascination with the concept grew (Sandberg, 1995; Berggren, 1995: 76; Shimuzu, 1995; Benders, 1996: 11).

The experiments in Japan (specifically Toyota's Tahara and Kyushu plants) moved away from leanness – but within constraints. Most importantly, the practice of short-notice overtime was not available, since work shifts were 'back to back', and this removed the time buffer at the end of the day (Berggren, 1995: 78). Their adherence to JIT was limited by their remote location (Sandberg, 1995: 22; Benders, 1996: 15). They allowed greater emphasis on 'internal' buffers, and the Toyota plant at Kyushu had not one moving assembly line, but a series of 'mini-lines' that were linked by buffers (Shimuzu, 1995: 399; Benders, 1996: 18). The lines could be stopped and started independently of each other, thus minimizing losses from down-time, and alleviating the stress that comes from halting the whole plant's production. They made significant changes to the *satei* (personnel evaluation) system, by lowering the proportion of payment that is determined by the individual evaluation, and in some cases removing the productivity-linked component (Shimuzu, 1995: 395–6; Benders, 1996: 21). They made numerous ergonomic improvements, to lessen the risk of injury (Shimuzu, 1995: 397, passim). It remains to be seen if these plants become more typical of auto production in Japan, but they do illustrate that the Toyota production system is capable of considerable social shaping in an 'anti-lean' direction. On the other hand, the experiments also reveal some of the limits of that shaping. Most notably, although some of the experiments shifted away from automation, at least in trim and final assembly, the basic work process remained essentially unchanged. In particular, there was no lengthening of work cycles, and the moving assembly line remained (Sandberg, 1995: 22).

The case of Australia is interesting but more complicated. It is tempting to see the union movement in Australia in the 1980s and early 1990s as having considerable power resources with which to shape the course of work reorganization and industrial adjustment, and this indeed was the interpretation of many commentators (e.g. Kyloh, 1994; Archer, 1992). However, there is considerable evidence of work intensification in a range of surveys, some of them conducted by government departments (DIR, 1995; 1996), some by independent research organizations (ACIRRT, 1998). Union density has fallen, from 51 percent in 1976 to 31.1 percent in 1996 (ABS, 1997), in part because of the failure of unions' 'involvement' in restructuring. While unions did indeed hold some influence over work reorganization in Australia, especially from the late 1980s, this influence acquiesced to work reorganization that amounted to work intensification. In the late 1980s the union movement as a whole did not make an accurate assessment of the dangers posed by 'lean production' (Hampson et al., 1994). The influential doctrine of post-Fordism did not properly distinguish models of work taking shape in Sweden, Germany and Japan, since they were all 'post-Fordist' (e.g. Mathews, 1989: 37; Curtain and Mathews, 1990: 73; Botsman, 1989). Important union strategic documents lacked a critical understanding of the Toyota production system's potential for 'leanness', and what made it different from European models of work (e.g. Anon., 1989a: 11–13; ACTU/TDC, 1987: 135, 155–6). The concept of 'lean production', embedded as it was in notions of 'best practice', gained considerable institutional momentum. A government International Best Practice Demonstration Programme was set up to provide funds to firms and workplace change consultants to implement 'best practice' work organization (Hampson et al., 1994; PCEK/T, 1990).

Even so, Australia's industrial relations system in the auto assembly industry did not prove to be fertile soil for at least the *extremes* of 'leanness', despite the fact that

Toyota made union assent to 'lean' working arrangements a condition of the investment at their new plant at Altona, Victoria (*Australian Financial Review*, 12 December 1991). First, the actual layout of the plant had some similarities with the Japanese 'post-lean' experimental plants described earlier. Trim and final assembly consisted of several mini-lines separated by buffers, and this permitted each to start and stop independently of the others. The concept of *heijunka* was prominent at the plant, according to management, and this somewhat tempered the pursuit of 'leanness'.[4] Second, extending the principles of JIT to suppliers risked disruption, as many could not meet strict delivery schedules, so a thorough component inventory was kept on the plant premises. Third, the company encountered considerable 'external' constraints as to selection, training and reward, and thus did not have a free hand to fully implement human resource management strategies supportive of 'leanness'. A pre-existing agreement with the main union, the Victorian branch of the Vehicles Division of the Amalgamated Metals and Engineering Union, gave priority to employees of the nearby Dandenong and Port Melbourne plants, which were being phased out of auto assembly, thus limiting managerial prerogatives as to recruitment and selection. Although Toyota itself was a registered provider of training, the firm's autonomy in that respect was somewhat limited by requirements that training be in line with national accreditation standards, in particular the Vehicle Industry Certificate (VIC), with a view to transferability of qualifications and the development of career paths (Anon., 1989b; 1989c; 1995). And Australia's award system, which determines a component of wages and working conditions centrally, prevented the implementation of individualized merit pay.[5] Workplace reform and restructured awards had in any case linked pay increments with competency standards and progression up skills ladders, integrated with the VIC (Anon., 1989b; 1989c; 1995). Interestingly, Toyota put in place suggestion schemes that gave cash rewards for useful suggestions, and these to some extent provided a degree of 'functional equivalence' to the *satei* system (interview with human resource manager, Toyota, 9 December 1994), which could encourage individual participation in *kaizen*. Fourth, the union had in 1991 just changed leadership in favour of the left, which was far more suspicious of 'lean' ideas and the post-Fordist ideology in which they were set than the right. Thus the union, while committed to the implementation of 'lean' principles by pre-existing 'structural efficiency' agreements, also sought to impede the full implementation of those principles.

Fifth, the company's ability to schedule short-notice overtime was contested. While the relevant 'Structural Efficiency Agreement' (Anon., 1989b: 18) agreed that 'overtime will be worked on a basis determined by the actual production needs of the enterprise', and the 1995 Workplace Agreement affirmed that 'Toyota reserves the right to assign work in excess of the basic working week' (Anon., 1995: 17), the agreement goes on to state that 'working pattern variations will be discussed with affected employees at least fourteen days prior to the variation being implemented' and limits overtime to 20 hours per calendar month (Anon., 1995: 17, 19). However, the agreement also refers to 'short-notice overtime', which is '*voluntary*'. Even so, 'if employees are *required* to work additional overtime on week days, they will be notified of the actual overtime needed on that day by the beginning of the second relief break. The actual overtime *required* will depend on 'the amount of daily overtime forecast and the production schedule volume which may have been lost due to unforeseen problems' and even 'there may be exceptional circumstances' in which 'shorter notice than that detailed above' is justified (Anon., 1995: 19, emphasis added). Reading between the lines, overtime was a contested issue which was not clearly regulated by the formula of words here. However, and this is the point, nor was it a matter of uncontested managerial prerogative, and thus it could not constitute the endless buffer which could support an emphasis on *kaizen*.

Thus, the Toyota plant at Altona, Australia, hardly conformed to the celebrated 'lean' model, and according to management did not seek 'zero buffers', but sought to balance the goal of inventory reduction against the advantages to be derived from 'levelled production' (interview with human resource manager, Toyota, 9 December 1994).

Conclusion

Advocates and critics alike of Japanese production methods have neglected important production concepts, the most important of which is *heijunka*. There is a tension between the approach to production emphasized in the *heijunka* concept, and that implicit in approaches driven by 'leanness' and the quest for *kaizen*. An emphasis on *heijunka* values continuity, balance and the avoidance of down-time; *kaizen* accepts disruption in quest of productivity improvements via innovation. This article has argued that the balance struck between the contending principles of *heijunka* and *kaizen* is shaped by the surrounding social settlement within which the industrial relations system and particular work arrangements are set. Strong, strategically adept unions and a supportive industrial relations system that can impede managerial prerogative will be less likely to allow extremes of 'leanness'. On the other hand, industrial relations systems where unions are excluded, lack power resources and/or are ill informed strategically are more congenial to the extremes of 'leanness'. This distinction may offer a rhetorical strategy for progressives to shape the actual outcomes of work reorganization. It seems that Womack et al. (1990) have given a less than comprehensive explication of the Toyota production system, and in so doing emphasized 'leanness' at the expense of the 'forgotten production concepts', in particular *heijunka*, *mura* and *muri*. *The Machine that Changed the World* is thus set within a long managerialist tradition with particular strengths in the USA (see Hayes and Wheelwright, 1984) that seeks to substitute for management's deficiencies in the organization of manufacturing by intensifying work at the expense of the conditions of workers.

NOTES

1   The idea was derived from American supermarkets, when empty shelf space indicates more stock is needed (Ohno, 1988: 25–6; Shingo, 1989: 90).
2   Interview given to the BBC programme *Nippon* (shown on Australia's Special Broadcasting Service, 22 October 1991).

3 The Supreme Court ruling on the Tanaka case is available at http://www/mol.go.jp/bulletin/year/1992/vol31-05/05.
4 The Toyota Australia Workplace Agreement (Anon., 1995: 6) lists 'balanced and levelled production' among key principles of the Toyota production system.
5 This information and much of the following was gleaned from two plant visits in 1993 and 1994, two semi-structured interviews with management and six with union representatives (8–10 December 1993, 9–11 December 1994).

REFERENCES

ABS (Australian Bureau of Statistics) (1997) *Trade Union Members*, Cat. 6325. Canberra: ABS.

ACIRRT (Australian Centre for Industrial Relations Research and Training) (1998) *Australia at Work: Just Managing?* Sydney: Prentice-Hall.

ACTU/TDC (Australian Council of Trade Unions/Trade Development Council Secretariat) (1987) *Australia Reconstructed.* Canberra: Australian Government Publishing Service.

Adler, P. (1993) 'Time and Motion Regained', *Harvard Business Review* January–February: 97–108.

Adler, P. and R. Cole (1993) 'Designed for Learning: A Tale of Two Auto Plants', *Sloan Management Review* Spring: 85–94.

Anon. (1989a) *The Australian Vehicle Manufacturing Industry: Award Restructuring. Report of the Tripartite Study Mission to Japan, United States of America, Federal Republic of Germany, and Sweden.* Melbourne: Ramsay Ware.

Anon. (1989b) *Structural Efficiency Agreement between the VBEF and Toyota: Non-Trade Group.* Victoria: Vehicle Builders' Employees Federation.

Anon. (1989c) *Structural Efficiency Agreement between Toyota Motor Corporation, and Vehicle Builders' Employee Federation, Amalgamated Metal Workers Union, Electrical Trade Union, Australian Society of Engineers. Support Mechanism: Training.* Victoria: Vehicle Builders' Employees Federation.

Anon. (1995) 'Toyota Australia Workplace Agreement (Port Melbourne, National Parts Division and Sydney and Regions)'.

Archer, R. (1992) 'The Unexpected Emergence of Australian Corporatism', pp. 377–417 in J. Pekkarinen, M. Pohjola and B. Rowthorn (eds) *Social Corporatism: A Superior Economic System?* Oxford: Clarendon Press.

Barker, J. (1993) 'Tightening the Iron Cage: Concertive Control in Self-Managing Teams', *Administrative Science Quarterly* September: 408–37.

Benders, J. (1996) 'Leaving Lean? Recent Changes in the Production Organization of some Japanese Car Plants', *Economic and Industrial Democracy* 17: 9–38.

Berggren, C. (1992) *Alternatives to Lean Production, Work Organisation in the Swedish Auto Industry.* Ithaca, NY: ILR Press.

Berggren, C. (1995) 'Japan as Number Two: Competitive Problems and the Future of Alliance Capitalism after the Burst of the Bubble Boom', *Work, Employment and Society* 9(1): 53–94.

Botsman, P. (1989) 'Rethinking the Class Struggle: Industrial Democracy and the Politics of Production', *Economic and Industrial Democracy* 10: 123–42.

Cole, R. (1989) *Strategies for Learning: Small Group Activities in American, Japanese and Swedish Industry.* Berkeley: University of California Press.

Coleman, J. and R. Vaghefi (1994) 'Heijunka: A Key to the Toyota Production System', *Production and Inventory Management Journal* 4: 31–5.

Curtain, R. and J. Mathews (1990) 'Two Models of Award Restructuring in Australia', *Labour and Industry* 3(1): 58–75.

Dertouzos, M., R. Lester and R. Solow (1989) *Made in America – Regaining the Competitive Edge*. Cambridge, MA: MIT Press.

DIR (Department of Industrial Relations) (1995) *Department of Industrial Relations, Enterprise Bargaining in Australia, Annual Report, 1994*. Canberra: DIR.

DIR (Department of Industrial Relations) (1996) *Department of Industrial Relations, Enterprise Bargaining in Australia, Annual Report, 1995*. Canberra: DIR.

Dohse, K., U. Jurgens and T. Malsh (1985) 'From "Fordism" to Toyotism? The Social Organisation of the Labor Process in the Japanese Automobile Industry', *Politics and Society* 14(2): 115–46.

Fucini, J. and S. Fucini (1990) *Working for the Japanese*. New York: Free Press.

Hampson, I., P. Ewer and M. Smith (1994) 'Post-Fordism and Workplace Change: Towards a Critical Research Agenda', *Journal of Industrial Relations* 36(2): 231–57.

Hayes, R. and S. Wheelwright (1984) *Restoring our Competitive Edge: Competing through Manufacturing*. New York: John Wiley.

JAW (Japan Auto Workers) (1992) *Japanese Automobile Industry in the Future. Towards Coexistence with the World, Consumers and Employees*. Tokyo: JAW.

Joint Committee of Trade Unions Supporting Mr Tanaka's Trial (1989) *Unfair Dismissal in the Hitachi Musashi Plant: Resistance to Zangyo and Karoshi*.

Jurgens, U. (1991) 'Departures from Taylorism and Fordism: New Forms of Work in the Automobile Industry', Ch. 11 in B. Jessop, H. Kastendiek, K. Nielsen and O. Pedersen (eds) *The Politics of Flexibility: Restructuring State and Industry in Britain, Germany and Scandinavia*. Aldershot: Edward Elgar.

Kato, Tetsuro (1994) 'The Political Economy of Japanese *Karoshi*', paper prepared for the XVth Congress of the International Political Science Association, 20–25 August, at http://www.ff.iij4u.or.jp/~katote/*Karoshi*.html.

Kenney, M. and R. Florida (1988) 'Beyond Mass Production: Production and the Labour Process in Japan', *Politics and Society* 16(1): 121–58.

Kenney, M. and R. Florida (1989) 'Japan's Role in a Post-Fordist Age', *Futures* April: 136–51.

Kjellberg, A. (1992) 'Sweden: Can the Model Survive?', Ch. 3 in A. Ferner and R. Hyman (eds) *Industrial Relations in the New Europe*. Oxford: Basil Blackwell.

Klein, J. (1989) 'The Human Costs of Manufacturing Reform', *Harvard Business Review* March–April: 60–6.

Kumazawa, M. and J. Yamada (1989) 'Jobs and Skills Under the Lifetime Nenko Employment System', in S. Wood (ed.) *The Transformation of Work*. London: Unwin Hyman.

Kyloh, R. (1994) 'Restructuring at the National Level: Labour-Led Restructuring and Reform in Australia', Ch. 10 in W. Genberger and D. Campbell (eds) *Creating Economic Opportunities: The Role of Labour Standards in Industrial Restructuring*. Geneva: International Institute for Labour Studies.

Mahon, R. (1994) 'From Solidaristic Wages to Soldaristic Work: A Post-Fordist Historic Compromise for Sweden?', pp. 285–314 in W. Clement and R. Mahon (eds) *Swedish Social Democracy: A Model in Transition*. Canada: Canadian Scholars Press.

Mathews, J. (1988) *A Culture of Power*. Sydney: Pluto Press/Australian Fabian Society and Socialist Forum.

Mathews, J. (1989) *Tools of Change: New Technology and the Democratisation of Work*. Sydney: Pluto Press.

Mathews, J. (1991) *Ford Australia Plastics Plant: Transition to Teamwork through Quality Enhancement*, University of New South Wales Studies in Organisational Analysis and Innovation No. 3. Sydney: UNSW.

Monden, Y. (1994) *Toyota Production System*, 2nd edn. London: Chapman and Hall.

Moore, J. (1987) 'Japanese Industrial Relations', *Labour and Industry* 1(1): 140–55.

NDCVK (National Defence Counsel for the Victims of Karoshi) (1991) *Karoshi: When the Corporate Warrior Dies*. Tokyo: NDCVK.

Nishiyama, Katsuo and Jeffrey Johnson (1997) '*Karoshi* – Death from Overwork: Occupational Health Consequences of the Japanese Production Management' (sixth draft for International Journal of Health Services, 4 February, http://bugsy.serve.net/cse/whatsnew/*Karoshi*.htm.

Ohno, T. (1988) *Toyota Production System: Beyond Large-Scale Production*. Cambridge, MA: Productivity Press.

Oliver, N. and B. Wilkinson (1992) *The Japanization of British Industry*. Oxford: Blackwell Business Press.

Park, P. (1993) 'Uniform Plant Loading through Level Production', *Production and Inventory Management Journal* 2: 12–17.

Parker, M. and J. Slaughter (1988) 'Management by Stress', *Technology Review* 91(7): 37–44.

PCEK/T (Pappas; Carter; Evans; Koop; Telesis) (1990) *The Global Challenge: Australian Manufacturing in the 1990s*. Melbourne: Australian Manufacturing Council.

Rosenberg, N. (1982) *Inside the Black Box: Technology and Economics*. Cambridge: Cambridge University Press.

Ross, P., G. Bamber and G. Whitehouse (1998) 'Appendix: Employment, Economics and Industrial Relations: Comparative Statistics', Ch. 12 in G. Bamber and R. Lansbury (eds) *International and Comparative Employment Relations*, 3rd edn. Sydney: Allen and Unwin.

Sandberg, Å. (ed.) (1995) *Enriching Production: Perspectives on Volvo's Uddevalla Plant, as an Alternative to Lean Production*. Sydney: Avebury.

Sayer, A. (1986) 'New Developments in Manufacturing: The Just-in-Time System', *Capital and Class* 30: 43–72.

Sewell, G. and B. Wilkinson (1992) 'Someone to Watch Over Me: Surveillance, Discipline and the Just-in-Time Labour Process', *Sociology* 26(2): 271–89.

Shimuzu, K. (1995) 'Humanization of the Production System and Work at Toyota Motor Co and Toyota Motor Kyushu', pp. 383–404 in Å. Sandberg (ed.) *Enriching Production: Perspectives on Volvo's Uddevalla Plant, as an Alternative to Lean Production*. Sydney: Avebury.

Shingo, Shigeo (1989) *A Study of the Toyota Production System from an Industrial Engineering Viewpoint*. Cambridge, MA: Productivity Press.

Slaughter, J. (1990) 'Management by Stress', *Multinational Monitor* January/February: 9–12.

Turner, L. (1991) *Democracy at Work: Changing World Markets and the Future of Labor Unions*. Ithaca, NY: Cornell University Press.

Unterweger, P. (1992) 'Lean Production: Myth and Reality', IMF Automotive Department, October.

Williams, K., C. Haslam, J. Williams and T. Cutler, with A. Adcroft and S. Johal (1992) 'Against Lean Production', *Economy and Society* 21(3): 321–54.

Womack, J., D. Jones and D. Roos (1990) *The Machine that Changed the World*. New York: Macmillan.

Lean Production in a Changing Competitive World: A Japanese Perspective

Hiroshi Katayama and David Bennett

Introduction

. . .

The purpose of this article is to examine the role and significance of lean production within the context of the current industrial and economic environment in Japan. It explores the contemporary pressures on Japanese companies and considers how they are demanding a response to the new conditions which are emerging as a result of the continuously changing economic, competitive and industrial situation. For its empirical evidence, it draws on the recent experiences of four Japanese manufacturing plants. The first is the final assembly plant of a major automobile manufacturer, acknowledged in the industry for its pioneering role in developing lean production; the second is an electronics plant of a telecommunications equipment company; the third is a plant manufacturing refrigerators; and the fourth makes domestic air conditioners.

Our work illustrates that Japanese companies can no longer rely on concepts developed during the 1980s. In order to remain competitive they must adapt to developments in the market and a changing industrial relations climate. Moreover, there is the paradox that Japanese companies' overseas operations are reducing the opportunities for their own domestic plants to rely on exports as their means of achieving large production volumes.

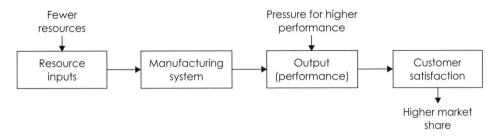

Figure 1   The essential elements of lean production

Lean Production in an Era of Change

From their five-year worldwide study of the motor industry in the 1980s, the authors of *The Machine that Changed the World* [1] assert that the lean production system is the superior way of producing manufactured goods. In making their assertion they draw mainly on the evidence of Japanese automobile companies which, they argue, have developed the means for designing and building cars in less time with fewer people and lower inventories than Western manufacturers.

The essential elements of lean production are shown in Figure 1. A key feature is that fewer resource inputs are required by the manufacturing system (less material, fewer parts, shorter production operations, less unproductive time needed for set-ups, etc.). At the same time there is pressure for higher output performance to be achieved (better quality, higher technical specifications, greater product variety, etc.). This should result in greater customer satisfaction which in turn provides the opportunity for the lean company to gain a market share larger than those of its competitors [2].

Within the automobile industry the consequence of creating a lean system of production has been demonstrated best by Toyota. Since starting to introduce lean principles around 1950, Toyota has transformed itself from being a minor producer of just a few thousand vehicles into one which produced 3.5 million vehicles in 1984, ranking it third in the world and only just behind Ford.

Despite the apparent superiority of lean production compared with conventional mass production systems, however, there are now questions being asked in Japan concerning its robustness as an approach to coping with future economic and market conditions. There are several factors to bear in mind concerning the apparent dominance of lean production. The first is that Womack and his colleagues conducted their research at the time of Japan's 'bubble economy' of the late 1980s during conditions of a bull stock market and low interest rates. Domestic demand for consumer products was at an all-time high level and the output from Japan's factories could also remain high. The main competitive objective of companies, therefore, was to increase market share by reducing costs, and thereby prices, as well as offering a greater variety of products with more features. The second point is that

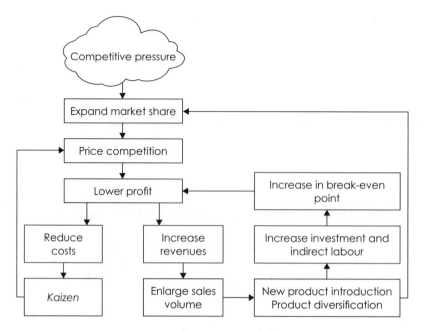

Figure 2   The past trend in Japanese manufacturing

Japan has a severe *shaken* vehicle inspection system which encourages owners to scrap their cars and buy new ones. There is little demand for second-hand vehicles and cars more than a few years old are a rare sight on Japanese roads. This has enabled automobile manufacturers to rely on a large domestic market which has been willing to accept the latest models readily, thereby increasing the rate of new product development. Domestic sales in Japan, at around eight million per year, account for about one-quarter of total world production and are two-and-a-half to three times larger than the market size in Germany, the UK or France, where sales are between two and three million per year. Also, the average model age of Japanese cars is less than two years compared with around four to five for a typical European or North American product.

The effect of the phenomenon just described is shown in Figure 2. The main competitive pressure on companies has been to expand market share, the principal means of achieving which has been through price competition. This in turn has reduced profits, thereby necessitating cost reductions and increased revenues. Cost reductions have been achieved through *kaizen* (continuous improvement) activities, which have further stimulated price competition, while increased revenues have necessitated larger sales volumes and required new products to be introduced and products to be diversified. This has required increased investment and more indirect labour, so increasing the break-even point and reducing profit.

Japanese industry was able to maintain this continuous cycle during the 'bubble' economy, but more recently the chain of events in Figure 2 has been broken. In particular the increase in revenues through larger sales volumes can no longer be a presumed step in the cycle with the increase in interest rates and levelling of disposable incomes. Moreover, the increasing value of the yen, brought about by the strength of the industrial economy, has reduced the opportunity for Japanese companies to rely on exports as a means of compensating for lower domestic sales.

As well as these economic factors which have broken the manufacturing cycle there are, in addition, a number of influences which have called into question the viability of lean production principles within the context of Japan's current situation.

External and Internal Environmental Influences

During the last few years a growing number of concerns have begun to emerge regarding the trend of Japanese manufacturing and the application of lean production methodologies and technologies. Some of these relate to the external environment of companies, while others relate to the internal production environment. Some of these have recently been documented [3].

One of the most apparent effects relating to the external environment, reported widely in the popular Japanese press, has been the increase in traffic brought about by the pressure for smaller, and thereby more frequent, deliveries of materials to factories. Not only has this been the cause of urban congestion, but at times it has also created long queues of delivery vehicles on the country's main highways, particularly the most important arterial route linking the main industrial centres, including Tokyo, Nagoya, Osaka, Kobe and Hiroshima. This situation has given rise to accusations that it has resulted in pollution and unnecessary energy consumption as well as being the cause of inconvenience to other road users.

Another effect relating to the external environment has been the public's reaction to the plethora of new products and variants that have appeared at an everincreasing rate. While this was once an attraction to consumers, the situation more recently is one in which they have become confused by the choice they are offered and they feel annoyed by the fact that new goods become obsolete almost as soon as they leave the store in which they were purchased. Many customers for automobiles, for example, are beginning to feel that despite the number of models on offer, very few are attractive [4]. Some evidence of this can be found in the number of well-established foreign models which can be seen on Japanese roads despite their high price compared with domestically produced vehicles. For example the British made Austin (now Rover) Mini, almost unchanged since its launch 35 years ago, is a particularly popular model in Japan.

An external influence of the global economy, the high value of the yen, was mentioned earlier. Another influence has been the setting-up of Japanese-owned factories abroad. This in turn has created a source of competition for Japanese parent plants in both foreign and domestic markets. For example, a subsidiary factory in South-East Asia can typically manufacture products at 50 per cent of the cost in Japan while a European plant can manufacture at around 80 per cent of the cost. The effect of this is that Japanese companies are increasingly importing products and parts from their overseas subsidiaries, causing a decrease in demand on domestic plants.

The main internal environmental factor affecting the application of lean production relates to the workforce. There is the question of the ageing population, which means that there are fewer younger workers employed in Japanese factories. In the past Japan had an abundant younger workforce which was adaptable to new technologies and, by virtue of the seniority-based pay system, provided relatively cheap labour. Today, Japan has achieved the longest life expectancy in the world and the number of young workers entering the labour market is starting to decline. The total size of the Japanese workforce is also expected to decrease, so Japan's problem in the future is likely to be a labour shortage rather than unemployment [3]. A particularly difficult problem that is already starting to become evident in many Japanese companies is the shortage of young workers and the relatively large number of older employees. As well as being less productive and versatile these older workers also increase wage costs, and it is now common for the average annual wage per production worker in a Japanese car factory to be around Y60 million (£40,000).

The ageing population is not the only reason why fewer younger workers are going into Japanese factories. The work itself is also proving to be a disincentive, being seen as exhausting and involving long working hours. The automotive industry is especially notorious in this respect and a report by the Confederation of Japan Automobile Workers' Unions [4] recognized an 'exhausted workplace' as being among the factors which it considered were causing harm to the industry's competitiveness. Of particular significance in this report is the suggestion that the Japanese automobile industry may not be competitive in the true sense of the word when taking into consideration the fact that employees work 2,200 hours per year. These are much longer working hours than are common in European or US plants and the question is posed: how competitive would a Japanese plant be if the work hours were shortened to a more typical 1,800?

. . .

The Need for a New Approach

Our analysis of automobile, printed circuit board (PCB), refrigeration and air-conditioning plants showed that each plant has developed its own unique approach to the design of its production systems and use of technologies and methodologies. The study highlighted a number of problems, for some of which solutions have been found while others remain to be resolved. The most common problem area relates to the demand for products and the need to adapt the production system to meet a more uncertain situation. In the auto plant this situation has arisen as a result of falling domestic sales and supply from overseas plants; in the PCB plant it is

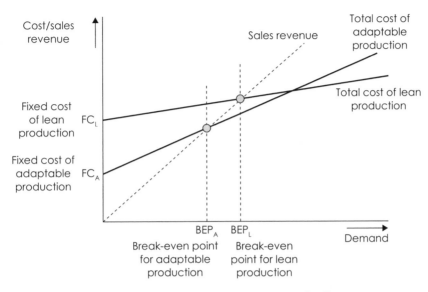

Figure 3   The relative costs of lean and adaptable production

due to the proportion of specialized products sold in small quantities; while in the air-conditioner plant it is due to the seasonality of sales and, again, the supply of its products from overseas plants. Only in the refrigerator plant is demand more predictable, although here there are problems to be resolved as its mix of products increases.

The overall message which comes from our work is that lean production in its currently defined form is proving to be deficient as a solution to many of the kinds of problem faced by these companies. What is needed is a more versatile design of production system which allows for changing circumstances; we can call this 'adaptable production'. The rationale behind adaptable production is illustrated in Figures 3 and 4.

Figure 3 shows the relative costs of lean and adaptable production. The variable costs of lean production are low as a consequence of the reduction in resource inputs and the drive for higher process performance from the manufacturing system. However, set against this low level of variable costs must be the high cost of fixed assets, indirect labour and indirect overheads (FC_L). This is caused, among other things, by the need to develop new products constantly and to acquire the facilities to produce them in the most resource-efficient manner. By contrast the variable costs of adaptable production are higher since it may involve more manual work, greater inventories and use of less efficient (although more flexible) equipment. Set against this, however, is the lower level of fixed investment (FC_A) since equipment will not need to be replaced as frequently and its acquisition cost is likely to be lower since it would be more general purpose in nature.

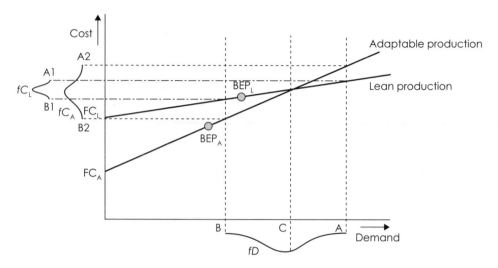

Figure 4   The cost sensitivity of lean and adaptable production

Looking at the sales revenue line in Figure 3 it can be seen that lean production potentially generates the greater profit at higher levels of demand. However, from the intersection point of the sales revenue line and the total cost lines of the two production system types it can be seen that the break-even point for adaptable production is at a lower level of demand than for lean production. This means that when demand is lower, adaptable production becomes the more profitable of the two systems. This point is further emphasized in Figure 4, which shows the cost sensitivity of the two system types. Here a possible distribution pattern of demand is shown (fD), together with the associated cost distributions for lean production (fC_L) and adaptable production (fC_A).

For a range of demand from A to B the cost distribution for lean production is relatively insensitive with a range from A1 to B1, while that for adaptable production is more sensitive with a range from A2 to B2. Thus when demand is lower, adaptable production is more versatile and has the capability of carrying lower costs and being more profitable. This occurs at any demand below C. In fact in this example the demand can reduce to B and adaptable production would still remain profitable (being above the break-even point BEP_A) while lean production would incur losses (since demand B is below BEP_L).

Of course if higher and more predictable levels of demand can be guaranteed then lean production will still be more profitable, but its cost advantage may not be as great as Figure 4 would at first seem to indicate. This is because *kaizen* activities can be applied to both systems, and economy of scale benefits would also be achieved in adaptable as well as lean production. Hence the cost lines will probably be non-linear as shown in Figure 5.

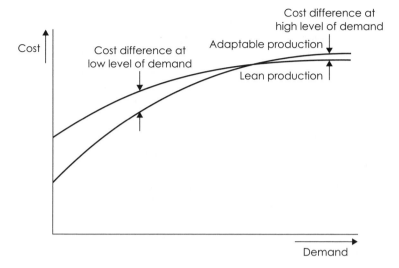

Figure 5   The effect of non-linear costs

The Characteristics of Adaptable Production

The position of adaptable production on Figure 3 might suggest that it is equivalent to the batch or job production systems as identified earlier by Bennett [5] or the project, jobbing and batch types of process identified by others such as Hill and Slack et al. [6, 7]. However, it is not simply one of the alternative systems or processes in the traditional sense; rather it is a production concept based on gathering together the technologies and methodologies which are compatible with the objective of adaptability rather than resource and process efficiency. Adaptable production is not the same as 'agile manufacturing' [8], which is still based on the idea of frequently changing products and making investments in equipment to facilitate the production system's agility. However, there may still be some common features between these two concepts. From a synthesis of the key points drawn from our work, some of the features of adaptable production would be as follows:

- *Production costs are more sensitive to changes in demand*   As mentioned earlier, this is an essential feature which enables adaptable production to remain profitable over a wider range of demand situations than lean production.
- *Systems enable production rate to be adjusted to accommodate changes in demand* Adaptable production will have lower fixed costs and higher variable costs than lean production. Adjusting the amount of direct labour and materials is the usual means of varying production cost but adaptable production will also have equipment with the ability to be 'volume flexible'.
- *System software can support changes in production rate and product mix*   Software systems for lean production are often designed to support constant production

rates and a stable product mix. Software for adaptable production will need to exhibit flexibility capabilities commensurate with the range of quantities, products and variances which are likely to occur in the future.

- *Lower fixed costs on new product development activities and the acquisition of new production facilities* Less frequent changes to products will require fewer new product development projects and fewer equipment replacements.

- *Use of human operators as a flexible resource* Flexible machines are expensive and lead to high fixed costs, thereby reducing the adaptability of the whole system. Use of manual operations can make production systems both flexible and adaptable.

- *Prevalence of mechanisms to support manual work* An argument against manual work is that it may result in lower productivity and quality than using automated equipment. However, intelligent use of mechanisms to support manual work can often raise productivity to a level close to that of automated systems, while appropriately designed tools, fixtures and *poka yoke* (or foolproof) techniques can enable high quality levels to be achieved.

- *Production systems support job enlargement and job rotation* *The Machine that Changed the World* is particularly critical of methods of work organization which the authors call 'neocraftsmanship' where long cycle times provided greater job enlargement. They argue that such forms of work organization can never reach the productivity levels of lean production. However, this fails to recognize the possibility of using alternative forms of work organization as a means of changing the rules of competition [9]. The idea of a new production concept has been proposed which links the 'modern sociotechnology' form of work organization with lean production to create 'lean sociotechnology' [10].

- *Use of technological solutions to increase the variety of upstream products and flexibility of upstream processes* To date, most of the emphasis on achieving flexibility in production systems design has been on downstream processing and assembly operations [11]. Adaptable production requires that equal emphasis is placed on developing the flexibility of 'front end' products and 'enabling' processes such as planning and programming of production.

- *Grouping of parts and products into families to reduce work-in-process variety and shorten set-up times* Group technology is a powerful tool for allowing small numbers of parts to be manufactured economically. However, in recent years its basic philosophy has tended to be forgotten as the focus of attention has moved to production technologies such as flexible manufacturing systems (FMS). Adaptable production will recognize the underlying principles of group technology in its design.

- *Modularization of product designs to enable efficient production of greater product mixes* High product variety can be achieved without necessarily embarking on completely new designs. Standardized modules of established and reliable design can be incorporated into new products, thereby allowing greater mixing of products within an uncertain demand environment.

- *Planned mixing of different product complexities to smooth production load* Mix production can allow a variety of products to be manufactured without large inventories. However, to minimize system losses during manufacture the sequence of products needs to be carefully planned. In adaptable production the changes in mix require the sequence to be re-planned quickly to avoid inefficient operation. To ensure the best result a new sequence can be tested using simulation before being implemented in practice.

- *Extensive use of* kaizen *activities and methodologies such as TQM and TPM (total productive maintenance)* The benefits of lean production are often achieved not by the underlying system but by the associated improvement techniques and methodologies. However, improvement techniques are not exclusive to lean production. They are equally applicable to adaptable production and should be rigorously applied to ensure that it remains competitive.

Conclusions

Lean production has undoubtedly proved to be a competitive and effective method of manufacture within the context of the Japanese 'bubble' economy. However, the more recent recession, coupled with the threat from imports, has cast doubt on whether lean production will be the most appropriate system, given the changes that have occurred in more recent years.

A particular weakness of lean production is its inability to accommodate the variations or reductions in demand for finished products which have occurred in many Japanese companies. Only small changes in demand will often take production to below the break-even point. Therefore the new economic and competitive situation which is emerging calls for systems of production which can manufacture goods profitably across a range of levels of demand.

Adaptable production offers such an alternative by embracing features which enable it to operate with lower fixed costs and thereby benefit from a higher variable cost element. The additional features of adaptable production help to improve its ability to produce a mix of products and number of varieties efficiently while still remaining competitive as well as strategically viable.

REFERENCES

1   Womack, J.P., Jones, D.T. and Roos, D., *The Machine that Changed the World*, Rawson Associates, New York, NY, 1990.

2   De Meyer, A. and Wittenberg-Cox, A., *Creating Product Value: Putting Manufacturing on the Strategic Agenda*, Pitman, London, 1992.

3   Miyai, J., 'The redesign of Japanese management systems and practices', *APO Productivity Journal*, Summer 1995.

4   Confederation of Japan Automobile Workers' Unions, *Japanese Automobile Industry in the Future*, JAW, Tokyo, 1993.

5   Bennett, D.J., *Production Systems Design*, Butterworth, London, 1986.

6   Hill, T.J., *Production and Operations Management: Text and Cases*, Prentice-Hall, Hemel Hempstead, 1991.

7   Slack, N., Chambers, S., Harland, C., Harrison, A. and Johnston, R., *Operations Management*, Pitman, London, 1995.

8   Kidd, P., *Agile Manufacturing: Forging New Frontiers*, Addison-Wesley, Wokingham, 1994.

9   Bennett, D.J. and Karlsson, U., 'Work organization as a basis for competition: the transition of car assembly in Sweden', *International Studies of Management and Organization*, Vol. 22, No. 4, 1992.

10 van Bijsterveld, M. and Huijgen, F., 'Modern sociotechnology: exploring the frontiers', in Benders, J., de Haan, J. and Bennett, D. (Eds), *The Symbiosis of Work and Technology*, Taylor & Francis, London, 1995.

11 Bennett, D.J. and Forrester, P.L., *Market-Focused Production Systems: Design and Implementation*, Prentice-Hall, Hemel Hempstead, 1993.

1.6

Integrating the Supply Chain: Industrial Relations Implications in US Grocery Distribution

John Lund and Christopher Wright

Introduction

While the role of technology has long been recognised as an important factor shaping industrial bargaining power (Sayles, 1958; Kuhn, 1961), recent technological changes resulting in far greater levels of industry integration and potentially greater vulnerability to industrial disputation have been largely ignored by contemporary researchers. In particular, the trend towards ever-increasing integration between and across enterprises and industries, through the dissemination of new 'supply chain management' (SCM) information technologies, offers employers the possibilities of increased productivity and customer responsiveness, while at the same time also raising the potential for increasing enterprise interdependence and vulnerability to industrial action. While there has been considerable discussion from an engineering and logistics perspective about SCM, the *absence* of consideration given to the industrial relations implications of these technologies, particularly in the non-manufacturing sector, as well as related outcomes such as outsourcing, casualisation, work intensification, and strikes is an important oversight given the potential for these technologies to seriously reshape employer–union dynamics. This new integrating technology has been driven by a preponderance of engineering, information technology and accounting expertise, while the industrial relations implications have been largely ignored. By contrast we argue in this article that the industrial relations implications of SCM are in fact highly significant and offer both opportunities and threats for employers, workers and trade unions who operate in increasingly integrated work settings.

The article begins by briefly examining the concept of supply chain management and academic studies which have sought to examine this concept in terms of the implications for human resource management and industrial relations. Next we focus on the major developments in supply chain management within US grocery distribution, an industry sector that is particularly advanced in the application of supply chain integration. As we note, a plethora of consultants and information technology enterprises now aggressively market a wide range of products and services designed to help firms manage their supply chain more effectively. Despite a growing management fashion for supply chain integration within the US grocery distribution sector, the industrial relations implications of these fundamental technological changes are uncertain. We examine several scenarios through which the dynamic of supply chain integration may reshape industrial relations within this industry, focusing in particular on the potential for trade unions to use greater industry integration as a lever for organising and bargaining, as well as considering employer strategies which seek to further fragment union bargaining power. We conclude by outlining the broader implications of this study for industrial relations change more generally, as well as formulating questions for further research.

Supply Chain Management, Industry Integration and Industrial Relations

One of the defining characteristics of recent industry restructuring has been the movement towards the increased integration of productive relations between enterprises within 'production networks', or more broadly within a process of 'systemic rationalisation' (Altmann et al., 1992; Harrison, 1997; Altmann and Deiß, 1998). Researchers argue that traditional internal strategies of corporate rationalisation are insufficient in the current era of rapid economic change, and that dominant companies now seek to maximise productivity across the entire production or supply chain.

Viewed from this perspective, the rapid growth in management interest in supply chain management (SCM) appears to involve far more than a simple adherence to the latest management fad. Like earlier innovations in management practice such as just-in-time (JIT), total quality management and business process reengineering, advocates of SCM promote a continued focus on the need to reduce inventory levels and eliminate waste in operational processes, maximise quality at source, and develop closer, long-term supplier relationships (Sayer, 1986; Cox, 1999). However echoing the insights of Altmann et al., what distinguishes SCM from these earlier concepts is that unlike the traditional focus on improvements in internal enterprise efficiency, SCM seeks to improve competitive performance through the closer integration of external enterprise relations. Hence an optimised supply chain involves 'an integrated collection of organisations that manage information, product and cash flows from a point of origin to a point of consumption with the goals of maximising consumption satisfaction while minimising the total costs of the organisations involved' (Kiefer and Novack, 1999: 18). SCM as a philosophy seeks to eliminate waste and duplication of services, compress the product flow cycle time (from producer to customer), improve information and cash flow, increase flexibility in responding to changing customer specifications, and reduce costs and enhance revenues across the supply chain while maintaining or improving customer acceptance and quality (WERC, 2000a). This macro focus on cross-enterprise relations has been accentuated by recent improvements in information technologies which now offer the potential for 'real-time' information transfer not only within a single enterprise but across enterprises and industries. Ideally, any 'node' (growers, manufacturers, wholesalers or retailers) can now log into a common information exchange and track, in real time, processes that are occurring elsewhere in the supply chain, offering unparalleled opportunities for customer responsiveness, and cost and productivity improvement.

While extensive academic analysis of cross-organisational integration has focused primarily on the technical and economic dimensions (for example Womack et al., 1990; Womack and Jones, 1996), far less attention has been directed to the industrial relations implications of such technologies. Studies which have addressed the labour relations side of supply chain integration, and earlier related workplace innovations such as JIT and lean production, have tended to focus upon three principal topics. First, a significant literature has developed around the need for changed human resource practices in order to promote new employee skills and behaviour. For example, a variety of studies have examined the need within increasingly interrelated and flexible enterprise relations to promote a customer orientation amongst employees, increase job flexibility, and develop workplace cooperation through the use of teamworking and quality management techniques (Hopkins, 1989; Inman and Mehra, 1989; Johnson and Manoochehri, 1990; Finkel, 1991; Hiltrop, 1992; Im et al., 1994). Second, a more critical body of literature has developed around the workplace implications of increasingly 'lean production' and the potential for such new forms of work organisation to intensify work effort and increase managerial control over the labour process (Sayer, 1986; Parker and Slaughter, 1988; Berggren, 1991; Altmann and Deiß, 1998; Wright and Lund, 1998). Finally, a third group of literature has focused upon the implications of closer relations between enterprises within a supply chain and how this might affect human resource and other organisational practices. In some studies such diffusion has been presented as the outcome of unequal power relations between enterprises resulting in the imposition of new human resource and production practices by dominant larger firms upon smaller dependent organisations (Greig, 1990; Roper et al., 1997). Alternatively other researchers have presented a more nuanced interpretation, in which supply chain relationships may act as a variable form of institutional innovation often subject to internal contradictions and conflict (Doel, 1999; Hughes, 1999; Scarbrough, 2000).

By contrast, the macro industrial relations implications of ever 'leaner' production have received far less attention from researchers. While studies of earlier JIT and lean production systems noted the heightened vulnerability of employers to worker resistance in an environment of reduced inventory and buffer stocks, this issue was rarely examined in depth and more often appeared as an explanation for the emphasis upon employee and trade union involvement, which were also seen as characteristic elements of the Japanese production system (Sayer, 1986). However, the increasing adoption of SCM techniques further accentuates issues of cross-enterprise integration, dependence and vulnerability to industrial disputation, which in turn have implications for the industrial bargaining power of strategically located groups of workers and the trade unions which represent them. One of the critical issues here is the potential for a shutdown or stoppage in one enterprise to have a domino-like effect throughout the broader supply chain, potentially wreaking havoc within and across industries. Nor are such scenarios fanciful hypotheses. In fact, as has been graphically demonstrated in a series of recent major strikes in the US automotive and package delivery sectors, the flow-on effects of industrial disputation and union bargaining within increasingly dependent supply chain relations can be significant. For example, in 1998 strikes at two General Motors parts manufacturers forced the shutdown of virtually all of GM's North American operations, resulting in the longest US auto strike since 1970, idling over 200,000 workers for 67 days (Blumenstein, 1998). In this case, just-in-time production methods had radically reduced inventories and squeezed much of the slack out of the supply chain, with many GM assembly plants holding less than a day's supply of parts. Under such a lean production system, since many suppliers delivered parts to assembly plants several times per day, a breakdown anywhere in the supply chain could cause downstream plants to shut down almost immediately (Sendler and White, 1998).

The strategic location of workers engaged in distribution and transportation functions suggests these workers may have an even more critical role to play within increasingly integrated and time-responsive supply chain relations. One example of this potential was demonstrated in the August 1997 United Parcel Service (UPS) strike. The 15-day national strike by the International Brotherhood of Teamsters, the US's largest trade union, against the country's largest package delivery company over stalled negotiations for a new collective contract, captured widespread media attention and the union's victory was seen by many observers as a turning point for American trade unionism (Rothstein, 1997). However, this dispute also revealed the way in which the reorganisation of distribution and supply chain integration had radically increased the bargaining power of trade unions representing transport and distribution workers. Reviewing the implications of the UPS strike, Coleman and Jennings (1998: 63) argued the dispute highlighted how 'management is only as strong as the weakest link in its supply chain, and union unrest at any point in this process seriously undermines JIT inventory management'. Examples such as these raise questions about the extent to which employers are aware of such vulnerability, and if so what strategies they might implement to reduce this threat, as well as trade union awareness of the increased bargaining power conferred by these new integrating technologies. In the sections that follow we explore the growth of SCM technologies within a specific industry and what the industrial relations implications of such technical diffusion might entail.

Tightening the Supply Chain within Grocery Distribution

The concept of SCM has grown rapidly in popularity in North American industry over the last five years. Available evidence suggests many businesses are expending significant resources on trying to improve supply chain integration. For instance, a 1998 survey by Deloitte and Touche of 200 North American manufacturers and distributors found that 97 per cent ranked SCM as important to the long-term success of their business, but that only 33 per cent ranked their own performance as better than industry average and just 1 per cent felt they were world class in terms of SCM (WERC, 1998a). Underpinning this rapid growth in interest in SCM has been the emergence of a thriving industry of consultants and vendors selling the merits of greater supply chain integration. These include large international software companies such as SAP, Oracle, Baan and J. D. Edwards which have added SCM features to their traditional enterprise resource planning (ERP) softwares, SCM specialist firms such as i2 and Manugistics, as well as leading management consultancies such as Accenture and PricewaterhouseCoopers which have included supply chain integration as part of an ever growing range of business services. However, the high cost of implementing SCM software and systems has meant that most enterprises using these technologies have been larger firms, with one report finding that over half of the users of SC software are companies with annual revenues of $1 billion (USD) or more, while another 30 per cent of customers have revenues between $250 and $999 million (WERC, 1998b).

One industry in which supply chain integration has been a long-term concern and where practice is particularly developed is grocery distribution. In the United States, grocery distribution is a highly competitive industry with tight margins based around regional markets. As outlined in Table 1, the top ten grocery distribution firms include the country's largest supermarket chains as well as a number of wholesale companies.

Over the last 20 years, US grocery distributors have implemented a range of strategies seeking to reduce costs and improve efficiency within their operations. Originating in the early 1990s in response to the declining profitability of the US grocery industry against new mass retailers, supply chain management achieved prominence with the publication in 1993 of an influential report by Kurt Salmon Associates which stressed the need for grocery retailers to reduce inventory and cost through what was termed efficient consumer response (ECR) (Kurt Salmon Associates, 1993). ECR, like related manufacturing concepts such as quick response, attempts to shift the supply chain from a 'push' to a 'pull' system whereby stock replenishment occurs in a 'just-in-time' manner based upon greater information sharing and alliance building across all parties within the supply chain. Here the drive towards closer real-time integration between suppliers, warehouses and customers results in greater horizontal integration of the broader supply chain as well as significant vertical integration within individual business units such as grocery warehouses.

Figure 1 Supply chain

Table 1   Leading US grocery and food distribution companies

Name	Sales (million)	Employees	Sales growth
Wal-Mart Stores Inc.	$191,329	1,244,000	15.9%
The Kroger Co.	$49,000	312,000	8.0%
Albertson's Inc.	$36,762	235,000	1.9%
Safeway[a]	$31,977	192,000	10.8%
ALDI Group[a]	$27,500	N/A	10.0%
Ahold USA Inc.[a]	$27,023	146,642	32.9%
Supervalu Inc.	$23,194	62,100	14.0%
Sysco Corporation	$21,784	40,400	12.9%
Walgreen Co.[a]	$21,207	116,000	18.9%
IGA Inc.[a]	$21,000	92,000	16.7%
Fleming Companies Inc.[a]	$14,444	29,567	1.4%
McLane Company Inc.	$10,542	10,000	20.3%
C & S Wholsale Grocers Inc.[a]	$7,000	5,000	15.7%
Nash Finch Company[a]	$4,016	13,537	2.6%
Richfood Holdings Inc.[b]	$3,968	15,141	23.9%
Spartan Stores Inc.	$3,506	13,000	14.9%
Associated Wholesale Grocers Inc.[b]	$3,370	3,300	6.0%
Unified Western Grocers Inc.[a]	$3,067	4,000	62.0%
Roundy's Inc.[a]	$2,991	9,071	9.7%
H. T. Hackney Co.[a]	$2,000	3,000	22.7%

[a] 2000 data; [b] 1999 data
Source: Hoovers Online, http://www.hoovers.com/, accessed 27 August 2001

Figure 1 presents a simplified schematic portraying the supply chain from the focal point of the warehouse or distribution centre (DC), following the flow of product from producer to customer. As highlighted in this schematic, warehouses play a pivotal intermediate role between supplier and customer. Strategies such as ECR seek to increase customer value at one end of the supply chain while maintaining low prices by integrating internal and external operations of procurement, manufacturing and logistics throughout the rest of the supply chain. One mechanism for doing this is to eliminate unnecessary steps in the supply chain and effectively trade off inventory for information, so that inventory is reduced effectively into a continuous flow operation (Handfield and Nichols, 1999: 1–11).

As an example, one industry analyst describes the plight of a dead chicken in a typical grocery supply chain. From the moment it leaves the food processor to the time it's purchased by the consumer, the chicken may actually be handled more than 30 times. These points of contact may occur within a single link (or 'node') of the supply chain; a typical supermarket distribution centre alone may touch a case of frozen chicken parts an average of 4.3 times, beginning on the receiving dock, putting it away into storage, moving it into an active slot, picking up from the slot

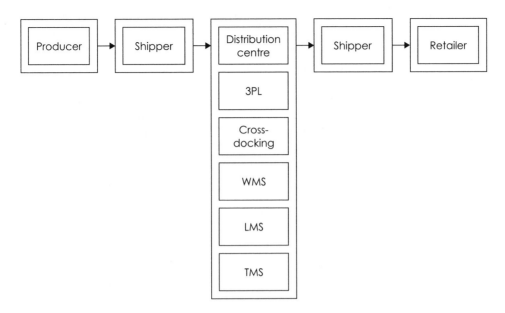

Figure 2   Engineering and IT technologies deployed in grocery warehousing

and loading a full pallet of frozen foods to a trailer for shipment to a grocery store (WERC, 1995). Add up the number of times the chicken is 'handled' by shippers, grocery store workers and packing plant workers and it's not difficult to come up with 30 points of contact. Not only are these points of contact time-consuming, but they are also expensive in terms of maintaining inventory, labour costs, spoilage and damaged product.

However, what might appear simple in concept is often quite difficult to achieve in practice, and the more general strategy of improved supply chain integration is actually reliant upon a series of more micro organisational and system changes.[1] Within the 'four walls' of grocery distribution centres a series of reforms have been implemented in an effort to facilitate broader supply chain integration. The schematic presented in Figure 2 outlines the more prominent engineering and IT technologies developed and deployed within the grocery warehouse industry to improve productivity and quality, drive down inventory, increase inventory turns, and reduce order cycle times and costs. These technologies include third-party logistics (3PL), cross-docking, warehouse management systems (WMS), labour management systems (LMS) and transportation management systems (TMS).

Outsourcing and 3PL

One response to the infrastructure, acquisition and implementation costs of SCM solutions has been to contract out some or all of the supply chain activities (particularly transportation and warehousing) to third-party logistics (3PL) providers. A recent study by the Warehouse Education and Research Council (WERC, 2000b) found a growth in the use of 3PL warehousing of 7.6 per cent over the previous year. Of those firms using 3PL providers, 82 per cent reported they were satisfied with this outsourcing solution. Logistics costs decreased an average of 9 per cent, logistics assets reduced an average of 21 per cent, order cycle time reduced from 8.8 to 6 days and overall inventories decreased by 9.9 per cent (Lieb and Randall, 1999; WERC, 2000b). Another indication of the growth in outsourcing of warehousing and distribution functions is the large number of specialist 3PL companies that now offer these services, with one Internet listing providing links to 119 such companies, many of which specialise in grocery and food distribution (Armstrong and Associates, 2001). Leading 3PL companies include Exel, GATX Logistics, Tibbett and Britten, Kenco, and USCO Logistics (Johnson, 2001). As we argue later in this article, such outsourcing of trucking and distribution centres constitutes one of the largest single threats to unions representing workers in the grocery warehouse industry and appears likely to become an increasingly common strategy amongst companies which perceive unionised labour as a serious threat to increasingly integrated and vulnerable supply chains.

Cross-docking

A second trend within grocery distribution has been the growing use of 'cross-docking' which is seen by advocates as an integral part of the ECR model of supply chain integration. This involves shipping of a product, once manufactured or received, as soon as it is *available* to be shipped, without putting it away for storage, thus eliminating the intermediate steps of putaway, replenishment and order selection and significantly reducing inventory carrying costs and storage space. In other words, the product is received, and moves directly across the dock to be loaded onto an outgoing truck. While simple in concept, it is a difficult strategy to implement, requiring highly sophisticated information systems, planning and excellent relationships across the supply chain. However, proponents of cross-docking suggest logistics cost savings may average as much as 25 per cent over conventional warehousing operations (Cooke, 1994; WERC, 1995; 1999).

Warehouse management systems

A third development has been the introduction of what are known as warehouse management systems (WMS). These are a suite of hardware and software tools including electronic data interchange, radio-frequency communication with forklifts and equipment, bar coding capability to improve accuracy of putaway, replenishment and selection, control of conveyors and sortation systems, inventory management and order generation capabilities. A WMS is a necessary precondition for integration into supply chain management, as it is able to coordinate and control product movement throughout the distribution centre prior to receiving and through the shipping phase (WERC, 1998b). However WMS systems are not cheap; purchasing a WMS can easily exceed $1 million including licence, installation and training. This up-front cost must be balanced against claims from WMS vendors of labour savings of as much as 20 per cent (Cooke, 1998).

Labour management systems

The fourth element of increasing integration in grocery warehousing is labour management systems (LMS) which have in fact been in existence since the late 1970s based upon traditional industrial engineering techniques. These systems utilise information about orders, product location and availability from a WMS in order to generate allowed times for order selectors and forklift operators to pick orders, putaway product or replenish slots. LMS are also used for real-time computer monitoring of work performance, comparing allowed versus actual time for each job task, and generate performance indices which can be linked to incentive pay or disciplinary action (Wright and Lund, 1996; 1998). LMS systems are developed by a variety of consultants and are also sold by several SCM consultants. Vendors claim that an LMS system, properly implemented, can improve warehouse productivity by an average of 15 per cent (Gilmour, 2001).

Transport management systems

Finally, the fifth element of grocery warehouse integration, transportation management systems (TMS), route shipments, select carriers, and perform cube analysis to find the best method to load a trailer. TMS can also coordinate inbound shipments and manage delivery requirements and even track the status of incoming and outbound trucks and trailers, including those waiting in the yard (Cooke, 1998). Depending upon the vendor, TMS packages can control all aspects of the transportation cycle including automating the load building, routing, rating and payment processes.

While TMS or LMS systems can be purchased separately, a number of vendors have begun to bundle TMS, LMS and WMS. While consultants and vendors more familiar to the grocery distribution industry currently offer these software bundles, traditional ERP firms such as SAP, i2, Manugistics and Baan have also begun to offer bundled WMS-TMS-LMS software packages (WERC, 2000c). One vendor, McHugh Software, which recently acquired an LMS consultant, Gagnon and Associates, offers a package called LES (Logistics Execution Systems) which includes TMS, WMS and LMS 'preconfigured' for the buyer's enterprise and 'logistics needs' (Small, 1998). To give some indication of the uptake of SCM technologies in the grocery warehousing sector, one of these consultancies, OMI, claims that 58 per cent of North America's top 100 retail grocery organisations and 46 per cent of the wholesale grocery firms use at least one form of their software (OMI, 2000).

Industrial Relations Implications of SCM in US Grocery Distribution

Clearly, US grocery distributors and supermarket retailers are in the process of a significant investment of money and resources aimed at better integrating supply chains within and between business units; the stakes are high – increased market share and greater profitability. However the potential for such changes to impact upon prevailing industrial relations dynamics has, at least publicly, received little comment. This is particularly surprising given that the major trade union representing workers in the transport and distribution side of the industry, the International Brotherhood of Teamsters, was the union at the centre of the recent national UPS strike (Rothstein, 1997), which as noted earlier highlighted some of the limitations of increasing supply chain integration. The Teamsters are the largest trade union in the United States, organising 1.4 million workers across a diverse range of industries, and enjoy a reputation for strong bargaining and organising. Indeed during the 1930s the union's organising strategy focused on 'leap-frogging' and secondary boycotts throughout the supply and distribution chain which extended union coverage across regions and occupations (truck drivers, warehouse and dockworkers) (Belzer, 2000: 23–4). As we note in the following section, there is growing evidence of a resurgence of this organising strategy, with prominent examples such as the Teamsters forming an alliance with the United Food and Commercial Workers Union (UFCWU) to organise the distribution centres, logistics and stores of the largest North American retailer, Wal-Mart (Westervelt, 2001). Moreover, as the following two examples demonstrate, the Teamsters also appear to have a growing appreciation of their organising and bargaining leverage within increasingly integrated supply chain relationships.[2]

The Associated Wholesale Grocers campaign

On 1 April 2000, approximately 1,300 Teamsters warehouse workers and drivers located in Kansas City and Springfield, Missouri were locked out by Associated Wholesale Grocers (AWG), the largest cooperatively owned grocery company in the US. In February, the company had given two months redundancy notice (required by US law) and announced to the unions that they were planning to contract out the two distribution centres and all logistics operations to several different firms, including Elite, a wholly owned subsidiary of the British Tibbett and Britten Group. With the implementation of this outsourcing plan, the company estimated it would save approximately $43 million in operating costs (Heaster, 2000c). According to union officials, it is also likely that this early announcement was an attempt to goad the union into an unlawful wildcat strike which would breach the labour agreement and give AWG a significant advantage; however, the union did not respond. The 3PL companies, using the existing distribution centre facilities, hired striker replacements and a number of picket line confrontations erupted (Kallaos, 2000).

However a conscious decision was made by the Teamsters leadership not to run a traditional labour dispute; this was done in several ways. First of all, the union ran an effective media campaign, which began with press breakfasts several months before the strike began. Secondly, the union printed and distributed huge quantities of flyers asking patrons of stores supplied by AWG not to patronise these stores. This resulted in a highly effective consumer boycott in which one of AWG's largest customers, Dillon Stores, announced it would cease doing business with AWG one year before its contract was due to expire; Dillon accounted for approximately 14 per cent of AWG's business (Kallaos, 2000). Thirdly, the union picketed the Oklahoma City AWG warehouse, where the contract had still not expired; under US labour law, unless the labour agreement specifically allows sympathy strikes, they are generally illegal. However, nearly 200 of the Oklahoma City workers at AWG's distribution centre refused to cross the picket lines. Fourthly, the union ran an effective community campaign, holding mass rallies and marches, including a rally with nearly 8,000 people on a Saturday morning at Southwest Missouri State College. Finally, the union filed unfair labour practices charges against AWG alleging that they had failed to negotiate with the union in good faith. Under US labour law, if the National Labor Relations Board (NLRB) finds in their investigation of an unfair labour practice charge that such unlawful bad faith bargaining occurred and contributed to the labour dispute, the displaced workers are entitled to automatic reinstatement at the conclusion of the strike, as well as back pay and benefits with interest. In this case, the NLRB did find such a breach of the employer's bargaining duty and although a written complaint was never issued, the mere announcement of this finding and the suggestion that the Labor Board was considering to file for injunctive relief[3] was sufficient to prompt the parties into reaching a settlement (Heaster, 2000c).

This prompted a settlement to the dispute in which the union signed an unusual eight year collective bargaining agreement with Tibbett and Britten.[4] In this agreement the Teamsters Union recognised AWG's right to outsource its operations, but reduced the number of 3PL providers from four to one (a move that is still estimated to save AWG $30 million over the eight year term of the new labour agreement) and agreed to back pay awards of $3.5 million to the reinstated strikers. Tibbett and Britten plc is a British company and 3PL, which has run operations first in Canada and then for Kroger and Safeway in the US. It is currently estimated to run about 30 different contracts in the US with about 12,000 employees and 1999 annual sales of $630 million in the US. Tibbett and Britten is reputed to enjoy good relations with the Teamsters and estimates that approximately half of the North American operations it runs as a 3PL are unionised. The business manager of Teamsters Local 245 stated that the Tibbett and Britten managers he has dealt with are 'reliable, straightforward and fair' and the number of grievances with the employer have significantly dropped from the days when AWG managed the warehouses (Heaster, 2000a; 2000b; Anon., 2001).

Kroger–Fred Meyer and Tolleson, Arizona

Another example of a union response to an employer subcontracting out to a third-party logistics provider involved Teamsters Local 104 in Phoenix, Arizona. In March 1999 the Kroger Company, the second largest grocery company in the US, purchased Fred Meyer Ltd, shutting down two of its Phoenix warehouses and consolidating them with another Fred Meyer distribution centre in Tolleson, which was previously a non-union facility. Kroger laid off the entire workforce at both warehouses, putting 450 Teamsters members out of work. Local 104 successfully pressured Kroger to hire the laid-off workers, and Kroger brought 207 back but for substantially less pay ($4 per hour average), removed the guarantee of a 40 hour work week with two consecutive days off, and eliminated their pension and welfare plans. The recalled Kroger workers also lost their seniority. Meanwhile, negotiations with the new distribution centre management went on for 13 sessions over six months, but with no collective agreement resulting. On September 30, two days before the strike, Kroger announced the sale of the Tolleson facility to a 3PL provider, Central Services Integrated, a subsidiary of Security Capital Industries, which handles storage and distribution for companies such as Nike, Xerox and Federal Express (Holthouse, 1999).

In this case, the employer did not lock out the union, but instead the union went on strike on 2 October 1999 for nearly twenty-one weeks. Once again, the employer hired replacement workers and the union established an around-the-clock picket line at the Tolleson facility. As in the case of AWG, the union used a variety of traditional and non-traditional tactics, including a consumer boycott which resulted in actions as far away as Los Angeles, and picketing of other Kroger warehouses. However the key ingredient to the union's success in this dispute was a November NLRB finding that the strike 'was caused by the unfair labor practices of Kroger'. This finding converted the strike from an economic to an unfair labour practice strike, and under US labour law guaranteed all 450 strikers their jobs upon returning to work and entitled them to back pay for wages and benefits lost during the strike. Interestingly, as was the case with AWG, the NLRB did not issue a written complaint and no unfair labour practice hearing was ever held; rather the unfair labour practice finding was a spur to settlement and the resulting collective agreement was overwhelmingly ratified. The new agreement included a letter of agreement with Kroger stipulating that should the company move any work from the Tolleson facility to another warehouse within the local union jurisdiction, the terms of the agreement must be honoured. The new agreement restored full coverage to the Teamsters' medical and pension plans and restored the 40 hour work week as well as seniority of strikers and their return to work (Anon., 2000a).

The Wal-Mart threat

Despite these two significant union victories against warehouse outsourcing, and a resurgence in traditional and non-traditional bargaining tactics, there is one company which has grown dramatically through aggressive use of supply chain integration and which represents a significant threat to unionised labour in the US grocery industry. Wal-Mart is the largest retailer in terms of global sales in the world and dominates American retailing through a sophisticated use of SCM techniques and 'lean' supplier relations which provide an aggressively low cost structure (Kaufman, 2000; Burt and Sparks, 2001). Such has been Wal-Mart's retailing success that the firm is seen as an industry forerunner in the use of sophisticated supply chain information systems and thinking. Unions also argue that the company is 'violently anti-union' and that its non-union workforce give the company a significant labour cost advantage (Ortega, 1999; Bernstein, 2000; Zellner and Bernstein, 2000).

Representing nearly 25 per cent of the US grocery retail market, Wal-Mart can afford to use groceries as loss leaders to lure customers away from traditional grocers; their annual sales are already four times that of primarily union-represented grocery employers such as Kroger, Safeway and Fleming. Wal-Mart has also recently announced its intention to open 700 'supercentre' locations throughout the US in 2002; by 2005, it hopes to operate nearly 1,400 such supercentres around the country. In addition, it will have 78 distribution centres which will employ 25,000 workers. By comparison, Supervalu has 55 distribution centres, yet Wal-Mart's distribution capacity is *double* that of Supervalu (Anon., 2000b).

The Wal-Mart effect has already been felt by all players in the grocery industry. As mentioned earlier, as part of their broader organising strategies in grocery distribution, the Teamsters have formed an alliance with the UFCWU and launched a major organising campaign aimed at Wal-Mart distribution centres and stores (Cookson, 2001). The initial focus of this organising drive has been on Wal-Mart's operations in the union stronghold of Las Vegas, although high labour turnover and the company's history of successful union avoidance suggest even such a coordinated campaign will prove extremely difficult (Westervelt, 2001). The threat of Wal-Mart's move into grocery retailing and expansion across the US has also prompted counter-vailing trends amongst more established grocery chains. One indicator of this has been significant consolidation in the industry with the acquisition of many smaller regional supermarket chains by the larger national companies such as Kroger, Safeway and Albertson's (Ingram, 2000). Wal-Mart's lower non-union cost structure is argued to place further pressure on the older established retailers to seek further cost reductions. Wal-Mart distribution centre workers are paid an average of $11.70 per hour, against an industry average which is over $13.00 per hour (Anon., 2000b). As one executive from a rival grocery company conceded, 'When a competitor comes in, you have to mimic their operations, and you get reduced to the lowest common denominators' (Kaufman, 2000). Hence while Wal-Mart presents an apparent opportunity for union organising given its centrality within the retail supply chain, the company also provides a competitive threat and model for other grocery retailers based around low cost, non-union operations.

Discussion and Conclusions

Supply chain integration poses a distinct set of challenges and opportunities for employers and unions alike, particularly in the grocery distribution and logistics industry. For employers, the promise of 'seamless' integration with other nodes of the supply chain presents a significant potential for cost savings, improved profitability through increased inventory turns, lower inventory costs and increased market share. The workplace implications of the shift towards greater supply chain integration within the 'four walls' of distribution centres include initiatives such as the outsourcing of operations to third-party logistics providers, cross-docking, WMS, LMS and TMS. However, as our article has demonstrated, employers must also factor in the potential cost of labour disputes and supply chain disruption into their cost calculations.

Unions are presented with some tantalising possibilities as well as perhaps insurmountable challenges. As the AWG and the Arizona cases highlight, a well-planned and coordinated campaign involving picketing, consumer boycotts, media, community and corporate campaigns, as well as picketing allied employers, can impact upon the nodes of the broader supply chain. As the case of Dillons and AWG highlights, picketing grocery store customers of a wholesale distributor can force grocery stores to 'take their business elsewhere', which can be devastating in such a highly competitive industry. Picketing distribution centres can also have a major impact, resulting in Teamsters-represented drivers ceasing deliveries and pickups. Clearly at the macro (supply chain) level, union tactics can effectively increase bargaining leverage. Similarly, they can enhance the union's ability to organise non-union distribution centres simply by flexing this economic muscle and by negotiating for employer neutrality and card-check contract language to get quick employer recognition of the union at facilities owned by the same company. Despite these advantages, the Wal-Mart example provides evidence of the potential for increasing supply chain integration and industry concentration to undermine union organising efforts and promote a lowest common denominator approach, resulting in the diffusion of non-union low wage labour relations throughout the industry.

In addition at the micro-level, unions are also likely to face difficulties in challenging supply chain related information technologies and their consequences such as LMS, WMS and cross-docking. US labour law reserves a large area of discretion to managers to run their business under the rubric of 'management rights', basically allowing employers the unfettered opportunity to select new technologies and reducing unions to the position of bargaining the 'effects' of such technology in terms of redundancies. One alternative at this level may be for unions to advocate the adoption of 'high trust' systems of employee involvement such as total quality management and work teams, in order to blunt the worst excesses of these technologies. On the other hand, as the AWG and Kroger–Arizona cases demonstrate, unions may be more effective in dealing with the 3PL/outsourcing issue not simply through strikes and other tactics, but in negotiating contract language, as in the case of Kroger–Arizona, which guaranteed that if an existing operation in a geographical area is outsourced, then the terms of the current collective bargaining agreement will remain in effect. Such 'work preservation' language is legal in the US and is quite common in the retail industry. Additionally, unions may also be able to blunt the effect of labour management systems (LMS) by negotiating contract language governing how production standards are established, and how they are enforced or tied to incentive pay, and by placing other safeguards in effect (Wright and Lund, 1998).

Increasing supply chain integration will clearly have a major impact upon labour relations, particularly in strongly unionised industries. There is potential for both unions and employers to exploit the strategic advantages that increasing supply chain integration brings; however it is still too early to determine how these changing dynamics will be played out. We anticipate that key factors shaping union bargaining power will include areas such as the extent of unionisation throughout the supply chain, the degree of fragmentation of bargaining structures, and the shape and nature of inter-union relations and demarcations. In terms of employers, awareness of potential supply chain vulnerabilities is likely to lead to a variety of responses including union avoidance and outsourcing, or alternatively attempts at building more cooperative union relationships. The task of future research will be to document more closely shifts in the balance of power between labour and management, the factors which contribute to these shifts, and their industrial relations outcomes.

NOTES

1   In terms of the problems of implementing greater supply chain integration, one international comparative study found the US grocery industry compared unfavourably to the UK industry in terms of supply chain efficiency. Factors explaining this difference included a greater emphasis upon price competition, conflict between suppliers and retailers, commodity purchasing and slower adoption of information technology (Fernie, 1995).
2   As the National Labor Relations Board did not issue a formal decision in either of the following two disputes, a range of source materials have been used to document the disputes including union documents, newspaper reports, and interviews with officials of the relevant Teamsters locals.
3   Under the National Labor Relations Act, the NLRB may in certain unfair labour practice cases seek injunctive or Section 10(j) relief.
4   Labour agreements that are eight years in length are extremely rare in the US, where the average length is generally three years.

REFERENCES

Altmann, N. and M. Deiß (1998), 'Productivity by Systemic Rationalization: Good Work – Bad Work – No Work?', *Economic and Industrial Democracy*, 19, 1, 137–159.

Altmann, N., C. Köhler and P. Meil (1992), 'No End in Sight – Current Debates on the Future of Industrial Work' in N. Altmann, C. Köhler and P. Meil (ed.), *Technology and Work in German Industry*" (London: Routledge, pp. 1–11).

Anon. (2000a), 'Teamster Strike at Kroger Ends, Members Gain Unprecedented Job Security', *Teamsters Online*, 16 February, <http://www.teamster.org/00news/nr%5F000216%5F2.htm>, accessed 2 August 2001.

Anon. (2000b), 'Wal-Mart: Driving Down Standards in the Food Industry', *Teamsters Online*, 11 July, <http://www.teamster.org/00news/nr_WW_1.htm>, accessed 2 August 2001.

Anon. (2001), 'Looking Back One Year After Associated Wholesale Grocers Strike', *Associated Press State and Local Wire*, 2 April.

Armstrong and Associates (2001), 'Third Party Logistics Services Providers', <http://www.3plogistics.com/Links.htm>, accessed 2 August 2001.

Belzer, M. H. (2000), *Sweatshops on Wheels: Winners and Losers in Trucking Deregulation* (New York: Oxford University Press).

Berggren, C. (1991), 'Lean Production – the End of History?', *Work, Employment and Society*, 7, 2, 163–188.

Bernstein, A. (2000), 'Labor Finally Puts a Target on Wal-Mart', *Business Week Online*, 6 December.

Blumenstein, R. (1998), 'GM is Closing Rest of North American Operations', *Wall Street Journal*, 25 June, A2.

Burt, S. and L. Sparks (2001), 'The Implications of Wal-Mart's Takeover of ASDA', *Environment and Planning A*, 33, 8, 1463–1487.

Coleman, B. J. and K. M. Jennings (1998), 'The UPS Strike: Lessons for Just-in-Timers', *Production and Inventory Management Journal*, 39, 4, 63–68.

Cooke, J. (1994), 'Cross Docking Rediscovered', *Traffic Management*, 33, 11, 51–53.

Cooke, J. A. (1998), 'Software is IT!', *Warehousing Management*, 5, 5, 54–55.

Cookson, B. (2001), 'Teamsters Make Run At Wal-Mart', *Business Journal of Kansas City*, 27 July.

Cox, A. (1999), 'Power, Value and Supply Chain Management', *Supply Chain Management: An International Journal*, 4, 4, 167–175.

Doel, C. (1999), 'Towards a Supply-Chain Community? Insights from Governance Processes in the Food Industry', *Environment and Planning A*, 31, 69–85.

Fernie, J. (1995), 'International Comparisons of Supply Chain Management in Grocery Retailing', *Service Industries Journal*, 15, 4, 134–147.

Finkel, L. M. (1991), 'Just-In-Time Principles Can Strengthen Dispute Resolution', *Employment Relations Today*, 18, 2, 167–173.

Gilmour, D. (2001), 'Creating a Labor Trifecta', <http://www.mchugh.com/Knowledge_Center/articles/Labor_Trifecta.htm>, accessed 2 August.

Greig, A. (1990), 'Technological Change and Innovation in the Clothing Industry: The Role of Retailing', *Labour and Industry*, 3, 2/3, 330–353.

Handfield, R. B. and E. L. Nichols (1999), *Introduction to Supply Chain Management* (Upper Saddle River, NJ: Prentice Hall).

Harrison, B. (1997), *Lean and Mean: the Changing Landscape of Corporate Power in the Age of Flexibility* (New York: The Guilford Press).

Heaster, R. (2000a), 'British Venture a Big Area Employer; Success in AWG Strife Adds to Contractor's Prominence', *Kansas City Star*, 22 July, C1.

Heaster, R. (2000b), 'No Clear-Cut Winner, Loser in AWG's Battle with Union', *Kansas City Star*, 13 June, D16.

Heaster, R. (2000c), 'Teamsters Settle Dispute With AWG', *Kansas City Star*, 2 June.

Hiltrop, J. M. (1992), 'Just-in-Time, Manufacturing: Implications for the Management of Human Resources', *European Management Journal*, 10, 1, 49–56.

Holthouse, D. (1999), 'Strike Two', *Phoenix New Times*, 9 December.

Hopkins, S. A. (1989), 'An Integrated Model of Management and Employee Influences over JIT', *SAM Advanced Management Journal*, 54, 2, 15–20.

Hughes, A. (1999), 'Constructing Competitive Spaces: On the Corporate Practice of British Retailer–Supplier Relationships', *Environment and Planning A*, 31, 819–839.

Im, J. H., S. J. Hartman and P. J. Bondi (1994), 'How Do JIT Systems Affect Human Resource Management', *Production and Inventory Management Journal*, 35, 1, 1–4.

Ingram, B. (2000), 'Labor Laboratory', *Supermarket Business*, 55, 8, 15 August, 1, 10–12.

Inman, R. A. and S. Mehra (1989), 'Potential Union Conflict in JIT Implementation?', *Production and Inventory Management Journal*, 30, 4, 19–22.

Johnson, J. R. (2001), 'Warehouse Plays Prominent New Role', *Supply Chain Management Review*, Jan/Feb.

Johnson, T. W. and G. H. Manoochehri (1990), 'Adopting JIT: Implications for Worker Roles and Human Resource Management', *Industrial Management*, 32, 3, 2–6.

Kallaos, T. (2000), 'AWG Replacements Flying In', *Springfield News-Leader*, 5 March.

Kaufman, L. (2000), 'As Biggest Business, Wal-Mart Propels Changes Elsewhere', *New York Times*, 22 October.

Kiefer, A. W. and R. A. Novack (1999), 'An Empirical Analysis of Warehouse Measurement Systems in the Context of Supply Chain Implementation', *Transportation Journal*, 38, 3, 18–27.

Kuhn, J. W. (1961), *Bargaining in Grievance Settlement* (New York: Columbia University Press).

Kurt Salmon Associates (1993), *Efficient Consumer Response: Enhancing Consumer Value in the Supply Chain* (Washington, DC: Kurt Salmon Associates).

Lieb, R. C. and H. L. Randall (1999), '1997 CEO Perspectives on the Current Status and Future Prospects of the Third Party Logistics Industry in the US', *Transportation Journal*, 38, 3, 28–41.

OMI (2000), 'About OMI International', <http://www.omiintl.com/news_a&p.asp>, accessed 2 August 2001.

Ortega, B. (1999), 'Organizing Wal-Mart: An Anti-Union Company Bests Labor', *Working USA*, 2, 5, 39–53.

Parker, M. and J. Slaughter (1988), 'Management By Stress', *Technology Review*, 36–44.

Roper, I., V. Prabhu and N. Zwanenberg (1997), '(Only) Just-in-Time: Japanisation and the "Non-Learning" Firm', *Work, Employment and Society*, 11, 1, 27–46.

Rothstein, R. (1997), 'Union Strength in the United States: Lessons from the UPS Strike', *International Labour Review*, 136, 4, 469–491.

Sayer, A. (1986), 'New Developments in Manufacturing: The Just-In-Time System', *Capital and Class*, 30, 43–72.

Sayles, L. R. (1958), *The Behaviour of Industrial Work Groups* (New York: Wiley).

Scarbrough, H. (2000), 'The HR Implications of Supply Chain Relationships', *Human Resource Management Journal*, 10, 1, 5–17.

Sendler, E. R. and G. L. White (1998), 'Auto Makers Battle Y2K Bug in Vast Supplier Network', *Wall Street Journal*, 30 November, 4.

Small, S. (1998), 'Taking On the World', *Warehousing Management*, 5, 8, 12.

WERC (1995), 'Cutting Costs with Crossdocking', *WERC Sheet*, September.

WERC (1998a), 'The Best From the Rest', *WERC Sheet*, October, 6–7.

WERC (1998b), 'Beyond WMS', *WERC Sheet*, March, 1–3.

WERC (1999), 'WMS and ERP – A Perfect Match?' *WERC Sheet*, June, 9–10.

WERC (2000a), 'Measuring Supply Chain Performance', *WERC Sheet*, January, 7.

WERC (2000b), 'New Study Looks at Outsourcing', *WERC Sheet*, November, 4–5.

WERC (2000c), 'WMS + TMS = Success', *WERC Sheet*, February, 1–4.

Westervelt, E. (2001), 'Unionization of Wal-Mart', *National Public Radio*, 27 March, <http://www.npr.org/ramfiles/me/20010327.me.12.ram>, accessed 10 December.

Womack, J. P. and D. T. Jones (1996), *Lean Thinking: Banish Waste and Create Wealth in Your Corporation* (London: Simon and Schuster).

Womack, J. P., D. T. Jones and D. Roos (1990), *The Machine That Changed the World* (New York: Rawson Associates).

Wright, C. and J. Lund (1996), 'Best Practice Taylorism: "Yankee Speed-Up" in Australian Grocery Distribution', *Journal of Industrial Relations*, 38, 2, 196–212.

Wright, C. and J. Lund (1998), ' "Under the Clock": Trade Union Responses to Computerised Control in US and Australian Grocery Warehousing', *New Technology, Work and Employment*, 13, 1, 3–15.

Zellner, W. and A. Bernstein (2000), 'Up Against the Wal-Mart', *Business Week Online*, 13 March.

1.7

Intangibles: The Soft Side of Innovation

Pim den Hertog, Rob Bilderbeek and Sven Maltha

Knowledge, De-materialization and Service Activities

Knowledge-based economies are entangled in an ongoing process of 'de-materialization': the cost structure of goods is increasingly dominated by intangible elements.[1] Common 'intangible' components of production are, for instance, quality (assurance and control), research and development, (product and/or process) design, marketing, logistical planning, distribution, licensing, training and servicing. Many of these components predominantly have a service character.[2] Moreover, most of them are geared towards understanding client needs better and interacting more closely with users. As a consequence, the production of material products often constitutes only a limited and decreasing part of the total process of generating added value. The American service sector guru Quinn estimated that 'within manufacturing, 75 to 85% of all value added, and a similar percentage of costs, are due to service activities. The major value added to a product is typically due less to its basic commodity value than to styling features, perceived quality, etc. added by "services" activities inside or outside the producing company'.[3]

Both within and between firms, this de-materialization process reflects three parallel phenomena:

- increasing interdependence and intertwining of industrial and service activities;
- the continuous process of specialization and differentiation, within both individual firms and economic sectors;
- emerging economic networks of highly interdependent firms in a mutual subcontracting, outsourcing and cooperation relationship.

On a macro-level (the economic system as a whole), de-materialization is reflected in an increasing dominance of the service sector. At present, the majority of the working population in most advanced economies have a job in the service sector. Many modern economies show a dominant contribution of the service sector to GDP.

Competitiveness depends increasingly on investing in intangibles adequately, given their innovative role in modern production processes. Or, as Quinn puts it provocatively: 'Value added is increasingly likely to come from technological improvements, styling features, product image, and other attributes that only services can create . . . Products themselves are only physical embodiments of the services they deliver.'[4] Therefore, decision making within company strategies and public policies requires an adequate consideration of investment in intangibles. Therefore, it is essential to have a clear vision on intangible investments as a concept.

Defining Intangible Investment

In general, definitions of investment traditionally refer to the acquisition of durable physical goods, such as machines, means of transport and buildings which can be used in production processes more than once. Accordingly, statistical data as well as economic analyses of investment usually focus on investment in material fixed assets. Thus far, investments in *immaterial* assets still constitute an underexposed aspect of innovation theory. Apart from investments in research and development (R&D), patents and licenses, as well as education, the statistical identification of intangible investments is still in an experimental stage. This complicates an adequate assessment of the innovative potential of intangibles.

Research and statistics on intangible investments show a tendency to focus particularly on R&D expenditures. This is mainly caused by limited availability of internationally comparative statistics on other components of intangible investments. This myopic view is likely to be a reflection of the prevailing interpretation of innovation as a process primarily driven by investments into 'hard' technology-oriented R&D. However, R&D-based indicators are not capable of sufficiently reflecting economic creativity and innovation. Adequate measurement of successful market introduction of innovative products or processes requires much more than R&D alone.[5]

The influence of investment in *non-material* goods on economic welfare has clearly increased substantially over the last decades.[6] In itself, this justifies an open mind towards the role of intangibles in the economic process, particularly in innovation. As opposed to fixed assets, intangible assets are said to have the potential of giving a *permanent* impulse to economic growth. A common definition of intangible investments refers to *expenditures on education and production or acquisition of disembodied know-how*. In contrast with material investment, immaterial assets have the potential to give a permanent impulse to economic growth. Knowledge is considered non-rival and only exclusive to a limited degree. Ideas are looked upon as mostly non-rival because different people may use them for free at the same time. Moreover, using ideas does not exhaust the resource or exclude others from using it.

Table 1   Components of intangible investments according to the OECD, 1992

- R&D expenditure
- Know-how
- Industrial patterns and design
- Patents and licenses
- Artistic creations, copyright
- Rights to receive royalty payments
- Training and other investments in human resources
- Market share
- Product certification
- Customer lists, subscriber lists and lists of potential customers
- Product brands and service brands
- Software and similar products

Source: OECD, *Technology and the Economy*, TEP, Paris, 1992

This combination (non-rivalry and difficult to exclude) gives knowledge positive externalities.

Accordingly, the OECD[7] uses a broader definition of intangible investments, covering *all long-term outlays by firms aimed at increasing future performance other than by the purchase of fixed assets*. A further subcategorization refers to intangible investments in technology, enabling intangible investments and market exploitation and organization. However, up till now no consensus has been reached on a full list, system or categorization of intangible investments (Table 1).

A recent attempt to assess the development of intangible investments in 10 countries includes several of the components mentioned above. Unfortunately it focuses exclusively on those categories on which international comparable data are available. This comparative study shows a variation of intangible investments in these countries between 8 and 11% of GDP in 1992. Tangible investments for the same year accounted for 14 to 24% of GDP (Table 2).[8]

There are however serious data flaws which prevent a more complete assessment of the magnitude of intangible investments. Not only are some categories of intangible investments excluded, but some of the categories included are not fully covered (e.g. software and marketing). Therefore, the available figures are believed to be an underestimation. Nonetheless, the figures at least show other categories than R&D to be taken into account.

Illustrations from Five Industries

The OECD list presented in Table 1 clearly adopts an economic perspective. It is likely to underexpose the significance of intangible factors such as reputation, image and the ability to create appealing formulas and concepts like those of Benetton, McDonald's, Ikea, CNN and Swatch. Insights from modern strategic management

Table 2 Some components of intangible investments for 10 countries, as a percentage of GDP, 1992

	Education[a]	R&D	Technology payments[b]	Software[c]	Advertising[d]	Sum
Austria	5.4	1.5	0.23	0.39	0.76	8.3
Belgium	5.2	–	1.2	0.61	0.6	7.7
Denmark	5.9	–	–	0.54	0.81	7.3
France	5.2	2.4	0.21	0.59	0.7	9.1
Germany	3.4	2.5	0.51	0.44	0.9	7.7
Netherlands	5.5	1.9	0.44	0.78	0.89	9.4
Norway	7.3	1.9	0.16	0.53	0.75	10.6
Sweden	6.4	3.0	–	0.62	0.71	10.8
UK	4.6	2.2	0.23	0.61	1.1	8.7
USA	5.2	2.8	0.08	0.8	1.23	10.1

[a] Only public investments (by the government) are included here. Investments of private firms into education and training are not included.
[b] Based on (international) technology balance of payment data. Apart from excluding investments made in a national context, copyrights are not included either.
[c] Since software development costs for own purposes are not included, these figures are believed to be an underestimation.
[d] Based on investments into advertising, not covering all marketing related costs. CBS/CPB estimate that for the Netherlands marketing costs are twice as high as reported here.
Source: CBS and CPB, *Immateriële Investeringen in Nederland: Een Internationale Positiebepaling* (Immaterial investments in the Netherlands: determining the international position). Voorburg (NL): Netherlands Statistics/Central Planning Office, 1995, p. 11

theory show that investments in new concepts and commercial solutions are more decisive for competitive strength than the availability of new technologies.[9] These soft factors, which have a fairly high service component, are often by definition hard to measure. However, increasingly intangibles develop into decisive driving forces behind innovation processes in both manufacturing and service sectors. This point will be illustrated in the next sections, showing, in a qualitative way, how intangibles promote innovation in five industries: clothing and fashion, flowers, beer, publishing and financial services.[10]

Clothing and fashion industry

Since the 1950s the clothing industry has undergone many changes worldwide. Local family companies, such as Benetton, have evolved into multinational companies serving international markets. Many Western European production facilities have moved to low wage countries in Asia and Eastern Europe. Outsourcing labor to third world countries marks the fall of national textile industries in several European countries. Some parts of the upmarket segment of the clothing and fashion industry have survived this shake-out by anticipating changing consumer preferences and producing high-value-added products. Through acquisition of foreign fashion stores and multiplexing retail formulas, huge worldwide distribution chains emerged.[11] Over the years companies such as Levi Strauss (US), Boss (Germany), Benetton (Italy), Hennes & Mauritz (Sweden) and Swatch (Switzerland) have developed into dominant players in European and world clothing and fashion markets.

The driving forces behind market success and innovation in the clothing and fashion industry are highly intangible. Whereas, for example, the textile industry has become very capital-intensive (substitution of labor), the clothing industry has rapidly developed into a *knowledge-intensive* and high-value-added industry.[12] Intangible factors such as image, lifestyle and satisfaction play a dominant role in product design, the distribution and the overall company concept. The significance of investment in intangible assets such as advertising, staff and store formulas is therefore unambiguous in this sector. Three intangible factors are dominant:

1 *Design, advertising and distribution* Upmarket clothing and fashion industry segments developed successfully on the basis of intangible assets like design, new business concepts, aggressive advertising and efficient distribution systems. In particular, investing in strong store formulas proved to be a success factor.
2 *Knowledge-intensive and high-value-added production* Cheap labor is no longer the key to successful international market penetration. High investment in human capital, design and an effective infrastructure have become important strategic tools. In addition, close cooperation via subcontracting relationships in the clothing industry enables firms to optimize production and distribution strategies.
3 *Responsiveness to consumer preferences* In the clothing industry, sensitivity to changing consumer behavior, the quality of department stores, as well as their atmosphere, are crucial success variables. Successful retail chains use explicit retail formulas for store design. In this context, the combination of collection and presentation plays a key role in attracting customers to a product. The formulas aim at creating awareness among potential customers, matching strong individual consumer identities.

Flower industry

'Flowers from Holland' is a well-known marketing phrase for Dutch flowers in foreign markets. For a long time the Netherlands has dominated the international market for cut flowers. Cut flowers still are the number one export product.[13] A large regionally concentrated community of breeders and related industries and services produce high quality flowers. Production covers numerous varieties in (mainly) sophisticated greenhouses that use modern process equipment. High productivity levels compensate for less favorable conditions (i.e. climate).

Growing flowers is by definition a highly capital-intensive industry. Nonetheless, these factors and major context changes[14] indicate the increasingly decisive role of intangible investments in this industry. Apart from material factors influencing its competitive position, there are three categories of *intangible* factors that determine the sector's innovative potential:

1 *Knowledge and education*   The flower industry flourishes through a network of well-educated, innovative breeders, supported by a strong and open knowledge infrastructure. In this structure, universities and public and private research institutions cooperate and disseminate knowledge efficiently. The breeders themselves are open to innovation. They share information on new developments, varieties, etc. as much as possible.

2 *Distribution and logistics*   The flower industry benefits from a well-organized logistic system. In this system a key role is attributed to the auctions integrating growers, strong wholesale traders, and critical and trendsetting customers via numerous sales outlets. Given the massive supply and demand volumes, prices at auction are in fact world prices. Logistics are crucial since cut flowers are perishable: they need to be packaged, transported, repackaged, traded, distributed and sold to the customer as quickly as possible.

3 *Image, design and quality*   Flowers are by definition an emotive product subject to fashion, image and customers' feelings. The ability to assess long-term trends in fashion, interior decorating, gardens and especially colors is crucial for product developers and breeders to anticipate the newest trends. This ability (to assess) is continuously put to the test by censorious and trendsetting users in the domestic market. The increasingly differentiating and unpredictable taste of consumers complicates this early assessment even more. Tighter environmental laws and environmental groups put the industry under further pressure. Consequently, there is a growing tendency to invest in new process equipment, packaging, the image of flowers, the flower industry and quality control systems.

Beer industry

Developments in the beer industry are dominated by a proliferation of acquisitions by the big brewing companies with global ambitions and new partnerships with local breweries. Heineken and Guinness, the Dutch and UK brewers, moved into international markets after the Second World War. Only recently, however, have other big brewers such as Anheuser-Busch of the US attempted to turn themselves into global powers. Whereas the market for soft drinks is thoroughly internationalized, the beer market is still fragmented: three brands (Coca-Cola, Pepsi-Cola and Seven-Up) control 70% of the soft drinks world market; the 20 biggest beer brands barely reach 26% in their market. Prime driving forces are the struggle for market share, economies of scale in the home market, and the search for entrances to new markets through local brands and their distribution networks.

The following intangible factors play a decisive role in the sector's development:

1 *Premium brands* Brewers consider premium brands as the key to market share. This applies both to catching bored consumers in the saturated North European and North American markets, and to hooking new drinkers in the expanding markets of Latin America, South East Asia and parts of Eastern Europe. The world's top major brewers are very active in expanding their market share by taking over local breweries. Brand familiarity and premium image are crucial. In the absence of completely new ways to make beer, innovative products such as 'ice' beers are an additional tool for reviving mature markets.

2 *Market differentiation* As consumers migrate away from the bland megabrands to tastier prestige labels, the big breweries tend to discount their famous-name beers heavily in order to lure consumers. At the same time they develop or buy unusual high-priced new types of beer, in particular import beers and microbrews. As a result of this differentiation strategy, many brewers expand their product range. Not only do they sell the standard mass market beer, they also offer a broad range of special and near beers, each aiming for a niche in the beer market that is differentiating as well.

3 *Innovative marketing* Apart from launching innovative products, brewers tend to focus on more creative marketing strategies. Among these are efforts to develop, test, and deliver new products more quickly and efficiently. Faster cycle times and more locally oriented marketing may give brewers a competitive lead. Related changes in the sales organization and the production system reflect development towards a more differentiated beer market.

Publishing services industry

Most publishers still concentrate on folio publishing (books, journals, magazines, newspapers, etc.). In many cases, non-folio publishing and new media are challenges to which the majority of publishers still have to respond. Nevertheless the context in which publishers have to operate is changing rapidly:

- digitization and medium-neutral information storage;
- the emergence of multimedia and interactivity;
- technological innovation allowing for more personalized media;[15]
- globalization, re-regulation and liberalization.

As a result of these changes, publishing has become part of a much larger and more complex industry with a variety of enabling technologies, players and delivery systems: the info-industry. New (combinations of) media, distribution channels and facilitating technologies are developing; contributing industries increasingly integrate and new players enter the field of publishing. The worlds of telecommunications, media and publishing, consumer electronics, computing, distribution and office equipment tend to overlap more and more. This convergence causes electronic media to develop rapidly; there is an increasing need for content. Consequently, the production and recycling of content is in the hands of a broad and growing range of firms. What they have in common is the capability to develop, produce and deliver new interactive information services: telecoms operators, music and film producers, entertainment companies, computer manufacturers and software firms. As a result, they have the potential to enter what was traditionally thought of as the exclusive domain of publishing. Content providers are no longer necessarily publishers; and, publishers increasingly merge into integrated communications companies.[16]

The highly intangible core function of a publisher or info-industry company addresses the ability to communicate the intellectual product of an author (broadly defined) to the end-user by the best means possible. A publisher's main considerations are how to find, process and manipulate information, how to store it, how to update databases, how to format information for a user and how to transport it. Intangible factors, creativity and knowledge-intensive activities play a pivotal role in the process of value adding in the info-industry. Two factors are highlighted here:

1   *The ability to produce, repackage and market content*   The reputation for the ability to create original content on the basis of text, sound, images, graphics and related copyrights is evolving into a most valuable asset in the info-industry. As the number of players increases and the capacity to reach the user is no longer a scarce item (e.g. multi-channel broadcasting), the need for content is growing rapidly. Simultaneously, the ability to use and repackage content at various times gains importance (both in the same form through different channels and recycled through transformation into different types of media products).[17]

2   *The ability to focus on and deliver content to specific user groups*   This requires an intimate knowledge of potential customers or target user groups. In addition, knowledge of the best way to reach these potential customers is a necessity. Increasingly, info-products are customized to the specific requirements of certain user groups and distributed in innovative ways.

Financial services industry

An ongoing process of mergers and acquisitions in the financial services sector has led to an increasingly bipolar development of the sector's structure worldwide. On the one hand there is a decreasing number of huge financial conglomerates, each offering a broad range of financial services.[18] Many of these 'financial supermarkets' aim at full financial service delivery, ranging, for example, from simple cash management services to highly specialized asset management. As far as *national* financial markets still exist, these *All-Finanz* providers tend to dominate national markets. On the other hand there is a wide range of smaller financial service companies. Often these SME (small and medium enterprises) financial service providers operate in a (few) market niche(s) on the basis of specialization and focus on specific client target groups. For this category, customer vicinity is a substantial comparative advantage, in particular in high-quality (and often high-value-added) market niches.

Furthermore, the blurring of financial market boundaries has led financial services to be increasingly interwoven with other economic sectors. In particular the larger financial service companies more and more often tend to offer a combination of banking and insurance services: banks and insurers merge into *bancassurance* providers, aiming at integrated financial provision of services. This integration process goes hand in hand with redesigning the organization of financial service companies.

Moreover, as a result of deregulation and liberalization, an increasing number of financial service providers operate in global markets. Whereas some parts of the financial market (e.g. the capital and stock markets) have been genuinely international for a long time, 'foreign' competitors now increasingly penetrate traditionally closed, national financial markets. This leads to intensified competition. The wave of (international) mergers and acquisitions has strengthened this process. Rationalization and cutting the operational costs of the financial service delivery process, largely facilitated by substantial investment into information and communications technologies, have developed into competitive factors.

Against this background, financial service providers are fairly active in investing in the following intangibles which serve as a basis for further innovations:

1   *Organizational transformation*   This aims at better client orientation, not least because of tightened competition. Information and communications technologies facilitate flexible, multi-channel, tailor-made financial service delivery. As a result, new financial products and service formulas emerge beyond pure financial service delivery.

2   *(Re)training*   These transformation processes force banking and insurance companies to invest substantially in training and retraining. Enabling employees to work with new technology-based applications, (re)training and organizational restructuring are vital for client-oriented service delivery. Therefore human resource management is developing into a core management field.

3   *Distribution channels*   Organizational redesign processes often specifically aim at broadening the channels for distributing financial services. In fact, distribution of financial services has turned into a key management area. The rise of call centers reflects the segmentation in financial services delivery. The use of standardized distribution channels for delivering standard, low-added-value financial services in a highly competitive market is one approach. An alternative is tailor-made client-focused delivery of high-value-added financial services to specific target groups, and further differentiation towards more specific market segments.

4   *New communication patterns with less predictable clients*   Technology-based innovations in the financial sector create new and often more differentiated communication and distribution channels to customers. The potential of these channels leads to a broadening range of feasible communication patterns. As competition gets more intense, banks and insurers have increasingly to regard client wishes as a determining factor. Like the chipcard, on-line banking is a promising distribution channel for banks, but consumers' whims and unpredictability are making it difficult for them to handle these developments convincingly.

5   *Active advertising and marketing strategies*   Traditionally, the financial sector had a rather moderate attitude towards advertising and marketing. As competitive pressures increase, banks and insurers tend to spend more time on creating an

image as a means to attract new clients. No longer are advertising and marketing exclusively based on concepts like reliability and solidness (though still essential to financial service providers). The emphasis is slowly shifting towards more challenging concepts like entrepreneurial attitude and cosmopolitanism.

Intangibles as Driving Factors Towards Innovation

Intangible factors playing a predominant role in innovation in each of the above-mentioned industries are summarized in Table 3.[19]

What lessons can be drawn from these sectoral cases? Clearly, they show the soft side of innovation: innovative products and services are not exclusively the result of 'hard' R&D as a reflection of the technological innovation process. On the contrary, apart from technology-based innovations an often substantial contribution to innovation comes from intangible service functions. These include design, marketing, human resources, the organization and management of knowledge, the ability to organize the interface with users, and modern distribution concepts. Considering the predominant intangible factors underlying innovation in the industries above, there seem to be several commonalities (see Table 4).

All these intangible driving forces behind innovation are directly related to service functions. This, in turn, illustrates the facilitating role of services in innovation processes, be it in manufacturing or in non-industrial economic activities.

Table 3 Predominant intangible factors in innovation in five industries

Industry	Intangibles in innovation
Clothing and fashion	• Design, advertising and distribution • Knowledge-intensive and high-value-added production • Consumer behavior
Flower	• Knowledge and education • Distribution and logistics • Image, design and quality (R&D, advertising, marketing)
Beer	• Premium brands (advertising/marketing) • Market differentiation (marketing) • Innovative marketing
Publishing	• Ability to produce, repackage and market content (marketing) • Ability to focus on and deliver content to specific user groups (marketing)
Financial services	• Organizational transformation • (Re)training • Distribution channels • New communication patterns with less predictable clients • Active advertising and marketing strategies

Table 4 Main categories of immaterial investment in the sector case studies[20]

	Intangible investment in:
Organization:	Transformation towards flexible, adaptive client-oriented organizational structure
Knowledge:	Knowledge-intensive production, education, (re)training
Product:	Brand names, images and design
Market:	Innovative advertising and marketing strategies, oriented towards specific user/consumer groups
Distribution:	Channels for tailor-made delivery of services/products, and communication with less and less predictable consumers

Source: Bilderbeek et al., 1995, p. 83: see note 19

An important impact on innovativeness appears to derive from two major factors in particular:

- the ability to make optimal use of available human resources ('organization' and 'knowledge');
- the ability to communicate with (potential) clients and users ('market', 'distribution', 'product').

Consequently, understanding of the nature of innovation processes requires a focus that includes the contribution of intangible investments. Accordingly reformulated innovative business and policy strategies will better reflect the growing role of service functions in innovation processes, and particularly of knowledge-intensive services.

Future Implications

Considering the growing significance of intangibles in innovation processes, the obvious question is whether there are serious implications for both future policy and business strategy development. If so, how could these be better geared towards making the most of the soft side of innovation?

As far as the development of future business strategies is concerned, the picture is rather mixed. On the one hand many firms still innovate along traditional lines, emphasizing *technological* innovation and R&D as prime drivers. On the other hand, a growing number of firms use broader innovation concepts, including the 'soft side' of innovation. Service companies, traditionally considered as 'followers' in (technological) innovation, are relatively well represented in this latter category. The cases mentioned above clearly illustrate the de-materialization of production processes; intangible components of investment like reputation, image and service formula play an increasingly decisive role as competitive success factors. Broadening the innovation concept towards the intangible, 'soft' side of innovation will offer good opportunities for firms to transform into learning organizations, as a step towards the knowledge-based economy.

However, strengthening overall competitiveness requires a much more proactive approach, as it does from an industrial and technology policy-making point of view. Present-day innovation and technology policy development still shows a strong manufacturing orientation. The substantial contribution of service functions to innovation is still largely ignored. At present a focus on 'hard', mainly technological components and innovation indicators such as R&D investments dominate the ongoing debate on innovation practices and innovation policies. As a result, incomplete and partial approaches to innovation practices dominate, as they do in prevailing industrial and innovation policies. In spite of growing awareness that future policy development should be more adequately directed towards the specificities of service innovation, the actual 'tertiarization' of innovation and technology policy development itself has yet to begin.

Such a tertiarized innovation and technology policy approach should arise from the often fuzzy and intangible character of service innovations, related to factors like:

- the interaction within and between networks of producers, suppliers and users in co-development and externalization processes;
- the complexity of many innovations: often a combination of innovations in the service delivery process, in products, markets and processes;
- the opportunities to appropriate the benefits of service innovations;
- the relatively fuzzy and broad concept of R&D in service innovation.

Intangibles include a wide variety of factors, ranging from human resources, organizational concepts, software, marketing and advertising, distribution and logistics, to image, design and brand names, and reputation. Given this broad range, the question arises of which components of intangibles may contribute to a large impact on innovativeness and competitiveness, and which may not. At this point it is not quite clear what it is that each of the components of intangible investments contributes to innovation. Future policy development requires a better insight into the potential contribution of each of these intangibles to strengthening innovation-based competitiveness.

A broad and knowledge-oriented vision of intangible investments, including these soft but essential components, is therefore to be favored. More needs to be done in the field of defining intangible investment adequately as an innovation factor. Specific attention should be paid to the following aspects:

- the linkage between innovation processes on the basis of intangibles and the use of the public knowledge infrastructure;
- the availability (or the lack) of an innovation toolkit, geared towards the specific characteristics of innovation processes on the basis of intangibles;
- knowledge management, within both innovating firms and institutions of the knowledge infrastructure, as an instrument for boosting intangibles as an innovation factor.

Conclusion

Given the substantial contribution of service functions to innovation and the prevailing manufacturing orientation of present-day industrial and innovation policy approaches, there is an apparent urgent need to 'tertiarize' these policies. Intangibles have proved to be an often essential input into innovativeness and therefore deserve more explicit attention in future industrial and technology policy-making processes. Thus far, intangible investments are still a widely underestimated area of the knowledge-based economy. A better integration of the service function focus into existing policy approaches promises to offer a good perspective for strengthening innovation-based competitiveness.

NOTES

1 Here, the term 'de-materialization' is not being used as a reference to the absolute decrease in materials required for certain activities (in the manner of Bernardi, Oliviero and Riccardo Galli, Dematerialization: long-term trends in the intensity of use of materials and energy, *Futures*, 1993, 4, 431–448). In this article, we associate de-materialization with the increased share of intangibles.

2 For a discussion of the prospects for services in the new industrial economy, see Miles, Ian, Services in the new industrial economy, *Futures*, 1993, 6, 653–672.

3 Quinn, J. B., Technology in services: past myths and future challenges, *Technological Forecasting and Social Change*, 1988, 34 (4), 340. And: Quinn, J. B., T. L. Doorley and P. C. Paquette, Beyond products: services-based strategy, *Harvard Business Review*, March, 1990, p. 58.

4 Quinn, 1988, p. 330.

5 Hertog, P. den, T. J. A. Roelandt, P. Boekholt and H. van der Caag, 1995, *Assessing the Distribution Power of National Innovation Systems. Pilot Study: the Netherlands.* Apeldoorn (NL): TNO Centre for Technology and Policy Studies (STB 95/051). See also Jacobs, Dany, 1996, Hot air: added value in the knowledge economy. To be published in *STI Review*.

6 The ratio of immaterial/material investment in the Netherlands increased from less than 40% to more than 50% in the period 1970–1991 (see Minne, Bert, 1995, *Onderzoek, Ontwikkeling en Andere Immateriële Investeringen in Nederland* (Research, development and other immaterial investments in the Netherlands), Onderzoeksmemorandum, nr. 116, Den Haag: Central Planning Office, p. 5, 11).

7 OECD, 1992, *Technology and the Economy: The Key Relationships*, TEP, Paris: Organization of Economic Cooperation and Development. More recent OECD documents take more explicitly the knowledge-based economy as a starting point. See OECD, *The OECD Jobs Strategy: Technology, Productivity and Job Creation. Vol. 1: Highlights and Vol. 2: Analytical Report.* Paris, 1996.

8 See also Vosselman, W., *Statistische Onderzoekingen. Investeringen in Immateriële vaste Activa Door Bedrijven* (Statistical investigations. Investments in immaterial fixed assets by companies). M43. Netherlands Statistics, Den Haag, 1991.

9 See Peters, Tom, *Liberation Management*, Fawcett Columbine, New York, 1992.

10 These branches of industry, drawn from a study performed for the European Commission (cf. Bilderbeek et al., 1995: see note 19), have been selected with the aim to get an

overview of intangibles' role in a broad range of industries having a relatively strong end-user orientation in common. Considering that other industries show comparable innovation patterns, we think that the branches selected here reflect the general significance of intangibles in innovation practices. For a more thorough test, we consider a wider scope of industries including basic industries (e.g. steel, chemical industry) as recommendable.

11   Benetton for example nowadays has over 5,000 branches in 87 export countries.

12   d'Ercole, Michele, *Innovation in a Mature Industry: Evidence From the Textile and Clothing Sector*, MERIT, Maastricht, 1993.

13   In 1994 Dutch firms exported a total of 6.8 billion flowers worth Dfl 3.6 b (ECU 1.7 b); nearly 60% (70% in 1990!) of all flowers produced worldwide were traded in the Netherlands. The Dutch floricultural industry employed 71,000 workers in 1992. Apart from production (25,000), this figure includes auctions (4,500), the supply industry (6,000), wholesalers/exporters (13,000) and retailers (22,500). We will concentrate here on the flower industry in itself, although it is an inseparable part of the agribusiness industry as a whole.

14   Although the Dutch flower industry still dominates international production and trade in cut flowers, there are indications that the dominance is decreasing. Floriculture industry in general has been confronted with some major changes lately (like overproduction, increased imports from third world countries, signals about a declining image, and lack of quality control).

15   Data compression, digital broadcasting, interactive TV, home decoding, on-line publishing are relevant innovations here.

16   A growing number of mergers and acquisitions, joint and unforeseen forms of collaboration and a relaxation of rules regarding cross-media ownership led to integrated communication concerns like Bertelsmann, Canal Plus, Pearson, Reed–Elsevier, Time Warner, Hachette.

17   Stewart, C. and Laird, J., *The European Media Industry. Fragmentation and Convergence in Broadcasting and Publishing*. London: Financial Times Management Reports, 1994, p. 30.

18   International differences in this respect are quite substantial. For instance, legislative barriers are used to inhibit the formation of large banks across state boundaries in the United States, whereas the formation of large financial conglomerates is a distinguishing characteristic of the Japanese financial sector.

19   For a more detailed insight into the role of intangible elements in the innovation process, see Bilderbeek, Rob, Dany Jacobs, Sven Maltha and Pim den Hertog, *Immaterial Investments as an Innovative Factor*. Research for EC DG III A.3. Apeldoorn (NL): TNO STB Centre for Technology and Policy Studies, 1995, Ch 4.

20   This table regroups the intangibles mentioned in Table 3 under a limited number of main headings.

The Environmental Challenge for Supply Chain Management

Q. J. Leiper, P. Riley and S. Uren

The environmental agenda for the UK construction industry has evolved from considerations related to waste minimization, environmental engineering and environmental project management to the more complex issues of sustainability and the life-cycle impacts of products and services used and consumed in the creation, maintenance and operation of the built environment. This represents a significant challenge for the construction sector – where the supply base is large and fragmented, and where most projects have their own unique requirements.

Only relatively recently have organizations begun to address and manage the environmental impacts of their suppliers and products and to realize that the application of established supply chain management techniques is essential to the delivery of sustainable construction. A UK government-sponsored initiative, Business in the Environment, has suggested that there are four key activities involved in best practice for environmental supply chain management (ESCM):

1 purchasing to environmentally sound specifications;
2 seeking out alternative products and services which are 'greener' than those in current use;
3 monitoring the commitment and performance of suppliers in environmental management;
4 working in partnership with suppliers for environmental improvement and cost-effectiveness.

This paper outlines how principles of the best practice ESCM initiative have been applied in current environmental practice in the major construction and services group, Carillion.

Carillion's ESCM Position Statement

Carillion was created in 1999 following the demerger of the Tarmac group into two separately listed businesses. The building products and materials division of the group became the new Tarmac; and the construction services division, with a turnover of £1.9 billion, a staff of 15,000 and working in 30 countries on 600 sites or offices, became Carillion. Carillion operates in all sections of the civil, rail and building construction markets, and is therefore involved in ground and geotechnical-related activities, ranging from tunnelling and deep station excavations on the Jubilee Line in London to a 26 m high embankment on the Manchester Runway 2 Project.

The UK construction sector has a poor environmental record, regularly appearing high in the league table of water polluters. Construction companies have also faced criticism for their involvement in major projects seen as damaging to the environment. It was the disruption of Tarmac's 1994 annual meeting by activists protesting at its involvement in the M3 motorway extension through Twyford Down that led to the chairman Sir John Banham's acceptance of the environment as a business issue.

The company's external spend with suppliers accounts for £1.2 billion of the £1.9 billion turnover and is with over 15,000 suppliers. Therefore, addressing the environment as a business issue has a significant dependence upon the effective management of a wide range of suppliers' environmental performance. Furthermore, when developing sustainable construction solutions, it is often the company's suppliers' suppliers, if not further up the supply chain, where the expertise has to be mobilized, or where the significant environmental and social issues have to be addressed.

A simplified version of the supply chain activities involved in providing all of Carillion's services is shown in Figure 1. Carillion needs to be aware of the environmental issues of supply at all stages of this chain: from the extraction of primary aggregates from a quarry; to the conversion of this material into building materials and the associated energy use and carbon dioxide production; to transportation of these materials and the associated air pollution this may cause; through to the waste streams from construction sites, and their final disposal. In private finance initiative (PFI) projects the supply chain is even more complex, as in these projects the company is often responsible for the subsequent maintenance of the completed development; thus the supply chain can extend to the choice of materials used to maintain these buildings.

In 1997 an internal task force was established to develop an acceptable framework for a position statement on environmentally aware supply chain management for the group. In this process it identified the main drivers for ESCM as

- continuity of supply;
- risk management;
- environment management systems;
- market opportunities.

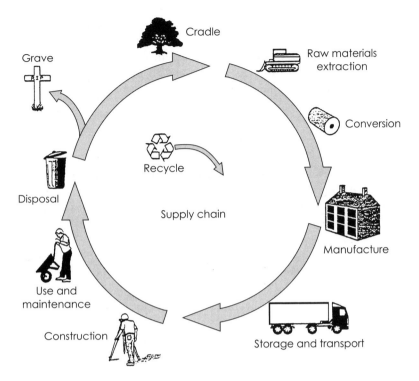

Figure 1 Supply chain cycle

Continuity of supply

A supplier who is not managing their environmental performance may be at risk of disruption due to non-compliance, pressure group action and other liabilities. This could ultimately put their ability to supply at risk as a result of costs associated with compliance affecting the business viability, or even force closure. In addition, if suppliers are not aware of the pressures on the environment and future legislative or market shifts, they are liable to become uncompetitive and are therefore a risk to the companies they supply.

Risk management

Examining and managing the effects of the supply chain can greatly reduce the risks both to the environment as a result of pollution and to an organization as a result of legislative non-compliance. For Carillion, where up to 80% of turnover is bought out, the potential risk of non-compliance with environmental legislation is significant. Even problems an site with dust or noise, for example, would be blamed on Carillion, not on the supplier carrying out the work.

Environmental management systems

Supply chain management is a crucial part of any environmental management system (EMS). The cooperation of suppliers is necessary to manage effectively all the impacts from an organization's operation.

Market opportunities

Market opportunities can be gained through both meeting stakeholder requirements and differentiating a product or service from that of a competitor. Six of Carillion's ten most important customers, including Railtrack, BT, Sainsbury's, and British Airports Authority, are seeking information about the environmental performance of their own suppliers.

The position statement (see Table 1) was published in 1998 in Tarmac's third corporate environmental report and incorporates the following:

- best practice principles from the *Business in the Environment* recommendations;
- research conducted by the task force;
- benchmarking with companies such as the Body Shop and the DIY chain B&Q.

Table 1   Carillion environmental supply chain management position statement

---

Carillion is committed to minimizing the environmental impacts of its operations, to improving the built environment and to achieving world-class performance in environmental management. It is recognized that meeting these goals will require the active involvement of all supply chain participants including customers, suppliers, subcontractors and designers.

The company will achieve best practice performance in environmentally aware supply chain management by:

- Identifying the significant impacts of materials and services in use and purchasing these to specifications which are compliant with legislation and environmentally sound.
- Considering, and encouraging other supply chain partners to consider, environmentally positive alternative specifications.
- Demonstrating efficient use of energy, water, packaging and raw materials and taking appropriate opportunities to minimize waste and to reuse and recycle.
- Assessing the environmental commitment of suppliers and subcontractors, monitoring their performance and providing feedback and advice on performance and improvement opportunities.
- Working in partnership with other participants in the supply chain to achieve continual improvement in performance and cost-effectiveness.
- Providing relevant training.
- Establishing systems, targets and action plans for the effective environmental management of the supply chain, communicating these to other participants and reporting on performance.

The implementation of the position statement has required each of Carillion's businesses to consider the risks of its own supply chains and to identify high-risk suppliers. To help the businesses, the ESCM task force developed a one-day training course, run jointly with Stanger Science and Environment, an environmental consultancy assisting Carillion with its environment programme and the purchasing function.

Purchasing to Environmentally Sound Specifications

Historically, the introduction of environmentally sound specifications has been driven by enlightened clients because the design and specification for a project has largely been undertaken by the client's consultants. However, with the increase in design-and-build contracts and PFI projects, the company has greater influence over the design and specification process and therefore the introduction of environmentally sound specifications. One of the main areas the company has been addressing has been the use of sustainable timber.

In January 1997, Carillion became the first construction and building materials company to join the WWF 1995+ group. This group is made up of over 80 companies working in partnership with the World Wildlife Fund for Nature (WWF) to improve the quality of the management of the world's forests and to encourage the use of sustainable timber. The group's target is for members to purchase substantial volumes of wood from forests certified as well managed. At present, only the Forest Stewardship Council (FSC) can provide this certification.

Carillion, and the construction industry as a whole, are major consumers of timber and timber-related products. Carillion alone spends £50 million on timber annually. The target is to source 80% of this spend from accredited forests by 2002 and is therefore a positive step towards reducing the environmental impacts associated with the supply of this product. The target is challenging due to the current limited supply of FSC-certified timber to the appropriate quality, requiring the company to understand and influence the supply chain.

For example, the company had to work closely with the window joinery manufacturer for a social housing project in Bradford to secure suitable FSC timber from Scandinavia. Historically, the joinery manufacturer would have been left to source the material from its preferred timber merchant. Since joining the WWF group, Carillion has investigated the credentials of over 30 major timber suppliers and has established the Forest Tracker database to record the environmental credentials of suppliers. This illustrates the ground work with the supply chain that may be necessary before environmentally sound specifications can be effectively applied. However, once they are in place, business advantage is obtained by being able to mobilize such options where competitors cannot.

Greener Products and Services

The issues surrounding the selection of greener alternative products are complex, as there are often play-offs between alternatives rather than clear choices. To aid internal decision-making and inform clients, the company is developing internal guidance documents on various products and materials, beginning with aggregates, timber, PVC and ozone-depleting substances.

Green procurement through optimizing the use of rock, aggregates, fill and soil arising from a construction site or from local sources has been common practice for the construction sector for some time, due to the significance of transportation costs and the introduction and increases in landfill tax in the UK. Recent efforts have been focused on challenging existing primary material bias specifications and practices and substituting recycled materials. Two examples of the supply chain working in practice follow.

Morrison's Supermarket, Bradford, UK

In conjunction with the supplier, Tarmac Quarry Products, 11,000 t of an alternative recycled concrete asphalt and type 1 sub-base was successfully offered to the client for the new build of its supermarket at Girlington, Bradford. In addition, the recycled material came from a location closer than the source of primary material.

Coastal defence, Humber and Severn Estuaries, UK

At the Hessle project on the Humber estuary, 10,000 t of the existing rock armour was either reused or crushed and used on site as bed stone material, and all 50,000 t of primary source rock armour, which was in 6–7 t blocks, was brought to site by rail. At Minehead on the Severn estuary, Carillion worked in conjunction with the client to achieve delivery of the 100,000 t of rock armour by rail by utilizing the 20 mile long West Somerset Railway, a preserved steam railway line. This eliminated the need for over 6,000 lorry movements through rural villages on secondary roads and their associated air and noise pollution.

Commitment and Performance of Suppliers

Most organizations focus only on the performance of their suppliers. The monitoring generally carried out is by means of a questionnaire to suppliers, which is resource-intensive and unfocused. This is then followed up by a requirement for them to introduce an environmental management element into their existing management systems.

After considerable research, benchmarking and consultation, Carillion has decided not to implement a questionnaire-based supplier evaluation system and has developed a risk-based approach to ESCM. This approach involves an examination of strategic risk, arising from the suppliers used, and tactical risk, from the products and services used. It tailors the action being taken to specific risks and impacts, both downstream, such as emissions, discharges and waste, and upstream, such as mineral extraction and forest management. The supplier risk approach does allow for consideration of suppliers' environmental awareness and the degree to which this is incorporated in their management systems, but utilizes third-party accreditation that is described later.

Risk-Based Approach to ESCM

The overall risk-based approach being applied to ESCM is illustrated in Figure 2 and the series of tools identified for each stage is highlighted in Figure 3.

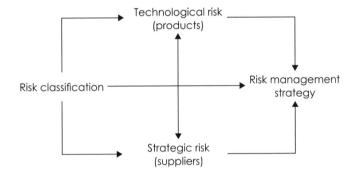

Figure 2   ESCM risk-based approach

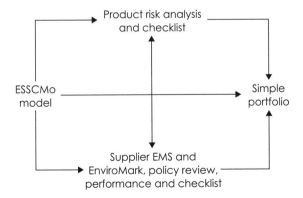

Figure 3   ESCM risk-based approach tools

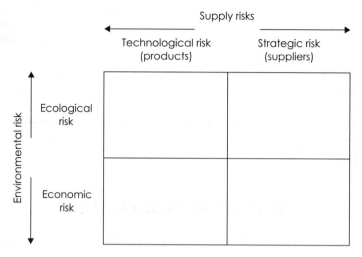

Figure 4   ESSCMo model

Risk classification

Risk classification is undertaken using a model derived from the Environmentally Sound Supply Chain Management (ESSCMo) project based at the Centre for Research in Strategic Purchasing and Supply, University of Bath, UK. The model, illustrated in Figure 4, facilitates the identification of both product and supplier risks, and their classification as either ecological or economic risks.

Product risk analysis

Through consideration of both the probability of the occurrence of a product risk and its impact, product risks are ranked and can be compared to the scorings of other products to influence prioritization of issues to manage. Supply chain mapping is also applied to identify where the risks lie in the supply chain. A simple illustration for ironmongery is shown in Figure 5. This shows that the significant impacts are often stages removed from Carillion's first-tier suppliers. They can be more pronounced in developing countries and raise further social and ethical issues, such as working conditions and debt bondage.

Supplier risk analysis

Supplier risks are assessed using a variety of tools. These range from a 20-point scoring scheme for assessing suppliers' environmental policies, through supplier awareness and management system assessment, to performance management.

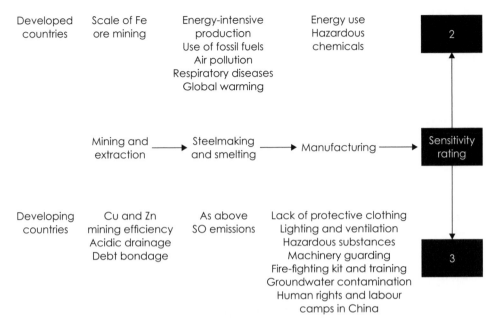

Figure 5 Environmental impact of ironmongery supply chain

The Carillion strategy of not issuing its own supplier questionnaires led it to become one of the founding patrons of the EnviroMark accreditation process, designed to help smaller businesses progress towards ISO 14001. The EnviroMark certification starts at bronze level, which is focused upon legislative compliance, through to diamond level, which is pre-certification to ISO 14001 Environmental Management Systems (EMS). This has the significant advantage of being a third-party accreditation which suppliers can use with other customers to demonstrate their level of competence on environmental issues, allows progression to a fully fledged environmental management system certification, and does not involve Carillion resources in the evaluation. Carillion also supports the equivalent scheme, Project Acorn, being delivered by BSI with support from the DTI.

Risk management strategy

The inputs from the ESSCMo model, product risk analysis and supplier risk analysis are combined and plotted on a portfolio matrix to prioritize the areas for action (see Figure 6). Where high-risk suppliers of high-risk products are identified, Carillion's business purchasing managers are being encouraged to shift to either a low-risk supplier or a low-risk product – or both, if the option is available. High-risk suppliers will be encouraged to change their practices rather than be delisted immediately.

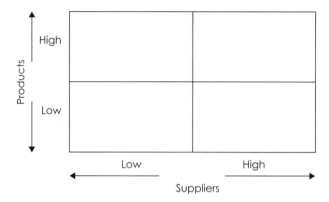

Figure 6   ESCM portfolio matrix

Working in Partnership with Suppliers for Environmental Improvement

The main focus of EnviroMark-related activities has been working with small to medium enterprises (SMEs). They help them manage their environmental performance and thus supply environmentally superior goods and services to larger companies through the EnviroMark Healthcheck and accreditation processes and SME training courses. Carillion has trained 21 suppliers in conjunction with the EnviroMark accrediting organization and progressed 34 suppliers through its Healthcheck process as the basis for them pursuing EnviroMark accreditation. These suppliers had been identified as higher-risk suppliers of higher-risk products. Carillion is now in the process of monitoring supplies through the BSI Project Acorn programme.

In addition, the company has been working with The Natural Step – the sustainable business initiative promoted in the UK by Forum for the Future – to extend ESCM to include the social and ethical dimensions of supply. Carillion has two pathfinder projects with The Natural Step (TNS): the PFI Princess Margaret Hospital in Swindon involving 15 volunteer suppliers; and the Ravenscliffe Estate social housing project in Bradford. It has committed to use the experience from these and other TNS pathfinder projects to apply the principles and approaches on all new PFI projects.

Conclusions

The trend to increase construction contractors' responsibility for design and detailed specification has increased the opportunity to introduce green products and services, and environmentally sound specifications. This in turn has served to highlight the challenges entailed in their delivery and the need to understand and influence the supply chain accordingly.

The delivery of environmentally aware and sustainable construction solutions is dependent upon the contractor working with a focused section of its supply base to achieve the necessary supplier commitment and performance.

The effective delivery of best practice ESCM is possible in a cost- and resource-effective manner through the introduction of a series of basic tools and techniques, by using a risk-based approach, understanding and managing the supply chains, and using third-party organizations to undertake evaluation, training and accreditation.

Increasingly, considering environmental issues alone will be insufficient. Broader social and ethical issues need to be addressed in order to deliver genuine sustainable construction solutions.

The challenge remains, however, to engage the many clients, suppliers and individuals who have not yet experienced or perceived the benefits of a business philosophy centred on environmental awareness and the concept of sustainability.

REFERENCES

1 *Environmental Data Services ENDS Report 294*, p. 11.
2 BS EN ISO 14001 (1996). *Environmental Management Systems – Specification with Guidance for Use*. British Standards Institution.
3 Bowen, F. E., Cousins, P. D. and Lamming, R. C., The Role of Risk in Environment-Related Supplier Initiatives. *Proceedings of the International Annual IPSERA Conference, April 1998.*

Part 2

Inter-Organizational Relationships

This part explores inter-organizational relationships (IORs) within product systems. Very many different types of IOR are set up (or come into being by default) in this context, ranging from traditional arm's-length relationships to collaboration and strategic alliances. In terms of size, they encompass everything from dyadic partnerships to networks with many members, large organizations and small ones. They may be cross-cultural, extending across the globe, or primarily local in character, lasting for decades or for just a few months. In almost all cases they are complex and require sensitive management. The chapters in this part illuminate such dimensions and tease out some important lessons for the practice of supply chain management.

With the increasing liberalization of markets, smaller firms with unique products and services have new opportunities to develop distinctive niches and to establish strategic supply relationships with larger buyers, sometimes across cultural divides. For some western SMEs, building a long term relationship with a Japanese buyer has been a critical factor in their success. The challenge for the supplier is in adapting to Japanese style buyer–supplier practice. Cooray and Ratnatunga (Chapter 2.1) study such a culturally sensitive partnership between a large Japanese buyer and a specialist SME Australian supplier. They examine differing perceptions in areas such as product features and customer-driven quality, business procedures and controls, and the correlation between effort and rewards. A notable recommendation for achieving congruence between the expectations of the two sides is the development and effective management of the critical role of 'link-pin' – in this case a member of staff in the Australian company who was familiar with the Japanese language, markets and business culture. She was able to act as facilitator or mediator to manage the 'formal linking processes' in the adjustment of the two parties to their longer term buyer–supplier relationship.

Handfield et al. (Chapter 2.2) and Liker and Wu (Chapter 2.3) continue the theme of relationships with suppliers. They both underline the importance, and the impact, of those relationships on supplier performance.

Handfield et al. investigate good practice in supplier development strategies. When suppliers fail to meet the expectations of a large customer, that customer may

'(1) bring the outsourced item in-house and produce it internally, (2) change to a more capable supplier, or (3) help improve the existing supplier's capabilities'. The third option is 'a long-term business strategy that is the basis for an integrated supply chain'. It involves commitment of resources by both parties and a varied programme of activities. The authors find that achieving a transformation in which suppliers become attuned to continuous improvement is not easy and that patient, sustained management of the relationship brings rewards.

Liker and Wu undertake a comparative analysis of supply chain performance in the American automotive sector, examining the relationships of suppliers to their US automaker and Japanese implant customers. It reveals that a buyer's lean practice and internal policies can have a profound effect on its suppliers' ability to optimize operations. The Japanese implants have 'brought the goals of lean manufacturing to their supply base in the United States and are much more successful in these practices than their US competitors'. The authors explore the reasons for the success of the Japanese companies in motivating their suppliers and the relative failure of the US companies to reach the same standards of supply chain performance.

Next, Harvey (Chapter 2.4) considers recent developments in retailing in the UK, raising some key questions about change in the nature of competition in this sector, and the connection between such change and innovation. In discussing the assertion that UK supermarkets now provide the model for food retailing across Europe, he highlights advances in SCM as leading innovation, for example with the introduction of an extensive chill chain for the supply of fresh produce. He argues that competition policy needs to take into account the long term impact of innovation, as well as short term pricing. He also touches on associated issues relating to quality of life.

Den Hond (Chapter 2.5) addresses innovation in SCM, focusing his interest around the product end-of-life phase. He contrasts theories of 'similarity' in innovation processes – that firms operating under similar conditions innovate in similar ways – with 'heterogeneity', that 'innovation processes are seen as socially constructed, following a unique historical path or trajectory in which not only technological or other problems, but also the visions, objectives and expectations of innovators and other social actors, play a role'. This stresses variety in innovation 'in terms of strategy, structure and performance, among firms that operate within the same contexts'. The chapter explores the innovatory response of the European automotive industry to regulation designed to increase the percentage of materials that are recovered from vehicle recycling and to systematize the recovery processes. It describes a case study of eight companies which aims to map their approaches to innovation in this field with respect to the 'similarity' and 'heterogeneity' theses. It concludes by proposing a third way: 'that sources of variety stem from managerial discretion in directing and coordinating the innovation process . . . the choice of a specific solution and mode of coordination by individual firms depends on the relation between the resources needed for this solution and the core competencies of this firm. The relation is described in terms of complementarity of resources and activities, perceived technological opportunity, and appropriability conditions.'

Berry et al. (Chapter 2.6) draw attention to the key role of management accounting in supply chains and its influence on IORs. They explain the link between the history of scientific management and the rise of management accounting, which provides a basis for decision making through analysis of activity-based costing, traditionally in vertically integrated organizations. Taking a more holistic view of the attribution of costs and benefits shared amongst supply chain partners leads to measures such as total cost of acquisition or total cost of ownership.

The authors' research questions are: 'What is the observed contribution of management accounting to the management of supply chains? What are the explanations for that contribution?' They explore four ideal-type models of relationships, using inter-firm supply chain case studies. They find that supply chain thinking and development is 'having a major impact upon the practice of management accountants in organizational management. Management accountants were contributing to the strategic management of the inter- and intra-firm supply chain . . . [they] are active partners in the new management teams' cultures – a development which follows the logic of the evolving supply chains as well as holding to the logics of hierarchy. Management accountants are getting involved in cost management for efficiency and effectiveness, and in strategic issues through their involvement in multi-functional teams which look at processes and functions . . . we can see the emergence of logistic modelling . . . When integrated with accounting and marketing data, this will provide the basis for new process driven integrated information systems.' However, they note that: 'The processes of change are episodic, based in *ad hoc* projects, and innovations in management practice and management accounting responses.' Further exploration of theory and practice in this area remains to be undertaken.

Some ethical issues for companies engaged in supply chain management were raised in Part 1, with Kaplinsky (Chapter 1.3) emphasizing the need for integrity in value chain governance and Hampson (Chapter 1.4) describing the need to counter 'management by stress'. Winstanley et al. (Chapter 2.7) deal with the controversies surrounding human resource management in the globalized supply chain, focusing particularly on ethical approaches to child labour. They examine 'what companies can do to improve working conditions down an international supply chain, and, more specifically, how they can tackle and implement policies of "no child labour"'. Using vignettes of companies, they explore the practical implications of the 'Three-I' model of corporate approaches to human rights developed earlier by one of the authors: ignorance, indifference, involvement. The last, where companies consider their responsibilities in this area seriously and take action, may lead to a response of either engagement or disengagement. Their main case study, of an international sports footwear brand owner, 'outlines the difficulties faced by a company . . . that decides not to disengage with suppliers in a certain area, or with the factories of that area, but does attempt to disengage from utilising "child labour"'. Among the issues encountered by the company in implementing its own ethical code of conduct – the Standards of Engagement – and, in particular, trying to provide educational support for underage workers, were the range and complexity of relationships within the supply chain, which make it difficult to agree a common approach with all the key stakeholders, as well as culture and gender. The authors conclude that the cost of addressing human rights issues does not deter companies from reaching into developing countries to reduce supply chain costs, estimating the former at about 5 per cent of the savings made from such globalization. They warn of the need for demands surrounding child labour to be carefully framed to 'focus on the context in which it is being addressed, consider for whose benefit . . . [it] is being made, and produce workable arrangements that can be implemented over the long term to develop sustainable rather than short-term solutions'.

Buyer–Supplier Relationships: A Case Study of a Japanese and Western Alliance

Shiran Cooray and Janek Ratnatunga

Introduction

Today's business world is one of inter-corporate relationships, found in an increasing variety and complexity of forms – joint ventures, licence agreements, franchising, research/technology consortia and strategic supplier networks.[1] Many of these relationships are between parties from very different national and organisational cultures, and often it is this very difference that creates the value proposition behind such partnerships. A firm valuing independence and innovation, and finding such qualities are not fostered in its own business climate, may seek an alliance with a firm from an alternative business culture. But such partnerships can face significant barriers to long-term success, mostly arising from the different perceptions and expectations of each party, which have been formed by the unique economic, social and cultural environment of their country of origin. These differences may include issues of product features, customer-driven quality, business procedures and controls and rewards expectations. However, for the partnerships to flourish, these barriers must be overcome, and some productive compromises must be found between different styles of business achieved; simply imposing one partner's business culture on the other would negate the very value proposition that underpins the choice of a partner from a different culture.

This research study considers how some of these control issues played out at a single site where an Australian firm with a unique high-tech product entered a partnership as a supplier to a large Japanese firm. The relationship established can be characterised as a buyer–supplier *partnership* with the Western firm responsible for product development and the Japanese firm responsible for market development. The study examines the sources of the difficulties that arose and the alternative modes of adjustment that were employed to secure a successful partnership despite the differences in both scale and background business culture of the partners.

Monitoring Buyer–Supplier Relationships

Previously viewed merely as 'procurement', supply is now seen as a strategic part of a value chain that stretches from the supplier to the end-customer. Suppliers are no longer individual, transient providers, chosen purely on the basis of lowest cost, but networked 'business partners', selected to allow organisations to improve continuously and deliver value to their stakeholders.

While Japanese buyer–supplier relationships vary among firms and across industries, with firms as different as Toyota, Canon and Nintendo naturally adopting different approaches to dealing with their suppliers, certain commonalties (discussed extensively by Nishiguchi[2]) can be noted. An understanding of these is vital to developing successful relations with a Japanese firm.

Once a Japanese buyer has selected component suppliers, they will be retained during the life cycle of the specific model: this was the approach taken by the Japanese in this case. Personnel from the buyer firm will typically be in charge of training supplier staff on the buyers' production and quality procedures, and also go beyond this formal role to make a comprehensive evaluation of the whole firm. This evaluation is critical to the relationship, as the buyer firm 'tests' whether a long-term relationship with the supplier is viable, and can obviously be made problematic if there are communication difficulties between the two sets of personnel. If the supplier firm can pass this test, the future prospects for a valuable long-term relationship are extremely good.

Western firms need both to understand the unique characteristics of Japanese buyer–supplier relations and to develop specific ways of handling them. However, the Japanese model must not be allowed to dominate, as the point of the strategic partnership is to utilise the particular strengths of Western firms. Their less-structured approach, the lack of formal controls and freer communication are perceived as underpinning the innovative environment that the Japanese value as their reasons behind seeking the alliance. According to Turnbull, Oliver and Wilkinson:[3]

> It is argued that the Japanese model involves very high intra- and inter-organisational dependencies . . . Pursuit of the pure Japanese model . . . risks sweeping away potential strengths of the existing structure.

Structure of Research

The study was conducted by two researchers (one based in Australia, the other in Japan) and included a one-and-a-half month field study in the supplier firm. The literature provides ample evidence of the appropriateness of generalising from the findings of single-site case studies.[4] Permission was obtained to attend relevant meetings, to interview personnel and to examine documentation (including, in this case, supply contracts). This access, once gained, had to be continuously maintained through appropriate negotiation. During a period of intense activity just prior to the delivery of the product, the on-site researcher also acted as a *de facto* facilitator in the change management process, enabling him to observe the success or failure of various alternative strategies implemented to enhance the buyer–supplier relationship. This article also examines the factors affecting the success of these relations over both the short and the long term, and the strategies for managing such relations.

Business Context and Relationship Environment

The Australian firm was a venture started by two founders with a Western business background, one a technical visionary and the other a marketing wizard. Started 7 years previously to develop an add-in product for a major piece of office equipment, the company had enjoyed continuous growth, with staffing at the development facility having grown to about 50, including a small administrative staff. Virtually all were highly talented and technically oriented personnel, who enjoyed the free culture established by the founders. There had been staff turnover, but a core team of developers including the lead architect remained with the company.

One year prior to the contract with the Japanese firm, the Australian firm had merged with a US based firm, allowing it to offer its products to a wider market, and further strengthening the company's 'Western' management orientation. Although this relationship was instrumental in winning the current contract, in terms of organisational controls the Australian operation had been largely untouched by the merger, continuing to operate very much as an independent entity.

The Australian company had developed a unique product – an add-on element to a major piece of office equipment – and had entered into an agreement with the Japanese buyer to customise it to fit with the buyer's own product. The buyer firm was one of the top three suppliers in the world of this end-product, and amongst the top 50 Japanese firms in terms of sales. The market for the particular end-product in question was maturing, and the buyer firm saw the Australian add-on product – a hardware/software combination – as one way of enhancing the main product. A competitor US based firm (the market leader) was already supplying the Japanese firm with a proprietary solution, but it was expensive, and the US supplier was reluctant to provide detailed information about the product to the Japanese buyer. In contrast, the Australian firm had found a novel way of delivering the same functionality using a large component of generic hardware and software. This solution was cheaper, allowed for more rapid product introductions and reduced the dependency risk for the buyer firm, as information was more easily shared.

The Japanese buyer had maintained a long-standing relationship with the previous US supplier, and was very satisfied with that add-on product's quality and performance. From its perspective, however, the relationship with the US firm was not ideal, the Japanese side feeling that the strongly placed US firm was inflexible, its unwilling-ness to share information giving it too much negotiating power. Conversely, the

Australian supplier, relatively weak in this market, was perceived as being more 'balanced' at the negotiating table. The Japanese buyer firm was attracted by the Australians' product innovations and information sharing approach, and selected them as supplier when a new product was planned.

However, the window of opportunity was small, as it was felt that competitors would soon start closing in. Establishing a long-term relationship was seen as crucial for mutual business success, securing continuity of supply for the buyer and generating much-needed R&D funds for the supplier.

At the start of the relationship, teams of engineers from the buyer firm, ostensibly responsible for quality assurance, were located in the supplier firm, and researchers categorised two levels of relations between the two firms.

1　*The Strategic level*　Top supplier managers and the buyer's divisional head agreed on the overall direction of the relationship, and also strategic issues such as product schedules and pricing. Relations at this level were very smooth: top supplier managers had visited Japan several times and developed trust and a good understanding with the Japanese side.
2　*The Operational level*　In contrast, interactions between the supplier's product development, quality assurance and production groups and the buyer's quality assurance team were contentious and relations were sour at times. The analysis of buyer–supplier relations in this article mostly focuses at this level.

The initial impression obtained from discussions with the Japanese team was that they felt the Australian side was not very responsive to their requirements, and that a Japanese supplier would have treated them much better. At the strategic level, the Australian managers could not understand why these feelings existed as they had spent money and time lavishly in entertaining the Japanese buyer team, and believed that they had done everything they could to make them happy. Meanwhile, at the operational level, the Australian opinion was that the Japanese made unreasonable demands about product quality and time schedules, and generally interfered in matters beyond their boundaries – in effect, the Australians felt, trying to control the whole supplier firm. A detailed look at the underlying causes of this friction reveals several areas of mutual misunderstanding.

Differing views of the product's features

The product development and design had been completely carried through by the Australian supplier, and so a significant irritant for those at the supplier operational level was the constant reference (including demonstrations) by the buyer's quality assurance (QA) team to a competitor product's functional superiority. At the strategic level the Australian firm had promised the Japanese firm both a superior product and an open and frank discussion of problem issues. But this had not been communicated to its own operational people, who thus saw the Japanese comparisons as negative and confrontational.

The real issue was that the Australian supplier did not understand that creating competition between the two potential suppliers for a similar product is normal behaviour for a Japanese buyer, and that they as a 'competitor supplier' needed strategies for handling such situations. At the strategic level, top supplier managers had a good understanding of this issue, and could clearly show the advantages of their product over that of the competitor. But this understanding had not been communicated to staff at the operational levels, at least half of whom were contract workers, who had infrequent communication with top managers and relatively low commitment to customer satisfaction.

Differing perceptions of customer-driven quality

A significant issue between the firms was perception of *quality*, made all the more important since the buyer's QA team was continuously monitoring product quality on-site at the supplier premises. Supplier staff mostly understood quality as satisfying the *specifications* – as long as the product could do what was intended, it was satisfactory – while the buyer side regarded quality as a matter of *customer satisfaction*, which included even its appearance. Many misunderstandings ensued, with supplier staff being particularly irritated by the Japanese making demands on their time over what they perceived to be very minor issues. When the Japanese QA team, aiming at end-user perceived perfection, showed aspects of the product they felt would not make a good impression on a Japanese customer, these were not taken seriously by Australian staff content with the technical perfection of the product and impatient of 'minor' cosmetic issues. Attempts were made to put the blame on third parties such as the operating system, which were only partly justified, and the whole interaction clearly indicated culturally different definitions of 'non-performance'.

Further examples of this 'cultural gap' involved the approach to developing different-language versions of the product, where the Australian side underestimated the need to invest in successful localisation for the Japanese market, and the fact that their attitude to product set-up assumed levels of technical competence in the end-user which were at odds with what the Japanese side felt their customers could be expected to possess.

Such cultural differences are well understood by those concerned with international buyer–supplier relations. The East-Asia Analytical Unit of the Australian Department of Trade and Industry conducts highly focused research on various aspects of Japanese industry and commerce. Its 1997 analysis of the Japanese consumer reported that:[5]

> Japanese consumers seek quality, reasonably priced products. Minor faults, for example in presentation, unimportant in other markets, can make products unacceptable in Japan.

Unfortunately these well-established insights were not communicated to staff at the supplier's operational level.

Differing business procedures

The key differences in this area were the acceptable levels of information disclosure, of involvement in the partner firm's processes and of formal controls. A significant part of the Japanese buyer's unhappiness with its previous US supplier was its reluctance to share product and cost information it considered proprietary. But it is often noted that Japanese buyers seek more information than Western buyers do,[6] and that this may be a key factor in the success of relations with a Japanese buyer. As they only had to quote a price to win the contract, the Australian firm initially found it difficult to understand the advantages of disclosing further information, especially cost data. But Japanese firms consider the provision of such higher levels of information to be a factor affecting the success of long-term relations, particularly as far as helping their suppliers in terms of continuous improvement. Such 'helpful' suggestions were not always welcomed by the Western firm in this case.

Differing perceptions of control structures

The approach to the introduction of a control framework showed another key area of cultural differences. A simple classification of business procedures defines *formal controls* as explicit procedures, including regular benchmarking of supplier prices, formal supplier evaluation systems using financial and/or non-financial performance measures, legal provisions to meet performance standards, etc., that seek to maintain or alter patterns of behaviour in organisational activities. *Informal controls*, on the other hand, rely on the application of interpersonal and social norms to affect behaviour, and include trust, socialisation processes, etc. It is expected that in most buyer–supplier relationships the *control mix* will comprise some combination of such formal and informal controls.[7]

Little is known of the how the mix of inter- and intra-firm relationships and control mechanisms operates in supply networks. Surveys tend not to distinguish between official controls and controls-in-use: legal remedies for non-performance in supply contracts may not be evoked because they are seen as a 'last' rather than a 'first' resort – and 'non-performance' may also have different cultural interpretations. Controls tend to be seen in isolation of each other. As far as the interrelationship of formal and informal controls is concerned, some studies claim that 'trust' in recurrent relationships replaces other control mechanisms,[8] while others suggest that high levels of trust co-exist with elaborate control mechanisms.[9]

This study suggests that the fundamental cultural difference in the expected level of formal control systems is directly related to the duration of the strategic buyer–supplier relationship (see Figure 1). The Western firm in the study expected initially a low level of formal control, and much more reliance on informal mechanisms such as trust. Believing that the required key performance indicators and benchmarks would only be established reliably after observing trends over time, the Western firm expected that, as the relationship matured, it could put more faith in formal control

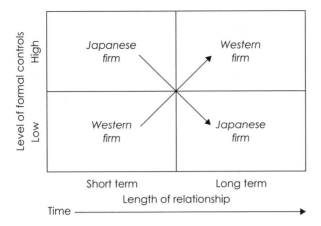

Figure 1   Time–control divergence

systems. Hence, as the arrows in Figure 1 indicate, the Western firm expected to increase the level of formal controls over time.

In contrast, the Japanese policy is to rely on a high level of formal controls at the start of a relationship. If the partner firm meets these initial benchmarks, trust is earned and the degree of formal control is relaxed. Hence, as the arrows indicate, the Japanese firm would expect to *decrease* the level of formal controls over time.

The effect of temporality on the level of control has been investigated by Heide and Miner, and more recently by Ring and Van de Ven.[10] The latter authors have suggested that informal psychological contracts increasingly compensate or substitute for formal contractual safeguards as reliance on trust between partners increases over time, echoing the Japanese firm's observed view of the changes in the use of formal controls over time.

The Australian firm's approach suggests that in the face of performance uncertainty, both contracting parties may agree, explicitly or implicitly, to suspend the use of formal controls at the start. However, as knowledge of input–output relationships increases over time, firms would substitute formal for more informal controls in order to minimise potential losses.

The Japanese buyer firm in this research study was very large, and had refined formal procedures perfected over a long period for most tasks, including quality assurance. In contrast, the supplier firm was relatively new and had a very informal atmosphere where people from product development, production, quality assurance, marketing and top management interacted continuously with each other. There were few established procedures and protocols, although attempts were being made to make some activities more formal. The visiting Japanese QA team attempted to maintain congruence between their ways of doing work and that of the supplier, and on many occasions were observed insisting on informally 'helping' the supplier firm in process improvements,[11] despite the fact that this was beyond their agreed brief.

While an informal atmosphere is certainly a good way of increasing communication within a firm, when issues of quality and lead time are paramount and when working with a customer accustomed to formal procedures, it is important that at least some formal controls are adopted. But, with informality almost a religion at the Australian firm, when the researcher (acting as facilitator) indicated the need for a level of formal procedures, the Western response was negative.

In this case, immature buyer–supplier business procedures involving a number of non-value-adding activities also delayed product completion, a further cause of irritation between the parties. The product launch was delayed by over three months, and the chance of developing a strong early lead over the market competitor was considerably weakened.

Differences in the effort–rewards structure

The Japanese buyer is a household name in the worldwide consumer electronics market. In contrast, the Australian supplier is a high-tech SME, and considered all its relationships from this perspective. It boasted strong entrepreneurial personalities and engineering dominance in management on the one hand, but had little marketing and international business exposure and experience on the other hand, and (an inevitable reality for many SMEs) possessed limited resources.

The Australian operational managers felt that the Japanese insistence on formal controls resulted in much non-value-adding activity. They perceived that, since their costs were higher than expected during the initial phase of the relationship, their rewards would be lower than expected. From the observations made in this case, we believe that it is essential for Western suppliers to understand the effort–rewards structure in Japanese buyer–supplier relations (see Figure 2).

In terms of cost–benefit, the supplier perceived that rewards would be much lower than effort during the initial stages. Since short-term working capital was very tight, price became an important factor: the supplier felt that, even though this was a long-term contract, it needed a better short-term return, especially for its engineering efforts. They soon realised that the profit rewards from a relationship with a Japanese buyer can take some time to realise. This was a very difficult period for the supplier, as the buyer firm was still continually evaluating whether it intended to establish long-term relations with the supplier.

Our view is that this is typical of such buyer–supplier relations, especially those between an SME and a large firm. The smaller supplier may not earn any profit on the initial contract, as was the case here. But once the proper relationship is in place, the supplier will hope that rewards will exceed effort. The most successful suppliers will reach the 'switching point' (as shown in Figure 2) swiftly; the least successful suppliers may never reach it at all.

In our field study firm, we estimate that this switching point will occur when the need for stationing a buyer's QA team at the supplier site ceases. At this point, the supplier firm will have a high enough level of knowledge of the buyer's requirements that they will be able to handle quality issues by themselves. The buyer firm

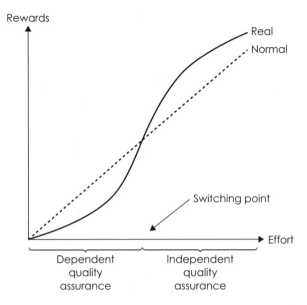

Figure 2   Effort–rewards structure in Japanese buyer–supplier relations

will accrue large savings from withdrawing their team and through improved quality, and these savings will be passed on to the supplier firm. However, at the time of writing this case, this point had not been reached.

Modes of Adaptation between Japanese Buyers and Australian Suppliers

The previous section identified several difficulties between the two partners, arising from uneven expectations. One could argue that these difficulties arose due to the specific corporate cultures of the two firms. However the authors are of the view that the two firms displayed typical national characteristics rather than any unique firm attributes, and (based on the theory discussed earlier) their observations are generalisable in understanding buyer–supplier relations between Western and Japanese business organisations.

The researchers recognised that, for such relationships to be fruitful, some degree of congruence in buyer–supplier expectations needs to be achieved. Although language difficulties and work hour patterns[12] may make complete congruence unrealistic – even unnecessary – the issue is one of reaching a level of congruence that will facilitate relations. The best way of achieving congruence of expectations between such parties is to educate Western staff about the expected norms of the Japanese buying environment, and the Japanese buyer on the merits of the Western approach to work. Mutual understanding in these areas is essential to minimise conflict, and can be approached in a variety of ways.

Supplier firm staff visiting the buyer firm

Although the supplier firm's staff visited the Japanese on a number of occasions and had a chance to interact with their counterparts, these visits were short and only involved managerial levels and above. The frequent interactions at this strategic level yielded smooth relations, but as these managers took no interest in addressing the operational issues identified, the visits were of limited use in achieving mutual understanding across the firm as a whole. We recommend a good balance of visits at both the strategic and the operational levels.

Buyer firm staff visiting the supplier firm

Although the buyer's quality assurance team was stationed at the suppliers for 4 months, they made virtually no contribution towards resolving the difficulties they identified, mainly because of communication difficulties. The Japanese team was unable to find an acceptable way to educate the supplier staff on the requirements of the Japanese market, and, rather than resolving issues, some of their attempts led to further misunderstanding.

Hiring an external consultant

It is paramount, therefore, that good communication links are established prior to extended visits by operational teams: in this case, the lack of awareness of potential problems meant that internal managers made no effort to head them off. We recommend that this function be undertaken by a person who speaks both languages fluently, and who is perceived to be independent.

An ideal way to resolve potential buyer–supplier relationship problems would be to hire an outside consultant to handle the task of mutual education outlined above. External consultants have the advantage of an independence of opinion that can be respected by both parties. However, where the issues involved need more direct and sustained intervention, a part-time external consultant may not be ideal.

Hiring knowledgeable staff

A more successful option would be for the supplier firm to hire staff familiar with both the Japanese language and the Japanese market on a more full-time basis. In this case, a turning point in relations between the buyer and the supplier came when the Australian firm hired a quality engineer with previous experience in Japan and a good knowledge of both language and market requirements. She quickly became much sought after, as both sides used her to assist inter-team communication, and top managers invited her to participate in strategic negotiations. Her capable handling of this wide brief allowed relations between the parties to become much smoother. Her day-to-day interaction with product developers and other staff led to improvements in their understanding of the Japanese requirements, and this was particularly evident in her efforts at fixing even very minor problems, which would previously have been considered a waste of time, and been left to the Japanese QA team to identify.

However problems soon developed associated with the mismatch between her role as it developed and her position in the organisation. Originally hired to test the product under Japanese operating systems, she soon accrued levels of understanding and influence beyond that of her superiors, a situation which bred considerable resentment,[13] including even the suspicion that she was passing confidential information to the Japanese side. Despite her beneficial effect on communications she eventually left the firm, realising that her role would also be in demand in other firms.

It is evident that hiring a staff member familiar with the language and the requirements of the Japanese market is the best approach to *adjustment* between Japanese buyers and Western suppliers. In this case her understanding of the Japanese environment earned her the respect of the Japanese, who were then willing to accept her explanations of the Australian style of work. Most of the supplier staff considered her a vital resource and also came to accept her explanations of Japanese requirements, despite the problems that developed later. Her role is of the type of *link-pin* suggested by Likert and Likert.[14]

However, on this occasion, the *organisational positioning* of the link-pin was clearly inappropriate, and the researchers identified that an independent position in the firm – perhaps just below project manager – would have been more suitable, with departments being required to negotiate for her services. (Such an arrangement was, in fact, considered, but unfortunately not enacted.)

Conclusion: Key Issues in Japanese Buyer–Supplier Relations

This article has examined issues relating to the monitoring of buyer–supplier relationships, focusing on how an Australian high-tech product supplier adapted to the requirements of a large Japanese buyer. The field study shows that, despite the existence of substantial differences between the firms, it was possible to develop a fruitful long-term relationship.[15]

Four key issues were isolated by the researchers as being fundamental to the success of these cross-cultural buyer–supplier relationships.

- Good relations at the strategic level are essential to the success of activities at the operational level. Their absence will lead to fundamental instability, which will in turn affect activities at the operational level. But communication between these two levels is also important: in this case, due to weak intra-firm communication, strategic level personnel did not make a significant contribution towards ensuring successful relations at the operational level. This resulted in many differences of perception in terms of product functionality and quality.

- Secondly, understanding the role of formal controls in different business cultures is important, especially in terms of the relationship between the levels of formal controls and the longevity of the strategic partnership. The study found that approaches to the need for formal controls were relative to the maturity of the partnership, and that the Japanese and Western firm approached the introduction of formal controls in a diametrically opposite manner (see Figure 1). Successful strategic partnerships must achieve a 'balance' between these two approaches.

- Thirdly, it is essential for Western suppliers to understand the effort–rewards structure in Japanese buyer–supplier relationships. In the Japanese–Western buyer–supplier relations as observed in this case, the rewards for the supplier were much lower than effort during the initial stages. Once the relationship has passed a certain 'switching point', however, rewards should exceed effort (see Figure 2). Successful suppliers who can circumvent those business cultural issues that cause delays and achieve swifter understanding of the buyer's requirements will reach this switching point faster than those who make no or unsuccessful efforts in these regards.

- Fourthly, the effective use of a link-pin and the establishment of effectively managed formal linking processes may be ultimately the most important factor in the success of such strategic partnerships. This aspect was a success as well as a failure in our field study firm. The development of good communications at all levels, the balance between formal and informal controls, and the speed with which the switching point is reached will very much depend on the role of the link-pin and how well the linking processes are encouraged within such a strategic partnership.

NOTES

1   For fuller discussion, see P. S. Ring and A. H. Van De Ven, Structuring cooperative relationships between organizations, *Strategic Management Journal* **13**, 483–498 (1992); and C. Handy, *The Age of Unreason*, Random House, London (1991).

2   See T. Nishiguchi and J. Brookfield, The evolution of Japanese subcontracting, *Sloan Management Review* **39**(1), 89–101 (1997).

3   See P. Turnbull, N. Oliver and B. Wilkinson, Buyer–supplier relations in the UK automotive industry: strategic implications of the Japanese manufacturing model, *Strategic Management Journal* **13**, 159–168 (1992).

4   In terms of previous single-site case studies, the literature is quite substantial. Recent work has been done in retailing by A. S. Sohal and E. Lu, The quest for quality in Safeway Australia, *Asia Pacific Journal of Quality Management* **4**(3), 44–61 (1995); in catering services by Z. Y. Chang, W. Y. Yeong and L. Loh, Critical success factors for in-flight catering services: Singapore airport terminal services' practices and management benchmarks, *The TQM Magazine* **9**(4), 255–259 (1997); and in education by S. Schauerman and B. Peachy, Strategies for implementation: the El Camino College total quality management story, *Community College Journal of Research and Practice* **18**(4), 345–358 (1994). Further, the much quoted literature on the balanced scorecard is

drawn from a number of detailed single-site case studies, especially in R. S. Kaplan and D. P. Norton, The balanced scorecard: measures that drive performance, *Harvard Business Review* January–February, 71–79 (1992). The authors considered it acceptable, therefore, to conduct a single-site case study.

5 See Department of Trade and Industry, *New Japan? Changes in Asia's Mega-Market*, a report by the East Asia Analytical Unit (July 1997).

6 See M. Munday, Accounting cost data disclosure in buyer–supplier partnerships: a research note, *Management Accounting Research* **3**(3), 245–250 (1992).

7 See K. G. Provan and S. J. Skinner, Interorganizational dependence and control as predictors of opportunism in dealer–supplier relations, *Academy of Management Journal* **32**(1), 202–212 (1989); and J. McMillan, Managing suppliers: incentive systems in Japanese and U.S. industry, *California Management Review* Summer, 38–55 (1990). Also see Ring and Van De Ven (1992) (Note 1) and their later work in P. S. Ring and A. H. Van De Ven, Developmental processes of cooperative interorganizational relationships, *Academy of Management Review* **19**(1), 90–118 (1994).

8 For fuller discussion see J. C. Jarillo, On strategic networks, *Strategic Management Journal* **9**, 31–41 (1988); and A. Parke, Strategic alliance structuring: a game theoretic and transaction cost examination of interfirm cooperation, *Academy of Management Journal* **36**, 794–829 (1993).

9 See Ring and Van de Ven (1992) (Note 1).

10 See discussion in J. B. Heide and A. S. Miner, The shadow of the future: effects of anticipated interaction and frequency of contact on buyer–seller cooperation, *Academy of Management Journal* **35**(2), 265–291 (1992); and L. D. Browning, J. M. Beyer and J. C. Shetler, Building cooperation in a competitive industry: Sematech and the semiconductor industry, *Academy of Management Journal* **38**(1), 113–151 (1995). Also see Parke (1993) (Note 8) and Ring and Van de Ven (1994) (Note 7).

11 See discussion by Heide and Miner (1992) (Note 10) and more recently by Ring and Van de Ven (1994) (Note 7).

12 When the product launch was running behind schedule, the Australian project manager encouraged operational staff to do weekend work, but the reception was negative. Meanwhile the Japanese team was doing weekend work voluntarily.

13 The relation between language and power in a multinational firm is discussed in R. Marschan, D. Welch and L. Welch, In the shadow: the impact of language on structure, power and communication in the multinational, Working Paper, Department of Marketing, University of Western Sydney, Nepean (1998). In this paper an almost identical situation is reported.

14 See for full discussion R. Likert and J. Likert, *New Patterns of Management*, McGraw-Hill, New York (1976).

15 A study by K. Langfield-Smith and M. Greenwood, Developing co-operative buyer–supplier relationships: a case study of Toyota, *Journal of Management Studies* **35**(3), 331–353 (1998) reports the case of Toyota Australia developing Japanese style buyer–supplier relations with its suppliers in Australia.

Avoid the Pitfalls in Supplier Development

Robert B. Handfield, Daniel R. Krause,
Thomas V. Scannell and Robert M. Monczka

As manufacturing firms outsource more parts and services to focus on their own core competencies, they increasingly expect their suppliers to deliver innovative, quality products on time at a competitive cost. When a supplier is incapable of meeting these needs, a buyer has three alternatives: (1) bring the outsourced item in-house and produce it internally, (2) change to a more capable supplier, or (3) help improve the existing supplier's capabilities.

All three strategies can work. The choice often depends on price, volume, or the strategic nature of the procured item. For low-value-added, nonstrategic commodities, the cost of changing to a new supplier is low, and switching may be the best option. At the other extreme, when an underperforming supplier provides an innovative product or process technology (that may be of sustainable long-term advantage to the buyer), the buyer may wish to protect this potential advantage and bring the work in-house by acquiring the supplier. In those cases that lie between these two extremes – and even at times including these extremes – the best option may be 'supplier development'.

We define supplier development as any activity that a buyer undertakes to improve a supplier's performance and/or capabilities to meet the buyer's short-term or long-term supply needs. Buying firms use a variety of activities to improve supplier performance, including assessing suppliers' operations, providing incentives to improve performance, instigating competition among suppliers, and working directly with suppliers, through either training or other activities.[1]

Supplier development requires both firms to commit financial, capital, and personnel resources to the work; to share timely and sensitive information; and to create an effective means of measuring performance. Thus, this strategy is challenging for both parties. Buyer executives and employees must be convinced that investing company resources in a supplier is a worthwhile risk. Supplier executives must be convinced that their best interest lies in accepting direction and assistance from their customer. Even if the two companies mutually agree that supplier development is important, success is not a foregone conclusion.

Although difficult, supplier development can be an important 'cornerstone' in the deployment of a truly integrated supply chain. The average manufacturing firm spends over 50 percent of its revenues on purchased inputs.[2] With companies continuing to increase the volume of outsourced work across industries,[3] this percentage is likely to rise. Consequently, suppliers will have a greater impact on the quality, cost, technology, and delivery of a buying company's own products and services, and thus on its profitability. The direct effect of supplier performance on a buyer's bottom line highlights the importance of optimizing supply chain performance. Thus, we propose the following.

Continuous long-term improvement of supplier performance is only achieved by:

1   identifying where value is created in the supply chain;
2   positioning the buyer strategically in line with value creation;
3   implementing an integrated supply chain management strategy to maximize internal and external capabilities throughout the supply chain.

We believe that improved supplier performance will not be realized or sustained unless buyers recognize procurement and supply chain management (SCM) as sources of competitive advantage and align their SCM strategy with their overall business strategy.[4] Any performance improvements gained without this strategic alignment are likely to be short term and perhaps only tactical in nature. Some companies with successful supplier-development programs suggest that first addressing easy-to-fix supplier problems helps build momentum. However, it is best to view supplier development as a long-term business strategy that is the basis for an integrated supply chain. The first step, therefore, is to successfully implement supplier-development programs. This study addresses the pitfalls that impede such efforts.

. . .

We begin by describing a process map that many firms intuitively employ. We found that, although most firms are able to identify suppliers requiring development, relatively few are completely successful in their supplier-development efforts. Then we explore the most significant pitfalls in supplier development and present strategies used to avoid them. Our goal is to provide general guidelines for supplier-development efforts.

A Process Map for Supplier Development

After scanning supplier-development strategies used in more than sixty organizations, we developed the following seven-step generic process map for deploying these initiatives.[5] Other case studies of supplier-development efforts describe variations of this model.[6] Most of the organizations studied deployed the first three or four steps, but they were less successful with the remaining steps.

Step 1: identify critical commodities

Not all companies need to pursue supplier development. Some may already be sourcing from world-class suppliers because they have made effective sourcing decisions and supplier selections. Or their purchases may be so small in proportion to total costs or sales that investing in suppliers is neither strategically nor financially justifiable. Therefore, managers must analyze their situation to determine whether supplier development is warranted,[7] and, if so, which purchased commodities and services require the most attention.

To focus the effort, a corporate-level executive steering committee must assess the relative strategic importance of all goods and services that the company buys and produce a 'portfolio' of critical commodities (products or services essential for success in a targeted industry segment). This assessment is an extension of the company's overall corporate-level strategic planning and should include participants from the functions affected by sourcing decisions (finance, marketing, information technology, accounting, production, and design). (See Figure 1, a matrix used to assess the relative importance of company purchases.)

After classifying commodities accordingly, the resulting portfolio consists of clusters of 'noncritical supplies', 'bottleneck supplies', 'leverage supplies' and 'critical strategic

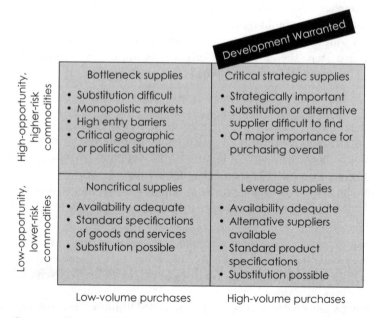

Figure 1 Commodity portfolio matrix

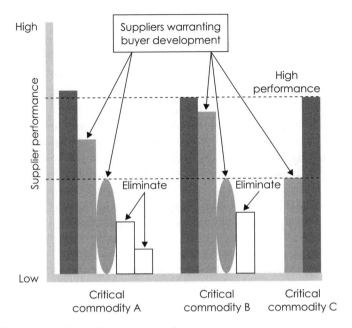

Figure 2 Pareto analysis of supplier performance

supplies'. Commodities in the 'strategic supplies' category are considered strategically important, difficult to substitute or purchase from alternative suppliers (often due to an oligopolistic market), important to purchasing overall, and purchased in relatively high volumes. These commodities become the targets for individual study by dedicated commodity teams.

Step 2: identify critical suppliers

Next, managers must assess how suppliers of strategic supplies are performing to determine which ones to develop. A common approach involves a Pareto analysis of current supplier performance (see Figure 2). In this case, the underlying axiom is that 20 percent of suppliers is responsible for 80 percent of the poor performance. Thus, Pareto analysis is useful in identifying suppliers with potential for development, as well as those that are underperforming, low-volume suppliers.

Identifying poorly performing suppliers requires systematically analyzing supplier performance data. Many leading companies monitor supplier performance on a plant-by-plant basis, ranking suppliers from best to worst. They target suppliers that fail to meet minimum performance objectives in quality, timely delivery, cost, technology, or cycle time for analysis and eventual supplier development. The buying firm meets with supplier representatives to determine the cause of the problem(s) and the required corrective action(s). If supplier development is warranted, both firms must harness the resources to drive the improvements. If improvement is not forthcoming, the item(s) may be sourced from an alternative supplier.

Step 3: form a cross-functional team

Before approaching suppliers to ask for improvements, a buyer must first develop internal cross-functional consensus for the initiative. Such consensus shows the supplier a 'unified front' and ensures that all buyer functions send the supplier consistent messages. Purchasing executives continually emphasize that improvements begin from within through 'buyer-focused' activities. A buyer must have its 'own house in order' before expecting commitment and cooperation from suppliers. Furthermore, to optimize supplier contributions, a buyer must first establish its supply chain strategies and roles of procurement so that its business objectives are clear.

Step 4: meet with supplier top management

Next, the buyer's cross-functional commodity team approaches the supplier's top management group and establishes three keys to supplier improvement: strategic alignment, measurement, and professionalism. Strategic alignment requires not only an internal business–technology alignment but also a buyer–supplier alignment that focuses on each customer's requirements throughout the entire supply chain. Supplier measurement requires a total cost focus as well as credibility and participation of purchasing and other key technical functions (such as engineering, quality, information systems, and manufacturing) in both organizations. Approaching a supplier's top managers with a good business case for improvement sets a professional tone that reinforces the relationship, fosters communication, provides specialized expertise, and develops trust.

Step 5: identify key projects

After identifying promising opportunities, managers must evaluate them in terms of feasibility, resource and time requirements, and potential return on investment. The goal is to decide whether they are achievable, and if so, what the goals should be. Additional criteria used to evaluate opportunities include willingness and ability of supplier (and buyer) to implement changes, duration of product/service life, strategic importance of the product/service and its impact on the business, return on investment, impact analysis, and standardization.

Step 6: define details of agreement

After identifying a potential improvement project, the parties need to agree on the specific metrics for monitoring its success. The metrics may include percent of cost savings to be shared, percent of quality improvement to be achieved, percent of delivery or cycle-time improvement desired, key product or service performance targets, technology availability, and system implementation targets. The agreement must specify milestones and deadlines for improvements as well as the role of each party – who is responsible for the project's success, and how and when to deploy the allocated resources. Upon reaching an agreement, the project begins.

Step 7: monitor status and modify strategies

Top maintain momentum in the project, managers must monitor progress and constantly exchange information. Revisiting objectives after attaining a milestone may bring to light the need for new or revised objectives. The parties may need to modify the original plan because priorities may change and additional resources may be needed. In short, the strategy must be revisited to stay 'in sync' with events.

Falling Short of the Model

. . .

Our evidence indicates that supplier development works – some of the time. We asked managers to describe the benefits realized from their most successful supplier-development efforts. The distribution of the percentage increases in buyer satisfaction clearly indicated that not all supplier-development efforts were equally successful. While most buying firms reported increased satisfaction in such areas as total cost, quality, delivery performance, product innovation, and cycle time, a few reported that supplier development actually led to *decreased* satisfaction – and those projects were their most successful efforts!

To better understand these results, we interviewed managers of several electronics and automotive companies in the United States, the United Kingdom, Japan, and South Korea. We found that many had identified the critical commodities and suppliers requiring development, and, in many cases, had formed cross-functional teams to initiate supplier-development efforts. However, the efforts fell short of their expected outcomes because of pitfalls they encountered in the final three stages of the generic process outlined earlier – that is, identifying key projects, defining the details of the agreement, and monitoring status and modifying strategies when necessary.

On the basis of our survey of 84 companies as well as the field interviews, we divide these pitfalls into three categories: supplier-specific pitfalls, buyer-specific pitfalls, and buyer–supplier interface pitfalls. Next we elaborate on each category.

Supplier-Specific Pitfalls

We found that six of the top ten pitfalls fell into the supplier-specific category. Failure to implement improvements stems chiefly from the suppliers' lack of commitment or lack of technical or human resources.

Lack of supplier commitment

In early meetings with a supplier's top managers, a buyer's team must clearly delineate potential rewards for the supplier organization; otherwise, supplier management may not be fully committed to the effort, unconvinced that development will benefit their organization. They may even agree to initial proposals but fail to implement them due to this insufficient dedication. The following are solutions companies have used to avoid this lack-of-commitment pitfall.

Show them where they stand   Varity Perkins is a producer of diesel engines used in automotive and construction vehicles. Previously, Perkins sent suppliers a 100-point quarterly report that assessed their performance in the areas of quality, delivery, and price competitiveness. Perkins did not, however, use the data in any manner, and suppliers did not take the assessments seriously.

Perkins recently revised its supplier-evaluation system to show suppliers the areas needing improvement. The new report shows a supplier's performance history in each area, its performance as compared to other Perkins suppliers, and its deviation from the mean performance. The report also includes graphs and other visual media. Perkins changed the metrics to reflect what it considers more important.

For example, to illustrate the impact of a supplier's performance on Perkins' daily operations, Perkins moved from weekly to daily delivery performance measurements. In one case, the *average* on-time performance for one supplier had ranged from 90 to 95 percent. However, daily measurements revealed that on-time performance dropped to 26 percent. Not long after implementing the new report, this supplier's daily on-time delivery rose to 90 percent.

Tie the business relationship to performance improvement   Perkins' reporting system became the foundation for its supplier-development program, which concentrates on results. By allowing suppliers to view their performance relative to competitors' performance, Perkins expects suppliers to recognize the potential benefits of supplier development. However, if a supplier's performance does not improve, Perkins considers reducing orders from that supplier.

Solectron is a contract manufacturer serving major original equipment manufacturers (OEMs) such as IBM, Hewlett-Packard, Sun Microsystems, and Cisco. Solectron ensures that its suppliers know the criteria used to measure their performance and that they understand the level of performance required to maintain their business relationship. The specific improvement targets set in a supplier-development effort become the primary measures for determining whether the business relationship will continue. Solectron employs set measures used to gauge supply chain excellence: reliability, mean time between failures, fulfillment lead time, just-in-time performance, schedule flexibility, commodity allocation, inventory risk reduction, and cost. When a supplier and Solectron cannot make progress on jointly developed improvement targets, Solectron either reduces or eliminates its business with that supplier.

Illustrate benefits first-hand Varity Perkins' supplier-development efforts are closely integrated with '*kaizen* events' – focused shop-floor-based improvement projects designed to realize significant operational results in a short time at minimal expense. Perkins managers will not plan a *kaizen* event with a supplier unless the supplier is fully committed to the process. To gauge commitment, Perkins invites the supplier's managing director to one of Perkins' weekly internal *kaizen* events. If the director is enthusiastic after the event, Perkins arranges to hold a *kaizen* 'awareness session' for the supplier's senior managers at the supplier's facility.

In general, commitment for supplier development at Perkins means: (1) the supplier is committed to continuous improvement, (2) both parties agree on cost-reduction targets, and (3) both identify specific opportunities for a *kaizen* event within the supplier's manufacturing process. Perkins asks the supplier to commit its workforce to the project – typically eight to ten operators for 1 week.

Perkins also will not run a supplier's first *kaizen* event until the supplier agrees on benefits sharing. Perkins no longer requires an equal split on savings, because true savings often cannot be determined for 6 months. Instead, Perkins requires that a supplier agrees not to raise prices the following year unless it experiences an increase in raw material prices.

To foster supplier commitment, the teams generally choose a project that is fairly simple and likely to succeed for the first *kaizen*. Often, it is where they can obtain the 'biggest quick fix' and the 'greatest good'. To illustrate the potential benefits, in one unusual case, Perkins actually performed a *kaizen* assessment on a competitor's area in a supplier's plant.

Honda of America Manufacturing uses another approach to garner supplier commitment by illustrating benefits: target pricing to identify cost-saving opportunities. Honda breaks down costs to the component level, then asks suppliers to provide a detailed breakdown of their costs, including raw materials, labor, tooling, packaging, delivery, and administration. By comparing cost breakdowns, Honda suggests ways suppliers can improve performance and thereby reduce costs. Honda jointly develops cost tables with suppliers and uses them to find differences (line item by line item) across all cost elements. Potential 'bones of contention' are generally the supplier's profits and its overhead. Honda expects suppliers to receive a fair profit, of course, but the level may depend on the size of the purchase; no fixed profit level is used in negotiations.

The purchasing department then aggregates the costs and compares them to the target cost. If total cost exceeds target cost, the design requires change to reduce the cost. Although the supplier's profit margins might be an easy place to look for cost savings, Honda realizes that doing so would squander any trust it may have earned. Therefore, Honda generally does not target supplier profits as an area for cost reduction.

Ensure follow-up through a supplier champion Johnson Controls Inc. (JCI), an automotive interior components manufacturer in the United States, found that many suppliers attending its training sessions failed to implement the tools and techniques presented. Therefore, JCI initiated a Supplier Champions Program (SCP) to ensure that suppliers become proficient in areas important to JCI customers. In the SCP, one supplier employee is designated as the supplier champion. That champion's job is to understand JCI expectations, demonstrate an acceptable level of competence in the tools and techniques, and be capable of disseminating that knowledge to the rest of the organization. If a champion moves out of his or her role, the supplier must designate a new champion, who trains with the outgoing champion and becomes certified in the appropriate training sessions. Certification generally requires a champion to submit several improvements undertaken by the supplier, such as process-flow mapping, failure-mode-effects analysis, quality-control planning, best-practice benchmarking, or process auditing.

Insufficient supplier resources

Some suppliers lack the engineering resources, equipment, information systems, employee skills, or training resources required to implement the improvement ideas identified in a supplier-development exercise. To surmount this potential pitfall, many companies we studied invested significant effort in boosting their suppliers' infrastructures using the following techniques.

Keep initial improvements simple To minimize significant investments, Varity Perkins' initial supplier-development efforts focused on high-impact areas that could be improved quickly. Each *kaizen* effort was limited to 1 week, was constrained to moving only a specific number of machines, and generally involved only about eight machine operators. Because Perkins managers believe that optimal solutions are never reached in the first effort, they feel it is more important to perform a *kaizen* event quickly. Even though further improvements might be possible by allocating additional time and resources, spending significant funds on capital equipment is contradictory to the *kaizen* philosophy of striving for simple, effective, and low-cost solutions. *Kaizen* events lasting more than 1 week become production 'reengineering' that might yield significant benefits. However, undertaking many small *kaizen* events often uncovers significant benefits without major resource commitments.

Draw on the buyer's resources Managers from National Computer Resources Inc (NCRI) reported that timely and accurate information was critical to decision making and, ultimately, to improving supplier performance. Thus, an important focus of National Computer supplier-development efforts has been to persuade suppliers to commit to electronic data interchange (EDI – the electronic transmission of data between supplier and buyer using a strict format). National Computer has helped suppliers that produce lower-level components (but are without the resources to implement EDI themselves) by getting them online, providing training, and making hardware and software recommendations.

. . .

Solectron renegotiates contracts every 6 months because of rapidly changing technologies and a highly competitive environment, even though the firm considers suppliers to be long-term partners and they assume that their contract will be renewed. The renegotiation has two goals. One is to inform the suppliers of probable order quantities 6 months in advance; the other is to garner price decreases from them.

Solectron plans to write price-adjustment clauses into these contracts to capture supplier cost decreases automatically during the contract period, rather than at the beginning of each new contract. However, the firm has not implemented this change, because suppliers' information systems are not integrated with Solectron's. Therefore, Solectron is considering providing suppliers with access to its databases. By doing so, Solectron will be able to forgo frequent renegotiations and will expect to receive real-time price reductions from suppliers.

Offer personnel support   Bavarian Motor Works (BMW), the car manufacturer, does not provide financial support to suppliers; however, it has provided the services of its employees when suppliers request assistance. BMW has sent maintenance engineers and procurement, logistics, and quality personnel to suppliers – sometimes for several weeks at a time. During its initial start-up in the United States, BMW had to focus on problem-driven projects. It still relies on a Pareto-driven approach to assisting suppliers. It identifies problems early and prevents them from worsening, which minimizes expending a supplier's resources and the need for BMW to undertake supplier improvement efforts.

Hyundai Corporation, the large Korean automotive manufacturer, realized that smaller suppliers with limited resources could not consistently recruit and retain the most skilled engineers. Therefore, most Hyundai *kaizen* processes focus on small suppliers. Hyundai sends engineers from its own shops to essentially 'live' at supplier facilities, performing time/motion studies and teaching layout design to improve the supplier's productivity. Hyundai encourages these suppliers to learn, apply, and eventually teach their own suppliers the knowledge that Hyundai transfers to them.

Honda invested significant resources in its supplier-support infrastructure. Of the 310 people in Honda's purchasing department, fifty are engineers who work exclusively with suppliers. In one case, a small plastics supplier did not have the capacity to produce the required volume, so the quality of their parts began to deteriorate. Honda sent four people to the supplier for 10 months, at no charge to the supplier; additional services were even offered as needed. The supplier improved and became a well-established Honda supplier. Although engineering support has played a large role in the success of Honda's supplier-development program, the company generally does not invest directly in a supplier's equipment. In some cases, however, Honda will own a percentage of a supplier's equipment for capitalization purposes and allow the supplier to repay the investment over time.

Build training centers   To fulfill suppliers' training inadequacies, JCI built a facility dedicated to providing extensive training to internal groups, suppliers, and customers. JCI requires that all potential suppliers take JCI's Supplier Principles Program; hundreds of people have completed the program. During the first 11 months of 1997:

- Suppliers spent 765 hours at Principles Program classes at the JCI facility.
- JCI supplier development engineers spent 1,283 hours involved in management and process training at suppliers' facilities.
- Supplier-development personnel spent 573 hours solving technical problems at supplier sites.

Occasionally, a government may even lend support for industry collaboration. The cost of Hyundai's training center (which provides specialized supplier training) is shared evenly between Hyundai and suppliers, but the Korean government provides tax benefits for building such centers and makes the shared training fees tax-deductible. The Korean government prohibits significant investment by a company in its supply base, so Hyundai only directly invests in supplier improvement in rare circumstances. However, the company is permitted to make machinery and equipment that it manufactures available to suppliers at a good price, facilitating the exchange of advanced technology.

Buyer-Specific Pitfalls

Buyers are reluctant to commit fully to supplier development primarily when they see no obvious potential benefits. Small-quantity purchases from numerous suppliers may not justify the investment in one particular supplier. Or a supplier may not be important enough to justify such an investment. Lack of immediate monetary benefits or the wavering support of top management may also lower a buyer's commitment. Finally, lofty expectations that go unrealized may reduce enthusiasm for future supplier-development efforts. Following are some tactics for avoiding such buyer-centric pitfalls.

Consolidate to fewer suppliers   One way to illustrate the value of investing in a supplier-development effort is to consolidate to fewer suppliers, thus making the remaining few more important to the buyer's success. Several purchasing managers noted that one way to increase the order size with key suppliers is to standardize parts, even for 'design-to-order' operations. For example, IBM's Networking Hardware Division, which produces customized networking solutions for customers, constantly strives to increase parts commonality. Currently, over 50 percent of purchased components for each major network hardware project is standard items. IBM personnel only order unique componentry when it will provide market advantage; otherwise, they standardize to leverage purchases worldwide.

Concurrent with the drive to standardized parts, many purchasing managers optimize their supply bases and use single suppliers to achieve economies of scale. For example, Daewoo Corporation uses single sourcing whenever possible. It only turns to two or more suppliers when labor disputes are likely. Similarly, National Computer, Doosan Corporation of Korea, Honda America Manufacturing, and Rover have made, or are planning, moves toward single sourcing within product platforms, while maintaining multiple sources across product lines. This strategy allows them to leverage purchasing volumes globally while simultaneously reducing the risk of insufficient supply. Reducing suppliers lowers administrative costs and provides the incentive to conduct supplier-development efforts with the fewer remaining suppliers.

Keep a long-term focus Solectron's competitive strategy relies heavily on its supply chain management competencies. Thus, Solectron looks beyond the price of the goods it purchases and examines how its most important suppliers impact the quality and technology of its own products. Solectron requires suppliers to provide 'black box' designs that can be integrated into Solectron products by its designers. Solectron uses total cost and long-term strategic impact as criteria for justifying investments in its suppliers. Currently, Solectron is developing an integrated information system across suppliers, OEMs, and distributors, which it calls World-Wide Materials System. This system will allow commodity managers better to identify and justify supplier-development opportunities because it will help them better to manage supplier–performance alignment, measurement, commodity team analysis, and supplier negotiations and reviews.

Determine cost of ownership Many companies we studied use total-cost-of-ownership data to measure the cost of doing business with a particular supplier. For example, Sun Microsystems measures supplier performance in quality, lead time, delivery, flexibility, process and technology investments, and level of support provided to Sun. The total points achieved by a supplier across these categories is multiplied by a price index, which compares the supplier's performance to the price-reduction goals set by Sun. The best score a supplier can receive on the price index is 1.0. A total-cost-of-ownership final score of 1.36 implies that the supplier costs Sun $1.36 for every $1.00 worth of value Sun receives from that supplier. By identifying where and how suppliers add (or detract from) value, Sun makes supplier-development decisions on the basis of total cost rather than purchase volume or monetary value alone.

Set small goals Varity Perkins' initial supplier-development efforts were relatively unsuccessful, partly because of unrealistic expectations. Thus, Perkins focused its *kaizen* improvement efforts on a smaller group of suppliers to garner a series of small wins. The effort was rewarded with incremental improvements that ultimately renewed the commitment of all parties. The goals for the supplier *kaizen* strategy were to:

- Highlight waste within a supplier's processes and demonstrate how incremental improvements could be made quickly through joint improvement activities.
- Achieve cost reductions at Perkins as a direct result of *kaizen* activities and share the benefits with the suppliers.
- Familiarize Perkins' purchasing, logistics, supplier quality assurance, and cost engineering staff with suppliers' products, processes, and training by having them participate in *kaizen* activities. This exposure then provided the basis for extending the improvement initiative outside of *kaizen*.

Make executive commitment a priority   Many of the managers we interviewed for this study reported that top management became convinced of the value of supplier development only when profits improved along with supplier performance. For companies such as Honda, which spends nearly 80 percent of cost of goods sold on purchased goods and services, such an argument is easy to make; for companies with lower percentages, the argument may be more difficult. Proving a specific relationship between supplier performance improvement and profits may not be easy; however, considering the total cost of *not* moving forward, there is a solid business case in terms of avoiding late deliveries, line shutdowns, and customer-warranty costs. Managers reported that optimizing their supply bases, together with parts standardization, freed up some resources over the long term and made supplier development more feasible. In addition, taking the total-cost approach to measuring supplier performance proved effective in demonstrating the cost of poor supplier performance. Thus, many of the strategies used by companies to avoid their own buyer-specific pitfalls to supplier development are complementary.

Buyer–Supplier Interface Pitfalls

Pitfalls may also originate in the interface between buyers and suppliers, in areas such as interorganizational trust, alignment of organizational cultures, and ineffective communication of potential benefits.

Lack of trust

One of the biggest challenges in supplier development is cultivating mutual trust. Suppliers may be reluctant to share information on costs and processes; the need to release sensitive and confidential information may compound this hesitation. Ambiguous or intimidating legal issues and ineffective lines of communication also may inhibit the trust building necessary for a successful supplier-development effort.

Delegate an ombudsman   To overcome suppliers' reluctance to share information, Honda has supplier ombudsmen who deal with the 'soft side of the business' – the human resource issues that are not associated with cost, quality, or delivery. Honda has discovered that often suppliers are more open with these ombudsmen because they are not involved in contract negotiations. If a supplier approaches an ombudsman with a problem caused by poor communication or misunderstanding between the two companies, the ombudsman is able to communicate the supplier's perspective to Honda's personnel while maintaining confidentiality as much as possible. Over time, suppliers come to trust the ombudsmen and appear more willing to share information in all areas, including costs.

Keep confidential information exclusive Sharing confidential information is especially difficult when dealing with new suppliers in high-technology areas. Thus, many companies require nondisclosure agreements and even exclusivity agreements (i.e. the supplier provides a specific product only to one buyer), especially when dealing with technologically advanced products that contribute to the buyer's competitive edge. Motorola, for example, has made confidentiality a part of its supplier-development agenda. The company even helps suppliers segregate Motorola product manufacturing from their other operations to prevent Motorola's competitors from seeing how these parts are manufactured.

Spell it out Since it does not plan a *kaizen* event unless a supplier fully commits to a relationship, Varity Perkins first insists on a signed agreement. Although some procurement staff at Perkins prefer a 'gentleman's agreement', *kaizen* leaders believe the only way to gain a supplier's trust is through written and signed terms, especially for the first few *kaizen* events. Perkins recently spent 8 months trying to convince a key supplier to consider a *kaizen*; the supplier's managers were reluctant because another company's recent *kaizen* failed to yield significant improvements. The lack of trust was compounded by Perkins' reputation for 'arm's length' relationships with suppliers, which manifested in Perkins frequently switching suppliers on the basis of price. Perkins is now aggressively trying to reverse this perception through its new purchasing philosophy, which emphasizes cooperative relationships with key suppliers and well-defined purchasing objectives beyond purchase price.

Minimize legal involvement JCI views suppliers as extensions of its company. The company forms alliances with key suppliers and develops close relationships between the two firms' senior executives. Alliance agreements include broad statements of operating principles and specify the roles each party should play, so formal contracts are rarely used. Instead, open purchase orders are employed on 90 percent of orders, and JCI commits to a certain volume of business. In interviews, the JCI team emphasized that they use only a single legal adviser to establish these relationships, and their contracts are written only for a 'supply agreement' – a memorandum that outlines general expectations and commitments. The only legal issues involve patent and intellectual-property agreements. So an important underlying success factor distinguishing JCI from its competitors is its continual emphasis in its corporate culture on its relationship-based strategy.

. . .

Poor alignment of organizational cultures

Occasionally, when conditions change, a once-successful supplier-development approach is no longer viable. Changes in supply chains or plant locations, or ambiguous expectations that do not take into account changing conditions, may adversely affect supplier development.

Adapt to local conditions   When setting up production in South Carolina, BMW quickly realized it would have to change its supplier-development approach to conform to North American supply conditions. In Germany, BMW uses a 'process consulting' approach, analyzing suppliers' processes for errors and insufficiencies. This approach works well in a mature supplier relationship, in which the supplier intuitively understands what the customer wants because the parties have worked together for many years. In the United States, however, BMW's new US suppliers had difficulty understanding BMW's requirements for quality and continuous improvement; this misunderstanding resulted occasionally in strained relationships. Consequently, BMW spent a great deal of time communicating with suppliers and showing them what BMW needed. Further, BMW had to change the message it sent to suppliers by emphasizing 'Your problems are our problems. You have good products, but you have to do better, and we are here to help you.'

BMW also found that, although a given supplier might be considered excellent in Europe, the supplier's subsidiary in North America might be incapable of meeting the same standards. For example, bumpers and body panels initially purchased in the United States often had small scratches and other minor imperfections that BMW considered defects. In setting expectations, BMW emphasized that it was not just a matter of 'right versus wrong', but a matter of effectively communicating quality criteria. Thus, BMW asked the suppliers to hold parts at certain angles under a light to look for scratches. For suppliers to understand these expectations and to align their business cultures with BMW's required face-to-face discussions with BMW.

Create an expectations road map   BMW strives to be 20 percent above the industry average in several quality-performance categories; management believes supplier development is a key contributor in this effort. One of the best ways to achieve this level of quality is to communicate BMW's expectations effectively. Thus, BMW recently published a *Supplier Partnership Manual* and held seminars for suppliers to present their 'Road Map to Quality'. The manual clearly delineates supplier responsibilities and expectations and is geared toward improving alignment between the corporate cultures.

Such road maps are an increasingly common way to spur buyer–supplier organizational alignment. They attempt to show companies where they are today and project where they should be in the short, medium, and long term. IBM's networking hardware division and personal computer operations share road maps with suppliers. Similarly, Sun Microsystems shares road maps with suppliers to drive their investment strategies, which will, in turn, drive Sun's supplier selection strategy. The alignment of a supplier's technology and Sun's technological needs is the basis for 'guaranteed' future business with Sun.

Insufficient inducements to the supplier

Buyers may ineffectively communicate potential benefits for investing in supplier-development efforts, thus losing a supplier's full commitment. It may be necessary to convey more motivating incentives.

Offer financial incentives   Hyundai Motor Company uses financial incentives to motivate suppliers to improve. The company rates supplier performance from 1 (highest) to 4 (lowest). Class 1 suppliers are paid in cash; Class 2 suppliers are paid net 30 days; Class 3 suppliers are paid net 60 days; and Class 4 suppliers are paid net 60 days and receive no new business. Because suppliers know how Hyundai evaluates performance, they take steps to ensure high levels of performance. This motivator has been especially important during the recent financial crisis facing Asian industries.

'Design in' motivation   Although Solectron is now generally able to offer large orders to suppliers, this was not always the case. To gain supplier cooperation in the 'low-volume years', Solectron emphasized that a supplier could become 'designed in' to its products and thus have a greater potential for future business. Designing a supplier's product into a Solectron product provides enough motivation for most suppliers to participate in supplier-development efforts. Solectron still uses this approach as a motivational incentive.

Offer repeat business as an incentive   Several companies interviewed were surprised to hear that a lack of special inducements was a pitfall to supplier performance improvement. For example, JCI managers believe that properly managed relationships require no explicit rewards or incentives for suppliers to improve their performance. JCI noted that its suppliers are not promised anything, but they expect contract renewal. If a supplier meets JCI expectations, it will continue to be a JCI supplier.

Lessons Learned

Although we gained many valuable insights while conducting this study, we summarize several that are particularly relevant to this discussion.

Most pitfalls occurred in steps 4–7 of the process model

If we were to view the major pitfalls in terms of stages of the process model, we would see that significant problems often arise:

- during meetings of buyer and supplier management teams;
- when defining key projects;
- when defining agreement terms and determining metrics for success;
- when monitoring project status and subsequently modifying strategies.

Thus, to avoid these pitfalls, the parties should openly address initial doubts and resolve the issues as soon as possible. Target projects that are too complex result in poor follow-through, due to either lack of resources or lack of commitment; firms must address this problem early. Furthermore, a buyer that does not commit sufficient resources for its proposed development effort is unlikely to convince supplier top management. So buyers must understand, support, and make clear their side of the bargain early on. Determining which costs to bear and which to share is also important. Finally, establishing metrics and timelines that provide a basis for follow-up and joint problem solving is critical to a project's completion. Confronting such difficult topics promptly can highlight the weaknesses in a poorly planned development project.

Unsupportive managers are a common pitfall   Many of the interviewed managers stated that suppliers are sometimes unwilling to accept help in the form of supplier development. Perhaps they are too proud. Perhaps they do not see the value in improving quality or delivery performance. Or perhaps they do not recognize they have a problem. Acknowledging that unsupportive managers are a potential pitfall, buyers can devise remedies, perhaps based on our findings, which provide the greatest overall benefits. Management attitudes significantly affect the success of a supplier-development effort, so they must be monitored and addressed continually.

Strategic emphasis is required on purchasing and supply chain management
A strong purchasing mission statement reflects and drives strategic emphasis and alignment. Consider the purchasing mission statement of a UK auto parts manufacturer: 'We are committed to procure goods and services in a way that delivers our aims and objectives of becoming the most successful auto parts business in the world.' This company pursues its mission through: (1) developing a world-class supplier base capable of meeting current and future needs; (2) obtaining the highest-quality, most cost-effective goods and services in a timely manner; and (3) establishing long-term relationships with supply partners that meet company standards, are committed to the manufacturer, and strive to continually improve in all areas. A strong supplier-development effort leads to improved strategic alignment between organizations and results in important transfers of tacit expertise and advanced technology.

Pitfalls may be related   A theme that underlies the findings in our survey and field interviews is that as companies work toward solving one supplier-development problem, they may concurrently progress toward avoiding other pitfalls. Although pitfalls may not correlate with each other in every case, it became increasingly clear during the field interviews that experiencing the pitfalls of one category (supplier, buyer, or interface) frequently had direct or indirect effects that led to other pitfalls as well.[8]

Relationship management is critical to success   Use of specific tools and processes (such as total-cost analysis, volume leveraging, resource support, formal and informal communication, linked information systems, incentives, and agreement on goals and objectives) can develop and strengthen relationships between buyers and their suppliers.

Initiating supplier-performance improvement is not an easy task. The objective is to transform suppliers so that continuous improvement becomes an integral part of their capabilities. Our findings suggest that such an accomplishment takes time and is only achieved by patient relationship managers who are tenacious enough to pay follow-up visits to suppliers and continually enforce a strong program of supplier evaluation and performance feedback.

NOTES

This article builds on a comprehensive research study which surveyed the processes that organizations use to develop their suppliers, and the obstacles to success. This focused on the electrical, electronics and automotive industries in the USA, UK, Japan and South Korea and looked at critical issues of procurement and supply chain strategy. Two hundred companies participated from the following sectors: industrial products (38%); services (14%); consumer durables (13%); consumer non-durables (8%); capital goods (2%); other (25%). The study was supplemented by the authors' survey of supplier development in 84 companies drawn from a wider range of industries.

1   D.R. Krause, R.B. Handfield, and T.V. Scannell, 'An Empirical Investigation of Supplier Development: Reactive and Strategic Processes', *Journal of Operations Management* (forthcoming); D.R. Krause, 'Supplier Development: Current Practices and Outcomes', *International Journal of Purchasing and Materials Management*, volume 33, number 2, 1997, pp. 12–19; K. Bhote. *Strategic Supply Management – A Blueprint for Revitalizing the Manufacturing–Supplier Partnership* (New York: American Management Association, 1989).

2   B. Burnes and P. Whittle, 'Supplier D.H. Development: Getting Started', *Logistics Focus*, volume 3, number 1, 1995, pp. 10–14; S. Tully, 'Purchasing's New Muscle', *Fortune*, volume 131, 1995, pp. 75–83.

3   T. Peters, *Thriving on Chaos: Handbook of Management Revolution* (New York: Knopf, 1988); J. Quinn, P. Anderson, and S. Finkelstein, 'Leveraging Intellect', *Academy of Management Executive*, volume 10, number 3, 1996, pp. 7–27; A Taylor, 'The Auto Industry Meets the New Economy', *Fortune*, volume 130, number 5, 1994, pp. 52–60.

4   M. Fisher, 'What is the Right Supply Chain for Your Product?', *Harvard Business Review*, volume 75, March–April 1997, pp. 105–116.

5   For a detailed description of the methodology and validation of this process model, see Krause et al. (forthcoming).

6   For example, see J.P. MacDuffle and S. Helper, 'Creating Lean Suppliers: Diffusing Lean Production through the Supply Chain', *California Management Review*, volume 39,

number 4, 1997, pp. 118–151; or C. Watts and C. Hahn, 'Supplier Development Programs: An Empirical Analysis', *International Journal of Purchasing and Materials Management*, volume 29, number 2, 1993, pp. 11–17.

7 B. Burnes and P. Whittle, 'Supplier Development: Getting Started', *Logistics Focus*, volume 3, number 1, 1995, pp. 10–14; Watts and Hahn (1993).

8 K. Fitzgerald, 'For Superb Supplier Development – Honda Wins!', *Purchasing*, volume 119, number 4, 1995, pp. 32–40.

2.3

Japanese Automakers, US Suppliers and Supply Chain Superiority

Jeffrey K. Liker and Yen-Chun Wu

Many manufacturers today are concerned with the inefficient manufacturing and delivery practices of their company's suppliers. Before pointing a finger accusingly at their suppliers, however, perhaps they should examine their own policies and procedures. Any manufacturer can learn this lesson from US automakers, their Japanese rivals that have set up operations in the United States and the automotive suppliers that provide parts to both groups.

In the 1980s and 1990s, Japanese automakers built significant production capacity in the United States, and their world-class manufacturing practices quickly became the new quality standard for the US automotive industry. These practices went well beyond the just-in-time (JIT) delivery of parts to a plant and included all aspects of lean manufacturing. The transplanted Japanese automakers, with their lean focus, realized that their success depended on developing a local supply base, which meant sharing with US suppliers the innovative manufacturing management practices and technologies that made similar plants so competitive in Japan.[1] Some skeptics claimed that lean manufacturing would never work in North America, considering the continent's size and transportation systems that might not be able to deliver materials reliably just in time. But Japanese companies in the United States seemed to prove otherwise. US automobile manufacturers began following the lead of their Japanese counterparts, transforming themselves in the lean direction and demanding JIT logistics from their suppliers.

Lean manufacturing and just-in-time delivery   Although much has been written about just-in-time (JIT) delivery and lean manufacturing, there seems to be some confusion about what they are and how to make them work.

Lean manufacturing is a philosophy of manufacturing that focuses on delivering the highest quality product at the lowest cost on time. It is a system of production and also takes a value stream focus. The 'value stream' consists of all the steps in the process needed to convert raw material into the product the customer desires. Any steps in the process that fail to do this are considered wasteful. By necessity, when the value stream passes between customers and suppliers that are located at a geographical distance, there is waste: product cannot simply flow from value-added process to value-added process. The goal of lean supply chain management, then, is to minimize this waste so product can flow as efficiently as possible. A key part of lean manufacturing is JIT delivery – getting the right part to the right place at the right time.

Secrets of supplier success   For automakers effectively to practice a lean approach, it would seem critical that suppliers make the transition from traditional mass production systems to lean systems internally and in their logistics practices.[2] In fact, this is only partly true. The logistics practices and internal management policies of the automakers – in other words, of the customers themselves – may have a more profound impact on the supplier's ability to respond with lean systems and thereby get the right parts to the right place at the right time.

The secrets of supplier success are as follows:

- Japanese manufacturers operating in the United States work with their suppliers to develop lean capabilities – at least for the particular production line that serves the Japanese assembly plants.
- The Japanese transplants level their own production schedules to avoid big spikes in demand, which enables suppliers to hold less inventory.
- Japanese transplants create a disciplined system of delivery time windows during which all parts must be received at the delivery plant.
- Japanese transplants develop lean transportation systems to handle mixed-load, small-lot deliveries. In some cases, that means building a cross-dock to redistribute large loads into smaller loads.
- Japanese transplants encourage suppliers to ship only what is needed by the assembly plant at a particular time, even if this means partially filled trucks.

The Study

The performance of US suppliers to the automotive industry in North America demonstrates the impact of customer policies on supply chain management: US suppliers perform at much higher levels when they are supplying Japanese automakers than when working with US automakers. To compare the policies and practices of the Big Three automakers and Japanese transplants, we surveyed supplier plants that made comparable products for US and Japanese customers. Production or logistics managers in supplier plants filled out questionnaires about their manufacturing and logistics practices with respect to their largest US automotive customer and their largest Japanese transplant customer. Because a supplier may operate several plants with markedly different internal and external logistics, we focused on the individual plant and treated multiple plants from the same supplier as separate cases. We examined not only how US and Japanese customers differed as a whole, but also how specific customers differed: Ford, GM and Chrysler for the US automakers; Honda, Nissan, Toyota and other transplants for the Japanese.

A total of 91 suppliers described their relationship with a Japanese customer and a US customer. We found that Japanese automakers have effectively brought the goals of lean manufacturing to their supply base in the United States and are much more successful in these practices than their US competitors. What follows is an examination of both the secrets of the Japanese transplants success and the ways in which US automakers, despite attempts to emulate lean manufacturing practices and supply chain logistics, are not performing up to the Japanese standard.

Methodology

Respondents were all suppliers to the automotive industry. We chose automobile manufacturing because of its richness and product complexity and because we had access to automotive suppliers for research.[3] In addition, it is broadly recognized that the auto industry is relatively advanced in adopting lean methods. Finally, recent research studies have documented that supplier relationships with US automakers are undergoing major changes with a movement toward adopting a model following some of the principles of Japanese supply chain management.[4]

We defined the study population as US first-tier automotive suppliers that manufacture individual parts and preassembled components and subsystems for US automobile manufacturers and Japanese transplants located in the United States. We excluded from the study suppliers of raw materials and semiconductors, chemicals, indirect materials, tooling and dies, or consulting and engineering services. We used the *1996 ELM Guide to U.S. Automotive Sourcing* to gather our sample. We selected, at random, companies with at least $100 million in annual sales, most of which are located in the Midwest region of the United States. We used this sales criterion to help limit our samples to larger first-tier auto parts suppliers that are directly affected by their automotive customers' purchasing policies and practices.

To provide insight beyond the quantitative data, we conducted preliminary site visits and interviews. We conducted the interviews on a convenience sample of suppliers (primarily located in Michigan and Ohio) that agreed to host a short visit. At least one week before our visits, we sent preliminary questionnaires to the plants requesting that managers fill out the questionnaires in advance so we could review and discuss the answers with the respondents. Such plant visits make it possible to identify the most knowledgeable respondents and to develop items for the questionnaires in simple, concrete terms in the language of the respondents. A questionnaire was then pretested at 10 sites and repeatedly modified to eliminate ambiguities and errors. On the basis of the plant visits, we developed a structured questionnaire to measure the variables of interest. We then returned to the original 10 sites with the final questionnaire and included these data in the study. We surveyed additional companies through the mail and follow-up telephone calls.

Qualified suppliers were first screened and selected at random, on the basis of our sample selection criteria. To enhance the response rate, we obtained permission from the plants' corporate headquarters and requested that they send a letter of support to the plants. Before mailing the questionnaire, we telephoned each plant to identify the appropriate respondents at each plant. Then we contacted each respondent directly to explain the purpose of the study, to answer any concerns about the study and to obtain their agreement to participate.

We collected the data required for this study from people whose primary responsibility involved production scheduling, materials management or outbound transportation. We encouraged the respondents to seek help on questions that could be answered more accurately by other functions, such as production, inventory, quality and transportation.

In all, we contacted 156 plants. Of these, eight plants were immediately dropped from the study because of plant shutdowns, serious labor issues or insignificant automotive sales; 11 refused to participate for reasons such as company policy, management unavailability and confidentiality restrictions. As a result, the questionnaire was sent to 137 plants, and we received 108 responses. Of these, five cases were dropped because we realized that they were not first-tier suppliers. Thus, the useable responses were reduced to 103 cases, resulting in a 72% response rate. Of those responses, 91 plants (88%) supply products to both US automakers and Japanese transplants.

Achieving Lean Manufacturing

Japanese automakers, when compared with their US counterparts, tend to emphasize long-term business relationships.[5] When Toyota, Honda and Nissan set up engine and assembly plants in the United States, they brought many of their Japanese suppliers with them – suppliers that had already mastered lean manufacturing and supply chain logistics. But under pressure from the US government, the automakers set out to find local supply sources that could meet their stringent cost, quality and delivery standards. This was not easy. The Japanese automakers faced a choice: accept poor performance or invest in their relationships with the US suppliers and teach them lean manufacturing. They decided to invest in supplier development initiatives.

Consider the case of Toyota and one of its suppliers, Johnson Controls, a company famous for its ability to build and deliver seats for Toyota just hours before the seats are to be installed on the assembly line.[6] Before working for Toyota, the supplier would hold a huge inventory of seats. After working for Toyota and transforming its plant in Georgetown, Kentucky, to lean manufacturing in 1992, inventory levels dropped from 32 days of inventory to 4.1 days. This required many internal changes such as reducing die setup times from 6 hours to 17 minutes.

Indeed, customer/supplier relations are a key determinant of successfully adopting and diffusing innovative manufacturing and purchasing practices among Japanese transplants.[7] Japanese transplants typically develop close relationships with a small number of suppliers and integrate those suppliers with plant production systems and JIT delivery systems through extensive information exchanges.[8] Our data show that the investments of Japanese automakers in developing their suppliers have been worthwhile. In the same supplier plants, production lines for their parts are leaner compared with production lines for their US competitors. With their US suppliers, Japanese automakers focus on holding low inventory levels, maintaining level production and building in quality.

An overview of Toyota and Honda supplier development initiatives

Because Japanese automakers know that a lean value chain is only as strong as its weakest link, they have invested significant time and capital in developing their suppliers. In the United States, Toyota and Honda are the masters of supplier development initiatives.

When Toyota and Honda first built their US assembly and engine plants, their managers quickly learned that they had to teach old-style mass producers the basics of lean manufacturing. Although US companies have long sponsored company training programs for their suppliers, Honda and Toyota do not believe in conference room training. They train their suppliers according to the concept of *gemba* (Japanese for 'go and see'): training occurs on the shop floor, transformation occurs through practice and action. Both Honda and Toyota identify significant parts of product lines and build 'model lines' in the suppliers' plants. Their advisors stay until they have achieved ambitious objectives for cost, quality and lead time.

For suppliers accustomed to experiencing only occasional slight improvements, the results have been astonishing. For example, the Toyota Supplier Support Center, a subsidiary of Toyota created to work with US suppliers, completed projects in 31 supplier plants between 1992 and 1997. The average improvement in productivity on the model lines in less than a year was 124%, and they reduced inventory by an average of 75%.[9] Honda developed a program dubbed BP (that is, Best Position, Best Productivity). By 1997, the automaker reported improvements from projects in 120 supplier plants of 47% in productivity and 30% in quality, and overall cost reductions of 7.25%.[10]

Keeping inventory levels low

One key to successful lean manufacturing is maintaining low inventory levels (see Table 1). Ideally, the time between when a customer needs a part and when the supplier builds it should be short. In traditional large-batch manufacturing, suppliers build products according to a schedule that does not take into account whether a customer actually needs those products. Suppliers are left with many weeks of inventory, and they may not have the specific product a customer wants. In small-batch

Table 1 Comparing performance indicators for suppliers

Performance indicators	Suppliers serving US auto plants (n = 91)	Suppliers serving Japanese-owned auto plants (n = 91)	Suppliers of:			Suppliers of:			
			Chrysler (n = 26)	Ford (n = 42)	GM (n = 23)	Honda (n = 22)	Nissan (n = 16)	Toyota (n = 37)	Others (n = 16)
Inventory turnovers[a]	25.4	38.3*	28.3	24.4	25.5**	38.4	49.2	52.4	26.8**
Work in process (work shift)	5.4	3.9*	3.0	3.9	7.2***	4.0	3.8	3.0	4.5
Finished-goods storage time (work shift)	5.5	4.4*	4.8	5.4	6.6*	5.3	4.9	3.2	6.0**
Inventory on the wheel (work shift)	3.4	2.3*	2.1	4.5	2.6*	2.8	2.08	1.61	3.8*
Inventory maintained at the customer's site (work shift)	4.0	3.7	3.5	4.8	3.1*	4.0	2.8	2.3	6.3**
Percentage change in manufacturing costs compared with previous year[b]	0.65%	−0.85%**	0.69%	0.58%	0.74%*	−0.9%	−0.7%	−1.3%	−0.7%*
Percentage of late deliveries	2.96%	1.38%***	4.45%	1.70%	3.04%**	2.11%	1.08%	0.44%	2.34%
Emergency shipping costs (per million sales dollars) in previous year[c]	$714	$371*	$1,235	$446	$616**	$423	$379	$204	$409***
Annual percentage of truckloads filled to capacity	68%	47%**	59%	83%	51%***	79%	19%	36%	46%**

*$P < 0.1$. **$P < 0.05$. ***$P < 0.01$. (The P value shows whether the comparisons are statistically significant or due to chance.)

[a] The ratio of annual sales to average inventory.

[b] Minus sign indicates a decrease in costs.

[c] To control the effects of annual sales, emergency shipping costs are normalized by the annual sales.

production, by contrast, products move rapidly through the suppliers' plant and to their customers. A small-batch capability obviously means lower inventory carrying costs, but there are other important benefits as well. Suppliers can respond quickly to changes in customer demand. They can identify any defects in products quickly and thus have fewer potentially defective parts that need to be sorted through and reworked.[11] With fewer people needed to perform wasteful activities, such as moving large batches of inventory from place to place in the plant, productivity rises.

The same supplier plants that make and ship a comparable product to both Japanese and US customers maintain lower levels of inventory for the Japanese transplants than they do for US automakers. Suppliers serving Japanese transplants achieve an inventory turnover of 38.3 (the ratio of annual sales to average inventory) as compared with 25.4 for their US customers. They also maintain much less work-in-process (WIP) inventory, finished goods and on-the-wheel (on-truck) inventory for their Japanese customers.

Important differences also emerge among Japanese and US customers. Among the transplanted Japanese automakers. Toyota has the least inventory and is widely regarded as the premier lean manufacturer with its Toyota production system. Chrysler leads its US peers, having invested earlier in JIT systems for getting parts to its assembly plants. Ford has the highest on-the-wheel inventory.

Although they continue to lag their Japanese counterparts, US automakers are improving. Whereas in the past weekly deliveries were common, there has been a significant shift toward daily deliveries and thus toward reducing inventory. Ford, for example, despite its high on-the-wheel inventory, has been moving aggressively toward more frequent, small-lot deliveries as part of its Ford production system.

One might expect that reducing inventory would increase the risk of missing deliveries to customers and shutting down the assembly line, which in turn would result in more expensive shipments by expedited trucks or even helicopters. Despite operating with far less inventory, however, Japanese transplants are not paying more for emergency shipping. In fact, Japanese transplants paid less in emergency shipping ($371 per million sales dollars) than US automakers ($714 per million sales dollars). Toyota's suppliers are the best performers at $204 and Chrysler's are by far the worst at $1,235.

Consider the myriad benefits of reducing inventory at one of Toyota's US suppliers. When Toyota began purchasing leather seats for its Lexus vehicles from Garden State Tanning (GST), the automaker found that GST could not keep up with demand.[12] The supplier often missed shipments and had to switch from scheduled ocean shipments to expedited air shipments of leather to Toyota's plant in Japan. Even though GST was paying for the emergency shipments, Toyota was not pleased with the supplier's performance. The automaker sent a team of Toyota production system specialists to GST. Working with everyone from the CEO to employees on the shop floor, the team moved equipment on the shop floor into one-piece flow cells, implemented *kanban* (instruction card) systems, developed standardized procedures for cutting leather and slashed inventories of cowhide.

The CEO of GST was convinced that the reduced inventory would ensure an increased number of missed shipments. To his surprise, as inventory fell from

Table 2 Scheduling and shipping

	Suppliers serving US auto plants (n = 91)	Suppliers serving Japanese-owned auto plants (n = 91)	Suppliers of:			Suppliers of:			
			Chrysler (n = 26)	Ford (n = 42)	GM (n = 23)	Honda (n = 22)	Nissan (n = 16)	Toyota (n = 37)	Others (n = 16)
Automakers that change the scheduling of orders									
Percentage change in parts order one week before part is needed	25%	16%**	16%	24%	37%*	10%	3%	7%	30%***
Percentage change in parts order two to three days before part is needed	15%	10%	3%	15%	30%***	2%	5%	3%	21%***
Percentage change in parts order one day before part is needed	10%	6%***	3%	10%	19%***	2%	1%	2%	12%***
Supplier shipments to automakers									
Number of daily shipments	2.4	3.6*	4.0	1.1	3.3*	3.5	2.8	4.7	3.1*
Automaker pressure on supplier to fill truck[a]	2.9	1.8***	1.9	3.6	2.1***	1.8	1.6	1.4	2.1
Percentage cost penalty by automaker for not filling truck	33%	8%***	14%	57%	13%***	8%	9%	6%	9%*

*P < 0.1. **P < 0.05. ***P < 0.01. (The P value shows whether the comparisons are statistically significant or due to chance.)
[a] 1 = no pressure from customer, 5 = tremendous pressure from customer.

112,000 hides to fewer than 40,000, emergency air shipments plummeted to nearly zero. At the same time, quality defects were almost eliminated, productivity more than doubled and lost-time accidents dropped from 242 per year to two. And the supplier achieved this in a two-year period without expending any capital.

Maintaining level production

The success of lean manufacturing also depends on a level production schedule; that is, the production of different items must be distributed evenly to minimize uncertainty for upstream operations and suppliers (see Table 2). Toyota defines level production as evenly 'distributing volume and specifications over the span of production' during the assembly process so that suppliers have a smooth, stable demand stream.[13] A nonlevel schedule (e.g. making a large batch of two-door cars and then switching to a large batch of four-doors cars) presents suppliers with spikes in demand. To deal with the spikes, suppliers are forced to maintain high inventory levels to ensure they are prepared for unexpected customer demand. Donnelly Mirrors calls the finished-goods inventory maintained for its nonlevel customers the customer's 'wall of shame'.

Providing suppliers with a predictable schedule – stable orders and regular demand – is particularly important in a lean logistics system with little inventory to cover unexpected fluctuations in demand. Japanese transplants outperform their US counterparts on this dimension. Their order demand is stable, reflecting more level schedules in their assembly plants. Honda, Nissan and Toyota stand out among their Japanese peers. Toyota is particularly sensitive to the importance of level production, a core principle of the Toyota production system. The automaker states that customers unable to level their schedule do not have the 'right' to use a JIT pull system.[14] Nonlevel customers are simply imposing their chaotic systems onto their suppliers, and the suppliers will pay the price in higher inventory, with all its related maladies and higher transportation costs for expedited shipments. The Big Three, however, are slower to learn this lesson. In fact, Chrysler alone is making improvements. Chrysler's suppliers can plan their production schedules much more easily than Ford's or GM's. They can hold less inventory and still consistently meet customer demand. The ability of Chrysler to level its schedule may help explain its lower inventory levels.

Much has been written about the 'bull whip' effect in which a small change in the schedule of the customer plant leads to a much larger disruption in the supplier plant and an even greater disruption for those companies that supply the supplier.[15] In short, maintaining a level production schedule has significant second- and third-order effects. The scheduling practices of the Japanese transplants and US automakers affect the ability of suppliers to maintain level production: the same suppliers maintain a higher degree of level production for Japanese transplants than they do for US automakers. And when first-tier suppliers have level production schedules, their second-tier suppliers are better able to cut their inventories and ship on a JIT basis.

Table 3 Lean manufacturing practices on supplier production lines

Lean manufacturing practices	Suppliers serving US auto plants (n = 91)	Suppliers serving Japanese-owned auto plants (n = 91)	Suppliers of: Chrysler (n = 26)	Ford (n = 42)	GM (n = 23)	Suppliers of: Honda (n = 22)	Nissan (n = 16)	Toyota (n = 37)	Others (n = 16)
Degree to which supplier has leveled schedule over time[a]	2.7	3.1*	2.7	2.8	2.6	3.1	3.0	3.2	3.0
Elapsed time until response to quality problem in supplier's plant (minute)[b]	6.2	6.2	6.7	4.0	9.6**	6.9	6.6	3.8	9.9**
Defective products shipped to customer (parts per million)	292	222	252	285	350	361	187	166	179
Products requiring rework or scrapping in supplier plants (parts per million)	23,634	13,591*	25,631	26,559	16,038*	12,866	8,756	7,888	18,578*
Frequency of die change[c]	3.1	3.5	2.9	3.5	2.5***	3.4	2.9	3.8	3.3**
Continuous flow[d]	3.5	3.6	3.4	3.3	3.9	4.0	3.3	3.6	3.5
Pull system[e]	3.2	3.4	3.4	3.2	3.0	3.8	2.8	3.6	3.3*

*$P < 0.1$. **$P < 0.05$. ***$P < 0.01$. (The P value shows whether the comparisons are statistically significant or due to chance.)

[a] 1 = once-a-month production, 2 = once-a-week production, 3 = once-a-day production, 4 = level production. (The time period within which the supplier schedules all the varieties of the product. 'Once a day' means running every version of the product, such as each color, every day.)

[b] After stopping the production line.

[c] 1 = monthly, 3 = daily, 5 = multiple times per shift.

[d] 1 = none, 5 = all. (Continuous flow means that, after processing each workpiece, it is sent to the next process for immediate processing.)

[e] 1 = based completely on production schedule, 5 = based completely on requests received from downstream process.

Japanese customers place much less pressure on suppliers to fill a truckload than US customers. In addition, only 8% of suppliers for Japanese customers, compared with 33% for US customers, are penalized if they do not fill a truck. Ford's suppliers are under particular pressure to load a truck fully, a finding that starkly contrasts with Toyota's suppliers. Examining the pressure on Ford's suppliers shows the ripple effects. Ford's low ranking on lean inventories, and particularly its high level of on-the-wheel inventory, can be partly explained by its truckload shipping policy. Ford wants to use all the space in its trucks to lower its transportation costs and therefore requires its suppliers to fill trucks on the basis of minimum weight requirements. Ford usually pays the shipping costs, but suppliers who fail to meet minimum targets must pay for the shipment themselves. Ford's policy encourages suppliers to fill trucks whether or not Ford needs the parts – a practice that refutes the core lean manufacturing principle of delivering the right part at the right place at the right time.

Incorporating quality

A focus on building in quality is another requirement for effective lean manufacturing. Instead of relying on a formal inspection process to uncover defects after they occur (which leads to costly repairs and wasted floor space in the repair areas), workers can stop the production flow immediately whenever they detect abnormalities (see Table 3).[16]

Although US and Japanese customers do not differ significantly in terms of the quality received from their suppliers, suppliers for the Japanese transplants reported significantly less scrap and rework than suppliers for the Big Three. In other words, suppliers delivered the same quality to their customers – but at a significantly higher cost in internal scrap and rework for their US customers. It seems clear that suppliers are more likely to build in quality when serving Japanese transplants and 'inspect in' quality when supplying US customers.

Insisting on quality from suppliers and penalizing them for not delivering are insufficient to prevent wasteful practices in supplier plants. For example, one US automaker set up a special warranty reduction department to identify parts that break down in the field causing high warranty costs and to help suppliers of those parts reduce the breakdowns. The automaker measured quality defects and threatened to stop dealing with suppliers that did not aggressively improve. The result was a significant reduction in defective parts delivered to the assembly plant. But there was little actual transfer of knowledge to the suppliers, and our data suggest that the suppliers were solving the problem through increasingly costly inspections of parts. Japanese automakers have elicited more effective performance on quality from their suppliers – without incurring the higher costs of extra inspection – by combining high-quality expectations with hands-on teaching of lean manufacturing methods.

Achieving Just-In-Time Transportation and Delivery

Lean manufacturing minimizes inventory and prevents waste, but critically depends on transporting and delivering parts – typically, small and frequent shipments by truck – in an orderly, timely manner and at low cost (see Table 4). Just as the Japanese transplants excel at lean management, they also stand out in regard to JIT logistics. Overall, suppliers for Japanese transplants achieve higher scores than those for the Big Three on all aspects of logistics performance except for the load factor (a measure of how often trucks are fully loaded). Suppliers to US plants ship 68% of trucks full to capacity, whereas the same suppliers fully load only 47% of trucks to Japanese suppliers. Differing customer policies are the reason: US customers penalize suppliers for partially filled trucks, whereas Japanese customers expect suppliers to ship *what* is needed *when* it is needed.

When it comes to their delivery and transportation systems, what are Japanese transplants doing right? They develop close working relationships with core carriers, set stringent delivery requirements, compensate for the longer distances in the United States by using innovative delivery methods, and adopt efficient loading practices such as mixed-product loading.

Developing close relationships with transportation carriers

Important as it is to develop close relationships with a relatively small group of parts suppliers, developing close ties with transportation carriers is equally critical for the efficient functioning of an automaker's lean transportation and delivery system.[17] By focusing on a small group of select carriers, known as 'core carriers', lean manufacturers receive proven, reliable service in such areas as consolidation, tightly scheduled deliveries, shipment tracing and effective communication.

For both the Japanese transplants and the Big Three US automakers, a few core carriers move a majority of the freight. But Japanese transplants use core carriers to a much greater degree than US automakers: the Japanese use 1.4 trucking firms compared to 4.3 firms for US automakers. Moreover, the highest percentage of freight carried by a single company working for a Japanese transplant is 92%, whereas among the US automakers the highest percentage is 75%.

Stark differences emerge when examining individual automakers. The contrast between Toyota and GM, for example, is startling: Toyota uses only one carrier, whereas GM uses seven. It is not surprising, then, that GM scores much higher on late deliveries and lower on on-time pickups than Toyota. With so many core carriers, how can GM develop its transportation suppliers to fit into its scheduling systems and make perfect delivery to GM a top priority? The lesson is clear: if an automaker outsources a transportation job to the lowest bidder, the result will be low price but not necessarily high-quality service. Within a lean enterprise, without the protection of large inventory reserves, reliable transportation service is critical.

Table 4 Lean transportation practices between suppliers and auto plants

Lean transportation practices	Suppliers serving US auto plants (n = 91)	Suppliers serving Japanese-owned auto plants (n = 91)	Suppliers of:			Suppliers of:			
			Chrysler (n = 26)	Ford (n = 42)	GM (n = 23)	Honda (n = 22)	Nissan (n = 16)	Toyota (n = 37)	Others (n = 16)
Percentage of shipments unloaded before scheduled delivery time	63%	34%***	78%	62%	49%	37%	31%	30%	33%
Percentage that use specific pickup time periods	74%	68%	73%	62%	95%**	63%	77%	61%	81%**
Percentage of on-time pickups	79%	89%***	79%	82%	72%	91%	98%	90%	79%*
Number of trucking companies used	4.3	1.4*	2.72	2.72	7***	1.47	1.31	1	1.19***
Largest percentage of freight hauled by one carrier	75%	92%***	74%	75%	76%	86%	96%	99%	94%***
Shipping distance (mile/kilometer)	356/573	376/605	376/605	361/581	332/534	293/472	401/645	379/610	456/734*
Loading time (minute)[a]	58	38**	55	65	44*	42	30	35	41
Percentage using side-loading trucks or trailers[b]	0%	19%***	0%	0%	0%	0%	0%	56%	0%***
Use of additional trucks or trailers	23%	35%*	22%	30%	12%*	66%	16%	33%	18%**
Percentage of single-product loads[c]	33%	16%**	11%	44%	34%**	19%	12%	13%	17%

Table 4 (cont'd)

Lean transportation practices	Suppliers serving US auto plants (n = 91)	Suppliers serving Japanese-owned auto plants (n = 91)	Suppliers of:			Suppliers of:			
			Chrysler (n = 26)	Ford (n = 42)	GM (n = 23)	Honda (n = 22)	Nissan (n = 16)	Toyota (n = 37)	Others (n = 16)
Percentage of mixed-product loads[c]	65%	65%	87%	53%	61%**	77%	82%	53%	56%**
Percentage of in-sequence mixed loads[c]	3%	19%***	2%	2%	5%	4%	6%	34%	23%***
Percentage of point-to-point deliveries[d]	57%	37%**	57%	64%	43%*	95%	0%	13%	38%***
Percentage of circuit deliveries ('milk runs')[d]	34%	45%	32%	32%	46%*	5%	92%	52%	44%***
Percentage of compound deliveries[d]	8%	18%*	12%	4%	11%**	0%	8%	36%	18%***

*$P < 0.1$. **$P < 0.05$. ***$P < 0.01$. (The P value shows whether the comparisons are statistically significant or due to chance.)

[a] Time to load a typical shipment onto a truck.

[b] Goods are loaded or unloaded from one or both sides of the truck rather than from the rear of the truck.

[c] Freight consisting of the same type of products (single-product load), different types of products (mixed-product load) or loaded according to the sequence of installation on the customer's production line (in-sequence mixed load).

[d] Freight is shipped directly to the customer (point-to-point), picked up at several places and then delivered to the customer ('milk runs') or passed through a consolidation center *en route* to an assembly plant to create smaller mixed loads (compound) as needed for assembly.

Developing relationships with carriers and demanding consistent, on-time shipping is a top priority.

Setting stringent delivery requirements

When customers establish stringent delivery requirements – regarding frequency, delivery within specific time periods and efficient loading and unloading – they motivate suppliers to meet those requirements by improving their operations and shipment activities.

Requiring frequent shipments from their suppliers is one key to the Japanese transplants' success. Infrequent shipments suggests that customers are receiving and holding large batches of inventory, which increases inventory holding costs, occupies valuable space and masks quality problems. Suppliers that serve Japanese transplants also make more frequent daily shipments than for US automakers – 3.6 shipments per day for the Japanese compared to 2.4 shipments for the Big Three. Chrysler's suppliers make an average of 4.0 shipments each day in contrast to only 1.1 shipments for Ford's suppliers. Toyota's suppliers lead all automakers, with 5.0 shipments per day (see Table 2).

To avoid chaos and congestion at their delivery docks, lean customers also require suppliers to unload their shipments within specific time periods. One lean company that makes aluminium gutters implemented a system of tightly scheduled windows of opportunity (i.e. time windows) for the pickup of finished goods. They also developed a highly disciplined system of organizing finished-goods inventory according to delivery times with standardized times and methods for loading and unloading finished goods. The company spaced deliveries throughout the day to ensure there was an even flow of work throughout the shift. The result: of 12 shipping docks that had always been congested, 10 docks were closed. The two remaining docks are used evenly throughout the day, and rarely are there any delays on the docks.

In regard to the unloading and timing of deliveries, we again see evidence that although US automakers have been embracing a lean philosophy on paper, they are missing key elements of the discipline needed to make it work. Only 34% of suppliers report that their Japanese customers allow truck drivers to unload freight before the scheduled delivery time. By contrast, a full 63% of suppliers say that US automakers permit early unloading. There are no significant differences in the use of pickup time windows at the suppliers of US and Japanese customers. However, trucking firms often fail to live up to suppliers' expectations – particularly those delivering to US customers. Trucking firms for Japanese transplants arrive at the suppliers' plants within the pickup windows 89% of the time compared with 79% of the time for US customers. Note that trucking firms for GM achieve only 72% on-time pickups even though GM 'requires' 100%.

Compensating for geographical distance

The sheer size of North America poses daunting geographical challenges for lean auto manufacturers. Toyota made the JIT approach famous in Toyota City, a rural area outside Nagoya in amidst a different geography. Land was plentiful, and suppliers dedicated to Toyota built plants around the assembly plant. Suppliers would receive a signal just a few hours before parts were needed on the assembly line and could ship exactly what Toyota needed many times throughout the day, building the parts just before they were shipped.

This approach clearly does not work when supplier plants are hundreds of miles away from assembly plants and it takes hours to make a delivery. Our results show a similar average shipping distance from suppliers to both groups of customers: 376 miles to Japanese customers compared with 356 miles to US customers. But Japanese transplants have found a way to compensate for the geographical distances they encounter in the United States. 'Milk runs', or compound deliveries, are the key. Traditional point-to-point delivery works well in lean manufacturing if a single plant provides enough products for an assembly plant to fill the truck many times every day. But if that is not the case, milk runs – that involve stopping at several suppliers or assembly plants – are preferable.

US customers tend to rely on single-product loads more than their Japanese counterparts: 33% of US customers used single-product loads compared with 16% of Japanese customers. In addition, 57% of freight haulers for US customers, compared with 37% for Japanese transplants, use point-to-point delivery. And 18% of freight for Japanese transplants is delivered via compound deliveries compared with only 8% for the US automakers.

Only 13% of the deliveries to Toyota plants from our sample of suppliers consists of single-product, point-to-point loads. Toyota has become the master of cross-docking in the North American auto industry. Cross-docks accept truckloads of product at one side of the warehouse and reconfigure them into different mixes of product on trucks leaving the other side. The automaker established a joint venture, called Transfreight, and taught the company how to use the Toyota production system to manage its cross-dock.[18] Full-truckload shipments come into the cross-dock from individual suppliers or milk runs. Transfreight then reconfigures the inventory into mixed loads and ships about 1.5 hours' worth of exactly the material Toyota needs in its assembly plants. Material flows through the facility, rarely spending more than a few hours in temporary storage. A similar approach is being adopted by Ford in its Nirvana project.

Adopting effective loading methods

In traditional manufacturing, taking extra time to load and unload a truck may incur additional labor costs, but those extra costs tend to be insignificant. In lean manu-facturing, by contrast, loading and unloading time is critical, because there are no inventory buffers on the assembly line. Inventory sitting on a truck being unloaded for an extra half hour can mean that the assembly line will be starved for parts.

Loading time for Japanese transplants is significantly less than for the US automakers. Suppliers for Japanese customers spend only 38 minutes loading a shipment, whereas suppliers for US customers spend 58 minutes. More specifically, Ford and Chrysler suppliers take almost twice as long loading as the suppliers of Nissan and Toyota.

Studies have shown that it can take less time to unload from a side-loaded truck, yet only trucking firms for Toyota use trucks equipped for side loading. In rear-loaded trucks, there is only a small space for removing parts, and workers must first remove parts at the rear of the truck before getting to parts closer to the cab. Side-loaded trucks provide broad access to parts stored throughout the truck. In addition, workers can be selective about the order in which they unload parts, unloading at the same time the parts going to similar storage locations in the assembly plant. Side loading, however, requires significant capital investment and cooperation from the supplier. It will not work if suppliers have raised shipping docks already set up for rear-loading trucks.

Use of sequenced loads also increases efficiency. Large products that are customized for different vehicles are brought to an assembly plant in the exact sequence needed for the cars being built on the assembly line. Instead of walking up and down the line to select the right seat for the next car coming down the line, assembly line workers need only to walk to one place and pick up the next item in sequence. This allows workers to focus on assembling the car rather than finding a part, but it also reduces the chances of selecting the wrong part for a particular car. Japanese automakers are more likely to use sequenced loads than their US peers. A total of 19% of freight for Japanese transplants is loaded in sequence compared with 3% for US automakers. Toyota's suppliers obtain the highest score at 34%.

An efficient truck transfer system that separates the roles of truck drivers and loaders can increase loading efficiency. This system involves leaving additional trucks or trailers at the supplier's plant so that the supplier can load products before drivers arrive at the dock. A truck driver can depart immediately with the loaded vehicle instead of waiting for it to be loaded. Suppliers to Japanese transplants are more likely to use additional trucks or trailers, particularly Honda for which 66% of its suppliers do this.

Conclusion

Our comparison of supplier plants with product lines serving both US automakers and Japanese transplants revealed that the actions of suppliers' customers significantly affected the ability of suppliers to be lean. In regard to supply chain management, the Big Three US automakers have publicly adopted some version of lean manufacturing and JIT logistics. The data showed, however, that they could still benefit from improvement. The same suppliers had much leaner operations within their plants and in their logistics when serving Japanese customers. By most measures, the suppliers that served Toyota were the leanest of all. This is not to say that US automakers were weak on all measures. There was variation across companies and, on many measures, the Big Three were equal with their Japanese competitors – most likely because the Big Three have been aggressively focusing on making improvements.

What did the Japanese transplants do to develop superior lean supply chains in North America?

1   They worked with their suppliers to help them develop lean capabilities – at least for the particular production line that served the Japanese assembly plants.
2   They leveled their own production schedules to avoid big spikes in demand, which enabled suppliers to hold less inventory.
3   They created a disciplined system of delivery time periods within which specific parts shipments must be received.
4   They developed lean transportation systems to handle mixed-load, small-lot deliveries. In some cases, this required building a cross-dock to accept large loads for redistribution into smaller loads.
5   They encouraged suppliers to ship only what was needed at the assembly plant at a particular time – for example, by not penalizing suppliers for shipments that did not completely fill a truck.

Is this phenomenon unique to the automobile industry? Clearly, the answer is no. Companies 'going lean' in aerospace, shipbuilding, computers, furniture, paint, telecommunications, aluminum products – to name only a few – face similar issues. Consider Miller SQA, a division of Herman Miller, that chose to make a lean furniture line that is 'Simple, Quick and Affordable'. To deliver quickly, as promised, the company needed to reduce lead time dramatically since their competitors were taking two to four months from receipt of a customer order to shipment to the customer. By systematically examining every step in the value chain and eliminating waste, Miller SQA was able to cut lead time to a few weeks and, in some cases, to just a few days. The company created a lean assembly plant for assembling the furniture and installed a metering center (a cross-dock) near the assembly plant. Pull signals are sent to the metering center, and parts are brought to the plant just a couple of hours before they are needed. Suppliers, who have developed highly reliable lean systems with the help of Miller SQA, are electronically connected to the metering center and receive pull signals telling them when to replenish the parts. Miller SQA cannot level its schedule because it builds furniture to order, but by developing lean suppliers, highly flexible assembly cells and information technology support, the company was able to assemble and deliver in record time more than 400,000 end items of almost perfect quality.

The power of creating a lean value chain is gradually being understood, and even Toyota is constantly improving its system. As the pace of e-commerce accelerates and customers expect deliveries to be as fast as computers, performance pressures will become more stringent. The central lesson of lean manufacturing is that speed does not necessarily mean increased cost and lower quality. Shrinking the time line can actually improve quality and reduce costs. But customers cannot achieve these benefits by simply expecting their suppliers to perform to a lean standard. Creating a lean supply chain requires a give-and-take partnership across all the links in the chain of value to the customer.

NOTES

1   R. Coie, *Managing Quality Fads: How American Business Learned To Play the Quality Game* (New York: Oxford University Press, 1999); T.M. Laseter, *Balanced Sourcing: Cooperation and Competition in Supplier Relationships* (San Francisco: Jossey-Bass Publishers, 1998); J.P. MacDuffie and S. Helper, 'Creating Lean Suppliers', *California Management Review* 39, no. 4 (1997): 118–151.

2   R.T. Lubben, *Just-In-Time Manufacturing* (New York: McGraw-Hill Inc., 1998); K. Suzaki, *The New Manufacturing Challenge: Techniques for Continuous Improvement* (New York: Free Press, 1987).

3   M. Bensaou and N. Venkatraman, 'Vertical Relationships and the Role of Information Technology: An Empirical Study of U.S. and Japanese Supplier Relationships in the Auto Industry', working paper, 95/20/SM/TM (Fontainebleau Cedex, France: INSEAD, 1995); J.H. Dyer, 'Does Governance Matter? *Keiretsu* Alliances and Asset Specificity as Sources of Japanese Competitive Advantage', *Organization Science* 7, no. 6 (1996): 649–665; T. Nishiguchi, *Strategic Industrial Sourcing: The Japanese Advantage* (New York: Oxford University Press, 1994).

4   M.A. Cusumano and A. Takeishi, 'Supplier Relations and Management: A Survey of Japanese-Transplant and U.S. Auto Plants', *Strategic Management Journal* 12 (1991): 563–588.

5   S.R. Helper and M. Sako, 'Supplier Relations in Japan and the United States. Are They Converging?', *Sloan Management Review* 36, no. 3 (spring 1995): 77–84; J. Womack, D.T. Jones and D. Roos, *The Machine That Changed The World* (New York: Rawson Associates, 1990).

6   K. Mishina, 'Johnson Controls, Automotive Systems Group: The Georgetown, Kentucky, Plan', Harvard Business School case no. 9-693-086 (Boston: Harvard Business School Press, 1993).

7   P.D. Jenkins and R. Florida, 'Work System Innovation Among Japanese Transplants', in *Remade in America: Transplanting and Transforming Japanese Management Systems*, eds J.K. Liker, W.M. Fruin and P.A. Adier (New York: Oxford University Press, 1999), 331–360.

8   S.M. Lee and A. Ansari, 'Comparative Analysis of Japanese Just-in-Time Purchasing and Traditional U.S. Purchasing Systems', *International Journal of Operations & Production Management* 5, no. 4 (1985): 5–14.

9   J.H. Dyer and K. Nobeoka, 'Creating and Managing a High Performance Knowledge-Sharing Network: The Toyota Case', *Strategic Management Journal*, in press.

10   D. Nelson, R. Mayo and P. Moody, *Powered by Honda: Developing Excellence in the Global Enterprise* (New York: John Wiley, 1998).

11   R.J. Schonberger and A. Ansari, 'Just-In-Time Purchasing Can Improve Quality', *Journal of Purchasing and Materials Management* 20, no. 1 (1984): 2–7.

12   J.K. Liker, *Becoming Lean: Inside Stories of U.S. Manufacturers* (Portland, Oregon: Productivity Press: 1997).

13   B.J. Coleman and M.R. Vaghefi, 'Heijunka: A Key to the Toyota Production System', *Production and Inventory Management Journal* (fourth quarter 1994): 31–35.

14   *The Toyota Production System* (Toyota City, Japan; Toyota Motor Corp., International Public Affairs Division & Operations Management Consulting Division, 1995).

15   H.L. Lee, V. Padmanabhan and S. Whang, 'The Bullwhip Effect in Supply Chains', *Sloan Management Review* 38, no. 3 (spring 1997): 93–102.

16   *The Toyota Production System* (1995).

17   J.J. Gentry, 'Role of Carriers in Buyer–Supplier Strategic Partnerships: A Supply Chain Management Approach', *Journal of Business Logistics* 17, no. 2 (1996): 35–55.

18   J. Karlin, J.K. Liker and M. Wheeler, 'Applying Toyota Production System Principles to Cross-Dock Operations', *Proceedings of Material Handling Institute of America Conference*, York, Virginia, May 2000.

Innovation and Competition in UK Supermarkets

Mark Harvey

Supermarkets: Innovative Saints or Anti-Competitive Sinners?

Three years ago, the Mintel International Group reported that supermarkets were more trusted by consumers than priests, politicians and teachers. This year their popularity ratings have slumped, suggesting that supermarket behaviour has changed, or that consumer opinion is fickle, or that swings in popularity can be readily engineered by the media (*The Guardian*, 1999b).

At the same time, the Office of Fair Trading (OFT) has been investigating the major food multiples for uncompetitive behaviour, high prices and excessive profits [1]. After some delay relating to the scope of the inquiry, the OFT has referred the practices of all major supermarkets to the Monopolies and Mergers Committee (*Financial Times*, 1999b). Disputes rage over the measures used to ascertain whether price variations and profit levels on turnover are reliable indications of anti-competitive behaviour, or whether return on capital employed is more appropriate (*Financial Times*, 1999a). The issue is far from trivial. If, for example, supermarkets are investing heavily in logistical infrastructure to enable them to bring to the shelf fresher and higher quality produce than other European or US retailers, then there must be a question as to whether like is being compared with like.

One of the major, and most innovative, areas of change has been the development of, and investment in, a whole new system of distribution, largely replacing wholesale markets, which has been undertaken by the major multiples. Each of them now has about 20 regional distribution centres, either in-house or contracted out, with advanced IT systems and dedicated 'cross-docking' transport fleets. In terms of product range, service, speed, freshness and quality this new system has little to compare directly with the system it has replaced. The UK, for example, is now endowed with a more extensive and integrated 'chill chain' for the new chill food goods than exists anywhere in continental Europe. This major infrastructural investment upstream of the supermarket outlet should rightly be compared for scope and efficiency with the system it replaced, and hence in terms of the return on the high rate of capital growth involved.

This change in the nature of the supply chain creates a difficulty in interpreting rates of return and competitiveness. It has another dimension because of the attitudes of some of the other participants in the supply chain. A series of television broadcasts and newspaper reports has given prominence to attacks from suppliers who complain of the overbearing power of the supermarkets, and the excessive share of added value they consequently capture from the food chain [2]. Prices of sheep or pork carcasses at auction are compared with price per kilo of meat on the supermarket shelf to suggest a quite astronomic mark-up of produce by the new tyrants (*The Guardian*, 1999a).

Finally, organisations representing the branded goods manufacturers (such as the British Brandowners Group) complain that the competitive threat posed by own-label manufacturers has stifled (their) innovation and investment in research and development. Major global players such as Unilever, Kellogs, Heinz and Campbells find themselves either constrained to produce under UK supermarkets' own labels, or risk losing shelf space to dedicated own-label manufacturers. Branding is therefore being undermined as an effective means of securing appropriate rents from the R&D and marketing investment in new product development in the competitive circumstances of 'copy-cat' behaviour by the retailers' own-label producers. So retail multiples stand accused of undermining the capacity of the food industry to engage in long-term investment in radical innovation.

Research undertaken at the ESRC (Economic and Social Research Council (UK)) Centre for Research in Innovation and Competition suggests that a rather broader view needs to be taken of what has certainly been a fundamental revolution in food retailing over the course of the last two decades [3]. There is a useful comparison to be made between German discount superstores, driving supply down a route of high yields of standard products at low prices, where price is the focus of competition; and the UK supermarkets creating a demand for product differentiation and high value added, where, it is claimed, quality is the focus of competition.

Recent years have seen the arrival of these discount stores, Aldi (German) and Netto (Scandinavian), on the UK food market, to complement Kwiksave and the other existing discount stores. Wal-Mart may well be next after its arrival in Europe [4]. But the strategy of discounting, and hence the market in which such firms operate, is quite different from that of the typical UK supermarkets. Product ranges are much smaller, and product differentiation within a product category much more restricted. The emphasis is on price and volume of turnover. UK supermarkets trade in a market which sells higher levels of convenience, greater choice in both price and quality, and wider product ranges (especially chill, own-label, and convenience foods) which are unavailable in discount stores. It is quite possible for supermarkets and discounters to survive, but it is incorrect to assume that they are directly competing with each other in the same market. As yet, discounting appears to have done little to erode the market of the large UK multiples. But policies which assume that the 'price of the standard shopping basket' is all that matters risk channelling competitive pressures down the discount route. The question is, what kind of a food market would there be if all were to be driven down the road of discounting, where emphasis is on price and a relatively limited range of relatively standard goods?

The UK supermarket is consequently now widely taken as a model for food retailing across Europe, in preference to the price–quantity focus of competition found in discount markets. It has pioneered many of the advances in supply chain management, by means of which innovation has been stimulated along the length of the supply chain. One effect of the concentrated power of the UK supermarkets has been its capacity to 'cream' the top of the quality range across a wide range of produce which is sourced from a wide geographical area. We now consider the changes that have characterised the emergence of this distinctive system of retailing in the UK.

Shaping Demand and Expanding the Product Range

A central aspect of the development of the new superstore is that in a society of wide income dispersion, exemplified in Europe by the contemporary UK, the large retail outlets organise and integrate many previously separate segments of consumer demand. They bring together high income consumers with low income consumers, so creating their own internal niche markets with distinctive marques at high prices, together with their own-label discount ranges. The consequence of creating a wide 'catchment' area of consumers, with a distinctive socio-economic profile, is that they can sell and target both high and low price items to the market they have created. They display a more extensive range of goods than was possible under previous retail organisation. Major stores now carry 25,000 to 50,000 products. To be sure, there are winners (especially consumers with purchasing power and transport) and losers (especially small retailers and low income, isolated or car-less consumers) as a consequence of the restructuring. Moreover, there is undoubtedly some truth in the assertion that superstores create a quasi-monopoly in their respective catchment areas. But the 'reshaping of demand' by the massive investment in the new superstores can only be envisaged in circumstances where 'first-mover advantage' in a new catchment area is decisive. The new consumer choice offered by wide product range is the necessary counterpart to the quasi-monopoly catchment area.

Reorganising Supply

In conjunction with the reorganisation of retail outlets, the big multiples also centralised their buying functions from the mid 1980s. There is no doubt that this was a key strategy which fundamentally altered the balance of power between retailers, their suppliers, and producers. Here again, as with any industrial restructuring, there are winners and losers. But some care needs to be taken in interpreting the effects, if only because of the counter-example of producer-dominated retail outlets in the car industry prompting similar investigations into trading practices. Two main consequences of the centralisation of buying power have been the development of higher levels of own-label produce in the UK than elsewhere in Europe and the emergence of dedicated long-term supply relationships. Both symbolise the extension of control of retailers over food supply. The losers are clearly the branded manufacturers, on the one hand, and the suppliers of fresh produce excluded from partnership and long-term supply relationships with particular retailers, on the other. Wholesale markets have virtually disappeared as channels for getting produce to the consumer.

So instead of an industry where producers and suppliers were sharply separated from retailers, the new organisation of the industry is characterised by the integrated supply chain. Large own-label manufacturers, such as Hazelwood or Northern Foods, have separate factories dedicated to the products of each major multiple, one factory producing under a Sainsbury label, another under Tesco, a third under Marks & Spencer, etc. Fresh produce suppliers likewise often enjoy a similar 'own-label' status with a particular multiple: in the Canary Islands, for example, a Tesco-designed pack of tomatoes leaves the grower with a Tesco label already stamped on it.

Revolutionising Logistics

The final major piece of restructuring of the UK food industry can be seen in the large-scale investment in the distribution infrastructure. Logistics have become critical in ensuring the expansion of fresh and chilled product ranges, but more generally the centralisation of distribution in regional logistical facilities by all the major retailers has brought about a continuing acceleration of stock flows (*Retail Distribution*, 1998). There has been a rapid technological and organisational innovation process of a major scale in the process of bringing food to the consumer. The major retailers either have constructed their own large-scale, high-tech facilities, or engage the major logistics companies (Wincanton, Excel, etc.) with equivalent facilities. Most of the major multiples deploy a combination of 'in-house' and contracted distribution systems.

Reconfiguring Innovation in Food

Putting these different aspects of restructuring together – the creation of the superstore, the centralising of buyer power, the development of supply chain organisation, and the construction of a new logistical infrastructure – the consequences of this revolution in retailing are fairly visible to the UK consumer. The chill and convenience food segment of the market is probably the most developed in Europe. The fresh produce supply has increased in scope, range, global sourcing and freshness. It is possible to discern a new style of product innovation, which can combine both quite radical technological innovation and high levels of transient novelty. A new sandwich filling to tickle the taste is not itself so much an innovation as is the constant capacity to produce variety. Convenience foods are a typical example of this kind of innovation, where design and cuisine are as significant as the infrastructural and technological innovation necessary to bring them to the superstore shelf.

We can perhaps contrast the innovation strategies of the big food product producers and the supermakets in the following way. Where the branded manufacturers can be described as 'conservative radicals', making few but major investments in new products, the own-label manufacturers typically produce more than 1,000 new products per year, many with very short life cycles, and so could more appropriately be dubbed 'variable geometry innovators'. Likewise supply chain organisation affords 'insider suppliers' the possibility of a longer-term attitude towards their own retail outlets, and a more co-ordinated approach to new product development and marketing. The supply chain is therefore a *different innovation environment* from a more arm's-length marketplace.

It is difficult to know which of the standard measures of competition are appropriate to assess such a complex process of industrial restructuring at a given point in time, when the outcomes of that restructuring are still uncertain. Certainly any simple measures on profit over turnover, returns on capital employed, let alone price per specified standard items, are woefully inadequate. It is also unwise to rely too heavily on views expressed by the inevitable 'winners' or 'losers' of the process of restructuring.

Who Is Competing with Whom?

One important consequence of the industrial restructuring is that the unit of competition has changed. Economists tend to treat the firm as the unit of competition. That may or may not have been suitable in an industry where there were discrete classes of retailer firms, manufacturers, and suppliers, each in competition with other members of their respective class. But the key unit of industrial organisation in the food sector now is the supply chain. The apportionment of added value along the chain is part of the financial and trading organisation of the chain. The 'front-end' competition between retailers carries with it a much broader scale of competition between the 'back-end' supply, processing, and distribution systems. Any narrower conception of competition threatens to overlook the scale and nature of the innovation processes that have transformed the range and nature of food now available for consumption as well as the major characteristics of industrial reorganisation.

What Is Competing with What?

Many of the traditional views of competition reflect the way the world was when producers ruled the roost. It is the price of the shopping basket approach: a product is made, and has a price tagged to it, with the retailer perceived to be simply taking their cut, but adding nothing of value. In this model, any price variation above the lowest is taken as prima facie evidence for possible oligopolistic practice by retailers. This view of competition is both obsolete and simplistic.

The OFT Report *Competition in Retailing* clearly recognises the separate contribution that retailers make. They are providing a service on top of the product, and that service has both a cost and a consequent additional price to the shopping basket. But the real difficulty in standing by a modified 'price of the shopping basket' approach [5] which includes the price of these additional services is that it fails to grasp fully the significance of a change in the focus of competition from price to 'convenience'. Surveys have shown that convenience [6], and its provision by retailers, is the prime consideration in determining whether a consumer sticks or switches 'loyalty' from one supermarket or type of shopping to another. Yet, when you unpack just what is meant by 'convenience', much of it has to do with how the consumer's own unpriced activity (shopping behaviours, travelling time, 'search costs') is or is not facilitated.

Take a couple of examples of 'convenience'. The shopper goes to one shop and does all his/her shopping, saving on both time and travel costs, but requiring the superstore to invest in space in order to be able to supply the total shopping basket. It may be possible to buy a smaller range of goods at lower cost from a discount store. But that is not the appropriate comparison. Shopping patterns in the UK are known to be different from much of Europe, with people going to a superstore less frequently, and spending less overall time, by doing the 'one big shop'. Moreover the 'value of time' and distribution of time may also be changing, as dual earner households may have an increased preference to shopping in fewer but more comprehensive 'bursts'. Second example: what cost is speed through the check-out? Clearly, supermarkets are competing on the provision of quick exits, in terms of both infrastructure and labour. They are selling a service for shopping on top of the price of the good. But their service, and the price tag attached, combines with the convenience of time saved for the shopper. The competition is on both price (of additional service quality) and an unpriced convenience.

Supermarkets are thus also facilitating reductions or qualitative improvements in the uncosted time expended by the consumer in the equally economically essential activity of shopping. The growth and development of infrastructure by the supermarkets for home shopping are an important further development of this, and the question remains, 'Who pays?' for the service of home delivery. Tesco has 200,000 customers on home shopping, and Asda and Sainsbury are reported to be investing heavily in order to gain their market share of what is expected to become a £2 billion to £3 billion market in the next few years (*Financial Times*, 1999d). There is thus new capital growth in a process of an extension of the 'competition for convenience' into the new areas of e-commerce.

Long-Term Innovation Dynamic or Short-Term Price War?

There can be little doubt that, over the past couple of decades or more, we have witnessed a radical transformation of the food that is consumed, and of the retailing, distribution and supply that have provided it. For taste (and was it ever just taste?), it may not pass the 'grandmother test' – but then nothing ever does. The different aspects of the changes, innovations which are both technological and organisational, suggest a long-term dynamic process in which concentration at the retailing end of the supply chain has been a key aspect. Of course, it is possible to speculate that the rate of change will slow down, and that the 'big four' retailers will sit on their relatively oligopolistic gains. But, it is equally possible that this process of long-term dynamic growth could be stalled by short-term price wars stimulated by a discounting model of retailing or a regulatory framework that takes a narrow view of competition as one simply of product and price, and of firm against firm.

One lesson from this is that competition is to be judged not in terms of the relationship between prices and costs at a point in time but rather in terms of the capacity to innovate over time leading to longer-term gains in quality, convenience and price. Innovation-based competition is naturally a dynamic process in which one looks for changes in the relative importance of rival firms over time. The fluidity of market shares is a good first test for competition in practice. Here the evidence is interesting. While Tesco increased its share of the overall grocery market from 16.2 per cent in 1991 to 17.7 per cent in 1996, its share of the market of the big four for food retailers increased from 28.5 per cent to 33.8 per cent over the same period. Sainsbury's share of the top four declined from 32.3 per cent to 29.1 per cent, while the share of the top four also declined from 56.9 to 52.4 per cent. Of the smaller multiples, Marks & Spencer and Somerfield also lost substantial market share. From this we can deduce that food retailing in the UK is competitive by virtue of the fluid market share test.

So when we look at the bigger picture of 'Who is competing with whom?' and 'What is competing with what?' it is clear that major changes have occurred in what the shopping basket is, what shopping is, and the availability and ranges of food products. Compared to a period when manufacturers and primary producers predominated, and used their own distribution systems or wholesale markets to get their products to market, we are staring now at a different landscape. This has been a long-term change in the structure of capital invested in the sector. Short-term measures of shopping basket prices at any one point in time are singularly inadequate for understanding the nature of competition or of consumer benefits in this new situation. With a narrow view of competition, it might be questioned whether this change in the nature of shopping, retailing, distribution and organisation of production amounts to competition at all. For instance, how can one compare Covent Garden Fruit and Vegetable Market with Excel Logistics? But, taking a broader view, one system of economic organisation has replaced (largely) another. And that certainly can be called competition.

By taking this broader view, it is clear that national regulatory frameworks on competition can have a significant effect on this process of major restructuring. A competition policy focusing on the price of the shopping basket might well inhibit the further process of restructuring, and limit the competition for convenience. While it is by now quite unlikely that we would ever be stranded in an exclusively discount desert, stimulation of short-term price 'spats' could certainly marginally restrict longer-term capital investment and restructuring.

But this 'competition for convenience' raises some interesting questions about quality of life. Restrictions on planning permissions for new out-of-town super- or hyper-markets can correctly enter those considerations which achieve a better balance between individual 'convenience' for some and social and ecological convenience for all. It is a dangerous assumption to make that retailers have a monopoly on what might be meant by convenience, and stand as the bargaining representatives acting on behalf of the individual consumer against the otherwise unrestricted powers of the manufacturers [7]. The most effective vehicle currently available for any expression of the countervailing power of consumers, whether individually or collectively, remains through the channels of consumer organisations, political institutions and regulatory frameworks. There are choices to be made about supermarkets, other than which supermarket one shops at. At the moment, unfortunately, the only choice that is publicly on offer is the rather narrow one of whether we want a populist discount type of food society or the 'overpowerful' middle-England super-market. The probable takeover of Asda by Wal-Mart pinpoints the political choices involved. The rumoured impending relaxation of planning permission for large superstores, in order to facilitate the entry into the market of a new and possibly powerful discounter, only serves to highlight the consequences of subordinating wider preference issues to a short-sighted orthodoxy of price competition. Wal-Mart or Tesco? Is that the only choice we are to make?

NOTES

1   Office of Fair Trading Report, London Economics, September 1997. *Competition in Retailing.* The report recognises the problems of defining markets in which different kinds of retailers, from discounters and supermarkets to small independent corner shops, coexist. However, ultimately it inclines to a modified use of the 'price of a shopping basket' approach.

2   BBC, Panorama, January 1999.

3   A group of researchers at the ESRC Centre for Research in Innovation and Competition has undertaken a series of interview programmes with different sectors of the food industry. As one of our empirical 'probes' we have investigated the innovation processes surrounding tomato products and the tomato food chain, from the seed to the supermarket. It is an ongoing research programme looking at innovation and its relation to competition in genetic engineering, logistics, retail markets, primary and secondary producers.

4   *Financial Times*, 1999c. The possibility is now an established fact following Wal-Mart's takeover of Asda.

5   This is the SSNIP test, as modified by London Economics, to include the additional costed components of retailer services, but nonetheless is based fundamentally on the 'price of a shopping basket model' of short-term consumer preferences, and the excessive profits that can be derived from monopolistic powers of a firm within a given market.

6   Nielsen Household and Shopping Survey, 1995.

7   The view of London Economics, in the OFT Report.

REFERENCES

Financial Times (1999a), 19 February.

Financial Times (1999b), 20 March.

Financial Times (1999c), 'The power of price cannot be discounted', 14 May.

Financial Times (1999d), 17 May.

The Guardian (1999a), 'Are our supermarkets out of control?', 4 January.

The Guardian (1999b), 'Verdict Research', 30 January.

Retail Distribution (1998), 'The Institute for Grocery Distribution Annual Report'.

The Similarity and Heterogeneity Theses in Studying Innovation: Evidence from the End-of-Life Vehicle Case

Frank den Hond

Introduction: Two Contrasting Theses

The innovation process is understood as a knowledge-based search for new products, processes, organizational routines and organizational structure. Technology development is an important means for companies to innovate, but innovation cannot be solely understood as technological innovation. Innovation is an important element for companies to increase their chances of long-term survival in a highly competitive business context. It may also be an important factor for companies to be able to respond to stakeholder pressure, for example, in relation to environmental issues. However, the very nature of innovation is still not fully understood, despite a vast body of literature. Since the first attempts to open up the 'black box' of innovation, it may be argued that at least two different streams of analysis have developed.

In one stream, the innovation process is seen as dependent on various contingencies such as market size, size of the firm and characteristics of the technology itself. While encompassing various bodies of literature, the central thesis emphasizes the 'similarity' of innovation processes among firms that operate under similar conditions. 'Globalization' is the strongest example of the similarity thesis. If the markets of an industry converge world-wide, if international trade fully liberalizes and if this industry is unrestricted by natural resource inputs, then it would be likely that a global style of doing business emerges. Examples of industries where the globalization thesis has been proposed include the agrochemical and pharmaceutical industries, the microelectronics and information-technology industries, as well as (parts of) international finance. The automotive industry is another example for which the globalization thesis has been advanced. According to the International Motor Vehicle Program (IMVP), there is one best way of designing, assembling and selling motor vehicles, which is described by 'lean production'.[1] Others contest their findings, and argue that it is an empirical question in which several factors influence what style emerges.[2]

Weaker examples of the similarity thesis posit that distinctive 'styles' of innovation may be identified at different levels of analysis, for example within specific geographical, industrial or market contexts. National systems of innovation,[3] industry characteristics,[4] and strategic groups[5] are examples of theories that match the similarity thesis. For example, Patel and Pavitt[6] find that a firm's industry influences its rate and direction of technological accumulation. Patel and Pavitt[7] find that 'uneven and divergent patterns of technological accumulation persist in OECD countries'. Porter[8] argues that a firm's innovative capability and competitive success in international markets may be enhanced by characteristics of its home country. The common thread in these and other studies is that the rate and direction of a firm's innovation strategy are characterized by one (or a limited number) of variables; firms operating in a similar situation develop similar innovation strategies.

In the other stream, innovation processes are seen as socially constructed, following a unique historical path or trajectory in which not only technological or other problems, but also the visions, objectives and expectations of innovators and other social actors, play a role. Thus, the contrasting thesis stresses the 'heterogeneity', in terms of strategy, structure and performance, among firms that operate within the same contexts. Firms are unique for several reasons. First, there is the possibility of 'strategic choice' in important contingencies such as (business) environment, technology and firm size.[9] Second, there is scarcity of the critical resources whose adoption and exploitation may bring the firm long-term competitive advantage.[10] Thirdly, most resources may be used to provide a variety of different services.[11] Finally, ordinary people, employees and managers may have different preferences previous experiences and cognitive styles, which make them assess and solve strategic issues differently. Heterogeneity has been pointed out as a phenomenon that reflects the need for companies to distinguish themselves from their competitors in order to realize sustained competitive advantage and long-term survival.[12] Technological innovation at the resource level is seen as an important source of heterogeneity. Firms develop new activities as they renew their resource base. Rather than the static representations of resources by Penrose and the resource-based view theorists (among others Barney and Wernerfelt), a more 'dynamic' frame of knowledge and capability building is appropriate to understand and analyse technological innovation at the resource level.[13] If different 'styles' of innovation may be identified, then they would relate to patterns in the exploitation and exploration of the firm's resources.

This paper seeks to understand how eight companies in the European automotive industry responded to regulatory pressure. In the late 1980s, public authorities at the national and EU levels questioned the environmental consequences of the amounts of waste that remain after the processing of end-of-life vehicles. During the 1990–1995 period, car manufacturers developed 'recycling strategies', i.e. coherent sets of actions to solve the problem of automotive waste by increasing the recycling rate of end-of-life vehicles.

If the similarity thesis holds, then commonalities within the empirical set of innovative response strategies can be related to the presence of contingency variables. However, if the heterogeneity thesis holds, and if Penrose's view of the firm as a unique bundle of related, productive resources is correct,[14] then the firm may only solve the issue by changing its activities or products, or developing new activities or products, such that the environmental consequences are reduced to acceptable levels. This would require the firm to pursue innovation at the resource level, and to change its activities by integrating such innovations in their organizational routines. Most likely, this would result in a differentiation of responses.

The End-of-Life Vehicle Recycling Issue

The environmental issue considered is the need for car manufacturers to reduce the amount of waste from processing of end-of-life vehicles. Cars are among the best-recycled consumer products; about 75% of the vehicle weight (essentially metals) is recovered for recycling. However, 25% remains as waste. Today's end-of-life vehicles were designed about 15 years ago. Since then, the relative share of metals in their material composition has decreased, hence the amount of end-of-life vehicle waste is expected to increase. Plastic materials have increasingly substituted for metals, and numerous new parts composed of composite materials have been added to the vehicle in order to offer novel functions to the customer.

In the mid 1980s, public authorities in various European countries became concerned about the increasing amount of end-of-life vehicle waste and started to develop policy initiatives aimed at stimulating car manufacturers to reduce this waste stream through source reduction and increased levels of recycling. For example, the German Environmental Ministry issued a draft regulation in August 1990, in which the Ministry proposed that car manufacturers take back free of charge end-of-life vehicles from the last owner; that they establish a dense nation-wide network of collection sites for end-of-life vehicles; that they reuse parts and materials when economically and technically viable; that they disassemble end-of-life vehicles in order to realize precisely defined recycling targets; and that they include waste minimization objectives and the environmentally compatible treatment of end-of-life vehicles as objectives in the development and production of new models. Car manufacturers were allowed to charge a 'third party' on their behalf with the responsibility to take back and recycle end-of-life vehicles. Other national authorities in the European Union (EU) as well as the European Commission followed the German lead, but extensive negotiations between the automotive industry and the various regulators influenced the choice of a mode of regulation as well as its contents.[15]

Car manufacturers responded to the threat of regulation by setting up recycling schemes, some of them in cooperation with shredder, car dismantling or material

Table 1   Four stages in developing recycling strategies

Stage	Time period	Most important actors	Leading actors
0	1970s–1980s	Problem definition and identification of potential solutions	Car manufacturers, individually and via industry organizations
	Late 1980s	Research on plastics recyclability	Car manufacturers and plastics producers
1	1990–1991	Start of dismantling pilots and collective political lobby	Car manufacturers alone, or with car dismantling and shredder companies
2	1991–1992	Build-up of recycling networks via bilateral agreements with car dismantling companies	BMW, Ford, Opel
3	1991–1995	Build-up of recycling networks via framework agreements with shredder companies who act as 'third parties'	Volkswagen with Preussag; Mercedes-Benz with Preussag; Renault with Compagnie française des ferailles (CFF); Peugeot with CFF; Fiat with Falck

recycling firms. Politically, they joined forces in national and international lobbies in order to prevent the authorities from implementing their policy objectives through direct regulation. While accepting the need for solving the end-of-life vehicle waste issue, the automotive industry argued it needed full discretion in developing the most effective and efficient solutions. Technologically, car manufacturers explored three different search trajectories: (1) selective disassembly and recycling of parts and materials, (2) improved treatment and separation of shredder waste, and (3) metallurgical recycling. Different response strategies are thus observed, different search trajectories were adopted and different modes of cooperation were established. With hindsight, three distinctive stages can be discerned in the automotive industries' efforts to develop recycling strategies (Table 1).

Although end-of-life vehicle waste became an issue only in the late 1980s, the automotive industry had already concluded from various studies conducted in the 1970s–1980s period that changing material composition of vehicles since the mid 1960s might compromise end-of-life vehicle recycling practices in the long run and that vehicle disassembly and subsequent materials recycling might contribute to solving the potential end-of-life vehicle waste problem. Additional studies were commissioned to propose and evaluate potential solutions, including chemical recycling of plastics, vehicle disassembly and material recycling, and incineration of shredder waste. In the late 1980s, car manufacturers in Germany and France joined plastic producers in large-scale R&D projects on plastics recyclability. For car manufacturers, these R&D projects were related to the issue of automotive waste. Knowledge of the recyclability of specific materials (physical and chemical properties, costs and benefits) is essential given the problem definition and potential solutions. For plastic producers they were parts of larger R&D programmes on plastic recycling, since the issue of plastic waste threatened their business in other markets as well, notably in packaging.

It was not until the German Environmental Ministry made public its policy objectives that the automotive waste issue became a problem to be solved. A twofold industry response marked the beginning of the first stage. First, the automotive industry started a lobby through its industry organizations in order to prevent government regulation. The most important among these were the End-of-Life Vehicle Recycling Project of the German car industry (PRAVDA) and the lobby at the European level by the European Association of Car Manufacturers (ACEA). In consultation with other industry organizations, the industry developed alternative policy plans. Second, individual car manufacturers started so-called 'vehicle dismantling pilots' in 1990–1991. These pilots served multiple objectives:

- assessing the cost and potential benefits of vehicle disassembly;
- developing cost-efficient disassembly routines;
- developing and testing concepts for larger-scale end-of-life vehicle recycling;
- developing knowledge of design for disassembly and design for recycling;
- increasing the efficiency of current vehicle designs and assembly procedures;
- continuing research into material recyclability;
- creating markets for recovered automotive materials.

To a certain extent there was coordination of dismantling activities at the industry level through PRAVDA and ACEA. Although car manufacturers reported largely similar objectives for their respective dismantling pilots, the greater share of the activities was firm-specific. Several car manufacturers cooperated with companies outside the automobile industry, e.g. Volkswagen and Peugeot–Citroën with shredder companies and Mercedes-Benz with a steel works. BMW, Fiat, Ford Europe, Opel and Renault did not cooperate with other companies in their dismantling pilots. One of the most important conclusions drawn from this first stage was that if vehicle disassembly and large-scale recycling of automotive parts and materials were to provide a solution for the automotive waste problem, this would only be viable in a network of decentralized end-of-life vehicle recycling centres. In addition, car manufacturers developed design guidelines on how to improve vehicle recyclability and model-specific disassembly manuals as well as dedicated tools and equipment for draining the end-of-life vehicle and for the removal of specific parts and components. The first stage was characterized by the acquisition of relevant knowledge and the development of organizational capabilities.

During the second and third stages, car manufacturers started to implement their recycling strategies, building on the results from the previous stage. However, they did so in two groups following two different models. BMW, Ford Europe and Opel are in the first group. Fiat, Mercedes-Benz, Peugeot–Citroën, Renault and Volkswagen are in the second group. For strategic reasons, BMW also joined the second group at a later stage.

Car manufacturers in the first group started to implement end-of-life vehicle recycling in the 1991–1992 period. They did so by engaging in bilateral agreements with selected car dismantlers. Initially, these cooperations worked on a small scale and ran parallel to the dismantling pilots. They served to test under full market conditions the end-of-life vehicle recycling concepts as developed in the dismantling pilots. Results were apparently positive, since by 1995, BMW, Ford Europe and Opel had associated with several dozens of car dismantlers as 'recycling partners' in Germany (and in the case of BMW also in other countries) to implement the option of selective disassembly and recycling of parts and materials. The car dismantling partners take care of collecting the end-of-life vehicle and of administrative procedures for deregistration, and they remove hazardous substances from the vehicle. They are not being paid for these activities by the car manufacturer, the argument being that car dismantlers can increase their local market shares because the manufacturers' commercial network is obliged to deliver end-of-life vehicles to their sites. Consequently, disassembly activities for materials recycling remain limited. For example, BMW requires its recycling partners to disassemble a limited number of plastic parts and to deliver these without cost and in separate batches to its plastic parts factory. Still, these cooperations are important for another reason. The car manufacturer actively assists the car dismantler in modernizing its procedures by providing expert advice, insists on respecting environmental regulations, and introduces new tools and equipment.

In the third stage, a number of shredder companies and metal refinery firms entered the scene. They saw business opportunities in end-of-life vehicle recycling. Such companies had developed their own end-of-life vehicle recycling concepts and proposed to act as 'third parties' to take commercial responsibility for organizing end-of-life vehicle recycling. They started to implement the technological option of improved treatment of shredder waste. For example, the largest French shredder company, Compagnie française des ferailles (CFF), concluded framework agreements with both Renault and Peugeot–Citroën for organizing end-of-life vehicle recycling on an industrial scale, using its process for valorizing shredder waste in cement ovens. Since 1992, CFF has opened a number of end-of-life vehicle recycling sites in France. At these sites, CFF associates with local car dismantlers (via their industry organization) for taking care of vehicle drainage. In principle, disassembly of parts for materials recycling could take place at CFF's sites, but lack of outlets for recovered materials is the reason why this happens on a very small scale. In November 1992, Fiat concluded a framework agreement with Falck (a large Italian shredder company), several material recycling firms, and the Italian association of car dismantlers. Since 1994, the German companies Preussag, Thyssen-Sonnenberg and Klöckner have proposed comparable framework agreements to the German car manufacturers to which Volkswagen and Mercedes-Benz responded. Mercedes-Benz, the only company having explored the option of metallurgical recycling, has not (yet) succeeded in commercializing this concept. BMW also signed such a contract as a strategic move to prevent monopoly power, rather than abandoning the previous build-up of a dedicated network of car dismantlers.

		Stage 1: developing knowledge and capabilities	
		Dismantling pilot without a partner	Dismantling pilot with a partner
Stages 2–3 implementation of recycling strategy	Selective disassembly through a dedicated network	BMW, Ford Europe, Opel	—
	Improved treatment of shredder waste through a 'third party'	Fiat, Renault	Mercedes-Benz, Peugeot–Citroën, Volkswagen

Figure 1 'Styles' in developing and implementing a recycling strategy by European car manufacturers

Figure 1 summarizes the differences among European car manufacturers in the mode of cooperation during the knowledge and capabilities building stage (stage 1) and choice of technology in the implementation of recycling strategies (stages 2 and 3). The discussion of the implementation of recycling solutions indicates that European car manufacturers are not eager to take a major control over vehicle dismantling and recycling technologies. Rather, Fiat, Peugeot–Citroën, Renault and Volkswagen have engaged shredder companies to act as a 'third party' in developing large-scale end-of-life vehicle recycling activities. Mercedes-Benz has done likewise, as the company was unable to license its metallurgical recycling technology for upscaling and commercialization. BMW, Ford Europe and Opel have developed dedicated networks of car dismantling firms over whose dismantling activities they have close control. This provides them with the opportunity of buying recovered material cheaply.

Discussion I: the End-of-Life Vehicle Case and Similarity Hypotheses

How may such differences be accounted for? In this section, I forward several hypotheses that match the similarity thesis. Table 2 provides the background data for several of the hypotheses. I make extensive use of Whiston (1995).[16] Whiston is one of the very few researchers who advanced hypotheses of why car manufacturers develop diverging recycling strategies, without, however, testing them explicitly. His hypotheses come close to the various similarity hypotheses of innovation.

First, industry characteristics are considered. In Pavitt's taxonomy, the automotive industry is a 'production intensive' industry, dominated by economics of scale and a strong tendency to cost reduction.[17] From this perspective it may well be understood why car manufacturers have used the automotive waste issue to improve their vehicle

Table 2 Summarizing the similarity argument

	Production volume (1)	Market share Europe (2)	Level of vertical integration (3)	Market strategy	Country of origin
Volkswagen	d	c	c	All segments	Germany
Opel	c	c	b	All segments	Germany
Ford Europe	b	b	b	All segments	Germany/UK
Renault	c	b	a	All segments	France
Peugeot–Citroën	c	c	a	All segments	France
Fiat	b	c	c	All segments	Italy
Mercedes-Benz	a	a	c	Top segment	Germany
BMW	a	a	N/A	Top segment	Germany

(1) a = <600,000; b = <1,500,000; c = 1,600,000–2,000,000; d = >2,000,000 (data for production in Europe for 1995 provided by CCFA); (2) a = <6%; b = 6–12%; c = >12% (data for 1990 provided by CCFA); (3) a = 20–25%; b = 30–35%; c = 45–50%, expressed in percentage of value added (data for the mid 1980s, Chanaron, Note 19).

designs through the exploration of design for dismantling – or 'design for recyclability'. To the extent that reconsidering vehicle design through a new lens results in cost reduction, design innovations have been adopted. This perspective also sheds light on the reluctance of car manufacturers to engage in take-back and recycling activities, as they have traditionally not been in this business and expected small or negative returns of these activities. Take-back and recycling activities would increase the complexity of the business, which is at odds with current trends of outsourcing major parts of the production process, including the design and supply of parts and components. However, the intra-industry diversity in developing recycling strategies is too subtle to be captured within Pavitt's taxonomy.

Characteristics of the intra-industry structure may be advanced as hypotheses matching the similarity thesis. Differences in company size and levels of vertical integration would clearly be variables to consider. The size argument, when measured in units of production volume, can be qualified straightaway. Volkswagen is the leading mass producer in Europe, followed by Opel, Peugeot–Citroën and Renault. BMW and Mercedes-Benz are relatively small-scale speciality producers. Yet, as may be observed from Figure 1, there is no match between size and recycling strategies.

Regarding levels of vertical integration, Whiston advances that competitive gain could be created in the supply of material. Since some car manufacturers retain high levels of control and linkage over material and parts supply, the degree of vertical integration within a particular auto company is an important factor to be considered.[18] This hypothesis is problematic, because it is not sufficiently specified. With respect to vertical integration *per se* it is obvious that there are large differences between individual car manufacturers. By the mid 1980s, Fiat, Mercedes-Benz and Volkswagen had high levels of vertical integration, whereas those for Renault and Peugeot were considerably lower. Opel and Ford of Europe were in between these extremes.[19]

However, aggregate levels of vertical integration are not constant over time for individual car manufacturers. Currently, there is a trend to decreasing levels of vertical integration. Because it is changing, it would be hard to use this factor as the independent variable in a study. Moreover, vertical integration is a composite variable. Levels of vertical integration can be decomposed with respect to specific parts and components; design and production of some parts and components is fully integrated, whereas other parts are essentially bought in, including parts design and technical engineering. They may also vary among the various production plants of individual car manufacturers, because of cost differences. Thus, it would not be vertical integration in itself that is a significant variable for diverging recycling strategies, but rather the car manufacturers' motivations for choosing specific levels of vertical integration, most significantly, in vehicle design and engineering. In this case, however, the vertical integration hypothesis reverts to a heterogeneity hypothesis.

Regarding the strategic group hypothesis, Whiston speculates about the importance and influence of the car manufacturer's market segment or niche, its market share, and its particular product image or characteristics on developing a specific recycling strategy: 'It may well prove to be that the unit-cost of disposal of a single vehicle is fairly insensitive to the *absolute* price of the vehicle. In which case, in relative terms, manufacturers of more expensive luxury vehicles will obtain some comparative advantage. Alternatively, from a large mass-production standpoint, new design principles geared to improved recycling and disassembly procedures may also possess, in terms of economy of scale, some comparative advantage' (emphasis in the original).[20] This hypothesis would require detailed economic analysis, which, according to Whiston, is not feasible for the time being, given the 'too early stage of development [of vehicle take-back and recycling] to carry out or even attempt such an analysis'.[21] However, this hypothesis may also be qualified. According to this hypothesis, BMW and Mercedes-Benz would be expected to develop closely similar recycling strategies, but this is shown not to be the case. Moreover, the implicit (but incorrect) assumption in this hypothesis is that the car manufacturer itself will be undertaking dismantling and recycling activities. At the level of the car dismantler or end-of-life vehicle recycling plant, the combination of specialization into specific models or marques and economies of scale may well lead to a comparative advantage. However, the focus of dismantling and recycling (e.g. disassembly of reusable parts from total-loss vehicles vs dismantling for material recycling from worn-out vehicles) seems to be a prime choice for specialization for car dismantlers and end-of-life vehicle recycling plants. The semi-automated disassembly lines, as developed by e.g. Volkswagen, are dedicated to material recovery from worn-out vehicles and flexible for the dismantling of end-of-life vehicles of different makes.

Next, the hypothesis may be advanced that car manufacturers' recycling strategies depend upon the characteristics of national regulatory pressure, and that they are embedded in national industry structures. Indeed, the French and German authorities chose different approaches in initiating end-of-life vehicle recycling policies. The Germans aimed for direct regulation, whereas the French preferred a voluntary agreement.[22] The Italian and English authorities preferred closely similar agreements to the French, whereas the Dutch adopted an approach of their own.[23] This might lead to the conclusion that national regulatory styles were important variables in determining car manufacturers' recycling strategies. However, the German Environmental Ministry was unable to keep to its own preferred mode of regulation. In February 1996, the German Ministry accepted the same voluntary agreement as had been devised in France, because of fierce industry opposition to direct regulation. Car manufacturers did not simply comply with regulation, but tried to influence and shape the regulatory context to their interests, while simultaneously conserving a considerable space for developing such solutions to best serve their interests by collective and organizational learning, and to allow for competitive gain to be pursued. The analysis of the French and German cases (the two countries that host more than one independently operating car manufacturer) reveals that under the same political circumstances car manufacturers developed diverging recycling strategies. Nevertheless, it should be acknowledged that the 'third party' contracts with recycling and metal refining companies have a very national orientation. Although the German, French and Italian schemes are oriented toward the same technical goals, i.e. improved treatment of shredder waste, there are subtle national differences in the composition and operation of the various consortia.

Finally, little can be said regarding the 'globalization' and 'triad' hypotheses. The data used were collected in Europe only. The car manufacturers studied are all European companies, shown by the facts that their design and development work and their production and sales are to a very large extent realized in Europe. In this respect also Opel and Ford should be considered as European companies, operating quite independently from their American parent companies. It was appropriate to limit the case to Europe, as both the North American and Japanese companies lag behind the Europeans.[24] They watched what was happening in Europe and learned from these experiences.

It would appear from the above that neither of the discussed similarity hypotheses is fully capable of capturing the diversity of car manufacturers' recycling strategies. Therefore, I wish to turn to the alternative heterogeneity thesis in order to develop another explanation, one that is based on resource differentiation between the car manufacturing companies.

Discussion II: the End-of-Life Vehicle Case and the Heterogeneity Thesis

Regarding the heterogeneity thesis, Whiston argues that 'car manufacturers may differentiate themselves in order to gain competitive advantage in end-of-life vehicle recycling: those companies who at present are undertaking extensive product development, research, [and] new design, in compliance with any forthcoming disposal-legislation . . . *are preferentially priming themselves for new market opportunities*' (emphasis in the original).[25] Indeed, all European car manufacturers have developed some sort of recycling strategy, including those car manufacturers (and Japanese importers) not studied in this case. He continues to say that 'such a statement clearly depends . . . upon the extent to which any such knowledge gained is tacit or of a transferable-knowledge form'.[26] Two factors indicate that it is fairly difficult for a car manufacturer to gain a competitive lead in design for recycling. First, innovatory gain in the automotive industry usually lasts for a limited period of time due to a rapid and wide diffusion of knowledge and techniques across car manufacturers. Second, within the context of PRAVDA and ACEA, car manufacturers exchanged information and discussed a range of potential solutions, including design for recycling, thus reinforcing transfer of the relevant knowledge among them. As a consequence, Whiston suggests that '*ultimately* there will be little "competitive-edge" to be gained', and that currently 'it would appear that there is *not* a single pace setter; one manufacturer who is out in front' (emphasis in the original).[27]

Whiston thus rejects this hypothesis, a hypothesis that points towards the heterogeneity thesis. But he may well have been too quick in dismissing this hypothesis. The horizontal collaborative ventures in developing end-of-life vehicle recycling were primarily aimed at standardizing and optimizing dismantling procedures and at advancing knowledge in material recycling. Furthering design-for-recycling knowledge depended on dismantling pilots, but these pilots also provided highly valuable feedback on specific vehicle designs resulting in cost advantages. Thus, car manufacturers did try to develop 'innovatory gain' in compliance with any forthcoming regulation. The question then is why and how car manufacturers developed diverging recycling strategies in a situation of uncertain potential of innovatory gain.

The argument is that companies, in order to solve environmental problems, need to change their activities or to develop new activities, i.e. to innovate. Innovation theory holds that three factors stimulate companies to innovate: the growth rate and size of market demand, technological opportunity and appropriability conditions.[28] These factors have been used in empirical studies of environmental innovation.[29] Given the regulatory pressure on car manufacturers to find a solution to the end-of-life vehicle waste issue, market factors are not considered to be relevant in this specific case. However, if various innovative options were viable for solving environmental problems, it would be expected that firms would prefer to choose that option where technological opportunity is highest and where appropriability conditions are most favourable.

In addition to innovation theory, theory about the internal growth of the firm is relevant too. The Penrosian perspective suggests that firms would prefer to develop new activities by expanding the range of productive services that may be derived from the resources that they already control, rather than developing activities for which they do not yet have the resources.[30] If firms do acquire new resources for new activities, they would prefer those which are complementary to the existing stock of resources and activities, i.e. which enhance their value adding.[31] If various ways of changing activities are viable, the firm would prefer the most complementary.

Moreover, it may be argued not only that firms prefer to choose those options that are highly complementary and that have high technological opportunity and favourable appropriability conditions, but also that firms prefer to undertake such options themselves, rather than engage in some form of cooperative arrangement or market transaction with other companies. Indeed, several authors have proposed that choices about the mode of control over activities may be derived from such

Table 3 Complementarity, technological opportunity and appropriability determine the mode of coordinating the preferred option

	Complementarity	Technological opportunity	Appropriability of profit opportunities	Resulting mode of coordination
(a)	High	High	High	No cooperation – hierarchical control
(b)	High	High	Low	Close cooperation
(c)	High	Low	High	Prepare business plan
(d)	High	Low	Low	Specialized subcontracting
(e)	Low	High	High	No cooperation – diversification
(f)	Low	High	Low	Distant cooperation
(g)	Low	Low	High	Standard subcontracting
(h)	Low	Low	Low	No cooperation – 'keep the dog out'

factors as complementarity and appropriability.[32] If it is assumed that each option may be scored on a dichotomous scale of 'high' vs 'low', and if the factors are independent, then a $2 \times 2 \times 2$ matrix may be constructed that describes which mode of coordination would be preferred (Table 3).

In situation (a), the option is highly complementary to the firm's core activities; the firm sees opportunities for innovation in relation to its resources; and it believes it can appropriate the profits from implementing this option. In such a situation, the firm should not hesitate to develop this option and to integrate the required resources and activities within the firm's hierarchy, because in doing so the firm enhances its competitive power. Therefore, the firm is likely to pursue a strategy of direct control over the implementation of this option and the required resources are developed in-house. The extensive programmes for increasing energy and materials efficiency, such as 3M's 'pollution-prevention-pays' programme, would be an example.

If an option is adequately described by situation (b), the firm does not see profit opportunities or cannot readily appropriate any profits from implementing the option, despite high complementarity and high technological opportunity. Close control over developing and implementing the option is required, but the firm is unwilling to fully integrate these activities since they raise costs without much prospect of positive revenues. A strategy of 'close cooperation' would be more apt in this situation. However, the combination of high complementarity and low appropriability creates a risk of moral hazard; the firm may be 'held up' by its contract partner.[33]

When complementarity is high, and when the firm thinks that the opportunity for innovation is low but that it will have no difficulties in appropriating profits from implementing the option, such as in situation (c), the firm has to choose between prevailing technological opportunity or appropriability in its assessment. This situation may occur when there is a 'reverse salient'[34] or a 'technological imbalance'.[35] If the firm chooses to explore the few technological options in an attempt to reinforce its core capabilities, it faces uncertain and costly investments in R&D, which are likely to be integrated within the firm's hierarchy. However, if the perceived lack of technological options is considered more important than the appropriability of profits, the firm is likely to forgo profit opportunities. The decision between these two options depends on a detailed analysis of costs and benefits. Thus, the firm should develop a business plan for investing in technology development.

In situation (d) the option is still highly complementary, but the firm does not believe that there are opportunities for low-cost innovation in developing the option or for appropriating any profits from implementing this option. Because of high complementarity, close control over problem-solving activities is desirable, but the firm might be reluctant to invest in developing the required capabilities since it sees few chances for successful innovation. A likely strategy in this situation would be to contract another company to develop the required highly specialized technology ('specialized subcontracting'). Such a solution increases the firm's cost level, but the firm may not be able to escape these investments because of the high complementarity. As is the case in situation (b), there is a risk of moral hazard. Therefore, before implementing such an option, the firm is likely to try minimizing cost by using its power and influence. Generally speaking, end-of-pipe pollution abatement technologies fall into this category.

Another situation is (e). Any option here is characterized by low levels of complementary to the firm's core activities. However, the firm sees options for technology development that promise to create appropriable rents. The firm can choose to develop the capabilities that are required for undertaking the problem-solving activities, or not. If it does, it diversifies in relatively unrelated activities and the firm is likely to try to transform these activities in such a way as to make them part of the firm's core activities ('diversification').

However, in a situation of low complementarity, it is likely that the firm lacks the required capabilities for developing solutions by diversification. Therefore, diversification is a risky strategy, all the more so when appropriability of profit opportunities is uncertain or low, as in situation (f). It is more likely that the firm thinks that other companies can implement the option more efficiently, because the required resources and activities constitute their core. Then, the firm might engage in cooperative agreements with these companies in order to develop dedicated solutions, but because of low complementarity there is less need to exert close control over the cooperative agreement. Such a strategy could be called 'distant cooperation'.

If an option were characterized with low complementarity and low technological opportunity, yet high appropriability, as in situation (g), this would resemble the need to buy in standard technology. Because of low complementarity and low technological options, the firm is unlikely to develop such technology itself. However, if other companies have developed it, it is profitable for the firm to adopt it, because of the high appropriability of profits associated with using the technology. In this situation, the firm is likely to follow a strategy of 'standard subcontracting'. The purchasing of standard pollution abatement technology would be an example of an option with such characteristics.

Situation (h) is the last possible characterization of an option. In this situation, the option is not complementary and the firm does not see low-cost technological

Table 4 Assessment of the end-of-life vehicle recycling options along the complementarity, technological opportunity and appropriability dimensions

	Complementarity	Technological opportunity	Appropriability
Selective disassembly and recycling of parts and materials	High	High	Low
Improved processing of shredder waste	Low	High	Low
Metallurgical recycling	Low	High	Low

opportunities or appropriable profit opportunities. In such a highly constrained situation, implementing the option might be a threat to the firm's capabilities, if reallocation of scarce resources to problem solving implies a weakening of existing capabilities. Moreover, the firm is only interested in cooperation with other firms if it can develop low-cost solutions. Therefore, denying the problem, or trying to influence the political process in order to redefine the problem or potential solutions, are more likely strategies than engaging in developing and implementing the resources and activities for this option. This strategy is one of 'keeping the dog out'.

In order to explain the divergence in recycling strategies of European car manufacturers, I proceeded as follows in testing the relationships between complementarity, technological opportunity and appropriability. I thoroughly analysed the three options that emerged from the problem definition (selective disassembly of parts and materials, improved processing of shredder waste and metallurgical recycling) on the dimensions of complementarity, technological opportunity and appropriability. Table 4 summarizes the results of this analysis. Next I hypothesized for each option that the corresponding organizational arrangement would be chosen for implementation, assuming first that my analysis of the options was correct and, secondly, that car manufacturers proceeded in the same way. Finally, I compared which were the options of choice and which organizational arrangements were adopted in developing and implementing these options. It appeared from this comparison that the hypothesized relationships are confirmed by the empirical data (collected through extensive interviewing and document analysis). Thus, BMW, Ford Europe and Opel, pursuing the option of selective disassembly of parts and materials for recycling, adopted a strategy of close cooperation through a dedicated network of car dismantlers when it came to the implementation of this option, because profits from such activities would be low and hard to appropriate. The other car manufacturers implemented their preferred option of improving the processing of shredder waste through a strategy of distant cooperation by concluding framework agreements with shredder and metal refining firms as a 'third party'. They did so because the level of complementarity and appropriability of profits was considered to be low, despite a significant technological opportunity in improving the efficiency of the shredding process. Moreover, to the extent that car manufacturers identified cost-efficient solutions to improve their vehicle designs and assembly procedures during the first stage of dismantling pilots, they kept those solutions under their own close control.

Conclusion

Based on the similarity and heterogeneity hypotheses, different explanations for the variety of innovative responses in the case study are examined. The paper argues that neither national, nor industry-specific, nor market-specific styles of innovation provide satisfactory explanations for the observed variety of innovation processes in response to stakeholder pressure. The paper aims at making three theoretical points:

1   Depending on the level of detail in the analysis, different styles of innovation might in some cases be distinguished. I propose, however, that sources of variety stem from managerial discretion in directing and coordinating the innovation process. It is proposed that the choice of a specific solution and mode of coordination by individual firms depends on the relation between the resources needed for this solution and the core competencies of this firm. The relation is described in terms of complementarity of resources and activities, perceived technological opportunity, and appropriability conditions.
2   To the extent that innovation is about the acquisition, development or recombination of resources (including tacit, intangible resources such as knowledge, capabilities and experience) in order to undertake new activities, I propose that 'complementarity' is another innovation stimulating factor in addition to growth and size of the market, technological opportunity and appropriability.
3   If firms may choose among a variety of organizational arrangements in developing and marketing innovations, including internal integration, various modes of inter-firm cooperation and outsourcing, I propose that firms' perceptions of technological opportunities to innovate are an additional factor to complementarity and appropriability in the mode of governance choice.

NOTES

1   P. Womack, D.T. Jones & D. Roos, *The Machine that Changed the World* (New York, Rawson Associates, 1990).
2   R. Boyer & M. Freyssenet, 'The Emergence of New Industrial Models: Hypotheses and Analytical Procedure', *Actes du Gerpisa*, *15*, 1995, p. 75; W. Ruigrok & R. van Tulder, *The Ideology of Interdependence: The Link between Restructuring, Internationalisation and Trade* (Rotterdam, Erasmus Universiteit, 1993).
3   B.A. Lundvall, 'Innovation as an Interactive Process: From User–Producer Interaction to the National System of Innovation', in: G. Dosi, C. Freeman, R.R. Nelson, G. Silverberg & L. Soete (Eds), *Technical Change and Economic Theory* (London, Pinter, 1988), p. 349.
4   M.E. Porter, *Competitive Strategy* (New York, Free Press, 1980); K. Pavitt, 'Sectoral Patterns of Technical Change: Towards a Taxonomy and a Theory', *Research Policy*, *13*, 1984, p. 343.

5   R.E. Caves & M.E. Porter, 'From Entry Barriers to Mobility Barriers: Conjectural Decisions and Contrived Deterrence to New Competition', *Quarterly Journal of Economics, 91,* 1977, p. 241.

6   P. Patel & K. Pavitt, 'The Technological Competencies of the World's Largest Firms: Complex and Path Dependent, but Not Much Variety', *Research Policy, 26,* 1997, p. 141.

7   P. Patel & K. Pavitt, 'Uneven (and Divergent) Technological Accumulation Among Advanced Countries: Evidence and a Framework of Explanation', *Journal of Industrial and Corporate Change, 3,* 1994, p. 759.

8   M.E. Porter, *The Competitive Advantage of Nations* (London, Macmillan, 1990).

9   J. Child, 'Organisational Structure, Environment, and Performance: The Role of Strategic Choice', *Sociology, 6,* 1972, p. 1.

10 B. Wernerfelt, 'A Resource-based View of the Firm', *Strategic Management Journal, 5,* 1984, p. 171; J.B. Barney, 'Strategic Factor Markets: Expectations, Luck, and Business Strategy', *Management Science, 32,* 1986, p. 1231.

11 E.T. Penrose, *The Theory of the Growth of the Firm* (Oxford, Basil Blackwell, 1959).

12 R.R. Nelson, 'Why do Firms Differ, and How Does it Matter?', *Strategic Management Journal, 12,* 1991, p. 61.

13 See Penrose, *op. cit.,* Note 11; Barney, *op. cit.,* Note 10; Wernerfelt, *op. cit.,* Note 10; S.G. Winter, 'Knowledge and Competence as Strategic Assets', in: D.J. Teece (Ed.), *The Competitive Challenge* (Cambridge, Ballinger, 1987), p. 159; D.J. Teece, R.P. Rumelt, G. Dosi & S.G. Winter, 'Understanding Corporate Coherence: Theory and Evidence', *Journal of Economic Behavior and Organisation, 23,* 1994, p. 1; and D.J. Teece, G. Pisano & A. Shuen, 'Dynamic Capabilities and Strategic Management', *Strategic Management Journal, 18,* 1997, p. 509.

14 Penrose, *op. cit.,* Note 11.

15 T.G. Whiston, *Disposal and Recycling of Motor Vehicles: An International Perspective,* final version of a study commissioned by the Commission of the European Union DGXII (Brighton, SPRU, 1995); T.G. Whiston & M. Glachand, in: F. Lévéque (Ed.), *Environmental Policy in Europe: Industry, Competition and the Policy Process* (Cheltenham, Edgar Elgar, 1997); F. den Hond, *In Search of a Useful Theory of Environmental Strategy: A Case Study on the Recycling of End-of-Life Vehicles from the Capabilities Perspective* (Amsterdam, Vrije Universiteit, 1996); F. den Hond, 'L'expérience néerlandaise du traitement des automobiles en fin de vie', *Annales des Mines – Réalités Industrielles,* November 1997, p. 114; F. den Hond, 'Inertia and the Strategic Use of Politics and Power: A Case Study in the Automotive Industry', *International Journal of Technology Management, 16,* 1998, No. 7, pp. 641–654.

16 Whiston, *op. cit.,* Note 15.

17 Pavitt, *op. cit.,* Note 4.

18 Whiston & Glachand, *op. cit.,* Note 15, p. 71.

19 Chanaron, 'Productivity, Vertical Integration and Competitiveness: Some Methodological Reflections and Empirical Evidences', in: B. Dankbaar, U. Jürgens & T. Malsch (Eds), *Die Zukunft der Arbeit in der Automobilindustrie* (Berlin, Sigma, 1988), p. 283.

20 Whiston & Glachand, *op. cit.,* Note 15, p. 72.

21 *Ibid.*

22 Den Hond, 1998, *op. cit.,* Note 15.

23 Den Hond, 1997, *op. cit.,* Note 15.

24 L. Kincaid, C.A. Wilt, G.A. Davis, J. Lumley, F. Stoss & E. Carnes, *Vehicle Recycling and Disposal Policies in Industrialized and Developing Countries* (Knoxville, University of Tennessee, Center for Clean Products and Clean Technologies, 1996).

25 Whiston & Glachand, *op. cit.*, Note 15, p. 70.

26 *Ibid.*

27 *Ibid.*, p. 71.

28 W.M. Cohen & R.C. Levin, 'Empirical Studies of Innovation and Market Structure', in: R. Schmalensee & R.D. Willing (Eds), *Handbook of Industrial Organisation* (Amsterdam, Elsevier Science, 1989), p. 1059; A.K. Klevorick, R.C. Levin, R.R. Nelson & S.G. Winter, 'On the Sources and Significance of Interindustry Differences in Technological Opportunities', *Research Policy*, 24, 1995, p. 185.

29 R. Kemp, X. Olsthoorn, F. Oosterhuis & H. Verbruggen, 'Supply and Demand Factors of Cleaner Technologies: Some Empirical Evidence', *Environmental and Resource Economics*, 2, 1992, p. 615.

30 Penrose, *op. cit.*, Note 11.

31 G.B. Richardson, 'The Organisation of Industry', *The Economic Journal*, 82, 1972, p. 883.

32 D.J. Teece, 'Profiting from Technological Innovation', *Research Policy*, 15, 1986, p. 285; J. Hagedoorn & J. Schakenraad, 'Technology Cooperation, Strategic Alliances and their Motives: Brother, Can You Spare a Dime, or Do You Have a Light?', MERIT Research Paper 90.019, Maastricht, MERIT, 1990.

33 O.E. Williamson, *The Economic Institutions of Capitalism: Firms, Markets, Relational Contracting* (New York, The Free Press, 1985).

34 T.P. Hughes, *Networks of Power: Electrification in Western Society: 1880–1930* (Baltimore, Johns Hopkins University Press, 1983).

35 N. Rosenberg, *Perspectives on Technology* (Cambridge, Cambridge University Press, 1976).

2.6

Supply Chains and Management Accounting

A. J. Berry, J. Cullen and W. Seal

Introduction

Accounting has been developed around the needs of owners to have an understanding of their income and asset position. Mostly this problem has been handled via the practices of financial accountants who concentrate upon issues of reporting to shareholders of the stewardship of their board of directors. From this stance, the recognition of the owners' claims and liabilities is a central concern, a concern which is reflected in the recognition of the financial boundaries of the firm and in attention to accounting for control. Such control accounting is based upon a model of vertical integration of activities with the structure of the balance sheet. The origins of management accounting lie in the history of scientific management with its special emphasis upon the pursuit of efficiency. This emphasis has led to the development of management accounting to support decision making. These two issues, control and decision, reflect the role of accounting in reporting and measurement of performance and the construction of accounting models and processes for planning, budgeting and decision making. They are inextricably linked together.

The relevance debate launched by Kaplan (1984) argued that the accounting practices in use were contributing to efficiency, but by virtue of their inherent models, they were contributing to ineffectiveness and to uncompetitiveness as they did not focus managers' attention upon the need to consider the whole cost structure and how that could be managed. In some ways this was an old debate rekindled. But the significance of the differences between cost management and measurement in (traditional) accounting terms, in cost management for system optimisation and strategic cost management were clarified. The development of activity based costing and target costing went some way to address the accounting cost issues.

The rapid changes in technology and organisation of production with attention to lean production (Womack et al., 1990), closer supplier relationships (Lamming,

1993), world class manufacturing and flexible specialisation has transformed manufacturing and the provision of services. In the case of Japan (Sako, 1992; Akoi,
1988; Okimoto, 1986) this also involved a network of long term relationships
between customers and suppliers. According to Harland (1996), the term 'supply
chain management' seems to have originated in the 1980s and covers the internal
business functions of purchasing, manufacturing, sales and distribution. Since then
the concept has been externalised beyond the boundary of the firm to incorporate
managing operations across organisational boundaries (Harland, 1996). Sako (1992)
identified four main theoretical approaches to the study of supply chains:

1   transaction cost economics, following Coase (1937) and Williamson (e.g. 1979);
2   relational contract theory, influenced by Macaulay (1963) and Macneil (1974);
3   a sociological approach to networks, e.g. Granovetter (1985), Frances and Garnsey
    (1996);
4   networks as management strategies, e.g. Miles and Snow (1986), Nohria and
    Eccles (1992).

In the study of accounting issues in schema 1 Gietzmann (1996) argues that cooperative strategies require a re-examination of the accounting governance systems
which assume arm's-length transactions. These assumptions may act as a major
obstacle to the formation of alliances or partnerships where information exchange is
essential (Stuart and McCutcheon, 1996). The idea of partnership is antithetical to
that of arm's-length adversarial contractual relationships. Success in partnerships
(Mohr and Spekman, 1994) requires commitment, co-ordination, trust, sharing of
risks and information, communication quality and participation, and joint problem
solving of disputes. Such partnerships may achieve reduction of transaction and
production costs (Williamson, 1975; Dyer and Ouchi, 1993). Trust, while advocated
by many authors (Pruitt, 1981; Stuart and McCutcheon, 1996), was recognised
as needing time and care to build (Turnbull et al., 1992). Such partnerships are a
considerable organisational innovation (Teece, 1996) and may be a viable and advantageous route to achieving the benefits of vertical integration (Johnston and
Lawrence, 1988). Much of the literature discusses the successes for both customers
and suppliers in partnerships resulting in a win–win situation (Kanter, 1994; Macbeth
and Ferguson, 1994) and joint successes (Helper and Sako, 1995).

The Management Accounting Problem

Lean production requires changes in the organisation of production and the collection
of cost accounting data by the customer and by the supplier (Lamming, 1993).
Lamming also noted the success of Japanese suppliers and assemblers in the control of the return on assets (RoA) achieved by each company in a partnership and
the poor quality of similar UK data. In his view, 'lean accounting would provide the
means for such information, upon which lean production might be based in the search
for reducing costs, improving value and gaining a better understanding of the
behaviour of both' (1993, p. 200). As supply chains develop, via out-sourcing

and/or partnerships, lean supply arrangements (Saunders, 1994) are needed as a greater part of the cost of production is entailed in the supplied goods. Saunders notes that 'costs are an important dimension of performance in supply chains and it is a factor that needs to be managed on an integrated basis' (1994, p. 213). He argues for a more proactive role for purchasing and supply management and for a more holistic and systematic approach, leading to a 'total cost of supply' or 'total cost of ownership' which can be used in identifying the real costs of buying and for considering benefits from improved supply arrangements.[1] He proposes the use of activity based costing, target costing and open book policies to aid supply chain effectiveness. The conflict between partnership and the asset management basis of accounting was recognised by Gietzmann (1996). Gietzmann argues that some modification of accounting governance seems to be necessary, based upon trust and commitment. But the adoption of Japanese supply chain and accounting practices has been found to be difficult because UK firms may be attempting to introduce practices or techniques without the necessary attention to governance issues (Gietzmann, 1996).

The vertical integration role of accounting linked to the balance sheet has been reinforced by the functional structures common in organisations, in which each function has its own budgets. The integration of functional operations normally takes place in the discussions and debates in the organisation's planning and budgeting cycle. However, it has been argued[2] that supply chains are essentially horizontal processes which require integration along the chain. The search for more effective cost models of operations was given impetus by the recognition of cost drivers (Porter, 1985), the factors which determine the cost of an activity, e.g. economies and diseconomies of scale, learning or experience effects, patterns of capacity utilisation, linkages, interrelationships, integration, timing of market entry, discretionary policies, location and institutional (legal and regulatory) costs. These create the possibility of analysing the costs in value chain analysis and the search for competitive advantage. This new focus upon a wider array of sources of costs improves on the position where 'accounting systems do contain useful data, but they often get in the way of strategic cost analysis' (Porter, 1985, p. 63). However, the inward vertical integration models of accounting ignore value created outside the firm's boundaries (Partridge and Perren, 1994).

Subsequent research emphasised that the identification of cost drivers, and analysing costs through the value chain, are essential components in the search for competitive advantage (Shank and Govindarajan, 1992; Hergert and Morris, 1989; Bromwich, 1991; Partridge and Perren, 1994). Activity based analysis provides information along the chain of value adding activities within a 'total cost management' approach which contains three elements: activity based costing (ABC), process value analysis and performance measurement (Quillian, 1991). Quillian notes that such an approach 'can act as a catalyst for integrating isolated logistics functions, leading to substantial improvements in costs, cycle times, inventories and levels of customer service' (1991, p. 9). Complementing this supplier study, Lere and Seraph (1995) examined the supply issues from the purchaser's perspective, noting how ABC can be used as a basis for price negotiation and as a means of exploring with suppliers how they have arrived at a price. Their model was designed to identify the costs triggered by purchasing parameters such as product design specification, lot size, delivery schedule, shipments, number of design changes, level of documentation, inspection, allocation of overhead costs and calculations of cost per unit. These two studies taken together suggest that suppliers and buyers could usefully jointly examine these issues to gain common efficiencies but it does not indicate how any savings could be shared.

For assemblers who purchase as much as 80% of their parts by value, the issues of supply effectiveness and efficiency are crucial contributors to competitiveness. For example, in the case of Nissan, 'achieving total cost control throughout the whole supply chain has represented a critical challenge' (Carr and Ng, 1995, p. 348).

These authors report that Nissan used a multidisciplinary team approach to supply cost management. Of special note was the very limited role of accountants in these processes, which were built upon value engineering and 'value analysis to continually review product costs and manufacturing process' (1995, p. 356). In Carr and Ng's study, the degree of openness of the books – or transparency – was limited (see Lamming, 1993). Two major suppliers showed 'a greater concern as to whether Nissan would exploit its position of power, particularly in the light of its tougher circumstances' (1995, p. 361).

Accounting measures of performance are based upon either profitability or cost. Supply chain advocates speak mostly about costs, but they also emphasize partnership. The latter is intended to bring benefits to all participants in a shared destiny. It would be necessary to at least align performance with the shared destiny principle (Harland, 1996), and with some agreement as to the measures to be used (Hope and Hope, 1995). This might be achieved by applying the concept of the balanced scorecard to the problem, combining its four elements (customer, internal business, innovation and learning) with the financial perspective.

Much of the supply chain literature has its origins in studies of Japanese companies, especially in the motor industry. Whether the social structure of Japanese industry is crucial to the operation of these supply chains is unclear, but it is argued (Whitley, 1994; Scott, 1995) that the wider patterns of values and beliefs shape and construct the economic arrangements of corporations and markets. Japanese and Asian cultures are viewed as having a more dependent culture than the UK and this is held to explain some aspects of inter-organisational behaviour, where 'trust' is implied but may actually be more a matter of social obligation.

By contrast, much of the logistics and economics literature on supply chains appears to be rather technical in nature, and it may be not be easily applied in Anglo-Saxon contexts. The issues of dependence, power and dominance in network formation and functioning were addressed by Zheng et al. (1997). In the pharmaceutical and automotive industries, they found that the final manufacturer was dominant; in the retail consumer goods sector the final retailer exercised considerable power; while in electronic components there was no one dominant actor. However, Castells argued that the trend to supply chain integration and networking does not mean that the UK is shifting to an Asian model of the corporation:

Countries and institutions continue to shape the organisational requirements of the new economy, in an interaction between the logic of production, the changing technological base, and the institutional features of the social environment. The architecture and composition of business networks being formed around the world are influenced by the national characteristics of societies where such networks are embedded. (1996, p. 194)

Further, as was noted by Turnbull et al., there is a lack of trust (or, in our terms, social obligation) in the UK, and this extends to Japanese style techniques:

After more than ten years of price freezes, volume cuts, multiple sourcing and the like, many suppliers view the latest moves to JIT as another means by which the vehicle assemblers intend to put the squeeze on. (1992, pp. 167–8)

This evidence of the expectation of power is paralleled by that of Frances and Garnsey (1996), who noted that UK large food stores use accounting techniques as control mechanisms beyond their own boundaries, by which suppliers lost more degrees of freedom, and which gave rise to barriers to entry and an increase in market power and concentration.

Trust is not such a simple concept, nor is it readily created. Sako (1992) notes three types of trust:

- *contractual trust* relating to the keeping of promises;
- *competence trust* that partners have the ability to carry out the work;
- *goodwill trust* allowing more discretion and implying the possibility of more commitment.

In these cases, trust appears to be about acceptance that the other party will behave well and not exploit any offers.

The Research Problem

What is the observed contribution of management accounting to the management of supply chains? What are the explanations for that contribution?

The rationale for the existence of firms has been postulated as being dependent upon transaction costs (Williamson, 1979), with empirical findings of economic activity being organised by one firm in a mode of hierarchy or by many firms in a market. Between these two ideal types lie a number of possibilities of alliances or what are sometimes called hybrid forms. As this study is concerned with supply chains within firms (the intra-firm case) and between firms (the inter-firm case), we prefer to work from models of relationships between entities. These can be characterised in four ideal types:

1   The *autonomous firm* in the arm's-length market relationship of free buyers and sellers. This is a condition where firm A is independent from firm B. This applies to the inter-firm case but not the intra-firm case. The next three ideal types apply equally to both the intra- and inter-firm cases.

2   *Serial dependence*, where the output of firm A goes directly into the production system of firm B.
3   *Reciprocal dependence*, where firm A and firm B are dependent upon each other such that firm A and firm B affect each other's behaviour.
4   *Mutual dependence*, where the behaviour of firm A and firm B is interlinked.

It may be that in the inter-firm cases, these four ideal types represent the process of creating a managed supply chain through three stages of transition: from autonomy to serial dependence, where the units are tied together; from serial dependence to reciprocal dependence, where the interplay of one upon the other is recognised and managed; and from reciprocal dependence to mutual dependence, where joint behaviours of full partnership are evident. This latter is the idealised state of supply chains which corresponds to the 'Japanese' model.

It is suggested that the development of management accounting will closely follow the position of the firms in terms of the degree of autonomy or dependence in which each finds itself. We expect that in autonomous firms there will be no attention to inter-firm supply chain accounting.

In inter-firm cases we expect to find the following:

- Serial dependence – accounting is handled by the dominant actor.
- Reciprocal dependence – accounting has developed to include some attention to each other's costs.
- Mutual dependence – the accounting approach represented in a joint construction of a financial representation of the supply chain.

In intra-firm cases, we expect to observe common accounting policies and practices. We also expect to find the following:

- Serial dependence – accounting handled within common transfer pricing policies.
- Reciprocal dependence – accounting procedures reflecting interaction between units.
- Mutual dependence – accounting set within the context of wider business considerations.

For this project we construe management accounting to have five main elements: the cycle of planning and control; costing practices; cost management; supply chain issues; the changing role of the management accountant.

Field Studies

The design and intent of this project was to observe management accounting practice in the UK in relation to the development of supply chain management in the context of changing organisational approaches to the provision of goods and services. The research methods were based upon a search for collaborating companies. These were sought in three ways: via ISCAN (Innovative Supply Chains and Networks);

Table 1 Development of supply chains

		Inter-firm		Intra-firm
Management of suppliers (serial dependence) (Lamming: stress)	(1)	A B 'CMG' X D E F		No evidence in this study
Collaboration with suppliers (reciprocal dependence) (Lamming: resolved)	(2)	G H/T	(4)	M N S
Systemic management of a chain (mutual dependence) (Lamming: partnerships)	(3)	J K L	(5)	W R
Average turnover		£700m		£2540m

via the research team's cold calling; and via the CIMA (Chartered Institute of Management Accountants) Employers Exchange group. Some sixteen companies, from four sectors, were able to collaborate, rather less than one-third of those which were contacted. From these we were able to write three inter-firm cases, one at each of the stages of serial dependence, reciprocal dependence and mutual dependence. These and the other companies were interviewed using a semi-structured schedule which, together with documentation, formed the basic data collection. Their location in terms of their stage of supply chain development is shown in Table 1.

Decision and Control Cycle of Planning, Budgeting and Reporting

In virtually all of our case study companies, routine management accounting cycles remained in place despite accounting innovations. In most situations there was little impact on the routine structures of financial planning, budgeting and reporting. Despite identifying the need to understand processes, and introducing *ad hoc* systems to provide such information, there was still a tendency to provide routine monthly reports under traditional functional responsibility headings. However there was also evidence, consonant with the stages of development model, of new horizontal integration processes being created alongside the typical vertical integration procedures of management accounting.

One major issue in this new enviromnent is that time cycles of order fulfilling are becoming much shorter and out of harmony with the common monthly and annual cycles of management accounting. There was evidence of attention directing elements of managing being bypassed by physical on-line real time observations and action taken without 'formal' cost analysis.

Supply chain thinking is based partly in the concept of cost management extending from within the firm to take in upstream processes and inputs to the firm. Hence cost management has extended from production to embrace accounting and procurement. There was evidence of techniques such as horizontal information systems, *kaizen* costing, benchmarking, open book accounting, value engineering and target costing. The changes in management accounting practice broadly fitted the stages of development model. Cost management for efficiency and for effectiveness was broadly changing in line with the stages of the development model with more impact as the nature of the interdependence became mutual.

Costing Practices: How Costs are Measured

Costing Models

Standard costing   The use of standard cost was much wider than we had expected. The common reasons for this were that the costs were used to measure product profitability. It appears that the advent of supply chain management has had no effect upon this. The use of such costs was in the context of some new understandings about how costs are incurred and how they can be managed or reduced. To some extent the speed of change and the changes in time cycles have led to standards not being used for detailed variance analysis; but analysis of cost movements was common among our companies.

Variable and marginal costing   There was little evidence of the recognition and use of marginal and variable costs except in circumstances where the cost of a principal material input so dwarfed other costs that the material cost was an estimate of variable costs. Company W had developed an approach to understanding variable costs; they reported a good understanding of their own internal costs but some difficulties in recognising the variable costs of external contractors who provided some logistic and other services.

Life cycle costing   There was little evidence of this practice in any of the research companies.

Activity based costing   ABM/C has been applied in the major companies who are mostly involved in the intra-firm supply chain. The expectation that ABM/C, which attends to the horizontal flows, would find a ready application in the inter-firm supply chain was not observed. The inter-firm supply systems in this research were not in a position to build cost models and analysis along the chains.

Cost control procedures   While there were active cost management procedures in many of the companies, these were part of ongoing management and not directly

related to supply chain management. It may be argued that supply chain manag
itself was seen as a cost control approach. However the cost management proce
were stimulated by supply chain management via attention to the internal cost.
especially to the input costs and the costs of procurement.

Resource focus

Cost of suppliers   There was little or no evidence of analysis of the benefits and
costs of changing the process of managing suppliers; decisions were taken on the
self-evident proposition that simplification of the numbers of suppliers combined
with staff reductions would have positive outcomes. There was anecdotal evidence of
the influence of consultants, of stories of other companies and trade press articles
together with the imperative to reduce cost. It appears that few companies had the
accounting procedures to record and track the costs of purchasing. But the developments do follow the stages model in that the more the manner of supplier management
changes as expected, so the chain becomes more related to partnerships.

Of course, the central thrust of much supply chain thinking is to reduce costs and
improve the reliability and quality of goods and services in shorter time cycles. The
observed developments fit those ideas. The cost of suppliers was a major element
in the management of the supply chain. In the inter-firm case it was observed that
the shift to understanding serial dependence led to a mode of dominance back
up the chain. In the step to reciprocal dependence, reduction of the number of
suppliers to one or two for a given need creates a new mode of dependence, which
has to be managed. This led to the observation in the inter-firm case that reduction
in the number of suppliers was followed by collaboration with those remaining. It
appeared that an efficiency frontier had been reached via reduction and simplification; the next stage was to build collaborative advantage. The intra-firm companies
were following the same processes but in a more sophisticated way. What was of
particular interest was that these processes took place with very little formal cost–
benefit analysis and little impact upon management accounting calculus.

Cost of stock holding   All companies were aware of the need to calculate this and
all were involved in it. The use of lean production concepts to reduce cycle times
was common: for example, company E had an active programme of cost and lead
time reduction.

Connecting methods

Target costing   The expectation that supply chain management would lead to a
recognition that target costing, in relation to the positioning of product in market,
would become a central theme in management accounting change was not borne
out, except in the case of the Japanese owned company B. It was under consideration
by the Japanese influenced company D.

Throughput costing   No evidence of this in any of the case companies.

Cost management methods for considerations of efficiency   It was considered that supply chain management might offer the possibility of developing optimisation analysis of supply chains to enable cost minimisation to be managed. This requires sufficient knowledge of the marginal costs of the production processes across the chains. Only the intra-firm companies W and R had knowledge of marginal cost and the models of the processes and hence were able to consider this issue. W and R were able to consider the relationship of different supply chains in their complex systems. As far as we could understand from the companies, few, if any, of their supply chains suffered capacity constraints. Where capacity was problematic it was in R where different supply chains were using the same production and distribution facilities.

It is observed that cost management is central to supply and supply chain management; especially noting that, as companies move to lean manufacturing etc., there is a tendency to purchase sub-assemblies which are described as material inputs (Saunders, 1994; Lee and Seraph, 1995). It is not necessarily the case that the overall relationship of labour and material costs has changed, but in relation to the final assembler, it appears to have changed.

However as the proportion of input costs in relation to input plus transformation costs increases, then the focus of cost management has moved from production and management accounting to include procurement and management accounting. (The CMG case illustrated this movement through the management of input costs crossing the boundary of the firm into the suppliers' operations.)

Considerations of strategic decision making   It appears to be the case from these companies that the benefits of vertical integration (co-ordination) via hierarchy (even if it is also pluralist in nature) are that many stages of a complex supply chain can be managed in-house. However, because these larger multinational companies operate across many regions, countries, and markets, managing in-house was observed to be of considerable complexity. The use of supply chain management as a strategic tool to generate a new mode of strategic integration was evident in companies S, W and R (all intra-firm cases). The evidence was that it was not possible to develop the same strategic integration in the inter-firm cases. This may well act as a barrier to supply chain effectiveness.

Supply chain processes

Applicability of ABC etc. to supply chains   Our findings fitted with the earlier evidence on ABM/C. The further along the stages, then the greater the likelihood that the techniques could be applied.

Open book accounting   As expected, the use of 'open books' reflects development through our supply chain stages. In market or serial dependence, the books are closed. As reciprocal dependence develops, then the books become open to facilitate chain relationships. The degree of openness should not be overstated, however; these were specific to particular cases, and were not a general invitation to access companies' accounts. In the case of company D, it was more a matter of limited disclosure and protection at the same time. In H/T, discussions about the nature of open book accounting were interesting. Often, open book accounting is perceived as a mechanism whereby the supplier opens its books to the customer. It is important to recognise that the need to share information must be two way: there is a need for the customer to open its books to the supplier. In case H/T, it was accepted that customers must share data (including cost and value added calculations) with the supplier about the procedures between delivery of components and their subsequent use in the assembly process. In the H/T case, there was a willingness to look across company boundaries and to allow open book analysis within pre-agreed limits.

Performance management   The data show a significant impact from supply chain management on performance measurement and management. As firms move along the supply chain stages, the degree of attention required, and given to, this issue increases. The challenge presented in the later stages is whether to continue with 'bolt-on' additional supply chain performance measurements. An alternative is to change the whole organisation radically to a supply chain management approach which integrates a process driven structure with an integrated information system.

Supply chain reporting, including balanced scorecard   The main focus of reporting had not changed; but the impact of supply chain development at each stage was leading to consideration of the need to report along, and about, the chain. The CMG case gives an example of the development of additional information systems.

Role of accounting in strategic management of supply chains   There was little evidence of the actual role of management accounting in the strategic management of the supply chain, except via special projects and the involvement of management accountants in the work of strategic management.

Connection to other horizontal information systems   The stages of supply chain development place greater demands upon the integration of accounting data with other information. The end point of such integration was not observed, but the connection to process driven integrated information systems is visible in the developments at companies R and W and is under consideration in company S.

Electronic data interchange (EDI)   This study was not primarily concerned with EDI. However, much change was observed, with the early stages of supply development using simple linking exchanges such as ordering and scheduling. At the most developed companies, the use of EDI was via complex logistics systems in which there were options to add systems for accounting.

Relational contracting and shared destiny   Company D is a supplier to a number of multinational companies in the automotive business and hence had experience of several approaches to being brought along with the customer's idea of managing a supply chain. It seemed that relationships with these companies differed. They were affected by many years of trading experience. Where their customers had been hard bargainers, it was likely to take many years before company D would be more than sufficiently co-operative. They assumed that the approaches from the hard bargainers were another form of extracting compliance and cost reduction, or of the hard bargainers extracting more of the profit from the system. Protestations of a new beginning were not believed. In contrast, customers with some understanding of collaboration were given more attention. There was more readiness to share productivity and product technology improvements with these customers and with parallel suppliers. However, company D was unwilling to open its accounting books in any great detail, and was certainly unwilling to enter into detailed discussions of its cost structures with any of its customers. This suited one customer which had concentrated on decremental costing in preference to examining cost structure.

Changes in the role of the management accountant

The management accountants were responsible for the integrity of the design of the accounting systems in use, and for the integrity of their basic data capture and classification. This was very much affected by supply chain drivers, such as the adoption of customer and service orientations, lean manufacturing, world-class manufacturing, shorter production cycles, shorter production runs, greater variety.

Two major issues emerge from the evidence. The first is that the technical or professional role of the management accountant is becoming more complex as there is a need to integrate accounting with logistics driven manufacturing and to work across organisational boundaries with different technical issues and histories, to co-operate with the development of balanced scorecard approaches to information management and provision. The second is the rapid change in the role which the organisations require of management accountants. This new institutional role demands the ability to work effectively in cross-functional teams, to work across and outside the boundaries of the organisation with suppliers, and to link technical issues to managerial roles and problems.

All of this expansion in scope for the management accountant must be accomplished without diminution of the professional capability to assure the integrity of accounting systems and procedures, and the ability to provide sound interpretation of the information provided.

The evidence suggests that the advent of supply chain management has led to a significant increase in organisational striving for functional integration. The use of multi-functional teams had become very common. This was taking place in the context of 'delayering' so that the complexity of work that a team was expected to handle was also increasing. It appears that the full development of intra-firm supply chains can produce very radical changes within organisations. Changes among the inter-firm companies were more limited, but radical solutions to the problems of closer integration among the companies within a supply system cannot be ruled out. The solution in one textile firm (not included in this study) was to physically separate its manufacturing plants so that it could dedicate a plant to a customer and then work across boundaries to integrate their systems, production and distribution.

Discussion

This study has made observations in the context of rapid change in which our classifications caught almost all companies in varied states of transition. All the companies were undertaking a variety of changes, with the potential to affect each other, and to affect management accounting. There was a significant increase in changes in working. Changes in the inter-firm companies were limited, but became more evident as they progress through the transition stages identified above. In the intra-firm cases, some radical restructuring was evident. The potential for dramatic impact was observed to be greater in the mutually dependent modes than in the reciprocal dependent modes.

Management accounting cycle

None of our companies reported any changes to their financial planning and reporting cycles arising specifically from supply chain factors. There was evidence of working for greater integration of planning processes and of additional reporting for supply chain issues.

The common periodicity of monthly and annual cycles of management accounting is challenged by the shortening cycles of order fulfilment (ordering, procurement, manufacture and delivery). Hence there was evidence that the common accounting cycles were too slow to be of use in the monitoring and management of the order fulfilment process. This was being more effectively monitored using physical measures. The evidence from most of the companies suggests that the time cycles of operations are shortening and that production budgeting is becoming focused over 3/4 months (company D) with an ability to change overhead rates on an eight week cycle.

It was common for management accounting to be constructed on the basis of the organisation's structures of responsibility and accountability. Here, management accounting and control was a basic procedure for vertical integration of financial behaviour. In some of the multinational companies in our study, especially in the intra-firm cases, it was observed that there was considerable use of quasi-economic controls such as return on investments, return on assets, residual income and its variants, as means for introducing financial market related disciplines into company divisions. Here integration between functions was achieved through the use of transfer pricing within a corporate policy.

Supply chain thinking complicates the locus of responsibility and accountability in a manner very similar to the arguments used in relation to programme planning and budgeting. It was observed in one intra-firm company that new, supply chain related, demands forced operational integration and redefined both the structures of responsibility and accountability, and the required financial decision rules for transfer, thus affecting the measures of performance. This had a direct impact on managers who had become accustomed to performance related pay based on their divisional performance. Consequently, there were significant problems in integrating the intra-organisational supply chain.

In general this problem was based on the management accounting and control procedures being used for short, medium and long term integration. In the newer world of supply chain thinking, the vertical integration of management accounting and control cycle still exists for the longer term (as does financial reporting). However, there was evidence from two companies of an emerging shift to systems of information and control for intra-functional integration for the short and medium term.

Performance management

The observed supply chains were mostly focused on specific supplier links, company by company. It was noted that performance management was a major problem. As the inter-firm supply chain developed through the transition stages, so performance management became more central, even if the procedures were rather bolted on, with joint management and sharing of surpluses being found in the mutually dependent stage. In the case of the intra-firm supply chains, there was considerable impact as the new and emerging horizontal and logistics models led towards more systemic management processes. This produced conflict between the divisional performance tradition and the new process driven management. Cases W and R illustrated this since the supply chain was well specified and managed by the supply chain team while the management of the geographic and functional organisations had not changed. A construction company J, whose whole strategic focus was aligned to creating partnerships, used a version of the balanced scorecard to measure performance in partnership situations. There was evidence that the evolution through the supply chain stages had a parallel impact on reporting procedures.

Costing

Our findings demonstrate that there has been little conceptual change in cost models. Standard costing for products was common, with little use of: variable, marginal, or target costing (except where influenced by Japanese management); life cycle costing; activity based costing; or throughput costing. So the management accounting practices were observed to be very 'traditional' in their connection to product cost and margin calculations, stock valuation and working capital analysis. These observations were largely indifferent to the inter- and intra-firm classifications of supply chains, and to the stages of supply chain development.

Cost of resources

Suppliers costs were a major element in the management of the supply chain. In the inter-firm case it was observed that shifts towards serial dependence led to a mode of dominance back up the chain. In the step to reciprocal dependence, reduction of the number of suppliers to one or two for a given need has created a new mode of dependence, which has to be managed. This led to the observation that, in cases of mutual dependence in the inter-firm category, reduction in supplier numbers was followed by collaboration with the remaining members. An efficiency frontier appears to have been reached via reduction and simplification; the next stage was to build collaborative advantage. The intra-firm companies were involved in the same processes but were able to apply more sophisticated approaches. These processes took place with very little formal cost–benefit analysis and little impact upon management accounting calculus. However the processes did reflect the role of management accountants in the management of the companies (see below).

Cost management

Efficiency   It was noted that cost management was central to supply chain management. This reflects the observation by Saunders (1994) and Lere and Seraph (1995) that, as companies move to lean manufacturing, there is a tendency to purchase materials inputs as sub-assemblies. (The *overall* relationship of labour and material costs may not change, but it changes for the final assembler.) However as the proportion of input costs in relation to input plus transformation costs increases, then the focus of cost management moves from production and management accounting to include procurement and management accounting. (The CMG case illustrates this movement, with the management of input costs crossing the boundary of the firm and extending into the suppliers' operations.)

In addition, there was evidence in some companies that the penetration of management accounting into the micro detail of organisational work was being pushed back up through the hierarchy – albeit one that was 'flattening'. This occurred because the companies could use physical measures as a basis for decisions, having in their minds an understanding of the consequences of costs. The point at which physical and accounting measures were integrated was shifting in the intra-firm and, to a lesser extent, in the inter-firm cases into procedures for functional horizontal integration.

Effectiveness (optimisation)   It was conjectured that management accounting procedures based on a more systemic approach to cost management would find a ready application in the inter-firm and intra-firm supply chains because they were developed as a means of moving away from the single overhead rate calculations. In fact, there was little evidence of application of BPR, ABM, ABC to inter-firm or intra-firm supply chains. It is suggest that this occurred because the inter-firm cases were not managed across organisations. Rather, they were managed link by link, with little or no consideration of the sequence of links in the chain. In the H/T case, the firms did examine processes across organisational boundaries and accounting information, but this involved only a single link.[3] The intra-firm chains should have been more amenable to these approaches; but those classified as in reciprocal independence were not changing rapidly, while those in mutual dependence had moved on to more sophisticated modelling.

Strategic cost management   There was little or no evidence from the inter-firm cases of the impact of supply chains on the use of management accounting for strategic management. We did not observe any evidence of the development of strategic management accounting[4] in the inter-firm cases except in so far as management accountants were involved in strategic management. It was observed that there was a strategic intent in supply chain management in the companies studied in that strategic management sought to get a grip on input costs. In the intra-firm cases of mutual dependence, we observed the firms to be close to the provision of an integrated logistics, procurement, production and market model. This included accounting data, thus creating an on-line strategic management tool.

Supply chain processes

The use of open book accounting followed our stages of supply chain development. It should be noted that all our observations of open book accounting in the inter-firm cases demonstrated quasi-openness rather than full openness. It seems to be the case that, as dependence moves from serial to reciprocal and then to mutual dependence, a greater openness is evident. This sharing in both directions is an essential aspect of mutuality. It was also observed that open books were not always achieved in the intra-firm cases.

Horizontal information systems in two inter-firm cases, CMG (serial dependent) and H/T (reciprocal dependent), were very much project based, but these were regular additions to current procedures. Horizontal information systems were most developed in the mutually dependent intra-firm chains. The mutual dependence intra-firm cases had developed very sophisticated logistic models of procurement, production and distribution that extended to the flows in their suppliers' factories. However, marketing and accounting data were not yet integrated into the supply chain. This was to be a next major step.

The inter-firm case companies were managing link by link and made limited use of EDI. This technology has been used in partnership arrangements between organisations in the retail, financial and manufacturing sectors, albeit mainly in dyadic relationships. There was no conclusive evidence of EDI being used systemically along the supply chain.[5] In the intra-firm cases, supply chain development was leading to a revolution in the use of EDI as an internal vehicle for integrating supply chain management.

The H/T case was undertaken specifically to explore the issue of management accounting and the shared destiny principle. The evidence suggests that accounting and management accounting aid the development of alliances; Marson and Massey (1999) argue that accounting can and does play a constitutional role in this respect.

There was evidence from the case studies that once they are through the first stage of developing cost management and supplier management, companies begin to build upon their experience of managing serial dependence to move towards reciprocal dependence. Our respondents – managers, purchasing managers and management accountants – acknowledged that the next stage would include relational contracting, encompassing a wider sharing of accounting information. However in the more adversarial culture of the UK, the evidence from case D suggested that this step would require some time to elapse before histories of dominance by customers could be set aside and invitations to greater collaboration would be accepted. Companies at the mutual dependence stage were engaged in relational contracting – as was illustrated by case J.

But company D was especially interesting in that it behaved differently with different customers. Where there was a history of customer dominance, little movement was seen. In the case of companies without such histories, relational contracting had developed to include the sharing, with customer and competitive suppliers, advances in technology together with procedures that enhanced quality and reduced costs. In a like manner, company D was able to benefit from its competitors' advances.

The supply chain roles of management accountants

The major issues were:

- maintenance of technical contribution, and the technical integrity of the accounting procedures;
- a shift from the technical or professional role to include a managerial role;
- a shift from a professional functional contribution to membership of managerial teams with a need to be a constructive member of teams;
- evidence of management accountants being appointed as supply chain accountants.

There was a note of warning in that there was some experience of pushing younger (about 28 years) qualified management accountants into team and managerial roles in very complex organisations, before they have full confidence in their maturing technical and professional capabilities.

In the intra-firm cases, management accountants had to work across organisational boundaries.

The cutting edge: intra-firm examples

In general, the greatest impact of supply chains upon management accounting was in the intra-firm chains in multinational companies. These examples were the product of a convergence of a number of ideas and technologies, including the following.

- computing power;
- the building of very complex logistics models;
- satellite communications technology (fast and always available);
- the capacity for local access to global systems;
- the application of systemic thinking as a mode of integration;
- moves towards the creation of lean manufacturing and world-class manufacturing;
- the need for rich information for decision and control and analysis;
- the capacity to manage beyond the legal boundaries by modes of dominance – serial dependence, reciprocal dependence and mutual dependence.

These are coming together to establish process driven integrated information systems (PDIIS). However these new (if embryonic) systems are being introduced alongside the extant systems and have not displaced them. But, if the organisation structure is radically changed to being process driven, then the older systems will have to be changed. New (or emerging) PDIIS need to be embedded before the old systems are disembedded. They do not replace the need for local operating information systems, but when integrated with accounting, they provide a potential tool for strategic analysis and management. Two of our companies were close to such possibilities, with several more seeking to move in that direction – i.e. from reciprocal to mutual dependence.

This new ideal type of PDIIS improves the capability of hierarchic firms to enhance their flexibility and to achieve complex co-ordination. Such capability is unlikely to be attained in the inter-firm cases, although suitable platforms will soon be available.

Conclusions

In the inter-firm cases, 'the supply chain' was almost always managed as a set of discrete links, with little or no attention to managing the whole chain. This reflects the construct of supply chains as observed sets of connections but not as manageable sets of inter-firm behaviours. This absence of integration of management accounting along the chain reflects the issues of ownership and asset protection. The experience of these companies in supply chains in the UK was that they were not surrendering to the image of the integrated supply chain; rather they were managing their destiny by engaging in a series of dependent relationships to their own mutual advantage. This fits with the arguments of Scott (1995) that economic arrangements will reflect the (changing) social structure. We have observed companies and cases in a domain of considerable past, present and expected future changes in supply chains and in management accounting practices. Table 2 summarises the stages of development of management accounting responses.

While much of the practice of management accounting was rather 'traditional', it was observed that the supply chain impact on management accounting practices

Table 2 Development of management accounting responses

Business focus of supply chains	Focus of cost management		
	Accounting for efficiency	Economic optimisation (effectiveness)	Strategic
Finance and operations	Reduction of cost of management Reduction of cost of supply/suppliers Cycle time and working capital reduction	Little	None
Management of future business configurations	As above	Organisational innovation Active reconsideration of supplier's contribution to design/development of products/services (balanced scorecard)	Little
Strategic development	As above	As above	Intra-firm: PDIIS as a strategic tool Inter-firm: a virtual PDIIS – but is it strategic?

followed the stages of supply chain development, and that these changes in practice were easier to implement in the intra-firm cases. Clearly, management accounting developments were central in shifts towards reciprocal and mutual dependence. This process is more difficult in the somewhat conflictual and autonomy-preferring Anglo-Saxon context, but supply chains challenges are changing behaviour.

Management accounting as a set of ideas informed all cost management practices in both inter-firm and intra-firm cases. Management accounting may be becoming redundant as a separate set of processes but will continue to make a vital contribution to the management of integrated information systems in inter-firm and intra-firm supply chains.

The advent of the new systemic thinking and technologies noted in the intra-firm examples above makes possible the enactment of the basic ideas of programme, planning and budgeting systems as modes of inter-functional (horizontal) integration across different parts of complex organisations. It is also the case that the advent of supply chain management in the inter- and intra-company cases means that there are shifts in the:

• score-keeping role to include extra organisational data;
• attention-directing role as this becomes shared across organisational boundaries;

- problem-solving role because the rich data structures must be designed with a variety of analytic intents.

The shortening of time cycles leads to the seeming redundancy of the attention-directing role, as action follows from physical data rather than accounting data. Here the accountant, as a member of the team, must be able to infer the impacts upon accounts, and to advise, on-line in real time, on desirable actions.

So while management accounting practice might appear to be traditional (if open to a radical challenge), supply chain management practice was quite the opposite. Supply chain thinking and development was observed to be having a major impact upon the practice of management accountants in organizational management. Management accountants were contributing to the strategic management of the inter- and intra-firm supply chain. It was very clear from three case studies that management accountants are active partners in the new management teams' cultures – a development which follows the logic of the evolving supply chains as well as holding to the logics of hierarchy.

Management accountants are getting involved in cost management for efficiency and effectiveness, and in strategic issues through their involvement in multi-functional teams which look at processes and functions. The career stages at which management accountants can take on these wider team and institutional roles is not clear but, in a few cases, there is evidence of management accountants being forced into too much complexity too quickly.

From these research findings we can see the emergence of logistic modelling in the intra-firm cases. When integrated with accounting and marketing data, this will provide the basis for new PDIIS. The processes of change are episodic, based in *ad hoc* projects, and innovations in management practice and management accounting responses.

It is possible that once the PDIIS are more widely available, they will impact at the inter-firm level. Table 2 provides a framework for describing the possible path of change in management accounting practices as process driven integrated information systems are developed. From the routines of hierarchic systems, via a series of complex, *ad hoc* projects, the technology for PDIIS is slowly being created. At the moment, the existing systems – which require great expertise and support as organisations change – are being maintained and remain embedded. The new systems need to become embedded in parallel and proven in practical use before any disembedding can take place. It is not that managers and accountants are risk averse; rather, the technical and managerial utility of such new systems requires substantial testing of robustness before they can take over.

It is clear from our conversations with companies that the costs of such systems are immense; sums of the order of £10 million (and perhaps more) were mentioned. But as consultancy firms are working very busily in these fields, it can be but a matter of time before these systems can be extended to the inter-firm level, though the question of who should pay will be difficult to resolve. However, they could be made available on common carrier terms and leased.

This research project has made some progress in understanding the consequences of supply chain management at the inter-firm and intra-firm levels for management accounting and for the practice of management accountants. However, it also appears to us that we have only scratched the surface of the significance of the emerging practice of management accountants. More will be learnt after the usefulness and validity of a number of management accounting practices are tested in the fire of experience.

NOTES

1   Saunders (1994) notes the costs of assisting suppliers with negotiations, make or buy decisions, product development and modification, comparison of home or overseas sourcing, analysis of product costs including overheads.
2   The 1960s literature on programme, planning and budgeting systems demonstrated how difficult it was to change from vertical to horizontal accounting information systems.
3   Lamming at Bath and current studies of the ceramic industry at Keele make similar observations.
4   In the sense that strategic management accounting refers to strategic decisions about cost structures in relation to competitor cost structures.
5   See Marson and Massey (1999) which explores this issue outside of our case companies.

REFERENCES

Akoi, M. (1988) *Information, incentives, and bargaining in the Japanese economy*, New York, Cambridge University Press.

Bromwich, M. (1991) 'Accounting for strategic excellence'. In: Okonomistyring OG strategic – nyeideer nye erfarinjer (pub. systime Denmark).

Carr, C. and Ng, J. (1995) 'Total cost control: Nissan and its UK supplier partnerships', *Management Accounting Research*, vol. 6, pp. 347–365.

Castells, M. (1996) *The rise of the network society*, Blackwell Publishers.

Coase, R. (1937) 'The nature of the firm', *Economica*, vol. 4, pp. 386–405.

Dyer, J. H. and Ouchi, W. G. (1993) 'Japanese-style partnerships: Giving companies a competitive edge', *Sloan Management Review*, Fall 1993, pp. 51–62.

Frances, J. and Garnsey, E. (1996) 'Supermarkets and suppliers in the United Kingdom: System integration, information and control', *Accounting, Organisations and Society*, vol. 21, no. 6, pp. 591–610.

Gietzmann, M. B. (1996) 'Incomplete contracts and the make or buy decision: Governance design and attainable flexibility', *Accounting, Organisations and Society*, vol. 21, no. 6, pp. 611–626.

Granovetter, M. S. (1985) 'Economic action and social structure: The problem of embeddedness', *American Journal of Sociology*, vol. 91, no. 3, pp. 481–510.

Harland, C. M. (1996) 'Supply chain management: Relationships, chains and networks', *British Journal of Management*, vol. 7, Special issue s63–s80.

Helper, S. R. and Sako, M. (1995) 'Supplier relations in Japan and the United States: Are they converging?', *Sloan Management Review*, Spring 1995, pp. 77–84.

Hergert, M. and Morris, D. (1989) 'Accounting data for value chain analysis', *Strategic Management Journal*, vol. 10.

Hope, T. and Hope, J. (1995) *Transforming the bottom line: Managing performance with the real numbers.* London, Nicholas Brealey Publishing.

Johnston, R. and Lawrence, P. R. (1988) 'Beyond vertical integration – the rise of the value-adding partnership', *Harvard Business Review*, July/August, pp. 94–101.

Kanter, R. M. (1994) 'Collaborative advantage: The art of alliances', *Harvard Business Review*, July/August, pp. 96–108.

Kaplan, R. S. (1984) 'Yesterday's accounting introduces production', *Harvard Business Review*, July/August, pp. 95–101.

Lamming, R. (1993) *Beyond partnership: Strategies for innovation and lean supply*, New York, Prentice Hall.

Lere, J. and Seraph, J. (1995) 'Activity based costing for purchasing managers' cost and pricing determinations', *International Journal of Purchasing and Materials Management*, Fall, pp. 25–31.

Macaulay, S. (1963) 'Non-contractual relations in business: a preliminary study', *American Sociological Review*, vol. 28, no. 2, pp. 55–67.

Macbeth, D. K. and Ferguson, N. (1994) 'Partnership sourcing: An integrated supply chain approach', London, Pitman, *Financial Times.*

Macneil, I. R. (1974) 'The Many Futures of Contract', *Southern California Law Review*, vol. 47, pp. 691–816.

Marson, J. and Massey, P. (1999) 'The strategic use of IT in the supply chain', *Journal of Financial Information Systems.*

Miles, R. E. and Snow, C. C. (1986) 'Organisations: New concepts for new forms', *California Management Review*, vol. 28, no. 3, pp. 62–73.

Mohr, J. and Spekman, R. (1994) 'Characteristics of partnership success: Partnership attributes, communication behavior, and conflict resolution techniques', *Strategic Management Journal*, vol. 15, pp. 135–152.

Nohria, N. and Eccles, R. G. (1992) *Networks and organisations: Structure, form and action*, Harvard Business School Press.

Okimoto, D. I. (1986) 'Regime characteristics of Japanese industrial Policy'. In: Hugh Patrick (ed.) *Japan's high technology industries*, Seattle, University of Washington Press.

Partridge, M. and Perren, L. (1994) 'Cost analysis of the value chain: Another role for strategic management accounting', *Management Accounting*, July/August, pp. 22–28.

Porter, M. E. (1985) *Competitive advantage: Creating and sustaining superior performance*, New York, The Free Press.

Pruitt, D. G. (1981) *Negotiation behavior*, New York, Academic Press.

Quillian, L. (1991) 'Curing "functional silo syndrome" with logistics total cost management', *CMA Magazine*, June, pp. 9–14.

Sako, M. (1992) *Prices, quality and trust: Inter-firm relations in Britain and Japan*, Cambridge University Press.

Saunders, M. (1994) *Strategic purchasing and supply chain management*, Pitman for the Chartered Institute of Purchasing and Supply.

Scott, W. R. (1995) *Institutions and organisations*, Sage.

Shank, J. K. and Govindarajan, V. (1992) 'Strategic cost management and the value chain', *Journal of Cost Management*, vol. 5, no. 4, pp. 5–21.

Stuart, F. I. and McCutcheon, D. (1996) 'Sustaining strategic supplier alliances', *International Journal of Operations and Production Management*, vol. 16, no. 10, pp. 5–22.

Teece, D. (1996) 'Firm organisation, industrial structure, and technological innovation', *Journal of Economic Behaviour and Organisation*, vol. 31, pp. 193–224.

Turnbull, P., Oliver, N. and Wilkinson, B. (1992) 'Buyer–supplier relations in the UK automotive industry: Strategic implications of the Japanese manufacturing model', *Strategic Management Journal*, vol. 13, pp. 159–168.

Whitley, R. (1994) *Business systems in East Asia: Firms, markets and societies*, Macmillan.

Williamson, O. E. (1975) *Markets and hierarchies: Analysis and anti-trust implications* New York, Free Press, Macmillan.

Williamson, O. E. (1979) 'Transaction–cost economics: The governance of contractual relations', *Journal of Law and Economics*, vol. 22, no. 2, pp. 3–61.

Womack, J. P., Jones, D. T. and Roos, D. (1990) *The machine that changed the world*, New York, Rawson Ass.

Zheng, J., Harland, C., Johnsen, T. and Lamming, R. (1997) 'Features of supply networks', paper presented at the BAM conference, London, 1997.

Approaches to Child Labour in the Supply Chain

*Diana Winstanley, Joanna Clark
and Helena Leeson*

Introduction

As organisations become increasingly global, it is becoming more and more difficult to ensure ethical integrity in the supply chain, and to take an ethical approach to managing the workforce that extends beyond organisational, national and cultural boundaries (Legge 2000). Moreover, organisations which have attempted to tackle these issues, such as those in the sportswear, football stitching and carpet industries, rather than being applauded for their actions, have become media pariahs, castigated for their failures and for the emptiness of their actions, which are assumed cynically to be intended for PR purposes alone.

For example BBC's 'Panorama' programme 'No Sweat' (BBC 2000) utilised investigative journalism to uncover child labour and other exploitative labour practices in a factory in Cambodia despite the fact that both Nike and Gap have codes of conduct addressing these issues. Student campaigns against Nike in the United States are claimed to be the biggest student protest in the US since the opposition to the Vietnam War, and the 'Just Stop It' campaign which has targeted Nike for its poor labour practices in developing countries is becoming as well known as the company's 'Just Do It' trademark. It is also becoming more and more common for workers themselves to draw abuses to the attention of international bodies either directly or via the media. The 'Saipan Sweatshop Litigation' is perhaps the most high-profile example of this, where three major lawsuits were filed in the US challenging unlawful sweatshop conditions in Saipan, a US commonwealth protectorate in the Western Pacific. The lawsuits claimed violations of the laws against involuntary servitude, misleading labelling, and misleading advertising practices as well as other abuses. Leading brand names such as Gap, Levi Strauss, Sears, Calvin Klein and

Tommy Hilfiger were named. In March 2000 seventeen US retailers agreed to pay a total of $8 million in settlement and adhere to a rigorous system of independent monitoring; more cases remain pending (Sweatshop Watch 2000). Adidas-Salomon (the trademark being 'Adidas-Salomon'), one of the companies discussed below, has itself received adverse publicity with regard to employment of child labour in supplier factories in Indonesia. Worker representatives took the case to the European Parliament, claiming that factories manufacturing Adidas clothes were using child labour and forced overtime, and were guilty of sexual harassment. A worker in an Adidas supplier factory in Bangkok, Thailand made similar allegations a year ago.

However, despite the criticisms, some companies have attempted to take a more active stance in their management and deployment of human resources. In this paper we look at some of the problems of globalisation for human rights and for child labour in particular, and explore the alternative approaches that can be taken. We use a case study of Adidas-Salomon to identify the issues faced by companies adopting an 'involvement' strategy to human rights.

The Problems of Globalisation and Regulation of International Supply Chains

As Bairoch (1996, quoted in Collier 2000) claims, globalisation is nothing new. Goods, people and capital have been globally mobile since before the First World War (Collier 2000). Collier argues however that globalisation as we define it today is different in that it contains 'the idea of access to resources', and globalisation can therefore be understood as 'the process of economic, political and social change that occurs when all agents in a system have access to a common pool of resources'. One of these resources is people, and access to international labour is often motivated by cost reduction and economic logic. Labour is simply cheaper in some parts of the world than others. Not only does this mean lower wages further down the supply chain of these global organisations, but it may involve poorer working conditions and limitations on access to basic human rights. Abuses of human rights may be tolerated by economic interests, or firms further up the supply chain may intervene to attempt to impose a basic floor of standards. However, this is notoriously difficult where local cultural practices reinforce practices which would be unacceptable in the developed world.

Are sweatshop practices an inevitable stage in societal development? Hartman et al. (2000) argue to the contrary by drawing the analogy of doctors not having to practise blood letting before being able to practise modern medicine. They suggest that:

> Progress occurs when one age can build on the developments of another . . . in the past the barrier was knowledge; currently the barrier is the willingness of advanced economies to help developing economies. (2000: 85)

Whereas most developed economies have relatively well-regulated and well-enforced labour laws, this cannot be said of many developing economies. Whilst the need for foreign investment is essential in order to promote economic prosperity, a significant competitive advantage of most developing countries is the availability of a vast and cheap labour force. Exploitation of this competitive advantage all too often results in exploitation, often to an extreme, of the workforce itself.

This raises the question as to what frameworks exist for accountability and regulation, given the weakness of national governments and nation states to address workplace human rights. Despite the existence of international organisations (UN, World Bank, WTO) which have a stake in promoting human rights, they are in practice as ineffectual as nation states. There are also organisations and initiatives explicitly set up to promote social responsibility in this area. The Global Reporting Initiative and AccountAbility have established quantitative standards against which companies can measure their performance. The Ethical Trading Initiative is an alliance of UK companies, NGOs and trade unions which works to support the maintenance of its employment standards and best practice sourcing. Initiatives such as these, aimed at enabling companies to perform better on human rights, continue to be developed.

Corporate Approaches to Child Labour

This paper looks at what companies can do to improve working conditions down an international supply chain, and, more specifically, how they can tackle and implement policies of 'no child labour'.

From 26 interviews at 21 companies, Leeson (2000) has identified a 'Three-I' model of the different corporate approaches to human rights (see Figure 1).

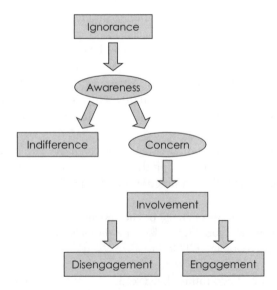

Figure 1   The 'Three-I' model of corporate approaches to human rights

1 *Ignorance* Many companies are not even aware that there may be human rights implications of their policies further down the supply chain. These companies do not see human rights as a key business concern, and may not even take steps to determine the level, if any, of their involvement in human rights abuses.

2 *Indifference* Some companies are aware of human rights issues, and of violations with which the company's name has, however tenuously, been linked. However, for one or more reasons they have chosen not to act, or have acted only with reluctance, in support of those whose rights are being abused.

3 *Involvement* Some companies are aware of human rights issues, and of their own responsibilities in relation to these. They may actively take steps to identify and monitor human rights issues down their supply chain, seeking out information on the issues. As well as assessing the situation, they may also take steps to respond to their perceived responsibilities in the area. Companies can be roughly divided according to the type of response they make.

   • *Disengagers* These endeavour to resolve specific problems in a methodical task-by-task fashion. If satisfactory resolution is not achieved in the short to medium term the company may well 'disengage' from the country/project/supplier concerned, and do business elsewhere.

   • *Engagers* These endeavour to address the wider context in which human rights violations may be occurring, and work for a pragmatic compromise if a satisfactory resolution is not achieved. Instead of disengaging with factories or parts of the world which may bring them into contact with child labour, the organisation becomes involved in tackling the child labour issue. Instead of taking a narrow approach focusing on the child labour in the factories alone, these companies may adopt wider and more comprehensive anti-poverty and educational strategies which reach out from the factory to work with the local community and other groups in the area. This may involve a long-term approach.

Table 1 identifies the risks and rewards for companies taking involvement and indifference approaches to human rights respectively. This paper focuses only on those companies taking the 'involvement' route. However, for these companies the choice between engagement and disengagement strategies is not easy. We illustrate this by two different approaches to the problems of regulating child labour in the football stitching industry in Sialkot.

Reebok: disengagement strategy

Reebok opted for a 'zero tolerance' strategy which was akin to a disengagement strategy (Leeson 2000). It collaborated with its peer companies, as represented by the Soccer Industry Council of America (SICA). A task force on global manufacturing processes was set up, which reported that, whilst conditions in Sialkot were better than the original publicity had suggested, children were making up around 20% of the labour force involved in football production.

Table 1   The risks and rewards of taking the involvement and the indifference approaches to human rights

Stakeholder	Involvement	Indifference
Staff	✔ High morale ✔ Increased loyalty ✘ May cause cultural offence ✘ Wages may be higher than prevailing	✔ Non-judgemental concerning cultural norms ✘ Staff seen as expendable
Suppliers	✔ Visibility of supply chain ✔ Supplier commitment ✔ Improved product quality ✘ Reduced choice of source ✘ Possibly increased cost	✔ Unlimited supply choice ✔ Access to low competition markets ✘ Risks from civil unrest ✘ Suppliers at risk from dangerous workplaces etc.
Customers	✔ Supply reliability avoids stock-outs ✔ Reputation for caring builds loyalty ✘ Price may increase	✔ Cheap and diverse products ✘ Reputation for amorality
Home government	✔ Respect for supporting implicit boycotts ✘ Seen to be involved in politics	✔ Trade missions to difficult countries ✘ May cause embarrassment in foreign policy matters
Community	✔ Support from locals reflecting safe environment, support against oppression ✘ Conflict with oppressive groups	✔ Support from local enforcement groups ✔ May gain 'free' labour ✘ Lawsuits for environmental/ health damage ✘ Direct action from local groups

The Reebok answer was to remove children from the supply chain. The company invested both time and finance in creating stitching factories that they could guarantee would be free of child labour. The factories, operated by Reed and Associates and Moltext Rubber, are housed in purpose-built premises, and are highly regulated and randomly inspected by Reebok representatives to ensure both that children do not work within the factories, and that panels do not leave the factories for assembly in an uncontrolled location. In accordance with the 'Atlanta Agreement' all stitchers must be registered. Reebok has contributed $1 million to support educational opportunities for children in the area (Gaines 1996). The company acknowledges that the approach has increased costs significantly (one source suggested by as much as 50%), but states that all costs are borne by the company and not passed on to the consumer. Reebok is so confident that its footballs are made only by adult labourers that it has introduced its own mark – 'Guarantee: Manufactured without Child Labour'.

However, the efficacy of the Reebok approach has been questioned. FoulBall, a US-based pressure group, has alleged that whilst the stitching centres are indeed child labour free, the final shipments of footballs may include both adult and child stitched footballs – a practice known as 'mixing' (McCurry 1998). Also, orders in Sialkot have dropped, and smaller suppliers face bankruptcy (Lloyd Roberts 1998).

The Pentland Group: engagement strategy

In 1995, they year in which the scandal broke, Pentland's CEO Stephen Bubin had become president of the World Federation of Sporting Goods Industry and had declared an interest in human rights issues. At about the same time the company took over Mitre, and found itself the owner of a company deeply embroiled in the child labour story. Rubin acted quickly, and by the end of 1995 the Pentland Group board had published both a human rights policy statement and an environmental policy statement. He then recruited a former Director of Anti-Slavery International to create and implement a set of practical processes through which to execute the company's policy.

Seeing the problem as being as much about underlying poverty as about child labour, Pentland began to explore alternative approaches. The company recognised that by introducing new factories where stitchers worked together, not only would children be removed from the industry, but in all probability so too would women, who would be culturally prohibited from working in the same room as the men. The denial to families of income from both children and women had the potential to be catastrophic. Furthermore, the loss of income would simply move children out of the relative safety of the stitching industry and into entirely unregulated and physically more dangerous industries such as brick-making.

Pentland devised a compromise approach in which a number of women's homes would be nominated as stitching centres: 10 to 15 women would be registered and the women would work together. An agreement was drawn up with local NGOs and with the ILO that monitors would visit the new 'stitching centres', at appropriate notice, to ensure that conditions remained safe and that children were not working at the time of the monitor's visit. Pentland is also sponsoring literacy classes for the women enabling them to gain significant autonomy within the community and to be paid directly.

Strategy comparison

The Reebok disengagement approach brings less negative publicity. However, the disadvantages relate to the difficulties of policing such a policy. Also, there is little impact on the causes and conditions of child labour itself, since the focus is on eliminating it from the supply chain. By contrast, the Pentland Group took a wider engagement strategy to deal with child labour.

The Pentland approach, although logical, has received far from universal support. Conversely the Reebok approach, which has clear benefits for the reputation of the company, has been adopted by companies such as Nike. Manufacturers are reluctant to use the home-stitching approach as there exists a clear risk, possibly even an expectation, that children will work with their mothers stitching footballs. Similarly, the NGOs to whom the companies turn for advice must also satisfy their membership constituencies, which demand that children should not be exploited, but which in many cases fail to distinguish between child labour and child work.

The term 'child work' is seen by many as something which is legitimate, and encompasses for example children doing paper rounds in the UK, or tending family animals in Vietnam. Child work is seen as important in developing responsibility and independence, as well as bringing status and contributing to the household economy. On the other hand, the term 'child labour' goes beyond this to incorporate elements of exploitative and hazardous work and 'work that is harmful to children because it prevents them from getting an education, because it damages their health or because it subjects them to physical, sexual or emotional abuse, or exploits them in other ways' (King and Marcus 2000).

It may be simplistic to say that Pentland has responded to the needs of the community stakeholder whilst Reebok has responded to peer group and consumer pressure. Reebok has declared 'zero tolerance' for child labour, but the question remains, to whose benefit is such a declaration? This paper does not intend to establish right and wrong, but instead seeks to provide more information about the issues that need to be faced when adopting an involvement strategy for child labour. The following case study of Adidas illustrates in more detail some of the complexities of taking an engagement approach.

A Case Study of Adidas-Salomon's Approach to Child Labour in Vietnam

This case study outlines the difficulties faced by a company such as Adidas-Salomon that decides not to disengage with suppliers in a certain area, or with the factories of that area, but does attempt to disengage from utilising 'child labour'. The company adopts a targeted approach, but one which does attempt to go beyond merely strict monitoring and regulation. This mixed approach, which in many ways is between that of Reebok and the Pentland Group, but has more similarities with the former, focuses on the development and implementation of the Standards of Engagement (SOE). The information for this case study has been gathered through interviews with Adidas-Salomon staff and other key informants, in a one week trip to see the operations in Vietnam, including visits to three of the six footwear factories which supply Adidas, through attendance at staff SOE training sessions, as well as through general observation and the use of public documents.

The Adidas company (now known as the Adidas-Salomon Group, here known as Adidas) was founded in 1949 as a family business producing high quality sports footwear, with its headquarters in Herzogenaurach, Germany. Worldwide it now works in 50 countries, owns and manages 11 factories and has contracts with over 1,000 supplier factories which produce the whole range of sports products with the brand name Adidas or Salomon.

The first shoe production for Adidas in Vietnam began in January 1996. Of the three main supplier countries, Vietnam produces 18–20% of Adidas footwear, Indonesia 25–30%, and China 50%, with 3–4% of production going to Germany, Korea and Taiwan. Moreover 99.5% of Vietnamese production is for export, by far the biggest markets being the United States and Europe. Worldwide production is 8 million pairs of shoes per month. Although it would be practicable for Adidas to source all their shoes from China, it chooses to source from a number of countries in order to spread the risks, both political and economic. Should the need arise to leave any one supplier country, for example because political unrest could make it impossible to operate there, the risk is minimised by having operations in other countries which could take on the work.

As a newly emerging market economy Vietnam offers a large, young labour force currently willing to work for extremely low wages. Of Vietnam's population of 76.3 million (1999 census), 65% are under the age of 25, i.e. born after the end of the war with the US. Real economic reform started in 1989, and by 1994 Vietnam switched from being a major importer of rice to being the world's third largest exporter. By sector, industry claims the highest percentage of foreign direct investment (FDI) commitments at 37.8% (Economic Intelligence Unit 2000).

The company has contracts with six footwear factories in Vietnam which assemble 1,600,000 pairs of shoes per month. Taking into account the fact that every shoe comes in a range of sizes and colours, Adidas in Vietnam produces 3,000 different models at any one time. In turn each factory subcontracts to other suppliers for the production of the rubber soles for the sports shoes. Components for each shoe come to the factory from up to five different countries worldwide. Of the six factories the smallest employs 3,500 staff and the largest 14,000. Because assembly lines of this sort are relatively new to Vietnam and are found in newly industrialised zones, many of the factories are recently built and, though not luxurious, have the benefit of being light, spacious and reasonably well equipped with basic facilities.

In Vietnam, the factories are all foreign owned enterprises – they are Taiwanese. It is not by accident that Adidas chose to work with Taiwanese managed factories, as the Taiwanese are perceived to have a 'better business approach than their competitors' (one Adidas manager). However this makes the situation more complex and challenging when it comes to regulating their Standards of Engagement.

Adidas began to be aware of social and human rights issues in the supply chain in the 1990s, primarily as a result of bad publicity for the sports industry as a whole at that time, and of the focus on itself and its competitors at the time of the 1998 World Cup when the story of child labourers stitching footballs in Sialkot, Pakistan, hit the headlines. This risk to reputation catapulted Adidas from ignorance into the involvement category of corporate responses (see Figure 1). It set up a 27-strong Department of Social and Environmental Affairs, its mission being:

To enhance the values of the Adidas-Salomon brand by promoting socially responsible, safe and environmentally sustainable practices for the company and its business partners.

It also developed a code of conduct, now evolved into the Standards of Engagement. The 'core values' of the Adidas brand upon which the Standards of Engagement are based are: 'Authenticity, Inspiration, Commitment, Honesty'. The department as such has no budget and has to bid for funds to implement any programmes which are in addition to the tasks that full-time staff are contracted to perform. Earlier work focused on environmental issues and health and safety, and the wider issues of social responsibility have only recently begun to be addressed.

The role of the department is to oversee the implementation of the Standards of Engagement, which themselves are based on the ILO's Conventions and the model code of conduct of the World Federation of Sporting Goods Industries (WFSGI) of which Adidas is a member.

On child labour the SOE state:

> Business partners shall not employ children who are less than 15 years old (or 14 years old where the law of the country of manufacture allows), or who are younger than the age for completing compulsory education in the country of manufacture where such age is higher than 15.

Adidas does not intend to use the SOE as a marketing tool, recognising that the risk of making claims which cannot be substantiated is too great. At the time of the research (2000), Adidas had introduced a minimum age of 18 in the six factories, but had identified their key challenges as:

- consistency with SOE and justification of the decision to set this age limit (given that the SOE age limit was significantly lower);
- how to work with the existing staff who were under 18.

It is perhaps surprising that Adidas chose to set their minimum age in these factories at three years above the SOE requirement. Vietnamese labour law requires that no one should be employed unless they have completed primary education, and in effect this means that a child should be in full-time education until the age of 15 or 16; thus Adidas's minimum age exceeds this by two or three years. It could be thought that this is an over-ambitious and over-zealous reaction of a company sensitive to media interest. Adidas considered this was appropriate considering the kind of tasks required in the footwear industry, and the policy was arrived at after discussion between Adidas SOE representatives and Adidas and factory managers.

Also, it does give them a safer margin of error for tackling child labour in a country where it is notoriously difficult to gain conclusive evidence of staff ages. For example, in carrying out an audit of recruitment and labour practices in all six factories, the Adidas labour monitor identified a number of underage workers in the Nan Kang Shoe Factory. Most of these young workers had been accepted on the workforce by presenting false documents (those of an aunt or older sister). In all,

Adidas in the Nan Kang Shoe Factory (employing 3,500) identified 12 girls between the ages of 14 and 15, with most of them having been in the factory at least a year and some as long as three years. Several had therefore been employed when they were only 12 years old. In addition the audit identified 130 workers between the ages of 16 and 17. They were then faced with the decision as to what to do with these underage workers, and how to implement their SOE.

Adidas found there were a number of implementation issues they faced with relation to the SOE in Vietnam.

Range and complexity of relationships

Implementing the SOE in the footwear industry is relatively straightforward compared to some other industries, such as the garment industry, where supply chains are less well defined, and where the majority of the workforce is not confined to the factory floor. In this context, the key relationships are identified in Table 2, along with their level of engagement.

The more engaged a company is in implementing the SOE, the closer will be its relationship with all its stakeholders. Identifying the range of stakeholders is one of the first steps of successful implementation. Table 2 gives a broad indication of the extent to which Adidas in Vietnam engaged the stakeholders most immediately relevant to the practical implementation of the SOE. Initial implementation of the SOE had involved little or no participation by some of the key stakeholders, and although these relationships may change and strengthen over time, implementation would potentially be more sustainable if engagement with these stakeholders had been undertaken from the beginning.

The importance of developing stakeholder capability can be seen in relation to the role of the government. In an ideal situation the government would fully develop and implement law in this area. However, although Vietnam has a comprehensive Labour Code, as in many transition economies it is not implemented in practice. The potential is high for government officials to 'turn a blind eye' with regard to

Table 2 Levels of engagement of key stakeholders

High level of engagement	Limited level of engagement	Low level of engagement
Adidas staff	Factory workforce	NGO (national and international in Vietnam)
Supplier factories (factory managers, Taiwan management)	Subcontractors in Vietnam	Trade unions
One international NGO	Competitors Government 'Child workers'	Academic institutions Government departments Community organisations

health and safety and environmental practices. Although this can be seen as an advantage by factory owners, it contributes to the challenges which Adidas faces in trying to introduce and implement sustainable, socially responsible approaches. Lack of implementation of national legislation contributes to a lack of appreciation by the workforce of the necessity of some of the standards upon which Adidas insists. Similarly, a lack of enforcement of standards with regard to recruitment contributes to the fact that a large percentage of the migrant workforce has been appointed through agencies that are unscrupulous in charging employees at rates higher than their first month's salary. However, major international companies such as Adidas are in a position to exert considerable influence on legislative practices. Developing closer ties with government agencies at all levels can contribute to this and is part of a responsible approach to the implementation of appropriate standards of engagement.

Competitors are another stakeholder group that pose problems for engagement, but their involvement is vital for success. Fierce competition generated by the desire to use cheap labour to keep profits up and costs down has led to the need to contract work to suppliers rather than for buyers to own and manage their own factories. Consequently, all buyers seek suppliers who are competent in their particular business, and in the case of footwear factories, several buyers will contract with the same factory at any one time. Although specific areas of the factory and staff are dedicated to the lines of individual buyers, the fact that other lines are being manu-factured for buyers who may have different standards of engagement to Adidas presents significant challenges in terms of how effectively the SOE can be implemented in any one factory. Pressures of deadlines, last minute orders or the need to let staff go during slack periods has impacts throughout the factory, some of which employ as many as 14,000 staff at any one time. Of its six suppliers in Vietnam, Adidas engages with only one factory which produces their brand almost exclusively. Other factories also produce for a range of competitors. In such cases Adidas is in a position to insist that its SOE apply to staff working on its production line but can do little to ensure that such practices are implemented throughout the factory or to ensure that workers on Adidas lines do not seek overtime on other lines. All com-panies could benefit from a more uniform and systematic approach in this field even though to do so would entail breaking down some of the traditional barriers to communication between the competing agencies.

The staff, their families and the local communities are another group where stakeholder relationships could be developed, but where currently local culture and practices mitigate against stamping out child labour. The falsification of documents is just one example of the extent to which the family and community cultures underpin child labour. Although working for an Adidas supplier is better paid and more prestigious than many of the work alternatives available, it is not necessarily the case that more engagement with these wider stakeholding groups would help to stamp out child labour. Politicisation and the development of local groups working from the bottom up in campaigning with local NGOs seems to be one way in which awareness of these issues is developing in communities. But caution is needed before assuming that a stakeholder approach would reduce child labour.

Table 3   Range of nationalities and cultures: Adidas operation in Vietnam

	Adidas	Footwear factories	Supply chain	Retailers
Owners	German	Taiwanese	• Vietnamese • Taiwanese • Chinese • Korean • European	Primarily European and North American
Managers	European	Taiwanese/Chinese		
Senior staff	European/ Vietnamese	Chinese/Vietnamese		
Workforce	Vietnamese	Vietnamese		

Cultural issues

Cultural issues also have an impact on the implementation of the SOE. It cannot be assumed that the need for effective SOE implementation is commonly understood across a diversity of cultures. Table 3 identifies the range of cultures involved in the supply chain in Adidas's operation in Vietnam. An example of some of these cultural differences is found in operation in the Taiwanese factories where the practice is to 'name and shame' workers who contravene any of the factory rules by placing signed confessions of their wrongdoings on a public noticeboard. Such practices sit very uneasily with the Vietnamese culture of 'saving face' and contravene 'western' practices of confidentiality and disciplinary procedures. As such they are but one example of the difficulties all encounter when trying to 'walk the thin line between moral absolutism and cultural relativism' (Brakel 2000).

The success or otherwise of implementing socially responsible practices relies most significantly on the organisational culture of the company driving this change. Without organisational commitment at the highest levels, implementation of sustainable approaches will be limited. At more local levels this can be demonstrated in the interrelationship between different departments within an organisation. One of the greatest challenges for the Adidas SOE team in Vietnam is the need to gain credibility and acceptance amongst their colleagues in different departments of the organisation. Attitudes towards the SOE team vary, with some viewing it as operating a 'policing' role, and others viewing it as somewhat 'tokenistic' and not to be taken as seriously as departments more apparently involved in the production process. The culture and message become further diluted when we go further down the supply chain into other organisations, employing other national cultures, and out into the community.

Gender issues

Women traditionally represent the most underpaid segment of the workforce, and it is therefore no surprise to find that, where industry is attracted to countries because of the abundance of cheap labour, a large proportion of the workforce is made up of women. In the case of the footwear industry in Vietnam, women represent virtually the entire workforce on the factory floor (95%) but are not represented at all in middle and senior management levels. This gender imbalance in terms of roles is culturally the norm within Vietnamese society, and moreover, all the Taiwanese factory owners who were interviewed were adamant that women were the best choice for this type of work because they paid more attention to detail than men, were faster and more flexible, and retained levels of concentration over long hours. Within the social and organisational structures that exist it is not unreasonable to also draw the conclusion that women, in a male-dominated society and company, are easier to manipulate and dominate and will probably be willing to work for lower wages than men.

Not only is the workforce exclusively female, but it comprises almost entirely women between the ages of 18 and 25. This is not an accident; factory policy ensures that vacancies are advertised only for women between these ages. Apart from the likelihood that they will be able to travel, have the stamina to work long hours and have fewer responsibilities in the home at that age, an added advantage to employers, as they themselves recognise, is that women who work away from home are less likely to start a family until after the age of 25. Maternity leave is not seen to be a responsibility of the factories and there are no facilities for women with babies or young children. Essentially advantage is taken of the circumstances of what is primarily a migrant workforce.

Action taken by Adidas on underage workers: the educational programme

On inspection at the Nan Kang Shoe Factory Adidas found 12 workers between the ages of 14 and 15, and 130 between the ages of 16 and 17. The company was faced with the problem of what to do about those underage workers they had identified. A pure disengagement strategy might suggest they terminate their employment or even, if future factory audits did not show an improvement, terminate the supply contract altogether. However, neither of these actions would have been in the interests of the girls and the other factory workers, i.e. in the interests of the groups the SOE were designed to protect.

In the case of 12 girls aged 15–16, none of them had completed the required number of years of education, although all were literate and numerate to some degree. The two alternatives facing them were:

1   ask the girls to leave the factory on the basis that keeping them there contravened Vietnamese law and Adidas's own SOE;

2   take responsibility for ensuring that the girls received appropriate education without loss of wages.

On the basis that all the girls had been employees of the factory for a considerable length of time, Adidas decided to implement an education programme which would offer them full-time education whilst continuing to pay a basic wage. For the other 130 workers aged 16–17, Adidas committed to introduce a part-time education programme for them, to be conducted during work time.

At the time of one author's visit to the site, the educational programme for the 14 and 15 year olds had only just begun. It was the first week of lessons, and it was possible to speak to those involved with the design and implementation of the programme as well as to the students themselves. Adidas utilised the services of a US-based NGO with a track record of audit and project implementation in the field of corporate social responsibility to conduct the audit and implement the educational programme. This relationship was only partially successful as the NGO had only had a fairly superficial briefing as to what was expected and had no responsibility for any follow through on the project. The Vietnamese manager appointed to implement the education programme had developed education programmes before, but had only tenuous links with the NGO whose US consultant had not been to the factory to meet with staff, students and Adidas representatives, or indeed with the project manager whom they had appointed. Most of the supervision of the NGO part of the programme was carried out by the Adidas labour monitor.

The lack of expertise in implementation is a real one for all companies, and bringing in the support of an NGO with more experience of such work is a sensible solution. However, the Adidas case suggests that for a partnership with an NGO to work, there needs to be very clear communication about the aims and objectives, the work to be done, and the relative responsibilities of the different partners over the course of the project. The experience also suggests that more local involvement is important; however skilled the NGO may be, it is at a considerable disadvantage located far away in the US.

The conclusions reached by Adidas, the factory management and the NGO project manager were that the full-time education would be made available for the 14 and 15 year old girls on factory premises. It was considered undesirable to send them to local schools, because it would be more difficult to monitor attendance and there was a strong feeling that rather than going to school, the girls would seek employment elsewhere whilst potentially still drawing a salary from the Nan Kang factory. After individual assessment of education levels, three classes were arranged with three teachers, one class of seven, one of three, and one of two: these classes take place simultaneously in one large room in the middle of the factory. Lessons take place in the mornings only, the intention being that afternoons are set aside for supervised homework and study. The students are provided with lunch in the factory canteen (along with all the other workers), and are supposed to return to the classroom afterwards. Lessons are developed in line with the Vietnamese state curriculum, and each student has signed an undertaking to attend them over a two-year period. Their alternative is to leave the factory. It is the responsibility of the NGO to design and implement the education programme and the responsibility of the factory management to ensure that this takes place, to pay the teachers and the project supervisors and to pay the students the average monthly wage (i.e. the basic wage but not the possible bonuses and overtime which workers might be expected to earn if they are in full-time employment). The average factory wage is about $US35 per month. About 90% of production at the Nan Kang factory is for Adidas; thus there is a strong incentive to comply with the SOE that Adidas require. Failure to comply could result in loss of orders, or, at worst, withdrawal by Adidas from the partnership. Given the relatively small number of 14 and 15 year olds (12 out of a workforce of 3,500), the effect on profits is minimal. Although exact figures are not available, the factory manger estimated that implementation of the SOE programme in total might have cost only approximately 5% of profits.

The educational programme at the factory was visited twice by one of the authors. All the students were dressed in the factory 'uniform' and were being taught in a room located on the factory floor in full view of the other workers. The room itself is spacious and well equipped, well lit and cooler and more pleasant than the factory floor outside. Discussions with the students found that most of the group were from local families and therefore able to go home each evening. At least three came from further away (30 km or more) and during the week stayed in rented accommodation locally, going home at weekends. This is not representative of the majority of workers in the local factories who apparently come from much further away in the central and northern provinces of Vietnam. However, the factory manager confirmed that at the Nan Kang factory most of the workers lived within a 20 mile radius.

Although all the students could read, none appeared to be aware of the SOE even though they were very clearly displayed on large notices in the classroom in Vietnamese, Chinese and English. Their ignorance of these would also indicate that they perhaps have only a limited understanding of why they are involved in an education programme at all. It was clear that as the students broke for lunch, they had no expectation of returning in the afternoon, but the project manager confirmed this would be put into practice – their lack of attendance on the previous days had just been 'teething problems' in the early stage of the project. All the students claimed to be pleased to have the opportunity to return to studies, although it is unlikely they would have said anything else in the circumstances. According to the Adidas labour monitor, all were somewhat sceptical as to whether or not they would be paid for studying rather than working. The view of one of the factory managers was that they were 'in Paradise'.

On the second visit only 10 of the 12 students were present, although it was not clear why there was non-attendance, or what follow-up would take place. The project coordinator understood he had responsibility for developing an attendance register. At lunchtime all the students left, and still there was no expectation they would come back for the afternoon session. A discussion with one of the factory managers, the project coordinator and members of the SOE factory team and regional SOE manager highlighted many areas of confusion with regard to the perceived roles and responsibilities of different members of the project team.

The education programme addresses a very specific situation within one factory. As such the style of implementation tends towards the paternalistic and little account is taken of the wider context. This shows how difficult it is to implement a new practice when it goes against the local and prevailing culture and historical practices. However, it does show the need to act quickly in order to address the problems of underage workers. Lack of clarity in new procedures such as the educational programme could lead to its being undermined and falling quickly into disarray. Changing culture and practices needs the will to act with clarity and decisiveness.

In the case of Adidas's education programme at the Nan Kang factory, an evaluation must consider the girls' interests themselves, rather than just the reaction of potential consumers, or even more cynically public relations and the protection of home markets. It was the girls' interests that led to the programme being implemented rather than their employment being terminated. However, it is impossible to determine their best interests without a much greater understanding of the circumstances of the individuals concerned and without discussing a range of possibilities with them. More involvement of the girls and their families in discussion of the options, such as education at a school nearer home rather than in the factory, might have been helpful. Although holding classes in the factory means that attendance and progress can be monitored, children, many of whom have been working two or three years already, are suddenly isolated from other workers and given a different status. Lessons are carried out in a room which is on the factory floor where they can be observed by many of the other workers. The possibility of stigmatisation had not been considered.

The education programme at the Nan Kang factory is time-limited to two years during which period the girls will receive full-time education and get paid the basic factory wage. It is the responsibility of the factory as part of its contract with Adidas to implement the education programme, which includes monitoring attendance and paying the girls as well as ensuring that lessons take place. Agreements between Adidas and its suppliers are renewed on an annual basis. Should the company withdraw its custom from the Nan Kang factory at any stage in the next two years, it is by no means clear what would happen to the programme. Assuming the programme continues throughout the two years, it is still as yet unclear what sort of follow-up or support will be available to the students, should any of them have consistently low attendance or fail in their education.

In one sense Adidas has pursued an involvement strategy, but in practice it is a mixed approach which errs on the side of disengagement, i.e. of addressing a specific problem methodically in order to resolve it or ultimately disengage. The educational programme seeks to solve the problem of underage labour in the short term whilst in the longer term disengaging completely from the wider issue of child labour by ensuring that no workers under the age of 18 have access to work in supplier factories in the future. The contribution which a major international company could be making towards addressing some of the more fundamental issues of child labour in Vietnam is clearly not being made by Adidas.

Discussion

In this paper we have argued that managing ethical issues in the supply chain becomes more difficult as governments and nation states have less power to regulate abuses. In their place international bodies, campaigning organisations and cross-company arrangements are developing to take action in this area. At the company level there are a range of different responses that organisations can have to managing human rights, and specifically child labour issues in the supply chain, but we have suggested that the veil of ignorance is no longer available, and indifference is also becoming untenable.

Three factors have led to compelling commercial reasons for organisations at the top of the supply chain to become involved in dealing with human rights and child labour issues further down. One is a critical mass of media interest, triggered by key foci and events such as the 1998 World Cup, which has led to an ongoing education of consumers and organisations alike. Secondly there is the improved availability of information through media such as the Internet. Mass communication technologies such as the Internet have spawned a plethora of organisations and information sites such as Sweatshop Watch (http://www.sweatshopwatch.org). Thirdly there has been the development of a burgeoning infrastructure of NGOs and civil society organisations at the local, national and international level, which reflects a more general desire by society, consumers and producers to tackle the bottom line of exploitation. These organisations are playing a bigger part in the supply chain, whether it be because of distant 'outrage' campaigns, or because of more recent efforts to develop partnerships with organisations operating in third world countries in order to provide information, auditing and implementation support. In the case study provided, the author accompanying the trip was from Save the Children, and had a wealth of local Vietnamese experience to draw on when accompanying Adidas on their visits to implement the SOE (she had been a director of Save the Children in Vietnam for several years).

However, companies clearly face real problems in adopting an involvement strategy. We have identified the alternatives of disengagement and engagement, where the former is a more targeted and focused strategy for removing child labour from the supply chain, and if this limited approach fails, by removing the organisation from activities in factories or regions where child labour takes place. The alternative of engagement requires a broader longer-term approach to addressing child labour in its context, dealing with wider cultural, gender and poverty issues, which may mean the toleration of transitional arrangements, as well as the support and building up of local capability for changing practices. The case study found that in reality, even taking a limited disengagement strategy, a company such as Adidas faces considerable hurdles in trying to hold firm to a baseline of Standards of Engagement. Although the Standards of Engagement discussed in the case were not easy to develop, the greatest challenge is faced in implementation, and the case has highlighted one example, that of providing educational support for those underage workers found in the factories, where failure or success will depend on the strength of local support and arrangements, as well as the degree of 'embeddedness' in the company culture and in that of the organisations it contracts with.

Our experience leads to two conclusions. One is that it is easier for a company to work in partnership, both with other companies using the same suppliers, and with a variety of other stakeholders. Increasingly, NGOs and other international organisations can provide valuable advice and support in the process. The second is that changing local culture and practices is tremendously difficult, and as we have shown in the case, this is complicated by the huge variety of cultures that may be involved. Working at the local level to build up local capability and support through the workforce, local management and the community is therefore of vital importance, but it requires more extensive work than many organisations are prepared to commit themselves to.

Finally, although companies are responding to child labour issues in the supply chain due to commercial pressure, they also utilise these international supply chains to reach into developing countries because they are a source of cheap labour. Will addressing these human rights issues defeat the object of reducing costs in the supply chain? Apparently not: the costs of addressing these baseline abuses such as child labour equates to just a fraction (estimated at less than 5%) of the savings made by these international sourcing practices. In the past concern has focused on the damage done to first world employment where jobs are lost and working conditions deteriorate to compete internationally. When 'zero tolerance' of child *work* as opposed to child *labour* is promoted by governments of developed countries, the danger is that this becomes a tool for protection of home markets rather than a means of addressing the underlying issues of poverty in the supplier countries. The energy being put into focusing on improving conditions worldwide can only be of benefit to us all. At the same time, a declaration of 'zero tolerance' of child labour should focus on the context in which it is being addressed, consider for whose benefit such a declaration is being made, and produce workable arrangements that can be implemented over the long term to develop sustainable rather than short-term solutions.

REFERENCES

Bairoch, P. 1996. *Globalization Myths and Realities: One Century of External Trade and Foreign Investment*. London: Routledge.

BBC 2000. 'No Sweat: Gap and Nike'. Panorama Broadcast, 15 October.

Brakel, A. 2000. 'Professionalism and Values'. *Business Ethics: A European Review*, 9: 2, 99–108.

Collier, J. 2000. 'Editorial: Globalization and Ethical Global Business'. *Business Ethics: A European Review*, 9: 2, 71–75.

Economic Intelligence Unit 2000. Country Profile: Vietnam. Junex.

Gaines, S. 1996. 'Tackling Child Labour'. *Business Ethics*, 10, 15–18.

Giddens, A. 1999. 'Globalisation'. BBC Reith Lectures.

Hartman, L., Shaw, B. and Stevenson, R. 2000. 'Human Resource Opportunities to Balance Ethics and Neoclassical Economics in Global Labor Standards'. *Business and Professional Ethics Journal*, 19: 3/4, 73–116.

King, F. and Marcus, R. 2000. *Big Business, Small Hands, Responsible Approaches to Child Labour*. London: Save the Children.

Leeson, H. 2000. Towards an Understanding of the Corporate Approach to Human Rights. University of London, Birkbeck College, unpublished PhD thesis.

Legge, K. 2000. 'The Ethical Context of HRM: the Ethical Organisation in the Boundaryless World'. In Winstanley, D. and Woodall, J. *Ethical Issues in Contemporary HRM*, 23–40, Hampshire: Macmillan.

Lloyd Roberts, S. 1998. 'Stitching Footballs in Sialkot'. Newsnight, London, BBC, 12 February.

McCurry, D. 1998. 'Soccer Balls: Inflated with Hot Air?' Campaign for Labor Rights: Action Alerts, 22 December.

Sweatshop Watch 2000. 'Summary of the Saipan Sweatshop Litigation', May 2000. http://www.sweatshopwatch.org/swatch/marianas/summary5_00.htmlx.

Part 3

Change within Organizations

In this part we move from relationships *between* organizations to action *within* organizations, exploring how managers and other participants perceive, maintain and adapt their own internal supply systems to cope with change. A dynamic environment challenges a company to face a wide range of issues in positioning and repositioning itself within the supply chains in which it participates. The potential for, and pressures behind, internal change face managements with many difficult choices which are often viewed through the filters of management and academic fashion. The lean model has been particularly influential in supply chain reorganization at the inter- and intra-chain levels. But the model's reliance on interpretations of practice in some Japanese companies at a particular phase in economic development have made it the subject of some intense controversies, some of which are reflected in this section.

In the first chapter, Pilkington (Chapter 3.1) investigates the dichotomy between the adoption of 'best practice' models, still favoured by many manufacturing managers and researchers, and the realities of the need to develop integrated business strategy, as described in the business strategy literature. He points to the succession of management fads and how each in turn tends to be regarded as a universal panacea – until the next one comes along. Using Toyota and Honda as exemplars, the author reviews the rise of Japanese lean manufacturing techniques in the west, taking a critical view of the narrowness of their implementation: 'Either deliberately or by chance, the Japanese car manufacturers from whom the majority of best practice has been acquired have followed this integrated strategy model, building capability into inherited systems predicated on a market position . . . This alignment of manufacturing with the rest of the corporate strategy has been ignored in many firms pursuing best practices – where, for example, the manufacturing manager has been rewarded for reducing costs even when the rest of the organization has been trying to compete on product differentiation.'

The second chapter, by Fucini and Fucini (Chapter 3.2), is an extract from their book *Working for the Japanese: Inside Mazda's American Auto Plant*, and continues the theme of the adoption of Japanese practices within the factory. The authors focus on how Mazda (and Osamu Nobuto, the Japanese Chief Executive, in particular) coped with setting up a Japanese transplant in the heart of America's auto-stronghold – Detroit. Using the concept of a 'third-culture' plant, they explore many non-technical, human resource issues including workforce motivation and commitment, respect, thinking style, pace, communication channels, group dynamics and the criteria for success. They emphasize that cultural differences are really those which need heightened attention in this context, requiring long term, steadfast determination for such a venture to be successful. Many workers' voices are present in both the Fucinis' and Pilkington's chapters and the authors are astute at separating out the perspectives of the various players within each organization.

Many of the same organizational issues are explored by Bamber and Dale (Chapter 3.3), whose case study highlights an aerospace company which attempts, over a five year period, to adopt the Kawasaki production system (KPS) and ultimately fails to do so. To succeed, KPS requires specific adaptation for a particular organization and the commitment of a well educated workforce. Although some of the changes implemented were successful, the two major drawbacks were the redundancy programme and the lack of worker training, partly a legacy of the previous management regime. The chapter concludes by comparing the effectiveness of lean production methods in the automotive and aerospace sectors, and suggests that they are more appropriate in the former, where they may reduce the risks of speculative production, than in the latter where most products are made to order and there is a lesser element of risk from under- or overproduction. This chapter is particularly pertinent to contemporary manufacturing, as many organizations, including some automotive manufacturers, are considering moving more towards build-to-order, demand-led production, rather than the traditional 'build-to-sell', supply-led, 'push' retail model.

Lewis (Chapter 3.4) takes another critical approach to the long term implementation of lean production, examining its relationship to sustainable competitive advantage. He develops a set of four exploratory propositions and tests them by studying three SMEs providing component sub-assemblies to automotive OEMs. His results, on the generic versus specific contexts of 'lean', on its development trajectories and on the potential for innovation in a lean manufacturing environment, all suggest that the longer term implications of lean production are worthy of further investigation.

Emiliani (Chapter 3.5) discusses ways in which buyers can support the introduction of lean production across the whole of their SME supply networks. The chapter is based on a three year (1996–8) case study of Pratt & Whitney, a gas turbine engine manufacturer with a network of more than 100 SME suppliers of machined parts located in a geographic cluster. It illustrates the importance of appreciating the strengths, weaknesses, resources and constraints of SMEs which produce management behaviours that may cause misalignments between buyer and suppliers. Pratt & Whitney was successful in developing an understanding of lean production philosophy and practice amongst these SMEs using a mix of promoting regular electronic communication on business issues, training and education. Emiliani concludes: 'buyers that behave in ways that promote trust among all stakeholders will have discovered the foundation upon which lean production is built.'

The last three chapters in this part all deal with aspects of cost within the organization. The authors take different, but equally valid and important, approaches to their research. First there is Åhlström and Karlsson's (Chapter 3.6) observation of changes in a Swedish office equipment manufacturing company in the mid 1990s. It offers a detailed, longitudinal account of the difficulties of operating traditional management accounting systems in the newly adopted environment of lean manufacturing, for which they were not intended. The focus of the study is on the total process of change to a complex, new production strategy, not on the adaptation of the management accounting system itself. The authors stress the importance of the role of the management accounting system in the change process, but consider that: 'For the most part it serves as an impediment to the necessary changes, mainly due to its inability to accurately portray the results of these changes.' For congruence between management accounting systems and a lean production strategy, they recommend changes in those systems at three interacting levels: 'technically, through their design; formally, through their role in the organization; and cognitively, through the way in which the actors think about and use [them]'. All of these are crucial perspectives to consider.

Shank and Fisher (Chapter 3.7) review target costing as a strategic tool by focusing on one product, a specific type of paper in a paper mill. This case study of a project which was unexpectedly extremely successful 'illustrates the potential of using target costing as a proactive cost-reduction tool in place of ineffective standard costing'. Moreover, a value-added analysis contrasted with a standard form of cost reporting leads the authors to conclude that target costing enables the company to deliver better value to the customer. This study finds that fundamental cost breakthroughs are possible if appropriate new types of practice are adopted.

The final chapter is linked to this theme through an introduction on how target costing can be applied to total life cycle costs. Guide et al. (Chapter 3.8) discuss the growth and potential of recoverable manufacturing systems, broadening the topic to encompass industrial ecology, sustainable development and then recoverable systems. The chapter examines the waste hierarchy and the main complicating characteristics encountered in setting up recoverable systems. The authors warn that 'any firm that wants to do business in the EU must pay attention to providing environmentally friendly products'. The recoverables industry sector, although of high value in terms of materials flows, is still uncertain and unpredictable. This chapter provides an excellent introduction to understanding the complex nature of recovery of components in a world based increasingly on total product systems. The transparency of these processes is the only characteristic certain to continue to increase, as consumers and legislators drive home their demands on organizations which will need to change to meet these new principles. The ideas put forward in this chapter are linked directly to Chapter 1.1 where total product systems are shown to encapsulate the end-of-life phases of the product in order to ensure the system is sustainable in both resource and economic terms.

The chapters in this part use rich case studies to illustrate the importance of organizational and social learning in the sustainability of total product systems. It is clear that much research is still needed to understand, and then to reduce, the as yet unassessed social costs of total product systems in many areas.

Manufacturing Strategy Regained: Evidence for the Demise of Best Practice

Alan Pilkington

While analysts of production systems have benefited from their close attention to actual practice, they have tended to urge each new approach to manufacturing management as a panacea, at least until the next new method gains status.[1] However, manufacturing managers need to consider each advocated technique in the context of their firm's overall business strategy. They have to integrate the principles of their function with business-level strategy concepts such as generic strategies[2] and core competencies.[3] Strategic approaches to manufacturing management have been missing in the models of just-in-time production,[4] lean production,[5] flexible manufacturing,[6] and total quality control.[7] The conceptual separation of manufacturing practice from general business-level models results from the appeal of best-practice routes (normally Japanese and car manufacturing in origin) as an indiscriminate source of competitive advantage for all. Yet a number of researchers have sought to integrate manufacturing as a strategic weapon into corporate strategy.[8] Moreover, topical manufacturing management approaches have been proclaimed as best practice and have been assumed by manufacturing managers to generate competitive advantage in firms,[9] irrespective of their individual corporate strategies. Some conceptual models have been devised to explore the linkages between and among manufacturing strategy, business strategy, and performance,[10] but they are stylized and general. They do not deal with the reality of specific processes or with the practical reasons why manufacturing management techniques might not assist corporate strategy.

This article explores why manufacturing managers and researchers have remained embedded in the best-practice mode despite its rejection by the general strategy literature. The development of best-practice manufacturing techniques is analyzed by deconstructing the dominant theme of the 1990s, Japanese lean production.

Central to this deconstruction is the dichotomy between the suggested best-practice strategy and the actual practices of the exemplars. Did the Japanese car manufacturers, the source of many of the techniques, themselves follow the strategy of best practice?

The Emergence of Best Practice: the Rise of Japan

By the 1980s, researchers had turned their attention to Japanese firms in the hope of identifying the key to their success. As Figure 1 shows, the rise of Japan as the world's largest maker of cars was worthy of investigation, but conclusions were based mainly on particular Japanese operating methods such as JIT and TQM. By the 1990s, analysts were questioning the rise of single techniques for manufacturing supremacy, as faltering firms discovered that individual techniques required an overlapping complex of supporting systems. For example, it is now rare to find a discussion of JIT separate from issues of TQM,[11] and Japanese HRM (human resources management) practices are now included in the simultaneous engineering model of product development.[12] The Japanese manufacturing system is now often considered under one banner with a range of titles, but most widely known as *lean production*.[13] The argument that the Japanese had a better and imitable way of manufacturing was too powerful for managers to resist. But where did these best-practice models come from and why was the strategy element lost? To consider the influence of lean production it is necessary to dissect its background and appeal.

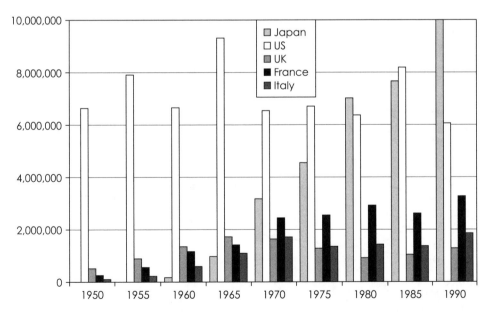

Figure 1 International car production volumes, 1950–90 (SMMT, *Motor Industry of Great Britain 1993: World Automotive Statistics*, London, 1993, p. 54)

Lean Production Exposed

The lean concept was proposed by the International Motor Vehicle Program's (IMVP) study of the world auto industry, as reported in *The Machine that Changed the World*.[14] This text was followed by others,[15] and they promoted the idea that Japanese car manufacturers had developed a new form of production – or, at least, a generic package of operating methods – that was more efficient than Henry Ford's mass-production system. As a result, lean production became the model for 1990s manufacturing, and many managers extended their existing Japanization (JIT and TQM) programs accordingly. Many manufacturing researchers accepted the lean model almost universally and extended it with the term 'mass customization'[16] and through studies in many different countries,[17] but they have done so largely without revisiting the basis of the original model.[18]

On reading the IMVP's accounts of lean production, it is clear that their system is based primarily on the operations of Toyota (previously recorded by Ohno,[19] Monden,[20] Shingo,[21] and Cusumano[22]), although it is portrayed as a generic system adopted by all Japanese firms. The focus on Japan as a manufacturing exemplar was not misplaced. However, as Figure 2 shows, the IMVP claim that the Japanese are twice as effective as American manufacturers is not entirely accurate.[23]

The performance of Japanese car manufacturers was worthy of investigation and the IMVP did reveal Toyota's production system to be significantly different from those of other players in the global market. With the exception of Honda, however,

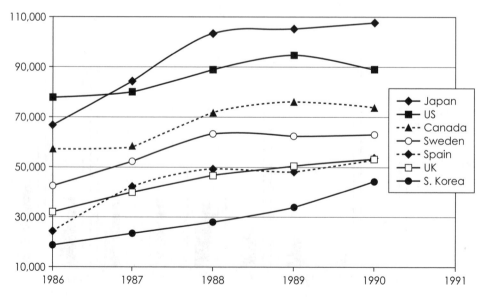

Figure 2 International value added per motor vehicle employee ($), 1986–90 (*Ward's Manufacturing Worldwide*, New York, 1996, pp. 617–18)

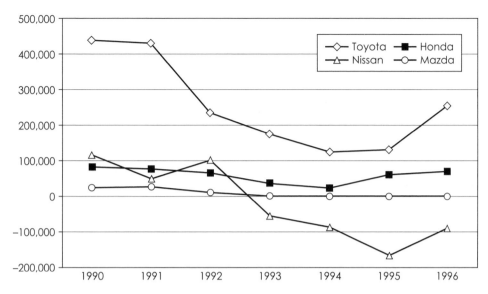

Figure 3 Net income for major Japanese car makers (million yen), 1990–6
(company reports and accounts, various years)

analysis of the remaining Japanese manufacturers shows levels of performance merely comparable to the rest of the world industry. There is also a growing amount of data that suggest that the success of the Japanese firms may have come to an end. Dwindling profits at Honda and Toyota, losses posted by Nissan, and the take-over of Mazda by Ford have raised serious questions (see Figure 3). External factors such as domestic recession and currency fluctuations have currently eliminated any advantage that even the best lean firms might have derived from their operating systems.

We need to take another look at the operating systems of individual Japanese car manufacturers to explain how Toyota and Honda differ from their competitors and how they were able to weather the economic storm more successfully. Also, if manufacturing managers are to understand how systems evolve from company specific circumstances, and if they are to appreciate their weaknesses as well as strengths, we need to understand the strategies that shaped the Toyota and Honda systems.

Manufacturing Strategy in the Japanese Car Industry

The IMVP study of Japanese operating systems aggregated data – apparently in order to protect individual firms' confidences – into a country-based analysis. When the individual systems of the Japanese firms are analyzed in more detail and in isolation from each other, it becomes clear that they are not similar at all. In Table 1, comparative measures of the operating structures of the Japanese car manufacturers reveal different strategies. Labor's share of value added is telling, as it can show how firms can minimize labor costs. Labor costs represent a large slice of the costs in car

Table 1 The manufacturing effectiveness of Japanese car manufacturers, 1990

Company	Ratio of stocks to plant and equipment	Value added/stocks	Labor's share of value added (%)
Honda	49.8	7.0	50.9
Toyota	13.5	14.1	42.2
Nissan	28.7	5.7	68.5
Mazda	13.9	8.1	64.9

Source: K. Williams, C. Haslam, S. Johal and J. Williams, *Cars: Analysis, History, Cases* (Providence, RI: Berghahn Books, 1994), pp. 18, 33, and 52

manufacturing, and so any reduction in labor content makes a significant increase in the productivity of the system. Toyota's system is highly efficient at using labor, allowing the firm great flexibility in investment and market strategies. Honda is also a leader in reducing the labor content of its vehicles, largely through investment in technology.

Toyota also has an advantage over its domestic competitors as a result of its stock levels, but the figures can be misleading, since Honda has a relatively poor value added to stocks ratio but its WIP levels are as low as Toyota's. This suggests that Honda and Toyota have very effective and efficient manufacturing systems that are able to move material through the plant at a high rate, using lower labor levels than other manufacturers in Japan and elsewhere. It is important not to dwell too long on these statistics, as perhaps researchers have in the past, but rather to examine how the operating systems of these firms function and how they have evolved.

Toyota's attention to labor reduction was first publicized by Cusumano, who described it as a waste reduction philosophy and compared it to the approach at Nissan.[24] He explained the differences by considering the relative historical performances and trajectories of each firm. Toyota's focus on waste was used across a range of products including sewing machines and prefabricated buildings, but evolved slowly from a system first used to free capital from work in progress at a time of crisis.[25] Unfinished goods were mounting up as poor deliveries caused shortages of key parts in the assembly operation. By reducing the level of stocks in the production process, and assembling each product in a batch of one, Toyota was able to identify the shortages and prevent the assembly of unfinished vehicles. The just-in-time system then moved on to the removal of labor from the production system. Its development is covered in great detail by Shingo[26] and in particular by Ohno,[27] one of its original engineers.

Apart from designing a system with low levels of labor costs, the heart of making the Toyota system work is the *kanban* – a system that links one production operation to the next, matching the production of parts closely to the demand established in the final assembly area. In essence, the Toyota system takes orders from customers (but only those which fit a predetermined plan) and then responds rapidly by assembling the car to the specification demanded. The level of vertical disintegration and a focus on removing labor costs from vehicle manufacture means that Toyota's suppliers also have to respond to changes in customer demands. The use of a highly tiered supply network that relies on many small family firms beyond the main suppliers helps Toyota insulate itself from labor costs. The costs associated with flexibility are much lower in the third and fourth tier suppliers than at Toyota itself. As a result, Toyota produces cars cheaply and carries very low levels of stocks, which move rapidly out to the customer. Nissan is perhaps the only other firm to follow the general lean model, but its attempt at introducing Toyota's JIT at a time of financial instability was not a total success and it has not been able to match the labor levels of its rival.[28] It has consequently been badly affected by the recent decline in the Japanese economy.

Honda similarly aspires to manufacturing efficiency and waste reduction targets, but the driving force behind its operations strategy is to support the quality of engineering design. Honda's founder, Soichiro Honda, was primarily an engineer who firmly believed that customer satisfaction was derived from the engineering excellence of his products. These were originally motorcycles, but he eventually moved into the more lucrative car market. This was despite resistance from the post-war MITI (Ministry of International Trade and Industry (Japan)), which sought to protect the existing players in the market from competition.[29] Honda's production systems, used for both motorcycles and cars, seek to minimize variations in the manufacturing process in an attempt to ensure that the vehicle meets the design specifications. The manufacturing strategy is to produce vehicles in large batches, not the batch-of-one/JIT approach favored by Toyota. Repetition is seen as the key to producing vehicles that conform to the engineering specifications. With such a strategy comes a focus on product specification simplification and stable production schedules that evolve slowly over a long period of time. This is quite unlike the rapid response of the Toyota system, but it shares some JIT techniques (notably the *kanban* system) to ensure the smooth running of the final assembly operation and the close links to component manufacturing areas and suppliers. Honda production lines often resemble those of Toyota, but they are supported by more raw material stocks and a planning system that is fixed up to six months in advance of manufacture. Honda has a relatively weak standing in its home market but has gained valuable sales overseas because of its ability to design and manufacture engines able to meet increasingly stringent emissions regulations, particularly in the United States.

It was Honda's engine technology and access to its manufacturing facilities and associated operating systems that the UK's Rover Group sought during the 1980s. Rover, which has been studied from many angles as a case of industrial decline,[30] proves to be an interesting case in the failure of 'Japanization'. Despite a decade of working closely with a world leader, Rover only achieved a stay of execution through the 1980s and early 1990s, and it was finally sold by its cash-starved parent BAe to BMW in 1994. Through Honda, Rover had access to what was believed to be one of the key exponents of lean manufacturing. If the Japanization theme were to be validated, Rover with its direct links to Honda should have successfully adopted the lessons of the Japanese experience. Why Rover was unable to revitalize its fortunes can only be explained by considering the original capabilities and context of the firm.[31]

The pressures of its downward financial performance, the spiraling decline of engineering resources, and a reliance on the highly competitive UK market during a period of economic recession were the key reasons for Rover's demise.[32] Apart from being restricted by its own capabilities, Rover had another barrier to learning from Honda: its failure to consider fully the strategy implications of its chosen manufacturing route. Rover's sales strategy was to target niche sections of the UK car market with distinctive and high-appeal vehicles, but Honda's manufacturing systems were not like the market-responsive Toyota-based lean model of Japanese production. Nonetheless, Rover did have access to Honda's highly efficient systems, yet the efficiency and conformity of Honda's own systems were sacrificed to meet the needs of the ailing UK manufacturer, struggling in a recession-bound, competitive market. Market conditions also squeezed the funding of new models, making its sale by BAe inevitable.

Mazda's production systems are perhaps closer to those of Toyota than Honda, but not because of any similarities in the firm or strategy. Mazda's goal was to take advantage of products that appeal to niches in the market, and its policies resulted from its small size relative to its competitors in the Japanese market and from a greater reliance on export markets. The standard approach to production-line design, as adopted at most car manufacturers, is for a facility to be dedicated to making one model. If the complexity of the process is increased to accommodate more than one model, then the risks involved and the complexity of managing such a facility lead to reduced efficiency. During the 1980s, Mazda developed production lines that could build fifteen models using the same facilities, believing that the reduced efficiency would be overcome by a reduction in break-even volume and higher-value products. The approach was based on the Toyota batch-of-one/JIT system, but expanded with the addition of labor-intensive operations to provide batch-of-one manufacture from any of the fifteen different models.[33] However, the strategy was only an engineering and manufacturing success as Mazda's commercial position continued to decline. Mazda now concentrates more on efficiency in its assembly systems, in keeping with the development of common models with its new owner, Ford.

More differences in the operating and manufacturing strategies of Japanese firms can be found in transplant factories. For example, the UK operations of Toyota vary from those in Japan, as do its other foreign operations and its joint venture with General Motors, NUMMI (New United Motor Manufacturing, Inc). The IMVP study itself indicated that NUMMI's productivity did not match the Takaoka plant because of the structure of the supply network. Similarly the Nissan plants in the US and UK look less like their lean parent plants in Japan and more like the simple final assembly plants that any overseas firm would establish in a new market.

In what is perhaps one of the most influential articles echoing and advancing the manufacturing strategy concept in the post-lean era, Hayes and Pisano argue that manufacturing's most valuable weapon is not imitation, but the flexibility that enables firms to achieve long-term strategic goals.[34] It was this process that led to the emergence of the Japanese car manufacturers as global players, as each one evolved different practices to achieve their own strategies, in turn determined by their own particular situation. When this idea is applied to the lean model, and the individual strategies of the Japanese car manufacturers are examined, it becomes clear they did not follow a single strategy, but each had their own approach, not all of them with the same levels of success.

The Japanese companies that have proved more resilient to their domestic recession have systems that are tailored specifically to support the business-level strategy of the firm. Toyota occupies a dominant position in the market and sells in large volumes – hence cost and production efficiency is the strategy that its production systems support. Honda has its historically derived engineering focus underpinning its rigid brand of leanness, while Mazda's low-volume, export-led, niche-market products led it to a discredited mixed-model-based production strategy. Nissan lost its leading position to Toyota, but, in seeking to imitate its great rival, it deviated from the IMVP pattern and compromised its efforts by integrating the approach into pre-existing practices. The Japanese themselves have not followed the best-practice approach, but rather adopted the capability and contingency-based strategy concepts of aligning production systems to corporate strategy.

How Successful Was Japanization?

If the best-practice strategy in manufacturing had been possible, we would have seen the significant adoption of Japanese operating models in western firms. Evidence on international manufacturing suggests that the Japanization theme has led to a degree of restructuring. Figure 4 compares the evolution of US and UK manufacturing industry and the automotive sectors during the Japanization era. The data use census information on the pattern and distribution of stocks to identify any changes as a result of Japanization. The work in progress (WIP) data show how the levels of in-process stock in the manufacturing operations have altered, and how there has been a steady reduction of WIP in automobile manufacturing operations, but with little overall change to the total manufacturing activities of both countries. This is despite the additional pressures from global recession. The success of Japanization in the car industry is to be expected, because market instability placed a premium on stock reduction techniques, and the arrival of transplant operations multiplied the number of firms assembling vehicles from subcontracted parts. However, car manufacturing firms, with a few notable exceptions in the US, have not returned to profitability.

Figure 5 shows the level of finished goods to all stocks, an indicator of whether manufacturing stocks have been entirely removed or merely pushed to another part of the chain. These data illustrate the penalty of the advances in WIP reduction, most evidently in the UK car industry where there has been a marked growth in the level of finished products as the stock is squeezed from one part of the supply chain downstream into the sales network. In the UK in 1973, the combined values of raw materials and WIP were twice that of finished goods (£623m to £240m), but in 1990 the situation is reversed (£1,353m to £2,526m). The lean model has much to

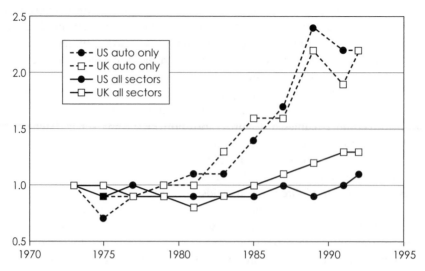

Figure 4   Value added to work in progress in automobile sector and all sectors, US and UK 1973–92, indexed ot 1973 (*US Survey of Manufactures, UK Census of Production*, various years). Indexing overcomes differences between the US and the UK in value-added calculations, automobile sector makeup, and government statistical classifications

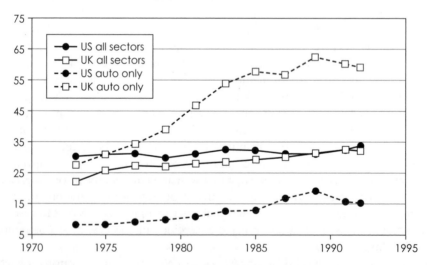

Figure 5   Finished goods as a percentage of all stocks in automobile sector and all sectors, US and UK 1973–92 (*US Survey of Manufactures, UK Census of Production*, various years)

say concerning the management of suppliers and the adoption of JIT, but many of the messages concerning finished products, order management, and customer delivery appear to have been diluted along the way as manufacturing managers picked the best practices while their sales departments persevered with existing systems.

In the UK car industry, traditional build-to-order systems have been severely tested by the move to lean production. The market was the scene of increasingly competitive practices that have forced a move towards sales-from-stock policies as a means of implementing aggressive strategies. This has not been so marked in the case of the US car industry where the market has traditionally been one where most vehicles are sold from stocks that have always been carefully managed.

Japanization has resulted in reduced stock levels as firms were persuaded to introduce JIT and supplier management programs. However, the overall result has been a shifting of liabilities from manufacturing and supply towards the sales networks. The firms that have been the most successful in reducing manufacturing stocks have experienced the largest increase in finished product stocks. The firms have pursued the Japanization theme without fully appreciating the strategy of those who developed it, and as a result many have gained little advantage for their efforts. The adoption of best practice may appeal to firms as a way of catching up with competitors, but competitors are continually advancing in production techniques. In some cases, the best-practice strategy can worsen a firm's situation as it selects practices unsuited to its operating environment. This ultimately was the position of Rover, where the Honda systems failed to deliver expected performance levels and even prevented the firm from pursuing its sales-led recovery.

The Re-emergence of Manufacturing Strategy

The Japanization story has shown that a best-practice strategy is unlikely ever to provide transformations in organizational performance, as the general strategy literature has been aware for some time with its development of contingency and competency models. Closer examination of manufacturing management theory, and its obsession with lean production, supports the case for integrating manufacturing and business-level strategy. Either deliberately or by chance, the Japanese car manufacturers from whom the majority of best practice has been acquired have followed this integrated strategy model, building capability into inherited systems predicated on a market position. This building of capabilities is a time-consuming and delicate process, as illustrated by the difficulties encountered by Mazda. This alignment of manufacturing with the rest of the corporate strategy has been ignored in many firms pursuing best practices – where, for example, the manufacturing manager has been rewarded for reducing costs even when the rest of the organization has been trying to compete on product differentiation.

The evidence presented tells us that the notion of lean production as a well-defined approach universally adopted throughout the Japanese car industry is inaccurate. There may be some factors that all Japanese firms have as a result of their national situation (for example, HRM policies and the tiered supply network), but these factors have been used to establish production systems that have radically different aims and procedures. The variations in business strategy and manufacturing philosophies of the Japanese car manufacturers reflect the impact of differing market forces on the companies – in particular, volume of sales, past experience, and the different capabilities of organizations. As the business-level strategy literature has been stressing for some time, competitive success comes from a strategy that challenges the norms and aligns all the business units into a common purpose. Merely trying to catch up, as the Japanization and best-practice strategies recommend, is insufficient in the long term.

Will chief executives become wary of the claims of manufacturing managers declaring that the adoption of best-practice production systems can reduce costs and generate competitive advantage? The attractiveness of system imitation and the need for quick results often prevents their integration with strategic considerations.

NOTES

1   S. Wheelwright and H. Bowen, 'The Challenge of Manufacturing Advantage', *Production and Operations Management*, 5/1 (1996): 59–77.
2   M.E. Porter, *Competitive Strategy* (New York, NY: Free Press, 1980).
3   C. Prahalad and G. Hamel, 'The Core Competence of the Corporation', *Harvard Business Review*, 68/3 (May/June 1990): 79–91.
4   R. Schonberger, *Japanese Manufacturing Techniques: Nine Hidden Lessons in Simplicity* (London: Collier Macmillan, 1982).
5   J. Womack, D. Jones, and D. Roos, *The Machine That Changed the World* (London: Macmillan, 1990).
6   J. Goldhar and M. Jelinek, 'Plan for Economies of Scope', *Harvard Business Review*, 61/6 (1983): 141–8; J. Meredith, 'The Strategic Advantages of the Factory of the Future', *California Management Review*, 29/3 (Spring 1987): 27–41.
7   R. Hall, *Attaining Manufacturing Excellence* (Homewood, IL: Dow Jones-Irwin, 1987).
8   W. Skinner, 'Manufacturing: Missing Link in Corporate Strategy', *Harvard Business Review*, 47/3 (May/June 1969): 136–45; T. Hill, *Manufacturing Strategy: The Strategic Management of the Manufacturing Function* (Basingstoke: Macmillan, 1985); E. Buffa, *Meeting the Competitive Challenge* (Homewood, IL: Dow-Jones Irwin, 1984); S.C. Cohen and J. Zysman, 'Why Manufacturing Matters: The Myth of the Post Industrial Economy', *California Management Review*, 29/3 (Spring 1987): 9–26; R. Hayes and S. Wheelwright, *Restoring Our Competitive Edge: Competing Through Manufacturing* (New York, NY: Wiley, 1984).
9   W. Skinner, 'Three Yards and a Cloud of Dust: Industrial Management at Century End', *Production and Operations Management*, 5/1 (1996): 15–24.
10 S. Kotha and D. Orne, 'Generic Manufacturing Strategies: A Conceptual Synthesis', *Strategic Management Journal*, 10/3 (1989): 211–31; P.L. Nemetz and L.W. Fry, 'Flexible Manufacturing Organizations: Implications for Strategy Formulation and Organization Design', *Academy of Management Review*, 13/4 (1988): 627–38; R. Parthasary and S. Sethi, 'The Impact of Flexible Automation on Business Strategy and Organizational Structure', *Academy of Management Review*, 17/1 (1992): 86–111; P. Ward, D. Bickford, and G. Leong, 'Configurations of Manufacturing Strategy, Business Strategy, Environment and Structure', *Journal of Management*, 22/4 (1996): 597–626.
11 S. Goyal and S. Deshmukh, 'A Critique of the Literature on Just-in-Time Manufacturing', *International Journal of Operations and Production Technology*, 12/1 (1992): 18–28; S. Smith, D. Tranfield, M. Foster, and S. Whittle, 'Strategies for Managing the TQ Agenda', *International Journal of Operations and Production Technology*, 14/1 (1994): 75–88.
12 C. Voss and G. Winch, 'Including Engineering in Operations Strategy', *Production and Operations Management*, 5/1 (1996): 78–91.

13 J. Krafcik, 'The Triumph of Lean Production', *Sloan Management Review*, 30/1 (1988): 41–52.

14 Womack et al., op. cit.

15 K. Clark and T. Fujimoto, *Product Development Performance* (Boston, MA: Harvard Business School Press, 1991); R. Lamming, *Beyond Partnership: Strategies for Lean Supply* (London: Prentice Hall, 1993).

16 S. Kotha, 'Mass Customization: Implementing the Emerging Paradigm for Competitive Advantage', *Strategic Management Journal*, 16 (1995): 21–43.

17 R. Kaplinsky, *Easternisation: The Spread of Japanese Management Techniques to Developing Countries* (Ilford: Frank Cass, 1995).

18 R. Delbridge and N. Oliver, 'Narrowing the Gap? Stock Turns in the Japanese and Western Car Industries', *International Journal of Production Research*, 29/10 (1991): 2083–95.

19 T. Ohno, *Toyota Production System: Beyond Large-Scale Production* (Cambridge, MA: Productivity Press, 1978).

20 Y. Monden, *Toyota Production System: Practical Approach Production Management* (Norcross, GA: Industrial Engineering and Management Press, 1983).

21 S. Shingo, *A Study of the Toyota Production System from an Engineering Viewpoint* (Cambridge, MA: Productivity Press, 1989).

22 M.A. Cusumano, *The Japanese Automobile Industry: Technology and Management at Nissan and Toyota* (Cambridge, MA: Harvard University Press, 1985).

23 K. Williams, C. Haslam, J. Williams, A. Cutler, A. Adcroft, and S. Johal, 'Against Lean Production', *Economy and Society*, 21/3 (1992): 321–53.

24 Cusumano, op. cit.

25 Ohno, op. cit.

26 Shingo, op. cit.

27 Ohno, op. cit.

28 G. Vasilash, 'Discovering Japan', *Production*, 103/1 (January 1991): 39–50.

29 T. Sakia, *Honda Motor: The Men, The Management, The Machines* (Tokyo: Kodansha International, 1984).

30 G. Robson, *The Rover Story: A Century of Success* (Cambridge: Stevens, 1984); R. Whipp and P. Clark, *Innovation and the Auto Industry: Product, Process and Work Organization* (London: Pinter, 1986); P. Dunnett, *The Decline of the British Motor Industry: The Effects of Government Policy, 1945–1979* (London: Croom Helm, 1980); K. Williams, J. Williams, and C. Haslam, *The Breakdown of Austin Rover: A Case-Study in the Failure of Business Strategy and Industrial Policy* (Leamington Spa: Berg, 1987); R. Church, *The Rise and Decline of the British Motor Industry* (Cambridge: Cambridge University Press, 1994); J. Wood, *Wheels of Misfortune: The Rise and Fall of the British Motor Industry* (London: Sidgwick & Jackson, 1988).

31 A. Pilkington, *Transforming Rover: Renewal Against the Odds, 1981–1994* (Bristol: Bristol Academic Press, 1996).

32 A. Pilkington, 'Learning from Joint Venture: The Rover–Honda Relationship', *Business History*, 38/1 (1996): 90–114.

33 A. Pilkington, 'Japanese Production Strategies and Competitive Success: Mazda's Quiet Revolution?', *Journal of Far Eastern Business*, 1/4 (1995): 15–35.

34 R. Hayes and G. Pisano, 'Beyond World-Class: The New Manufacturing Strategy', *Harvard Business Review*, 72/1 (January/February 1994): 77–86.

A Third-Culture Plant

J. J. Fucini and S. Fucini

Not long before the Mazda groundbreaking ceremony in 1985, Osamu Nobuto settled into a house on Grosse Ile, an island enclave of comfortable homes in the Detroit River about 15 miles south of Detroit city and 5 miles east of Flat Rock, that once served as a summer getaway for the pioneer princes of the automobile industry. Harry Bennett, the thuggish director of Henry Ford's security department and chief orchestrator of the Battle of the Overpass ambush, maintained a boathouse for his yacht on the island. The boathouse was said to have a secret escape tunnel below it and machine gun emplacements built into its upper walls, testaments to Bennett's underworld connections. 'Big Bill' Knudsen, the Danish immigrant who, as Ford's chief production engineer, oversaw the construction of the company's early assembly lines, and a man who would later leave Ford to become president of General Motors, purchased a large farm on the island's west side in 1917. The Fisher brothers, famous makers of vehicle chassis for General Motors, also built summer mansions on the island, as did Ransom E. Olds, the Lansing, Michigan, machine shop owner who founded Oldsmobile.

By 1985 Grosse Ile's legendary automotive estates had long been abandoned, turned into country clubs or divided into condominiums and apartments, but most of the island's homes, including Nobuto's, were impressive nevertheless. Nobuto's home was a handsome single-story pale yellow structure set back far off the road behind a large and carefully manicured lawn. Its spacious backyard bordered the Detroit River, affording a pleasant view of the wooded Canadian shoreline on the other side. In the summer of 1985, Nobuto would host barbecue picnics in the backyard for local high school students and community leaders as a gesture of neighborly goodwill. Ever mindful of the suspicion with which many in Detroit still regarded Japanese automakers, Mazda was eager to prove that the company and its executives could be good neighbors in America's Motor City. As a step toward this end, the company sponsored an exchange program for local high school students to study in Japan. It also presented the city of Flat Rock with two Mazda 626 automobiles (made in Japan) to use as police cars; donated $30,000 to the restoration of a local historical landmark – a building that once served as a stagecoach stop

– and promised to donate $100,000 annually to the city's general fund for ten years to make up for some of the revenue that would be lost as a result of the 100 percent tax abatement. 'We are very much aware of the diligent effort made by you and the entire Flat Rock City Council in providing an economic package that allowed us to choose Flat Rock as our plant location,' Nobuto wrote to Ted Anders when informing the mayor of Mazda's gifts to the city. 'We are honored by the faith you have placed in Mazda in taking such a courageous step. We will work hard to maintain your trust.'[1]

As the president of a major automaking venture, Nobuto was inevitably drawn into the fraternity of Detroit-area auto executives. This seemed to suit his forthright personal style. He joined many of the same professional associations as the city's other auto executives, participated in the same conferences and seminars, dealt with the same local suppliers, traveled in the same social circles, and negotiated with the same labor union. Yet, despite his successful assimilation, Nobuto would in many ways remain a world apart philosophically from his counterparts at American auto companies. Having come of age in postwar Japan, he had been trained to view the business of building cars from a perspective that differed sharply from that of Detroit's other auto executives. This philosophical difference was so fundamental that it was even evident in the very dissimilar ways in which Nobuto and his typical American counterpart went about evaluating the performance of an automobile plant.

The American manager, having been raised in a bottom-line environment, tended to look primarily or even exclusively at end results when assessing a plant's performance. How many cars was the plant producing a month? What was the defect rate? As long as he received satisfactory answers to these questions, the American manager considered a plant a success. Little effort was made by the American to evaluate how cars were being built or to look for steps that might be taken to improve a plant's production process and increase productivity. Such an evaluation would have been regarded as tampering with success by the American manager whose plant was meeting its production quota. 'If it ain't broke, don't fix it,' was an adage that had special meaning for American auto executives of Nobuto's age. Even if an American plant was plagued by a high defect rate, the American manager still preferred to attack the problem on the product rather than on the process level. Was every sixth car coming off the line with a crooked bumper? The American would send them to the redo shop to have the bumpers straightened. This took less time than stopping the assembly line to find the root cause of the problem, and in the short run at least, it allowed the plant to continue meeting its production quota, which made the manager look good to his superiors. The goal of the American manager was to keep cars rolling off the assembly line with no interruptions. Changes, even those that could improve the production process, were regarded as inherently disruptive and therefore undesirable.

Nobuto and other Japanese managers had been taught to evaluate their plants from a more-long-range 'process-engineering' perspective. Although they, too, were concerned with end results – the number of cars produced and the rate of defects – their primary focus was on the production process itself. No Japanese manager would consider his plant successful, regardless of how many vehicles it produced a month, if the process by which those cars were made was mistake prone or inefficient. The emphasis of the fluid and mutable process over the static and unchanging product made Japanese managers like Nobuto more adaptable than their American counterparts.

Even if a Japanese plant was succeeding in meeting its production quota, its manager would still continue to study the production process, looking for new ways to weed out inefficiencies, so that the same output could be achieved in less time or with fewer workers. The Japanese called this process of constantly seeking improvement *kaizen*. It was practiced with almost religious fervor at Mazda plants in Japan, where managers and workers seemed always to be holding meetings to discuss plans for 'kaizening' (i.e. improving) some part of the production process. Any *kaizen* suggestion that could shave one hundredth of a minute (0.6 seconds) off the time needed to assemble a car was said to be worthy of consideration. One *kaizen* suggestion would naturally beget others, since an improvement that hastened the work flow in one area of the plant put pressure on workers in the next area to catch up. If, for example, the workers who welded support pillars to cars devised a *kaizen* plan that allowed them to complete their welding ten seconds faster, the workers down the line who were responsible for grinding the welds smooth would have to come up with a way to take ten seconds off their job cycles to avoid backlogs.

When Nobuto and other Mazda managers spotted a defective vehicle coming off the assembly line, they were less concerned with correcting it – though correct it they did – than with finding the cause of the problem and developing a *kaizen* plan to prevent it from occurring again. They did not believe that quality control could be achieved by final product inspections. Such inspections would only show the results of a problem that had already occurred. As disciples of process engineering, Mazda managers were certain that if they exercised tight-enough control over the production process, the quality of their finished product and the efficiency of their operation would naturally follow.

The products that would be made at the Flat Rock plant managed by Nobuto were the Mazda MX-6 and the Ford Probe.[2] The latter was slated to be sold through the dealer network of America's number two automaker. Both cars would be built on the well-proven chassis of Mazda's popular 626 automobile, but each would have its own distinctive outer skin and interior cabin features. Both cars would be moderately priced, but the MX-6 would be slightly more expensive. A small but solid two-door coupé, it would have the alert, upright appearance of a German performance car. The Probe, a glassy, low-slung hatchback, would be sleeker and somewhat less serious in its styling. Ford was hoping that the Probe would win over some of the young middle-class consumers who had been buying sporty Japanese imports like the Toyota Celica. More than half the Probe's customers were expected to be women. Because Ford possessed much greater marketing strength than did Mazda in the United States, the two companies had agreed that 60 percent of all vehicles made at Flat Rock would be Probes. Later, after it became apparent that the demand for the Probe was exceeding all expectations, Ford's share of the plant's output would be increased, at times reaching as high as 70 percent.

The process of turning metal, plastic, and rubber into Probes and MX-6s would involve four basic steps. It would begin in Flat Rock's stamping shop, where large, thunderous presses would stamp out doors, roofs, bumpers, quarter panels, and almost one hundred other parts, cookie-cutter fashion, from coils of sheet steel. The stamped metal panels would then be transported to the body shop, where they would be welded to structural support beams shipped in from outside suppliers to form complete car bodies. More than 4,000 different welds would be performed on each vehicle, 84 percent of them made by gangly long-armed robots sent to Flat Rock from Japan. From the body shop, vehicle bodies would travel by monorail to the paint shop, where they would be dunked like doughnuts into a 350-ton tank of primer and then painted by multiple-axis robots and automated paint machines, each capable of applying 25 different colors of paint as well as sealers and undercoats.

After cars had been painted and dried in ovens, they would be taken by overhead conveyor to the trim and final assembly area. This would be the most labor-intensive shop in the Flat Rock plant, employing about one-third of its work force. Workers in 'trim and final' would perform jobs too minute or too delicate to be done economically by robots. They would drill in the engines; bolt on the tires; screw in the mirrors; and install the door handles, radios, ashtrays, and other components that go into making a finished automobile. These parts would be delivered to workers from a materials-handling department and a plastics-molding shop, both of which would border the trim and final area, as well as from several smaller subassembly stations located within trim and final itself. Of all the production areas at Flat Rock, trim and final would most resemble the archetypal image of an auto factory, with workers standing alongside a moving assembly line, performing routinized tasks with mind-numbing repetitiousness.

When Mazda's Flat Rock plant reached its full two-shift production schedule in 1989, about 45 Probes and 25 MX-6s would roll off its assembly line every hour – a rate of almost 1.2 one-ton vehicles a minute, 14 to 17 hours a day.

This output would be achieved with a work force of 3,500, fewer than 3,100 of them involved in actual production, the rest assigned to supervisory and administrative tasks. This would be a remarkable rate of efficiency by American standards. The General Motors Fairfax, Kansas, plant, a facility of roughly the same age and scope as Flat Rock, would require a work force of almost 4,100, roughly 3,800 of them involved in production, to build a little more than 65 Pontiac Grand Prix's an hour.[3] Part of Flat Rock's superior productivity would be due to the advanced technology employed at the plant; most would be the result of a management system brought to Flat Rock by Nobuto and the four hundred Mazda dispatches sent to Michigan from Japan.[4]

The system was a creation of the Toyota Motor Corporation, which introduced it in the early 1960s and quickly saw it adopted and expanded on by other Japanese manufacturers. Toyota itself had borrowed some ideas from American efficiency experts W. Edward Deming and Joseph M. Juran, but the system was really a natural outgrowth of the Japanese dedication to process engineering. It is a system built on the constant improvement and refinement of the production process; a 'kaizening' that strips away layer after layer of redundant manpower, material, and motions until a plant is left with the barest minimum of resources needed to satisfy its production requirements. The system tolerates no waste. It leaves virtually no room for errors.

The system is called *just in time* (JIT), a term that describes its formula for scheduling deliveries of parts and supplies to a plant. A more appropriate name would be 'just enough resources', because the system seeks to leave every plant with just enough – and *only* just enough – human and material resources to keep its production process going. A perfect JIT plant (none has ever existed) would be one at which the difference between the amount of resources *available* to meet a production quota and the amount *required* to meet the quota is zero. Such a plant would be perfectly 'balanced', according to JIT theory. All backup resources that push a plant over this balanced zero equation are considered waste or, in Japanese, *muda*. Under the JIT system no reserve inventory of parts and supplies is allowed to cover for disruptions in delivery schedules. The materials necessary for building cars are delivered to a JIT plant on what is almost an as-needed basis, usually shipped to the plant from outside suppliers several times a day in quantities large enough to last for three or four hours of production. No backup pool of workers is available to draw on when illness, injury, or vacations remove employees from the JIT work force. Nor is a JIT plant permitted to maintain a work force large enough to meet its labor demands during peak production periods. Under most of these circumstances, temporary employees are brought in to bring the work force up to the required level. A plant with a work force that included permanent employees who were not truly needed 100 percent of the time would be considered wasteful by JIT standards.

Time is another resource that is controlled carefully under the JIT system. No cushion of spare time is built into the production schedule of a JIT plant to account for human error and inefficiencies. Every step of the production process is clearly studied and kaizened to ensure the smoothest flow of work and materials and the most productive use of every worker's time. As Bill Judson, the newly appointed president of Flat Rock's UAW Local 3000, observed when he visited the Hofu JIT plant in 1986, Mazda has eliminated virtually all waiting time and wasted steps from the work routines of its hourly production employees. The workers Judson saw at Hofu were actively engaged in a production activity close to 60 seconds every minute. At the non-JIT American auto plants he was familiar with, workers maintained a 40- to 50-second-a-minute work pace, filling in the rest of their time waiting – waiting for a tool to turn up or for the next car to come down the assembly line. The 10- to 20-second-a-minute difference would not have given Hofu a significant productivity advantage had it applied to only a handful of workers. But when even a 10-second-a-minute differential is applied to a plant with 2,000 workers, the productivity gain will add up to 2,667 extra worker-hours over the course of an 8-hour shift, and 13,335 extra worker-hours over a five-day week. Assuming that every employee at the plant works a 40-hour week, the 10-second-a-minute productivity gain is equivalent to hiring 333 extra workers.

As Judson and other American visitors were to discover, Japanese JIT plants like Hofu (and later Flat Rock) were able to produce more cars per worker because they kept every worker productively employed more of the time.

The efficiencies created by strict control of inventory levels under JIT are often less obvious. The virtual elimination of backup inventories at a JIT plant appears at first to be less logical to many Americans than the Big Three's traditional 'just in case' strategy of maintaining a large cushion of spare parts and supplies to protect against unforeseen disruptions in delivery schedules. Deliveries from outside vendors will, after all, sometimes be delayed. The subassembly shops inside a plant that provide parts to the final assembly line (and are not allowed to build up reserve inventories of parts under a JIT system) will be slowed from time to time by absenteeism, injury, or worker error. The assembly line workers themselves, some of whom must fabricate their own parts while waiting for a car to arrive at their work stations (again with no backup parts inventory allowed), will occasionally fall behind in their work because of fatigue, boredom, or careless mistakes. With no safety net of spare parts to fall back on, the JIT plant is more vulnerable to these interruptions in the flow of work and materials. But the vulnerability that often appears to Americans to be a weakness is in fact one of a JIT plant's greatest strengths. This was true of Hofu, and everyone at Mazda believed it would be true of the Flat Rock JIT plant as well. Because interruptions in the flow of supplies are felt so severely and so suddenly, they cannot be ignored. With their entire production process thrown off balance by the supply problem, JIT managers and workers must move quickly to pinpoint the source of the delay and implement corrective action. (Their task is simplified by JIT's thinly stretched inventory levels, which leave a problem no place to hide, making it relatively easy to locate its point of origin.) Because problems occur routinely at a JIT plant, as they do at every plant, the unforgiving bare-bones inventory assures that attention will constantly be focused on the production process.

The removal of spare parts cushions provides a JIT plant with other, more tangible but less important advantages. It reduces the amount of capital that must be tied up in inventory, it reduces the amount of space that must be given over to in-plant warehouse facilities, and it reduces the paperwork and labor costs associated with stocking and maintaining large inventories of parts and materials.

Although individual American plants would make attempts to implement JIT systems in the early and mid 1980s, JIT was not compatible with the traditional product-engineering orientation of most American managers. Focusing as they did on end results, the Americans viewed a large spare parts inventory as essential to meeting their production quotas. Americans valued the security of knowing that simply by reaching into their vast reserves of extra workers and materials, they could overwhelm any glitches in the flow of supplies – at least in the short run – and continue to show the same results (a consistent output) despite inefficiencies in their production process. If the cushion of extra materials and manpower was large enough – and it usually was – the inefficiencies in an American plant could be carried along for years before they became impossible to ignore.

As a JIT plant, Flat Rock would have little space given over to warehouse facilities. The absence of backup inventories would make this unnecessary. Where Detroit's other American-owned automobile plants kept enough supplies on hand to cover several days or even weeks of uninterrupted production, Mazda would maintain less than a single shift's worth of inventory for most parts.

The number of workers at Flat Rock would also be kept low in accordance with JIT precepts. Mazda's production work force of 3,100 would be 500 to 1,000 workers smaller than the production work forces of comparable American stamping and assembly plants. Mazda would not expand its permanent work force during peak production periods only to lay off excess employees during slowdowns, as American plants did. Nor would it carry a cushion of extra employees to cover for worker vacations, absences, or injuries. When extra workers were needed temporarily to fill out the plant's work force, Mazda would be able to summon them from its support member pool (SMP), a group of American workers trained by Mazda, but not on the company's permanent payroll, who were available for short-term assignments.

Like workers at every Japanese-owned auto plant throughout the world, workers at Flat Rock would be organized into teams. Each Mazda team would consist of six to ten workers (or team members) and a team leader, who, like the workers under him or her, would be an hourly employee and a member of the UAW. The media has often presented a glowing image of the Japanese team plant as a place where workers and managers pull together in a spirit of mutual trust and respect as they pursue a common objective. Such shop floor fraternalism is, in fact, a key feature of the Japanese team system, but the organization of hourly employees into teams of cross-trained workers serves another, more practical function, allowing management to maintain a smaller work force by providing it with a readily available means of filling jobs vacated by absent workers without having to hire additional employees.

Mazda, for example, organizes teams around specific work areas: one team will be made up of workers who install different engine components, another of workers who apply different sealants and coatings to the underside of vehicles. The job of each team member is different, yet all jobs within a team share many common features. This makes it simple for Mazda to train team members to perform one another's jobs. With team members cross-trained, Mazda is able to move them freely from job to job within the team (or within similar teams) to fill in for injured, sick, or vacationing workers.

At Detroit's American-owned plants, management was not able to transfer workers freely to different job assignments. The traditional plant's UAW contract did not allow management this flexibility. But the 1984 'letter of intent' between the UAW and Mazda had exempted Flat Rock from traditional job classifications and work rules. Mazda was not only free to shuffle workers to different assignments within the team, it would have the power to transfer them to entirely different areas of the plant. A worker from trim and final assembly could be moved to the paint shop or body shop if the situation warranted such a move, just as could be done at Hofu.

Nobuto, and every other Mazda executive associated with the company's United States venture, knew that Flat Rock would need a dedicated effort from its American work force if the plant was to become a successful JIT operation. For all their great strengths, all JIT plants have the same Achilles' heel: they are easily derailed by a work force that offers anything less than a 100 percent commitment. Because a JIT plant cannot draw on backup inventories, any worker who does not complete his or her job cycle on time interrupts the flow of parts and supplies, throwing off the entire production process. If the subassembly shop worker making gas tanks slows his work pace or persistently makes careless mistakes, the main production line will soon be held up for a lack of tanks. If a materials handling worker dawdles when loading trim on his or her supply cart, or loads the wrong color of trim, the entire trim and final assembly shop will become logjammed. The fact that the standard work pace in a JIT plant approaches 60 seconds a minute makes it difficult for all but the most committed workers to complete job cycles on time. The relatively small size of a JIT plant's work force also increases its dependence on the dedication of workers. With fewer workers available at a JIT plant, the absence of each employee is felt more sorely. A JIT plant like Flat Rock thus requires employees who have the commitment necessary to show up for work when they have a headache, the flu, or a minor family crisis; employees who are willing to work through minor aches and pains; and employees who will take on added work to cover for absent team members without complaining. Steve Ross, the millwright who was among the first Americans hired by Mazda, recalled that during the question-and-answer segment of his orientation session on health benefits, one of the new hirees asked the Mazda trainer about the number of sick days allowed to Flat Rock workers. The trainer, an American, chuckled in amusement: 'You're not supposed to get sick here.'[5]

In Japan, with its strong hierarchical tradition and group orientation, assembling a work force with this level of loyalty and dedication had never been a problem for Mazda or any other manufacturer. Japanese culture, with its emphasis on self-sacrifice, respect for authority and social cooperation had, in fact, provided fertile ground for the development of a management system that required workers to commit themselves so completely to job and company. But the United States, with its strong social currents of self-gratification, individualism, and competitiveness, is in many respects the cultural opposite of Japan.

As Nobuto and Mazda's other Japanese dispatches drew up their plans for the company's United States plant, it was widely assumed that the biggest challenge they would face at Flat Rock would be to persuade the company's independent-minded American employees to accept the sacrifices imposed by JIT. The men of Mazda knew that to do this they would have to instill a sense of common purpose in their Flat Rock employees, encouraging the Americans to identify with the company and see themselves as part of a larger Mazda team. If the Americans came to regard the Flat Rock plant as their own, they would have more at stake emotionally in its success. Mazda advisors would explain to the Americans that the only way to ensure the success of the plant – their plant – in a competitive world market would be to implement the more efficient JIT system at Flat Rock.

To encourage workers to identify with Mazda, the company would go out of its way to cultivate an image of itself as a concerned, humanistic employer. In their talks to newly hired workers and in their many interviews with the Detroit media, Nobuto and other Mazda managers made frequent allusions to the company's lifetime employment policy in Japan (job security being presented as a tangible payback for JIT sacrifices). They discussed the company's commitment to providing employees with a safe, comfortable workplace, describing the ergonomic features that would be incorporated into the design of the new Flat Rock plant. They also pointed to the ongoing training programs that would be implemented at Flat Rock, and the Employee Fitness Center that was being built next to the plant, as examples of Mazda's interest in the development of the worker as a 'whole person'. 'People are people before they are assemblers, welders or managers,' Mazda's chief executive, Kenichi Yamamoto, said. 'Mazda does not take this philosophy lightly.'[6]

Mazda hoped to reinforce the sense of unity and common purpose at Flat Rock by exporting egalitarian team symbols from the company's Japanese plants to Michigan. These symbols were expected to help break down the barriers that historically had divided unionized American workers from their managers. The most conspicuous symbol was the blue-and-khaki Mazda uniform that would be worn by everyone at Flat Rock, from Nobuto to the newest hiree. Everyone at Flat Rock would also do calisthenics together in the morning and eat lunch together in a common cafeteria at noon. After work, managers would take workers to Fiorelli's, a local pizza parlor, for pizza and beer and some informal shop talk. There would also be more structured settings for worker–manager dialogue. If the worker had a problem, an idea, or a complaint, management's door would always be open at Flat Rock. The accessibility of Mazda management during the plant's start-up phase would surprise Forrest Green, a newly hired tool and die maker who had spent 16 years working at Ford. In the entire period he was at Ford, Green had rarely talked to a member of management other than his immediate supervisor. Most of the managers he encountered wore suits and ties and had an aloof, disdainful attitude toward workers. 'The few times I dealt with a plant manager, it was, "Yes sir, no sir", and that was it,' he recalled.

> One time, the Deuce [Henry Ford II] came to the plant for a tour, and they sent us all to the cafeteria for lunch before he walked in, so nobody would be there to bother him. At Mazda it was not like that at all – the Japanese were very down to earth. Nobuto would walk into the cafeteria and plop his butt down wherever there was a spot. He sat at my table a couple of times. We [the Americans at the table] were kind of nervous, but he was real easygoing and nice. We talked about baseball and golf and food. I got the impression that he was real sincere about not being high-handed with the workers. You'd hear stories about him, like the time some Ford people were going to visit the plant and someone told him he should wear a suit and tie, but he balked and said, 'No, I'm at work, so I'll wear my uniform.' You wouldn't get that at Ford when I was there.

The emphasis that Mazda placed on openness and communication would be reflected in the design of the Flat Rock plant itself. The four major shops at Flat Rock (stamping, body, paint, and trim and final assembly) would be located around a central administration area and computer control room. This 'four corner zone' layout, borrowed from Hofu, placed managers quite literally in the 'middle of the action', increasing their contact with the shop floor and making them more accessible to workers. At American plants, by contrast, administrative offices were located in front of the manufacturing area, separated from the noise and heat of the factory floor by a long and not-too-frequently traversed corridor.

The central administration area at Mazda's Hofu plant was an open office. Desks were stacked head-to-head in the style of a school lunchroom, with no dividers between them. The openness was supposed to encourage an even greater spirit of teamwork among the managers themselves. Mazda wanted to follow this open office design at Flat Rock, but its American managers, accustomed to a different sense of privacy, balked at the idea. The Americans wanted to have enclosed offices, or at the very least, shoulder-high partitions cubbyholing individual desks. As a compromise, Mazda agreed to put small dividers between the desks, which it still insisted on stacking head-to-head. The dividers would be high enough to afford some privacy when a manager was hunched over writing, but low enough to be talked over without craning one's neck. They would not impede open communication.

The modification of Hofu's open office design was only one of the ways in which Mazda would have to adjust its group-oriented management system to accommodate the more individualistic Americans. At Hofu the company maintained a Mazda infirmary for the treatment of workers, a discount supermarket on the factory premises, and worker dormitories. But Mazda could not even consider adding these amenities to the Flat Rock plant, since the Americans, who tended to be suspicious of an employer involving itself too deeply in the personal lives of workers, would have regarded this as paternalism. Even though Mazda would have a high degree of flexibility at Flat Rock by American standards, the company would still have to operate under more, and stricter, work rules than it did in Japan. The UAW, though it had agreed to relinquish most of its protective work rules and job classifications, was still an independent union. Unlike Mazda's company union in Japan, it had some teeth to bare when standing up to the company. Mazda had come to this realization at a couple of points during their negotiations with the American union. The company had wanted to make participation in its morning calisthenics program mandatory, but the union had rejected this, insisting that the exercises be voluntary. 'We didn't think it was right to tell workers they had to exercise,' said Bill Judson. 'The exercises were a good idea, but we felt it was something the workers should decide for themselves.'

The distinction between mandatory and voluntary, between instructions that were explicit and implicit, was something that Mazda's Japanese executives would have to learn to appreciate in America. In Japan, with its homogeneous population and close-knit groups, there is no real difference between 'should do' and 'must do' when a manager makes a request of an employee. Where an American worker would tend to regard the decision to participate in voluntary morning calisthenics, or take on a voluntary job assignment, as a matter of choice, the Japanese worker would consider it a matter of duty. Refusing the call to volunteer would be taken as a sign of the worker's disrespect toward management, a gravely serious offense in hierarchical Japan.

Nobuto recognized that Mazda would have to adjust its management style at Flat Rock, particularly the way in which it communicated instructions to workers, if it were to avoid misunderstandings with its American employees. 'My understanding is that in America there is a wide range of the way of thinking,' he had observed.

Compared to that, for Japanese, the range of thinking is rather narrow. Relatively speaking, in Japan you may find less things to be clearly written, clearly defined in writing, maybe partly because in Japan people work in the same place for many years, perhaps lifelong, you know. In Japan there is an expression, *a-un-no-kokyu*, unspoken understanding. Literally, it means even without explanations they can understand each other. That, however, is kind of ambiguous [for Americans]. That ambiguity can [cause] a problem [communicating with American workers]. But by clarifying, clearly defining, we can avoid such ambiguity.[7]

Nobuto and Mazda's other dispatches hoped to create what they called a 'third culture' at Flat Rock, one that shaped Japanese JIT and team concepts to the American temperament, without significantly altering the meaning of those management principles. Pouring Japanese clay into an American mold is how their objective could be viewed. The third-culture plant would be American in its external appearance, but its basic substance would always be Japanese.

Mazda's original group of four hundred Japanese dispatches would be responsible for training American hirees in the company's JIT-team system. Every American manager at Flat Rock would have his or her own Japanese advisor, a dispatch who would work side by side with the American to instruct him or her in Mazda's management methods. Every group of two to four teams (called a unit at Flat Rock) would have a Japanese trainer who would watch over new hirees until they became familiar with the daily factory routine, and answer questions that were not covered during their earlier ten-week orientation and training session. As the Americans learned their lessons, the Japanese would begin to leave. By September 1988, one year after Flat Rock began to make cars, only a few more than two hundred would be left. The Japanese said that they would eventually be turning over control of Flat Rock to the Americans. This would be the only way to have a true third culture at the plant. It was intimated that Nobuto would be stepping down as president in 1990 to be replaced by an American.

Denny Pawley was the man expected to succeed him. Pawley was the highest-ranking American at Flat Rock, joining Mazda in January 1986, before construction of the plant had been completed, as the vice president of manufacturing. At the time, he was one of a small minority of American plant managers with hands-on experience running a Japanese-style team plant. He had come to Mazda from General Motors, where he was manager of the Pontiac (Michigan) Fiero plant, which made the two-seat Fiero sports car. Opened in 1982, the Fiero plant began operations at a time when GM was groping for new ideas that could reverse the declining market share and quality problems that had plagued the company for almost a decade. The plant was regarded as an experiment by the world's largest automaker, in terms of both its product – a specialty car constructed of fiberglass – and its production process – it was one of the first team plants in America. Borrowing heavily from the ideas of its Japanese competitors, GM organized Fiero workers into teams of ten to twelve. Each team elected its own 'coordinator' and each was responsible for meeting its own production schedule and operating budget, performing its own safety inspections and housekeeping functions, and coordinating its own training program. GM also did away with all quality control inspections and time studies at the plant, allowing the workers to be responsible for the quality and productivity of their own operation. Every week, the plant was shut down for 30 minutes to allow workers to hold problem-solving meetings. 'Basically, we tried to pass responsibility for running each small piece of the operation down as low in the organization as we could,' said Pawley. 'It was very close to what you'll find at a Japanese plant. We worked closely with Doctor [W. Edward] Deming for over a year, and I read extensively about Japanese management systems.'

Pawley's familiarity with Japanese management methods attracted Mazda to him. It also attracted him to the idea of working for the Japanese automaker. Born in rural Waterford Township, 20 miles northwest of the city of Pontiac, he had been with GM for 21 years at the time he was contacted by a Mazda headhunter. He had begun his automotive career with some reluctance. His father, a plant layout engineer, his uncles, and, it seemed, just about every able-bodied adult male in his family, had spent their entire lives working for the Pontiac division of General Motors. He was determined to avoid a similar fate. After graduating from high school in 1959, he enrolled in Oakland University, becoming a member of the new suburban Detroit school's charter class. Two years later, he dropped out of school to get married, still vowing to stay away from the local car factory. 'I told myself, "I'm not going into that damn plant,"' he later recalled. 'So I went to work in the circulation department of the *Oakland Press* [the local newspaper] for three years and almost starved to death. Finally, I bit the bullet and talked to GM about a job.' Pawley began at GM as a cost and budget analyst, became a line foreman, and then gradually worked his way up the plant hierarchy – to general foreman, training director, department superintendent, general superintendent, production manager of the Fiero plant in 1982, and plant manager in 1984. Along the way he completed his college education, attending night classes at Oakland University and earning a degree in human resource development in 1982. By the time Pawley was offered the Mazda job, he was ready for a new challenge.

> Looking around me, I could see that if I stayed at GM for another ten or fifteen years, it would be just more of the same. I would move from this plant to that plant, but there would be no chance to do anything really new. Mazda was offering me a small increase in salary, but it wasn't the money that interested me, it was the opportunity to work with the Japanese. After studying the Japanese system at Fiero, I thought it would be something to really work with the Japanese, and learn from the true experts in the [automobile] business, so when the Mazda offer came, I jumped . . . The people at GM tried to convince me to stay, telling me what a big mistake I was making and saying I had this great career going for me, but I wanted the experience.[8]

Temperamentally, Pawley seemed ideally suited to a plant that emphasized open communication between management and labor. Stocky and confident, with meat-hook arms and a jaw that still looks square and strong, though the flesh around it has begun to sag with weight and age, he has a blunt, let's-not-stand-on-pretense style that is appreciated by American blue-collar workers. He did not talk down to workers and never pulled any punches. He said what was on his mind, looking you straight in the eye, and expected his workers to do the same. He was 'Denny', not 'Dennis', everywhere, not just on the shop floor like some managers who tried to affect a one-of-the-guys image. The basic Mazda work uniform suited him perfectly; a tie looked out of place hanging from his tree-trunk neck. 'When you first meet Denny you really like him and think he's a real have-a-beer-with-the-guys type of manager,' said Forrest Green, the tool and die maker. 'Then after you see him for awhile, you find out that you were right – Denny is very genuine.'

During Flat Rock's critical start-up phase, Pawley became almost a father figure for the plant's younger workers, most of whom had never worked in an auto plant before. He encouraged them as they struggled to adapt to the factory routine, trying to take what he called 'the fear' out of operating high-powered equipment on a rapidly moving assembly line. He told workers stories from his GM days, like the one about how foremen would walk through a GM plant with shirt pockets stuffed full of grievance slips that had been filed against them by workers. The foremen wore their bulgy pockets like badges of honor to prove that they were not soft, and to show the workers who was boss. It would be different at Flat Rock, Denny told the workers. He was taking almost personal responsibility for that.

'The big thick contracts you've got in your UAW [plants] across the country are there because management proved . . . they couldn't be trusted with general language,' he told the *Detroit News*. 'If five years from now we have a very traditional type of operating agreement in here, it won't be the UAW's fault, it'd be mine. Because I will have proved that they can't trust me and then they'll say, "OK, Denny, we tried it and you wouldn't do it, now here's some rules we're gonna live by." '[9]

Like Nobuto, Pawley believed that the Flat Rock plant would have to develop a third culture that combined elements of Japanese and American thinking. He was certain that the Japanese had developed a better way to build cars, with their emphasis on the production process and their organization of workers into teams. He agreed that Americans should learn to take a longer-range view of the production process, rather than charging head-on to deal with problems only on the results level. But the Americans' take-charge tradition would never allow them to be as patient as the Japanese. Sometimes direct action *was* the best response to a production problem, in Pawley's view. He was fond of recalling an incident that occurred at Pontiac in the late 1970s, when a car had slipped off the assembly line into the work pit below. Pawley, then a line supervisor, had calculated that the cost of stopping the line to save the car by easing it out of the pit was greater than the value of the car itself, so he called for a forklift operator to impale the car and move it out of the way. The car was demolished, but the line was hardly disrupted. Some workers at the plant could not believe that their supervisor was destroying a newly assembled car, but to Pawley there was no logical alternative.

Pawley had no doubts that American managers and workers could learn to cooperate with one another in a team system. The workers especially seemed to be crying out for a system that would give them some input into the making of plant decisions. But he doubted that an American team could ever be as serenely harmonious as Japanese teams, because Americans seemed to be much more independent. Nor did he believe that American workers, who had what he called a 'hit him square between the eyes' style of communicating, would ever adjust to the subtle, indirect style of Japanese managers.

These differences could only be accommodated, believed Pawley, if Flat Rock became a third-culture plant, one that was headed by an American, who could communicate with its American work force. He was convinced that Mazda would turn over control of the plant to American managers within three or four years. 'Every American here expects that,' he told the *Detroit News*. 'By then we will have illustrated our patience to learn the Japanese system and they damn well better let us implement it. I see no reason why they wouldn't. That's the reason they came here. They want the American mind as well as the American effort.'[10]

NOTES

1   Letter from Osamu Nobuto to Mayor Ted Anders, 3 June 1985.
2   In the fall of 1989, the plant would begin making a third model, the Mazda 626.
3   The comparison figures are from Gerry Kobe, 'Capital Performance! Mazda Flat Rock versus GM Fairfax: Does a Billion Bucks Mean Better Efficiency?', *Automotive Industries*, June 1988, p. 56.
4   'Dispatches' were Japanese managers seconded from Mazda's Japanese plants. Their role included team (and other) training and troubleshooting when production difficulties were encountered.
5   Hourly employees at Flat Rock were not given a specified number of 'sick days' to take at their own discretion over the course of a year. Workers received 60 percent of their base pay for 'excused absences' (that is, absences approved by management), which generally required a doctor's note.
6   Dale Thomas, 'The End of One Era; The Beginning of a New One,' *Mellus Newspapers*, 5 June 1985, section A, p. 3.
7   Ric Bohy, 'The Third Culture', *Detroit News*, 20 December 1987, section A, p. 17.
8   Telephone interview with the authors conducted on 21 April 1988.
9   Ric Bohy, 'The Third Culture', p. 17.
10   Ibid., p. 16.

3.3

Lean Production: A Study of Application in a Traditional Manufacturing Environment

L. Bamber and B. G. Dale

Introduction

. . .

In the early 1990s, the aerospace company who are the focus of this study initiated a lean approach to production using the Kawasaki production system (KPS). One of the key tenets of lean production is that its tools and techniques must be tailored to the individual organization. Kawasaki Heavy Industries are a Japanese conglomerate with interests in the aerospace sector and have employed the lean production philosophy to develop KPS, specifically for the aerospace environment; PriceWaterhouse are licensed to implement KPS (Butlin 1989). The host company decided to implement KPS because it offered the best fit with its own business and manufacturing processes; the implementation had full board-level sponsorship and support. Three consultants from Price Waterhouse were on site for most of the project duration and a senior manager from the host company was seconded full time to the team to facilitate knowledge transfer.

The purpose of this study was to evaluate the effects of this initiative on one of its products; the product in question was of low volume and high complexity. The research study was undertaken over a 5-year period. The primary research methods were semi-structured interviews with employees from all levels of the organizational hierarchy coupled with personal observations by one of the researchers during his employment at the plant. Secondary data were collected from study of relevant plant records and minutes of meetings.

The company, at the start of the study, employed some 1,200 people across various manufacturing processes, e.g. machining, painting, metal treatment, printed circuit board manufacture and population, and final product assembly. The manufacturing support functions included production engineering, production planning and purchasing. All the design and other non-manufacturing functions are located at a sister site. At the time of the KPS implementation the company was facing up to a new commercial situation. For example, its biggest customer, the UK Ministry of Defence, was drastically reducing its expenditure on weapons systems and new customers had to be found. Adding to these pressures, other leading Western defence contractors also faced falling expenditure in their home markets and were looking for export opportunities. This change in the global arms market conditions was a direct result of the ending of the cold war and the subsequent peace dividend. In response to these competitive pressures a number of US defence contractors had merged to form huge corporations with the resources to compete globally. European companies were responding to these pressures by forming mergers and joint ventures across Europe. Whilst discussing mergers with European defence contractors, the company came to realize that their manufacturing performance was below those of other companies in the industry and that action had to be taken to improve operational efficiency.

The company, in terms of Tracy and Wiersema's (1993) value disciplines, was seen as strong in product leadership, but lagging its competitors in operational efficiency and customer intimacy. It can design new and innovative products but cannot manufacture them efficiently. Various studies carried out by the company revealed that it had to make substantial improvements in operational efficiency if it was to become a world class manufacturer, as defined by Dale and Lascelles (1997). The company operated in a 'cost-plus' pricing environment (i.e. the cost of manufacturing a product was determined and a margin was then added to determine the price); consequently there was little incentive to drive down costs, resulting in low standards of manufacturing innovation and poor economic performance. A theory X management approach to employees, as typically described by Drucker (1955), Rose (1975), and Morgan (1989), also pervaded the site. In addition, none of the usual tools and techniques employed in lean production was used. Another key feature of lean manufacture is constant change and experimentation, whereas in the three decades preceding the adoption of the KPS there had been little change of any significance in this company.

Management Approach

Perrow (1972) summarizes the characteristics of the theory X approach to management using four main categories. These are mapped onto the charateristics displayed by the host company in Table 1.

The prevailing management view at the beginning of the KPS implementation was that the average worker has limited ability. This was reflected in the centralization of authority, extensive division of labour, separation of staff and line employees, and

Table 1 Examples of management characteristics

Theory X characteristics	Example of this characteristic at the host company
Centralized authority	The factory was organized along functional lines, apart from the 'projects' department. The functional organization was found to be ineffective and a 'projects' department was set up to pull the products through the system.
Clear lines of authority	The only means of communication and issue resolution was upward. For cross-functional issues, employees would usually go to their supervisor who, in turn, would consult his departmental head who would speak to other departmental heads, as appropriate.
Marked division of labour	There was a clear division of activity in relation to conception and execution. This is encapsulated in the following quote from a storeman: 'If you wear an overall here, they think you're stupid'.
Clear separation of staff and line	Until more recent times there had been a separate staff canteen to which employees had to be invited. Some toilet facilities still had 'Staff Only' signs.

splitting of the conception and execution tasks. Each department operated as a 'black box' where its own internal workings were kept secret and no explanation and justification were given, and any challenges were rebuffed with what Drucker (1955) terms 'esoteric wisdom'. It was clear that management did not expect line workers to think; this was the responsibility of the thinking departments (e.g. quality was the responsibility of the Quality Department and improving work methods was that of Industrial Engineering). Working practices and procedure were essentially dictated by these two departments. Even shop-floor supervisors were not expected to improve manufacturing procedures and processes. Any changes which they wished to make had to be done through the Quality and Industrial Engineering Departments. The approach to process improvement for people outside these two departments was at best unstructured, and it was difficult to get employees with the relevant expertise and power to make decisions. This division of work activities resulted in a ratio of direct to indirect workers of 1:2. The following comments reflect this situation:

If you wear an overall they think you are stupid. (storeman)

What do I think? I'm not paid to think. You tell me what to do and I will do it. Now go away. (shop-floor worker when asked what he thought about a suggested improvement)

They cannot do it, they are not up to it. (comment from the head of Industrial Engineering when it was suggested that supervisors carried out some of the tasks performed by industrial engineers)

The example below illustrates this separation of activities between staff and line processes.

A change to the batching rules in the cable assembly area was suggested by an operator. In the current procedure, wires were cut to length in large batches to minimize the set-up time per unit, and the wires which were not for immediate use were placed in the stores. When the next batch was needed, the pick list would go to the stores, and the wires were picked and sent to the production line. The stores manager agreed with the suggestion made by the operator as it would save his people having to put the wires away, update the computer system, cycle count and pick the wires when they were needed. The line supervisor supported the suggestion because it was less effective to have operators make out the 'paying-in' paperwork, and walk to and from the stores (the store was 500 m away from the wire cutting machine), than it was to set up the machine. The production planning manager was also in positive support of the suggested change because it meant one less part for which to schedule a number, check the availability, and create the necessary production paperwork.

The industrial engineer was responsible for determining batch sizes, and this change had to be agreed by him. He was unhappy with the proposed change because the standard cost of pre-cut wire would increase (this excluded the walking, making out of paperwork, etc.) and the machine utilization and efficiency would not be balanced between the pre-cutting area and the harness assembly.

In response to this line of objection, the supervisor argued that producing smaller batches would not present a problem because the machine was under-utilized and had excess capacity. However, the industrial engineer was unmoved by the arguments of the people who actually did the job. The industrial engineer had a disincentive to implement changes suggested by other people as it was his job to be the 'brains' of the organization and, like any rational individual, he was guarding his own position.

Employee Attitudes

Lean production requires a change in attitudes and behaviour not only by managers but also by employees. Managers must consider employees as being intelligent and willing and, in turn, the latter must respond by demonstrating initiative and commitment. The employees of the company have for many years turned up for work and waited to be told what to do and when to carry out the tasks. Under lean production, these same employees are required to look for potential problems, to seek out and eliminate waste, and to take responsibility for continuous improvement, quality assurance and maintenance.

In the implementation of KPS, the implications of continuous improvement on de-manning were not openly discussed with employees by management. For example, a union representative confronted a senior manager by asking about lifetime employment in the 'any questions' section of a 'communication meeting'. The response from the plant manager was: 'I would love to be able to discuss and offer lifetime employment, but I can't.' Indeed, not only were the de-manning implications of continual improvement not discussed, but during the implementation of KPS whole-sale redundancies were announced, approximately every 6 months. The cumulative effect of this was to take the workforce from 1,200 at the start of the implementation to a current figure of less than 300. Much of this was due to a downturn in the markets in which the company operated. The reality of a rolling redundancy pro-gramme meant that every employee had to go into his or her line manager's office every 6 months to be told whether or not they were to be made redundant. The low level of the order book and the announcement of these redundancies resulted in a considerable weakening of trade union power. However, the strength of feeling of the workforce was such that the union was able to organize that all employees walked out of the plant for a day in protest at the scale of redundancies. According to Dale et al. (1997), one of the greatest causes of failure with continuous improve-ment activities was the threat of redundancy and it was not surprising that, in this environment, the implementation of lean production practices floundered.

Other organizational changes, e.g. team working and problem-solving method-ologies, which are a necessary feature of lean production, were put in place and driven by the Price Waterhouse consultants, but as soon as they left this activity faded away.

In summary, continuous improvement did not become a way of life in the factory and there was no change in mindset of the majority of employees.

Education and Training

Two training courses were used to promote the techniques of lean production. One, based on the assembly of a plug, was used to demonstrate the principles of the pull system. In the exercise the assembly system was organized along lean production lines and demonstrated that as output increased, inventory decreased. The second course featured the use of simple tools and techniques, e.g. control charts and cause and effect diagrams; its aim was to provide people with the means of identifying and resolving problems. A large number of management and staff employees took these courses, but surprisingly they were not opened up to line workers.

Neither course attempted to teach the underlying principles of lean production, and the lack of involvement of line workers meant there was little commitment to the lean production concept. For example, stock was not seen as an absolute evil and people did not seek to eliminate it from the production process; indeed, the underlying principle was 'if in doubt, get it in'. The lack of understanding and education was evident even amongst senior managers, as demonstrated in the four examples below:

- The logistics manager decided on overtime for a number of his staff to ensure that all the requisite materials needed for production were obtained, irrespective of when they were required. This was so he could not be blamed for 'stopping' the line. The production planners were told by this manager, 'I will not discipline you for bringing parts and sub-assemblies in early'.

- The head of the Master Scheduling Department wanted the bill of materials to be decoupled to allow for 'strategic' stockbuilding.
- One production supervisor insisted on irregular *kanban* pulls and, on a particular weekend, six products were manufactured, whereas the normal 'drumbeat' of production was two products every two and a half days.
- The quality director did not believe in JIT: 'We had JIT 10 years ago, but the storemen had nothing to do and we had to set up a purchasing team to get materials in and give them something to do.'

It also proved difficult to break away from the traditional output-related performance and labour utilization measures; the hours taken to build a product were considered as the main performance measures for line supervisors. Under lean production, the emphasis is to encourage workers to make improvements to meet targets which may not be directly related to output and are less immediate, a typical key performance indicator for supervisors being the number of suggestions generated in their area. This change in the performance measurement system was not made.

Organizational Changes

The PriceWaterhouse consultants came to the company with the assumption that the average worker could perform many of the tasks currently undertaken by specialist professionals from the Quality, Industrial Engineering and Production Planning Departments. Whenever it was suggested by company management that shop-floor workers were not capable of performing tasks currently performed by specialists, this was challenged. This new attitude towards employees came to be the dominant mood in the factory.

As part of the KPS philosophy new organizational structures were put in place, based on the assumption that all employees are willing and able to improve efficiency. Authority was decentralized and pushed downwards; the division of labour was reduced and the distinction between staff and line eliminated. This had a dramatic impact on the number of vertical and horizontal organizational functions, and on relationships between functions, in particular through the introduction of link-pin structures, rather than the traditionally rigid organizational hierarchies. As a consequence, the functions needed within the factory were reorganized and whole functions were eliminated or reduced. These changes not only made the feedback loops quicker by reducing the problems of inter-departmental communication and inter-departmental politics, they also reduced costs by making the factory leaner. Prior to the introduction of KPS, there were up to eight layers of management between the operations manager and the shop-floor. As part of the move to KPS, the management structure was delayered and reduced to three levels; between the operations director and the shop-floor there is now only a head of manufacturing, a group leader and a team leader. As a direct result of this, the ratio of directs to indirects in the factory changed from 1:2 to 1:1.

The changes meant that tasks previously performed by staff could be transferred to line workers. For example, a reduction in quality inspectors through the introduction of 'product certification' (i.e. operators were trained to check and certify their own work) meant that line workers were made responsible for quality. However, little attempt was made to train operators to be responsible for machine maintenance and for ordering of parts. Another example of change was in the Projects Department. The factory had been organized by function (e.g. machining, mechanical assembly and electrical assembly). Production planning and control mirrored this organization with machine shop planners and assembly planners, and the task of the Projects Department was to pull the products through this matrix organization. As part of KPS the factory shop-floor was organized into dedicated product lines. This simplification meant that there was no need for the Projects Department.

New structures (e.g. continuous improvement activity groups, CIAGs, and integrated production teams, IPTs) were also established to provide a forum in which shop-floor employees and supervisors could suggest and implement improvements. Rigid hierarchies were replaced with more solution-focused and flexible hierarchies, whereby people had different reporting responsibilities depending upon the problem being addressed. For example, a production planner could be part of a defect review board team responsible for analysing and correcting defects, and he could be in an IPT responsible for a given production line.

The three major teams or 'link-pins' which were introduced – IPTs, CIAGs and defect review boards – are now described.

The IPTs are cross-functional and meet twice a day. Initially the team members reflected the existing matrix organization with members being drawn from each of the key functions; they also included a PriceWaterhouse consultant who would attend all the meetings and ensure that the team was functioning effectively. By integrating all functions in this way, the IPT had the expertise required to run the production lines on a daily basis. The IPTs have the knowledge and experience to solve any problems which may occur on a production line. All team members are located in the same office on the factory floor. The style of the IPT is open and transparent, and every member of the IPT is able to ask any other member a question. The IPT is chaired by the production manager and the members of the IPT report to him on a day-to-day basis, though nominally they are also responsible to their functional head.

The IPTs have pushed decision-making towards the shop-floor and have helped to reduce the distinction between staff and line, improving communication between the functions. It also means that any worker or supervisor only has to go to one place to discuss his problem and its resolution.

The CIAGs were formed to suggest and implement improvements in production line working methods. A CIAG comprises operators from a production line, their supervisor and a production engineer, and they meet once a week in the IPT room. Each CIAG was launched by a PriceWaterhouse management consultant and, as this consultant had a self-interest in its success, he/she was willing to drive its activities. Like IPTs, the meetings were conducted in an open environment with transparent decision-making, and any operator could make a suggestion to the production engineer and expect a response. Each CIAG has the expertise necessary to give a quick evaluation and feedback on any suggested productivity improvements. For example, the suggested improvement of pre-cut wires that had been rejected by the industrial engineer was put to the CIAG who discussed the problem and implemented the suggested solution.

Another cross-functional link-pin with the responsibility of solving product quality problems, known as defect review boards (DRBs), was introduced. Prior to this, the solution of quality problems had been the responsibility of the Quality Department. Each DRB consists of a supervisor, a production engineer and a logistics planner. If a defect occurs on the production line, the shop-floor operator makes it visible by putting the defective material or part on a table in the DRB room for examination. The key feature of the DRB is that all the people who are needed to solve a problem are present and have the means and responsibility to help the IPTs and CIAGs implement a corrective action. Like the IPTs and CIAGs, the DRB environment is open and transparent, thereby reducing the 'black box' approach to quality control.

In addition to the new organizational structures, other techniques (e.g. 'andon' or 'lights' system) were used to give shop-floor employees more power. At each workstation, push-buttons were installed that light up bulbs in the IPT office. When operators encounter a problem they stop the production line and push a button to highlight where the production line was stopped. The engineers respond to the flashing light by going to the production line to correct the problem.

All these changes have helped to facilitate an integrative and innovative approach to production.

Design for Manufacture

During its history the company has designed many innovative products and this is the main source of its competitive advantage. However, the products have not necessarily been designed for manufacture, and most are characterized by the introduction of a substantial number of design modifications whilst the product is being manufactured. For example, on one product there were about 50 modifications per week for some 6 months. This led to a 50% increase in the manpower of the production planning team to monitor what was actually being made. In addition to increased administrative overhead, the efficiency of the shop-floor was reduced. The introduction of design modifications meant that extensive rework of some materials was needed. For example, machined parts had to be remachined to change the dimensions, and assemblies had to be stripped and reassembled so that parts could be removed to be modified. The amount of time wasted in rework was so substantial that new cost collection codes were introduced to record the additional labour time. All this impacted on changes to production paperwork, operating schedules and supplier contracts.

As part of the lean production development, a design to manufacture initiative on all new products was launched with the intention to involve the manufacturing function as early as possible at the initial design stage.

Kanban

Improvement in production starts in the market place. The company is a make-to-order manufacturer, and in the short and medium term there is no need to respond to variable customer demand; in most of their contracts an agreement is reached with the customer on the delivery schedule. There is also the opportunity to negotiate delivery schedules, and if a 'drumbeat' is missed the sale is not lost as is the case in other environments. The validity of manufacturing in batch sizes of one, a key theme of lean production, is questionable in the company's environment. It can be argued that, in the environment in which the company operates, the minimum batch size should be the quantity of the customer's order, as there is no possibility of obsolete stock.

A key factor in the application of *kanban* is the setting of production drumbeats; the drumbeat is ultimately determined by the customer. To eliminate finished goods stock, the manufacturing rate should equal the market rate of demand, and to eliminate the stock of part-processed goods, the drumbeats of the different manufacturing areas should be equal.

Taking one particular product as an example of how *kanban* was applied, the delivery schedule agreed with the customer is to deliver six products a month, which equated to one product every 20 hours (based on an 8-hour working day). This means that every 20 working hours an assembled and tested product had to be completed. All the operations to be performed on this product were divided into 20-hour packages from final operations to the initial processing. By grouping work in this way, capacity workstations were balanced and it was difficult for stock to build up in the production process.

To eliminate inventory completely from the production system, the information provided by the *kanban* has to flow throughout the factory. For major sub-assemblies used in the product assembly, a number of 'infeed' or stocking areas were established. For example, one unit of each component with an attached *kanban* is held in an infeed area in the product assembly area. When the operator fits a component to a product, he pulls the unit from the infeed area, and the *kanban* is released and given to a manufacturing controller. This *kanban* is the signal for the manufacturing controller to replenish the stock that had been used.

During the introduction of KPS there was an existing project to implement an MRP II package. For many years production planning and control professionals believed that MRP II would plan the manufacture of exactly the right quantity of materials at exactly the right time (Plossl 1989). Indeed many of the company's production planning staff believed that MRP II scheduled materials into the factory 'just-in-time'. When *kanban* was implemented on low-value items through the 'two-bin' system, it was considered to be a 'discredited' reorder point system. Staff who had been with the company for some time commented that *kanban* was 'how we used to plan production' and this was the method that the more sophisticated MRP II had replaced.

The company attempted to combine MRP II and *kanban*. The former was used as the planning tool to communicate forward schedules with suppliers and the latter determined actual production. For some materials and components MRP II was also used as the control tool, as not all suppliers were willing to move to a *kanban* system. For example, an air-conditioning supplier needed 6 months lead time and had a large minimum order quantity. These units were high capital value and it was considered uneconomical to hold 6 months' worth of these units in stock.

There were limitations of *kanban* in the environment faced by the company. For example, the characteristics of the market in which the company operates are that the delivery cycle is usually greater than the production cycle; production is generally make-to-order, does not start until a contract is signed, and is not subject to unforeseen changes in customer demand. However, it was a very simple tool that the majority of employees did eventually understand, and was considerably cheaper to maintain than MRP II in terms of personnel and IT costs.

Layout

Much of the plant layout planning had been done before the decision to implement lean production. As part of the KPS implementation, the machines in the machine shop were grouped into dedicated product lines. A critical feature of cellular manufacturing is how it can respond to changes in the 'drumbeat' required by the market. The key to this is the multi-skilling of employees – the more skilled the worker, the more flexible and efficient the system (Burbidge 1963). As part of the KPS implementation, a flexibility matrix was drawn up that identified the workers, the skills needed and whether they had been trained in the required skills. There were some efforts made at cross-training workers to make them more multi-skilled. The shop-floor workers benefited from multi-skilling as it increased variety and reduced boredom. However, the redundancy programme meant that ultimately employees were reluctant to train in other people's jobs or to train other people how to do their jobs. Management did not pursue multi-skilling as there were very few significant changes in the drumbeat of production; the company was facing a substantial and permanent reduction in demand rather than 'wave-like' demand.

Suppliers

As part of the KPS programme, the company began a supplier development programme in which the first stage was to reduce the number of suppliers. The objective was to concentrate purchasing power so that the company could exert more influence on its suppliers to achieve better prices and service levels, including more frequent and defect-free deliveries.

Some of the company's suppliers had already implemented aspects of lean production and were using *kanban* information with their customers. Suppliers were required to guarantee the delivery of a component within five working days of the receipt of *kanban*. The company set up a two-bin system whereby 2 weeks' worth of stock was held in one bin and 2 weeks' of stock in a second bin, with a *kanban* positioned at the bottom of each bin. When all the stock in one bin was consumed, the *kanban* would be released to authorize the purchase of product. The *kanban* would go to the logistics planner who would fax an order or 'faxban' to the supplier who then had 1 week to deliver this product, whilst production would continue with the 2 weeks' worth of stock available in the second bin. The logistics planner hung the *kanban* on a board as a visible indicator of the deliveries which were due in the next five working days. When the order was delivered, the storeman would take the *kanban* off the board and put it with the stock.

A company can only become as lean as its suppliers, and in some high-performing companies there is a dedicated supplier development team (Lloyd et al. 1994). In this case, lack of internal expertise and credibility on lean production techniques meant that the company could not provide expertise to their suppliers. Consequently supplier development activity had a limited effect, being restricted mainly to the application of *kanban*, improved communications and some joint problem-solving activity.

Conclusions

The company needed a fundamental shift in its management approach to introduce lean production. Despite improved organizational structures, e.g. the IPTs, CIAGs and DRB, this reorientation was not possible during the widespread redundancy programme (i.e. a reduction in workforce numbers by three-quarters over a 5-year period). This was the biggest stumbling block to the adoption of lean production methods. The second biggest stumbling block was lack of employee education. For at least two decades people have been poorly managed in the company. The theory X orientation was most obviously manifested in the rigid hierarchical organizational design of the factory in which there was an extensive division of labour and central-ized decision-making in the hands of trusted employees. Unfortunately, the image of the lazy uncooperative worker is self-fulfilling and employees were seen as the cause of problems rather than the solution. There was no fundamental mind-shift and commitment to lean production, and as soon as the PriceWaterhouse consultants left, interest in the concept evaporated. The lack of education and training not only inhibited improvement within the factory, it also prevented the spread of lean pro-duction methods to suppliers. It is true to say that a company can only get as lean as its suppliers, and the company failed to properly educate its own employees, let alone its suppliers.

The elimination of waste through continual stressing of the manufacturing system demands organizational change – in particular, shorter feedback loops. The com-pany introduced many significant and useful organizational changes, in addition to delayering. However, reduced employee commitment to lean production methods due to the redundancy programme meant that these changes were not fully utilized.

However, the experience indicates that cross-functional teams are a key enabler of lean production.

Lean production is about focusing on objectives and being innovative in developing techniques that meet them. At companies such as those in automotive manufacture, it is assumed that the customer is lost if a drumbeat is not met. In the environment in which the company operates, the customer is not lost, and it was found that the best solution is to revert to a push system or to introduce false pulls. The main advantage of cellular manufacture layout is the ability to vary output effectively; this did not apply to the company's product as the drumbeat remained constant. However, this form of layout was effective in minimizing transportation and handling of product. Throughout the project, the company still favoured the trade-off between inventory holding and set-up, and were reluctant to experiment with reducing batch sizes; this reduced the impact of *kanban*.

From a technical perspective, manufacturing excellence is about choosing appropriate techniques from those available. There is an important and fundamental difference between the environment faced by the automotive manufacturing companies who have developed lean production and the aerospace industry. The former undertake make-to-forecast or 'speculative' production; the latter are usually make-to-order and undertake 'assured' production. Many of the tools developed as part of lean production, e.g. *kanban*, SMED and cellular manufacturing, were to reduce the risk of speculative production. Many aerospace companies are not exposed to the same risks, and it is concluded that many of the techniques of lean production are not as powerful in this environment as they are in the motor manufacturing environment.

REFERENCES

Burbidge, J. L., 1963, *Principles of Production Control* (London: Macdonald and Evans).

Butlin, C. 1989, Continuous improvement. *Proceedings of the BPICS Annual Conference.*

Dale, B. G., and Lascelles, D. M., 1997, Total quality management adoption: revisiting the levels. *The TQM Magazine*, 9, 418–428.

Dale, B. G., Boaden, R. J., Wilcox, M., and McQuater, R. E., 1997, Total quality management sustaining audit tool: description and use. *Total Qualiy Management*, 8, 395–408.

Drucker, P., 1955, *The Practice of Management* (Oxford: Heinemann).

Lloyd, A., Burnes, B., and Dale, B. G., 1994, Supplier development: a study in Nissan Motor Manufacturing (UK) and her suppliers. *Proceedings of the I.Mech.E.*, 208 (3D).

Morgan, G., 1989, *Creative Organisation Theory* (London: Sage Publications).

Ohno, T., 1983, *Just-in-Time for Today and Tomorrow* (Cambridge, MA: Productivity Press).

Perrow, C., 1972, *Complex Organisations* (New York: Newbury Award Records).

Plossl, G. W., 1989, You're now a class A MRP user – so what. *Production and Inventory Management Journal*, Third Quarter.

Rose, M., 1975, *Industrial Behaviour* (London: Penguin).

Shingo, S., 1981, *A Study of the Toyota Production System* (Cambridge, MA: Productivity Press).

Tracy, M., and Wiersema, F., 1993, Company characteristics and organisational performance. *Harvard Business Review*, Jan/Feb.

3.4

Lean Production and Sustainable Competitive Advantage

Michael A. Lewis

Introduction

A decade ago the lean production concept (Womack et al., 1990; Shingo, 1989) was viewed as a counter-intuitive alternative to traditional manufacturing models (Hayes, 1981; Krafcik, 1988). Today it is arguably the paradigm (Katayama and Bennett, 1996) for operations and its influence can be found in a wide range of manufacturing and service strategies (Womack and Jones, 1996). Yet despite its pre-eminence, the lean production model and the research that informed it raise a number of theoretical and methodological concerns (Williams and Haslam, 1992). Moreover, and especially problematic from a managerial perspective, there are questions surrounding its actual competitive impact (Oliver and Hunter, 1998). It is these questions that this paper seeks to address by combining a review of theory with case-derived empirical material.

This first section of the paper explores extant theory and suggests that it is necessary to separate lean production as an outcome from the organisational initiatives that are traditionally associated with it as a change process. In order to provide a platform for establishing the long-term competitive impact of the lean production model, the paper then develops a theoretical construct (centred around the resource-based view of the firm) explaining the mechanisms that underpin sustainable competitive advantage. During this largely theoretical debate, four research propositions are identified (*P1–P4*). In order to explore these propositions in some detail, three case studies were selected from a larger sample (all medium-sized auto component manufacturers making extensive use of lean production tools/techniques). The second part of the paper explores the research propositions in the light of the empirical evidence and concludes with recommendations for further critical and practical work.

Exploring Lean Production

The original International Motor Vehicle Program (IMVP) was a five-year (1985–1990) collaborative investigation (academics from various institutions funded by 36 automotive industry firms contributing to a $5 million research fund) into the performance of the global motor industry (Womack et al., 1990). The study 'revealed' the existence of a 2:1 productivity difference between car assembly plants in Japan and those in the West. The performance differential was ascribed to lean production practices that improved productivity through reduced lead times, material and staff costs, increased quality etc. These findings led to a great deal of industry 'soul searching' and perhaps inevitably further benchmarking studies, which appeared to confirm the initial IMVP results (Boston Consulting Group, 1993; IBM Consulting Group, 1993; Andersen Consulting, 1993).

Given such a backdrop, it is unsurprising that lean production practices aroused such intense interest. Enhanced productivity has universal appeal, regardless of whether it is Toyota seeking to survive the oil price shock of 1972–1973 or any Western manufacturer faced with increasingly intensive global competition. Indeed, lean production's originators, by formulating the 'operating problem' as an unceasing battle against waste (or *muda* in Japanese), were able to make it seem almost axiomatic that lean implied better. Since the original IMVP report, high-profile journal articles (Womack and Jones, 1994), another book (Womack and Jones, 1996) and annual 'Global Lean Summits' have continued the portrayal of lean production as a more or less universal set of management principles for the production of both goods and services:

> We've become convinced that the principles of lean production can be applied equally in every industry across the globe and that the conversion to lean production will have a profound effect on human society – it will truly change the world. (Womack et al., 1990, p. 7)

Reviewing the literature, however, reveals a number of concerns with the lean production model as it was initially derived. These can be summarised under three main categories:

1 Much of the interest in lean production principles was based upon the IMVP claim that Japanese manufacturers were twice as effective as their Western competitors. The measurement process (especially relating to the unit of analysis employed) has been criticised (Williams et al., 1994) and others have employed similar data to present an equally challenging but more confused picture. For instance, Table 1 shows how, at this level of aggregation, the USA was not performing as badly as the headline IMVP figures suggested. Such data might

Table 1   Value added ($) per motor vehicle employee, 1986–90 (indexed to Japan)

	1986	1987	1988	1989	1990
Japan	67,075	84,538	103,548	105,433	107,874
Sweden	42,776 (0.64)	52,413 (0.62)	63,433 (0.61)	62,723 (0.60)	63,229 (0.59)
UK	32,263 (0.48)	39,984 (0.47)	46,720 (0.45)	50,547 (0.48)	53,340 (0.50)
USA	77,787 (1.16)	80,403 (0.95)	89,034 (0.86)	94,912 (0.90)	89,219 (0.83)

Source: Pilkington, 1998

suggest, for instance, that IMVP highlighted the significance of the Toyota production system but that the remaining Japanese manufacturers exhibited 'levels of performance merely comparable to the rest of the world' (Pilkington, 1998).

2   In Europe, there has been a great deal of debate about how lean production principles will impact upon established production models, in particular those in Germany (Streeck, 1992; Culpepper, 1999) and Sweden (Sandberg, 1995). From a critical perspective, its effects upon the workforce (it often requires de-unionisation or single union agreements) have been fiercely attacked (Williams and Haslam, 1992; Garrahan and Stewart, 1992) and more managerially, the demands placed upon workers by lean systems have been highlighted as a problem with respect to ongoing staff recruitment (Cusumano, 1994).

3   Establishing the causal linkages between inputs and outcomes is notoriously difficult in any complex system. Even if one accepts that Japanese vehicle assemblers were (during the late 1980s and early 1990s) much more productive than their Western counterparts, any description of how these organisations achieved these superior outcomes must be filtered through any number of interpretative filters. For example, the predominance of Japanese exemplars raises legitimate concerns about cultural superficiality. In a similar vein, although benchmarking studies have benefited from close attention to actual practice, many have largely ignored wider economic and market conditions (Katayama and Bennett, 1996). The recent economic difficulties faced by Nissan (forced to merge with Renault), Honda and Mazda (bought by Ford) suggest that the lean production model may have reflected particular market conditions at a specific point in time.

The final point suggests that it is necessary to distinguish between lean as an outcome and the more ambiguous and uncertain process whereby an operation becomes lean. Figure 1 illustrates these twin aspects of lean production by representing them both as a transformation process.

Lean production as an outcome

This paper is concerned with the competitive impact of lean production at the level of the single firm. Within this unit of analysis, regardless of broader concerns over data

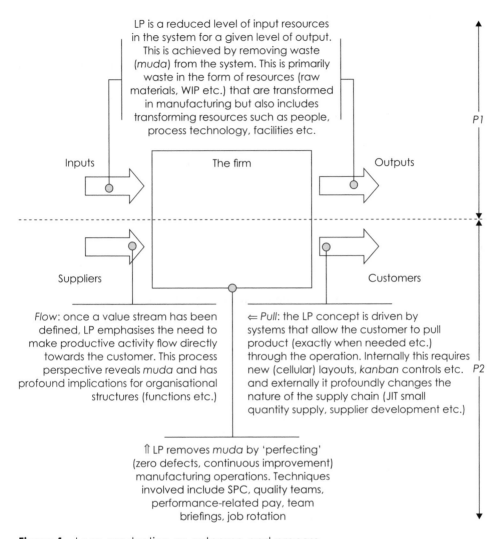

Figure 1   Lean production as outcome and process

comparability, it is self-evident that achieving similar (or higher) levels of productive activity with similar (or less) resource input is a positive outcome (not withstanding real concerns over employment conditions etc.). In our empirical investigations, therefore, it is important to look for evidence of the case companies being 'lean' and the impact that this has on their overall financial performance.

P1   If a firm has increased its overall effectiveness in converting resource inputs into outputs (measured against criteria, including in-process and finished goods inventory, delivery and quality performance, employee numbers, floor space etc.) this lowering of relative costs should result in improved overall business performance (measured by profitability or market share etc.).

This is of particular interest because recent investigations into the relationship between profitability and lean production adoption (Oliver and Hunter, 1998) found no statistical significance between high and low users except that high level users exhibited much higher volatility in profits.

Lean production as a process

The lean production model relates manufacturing performance advantage to adherence to three key principles (Womack et al., 1990; Womack and Jones, 1996):

1   improving flow of material and information across business functions;
2   an emphasis on customer pull rather than organisation push (enabled on the shop floor with *kanban*);
3   a commitment to continuous improvement enabled by people development.

As evidence of the paradigmatic nature of lean production, it is interesting to note how these originally counter-intuitive principles have become mainstream managerial concerns.

Yet beyond these general rules, the definition of lean production is actually rather vague and confused (Bartezzaghi, 1999). Attempts to empirically assess progress towards lean production have been forced to develop metrics linking together a wide variety of tools and techniques, many based on opposing principles. For example, Karlsson and Åhlström (1996) describe 18 different elements (each with their own sub-elements) of lean production, and the Andersen Consulting Lean Enterprise Research required firms to fill in a questionnaire that typically took five-and-a-half-days of managerial time to complete (Oliver et al., 1996). If no improvement technique is excluded then defining what actually constitutes the lean production process becomes extremely difficult

The sheer breadth of these 'real' descriptions might suggest that lean production is not easily imitated and, interestingly, evidence for this assertion can be found in the original IMVP work. This study was strongly influenced by Toyota and the work of Taiichi Ohno in particular. When this celebrated engineer wrote his book (Ohno, 1988) (after retiring from the firm in 1978) he was able to portray Toyota's manufacturing plants as embodying a coherent production approach. This was a powerful advertisement for Toyota's (and Ohno's) competence and appealed to the social scientists, industrial engineers and consultants seeking a systematic explanation for Toyota's success (Womack et al., 1990; Monden, 1983; Goddard, 1986; Harrison, 1992; Chang and Podolsky, 1996). However, this encouraged observers to deconstruct the system as described (focusing in on apparently key attributes such as *kanban* cards or *andon* boards etc.) and inevitably de-emphasised the impact of 30 years of 'trial and error'. All systems analysis should take into account the specific history and context of a system; yet it is now so widely accepted that lean production was 'born' in Japan, under the 'parenting' of Taiichi Ohno, that crucial formative influences remain largely hidden from view. To illustrate this, operating innovations claimed by Toyota (Ohno, 1988, p. 95), such as laying out 'machines in order of use', were widely employed in Ford plants of the 1920s (Williams et al., 1994). In our case research therefore, it is important not only to explore the link between lean outcomes and the tools/techniques that apparently delivered that outcome but also to consider where the firm started from (i.e. its history) and the specific implementation path it followed.

P2   Each firm will follow its own unique lean production development trajectory. This can be defined by its starting conditions and the specific implementation path followed (which techniques applied in which order etc.) to achieve the lean production outcome (compare with P1).

Lean Production and Sustainable Competitive Advantage

Competitive advantage can be defined as the result of a business being either a particularly able player in its market (i.e. being better, which could mean being lower cost or more lean) and/or differentiated in what it offers. In order to build a useful construct to explain how competitive advantage is created and sustained, and in order to build directly upon the previous discussion of lean production, another input (resources), transformation (process) and outcome (competitive advantage) model will provide the basic structure of our discussions. Figure 2 presents this model in more detail, illustrating how resources are deployed in business processes to create competitive advantage. The resource-based theory of the firm is then applied to explain how such advantage can be sustainable in the face of competitive pressures (Nanda, 1996). The central theme in this strategic management theory is that unique internal resources are as important as external market factors in determining competitive advantage because certain resources create effective barriers to imitation.

Although both the lean production and sustainable competitive advantage models are illustrated using basic transformation representations, there are some key distinctions between them. In exploring these distinctions we will develop the secondary set of research propositions that will guide the empirical work.

Sustainable competitive advantage, lean production and the competitive environment

Figure 2 illustrates how sustainable competitive advantage comes into being through the dynamic interplay between a firm and its external environment. So, for example, certain resources can be strategic, but only if they cannot be copied or replaced by

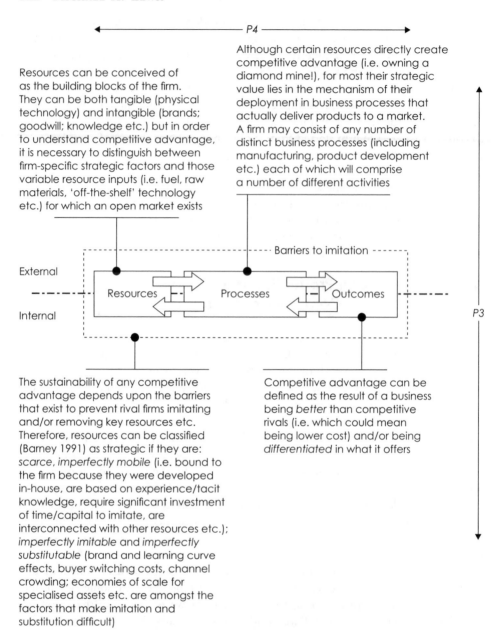

Although certain resources directly create competitive advantage (i.e. owning a diamond mine!), for most their strategic value lies in the mechanism of their deployment in business processes that actually deliver products to a market. A firm may consist of any number of distinct business processes (including manufacturing, product development etc.) each of which will comprise a number of different activities

Resources can be conceived of as the building blocks of the firm. They can be both tangible (physical technology) and intangible (brands; goodwill; knowledge etc.) but in order to understand competitive advantage, it is necessary to distinguish between firm-specific strategic factors and those variable resource inputs (i.e. fuel, raw materials, 'off-the-shelf' technology etc.) for which an open market exists

The sustainability of any competitive advantage depends upon the barriers that exist to prevent rival firms imitating and/or removing key resources etc. Therefore, resources can be classified (Barney 1991) as strategic if they are: *scarce, imperfectly mobile* (i.e. bound to the firm because they were developed in-house, are based on experience/tacit knowledge, require significant investment of time/capital to imitate, are interconnected with other resources etc.); *imperfectly imitable* and *imperfectly substitutable* (brand and learning curve effects, buyer switching costs, channel crowding; economies of scale for specialised assets etc. are amongst the factors that make imitation and substitution difficult)

Competitive advantage can be defined as the result of a business being *better* than competitive rivals (i.e. which could mean being lower cost) and/or being *differentiated* in what it offers

Figure 2   Defining elements of sustainable competitive advantage

external rivals. Equally, firms need not directly own strategic resources (i.e. when developing manufacturing processes, resources that have competitive significance are often 'owned' by suppliers). Similarly, all critical value creating processes stretch beyond the boundaries of the firm, involving actual and potential customers, and successful outcomes are only meaningful if they make the firm better and/or different.

Although the lean production model also stresses the generic importance of customers and suppliers, the attempt to create a series of 'operating principles' has required advocates to downplay the significance of the interaction between specific internal and environmental contexts. In the empirical research it is important to relate all lean production and sustainable competitive advantage findings to the specific external context of the firm (see *P2*).

> *P3* The success of lean production in delivering sustainable competitive advantage will be contingent upon the external context of the firm. Contextual factors might include: type of market (competitor activity, different demand profiles); dominant technology in sector; supply chain structure; etc.

There is already evidence suggesting that a more strongly contingent perspective on the lean production model is necessary. Some research (Katayama and Bennett, 1996) has claimed that lean production is incapable of responding to large oscillations in aggregate demand volumes, arguing that the Japanese economy at the time of the IMVP study was exhibiting very specific characteristics, creating conditions of high and stable domestic demand.

Lean production, sustainable competitive advantage, learning, complexity and failure

The sustainable competitive advantage model argues that resources (skilled staff, market information, technological data etc.) create value when enacted in processes. In turn, these processes allow the organisation to learn and thereby create new (or reinforce/extend existing) resources. Learning in organisations can take any number of forms (Huber, 1991) but for the purposes of this paper it is useful to distinguish between: the development of increasingly efficient and reliable routines; and increased resilience when faced with novel situations (Sitkin, 1991). It is the first of these that lies at the heart of the lean production process model, with its emphasis on 'perfection' through continuous improvement. When allied to the concepts of customer value stream and market pull, lean production suggests a very neat model of information and material flow. If the firm's competitive environment remains stable and modifies only slowly over time, then sustainable competitive advantage should be delivered through such adaptation. The final research proposition will explore the relationship between learning and lean production.

> *P4* The more successfully any firm applies lean production principles, the less it will engage in general innovative activity. The firm will focus instead upon continuously improving existing processes and adopting incremental changes.

Unfortunately, more and more markets are changing rapidly and the lean production view of continuous improvement might be trading short-term performance advantage for long-term viability. Evolutionary organisational theories suggest that if a firm cannot produce and retain enough diverse information, potential future choices will be severely restricted (Tamuz and Sitkin, 1989). Such information tends to be created through complex internal and external interactions that inevitably comprise complexity and failure – forms of *muda* that lean production seeks to eliminate (Emiliani, 1998).

Empirical Work

In order to retain the practical 'flavour' associated with most lean production work, the second part of this paper will investigate empirically the propositions developed above. A variety of different research designs were potentially applicable but case studies were felt to be the most appropriate (Yin, 1984; Bryman, 1989) because the intent was not to formally test hypotheses but to review four exploratory propositions. Once the decision had been made to undertake more than one case study, the problem of sampling arose (Eisenhardt, 1989). Whilst there are clear limitations to an opportunistic research strategy, initial access to cases was driven largely by availability, with a wide variety of points of entry employed (existing tangential research links, executive education, MBA classes/assignments). From the outset the intention was to investigate manufacturing companies (in one particular sector to minimise environmental 'noise') of a similar size (150–500 employees on a single site). Applying these criteria as an initial filter in informal conversations with managers generated a (potentially biased) sample population of 14 firms. To refine the sample further, a questionnaire based on a series of indices describing lean production tools/techniques (Womack et al., 1990; Oliver and Hunter, 1998; Schonberger, 1982; 1986) was sent to the 14 firms. Managers were asked to indicate whether these were present in their firm (Table 2).

These measures did not give any indication of implementation success but did provide an approximate metric for 'richness of adoption' – the dimension that was applied to select the final case set. After the returns had been reviewed (three companies failed to complete the questionnaire), it was found that three companies scored 14 per cent, four scored 38 per cent, one scored 42 per cent and three had adopted or were in the process of adopting more than 60 per cent of the techniques (i.e. companies A, B and C in Table 2). All are medium-sized businesses supplying component sub-assemblies to automotive OEMs. A and C had previously worked with the author on another research project and B was (at that time) the subject of an MBA project.

After three cases had been selected, initial interviews were conducted with the MD and manufacturing manager. These interviews (lasting approximately 1.5 hours) were largely unstructured and sought primarily to establish the general 'story' of lean production in those firms. The second set of interviews (see Table 3) was carried out between 9 and 11 months later and sought to understand how the lean production initiatives had developed over a comparable five year period. Interviews were conducted (lasting between 1.5 and 2.5 hours) using semi-structured question

Table 2 Lean production characteristics and the case studies

	Case A	Case B	Case C
Manufacturing processes			
Statistical process control	•	•	•
Kanban controls	•	•	•
Cellular manufacture	•	•	
Design for manufacture	•	•	•
Quality improvement teams	•	•	•
Set-up time reduction	•		•
Operator responsibility for quality	•	•	•
Human resources			
Single status facilities	•	•	
Performance appraisal for all	•	•	•
Team briefings	•	•	•
Performance-related pay		•	
Profit-sharing scheme		•	
Managerial job rotation	•	•	•
Company council or similar		•	
Supplier inputs			
Just-in-time delivery of supplies			
Quality assured supplies	•		•
Single sourcing of supplies	•		
Supplier development activities			•
Supplier involvement in design			•
Reducing number of suppliers	•	•	•
Financial stake in suppliers	•		
Total: 21 elements (100%)	71%	62%	62%

sets based upon the four research propositions. In total, 27 different managers and team leaders were interviewed. Attempts were made to include staff, customers and suppliers but given time constraints these proved impossible to co-ordinate. This inevitably introduces further limitations to the validity of any findings. In addition to the interview data, a number of secondary sources (accounts, results from a series of staff surveys etc.) were used.

Company A

A family owned, UK-based business, company A employs 430 people manufacturing electrical sub-assemblies for automotive control systems. In 1991 the firm had (at the behest of their largest customer) invested heavily in automation to improve quality and reduce unit costs. In this redesign it received a great deal of assistance

Table 3   The interview schedule

Interviews	A 1st visit	A 2nd visit	B 1st visit	B 2nd visit	C 1st visit	C 2nd visit
Managing director	×	×	×	×[a]	×	×
Manufacturing manager/director	×	×	×	×	×	×
Engineering/technical director		×		×		×
Marketing director		n/a[b]		×		×
Finance director		×		×		×
Production team leaders		2		1		2
Total number of interviews	8		10		9	

[a] By the time of the second round of interviews, the original MD had left the firm. The new MD was formerly a finance manager with one of their OEM customers.
[b] Company A had no distinct marketing group and as a result no senior marketing manager.

from the customer's supplier development units. The changes tied it into this OEM's production system (altering manufacturing and order fulfilment processes) but were seen as a great success. WIP levels reduced, quality improved and fewer people were employed making higher volumes. In 1992 and 1994 the firm won 'best supplier' awards.

By 1996, continued pressure on its automotive market margins encouraged the firm to explore new business opportunities – deciding on controllers for food dispensing systems. The product technology was similar but the systems had to be fixed in aluminium housings. In order to control both quality and delivery reliability, the decision was taken to acquire a local fabrications business. The explicit intent was to exploit its lean production expertise to 'bring this old metal-basher into the twenty-first century!' By 1998, after expending lots of investment on the site, 85 per cent of the original staff had left, inventory and defect levels were higher than before and throughput time had increased by almost 40 per cent.

Company B

Part of a multinational engineering corporation, company B employs 408 people in the manufacture of specialist fasteners. The site is located in Belgium, close to its key customers. Although its niche product had traditionally shielded it from much OEM cost pressure, by late 1990 it was clear (several senior managers attended an IMVP seminar) that the firm would have to become 'leaner'. Its new MD was convinced that the system was predicated upon staff development and his first action was to create a single-status facility (there had been three grades of lavatory). Teams were created, with daily briefings etc., and the senior team introduced individual performance and company profit-related pay structures. Whilst none of these changes represented quick fixes, by 1994 three annual staff morale surveys (conducted by a local university psychology department) indicated that staff perceived the culture of the company to be changing. More tangibly, devolving responsibility for quality to teams and operators reduced defect levels and their associated costs. Process redesigns, linked with voluntary redundancy, led to improved throughput times and reduced headcount. In 1995, the firm won a national training award in recognition of its efforts.

By late 1995, however, a problem had emerged. Despite the new pay structures, key members of staff (in particular team leaders) were being headhunted by other larger organisations willing to offer substantial (up to 3.5 times) wage increases. The human resource policy was based on low levels of staff turnover and struggled to replace key workers as they left. Staff expressed loyalty to the company in all surveys conducted, but in the face of such incentives still left.

Company C

Employing 560 people in north-east France, company C manufactures electronic components. In early 1993, it was under pressure from all key customers to improve cost and quality performance. Its manufacturing director expressed a great deal of cynicism about 'off-the-shelf panaceas' but the company was aware that significant variability in its supply chain (with many small suppliers) was creating problems in manufacturing. To 'get to the bottom of the problem' it decided to introduce statistical process control (SPC) and sent three managers and 25 staff on a course about the basics of control charting. After a couple of false starts (setting up inappropriate variables and controls etc.) measurements began to reveal that very high levels of defect occurred on a soldering process at specific times. This triggered local process improvements, and suppliers were provided with the relevant data and asked to explain their own problems so that company C engineers could help to rectify them. Using the initial introduction of SPC as a platform, the firm began to add many more of the elements that together define lean production.

Discussion: Lean Production as an Outcome Will Improve Business Performance (P1)

In order to establish the impact of lean production upon business performance, financial (drawn from published company accounts and converted *ex post* into euros) and operational data were obtained from each of the case companies (Table 4 summarises these data). Although for this type of investigation a much larger (and statistically significant) sample size would probably offer more valid conclusions,

Table 4 Lean production outcomes

	Case A		Case B		Case C	
	Pre-LP[a]	LP+5[b]	Pre-LP	LP+5	Pre-LP	LP+5
Gross annual profit (million euros) (1 euro ≈ £0.65)	5.04	3.6	3.15	3.1	3.75	8.75
Total sales (million euros)	36	40	28	35	25	48
In-process inventory (hours)	62	25	52	28	58	42
Finished goods inventory (hours)	30	14	42	22	47	42
Percentage on-time delivery	80	99.2	68	98	81	94
Percentage products defective (requiring rework/returned by customer)	1.7	0.05	0.9	0.2	0.6	0.03
New product development lead time (estimate, months)	36	8	28	12	38	20
Number of employees	580	430	640	408	542	560
Total productive floor space (approximate m²)	700	220	750	500	500	480

[a] Immediately before the lean production initiative.
[b] Five years after the lean production initiative.

proximity to these cases has revealed a number of potential problems with such an approach. Apparently straightforward headline figures are used, but a variety of factors including different accounting conventions (i.e. calculating total cost of sales for gross profit figures) and different ownership arrangements meant that the actual data are less reliable than they might appear. With these caveats, the data describe performance immediately before the lean production initiative and also five years later (not adjusted for inflation).

The research proposition suggested that improving productivity would lead to enhanced financial performance. If any firm's overall costs are reduced, then one would expect either its profitability or its sales figures (investing savings to grow market share) to increase. When examining the lean production operational data, it is A and B that have made the most dramatic operational improvements (i.e. −60 per cent and −46 per cent process inventory respectively) and yet they appear to have been unable to 'appropriate' these savings. They have had some sales growth but profitability has been squeezed (profit −29 per cent and −2 per cent respectively). Conversely, case C has seen both profit and volume growth (+233 per cent and +92 per cent) but has made much less progress towards lean production (i.e. −28 per cent in process inventory). When asked about this phenomenon, the finance director at A was very direct:

> [The OEM] steal it! Any real savings that we make are accounted for in next year's sales contract . . . we have preferred supplier status and a provisional 3-year rolling contract and our side of the bargain is keep reducing costs and improving performance.

This, combined with the cost of its investments (its automation programme and later its acquisition), has put severe pressure on the firm's profitability. More than one manager argued that the firm was only viable because it was family owned. In case B, although its product's unique features gave it some extra leverage with the OEMs, its lean production performance was primarily based upon reducing staff numbers. As its staff retention difficulties became more pronounced, their costs (wages, training, recruitment etc.) began to escalate and quality performance began to suffer.

Discussion with the managers at firm C revealed that their manufacturing director's deep cynicism about 'initiatives' had led them to question the rhetoric about supplier 'partnerships'. The firm believed that the biggest benefits from any cost savings it made would accrue to the firm with the greatest market power (Ramsay, 1995). This insight, together with its intention to remain independent, led it to build up its own market power through enhanced technical and production competences. By highlighting its constant evolution to the OEMs, even a small supplier like company C was in a strong position to continuously demonstrate the added value of the relationship (Lorange, 1996).

Discussion: Lean Production's Development Trajectory Is Unique (P2)

To explore the second research proposition, that lean production initiatives will follow unique trajectories in specific organisations, the interviews analysed the order in which different tools and techniques were implemented. Despite the large number of generic initiatives identified in each case, they all implemented various combinations of different tools and techniques. Figure 3 illustrates this as a series of building blocks.

There are two main observations to be made about these data. First, the number, duration and complexity of the lean production initiatives vary quite considerably. In both cases A and B (where 10 and 12 separate elements were identified), several interviewees commented upon the sheer number of initiatives. As one team leader at company B explained (translation by the author):

> Even if the [initiative] didn't directly affect me and my team, there were always lots of conversations about it. For nearly three years, I spent too much of my time in meetings.

The staff surveys (using Likert scales and qualitative focus groups) from case B offer further insight into the impact of so many changes. To begin with (1992, 1993) the initiatives were taken as a strong indication that the new MD was concerned with the staff and the long-term future of the firm. By 1995, the survey highlighted increasing frustration with 'yet more new ideas' and concern that they were acting as a substitute for overall strategy.

Second, the different starting points of each case had a significant impact on their outcome. Case A was driven initially by a series of investments in new technology.

Figure 3 The lean production trajectory at each case company

Case A

10 Managerial job rotation

9 Single-status facilities and performance appraisals

8 Devolved responsibility for quality to operators

7 Supplier development (rationalisation and financial stake)

6 Design for manufacture (DFM)

5 Automatic measurement and statistical process control

4 Tie production islands and cells together with kanban controls

3 Technology-led efforts to reduce set-up times

2 Quality improvement (supplier monitoring, teams/team briefings)

1 Automation and cellular manufacture

Case B

12 Cost pressures led to reduction in number of suppliers

11 Two-bin kanban system introduced

10 Cells introduced with redesign of key components (DFM)

9 Statistical process control introduced

8 Devolved responsibility for quality to operators

7 New terms and conditions for managers (job rotation)

6 Profit sharing scheme introduced for senior managers

5 Linked to appraisals, performance-related pay introduced

4 Performance appraisals introduced for all staff

3 Company council created with staff and team representatives

2 QI teams set up and regular briefings introduced

1 Single-status facilities in the factory (toilets etc.)

Case C

6 Simple kanban control (squares on floor) introduced

5 QI teams set up and responsibility for quality devolved to operators

4 DFM and redesign efforts to aid set-up time reduction

3 Rationalising supplier base but involving remaining in design

2 Changed managerial roles and performance appraisals; team briefings

1 SPC to monitor and improve supplier quality performance

The demands of 'leading edge' automation required the firm to rely heavily on both its customers and its key suppliers to provide implementation and operational expertise. Case B was driven by their MD's belief that human resources lay at the heart of any effective strategy. This focus allowed the firm to reduce its total labour costs by asking a great deal more from those that remained, but left it vulnerable to these staff leaving. Case C was more organisation centred.

Although the early initiatives resulted in cost savings by reducing the number of suppliers, the key driver was the 'scientific' use of SPC to obtain more information about performance.

Discussion: Lean Production Is Dependent upon the Context of the Firm (P3)

The next research proposition contends that external context has a major influence on lean production's ability to engender sustainable competitive advantage. The case material is drawn from a single market, thus preventing cross-sectoral comparisons, but it does highlight how market context determines whether lean production resource configurations will provide sustainable competitive advantage.

First, when a lean production strategy is being developed, certain unique resources can provide a direct source of competitive advantage. For instance, A and B have an advantage based upon the specificity of their locations (Williamson, 1985) (i.e. they are located close to their customer's assembly plants). Interestingly, such an advantage is also a source of risk because it can only be fully realised if there is a degree of trust between the firm and its customer. For instance, in the 1920s, General Motors wanted Fisher Body to build a new car body plant adjacent to its factory (Klein et al., 1978). Fisher Body refused because it feared that once the plant was built it would have little real choice other than to supply GM at whatever price it set (Collis and Montgomery, 1998). Equally, a location-based advantage will not be readily transferable to new markets. Company A's new marketplace was much more widely distributed and as a result its location advantage was lost, increasing its transport costs and diminishing its relative appeal.

Second, in B, reduced staff numbers proved capable of working 'harder and smarter' in order to deliver lean production. The skills, knowledge and experience necessary can be scarce and difficult to copy and hence provide a platform for sustainable competitive advantage. Unfortunately (for the firm) transferable skills have a market value and, if externally visible (i.e. after the national training award, B's managers toured Europe describing how good their staff were), then there is a risk of staff leaving to leverage this value. In this respect, different lean production trajectories have a very different impact upon the power relationships inside the firm (Oliver and Wilkinson, 1988; Marchington, 1979). All lean production programmes involve training (and hence some shift of 'knowledge power' to the staff) but in case B this was the focus almost exclusively. Subsequent problems with staff retention had a major impact on operating performance, and 'getting into a bidding war' (B's managing director, first visit) to retain these staff is time consuming and expensive and can have a major impact on morale in single status firms (1996 staff survey). The other cases placed greater emphasis upon structure (A's technology) and infrastructure (C's knowledge acquisition techniques), thus minimising the transfer of market value to individuals and the potential impact of their leaving.

Discussion: Lean Production Minimises General Innovative Activity (P4)

One of the core principles of lean production (Womack and Jones, 1996) is the 'scientific' refinement of operational procedures (Spear and Bowen, 1999). The final research proposition suggests that this refinement process will minimise more general innovation because this is primarily based upon broader experimentation and risk taking. Discussing this (in particular with engineering/technical directors) revealed variations in the scope of product innovation at each firm that were broadly in line with the different lean production approaches discussed earlier. Although no detailed design data were made available by any of the firms (e.g. percentage new parts), interviews established that:

- During the five years under investigation, A released eight 'new' products. Its automated production systems gave it mechanisms for rapid prototyping of new products providing they were close derivatives of the original dominant product design.
- Similarly, B's niche products needed 'refinement not revolution' (technical director, second visit), building on its continuous improvement culture. It introduced five new products during the five years under investigation.
- In the time frame of the study, C introduced one completely new product – although most of its innovative activity was focused on product support services. In March 1995 it embarked on a design-for-manufacturing (DFM: element 4, Figure 3) initiative which introduced some concurrent engineering practices; this led to the relatively rapid introduction (in December 1996) of two derivative products.

The only quantitative innovation metric was the estimate (modal response shown on Table 4) of product development lead time. These figures echo the rest of the operational performance metrics, whereby A and B achieved the strongest lean production innovation performance (i.e. lead-time reductions of 78 per cent and 57 per cent; C was only 32 per cent), but this did not translate into profitability.

There was also a marked contrast in how lean production affected the firm's overall innovation management approach. Contrasting cases A and C illustrates this:

- Over the time frame of the study, A made the most dramatic lead-time improvements. As a highly integrated 'partnership' supplier, it was subject to three OEM 'time-to-market' initiatives and this became a key performance indicator for the firm. As it developed its systems in close collaboration with key customers, its engineering and support functions became much more focused on these specific relationships. OEM product plans (and specific requests) drive all product innovation. Over five years, in the context of ongoing cost reduction pressures and lean production principles, any activity that does not contribute directly to this relationship was deemed to constitute *muda* and removed. The managing director (second visit) recognised that this had 'led to an atrophying of broader problem-solving skills . . . that was exposed when we entered a market where we claimed to be the experts'.

- In company C, changes in innovation practice were largely internally driven and (especially with the introduction of downstream support services) required additional IT, engineering, purchasing, marketing and HRM resources – increasing the overall complexity of the firm. Some of its initiatives took a deliberately wasteful route. For instance, introducing SPC was a long (18 months) and painful (i.e. understanding and overcoming fear of statistics) process. The lowest cost option would have been to bring in external consultants to set up the measurement system, but senior managers felt that this would minimise the organisational learning.

Conclusions

There are clear limitations to this research. Attempting to combine theoretical and empirical elements means that each area could have been more fully explored. Similarly, in condensing 50 hours of interview notes (some in French) into a series of observations and quotes, the researchers' own interpretation of events is a significant 'reality' filter. More specifically, despite the selection of similar sized cases from the same industry sector, the degree of divergence they exhibited raises concerns over comparability and the limited number inevitably reduces the generalisability of any findings. However, conclusions can still be drawn against each of the four research propositions and potential areas for further work can be suggested:

1 The case data confirm that becoming lean does not automatically result in improved financial performance, thus contradicting the first proposition. The critical issue appears to be the firm's ability to appropriate the value generated by any savings the firm can make. In markets (like automotive or supermarkets) where key firms exercise dominant market power, the benefits of lean production can very easily flow to these powerful players, although as case C illustrates, lean production does not automatically create these difficult conditions.

2 The case material illustrates why it has proved so difficult to define lean production precisely. Despite apparent similarity on the initial questionnaire, closer examination revealed the variation inherent in each of the initiatives and highlighted how important the starting conditions were. This offers strong support for the proposition that each firm is likely to follow a more or less unique lean production trajectory.

3 The single market context of the case studies prevented cross-sector comparisons from being drawn, but the case material still provided strong support for the 'context matters' proposition. It highlighted how some markets can render specific resources 'strategic' (e.g. location) and how certain job markets (e.g. those with skill shortages) can leave managers in a lean production system with a radically altered power dynamic *vis-à-vis* their key staff.

4 The final proposition suggested that firms would inevitably see a narrowing of innovative activity as they became more 'lean'. Although cases A and B provide some evidence to support this proposition, the relative performance advantage of case C appears to be based upon innovation. Over time, this resource development process involved technology push, short-term cost penalties and deliberately generated system complexity. This contradiction with lean production principles suggests that the proposition needs to be reformulated around some form of trade-off between degree of lean production and innovation.

The pre-eminence of the lean production paradigm reflects the academic and practitioner effort that has been directed towards establishing and transferring 'best practice' in operations. This paper has offered a theoretical critique of this generic approach and the empirical evidence presented adds further support, suggesting that contingency and complexity are the dominant characteristics of any successful implementation process.

Further work

The continued managerial popularity of the lean production model is sufficient justification for continued investigation of the phenomena and the above conclusions suggest a number of potential areas for further investigation:

- Accepting that individual implementations are essentially unique does not preclude the possibility of generating useful, contingent descriptions of the lean production development trajectory. The evidence presented in this paper suggests that this might be based around starting conditions (e.g. strategic objectives, business performance, managerial experience) and dominant resource types (e.g. technology, people, information-led).
- The effects of different market contexts (e.g. shipbuilding and aerospace) need to be explored. The automotive sector has probably been over-researched and arguably offers a relatively poor model for sustainable competitive advantage.
- The trade-off implied by proposition 4 – between lean and innovation – is comparable to the distinction between adaptation and adaptability (Boulding, 1978) in evolutionary theory. A number of operations authors have suggested that it is possible to create a strategically flexible production model that accommodates this apparent contradiction (Spina et al., 1996; Bartezzaghi, 1999). This requires substantial further investigation.

REFERENCES

Andersen Consulting (1993), *The Lean Enterprise Benchmarking Project Report*, Andersen Consulting, London.

Barney, J. (1991), 'Firm resources and sustained competitive advantage', *Journal of Management*, Vol. 17, pp. 99–120.

Bartezzaghi, E. (1999), 'The evolution of production models: is a new paradigm emerging?', *International Journal of Production and Operations Management*, Vol. 19 No. 2, pp. 229–50.

Boston Consulting Group (1993), *The Evolving Competitive Challenge for the European Automotive Components Industry*, Boston Consulting Group, London.

Boulding, K.E. (1978), *Eco-Dynamics: A New Theory of Social Evolution*, Sage Publications, London.

Bryman, A. (1989), *Research Methods and Organization Studies*, Routledge & Kegan Paul, London.

Chang, T.C.E. and Podolsky, S. (1996), *Just-In-Time Manufacturing: An Introduction*, 2nd ed., Chapman and Hall, London.

Collis, D.J. and Montgomery, C.A. (1998), *Corporate Strategy: A Resource-Based Approach*, Irwin, McGraw-Hill, New York, NY.

Culpepper, P.D. (1999), 'The future of the high-skill equilibrium in Germany', *Oxford Review of Economic Policy*, Vol. 15 No. 1, pp. 43–59.

Cusumano, M.A. (1994), 'The limits of lean', *Sloan Management Review*, Summer, pp. 27–33.

Eisenhardt, K. (1989), 'Building theories from case study research', *Academy of Management Review*, Vol. 14 No. 4, pp. 532–50.

Emiliani, M.L. (1998), 'Lean behaviours', *Management Decision*, Vol. 36 No. 9, pp. 615–31.

Garrahan, P. and Stewart, P. (1992), *The Nissan Enigma: Flexibility at Work in a Local Economy*, Mansell Publishing, London.

Goddard, W.E. (1986), *Just-In-Time*, Oliver Wight Publications, Brattleboro, VT.

Harrison, A. (1992), *Just-In-Time Manufacturing in Perspective*, Prentice-Hall, Hemel Hempstead.

Hayes, R.H. (1981), 'Why Japanese factories work', *Harvard Business Review*, July–August, pp. 57–66.

Huber, G. (1991), 'Organizational learning: the contributing processes and literatures', *Organization Science*, Vol. 2 No. 1, pp. 88–115.

IBM Consulting Group (1993), *Making It In Britain*, IBM Consulting Group, London.

Karlsson, C. and Åhlström, P. (1996), 'Assessing changes towards lean production', *International Journal of Production and Operations Management*, Vol. 16 No. 2, pp. 24–41.

Katayama, H. and Bennett, D. (1996), 'Lean production in a changing competitive world: a Japanese perspective', *International Journal of Production and Operations Management*, Vol. 16 No. 2, pp. 8–23.

Klein, B., Crawford, R. and Alchain, A. (1978), 'Vertical integration, appropriable rents and the competitive contracting process', *Journal of Law and Economics*, Vol. 21, pp. 297–326.

Krafcik, J. (1988), 'The triumph of lean production', *Sloan Management Review*, Vol. 30 No. 1, pp. 41–52.

Lorange, P. (1996), 'Interactive strategy alliances and partnerships', *Long Range Planning*, Vol. 29 No. 4, pp. 581–3.

Marchington, M. (1979), 'Shopfloor control and industrial relations', in Purcell, M. and Smith, R. (Eds), *The Control of Work*, Macmillan, Basingstoke.

Monden, Y. (1983), *Toyota Production System – A Practical Approach to Production Management*, Industrial Engineering and Management Press, Atlanta, GA.

Nanda, A. (1996), 'Resources, capabilities and competencies', in Moingeon, B. and Edmonson, A. (Eds), *Organizational Learning and Competitive Advantage*, Sage Publications, London, pp. 93–120.

Ohno, T. (1988), *The Toyota Production System*, English translation, Productivity Press, Cambridge, MA.

Oliver, N. and Hunter, G. (1998), 'The financial impact of "Japanese" manufacturing methods', *Manufacturing in Transition*, Chapter 5, Routledge & Kegan Paul, London.

Oliver, N. and Wilkinson, B. (1988), *The Japanization of British Industry*, Basil Blackwell, Oxford.

Oliver, N., Delbridge, R. and Lowe, J. (1996), 'The European auto components industry: manufacturing performance and practice', *International Journal of Production and Operations Management*, Vol. 16 No. 11, pp. 85–97.

Pilkington, A. (1998), 'Manufacturing strategy regained: evidence for the demise of best practice', *California Management Review*, Vol. 41 No. 1.

Ramsay, J. (1995), 'Purchasing power', *European Journal of Purchasing and Supply Management*, Vol. 1 No. 3, pp. 125–38.

Sandberg, A. (Ed.) (1995), *Enriching Production: Perspectives on Volvo's Uddevalla Plant as an Alternative to Lean Production*, Avebury, Aldershot.

Schonberger, R. (1982), *Japanese Manufacturing Techniques*, Free Press, New York, NY.

Schonberger, R. (1986), *World Class Manufacturing*, John Wiley & Sons, New York, NY.

Shingo, S. (1989), *A Study of the Toyota Production System from an Industrial Engineering Point of View*, Productivity Press, Cambridge, MA.

Sitkin, S.B. (1991), 'Learning through failure: the strategy of small losses', *Research in Organizational Behaviour*, Vol. 14, JAI Press, New York, NY.

Spear, S. and Bowen, H.K. (1999), 'Decoding the DNA of the Toyota production system', *Harvard Business Review*, September–October, pp. 97–106.

Spina, G., Bartezzaghi, E., Cagliano, R., Bert, A., Draaijer, D. and Boer, H. (1996), 'Strategically flexible production: the multi-focused manufacturing paradigm', *International Journal of Production and Operations Management*, Vol. 16 No. 11, pp. 20–41.

Streeck, W. (1992), *Social Institutions and Economic Performance*, Sage Publications, London.

Tamuz, M. and Sitkin, S.B. (1989), 'The effects of information processing on the availability of organizational information about potential dangers', *Proceedings of The American Sociological Society Annual Meeting*, June.

Williams, K. and Haslam, C. (1992), 'Against lean production', *Economy and Society*, Vol. 21, pp. 321–54.

Williams, K., Haslam, C., Johal, S. and Williams, J. (1994), *Cars*, Berghahn Books, Providence, RI.

Williamson, O.E. (1985), *The Economic Institutions of Capitalism*, Free Press, New York, NY.

Womack, J.P. and Jones, D.T. (1994), 'From lean production to the lean enterprise', *Harvard Business Review*, March–April, pp. 93–103.

Womack, J.P. and Jones, D.T. (1996), *Lean Thinking*, Simon and Schuster, New York, NY.

Womack, J., Jones, D.T. and Roos, D. (1990), *The Machine That Changed The World*, Rawson Associates, New York, NY.

Yin, R.K. (1984), *Case Study Research: Design and Methods*, Sage Publications, Newbury Park, CA.

3.5

Supporting Small Businesses in Their Transition to Lean Production

M. L. Emiliani

Introduction

The effective execution of supply chain management strategies requires the alignment of both internal and external stakeholders. Alignment is a highly sought-after goal, but one which is rarely achieved in western businesses (Mikami, 1982). This is due to a number of factors such as the temporal nature of business relationships, management turnover, inconsistent or confusing direction from senior management, poor morale, and systemic layoffs (Emiliani, 2000a). If internal alignment cannot be achieved, then how can external alignment with even first tier suppliers be achieved? In fact, it is more typical for the senior purchasing executive to force alignment by sending letters to suppliers demanding that they must immediately reduce prices by 10 per cent or risk losing all business (Karnitschnig, 2000).

Today, many large manufacturing companies managed in the western tradition seek to obtain alignment with first tier suppliers by engaging them in activities to improve their production capabilities (Handfield et al., 2000). Companies considered as leaders in lean production have long realized that entire supply chains (or supply networks), not just first tier suppliers, must mirror their production practices in order for just-in-time systems to function properly (Womack et al., 1990; Ohno, 1988). The buyer will often devote considerable resources to develop their suppliers at no cost to them (Bounds, 1996; Bounds et al., 1996). Senior managers at Toyota and Honda know implicitly that such investments are small and result in substantial improvement in overall performance including a reduction in total costs.

It has been much less common, however, for western companies to develop entire supply chains for a given type of product. This article presents the strategies and methods used by Pratt & Whitney, a manufacturer of gas turbine engines, for a three-year period (1996–1998), to develop the network of suppliers that produce small machined parts.

Overview of Small Machined Parts

The small machined parts supply network is part of an aerospace economic cluster located in the Connecticut Valley region (Porter, 1998), a 125 km corridor paralleling the Connecticut River, from Springfield, Massachusetts to Middletown, Connecticut. It came into being shortly after Pratt & Whitney was formed in 1925, with initial emphasis on machining processes. As the product technology advanced from piston to gas turbine engines in the late 1940s, a wide variety of supporting services were formed in order to produce more highly engineered parts with increased durability. The support services include processes such as electroplating, shot peening, brazing and welding, thread rolling, grinding, de-burring, plasma spraying, heat treating, and metallurgical testing. Most machining and support services businesses have been part of Pratt & Whitney's supply network for over 40 years.

Small machined parts consist of a few thousand part numbers in a wide variety of configurations, most less than 30 cm in diameter, and with an average price of less than $500 per unit. It was a highly fragmented spend of approximately $75 million per year which had never been managed strategically due to a historical bias in which these parts were perceived to be easy to make and a 'no-brainer' to procure. While these parts are certainly not the most complex to produce, there are, however, many systemic issues that resulted in chronic deficiencies in cost, delivery, and quality performance. In addition, small machined parts were considered to have a low level of importance relative to more expensive parts, and thus did not garner much attention from the design or project engineering communities.

It was clear from the outset that the small machined parts supply network was not well positioned to respond to the marketplace demand for significant improvements in cost, delivery, and quality performance that would arise after the 1989–1994 business downturn. More importantly, suppliers were not prepared for the change in production system, from batch-and-queue mass production to lean production, which P&W was undergoing since the early 1990s, and with which they in turn would be asked to follow suit.

The supply network for small machined parts consists of over 100 mostly small, family-owned businesses, with revenues between $2 million and $50 million and less than 150 employees. These businesses were established by entrepreneurs, many of which were former machine operators. It is not unusual to hear stories of how they started with just one machine and worked long hours every day of the week, for a decade or more, in order to grow their business.

The owners, many of them now second or third generation, are a remarkable group of people. Compared to large enterprises, small businesses tend to be responsive, resourceful, lower cost, and high quality.

But like any successful businessperson, the owners of small businesses have blind spots that can make it difficult to respond to changes in business conditions. For example, the management style tends to be top-down, with the owner making most of the decisions. They often find it difficult to delegate work to others, preferring instead to be directly involved in all activities. The owner may be so busy that they do not read *Aviation Week* or *The Wall Street Journal*, and thus lose touch with what is happening in the marketplace. In other words, they may possess a debilitating inward focus.

Owners and the management team may have a limited amount of formal education or may not recognize the shortcomings of their fundamental production processes or procurement practices – perhaps largely unchanged for 20 or more years. From the point of view of the owner, they are successful, and are not usually willing to listen to the new breed of young managers that switch jobs every two to three years. There may also be a historical bias against management practices developed in Japan and a general unwillingness to experiment. They will also likely view improvements made by a large company as unattainable in smaller businesses due to a perceived lack of resources. In addition, most owners have difficulty believing that their customer could begin to view their competencies as a commodity that can be purchased anywhere in the world (Emiliani, 2000b).

These management behaviors are not necessarily unique to small businesses. Nevertheless, they cause misalignments between buyer and seller that can take years to overcome. The trouble is, buyers do not typically give suppliers years to overcome them.

Supplier Development Strategy

The general strategy was built from the following viewpoint: the benefits of local supply networks greatly outweigh the disadvantages (Porter, 1998), and opportunities can only be understood through extensive personal interaction with suppliers – i.e. the owner and his or her management team. This included three key components: understanding which business practices or procedures make it difficult for suppliers to meet their customers' expectations; making commitments to resolve systemic problems; and evaluating suppliers' operations and recommending areas for improvement.

The focus was to improve suppliers' operations by helping them understand and implement the fundamentals of lean production which include 5S, total productive maintenance, set-up reduction, mistake-proofing, visual factory, standard work, and cellular production of part families. The cost, delivery, and quality improvements obtained by implementing lean production would eliminate overseas sourcing from consideration.

However, this goal was not made explicit at the time due to rapidly changing conditions in the marketplace and extreme emphasis on the cost reduction of purchased materials.

If suppliers were successful at reducing the price differential by 20 per cent or more (exclusive of freight) within three to four years, then senior management could be convinced that the small machined parts supply network was improving at a high rate, that the total cost was favorable for domestic suppliers, and that they were on the path to achieving world-class performance. This would make overseas sourcing considerably less attractive, and the buyer could continue to enjoy the benefits of a highly developed local manufacturing infrastructure.

The first challenge was to educate suppliers on what lean production was and then convince them to adopt new production practices. Suppliers also had to be convinced that lean production was not another fad, one of many that they had seen come and go over the previous 20–30 years.

Supplier Development Methods

The principal concern was how best to communicate with the supply network. While concentrated within the Connecticut Valley, the large number of suppliers made daily visits impractical. Part of the solution was e-mail. In early 1996, most suppliers had new computers and local area networks to support computer aided manufacturing, inspection records, deliveries, attendance, etc. However, only 5–10 per cent of the supplier network had e-mail. So the first step was to call the owner of every business and ask them to get an e-mail address, as well as Microsoft Office software, in order to support the exchange of text, spreadsheets, and presentations. Nearly every supplier honored this request, though some required additional prompting.

Though only a few suppliers had e-mail addresses, an activity was instituted whereby the supply manager would e-mail a note to suppliers, every other week, with relevant business information (Emiliani, 1996). This started out modestly, with short, half-page, communications regarding issues or upcoming events. As the distribution list grew, so did the e-mail note. Within a few months, the e-mail note expanded to several pages and typically included the following major sections: Cost, Delivery, Quality, Continuous Improvement, Training Opportunities, Master Production Schedule, Surplus Equipment, and Links to Valuable Websites. The notes established and reinforced performance expectations, and reinforced parallel on-site supplier development activities in which manufacturing engineers facilitated *kaizen* events.

The e-mail notes consistently emphasized lean production as the only means by which market-driven goals could be achieved. They presented cost, delivery, and quality as parameters that could be improved simultaneously, rather than at the expense of one another, as is traditionally the view in batch-and-queue mass production. They explained the benefits of lean production in relation to the suppliers' own interests, such as reducing inventories, increasing cash flow, improving operating margins, marketing, and competitiveness. The benefits to P&W and the end-use customer were also explained. They also included market data and trends from various internal and external publications. The e-mail notes provided context, interpreted events, and translated them into specific actions that people could take to improve performance.

They provided examples of set-up reduction and root cause analysis, and recommended important books or articles to read. They contained attachments such as presentations describing the fundamentals of lean production, performance measurement, and how to implement quality control process charts. One spreadsheet was developed to show the impact of set-up reduction on lot size, lead time, and customer satisfaction, while another was interactive and programmed to show the benefits of process improvements such as set-up reduction on financial performance. The e-mail notes were followed up by personal visits to scores of suppliers in order to witness their progress and reinforce the central theme of lean production. In fact, much of the content of the notes came from supplier visits in which lengthy conversations with senior managers revealed gaps in awareness of each other's business or knowledge of lean production.

The e-mail notes also announced affordable, high quality training in lean production offered by third party sources. Organizations not affiliated with buyers were very effective at spreading lean production in the Connecticut Valley, as the legacy of past business behaviors or operating priorities often makes it difficult for suppliers to trust their customers (Blois, 1998; Kim et al., 1999; Spekman et al., 1998). In addition, suppliers generally regard detailed operating practices and the results of improvement activities as proprietary information.

We also held formal supplier network meetings, but did things somewhat differently. For example, the agenda of most supplier conferences consists of topics that are presented solely from the viewpoint of the buyer. Our agenda contained items of concern to both P&W and the supply network. Responsiveness to suppliers' needs will always improve credibility. In addition, we gave the attendees some free gifts. But instead of giving out stickers, posters, and pens, we gave out books. Each attendee received a copy of *The Machine that Changed The World* (Womack et al., 1990), *Lean Thinking* (Womack and Jones, 1996), and P&W internal publications on continuous improvement (P&W, 1997a; 1997b). The supply network also received the book *Modern Approaches to Manufacturing Improvement – The Shingo System* (Robinson, 1990) in a subsequent mailing.

Several suppliers attended a lecture, 'The lean leap' by James Womack, at P&W's expense (Womack, 1997). In addition, suppliers were offered discounts on software, computer training, and professional skills development courses. They were also invited to participate in *kaizen* events and have their employees tour manufacturing areas so that they could witness firsthand the many improvements that had been made at P&W.

The e-mail notes were effective because they contained practical information, put issues into context, and explained the specifics of how to achieve challenging goals. This, coupled with P&W-facilitated *kaizen* events, third party training resources, and market conditions that could no longer be ignored, helped propel many suppliers in the aerospace economic cluster to adopt lean production practices.

The next step is to ensure that lean production does not become corrupted or misapplied, and thus turn into yet another passing fad.

Conclusions

There are many things that buyers can do in order to support the implementation of lean production across their supply networks. Since most businesses are small (i.e. <500 people), higher tier buyers seeking to create lean suppliers must inevitably interact with lower tier suppliers. The interaction will be productive if the buyer first asks for feedback from suppliers and makes commitments to resolve systemic problems prior to requiring the adoption of lean production practices. This is a very effective starting point, as it can help the buyer fix or eliminate wasteful business practices and also gain supplier buy-in for transitioning to lean production.

Small family-owned businesses generally exhibit management behaviors that are very different from large publicly owned businesses because they have different life experiences and are accountable to different stakeholders. A challenge for small businesses is to understand and respond to these differences without compromising their desirable attributes. Likewise, large businesses have a challenge to understand the strengths of small businesses and help them improve their weaknesses in a collaborative manner. This type of behavior is difficult to exhibit by those accustomed to western management practices because it is neither customary nor rewarded by investors (Emiliani, 2000a). So think of it as a moral imperative instead (Stainer et al., 1999).

The owners of small businesses will implement lean production if they can obtain affordable, high quality instruction on the philosophy and practice of lean production. The substantial differences between batch-and-queue mass production and lean production must be made very clear, including the implications for leadership and human resource management (Emiliani, 1998; Emiliani 2000a). Knowledgeable third parties can be important resources to facilitate implementation in an unbiased and less threatening manner. But it is not just the role of outside teachers to impart knowledge. The owners have a responsibility to read some of the great books and articles published over the last 20 years to gain added depth of understanding, teach their employees, and reinforce their leadership role. They would also benefit from the creation of a local network of like-minded people from similar-sized businesses that have made substantial progress in implementing lean production. Finally, buyers that behave in ways that promote trust among all stakeholders will have discovered the foundation upon which lean production is built.

REFERENCES

Blois, K. (1998), 'A trust interpretation of business to business relationships: a case-based discussion', *Management Decision*, Vol. 36 No. 5, pp. 302–8.

Bounds, G. (1996), 'Toyota supplier development', in Bounds, G. (Ed.), *Cases in Quality*, Dow Jones Irwin, Chicago, IL, pp. 3–25.

Bounds, G., Shaw, A. and Gillard, J. (1996), 'Partnering the Honda way', in Bounds, G. (Ed.), Cases *in Quality*, Dow Jones Irwin, Chicago, IL, pp. 26–56.

Emiliani, M. (1996), 'P&W supply chain e-mail notes', unpublished communications with the small machined parts supply network, 1996–1998.

Emiliani, M.L. (1998), 'Lean behaviors', *Management Decision*, Vol. 36 No. 9, pp. 615–31.

Emiliani, M.L. (2000a), 'Cracking the code of business', *Management Decision*, Vol. 38 No. 2.

Emiliani, M.L. (2000b), 'A critique of online business-to-business auctions', submitted for publication in *Supply Chain Management: An International Journal*.

Handfield, R., Krause, D., Scannell, T. and Monczka, R. (2000), 'Avoid the pitfalls in supplier development', *Sloan Management Review*, Vol. 41 No. 2, pp. 37–49.

Karnitschnig, M. (2000), 'BMW could use a little skid control', *Business Week*, 24 January, p. 134.

Kim, B., Kyungbae, P. and Kim, T. (1999), 'The perception gap among buyer and suppliers in the semiconductor industry', *Supply Chain Management: An International Journal*, Vol. 4 No. 5, pp. 231–41.

Mikami, T. (1982), *Management and Productivity Improvement in Japan*, JMA Consultants Inc., Tokyo.

Ohno, T. (1988), *Toyota Production System*, Productivity Press, Portland, OR.

P&W (1997a), 'Continuous improvement at Pratt & Whitney', unpublished work by Pratt & Whitney.

P&W (1997b), 'Achieving competitive excellence', unpublished work by Pratt & Whitney.

Porter, M. (1998), 'Clusters and the new economics of competition', *Harvard Business Review*, Vol. 76 No. 6, pp. 77–90.

Robinson, A. (1990), *Modern Approaches to Manufacturing Improvement – The Shingo System*, Productivity Press, Portland, OR.

Spekman, R., Kamauff, J. and Myhr, N. (1998), 'An empirical investigation into supply chain management: a perspective on partnerships', *International Journal of Physical Distribution and Logistics*, Vol. 28 No. 8, pp. 630–50.

Stainer, L, Stainer, A. and Gully, A. (1999), 'Ethics and performance management', *International Journal of Technology Management*, Vol. 17 Nos. 7/8, pp. 776–85.

Womack, J. (1997), 'The lean leap', a lecture by James Womack at Rensselaer, Hartford, 22 October.

Womack, J. and Jones, D. (1996), *Lean Thinking*, Simon & Schuster, New York, NY.

Womack, J., Jones, D. and Roos, D. (1990), *The Machine that Changed the World*, Rawson Associates, New York, NY., pp. 138–68.

Change Processes towards Lean Production: The Role of the Management Accounting System

Pär Åhlström and Christer Karlsson

Introduction

This is a study of a major change process – the adoption of lean production. Lean production is a complex managerial concept, which spans the entire company, from product development to strategies [1]. We can thus expect such a radical change to be fraught with difficulties, since major organizational changes are difficult to realize [2]. One area where such difficulties are likely to arise is the management accounting system, since the present management accounting systems were designed for environments unlike those which face today's companies [3].

The basic model underlying the traditional system assumes that the production setting is given and existing in a stable environment [4]. In contrast, lean production does not assume the production environment as given, in which 'optimal' decisions should be taken. Instead, the aim is to change the conditions of the production system. Thus, the adoption of lean production requires changes in the management accounting system. The need for making these changes has been known at least since the early 1980s [4, 5]. However, the nature of these changes is not obvious and is the subject of a continuing debate among management accounting scholars [6, 7].

While the debate on the nature of an appropriate management accounting system under a lean production strategy continues, many live with systems that are inappropriately designed to support the progress currently taking place within manufacturing. If we consider that an important role of the management accounting system is to act as a communication vehicle between production and other functions, a well-designed system should support the adoption of a new production strategy [8]. Consequently, an inappropriately designed management accounting system is likely to have a negative effect on the process of adopting a complex production strategy such as lean production.

Although much work has been done on possible solutions to the problem of obsolete management accounting systems, not much work exists on how these systems interact with, and affect, an attempt to implement lean production [8]. The research presented here was designed to study the process of adopting a complex production strategy. As an example of such a strategy, we have chosen lean production, however, our conclusions apply to other similar concepts.

The purpose of this article is to explore the role of the management accounting system in the adoption process. That is, the focus is on the changes taking place in the production system and the role of the management accounting system in these changes and *not* the management accounting system itself. Our research is exploratory in nature. We create hypotheses for further investigation as well as systematic experience for practitioners to learn from.

Methodology

Conducting exploratory research is facilitated by a longitudinal research approach with sustained participation in the organization [9]. Given our interest in studying an ongoing change process, we find the clinical methodology useful. The clinical methodology is characterized by the active participation of the researchers in formulating and observing organizational change [10]. The psychological contract that arises between the researchers and the organization gives the former access to data that are not usually available [11]. Through their high degree of penetration and involvement in the organization, researchers are able to gain access to a richness of data which is denied to other approaches. The sustained interaction with the organization also provides better opportunities for observing many aspects of the situation and for tracing through the connections between phenomena [9]. This offers a unique possibility for conducting exploratory research.

The study has been performed in Office Machines, an international manufacturing firm producing mechanical and electronic office equipment, mostly for export. Practically all the manufacturing activities are based in an industrialized European country, Sweden. We spent two to three days per week in the company, over a period of two-and-a-half years. Our role in the change process was to introduce academic knowledge and theories about production organization into the company, mainly in the form of seminars but also through daily interaction.

Three different methods were used during the empirical study – direct observation, interviews and content analysis of documents – to study a single phenomenon but overcome the weaknesses of a single-method design [12]. Interviews provide depth, subtlety, and personal feeling. Documents provide facts, but are subject to the dangers of selective survival. Direct observation gives access to group processes, and can reveal the discrepancies between what is said and what is actually done [13]. In addition to multiple methods, we have sought multiple data sources and multiple levels of analysis [14]. However, before beginning the case description, we would like to elaborate on the theoretical framework of this article.

Lean Production

Since our interest in this article is on the role of the management accounting system in the process of adopting lean production, it is first necessary to discuss the meaning of the term 'management accounting system'. As conceived of here, the management accounting system consists of all the information that is officially gathered to assess the performance of the company and to guide future actions. Thus, the term encompasses more than just the accounting system required for legal reasons; the management accounting system also includes what is often termed 'cost accounting' or 'cost measurement systems' as well as performance measurement. Furthermore, the management accounting system is not confined to monetary measures. It also includes non-financial measures, like quality and throughput times.

Lean production we see as consisting of five different parts: lean product development, procurement, manufacturing and distribution, as well as the lean enterprise [1]. As agreed on by the company and the researchers, the company in this study is currently implementing lean production according to this definition. However, henceforth we equate lean production with the activities that take place within the manufacturing function of a company, since it is there that the effects of the management accounting system are likely to be most discernible. Lean manufacturing consists of the following principles, which are elaborated below (see also [15] for a richer description):

- elimination of waste;
- continuous improvement;
- zero defects/JIT;
- pull instead of push;
- multifunctional teams;
- decentralized responsibilities/integrated functions;
- horizontal and vertical information systems.

A major purpose of lean production is to use fewer resources as compared with 'traditional' production systems [1]. A basic principle in achieving this is through the *elimination of waste* – everything that does not add value to the product, for example inventory, transportation and unnecessary movements [16]. The reduction of waste takes place constantly. The production system is being *improved continuously*; perfection is the only goal [17].

Although quality is in itself an important performance variable in lean production, it is also a prerequisite to attain high productivity [16]. *Zero defects* denotes how a lean company works with attaining quality, for instance through making quality assurance the responsibility of everyone, not only the quality control department. Closely associated is the principle of *just-in-time* (JIT), since fault-free parts are a prerequisite to achieve just-in-time deliveries. This implies that each process should be provided with the right part, in the right quantity (ultimately one part at a time), at exactly the right point in time [18].

Material is scheduled through *pull instead of push*. In a push system, a master schedule and more detailed production schedules control the production of the forecasted number of parts, whether they are needed or not. In this sense, material and parts are 'pushed' through the factory. The pull principle stands in stark contrast to this way of scheduling material. With pull, the starting point is a customer order, which goes to final assembly who orders parts from the preceding process. This process, in turn, orders parts from its preceding process, and so on. This means that nothing that has not been ordered is produced.

The most salient feature of work organization is the extensive use of *multifunctional teams* – groups of employees able to perform many different tasks. These teams are often organized around a cell-based part of the product flow. Each team is given the responsibility to perform all the tasks in this part of the product flow. Furthermore, *responsibilities are decentralized* to the multifunctional team which is expected to perform supervisory tasks through rotating team leadership among employees trained for the task.

A second principle concerning the multifunctional team is the *integration of different functions* into the team's responsibility. Tasks previously performed by indirect functions, such as procurement, materials handling, planning and control, maintenance, and quality control, are integrated into the team's tasks. Finally, *vertical and horizontal information systems* are used, since information is important for the multifunctional teams to perform according to the company's goals. Therefore, elaborate systems are necessary to provide timely information continuously, directly in the production flow.

A crucial starting point for this article is that the process of adopting these principles is likely to be affected by the management accounting system (as previously defined). The role of the management accounting system in the process of adopting lean production has been studied in an empirical case, to which we now turn.

Lean Manufacturing at Office Machines

The company in the study has two manufacturing facilities which were functionally organized; parts manufacturing was physically separate from assembly activities, which were organized along lines. The cost accounting system was designed to value inventory. Fixed costs were allocated to cost centres in relation to their use of fixed resources. From there, manufacturing costs were allocated to different products on the basis of direct labour costs. The measurement of manufacturing performance was mainly made through productivity, measured as the number of hours spent on operations compared with the standard number of hours.

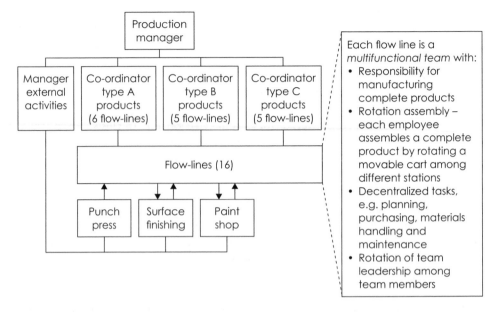

Figure 1   The vision of the organization under the lean manufacturing strategy

In November 1991 the company began the adoption of a new manufacturing strategy: lean manufacturing. Some of the major changes that were to take place included:

- Installation of flow-lines around families of similar products, containing both equipment and activities for parts manufacturing as well as for assembly.
- Physical relocation of manufacturing tasks and equipment between the company's two facilities.
- Inauguration of multifunctional teams responsible for producing complete products. Tasks previously performed by indirect personnel were integrated into the multifunctional teams' responsibility, for example production planning, materials control and handling, purchasing, maintenance, as well as quality control.
- Supervisory tasks were shared among team leaders, a role that would circulate among employees in the teams.

However, no changes to the management accounting system were planned. Figure 1 pictures the organizational structure under the new manufacturing strategy.

The first year of the project, 1992, was filled with preparatory work, such as analysis, information and training. April 1993 marked the beginning of the physical changes. These changes concerned three main areas:

1   *Relocation of manufacturing activities*   To prepare for the creation of flow-lines for all products, it was necessary to move different kinds of parts manufacturing and assembly activities from one facility to another.

2   *Rotation assembly*   As an intermediate step towards flow-lines, the assembly of some products was reorganized into rotation assembly. Instead of line assembly, each employee assembles a complete product, using a movable cart that is rotated among the different assembly stations.

3   *Flow-lines*   Finally, three flow-lines were created as a pilot project.

Observations from the Adoption Process

This section contains a selection of observations on the management accounting system's role in the adoption process. The way the description is made is important. Consistent with our methodology and to utilize the in-depth nature of our data, we have chosen to use a narrative format to indicate some interesting findings that later will be expanded into conclusions of more general interest. The observations are presented in the order in which they were made.

The inadequacy of the management accounting system

The changes in the organization that took place in April 1993 had profound effects on many areas. The issue that received the most attention initially was the drop in productivity. Since productivity was measured by the company as the number of hours spent on operations as compared with the standard number of hours, it now took longer to perform the same tasks than it did before the changes were implemented. In the analysis made by company management, this drop in productivity was attributed to several factors. One was the inclusion of indirect tasks into the team. However, no adjustment was made for this in the productivity measure.

As mentioned above, the management accounting system was traditionally designed. Quite soon it became clear that the system needed to be changed in a number of ways. However, the nature of these changes was not immediately clear; making changes was also a difficult task. In the early phases of the project, immediately after the pilot projects were launched, managers in the administrative function of the company expressed the view that 'no changes could be made in the manufacturing organization that could not be incorporated into the existing information system'. Thus, they gave priority to the computer system.

However, adjustments to the management accounting system became increasingly essential. The first adjustment was made to the productivity measure a few months after the physical change. A percentage to account for the indirect tasks now undertaken by the team was added to the standard number of hours. The motivation for adjusting the old measure was twofold. One reason was greater accuracy in reflecting the tasks performed by the team. The other reason was that the productivity measurement was important to many in the organization because it was traditionally used as *the* performance measure. Both managers at different levels and workers were accustomed to this measure.

The argument of losing control

Approximately at the same time as the adjustments to the management accounting system were begun, the managers in the administrative function expressed the opinion that they were 'losing control over what was happening in the organization', often saying that there was a risk of 'ending up in quicksand'. A proposed change in the cost accounting system was also resisted.

From the manufacturing function, there was a suggestion to simplify the reporting from the flow-lines. They no longer felt that there was a need to report the time it took to complete different tasks within the flow-lines. Since the lead times from when the material entered the group until it came out in the form of completed products had been lowered drastically, there was no need to keep track of details. This suggestion initially met with resistance from the administrative function. They still saw a need to keep track of the individual tasks performed by employees. Thus, there was a perceived need for having the employees making reports for the management accounting system every time they changed to another task, which could be several times a day. However, after a few months this view was reversed and the simplifying changes were begun.

Performance evaluation shifts to multiple factors

According to the lean manufacturing project's original plan, flow-lines were to be created from the beginning of 1994, but the company's board members postponed the decision to continue, since they were unsure of the value of the changes. A contributing factor was the decrease in productivity that occurred. Subsequently, however, productivity started to rise slowly. There was also a shift in attention in the evaluation of the flow-lines, since other performance measures besides productivity were being incorporated into that evaluation, for instance work in progress, quality and time accuracy, which all indicated positive outcomes of the change.

With both productivity and other performance measures showing that the changes thus far were beginning to pay off, the situation stabilized. In May 1994 the board decided to plan for the installation of flow-lines in the whole manufacturing operation. This led the managing director to inform all employees personally about the progress so far and the plans for the future. At these meetings, all performance measures were given the same attention.

The beliefs of important managers start to change

Around the summer of 1994 the managing director had problems interpreting the information he obtained from the management accounting system: 'I see that our total production costs are lower than before, and our operating margins are higher. We also keep our delivery times, and our products have a higher quality than before.

Still our productivity is lower than before the changes.' This led him to wonder whether the system measured the appropriate things.

This worry became pronounced in the autumn, when the management accounting system showed that the production department had consumed 32,000 hours more than budget. This report was sent to the board by the administrative department, which caused turbulence in the lean manufacturing project. The overrun was attributed to the drop in productivity that had followed the lean manufacturing project.

Analysis of the report pointed to variations in the product mix and work with new products not included in the budget as likely reasons for the number of hours spent exceeding those of the budget. However, most bewildering for the managing director was that the actual total manufacturing costs were lower than the budget costs. This made him really worried about what exactly the managing accounting system was measuring. This worry was highlighted one month later, when the figures looked better than ever before.

These difficulties in interpreting the data from the management accounting system led the managing director to question seriously the design of the productivity measure. There had been indications that this measurement had a number of shortcomings. One of these was susceptibility to faulty time standards. If actual time is compared with faulty standards, the productivity measurement can be deceptive.

A number of instances with faulty standards had been found. For this reason, there were suggestions for using the number of products manufactured in each flow-line and comparing this with the total number of hours spent in the flow-line. However, implementation of these changes was met with resistance from several persons in both the administrative function and the production function.

Changes in the management accounting system start

The managing director also proposed the design of a new cost accounting system in November 1994. In this system there would be no difference between direct and indirect costs in the flow-lines. Exactly what the workers spent their time doing was felt to be of less importance than them reaching their goals. All costs that were allocated to the flow-lines were to be split evenly between the number of products manufactured. This would be possible since the installation of flow-lines made it easier to trace costs, and also because each flow-line would produce family-like products. This suggestion was not met with resistance from the administrative function, as had been anticipated. Instead, discussions began on how this system should be built up and how it could be implemented. These discussions took place among representatives from the administrative function and the production function. However, the changes were more difficult than initially thought, due to problems of a technical nature. The management accounting system did not collect enough of the information needed for the change to be made. To make these changes would take quite some time.

Figure 2 summarizes the observations that were made during the process described previously. The focus is on the role of the management accounting system in the

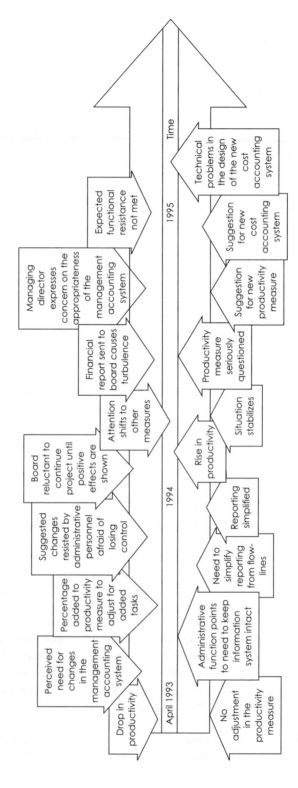

Figure 2 Summary of observations on the role of the management accounting system in the adoption process

adoption process. Abbreviated statements are placed at the approximate point in time when they were typically made. The reader should, however, bear in mind that these statements often represent observations made over a period of time. Figure 2 will be used later in our analysis section.

The Management Accounting System's Role in the Adoption Process

The first and perhaps most obvious thing that surfaces in analysis of the adoption process is that the management accounting system has had a profound effect on the adoption process. This will be elaborated on below. Our analysis of the adoption process is divided into three sections, where each section is based on a group of factors that have evolved from our observations.

The impetus for changing the management accounting system

Taken as a whole, the management accounting system has been a major impediment to the desired changes in manufacturing strategy. Perhaps the most important and obvious instance of this was when the productivity measure indicated increased costs for the new way of working in manufacturing, causing the appropriateness of the lean manufacturing strategy to be questioned. The way productivity was measured was not questioned, at least not initially. It was not until the productivity measure had reached a 'comfortable' level that other measures were incorporated into the evaluation of operations. When other measures, such as work in progress, quality, and time accuracy, showed positive signs, the way performance was measured became seriously questioned.

Thus, the process was such that the physical and organizational changes had to produce effects that reached a certain threshold before changes in the management accounting system were conceivable. This threshold mainly concerned productivity, since traditionally it was *the* performance measure in the company. The old measures were not discarded immediately after the physical and organizational changes. This can be interpreted as a need to maintain some stability in the face of drastically changed ways of working. The desire to compare performance over time also affected the decision to maintain the performance measurement system. Since uncertainty existed about whether the proposed changes would be beneficial, it was perceived as important to have the possibility of making comparisons with historical performance. The argument was that if the implemented changes did not produce the desired results, the decision could still be reversed.

Both these observations point to the inertia inherent in the management accounting system as having impeded the adoption process. However, one must also take into account that the role of the management accounting system is, to a large extent, to

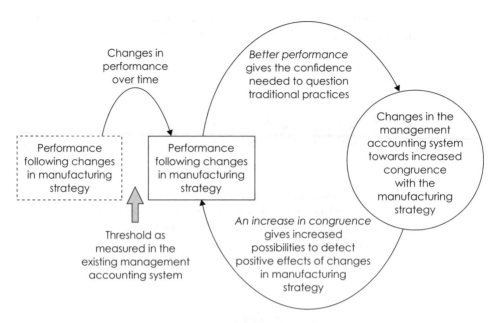

Figure 3   The impetus for changing the management accounting system

compare the present with the past. Thus, the system should not be changed too easily. Some stability must be maintained.

In the literature, there are assertions that management accounting systems can be driving forces in the type of changes referred to here [7]. However, their design then needs to be congruent with the chosen production strategy. This was not the case in the process studied. Instead, uncertainty of the appropriateness of a new strategy resulted in use of the old performance measurements under the new strategy. To change performance measurement as well as the organization required reaching a certain threshold in the old performance measurements. When that threshold is reached, and change in the management accounting system takes place, it is possible to imagine how the system can drive the changes. By measuring in a new way, the manufacturing strategy and the management accounting system can become increasingly congruent. This can be likened to a self-reinforcing loop: better results point to the appropriateness of the changes, which further leads to changes in the management accounting system, which now is able to detect more positive results and so on. Figure 3 depicts the relationship.

The importance of raising the level of the unit of analysis

When the threshold was reached at the company in this study and the management accounting system was changed towards increased congruence with lean manufacturing, there was one common denominator in the changes that took place: the level of the unit of analysis was raised. This is consistent with the aims of lean manufacturing. Achieving high load factors in terms of utilizing single machines and employees is no longer relevant. The output of the total system is important and the focus lies on the production of fault-free products in the right number at the right time.

The first instance where the level of the unit of analysis was raised concerns performance measurement. Although the traditional productivity measure was still kept, it was modified to incorporate an estimated percentage to account for indirect tasks now performed by the operators. This was one step towards raising the level of the unit of analysis, since the productivity measure included a larger part of the total production system. The suggestion was to raise the level of the unit of analysis further, by comparing the number of products manufactured to time used. What is more important, other measures than productivity were incorporated into the evaluation of manufacturing performance. Traditionally, the company relied predominantly on productivity. Over time, more attention was given to quality, time accuracy and work in progress.

The second illustration of how the level of the unit of analysis has been raised concerns the cost accounting system. When the flow-lines were created, it became less interesting to record in detail what was done to the product within the flow-line. The operations included in the flow-lines were no longer separated, but treated as a whole. The next step was to take all costs that are allocated to the flow-line, and to split them evenly between the number of products manufactured.

Taken together, these two instances show that raising the level of the unit of analysis in a management accounting system for lean production is done along two dimensions, as shown in Figure 4. The figure illustrates some important principles of lean production, as discussed above. The triangle symbolizes the organization. The core is the multifunctional team, which is made responsible for the production of a complete product from raw materials. The necessary machines are grouped according to the production flow and the indirect tasks are included in the team's responsibility. These teams are provided with strategic information, in order to be able to perform well.

The first dimension in raising the level of the unit of analysis is the horizontal, indicated by the arrow beneath the triangle. There is a need to shift the focus from single machines and/or operators to the whole production flow. The focus should be on the performance of the multifunctional team, not individual operators. Second, there is a vertical dimension, indicated by the arrow to the left of the triangle. There is a need to shift the focus from the operating level to the whole production system, including the higher levels. This is necessary since tasks previously performed by, and responsibilities belonging to, indirect personnel are integrated into the multifunctional teams.

The management accounting system influences the adoption process in three ways

Our analysis of the adoption process indicates that the management accounting system influences the adoption of lean manufacturing in three concurrent ways:

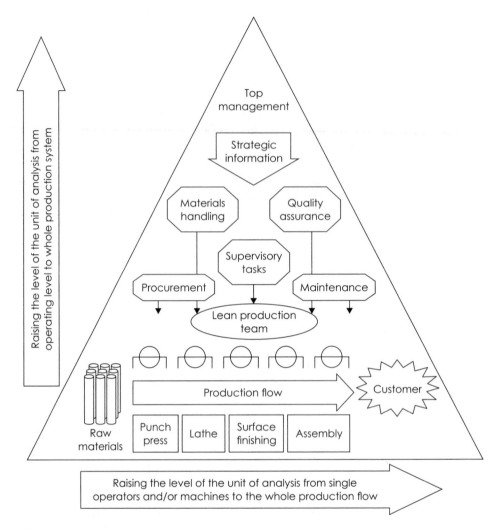

Figure 4 Raising the level of the unit of analysis in a management accounting system for lean production

technically, formally and cognitively. These three ways can be seen as coexisting and interdependent perspectives on an organization.

Technical influence. The technical perspective refers to the design of the management accounting system. Traditional management accounting systems are ill-equipped to function in a lean production environment. In this case, the turbulence caused by the mixed signals that the managing director received from the system around the summer of 1994 represents an instance where the design affected the process. A more recent example was when suggested changes in cost accounting principles were stalled because of the management accounting system's inability to record the desired data.

Formal influence   The formal perspective represents the formal role and purpose of the management accounting system in the organization, and this is sometimes difficult to separate from the technical influence. A common theme in the present case is that the administrative function, which includes the accounting department and the computer department, has had a 'controlling' role. For instance, they saw a trade-off between keeping control of operations and the changes taking place following the lean manufacturing strategy. In this trade-off they gave the highest priority to control.

As mentioned above, inertia is built into the management accounting system, since one of its tasks is to assess the performance of the company, much of which is done by comparing the present with the past. However, it is possible that management accounting systems can contribute to driving changes in manufacturing. One important feature of the Japanese view on management accounting is that it should play more of an 'influencing' role than an 'informing' role and be subservient to corporate strategy, not independent of it [19].

Cognitive influence.   The cognitive perspective concerns the way the management accounting system is used and how different actors in the organization think about issues related to management accounting. The cognitive influence is perhaps the most fundamental, since it is highly interrelated with the technical and the formal influences [20]. An example was when key actors' views on the management accounting system changed in the direction appropriate for lean manufacturing. Another example was the concern expressed by the managing director, when he questioned the appropriateness of the management accounting system. This observation represents an instance of unlearning, which is a prerequisite for learning [21].

A further example was when the administrative function resisted changes in the management accounting system, since they were afraid of losing control. Finally, we have the instance where focus continued to lie on productivity as the sole performance measurement, even though there were indications that the measure was not correct. Thus, the way people thought about the management accounting system and its role in the organization impeded attempts to change the system in the appropriate direction. It is also possible to see how the formal role of the mananagement accounting system affected the use of the information it supplied. Thus, the cognitive and the formal perspectives were mutually reinforcing.

Conclusions and Managerial Implications

From a production management point of view, it would be ideal if the management accounting system could support transitions towards lean production. However, traditional management accounting systems are likely to affect the adoption process negatively, since they are ill-equipped to interpret the changes made when implementing a complex production strategy.

This article reports the results of a study designed to explore the role of the management accounting system in the process of adopting a complex production strategy: lean production. We have found that the management accounting system indeed has a very important role to play in the adoption process. For the most part it serves as an impediment to the necessary changes, mainly due to its inability to accurately portray the results of these changes. In order for a management accounting system to support the adoption of lean production, we propose the following:

- The management accounting system can create impetus for changes in the direction of lean production, but not until traditional performance measures have reached a certain threshold (see Figure 3). Therefore, an important managerial task is to influence the location of this threshold, by making it easier to reach. The mere awareness of its existence is a good starting point.
- Another important way to create impetus for change is to raise the level of the unit of analysis in a management accounting system. First, there is a need to shift the focus from single machines and/or operators to the whole production flow. Second, there is a need to shift the focus from the operating level to the whole production system.
- When making these changes it is important to consider that management accounting systems affect the adoption process in three concurrent ways: technically, through their design; formally, through their role in the organization; and cognitively, through the way in which actors think about and use management accounting systems.

In order for a management accounting system to be congruent with lean production principles, all three of these perspectives need to be changed. Thus, it is not enough to implement a technical change in the management accounting system; if the formal role of the system does not simultaneously change, no lasting effects are likely. Perhaps most important is making sure that the cognitive perspective changes, since it affects the other two perspectives. If the values and beliefs of key actors do not change, the management accounting system is likely to continue to have an adverse effect on the possibilities for adopting a lean production strategy.

REFERENCES

1 Womack, J.P., Jones, D.T. and Roos, D., *The Machine that Changed the World*, Rawson Associates, New York, NY, 1990.
2 Moss Kanter, R., Stein, B.A. and Jick, T.D., *The Challenge of Organizational Change: How Companies Experience It and Leaders Guide It*, The Free Press, New York, NY, 1992.
3 Johnson, H.T. and Kaplan, R.S., *Relevance Lost – The Rise and Fall of Management Accounting*, Harvard Business School Press, Boston, MA, 1987.
4 Kaplan, R.S., 'Measuring manufacturing performance: a new challenge for managerial accounting research', *The Accounting Review*, Vol. 58 No. 4, 1983, pp. 686–705.
5 Kaplan, R.S., 'Yesterday's accounting undermines production', *Harvard Business Review*, July–August 1984, pp. 95–101.

6   Cooper, R. and Kaplan, R.S., 'Measure costs right: make the right decisions', *Harvard Business Review*, September–October 1988, pp. 96–103.

7   Kaplan, R.S. and Norton, D.P., 'The balanced scorecard – measures that drive performance', *Harvard Business Review*, January–February 1992, pp. 71–9.

8   Cooper, R., 'The role of activity based systems in supporting the transition to the lean enterprise', *Advances in Management Accounting; Research Annual*, Vol. 3, 1994, pp. 1–24.

9   Scott, W.R., 'Field methods in the study of organizations', in March, J.G. (Ed.), *Handbook of Organizations*, Rand McNally, Chicago, IL, 1965, pp. 261–304.

10 Stymne, B., *Values and Processes: A Systems Study of Effectiveness in Three Organizations*, Studentlitteratur, Lund, 1970.

11 Schein, E.H., *The Clinical Perspective in Fieldwork*, Sage, Newbury Park, Beverly Hills, CA, 1987.

12 Campbell, D.T. and Fiske, D.W, 'Convergent and discriminant validation by the multitrait–multimethod matrix', *Psychological Bulletin*, Vol. 56 No. 2, 1959, pp. 81–105.

13 Pettigrew, A.M., 'Longitudinal field research on change: theory and practice', *Organization Science*, Vol. 1 No. 3, 1990, pp. 267–92.

14 Pettigrew, A.M., *The Politics of Organizational Decision Making*, Tavistock, London, 1973.

15 Karlsson, C. and Åhlström, P., 'Assessing changes towards lean production', *International Journal of Operations & Production Management*, Vol. 16 No. 2, 1996, pp. 24–41.

16 Monden, Y., *Toyota Production System – Practical Approach to Production Management* Industrial Engineering and Management Press, Atlanta, GA, 1983.

17 Hayes, R.H., 'Why Japanese factories work', *Harvard Business Review*, July–August 1981, pp. 57–66.

18 Shingo, S., *A Study of the Toyota Production System from an Industrial Engineering Viewpoint*, Productivity Press, Cambridge, MA, 1981.

19 Hiromoto, T., 'Another hidden edge – Japanese management accounting', *Harvard Business Review*, July–August 1988, pp. 22–6.

20 Åhlström, P., 'Strukturella hinder vid implementering av lean production (in Swedish)', in Löwstedt, J. (Ed.), *Människan och strukturerna*, Nerenius & Santérus, Stockholm, 1995, pp. 129–52.

21 Nystrom, P.C. and Starbuck, W.H., 'To avoid organizational crisis, unlearn', *Organizational Dynamics*, Vol. 12 No. 4, 1984, pp. 53–65.

3.7

Target Costing as a Strategic Tool

John K. Shank and Joseph Fisher

Faced with increasing global competition, many firms are finding that cost-based pricing is becoming a relic of the past, whereas price-based or target costing is emerging as a key strategic tool. Consistent with the notion of price-based costing, several authors have argued that target costing is a superior approach to cost reduction and control when compared with typical standard-cost systems. Although many credit the Japanese with popularizing this technique, the idea and its early applications were evident in the philosophy of the Ford Motor Company in the early 1900s.[1] Today, as firms outside Japan start to integrate target costing into their management systems, there is little consensus on the technique's exact definition or when its use is most beneficial.

The logic of target costing is simple. The target cost is a financial goal for the full cost of a product, derived from estimates of selling price and desired profit. In a target-costing framework, product selling price is constrained by the marketplace and is determined by analysis along the entire industry value chain and across all functions in the firm. Top management sets the desired level of profit on the basis of firm strategy and financial goals. In many cases, the target profitability is based on desired return on assets or return on sales.[2] In contrast with cost-based pricing, product cost does not drive the estimated selling price. Instead, the target cost is the goal that a firm must achieve to meet its strategic objectives.

Common to most target-cost applications are a process that starts with competitive end-use market prices as the basis for determining acceptable manufacturing costs, and a belief that large-scale cost planning and reduction must occur early in the product life cycle. Several authors, in fact, assume that target costing is applicable only early in the product life cycle (i.e. during product specification and design). For example, Cooper states:

The purpose of target costing is to identify the production cost for a proposed product such that the product, when sold, generates the desired profit margin. The focus of target costing is to reduce the cost of a product through changes in its design. It is therefore applied during the design phase of a product's life cycle.[3]

The Consortium for Advanced Manufacturing–International defines the concept as follows:

Target costing represents a set of management tools and methods designed to direct design and planning activities for new products, provide a basis for controlling subsequent operational phases, and ensure that products achieve given profitability targets throughout their life cycle.[4]

These definitions imply that target costing is (1) driven by marker price and desired profits and (2) performed only early in the product life cycle. Some also argue that target costing is only applicable in certain industries. For example, Atkinson et al. state that 'target costing is a method of cost planning that focuses on products with discrete manufacturing processes and reasonably short product life cycles.' During the manufacturing phase of the product life cycle, such firms would incrementally improve processes by means of *kaizen* costing.[5] Many US firms use standard-costing systems to control costs at the manufacturing phase. The focus of *kaizen* costing is much different. In general, standard-cost systems focus on cost control (meeting the standard), whereas *kaizen* costing focuses on continuous improvement. That is, standard-costing systems focus on meeting the cost standard and avoiding unfavorable variances. In contrast, *kaizen* costing stresses continuous cost reduction. Atkinson et al. present a detailed analysis of how these methodologies differ.

In their view, combining target and *kaizen* costing under a single name is not beneficial since they rely on different cost-reduction techniques.[6] In contrast with target costing, *kaizen* costing does not explicitly focus on market prices or planned profitability, but is internally focused on continual incremental product cost improvements. Several authors have argued that up to 80 percent of a product's cost is fixed once it leaves product design, making major cost reduction difficult after the design stage. This implies that firms have little to gain by implementing target costing when products are in the manufacturing phase.[7]

The belief that target costing must he applied early in the product life cycle is based, in part, on the proposition that costs are fixed after a product is in manufacturing. In addition, increasingly shorter product life cycles also reinforce the supposition that major redesign loses its relevance when a product is being manufactured. These two propositions imply that any large-scale attempts at cost reduction at the manufacturing phase are pointless. Atkinson et al. point out that Japanese firms apply target costing most often with discrete (i.e. assembly) manufacturing processes that undergo regular model changes.[8] For example, Toyota, on average, changes models every four years, and Matsushita changes a disc player model every year. Although each model change can be viewed as a new product, many are actually modest modifications to the current product line. For example, when Toyota introduces a new Camry, it uses almost all the same manufacturing facilities and equipment to produce the new model, and a new Matsushita disc player may be almost identical to the previous model. Nevertheless, both manufacturers apply target costing to these product changes.

While target costing may be more easily applied early in the product life cycle, there is no conceptual reason why the methodology cannot be applied to existing products. We believe that target costing can also be applied at the manufacturing stages of the product life cycle. By defining target costing too narrowly, managers may conclude that this methodology cannot be applied for existing products and may continue with their current ineffective cost-management systems. There are many industries that do not fit the profile of little flexibility in manufacturing costs and short product life cycles. For these industries, target costing later in the product life cycle may still be a value-added exercise. Other researchers also see target costing as broadly as we do, suggesting that it can be applied throughout the full product life cycle. For example, Kato states: 'In reality, target costing is not a cost-quantification technique, but rather a complete cost-reduction program . . . Target costing is not a simple cost-reduction technique, but a complete, strategic profit management system.' And Horvath writes: 'Target costing is just a part of the cost-management function for a product throughout its life cycle. The cost target set must then be achieved, while meeting customer requirements, using various methods designed to identify cost-reduction potentials.'[9]

The Institute of Management Accountants also advises that firms can apply target costing to new products and to those being modified.[10] When sufficiently motivated, a firm can change production techniques, which may result in substantially different product costs and profitability. If managers were to believe that during manufacturing only incremental (i.e. slight) change is possible (through *kaizen* costing or controlling costs with standard-cost systems), firms might miss significant strategic opportunities. In fact, introducing a target-costing approach may drive product modification, rather than a planned modification prompting the initiation of target costing.

Next, we present a case study that demonstrates the relevance of target-costing techniques for a process-industry plant built in the 1890s that had been making largely the same products for fifty years. The firm's managers had used a standard-cost system for many years and, given the usual restrictive definitions of target costing, might have concluded that *kaizen* costing was most appropriate for this plant. However, competitive realities necessitated a major strategic change that employed target costing as an important ingredient in cost-reduction efforts leading to strategic revitalization.

Montclair Paper Mill

Three months after becoming president of the Montclair Papers Division of Mohawk Forest Products, Tom Winton was trying to understand why the Montclair mill's profitability was so low in order to formulate appropriate corrective actions. He focused on the manufacture of one product, Carnival Uncoated Cover Paper in Forest Green color, as representative of the mill's problems.

Montclair is the oldest and smallest of the ten mills owned by Mohawk. The mill's huge paper machines are some of the oldest in the industry, but, being well maintained, they still run well. The Montclair mill buys dry pulp, which it converts into coated and uncoated fine papers for premium applications, such as brochures, catalogs, magazines, annual reports, and labels. When creating viable strategies for Montclair's 1,500 products, its managers strive to exploit the mill's strengths and available market niches. Montclair's machines are 200 feet long by 20 feet wide (60.9 × 6.1 meters). They differ in width ('trim') and speed (feet per minute), which determines capacity. The machines can produce various colors, weights, and grades of paper, depending on pulp mix, additives, machine design, and machine settings.

It is widely believed in the papermaking industry that a firm can't make money unless mills run continuously – three shifts a day, 365 days a year. *What* a machine produces is secondary to the fact that it is *running*. Changing products 'on the run' (grade, weight, color, or texture) produces waste while the machine is achieving 'on grade' performance. Estimated at 30 percent of overall mill cost, waste includes lost materials, sewage disposal, operating costs during changeover, and opportunities missed. The common wisdom is: 'The fewer changes, the better.'

Narrow, old, and slow by parent-company standards, Montclair's machines are new, wide, and fast for a premium papers niche mill. Montclair's machines average ninety tons per day, whereas a typical premium papers machine produces from thirty tons to as little as ten tons per day. (A world-class commodity paper machine can produce 1,000 tons per day.) Management was not sure if Montclair's size configuration constituted a strategic asset or liability in the premium niches. That is, management was unsure if there are scale economies or diseconomies for machines of this size.

In the premium paper segment, converting – the process of creating finished products from the huge 'logs' of paper that come off the machines – is essential for a mill to produce exactly what each customer needs. The converting process includes coating, supercalendering, rewinding, slitting, sheeting, embossing, and packaging, with processes differing widely among products. Some paper is sold the way it comes off the paper machine; some products use nearly all the converting processes. At the Montclair mill the converting area operates like a job shop.

Most of the converting equipment at the mill is not considered state-of-the-art. However, even modern precision sheeters and sheet packers do not perform at their rated capacities because of the many changeovers that occur during the process. In addition, some operations add no value, such as the process during which a machine flips huge stacks of sheets 'face up' after a manual inspection operation flips them 'face down' one at a time.

Montclair maintains one of the largest premium paper warehouses in the United States, called the Distribution Center (DC), that holds more than 20,000 tons of finished goods comprising 1,000 products. Montclair sells about half of its 200,000-ton output each year through the DC and about half in manufacturing orders.

Dark or 'deep' colors are vital to product lines in the premium papers segment because they increase the visual appeal of a mill's swatch books – critical tools for

Table 1   Value chain analysis of one use of Forest Green Carnival[a]

Customer
(a) Reebok sales promotion brochure; 20,000 copies:
     Cost = $24,000 (printing = $7,000)

Printer
     Revenue = $7,000
     Cost =   5,900 (paper = $2,310 with 95% yield)
     Margin= $1,100

Paper merchant
     Revenue = $2,310
     Cost =   1,989 (paper = $1,466 per ton)
     Margin = $321

The paper mill – Ajax Paper Company
(a competitor of Montclair that won the order)
     Revenue = $1,466
     Cost =   ? (competitor cost analysis)
     Margin =   ?

---

[a] We do not consider stages 'upstream' from the paper mill, such as pulp mill and wood supplies.

marketing these papers to printers and graphic designers. The mill's 1,000-plus uncoated products differ in color, size, finish texture, basis weight, and package type. 'Merchant' distributors usually sell these uncoated papers to job-shop printers that contract with end-use customers.

The Montclair mill produces deep colors on one paper machine with frequent grade changes to produce a wide variety of weights, colors, and textures. The mill produces the darkest colors least frequently – demand for any one product (i.e. variants of color, size, or texture) being limited to about four to six tons annually. A typical specific deep-color order from a merchant is two tons, which requires only about forty minutes of machine time. As a result, management infrequently schedules production of deep colors to allow longer runs in order to amortize the high set-up cost and production waste.

Forest Green Carnival grade paper is a typical deep-color product. It is difficult to run, difficult to sell in large quantities, and difficult to position in the marketplace. (See Table 1 for a typical value chain analysis of one use of this product.)

The mill's standard cost for Forest Green Carnival was $2,900 per ton (see Table 2 for a cost report). Selling at $2,200 per ton, the Montclair mill was losing $700 per ton. With warehousing costs and a capital charge for the prorated share of mill investment added, the loss was $1,020 per ton (see Table 3). The managerial challenge was to determine what the mill could and should do about this problem product.

Table 2 Standard cost report for Forest Green Carnival (sheets pack)

Cost components	Price per ton
Fiber type and percentage of fiber mix	
Virgin hardwood (for opacity and smoothness) 63%	$425
Virgin softwood (for strength) 15%	475
Scrap (recycled waste) 22%	60
Weighted average cost of fiber	$352
Paper Machine (yield = 46%)	
Fiber ($352 ÷ 0.46 − $61 credit for scrap generated)	$704
Other materials and dyes ($550 ÷ 0.46)	1,196
Machine conversion[a]	376
Total	$2,276
Converting (yield = 88%)	
Paper ($2,276 ÷ 0.88)	$2,586
Sheeting and packing[b]	303
Pack and ship to the Distribution Center	11
Total	$2,900

[a] $520 per running hour ÷ 3 tons per hour ÷ 0.46.
[b] $600 per hour ÷ 2.25 tons per hour ÷ 0.88.

Table 3 Overall cost summary for Forest Green Carnival

Expense item	Cost per ton
Manufacturing cost	$2,900
Mill capital charge[a]	120
Distribution Center operating cost	25
Distribution Center capital charge[b]	145
Freight to merchant	30
Total	$3,220
Selling price[c]	2,200
Loss	($1,020)

[a] The mill has $160 million invested (including working capital). This is $800 per ton of annual throughput. To earn a 15 percent return on investment requires a mill-level profit of $120 per ton ($800 × 0.15). The 15 percent earnings rate is the mill-level proxy, before taxes, for a corporate-level 12 percent return on equity.
[b] $2,900 + inventory turnover ratio of 3 × 15 percent earnings rate.
[c] To merchant distributor.

Standard-Cost Methodology

Montclair's cost-analysis supervisor was convinced that the marketplace price for deep-color, uncoated cover grades was the problem, not Montclair's manufacturing process. The standard cost of $2,900 per ton for Forest Green Carnival was solidly constructed on:

- union wage rates for labor costs ('pattern bargaining' virtually assured comparable labor costs among the major firms, all of which were unionized);
- standard yield rates for all manufacturing steps, based on latest performance measured against long-standing norms at the Montclair mill;
- current market prices for all purchased components;
- generally accepted industry procedures for building the 'normal' cost of scrap into the standard cost, after deducting the offset for the market value of the scrap generated.

The standards were updated annually for changes in purchase prices, process flows, and yield targets. With more than 1,500 products manufactured at the mill, more frequent updating was deemed infeasible.

Manufacturing management and the division president, Tom Winton, accepted that the standard cost represented the best practices of the mill and thus was an appropriate basis for monitoring manufacturing performance. Standard costs were also helpful to simplify calculating the month-end cost of goods sold and the ending inventory for financial statements. Updated only once a year, the standard cost was stable from month to month. Management viewed this stability as a positive feature in monitoring monthly performance against the annual plan.[11]

In short, this was a typically derived standard cost for a product that was infrequently produced and hard to make. Also typical was the high level of skepticism among financial, manufacturing, and general management that a substantially lower cost was feasible in this mill.

Mill managers believed that the loss per ton was related to *price* rather than *cost*. They believed that the sales organization (see Table 3) was keeping the $2,200 per ton selling price artificially low to compete against firms operating small, fully depreciated, obsolete mills that might be employing nonunion labor or following a marginal cost-pricing strategy to keep their mills running. Sales managers considered pricing as a variable based solely on market competition. They were already selling Carnival grade at prices several hundred dollars per ton higher than competitors, such as Ajax Paper Company (see Table 1), because the market perceived Carnival as a high-price/high-quality specialty grade. Although some customers willingly paid the price premium, many did not, making further price increases infeasible. According to the sales force, the loss was not a sales problem. Manufacturing thought that costs were based on well-established production processes and materials requirements. The loss was, therefore, not a manufacturing problem. Financial management monitored mill-production performance using its well-substantiated standard costing. Thus, from its perspective, the loss was certainly not an accounting problem. None of the groups considered the mill's loss on Forest Carnival as originating with their processes or methodologies.

Target-Cost Methodology

Starting with a price acceptable to end-use customers, target costing involves deducting normal costs and margins along the value chain back to the mill (see Table 1). In this case, Ajax Paper had won out over Montclair with a bid of $1,466 per ton, thereby setting the prevailing price in the market.

The last step in netting back to an 'allowable' mill target cost is to deduct an allowance for a reasonable return on the investment at the Montclair mill. This is the residual income concept[12] that recently resurfaced as economic value analysis (EVA). Calculating 'economic earnings' can be a major challenge. Mill managers would have to make difficult choices about what to include in mill investment, how to value mill assets, how to allow for capacity utilization, and how to choose the required earning rate – all topics beyond the scope of this article. For our purposes, we estimate a capital charge of $120 per ton, on the basis of multiplying a fully allocated mill investment of $800 per ton (valued at replacement cost with full-capacity utilization) by an earnings rate of 15 percent (based on a factory-level proxy for the firm's cost of capital). With this step complete, we can calculate a competitive target cost for the Montclair mill (see Table 4). Because the Montclair mill sells to merchant distributors from the DC, we must also deduct from $1,256 the cost of getting the product to and through the DC, including a capital charge on invest-ment in the DC (see Table 5; data derived from Tables 2 and 3).

This clearly represented a depressing scenario for Montclair's managers. The product had a target manufacturing cost of $1,162 per ton, but a standard cost of $2,900 per ton – a daunting prospect for the mill, to say the least! Even more depressing was the fact that the problem lay deeper than just cost inefficiencies at the mill, as we demonstrate next.

Although it is not usually defined this way, it is possible to decompose standard cost into an 'ideal' cost (allowing for no waste, scrap, or conversion inefficiency)

Table 4 Calculating competitive target cost for the Montclair mill

	Cost per ton
Ajax selling price to the merchant	$1,466
Freight (paid by the mill)	(30)
Normal sales returns and allowances	(60)
Montclair capital charge	(120)
Montclair mill's allowable target cost	$1,256

Table 5   Distribution Center deductions from allowable target cost

	Cost per ton
Allowable target cost	$1,256
Ship to Distribution Center	(11)
Distribution Center operating cost	(25)
Distribution Center capital charge[a]	(58)
Target manufacturing cost	$1,162

[a] $1,162 ÷ an inventory turnover ratio of 3 × 15 percent earnings rate.

Table 6   Ideal cost and allowable variance for Forest Green Carnival

Ideal cost (perfect yield)		
Materials	$902	($352 ÷ $550)
Paper machine	173	($520 per hour ÷ 3 tons per hour)
Converting processes	267	($600 per hour ÷ 2.25 tons per hour)
Subtotal	$1,342	
Allowable variation		
Materials lost	$1,257	($2,159 − $902)
Lost paper machine time	254	($427 − $173)
Lost conversion time	36	($303 − $267)
Ship to Distribution Center[a]	11	
Standard cost	$2,900	

[a] No value added in this step.

and an 'allowable variance'.[13] Such a definition highlights part of the problem with standard costing – a 'normal' level of waste is sanctioned and buried in the allowable cost. (See Table 6 for a breakdown of ideal cost and allowable variance for Forest Green Carnival.) The Montclair mill's ideal cost would be $1,342 per ton versus a target cost of $1,162 per ton. That is, even if operations were perfect, the cost would still be $180 per ton too high!

Perhaps the market price of $1,466 per ton was 'unreasonably low', as mill management believed. When examined more closely, however, a competitor cost study not described here demonstrated that Ajax Paper Company probably earned a reasonable return on investment while charging $1,466 per ton, which translates to Montclair's $1,162 per ton manufacturing cost target (see Tables 4 and 5).

Montclair management's realization that an important competitor could be operating under a dramatically different mill cost structure seriously undermined the credibility of the assertion that a $2,900 per ton standard-cost reflected the best practices of the mill.

Target Costing in Action

As a result of this externally motivated, value-chain-driven analyis, managers decided to take action. After Montclair managers accepted that the allowable cost of $2,900 per ton was more than $1,700 per ton too high, they decided to reengineer the manufacturing process for the product. The target-cost approach forced management to remove its standard-cost blinders.

Once the mill management team accepted the challenge of reducing by more than 60 percent the manufacturing cost for deep-color grades, it focused on the four major cost components:

• fiber cost (changing the mix of recycled paper and virgin pulp to reduce raw materials cost);
• paper machine cost (getting on grade faster to improve yields);
• dye costs;
• conversion cost ('make' versus 'buy').

As we show, each area yielded substantial cost savings when a target-cost mindset replaced standard-cost dogma.

Fiber cost

A project team began a series of manufacturing trials showing that the mill could increase the percentage of recycled paper in the raw materials mix above the standard allowance of 22 percent – a figure largely based on levels of internal scrap generation. Experience proved that recycled percentages ranging from 30 to 75 percent would not detrimentally affect the quality of the finished sheet if the scrap paper were handled carefully. The results of the scrap-usage experiments were so impressive that the mill kept increasing its scrap percentage. As in other industries, steady application of the *kaizen* philosophy achieved positive results.[14]

Using 75 percent scrap in the raw material mix reduced the Montclair mill's fiber cost by 60 percent with no negative effect on paper quality. In addition, market acceptance of the paper was favorable because Montclair could tout its product's 'high recycled content'.

Paper machine cost

The dismal paper machine yield of 46 percent resulted from a self-reinforcing, negative cycle in the mill. Montclair management needed to schedule a four-hour run to achieve a yield as high as 46 percent (i.e. at least two hours to get the right shade and two hours of good production). But because the product had such poor yields, the mill scheduled a production run only about twice a year. Batching orders for six months allowed sufficient volume to justify a production run long enough to amortize the anticipated heavy changeover costs. The two-hour changeover time for Forest Green Carnival reflected infrequent product runs that did not enable crews to apply revised processes and improve yields. High losses meant that management was unwilling to run the product more frequently, thus causing the inefficient cycle to repeat itself. Breaking this cycle started a 'must improve, can improve' mindset driven by the target-cost study.

For Montclair, a root-cause analysis of the long changeover time revealed that the biggest time loss was getting 'on shade' for a designer-created color such as Forest Green. A project team tackled this problem by first observing that if the production run could start with a fiber mix closer to the desired shade, there was a dramatically reduced 'off shade' time. That implied starting with green fiber rather than white. This had never been possible when 80 percent of the fiber was virgin pulp that can only be purchased in one color – white. But increasing the percentage of recycled fiber in the raw material mix opened the possibility of buying green scrap paper instead of white. Since there was virtually no market demand for green 'broke' (scrap), the mill was able to buy essentially unlimited quantities at low prices. Broke dealers were perplexed as to why anyone would want colored broke! The thin demand for colored broke was because other mills (using their standard cost systems?) did not have color-mixing systems able to start with anything other than white fiber.

Another project team experimented with Montclair's computerized color-mixing system. Over the course of a year, they were able to develop proprietary software that allowed the color-mixing crew to get 'on shade' in 40 minutes instead of 2 hours by starting with green broke. The software they developed could take any combination of green shades of broke and mix to the exact Forest Green shade in only 40 minutes. This breakthrough derived from 'branch and bound' sort routines starting with a CD-ROM containing digital equivalents of 500,000 color shades. Reducing changeover time from 2 hours to 40 minutes raised the yield rate to 75 percent when producing 2 hours of good paper (120 minutes ÷ [120 + 40]).

Dye costs

Starting the papermaking process with up to 75 percent green fiber required much less dye to achieve the exact Forest Green shade. The newly developed proprietary software enabled getting on shade with an average dye cost of only $250 per ton instead of $500 per ton. Considering the 75 percent paper-machine yields, this reduced dye-related costs from $1,196 to $400 – an amazing $796 reduction in the cost per ton (see Table 7).

Conversion costs

Another project team tackled this cost component by seriously considering the make-versus-buy option. Based on a preliminary best-practices survey, a world-class

Table 7   Cost breakdown of other materials and dyes before use of green fiber

Materials (perfect yield)	Cost
Dyes	$500
Fillers	50
Subtotal	$550
Yielded cost (÷ 0.46)	$1,196

Table 8   Conversion cost reduction achieved in eighteen months

	Cost per hour	Tons per hour	Yield	= cost per ton
Before	$600	2.25	0.88	$303
After	$540	2.50	0.90	$240
Percent improvement	10%	11%	2%	20%

conversion cost of $150 per ton was deemed possible (as compared to Montclair's cost of $303 per ton). Each converting department was challenged to develop competitive programs or risk job loss to outsourcing. In fact, one salvage rework department was closed because improved 'first pass' yields eliminated much of the 'second pass' rework. Management also enacted a hiring freeze with the aim of absorbing all turnover in conversion jobs through productivity improvements. Over eighteen months, the $303 per ton conversion cost for Forest Green Carnival fell to $240 – a 20 percent reduction (see Table 8). Although no individual component in the calculation improved by more than 11 percent, a 20 percent overall improvement was possible thanks to the benefits of compound arithmetic! Interestingly, this dramatic reduction did not become the new 'standard', but was just the first step in a continuing *kaizen* effort to halve the original cost. The externally derived best-practice number of $150 per ton continued to be the benchmark.

By combining the improvements contributed by the four project teams, it was possible to envision lowering the manufacturing cost from $2,900 to $1,162 (see Table 9).
   Although the mill did not regularly achieve these benchmarks, the management team was greatly encouraged. A target-cost mindset could bring the lower numbers well within reach. The revised standard cost was lower by $1,738 ($1,162 versus $2,900) – almost a 60 percent reduction. Clearly, for this mill, the concept of 'achievable standard' was amenable to continuous improvement after incorporating a target-cost framework. The target-costing framework dramatically lowered

Table 9 Revised achievable standard cost and revised ideal cost of Forest Green Carnival

Cost component	Achievable standard cost	Ideal cost
Fiber		
Virgin hardwood (0.20 × $425)	$85	–
Virgin softwood (0.05 × $475)	24	–
Purchased scrap (0.75 × $45)	34	–
Subtotal	$143	–
Paper machine (75% yield)		
Fiber ($143 ÷ 0.75)	$190	$143
Other materials and dyes ($300 ÷ 0.75)	400	300
Machine conversion ($520 ÷ 3 ÷ 0.75)	230	173
Subtotal	$820	$616
Conversion process (90% yield)		
Paper ($820 ÷ 0.9)	$911	–
Converting[a]	240	216
Subtotal	$1,151	$216
Pack and ship to Distribution Center	11	–
Total	$1,162	$832

[a] $540 per hour ÷ 2.5 tons per hour ÷ 0.90 yield.

manufacturing costs, after which the mill continued to decrease costs through *kaizen* efforts.

The revised standard – $1,162 – was $180 *below* the $1,342 figure that had been considered the ideal cost in the first stage of the target-cost study. Yet, $1,162 still included 25 percent machine loss and 10 percent conversion loss. With substantial room for further cost reduction, the ideal cost dropped from $1,342 to $832 – a 38 percent reduction. Clearly, the concept of ideal cost is not an absolute, but is relative to how one thinks about the process.

Conclusion

The Montclair mill experienced a dramatic turnaround. Initially, the revitalization project teams faced a standard cost of $2,900 versus a target cost of $1,162, and an ideal cost of $1,342. After about eighteen months of price-based costing initiatives, Winton and mill management could see the possibility of an achievable target cost of $1,162 versus an ideal cost of $832. Thus, additional savings of $330 per ton remained a goal for future project teams to attain.

The following cost concepts featured prominently during the evolution of cost-reduction efforts at the Montclair paper mill:

- Ideal manufacturing cost (viewed from an internal perspective). No waste, no scrap, no inefficiency, no delays, perfect formulations, and perfect plant layout.
- Target cost (viewed from an external perspective). Ideal value proposition price to the end-user. From the ideal value proposition price to the end-user, subtract normal costs and margins along the value chain back to the manufacturer.
- Standard cost (tough but attainable). Ideal cost plus the allowable waste and inefficiency.
- Actual cost.

At the beginning of this field study, management focused too much attention on standard cost versus actual cost. There was heavy pressure to move standard cost toward actual cost in order to minimize unfavorable variances for public financial reporting. Management focused too little attention on ideal manufacturing cost, which is often dismissed as having dysfunctional motivational impact.[15] Target-costing received no attention. At the end of the field study, the most useful cost-management tool focused on ideal manufacturing cost versus target cost in relation to actual cost. The standard cost concept essentially dropped out of the picture.

The Montclair story illustrates the potential of using target costing as a proactive cost-reduction tool in place of ineffective standard costing. Although this account – as a single story – could be subject to 'small sample bias', it does not suffer from selection bias. The mill management team had no idea at the start of the target-cost project that results would be so dramatically positive. In fact, the prognosis for continued production of deep colors looked so bleak at the outset that the problem was viewed as more likely a make-versus-buy choice. Target costing forced Montclair's managers to rewrite the rules of the game by changing the way the mill delivered value to the customer. Because standard costing accepts the existing game rules and the existing value chain, we believe that fundamental cost breakthroughs are much more probable when using target costing.

We believe target costing is often too narrowly defined, which results in managers clinging to their current cost-management systems in the belief that target costing is irrelevant to their businesses. Cost-management practitioners need to seriously reappraise the prominence of standard costing as a cost-reduction or cost-control tool.

NOTES

1   M. Sakurai, 'Target Costing and How to Use It', *Journal of Cost Management*, volume 3, Summer 1989, pp. 39–50; P. Horvath, *Target Costing: State of the Art Report* (Bedford, Texas: Consortium for Advanced Manufacturing – International, 1993); J. Fisher, 'Implementing Target Costing', *Journal of Cost Management*, volume 9, Summer 1995, pp. 50–59; Institute of Management Accountants, *Implementing Target Costing*, 1994.
2   Fisher (1995).
3   R. Cooper, 'How Japanese Manufacturing Firms Implement Target Costing Systems' (*Claremont, California: Claremont Graduate School*, working paper, 1994).
4   Horvath (1993).

5   A. Atkinson, R. Banker, R. Kaplan, and S.M. Young, *Management Accounting* (Upper Saddle River, New Jersey: Prentice-Hall, 1997); J. Lee and Y. Monden, 'An International Comparison of Manufacturing-Friendly Cost Management Systems', *International Journal of Accounting*, volume 31, number 2, 1996, pp. 197–212.

6   Atkinson et al. (1997); see also R. Cooper and W.B. Chew, 'Control Tomorrow's Cost through Today's Designs', *Harvard Business Review*, volume 74, January–February 1996, pp. 88–97.

7   Cooper and Chew (1996).

8   Atkinson et al. (1997); Fisher (1995).

9   Y. Kato, 'Target Costing Support Systems: Lessons from Leading Japanese Companies', *Management Accounting Research*, volume 4, March 1993, pp. 33–47; Horvath (1993).

10 Institute of Management Accountants (1994).

11 J. Shank and K. Constantinides, 'Matching Accounting to Strategy: One Mill's Experience', *Management Accounting*, volume 76, September 1994, pp. 32–36.

12 D. Solomons, *Divisional Performance: Measurement and Control* (Homewood, Illinois: Richard D. Irwin, 1965), Chapter 3.

13 J. Shank and V. Govindarajan, *Strategic Cost Analysis* (Homewood, Illinois: Richard D. Irwin, 1989), Chapter 7.

14 S. Tully, 'Raiding a Company's Hidden Cash', *Fortune*, volume 130, 22 August 1994, pp. 82–89.

15 R.W. Hilton, *Managerial Accounting* (New York: McGraw-Hill, 1991); C. Horngren and G. Sundem, *Introduction to Management Accounting*, 9th edition (Englewood Cliffs, New Jersey: Prentice-Hall, 1993).

Supply Chain Management for Recoverable Manufacturing Systems

V. Daniel R. Guide Jr, Vaidyanathan Jayaraman, Rajesh Srivastava and W. C. Benton

Introduction

Over the past decade, firms have faced increasing pressures from consumers and from government regulations to become more environmentally responsible. Researchers have proposed a number of frameworks to explain and define the concept of an environmentally conscious corporation:

- industrial ecology;
- sustainable development;
- environmentally conscious manufacturing;
- total environmental quality management.

All these frameworks include one basic tenet: minimizing waste is key to a corporation becoming environmentally responsible.

There are many ways to minimize the environmental costs of manufacturing, but the prevention of waste products avoids many environmental costs before they occur. A system that focuses on the recovery of materials used to manufacture and deliver products can minimize the environmental impact of production. A material recovery system, referred to as a recoverable product environment and illustrated in Figure 1, includes strategies to increase product life, consisting of repairing, remanufacturing (including technical upgrades), and finally recycling products.

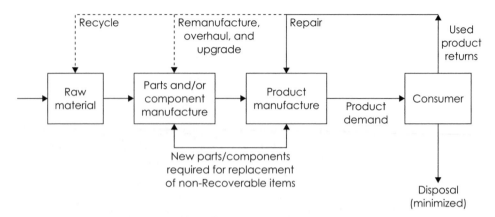

Figure 1   A recoverable product environment seeks to close the materials-use cycle by using repair and remanufacture operations to extend a product's life; recycling is used only when no value added remains

A major part of the recoverable product environment is the recoverable manufacturing system designed to extend product life through repair and remanufacturing. Recoverable manufacturing systems are environmentally friendly and profitable and have been reported for a number of products, including copiers, automobile parts, computers, office furniture, mass transit, aviation equipment, and tires.

Recoverable manufacturing is an environmentally, economically sound way to achieve many of the goals of sustainable development. Recoverable manufacturing operations account for total sales in excess of $53 billion per year, and based on a recent survey, Lund (1996) estimates that 73,000 firms in the United States are engaged in some form of recoverable manufacturing. The Environmental Protection Agency (EPA) cites remanufacturing as an integral foundation of reuse activities and reports that manufacturers use less energy and produce fewer wastes with these types of activities than with traditional methods. The EPA also reports on a number of firms successfully engaged in recoverable manufacturing, including Union Carbide (toner cartridges), Xerox (toner cartridges), Office Plan Inc. (office furniture) and Miller SQA (office furniture). A wide range of firms engage in recoverable manufacturing operations, including large multinational firms; Xerox estimates its total cost savings amount to over $20 million per year. Xerox practices asset recovery and remanufacturing for its photocopiers and toner cartridges in the United States and abroad. Deere and Company recently entered into a long-term agreement with Springfield Remanufacturing Corporation in which a joint corporation will remanufacture diesel engines and engine components for Deere products. Sales of remanufactured engines in 1996 exceeded $2.5 billion dollars; both engines and engine components have long been remanufactured worldwide. IBM Europe engages in a number of recoverable manufacturing operations and finds that they provide a green corporate image and are profitable. Digital Europe also finds that recoverable operations provide a number of benefits, including improved consumer image and profits from the operations themselves.

Firms based in Europe or doing business in the European Union (EU) have added incentive to engage in recoverable operations: legislative Acts. German Acts on packaging materials and recycling and waste control have had a profound impact on commerce in Europe. The German Recycling and Waste Control Act requires that manufacturers actively seek techniques and products that avoid waste and promote the reuse of nonavoidable wastes. In addition, firms must take back and recycle or reuse scrapped products at the end of their lives. This act applies to firms doing business in Germany, as well as to German companies. The EU is rapidly following German initiative, with Austria, Belgium, Finland, France, Italy, the Netherlands, Spain, and Sweden all passing stringent laws on reuse. Clearly, any firm that wants to do business in the EU must pay attention to providing environmentally friendly products. Given the profitability, legislative initiatives, and growing consumer awareness, the time is right for the formal development of recoverable manufacturing systems.

Industrial Ecology, Sustainable Development, and Recoverable Systems

In the early to mid 1990s, researchers espoused several frameworks for environmentally conscious systems development. Those in the industrial ecology movement saw the industrial system as an ecosystem that was not particularly efficient. The major problems they identified were those of toxic waste and the inefficient use of materials. Jelinski et al. (1992) envisioned the industrial system as a closed environment in which byproducts from industrial processes become inputs for other industrial processes. Frosch (1992; 1994) discussed the need for closed-loop industrial systems since natural resources are limited and any closed ecosystem, that is, the earth, can accommodate only a finite amount of waste. Piasecki (1992) called for the development of innovative management techniques designed to reduce waste, rather than reliance on technology. A great deal of the work in industrial ecology has concerned the development of technical solutions to problems associated with industrial processes rather than the development of managerial techniques. Industrial ecology is discussed in detail in the proceedings of the colloquium on industrial ecology at the National Academy of Sciences (1992) and by Ayres and Ayres (1996).

The sustainable development movement is concerned with such issues as the impact of population on ecosystems, food supplies, and production, and the development of sustainable economies. In this worldview, industrial activities play an important role in sustainable development, but society as a whole must change its consumption patterns and attitudes as well. A number of authors focus on the contribution of the corporation to sustainable development. These authors focus on strategies that allow the consumer, the corporation, and the environment to accomplish the goals of sustainable development.

Table 1   Differentiating factors for recoverable options, showing that repair, remanufacture, and recycling require varying amounts of effort to reuse materials and products. Recycling requires that there is no value, save materials, remaining in the product; repair and remanufacture require that some degree of valued added remains

Operations	Product identity	Degree of disassembly	Extent of transformation	Material value added	Labor value added
Repair	Unit	Diagnostic	None	Replace or repair defective parts	Limited
Remanufacture	Unit, component, or part	Complete	Limited	Replace unrecoverable parts Technical upgrades	Extensive
Recycle	None	Material	Complete	None added	Limited

Recoverable systems offer corporations potential advantages, including increased profitability through reduced requirements for materials and improved market share based on environmental image. In a recent survey of remanufacturing firms in the United States, Nasr et al. (1998) found that remanufacturing firms had high profit margins, around 20 percent. A recoverable manufacturing system seeks to minimize material waste by recovering the maximum content of returned manufactured products. This approach has several advantages – minimizing the amount of materials being landfilled and providing like-new units for only a fraction of the energy, materials, and labor required to manufacture a new unit.

A recoverable product system is composed of a number of highly interdependent subsystems (Figure 1). Firms have a number of options available for returning products to consumers in useable condition: repair, remanufacture, or complete recycling of the materials in the original product (Table 1). The correct choice among these options may be dictated by economics and by the condition and age of the returned product. A recoverable system is essentially a closed-loop industrial system with discarded items used in place of virgin materials to the greatest extent possible.

Several authors have recognized the need for recoverable manufacturing systems and see a need for supply chain management activities that explicitly consider the problems an organization faces in this environment.

Complicating Characteristics of Recoverable Manufacturing Systems

In a recent assessment of remanufacturing firms in the United States, Nasr et al. (1998) found a lack of technologies and techniques for logistics in general. However, we found that a number of tools and techniques are available to assist the practicing manager, and we identified seven major characteristics of recoverable manufacturing systems that complicate the management, planning, and control of supply chain functions. The seven characteristics are:

1   *The problem of uncertainty in timing and quantity of returns*   This reflects the uncertain nature of the life of a product. A number of factors, including the life-cycle stage of a product and the rate of technological change, influence returns. This characteristic has a marked impact on demand management and inventory control and management.

2   *The problem of balancing demand with returns*   This is also a function of a product's expected life and the rate of technical innovation. Muckstadt and Isaac (1981) first observed this characteristic in discussing repairable inventory, noting that organizations may not directly control repairable stock. Imperfect correlation between demand and returns may lead to excess stocks of unwanted units, components and parts and shortages of needed units, components and parts. This makes inventory management and purchasing complex and difficult to plan, manage, and control.

3   *The need to disassemble returned products*   This requires that firms know the degree and the method of disassembly in advance. Different options in product recovery require different degrees of disassembly; repair operations require only limited disassembly to remove and replace the nonfunctional part(s), but remanufacturing requires complete disassembly. Several authors have addressed the problem of determining the degree of disassembly. The disassembly process also adds complexity in coordinating production planning and control. Disassembly operations influence a number of decision areas, including production planning and control, information systems, and inventory control.

4   *The uncertainty in materials recovered*   This reflects the fact that two identical returned items may yield different sets of repairable or remanufacturable parts; recycling yield is less problematic since the condition of the item is of little concern. This uncertainty affects inventory planning and control, resource planning, and purchasing.

5   *The need for a reverse logistics network*   This concerns how products are collected from the end user and returned to a facility for repair, remanufacturing or recycling. This requirement is complex and requires decisions regarding the number and location of take-back centers, incentives for product returns, transportation methods, and third-party providers.

6   *The need to match parts*   This is of concern in repair and remanufacturing operations. Customers turning in a unit to be repaired or remanufactured may want the same unit back. Customer-driven returns are common in the aviation industry, which relies on third-party jet engine repair and remanufacturing facilities and whose customers require the same engine be returned. A unit may also be composed of a mix of common parts and components and serial-number-specific parts and components. This characteristic requires better information systems and complicates the scheduling of resources.

7   *Stochastic routings and highly uncertain processing times*   This is a concern at the operational level. Stochastic routings reflect the uncertain condition of units

Table 2   Comparison of the recoverable manufacturing environment and the traditional manufacturing environment by area of responsibility, showing that managers should consider the inherent uncertainties. All of the functional areas require the management of additional information

Factors	Recoverable manufacturing environment	Traditional manufacturing environment
Environmental focus	Seeks to prevent post-production waste	Environmentally conscious design and manufacturing, focus on pre-production Pollution prevention and remediation
Logistics	Forward and reverse flows Uncertainty in timing and quantity of returns Supply-driven flows	Open forward flow No returns Demand-driven flows
Production planning and control	Need to balance demands with returns Material recovery uncertainty Stochastic routings and processing times Manufacturing system has three major components: disassembly, remanufacturing, and reassembly	No such need Certainty in planned materials Fixed routings and more stable processing times Manufacturing system has two major components: fabrication and assembly
Forecasting	Forecast both core availability and end-product demand Must forecast part requirements because material recovery rates are uncertain	Forecast only end products No parts forecasting needed
Purchasing	Highly uncertain material requirements due to variable recovery rates Cores and parts and components, replacement parts, components	Material requirements deterministic Raw materials, new parts, and components
Inventory control and management	Types: cores, remanufactured parts, new parts, new and remanufactured substitute parts, original equipment manufacturer parts Must track and provide accounting for all part types	Types: raw materials, work-in-process, finished goods Must track and provide accounting for work-in-process and finished goods

returned. A part will have a maximum set of processes that should be performed to restore the part to specification. However, these routings represent a worst-case scenario; most parts will require only a subset of these processing steps. Highly variable processing times are also a function of the condition of the unit being returned. These additional forms of uncertainty make production planning and control and inventory control more difficult than they are in traditional manufacturing environments (Table 2).

While recoverable supply chain functions are more complex to manage than traditional supply chain activities, the rewards for a firm are correspondingly higher. Firms have reported improved customer service (Copeland Compressors, Digital Europe, IBM Europe, Rank-Xerox, and Xerox), lowered costs (Xerox), and improved customer image (Digital Europe, IBM Europe, and Xerox).

Uncertainty in Timing and Quantity of Returns

Uncertainty in the timing and quantity of returns affects inventory control decisions. It requires some additional activities to manage the complexities successfully Some researchers have considered the forecasting of returns of reusable containers (Goh and Varaprasad 1986; Kelle and Silver 1989b), but they are in an essentially closed-loop system. In the more general case, the planner must forecast the core availability (a core is an item available for repair or remanufacture), which depends on the product's stage in its life cycle. Early in the life cycle, when few units are in the field and they are new, one can expect a very low core recovery (return) rate. As the product matures, more cores should become available since the product has been in use for longer. The recovery rate of cores will not be 100 percent of sales of the product because units may be damaged in service or in disassembly, or customers may fail to return them. However, the product life cycle may still indicate the availability cycle for the cores, which should follow the product life cycle (or market growth curve) with a certain time lag. Uncertainty in the timing and quantity of returns makes planning for resource requirements into future periods difficult.

Balancing Returns with Demands

Inventory management is a challenge in a recoverable environment because of the need to balance return rates with demand rates and uncertainty in the timing and quantity of returns. Repairable inventory has been the subject of much research and comprehensive literature reviews. The repairable inventory problem is unique in recoverable systems since the assumption of perfect correlation between returns and demands is reasonable in many cases. However, many firms in recoverable manufacturing may have little control over the quantity, quality, and timing of returned products. Firms must also balance inventories of cores held and of repaired or remanufactured end items with actual customer demand. Without careful control and management of inventories, stocks may grow uncontrollably. Firms may need to dispose of used products to avoid carrying excess inventory. A number of inventory control systems have been proposed. Van der Laan (1997) discusses two independent demand inventory models.

In *periodic-review models*, inventory is reviewed at set intervals and decisions are made as to whether to order materials and by how much. Kelle and Silver (1989a) formulated a model for purchase quantities of new containers in a returnable network. However, they do not consider disposal of containers, remanufacturing lead times, or costs associated with repairs or remanufacturing. Inderfurth (1996; 1997) developed another periodic review model but allowed for nonzero remanufacturing and procurement lead times (deterministic) and disposal of inventory.

Continuous-review models require constant monitoring and updating of inventory levels and materials ordering based on trigger points from set inventory levels. Decision variables typically involve setting threshold values to trigger replenishment quantities and determine order quantities. Muckstadt and Isaac (1981) developed the first published model that explicitly considers the problem of imperfect correlation between returns and demands. The model does not allow for disposals, but it does account for nonzero lead times. Research by van der Laan (1997) and van der Laan, Salomon, and Dekker (1996) showed that models must consider disposal of items, or inventories may grow uncontrollably. Richter's (1996a; 1996b; 1997) continuous models address the deterministic case of the economic order quantity with disposal.

Salomon et al. (1994), van der Laan (1997), van der Laan and Salomon (1997) and van der Laan, Salomon, and Dekker (1995; 1996) developed push and pull strategies for joint production and inventory decisions for a mix of remanufactured and new items. Both strategies may consider disposal options (van der Laan and Salomon 1997), and findings indicate that strategy choice depends heavily on the cost-dominant relationship between remanufactured and new stocks. Van der Laan and Salomon (1997) also found that changes in demand and return rates make updating the model's parameters necessary. This implies that as products go through the normal life cycle, managers must revise the decision rules for effective management and control of inventories.

Core acquisition is an important activity in the supply chain for recoverable manufacturing firms, but virtually no researchers discuss that activity. Traditional manufacturing firms purchase only new parts and components and know the price, quantity, and supplier base. In contrast, core acquisition is highly uncertain. It is not the sole responsibility of purchasing: a number of functional areas manage it. They must obtain enough cores to meet demands and develop strategies to balance returns with demands. A firm may need to manufacture new items to meet demands when too few cores are available or purchase replacements when no traditional new manufacturing is possible. Clegg, Williams, and Uzoy (1995) developed a linear programming decision tool to help managers make these types of trade-off. Firms must also integrate traditional demand management activities, such as demand forecasting, with core acquisition activities to balance return rates with demand rates.

Firms must develop strategies for acquiring cores, since they may acquire cores from various sources, such as customers, core brokers and other third-party vendors, and original equipment manufacturers (OEMs). Each of the sources has its pros and cons. Firms may acquire cores directly from customers for remanufacture and return, in exchange for remanufactured units, or through simple purchase. Charging a core deposit could help reduce the uncertainty of return quantities since a sale would generate a return, but might not reduce timing uncertainty since demand rates would still be stochastic. By acquiring cores from third-party vendors and brokers, firms can acquire cores in larger lots and at a steadier rate. They can then plan remanufacturing more easily and achieve economies of scale in such areas as transportation and acquisition. The chief disadvantage of this approach is primarily that the firm has little control over the condition and age of returns.

OEM programs provide firms with a steady source of cores and economies of scale. They may lessen the exposure to obsolescence. The cores may be of known or unknown mix. However, firms can expect greater homogeneity for the cores than those from third-party vendors and core brokers.

Some firms are using innovative systems to ensure availability of cores. ReCellular, Inc., the major supplier of remanufactured cellular telephones in the world, has established working relationships with a number of cellular telephone manufacturers and service providers to improve availability of cores. The service providers return many used cell phones to ReCellular, which remanufactures and redistributes them. This helps keep costs low for service providers (for example, allowing them to provide free cellular phones with activation agreements), and provides ReCellular with a steady supply of cores. An agreement with the cellular telephone OEM Nokia led to ReCellular becoming the authorized North American service and remanufacture center. ReCellular Inc. has remanufactured over one million cellular telephones since 1991.

Firms need to develop formal core acquisition strategies to balance customer demands with returns and to avoid holding risky and impractical finished goods inventories.

Disassembly

Several distinct processes make up any recoverable manufacturing operation: disassembly and testing, remanufacture or repair, and reassembly. Each process is strongly dependent on the others so that control decisions must synchronize the entire system. The disassembly process provides inputs for many other decisions, including quantities of recovered materials, purchase requirements for replacement materials, disposal requirements, and the release of parts to the repair or remanufacturing shops.

Disassembly is complicated since, as Nasr et al. show (1998), few firms have access to OEM specifications and must perform reverse engineering. Reverse engineering is expensive, costing an average of $37,000 per product, and time consuming, requiring an average of 22.7 days. Two-thirds of the firms with access to OEM specifications still reported having to do reverse engineering. The firms surveyed indicated that by designing products for reuse, firms could save an average of $95,000 per year. Before beginning any disassembly operations, a firm must consider the recovery problem itself. Disassembly operations require labor, equipment, and overhead expenses. Firms need to balance the costs of disassembly with the revenues from material recovered. This is not easy because many benefits are difficult to quantify, such as improved corporate image, improved competitive position, and decreased liability from waste products.

A number of authors have addressed the problem of determining optimal disassembly: Navin-Chandra (1994) developed a software tool (ReStar) to determine the optimal level of recovery; Johnson and Wang (1995) developed another software system to provide optimal recovery levels; de Ron and Penev (1995; Penev and de Ron 1996) developed a method based on graph theory and dynamic programming; and Lambert (1997) developed a method based on graph theory. Each of these techniques is designed to help the practicing manager make informed choices about the economics surrounding the recovery problem. However, for the long-term solution, firms should design future products with reuse in mind. Several publications contain guidelines for new-product development.

Brennan, Gupta, and Taleb (1994) identified some problems with disassembly, including controlling and managing inventories of materials, the increased complexity in scheduling, resource allocation and availability, and locating and coordinating facilities for assembly, disassembly, and recycling.

Guide, Srivastava, and Kraus (1997a; 1997b) discuss the problem of materials explosion, one end item being disassembled into a large number of parts. Uncontrolled release of parts from disassembly operations may increase lead times for remanufacture and repair operations. Guide and his colleagues discuss various disassembly release mechanisms for controlling the release of parts. Although these findings are mixed, push policies seem best for inexpensive remanufactured parts.

Materials Recovery Uncertainty

Materials recovery uncertainty complicates resource planning, purchasing, and inventory control. Disassembly may provide variable yields of usable or repairable parts and components. Guide and Spencer (1997) describe a simple method for determining material recovery rates and discuss their major planning uses. Until the core has been fully disassembled and the parts cleaned and inspected, their suitability for reuse or rebuilding, as opposed to scrapping, is not known. The rates of recovery for parts vary. Firms should be able to forecast recovery rates for parts in order to plan for new parts to replace those they cannot recover. Recovery rates are clearly age, environment, and usage specific.

Purchasing is complicated by material recovery uncertainties and short lead times. Further complications may include substitutable parts, proprietary parts or technology, out-of-production parts, and little or no support from the original manufacturer. The purchasing function is particularly important when a firm aims to provide a wide range of reworked products and sufficient shop capacity to handle the flow, to hold the inventory and work-in-process, and to use equipment and labor efficiently. One of us conducted a survey of production planning and control practices in remanufacturing that indicates the importance of purchasing. When asked for the causes of late deliveries of customer orders, firms most often cited a lack of part availability, long lead times for order delivery, or OEM parts being very highly priced.

Although inventory control is more complex in a recoverable system than in traditional manufacturing, firms can use modified versions of some traditional tools and techniques. Material requirements planning (MRP) systems may be modified to help remanufacturing firms to manage and control dependent demand inventories. They may have to take into account the specifics of disassembly as a source of parts (Gupta and Taleb 1994) and to use discount factors for incomplete material yields (Flapper 1994) and modified bills of material (Krupp 1993). Inderfurth and Jensen (1998) analyze MRP policies with recovery options and compare them with traditional inventory control policies. Panisset (1988) discusses the implementation of an MRP system at a maintenance facility for locomotives and railroad cars. Guide and Srivastava (1997a) propose a specific structure for MRP mechanics and a method to calculate the safety stock needed to cover material recovery uncertainty. Safety stock does provide limited protection against material recovery variation. Guide and Srivastava (1997a) speculate that firms, when faced with uncertainty inherent in recoverable environments, may best use MRP for visibility in planning for purchased items.

Other work has focused on planning for and with recovered materials. Gupta and Taleb (1994) and Taleb, Gupta, and Brennan (1997) present a reverse MRP algorithm to aid in planning for parts recovered from disassembly operations. The reverse MRP system also serves as an inventory control tool, allowing managers to monitor the levels of recovered parts and components in stock. This approach may be practical since almost half of the firms Nasr et al. (1998) surveyed reported using a disassembly sequence that was the reverse of assembly. Flapper (1994) also presents an MRP-based algorithm, but with discount factors to reflect uncertain yield rates.

Reverse Logistics

Reverse distribution is the task of recovering discarded products (cores); it may include packaging and shipping materials and backhauling them to a central collection point for either recycling or remanufacturing. Handling the mechanics of reverse distribution requires professional attention. Distribution professionals must understand state and federal laws in the United States. In many European countries, recent legislation mandates take-backs of packing materials, consumer electronics, automobiles, and major consumer appliances. Competitive pressures are forcing many US firms to adopt similar practices, and environmental concerns will eventually lead to similar regulations in the US. Germany already has a law requiring product manufacturers to take back the pallets, cardboard boxes, stretch and shrink wrap, strapping, and all the other materials used to protect products during shipment. Germany and the Netherlands also prohibit dumping electronics products and major consumer appliances in landfills and prohibit firms from shipping such waste to countries that still allow landfilling. Other European countries are expected to adopt similar legislation. As US landfills approach capacity, the US Congress will likely enact legislation on recycling and remanufacturing.

Three key issues affect reverse logistics: (1) network structure, (2) planning for material flows, (3) the classification and routing of materials (Sarkis et al., 1995). The collection of goods from the marketplace is a supply-driven flow rather than a demand-driven flow. This flow is uncertain with respect to the quantity, timing, and condition of items. Thus predicting the quantity of goods available may be difficult.

Recovering goods is further complicated by the fact that (1) most logistics systems are not equipped to handle reverse product movement; (2) returned goods often cannot be transported, stored, or handled in the same manner as outgoing goods; (3) reverse distribution costs may be several times higher than original distribution costs (ibid.). High value products may justify high transportation costs; transporting low value products may not be economical. Demand for such products is probably unknown and exposes the network to even greater uncertainty.

Fleischmann et al. (1997) provide an excellent review of quantitative models developed for reverse logistics. Flapper (1995a; 1995b; 1996) provides an overview of the logistics problems firms face in recoverable operations. Kroon and Vrijens (1996) developed a mathematical programming model used for reusable containers. Spengler et al. (1997) describe mathematical programming models used in Germany for the reuse of building products. Several authors (Jayaraman, Guide, and Srivastava 1999; Kooi, Krikke, and Schuur 1996; Krikke, van Harten, and Schuur 1996) have developed generalized mixed integer programming models for use by any firm engaged in reverse logistics. Krikke (1998) describes several cases and models that link recovery strategies with reverse logistic network design. Both Digital and IBM have reported successful product take-back networks in Europe, and both firms expect continued success in the EU. Cooper (1996) reports on a number of successful third-party programs in the UK for returning consumer products.

Material Matching Restrictions

When customers require repair and return of the items they originally bought, the firm must coordinate disassembly operations with repair and remanufacture operations and reassembly. This practice is common in jet turbine remanufacturing, but many remanufacturers report offering it. To return the same unit to the customer, the firm must number, tag, and track parts, placing an additional burden on its information systems. Reassembly of the unit may be delayed by a delay in repairing any of its parts.

Guide, Srivastava, and Kraus (1997a) show that schedulers should use specific priority dispatching rules for particular product structure types to improve flow times and delivery performance. Guide and Srivastava (1998) show that schedulers should pay close attention to the interactions between part-type matching and disassembly release rules to insure consistent flow times and customer service.

Stochastic Routings for Materials and Highly Variable Processing Times

Stochastic routings for returned products and from variable processing times cause further uncertainty. Firms need to estimate the condition of the parts to be recovered from a core to schedule work centers and plan capacity. Shifting bottlenecks are common because the materials recovered from disassembly vary from unit to unit, processing times vary, and routings vary. Also, the end products in a recoverable environment do not require all new parts, and remanufactured components do not necessarily require all the operations associated with newly manufactured components.

Guide (1996) developed a bottleneck scheduling heuristic for a remanufacturing facility with a stable, dominant bottleneck resource. The system produces stable but long flow times; as a result the firm must carry greater inventory. Nasr et al. (1998) report that all the firms they surveyed reported that cleaning operations were bottlenecks, accounting for, on average, 20 percent of total processing time. A study by Guide, Srivastava, and Kraus (1997b) shows that a due-date-based priority dispatching rule combined with a simple disassembly release mechanism controls mean flow times and delivery performance very well. Guide, Srivastava, and Spencer (1997) present a capacity planning model that takes into account material recovery rates and stochastic routings. By maintaining sufficient capacity at each resource, a firm can better predict flow times and staffing requirements.

A planning function related to scheduling is order release. Order release policies determine when and how to release jobs to the disassembly shops. Proper control of order release can make shop loads more predictable and improve delivery performance. Guide and Srivastava (1997b) show that batching jobs (at the order release stage) increases variation in flow times and can degrade delivery.

The researchers cited previously all considered item-flow problems but not the complex problem of batching like parts for repair and remanufacture operations. Since whether or not a particular part will require an operation depends on its age and condition, routings for identical parts may diverge quickly. Carrying parts through unnecessary operations (but not doing any unnecessary work) may be a better choice than performing a large number of set-ups at each machine center. For resources with excess capacity, this is not an issue, but calculating required capacity at any resource is difficult. A simple rule of thumb is to batch common parts with standard usage rates and processing requirements. End-item-level batching decisions are complex, and the use of one-for-one order release seems reasonable in this environment.

Conclusion

Recoverable manufacturing is a growing area. As firms from different industries and process types start using recoverable manufacturing systems, more information will become available on the implementation of such systems and on handling the associated uncertainty.

REFERENCES

An extended reference list is contained in the original article.

Ayres, R. and Ayres, L. 1996, *Industrial Ecology: Towards Closing the Materials Cycle*. Edward Elgar, Brookfield, Vermont.

Brennan, L.; Gupta, S. M.; and Taleb, K. N. 1994, 'Operations planning issues in an assembly/disassembly environment', *International Journal of Operations and Production Management*, Vol. 14, No. 9, pp. 57–67.

Clegg, A.; Williams, W.; and Uzoy, R. 1995, 'Production planning and control for companies with remanufacturing capability', *Proceedings of the 1995 IEEE International Symposium on Electronics and the Environment*, IEEE, Orlando, Florida, pp. 186–191.

Cooper, T. 1996, 'The re-use of consumer durables in the UK; Obstacles and opportunities', in *Proceedings of the First International Working Seminar on Reuse*, eds. S. D. P. Flapper and A. de Ron, Eindhoven University of Technology, Eindhoven, The Netherlands, pp. 53–62.

de Ron, A. and Penev, K. 1995, 'Disassembly and recycling of electronic consumer products: An overview', *Technovation*, Vol. 15, No. 6, pp. 363–374.

Flapper, S. D. P. 1994, 'On the logistics aspects of integrating procurement, production and recycling by lean and agile-wise manufacturing companies', *Proceedings of the International Dedicated Conference on Lean/Agile Manufacturing in the Automotive Industry*, Aachen, Germany, pp. 749–756.

Flapper, S. D. P. 1995a, 'One-way or reusable distribution items?' Research Report TUE/BDK/LBS/95–04, Graduate School of Industrial Engineering and Management Science, Eindhoven University of Technology, Eindhoven, The Netherlands.

Flapper, S. D. P. 1995b, 'On the operational logistics aspects of reuse', *Proceedings of the Second International Symposium on Logistics*, Nottingham, UK, pp. 343–348.

Flapper, S. D. P. 1996, 'Logistics aspects of reuse: An overview', in *Proceedings of the First International Working Seminar on Reuse*, eds. S. D. P. Flapper and A. de Ron, Eindhoven University of Technology, Eindhoven, The Netherlands, pp. 109–118.

Fleischmann, M.; Bloemhof-Ruwaard, J. M.; Dekker, R.; van der Laan, E.; van Nunen, J. A. E. E.; and van Wassenhove, L. N. 1997, 'Quantitative models for reverse logistics: A review', *European Journal of Operational Research*, Vol. 103, No. 1, pp. 1–17.

Frosch, R. A. 1992, 'Industrial ecology: A philosophical introduction', *Proceedings of the National Academy of Sciences*, Vol. 89, pp. 800–803.

Frosch, R. A. 1994, 'Industrial ecology: Minimizing the impact of industrial waste', *Physics Today*, Vol. 47, No. 11, pp. 63–68.

Goh, T. N. and Varaprasad, N. 1986, 'A statistical methodology for the analysis of the life-cycle of reusable containers', *IIE Transactions*, Vol. 18, No. 1, pp. 42–47.

Guide, V. D. R., Jr. 1996, 'Scheduling using drum-buffer-rope in a remanufacturing environment', *International Journal of Production Research*, Vol. 34, No. 9, pp. 1081–1091.

Guide, V. D. R. and Spencer, M. S. 1997, 'Rough-cut capacity planning for remanufacturing firms', *Production Planning and Control*, Vol. 8, No. 3, pp. 237–244.

Guide, V. D. R., Jr. and Srivastava, R. 1997a, 'Buffering from material recovery uncertainty in a recoverable manufacturing environment', *Journal of the Operational Research Society*, Vol. 48, No. 5, pp. 519–529.

Guide, V. D. R., Jr. and Srivastava, R. 1997b, 'An evaluation of order release strategies in a remanufacturing environment', *Computers and Operations Research*, Vol. 24, No. 1, pp. 37–47.

Guide, V. D. R., Jr. and Srivastava, R. 1998, 'Inventory buffers in recoverable manufacturing', *Journal of Operations Management*, Vol. 16, No. 4, pp. 551–568.

Guide, V. D. R., Jr.; Srivastava, R.; and Kraus, M. 1997a, 'Product structure complexity and scheduling of operations in recoverable manufacturing', *International Journal of Production Research*, Vol. 35, No. 11, pp. 3179–3199.

Guide, V. D. R., Jr.; Srivastava, R.; and Kraus, M. 1997b, 'Scheduling policies for remanufacturing', *International Journal of Production Economics*, Vol. 48, No. 2, pp. 187–204.

Guide, V. D. R., Jr.; Srivastava, R.; and Spencer, M. 1997, 'An evaluation of capacity planning techniques in a remanufacturing environment', *International Journal of Production Research*, Vol. 35, No. 1, pp. 67–82.

Gupta, S. M. and Taleb, K. N. 1994, 'Scheduling disassembly', *International Journal of Production Research*, Vol. 32, No. 8, pp. 1857–1866.

Inderfurth, K. 1996, 'Modeling period review control for a stochastic product recovery problem with remanufacturing and procurement leadtimes', Preprint No. 2, Fakultät für Wirtschaftswissenschaft, Otto-Von-Guericke-Universität Magdeburg, Germany.

Inderfurth, K. 1997, 'Simple optimal replenishment and disposal policies for product recovery systems with leadtimes', *OR Spektrum*, Vol. 19, No. 2, pp. 111–122.

Inderfurth, K. and Jensen, T. 1998, 'Analysis of MRP policies with recovery options', Preprint No. 1, Fakultät für Wirtschaftswissenschaft, Otto-Von-Guericke-Universität Magdeburg, Germany.

Jayaraman, V.; Guide, V. D. R., Jr.; and Srivastava, R. 1999, 'A closed-loop logistics model for remanufacturing', *Journal of the Operational Research Society*, Vol. 50, No. 5, pp. 497–508.

Jelinski, L. W.; Graedel, T. E.; Laudise, R. A.; McCall, D. W.; and Patel, C. K. N. 1992, 'Industrial ecology: Concepts and approaches', *Proceedings of the National Academy of Sciences*, Vol. 89, pp. 793–797.

Johnson, M. R. and Wang, M. H. 1995, 'Planning product disassembly for material recovery opportunities', *International Journal of Production Research*, Vol. 33, No. 11, pp. 3119–3142.

Kelle, P. and Silver, E. A. 1989a, 'Forecasting the returns of reusable containers', *Journal of Operations Management*, Vol. 8, No. 1, pp. 17–35.

Kelle, P. and Silver, E. A. 1989b, 'Purchasing policies for new containers considering the random returns of previously issued containers' *IIE Transactions*, Vol. 21, No. 3, pp. 349–354.

Kooi, E.; Krikke, H.; and Schuur, P. 1996, 'Physical design of a reverse logistic network: A multi-echelon model', in *Proceedings of the First International Working Seminar on Reuse*, eds. S. D. P. Flapper and A. de Ron, Eindhoven University of Technology, Eindhoven, The Netherlands, pp. 205–212.

Krikke, H. R. 1998, 'Recovery strategies and reverse logistic network design', PhD thesis, Institute of Business Engineering and Technology Application (BETA), Universiteit Twente, Enschede, The Netherlands.

Krikke, H. R.; van Harten, A.; and Schuur, P. C. 1996, 'On a medium term product recovery and disposal strategy for durable assembly products', Working paper UT-TBK.OMST.WP.96.02, Universiteit Twente, Enschede, The Netherlands.

Kroon, L. and Vrijens, G. 1996, 'Returnable containers: An example of reverse iogistics', *International Journal of Physical Distribution and Logistics*, Vol. 25, No. 2, pp. 56–68.

Krupp, J. 1993, 'Structuring bills of material for automotive remanufacturing', *Production and Inventory Management Journal*, Vol. 34, No. 4, pp. 46–52.

Lambert, A. D. J. 1997, 'Optimal disassembly of complex products', *International Journal of Production Research*, Vol. 35, No. 9, pp. 2509–2523.

Lund, R. 1996, *The Remanufacturing Industry: Hidden Giant*, Boston University, Boston, Massachusetts.

Muckstadt, J. and Isaac, M. 1981, 'An analysis of single-item inventory systems with returns', *Naval Research Logistics Quarterly*, Vol. 28, No. 2, pp. 237–254.

Nasr, N.; Hughson, C.; Varel, E.; and Bauer, R. 1998, 'State-of-the-art assessment of remanufacturing technology-draft document', National Center for Resource Recovery and Remanufacturing, Rochester Institute of Technology, Rochester, New York.

National Academy of Sciences Proceedings 1992, Vol. 89.

Navin-Chandra, D. 1994, 'The recovery problem in product design', *Journal of Engineering Design*, Vol. 5, No. 1, pp. 65–86.

Panisset, B. 1988, 'MRPII for repair/refurbish industries', *Production and Inventory Management Journal*, Vol. 29, No. 4, pp. 12–15.

Penev, K. and de Ron, A. 1996, 'Determination of a disassembly strategy', *International Journal of Production Research*, Vol. 34, No. 2, pp. 495–506.

Piasecki, B. 1992, 'Industrial ecology: An emerging management science', *Proceedings of the National Academy of Sciences*, Vol. 89, pp. 873–875.

Richter, K. 1996a, 'The EOQ repair and waste disposal model with variable setup numbers', *European Journal of Operational Research*, Vol. 95, No. 2, pp. 313–324.

Richter, K. 1996b, 'The extended EOQ repair and waste disposal model', *International Journal of Production Economics*, Vol. 45, No. 1–3, pp. 443–447.

Richter, K. 1997, 'Pure and mixed strategies for the EOQ repair and waste disposal problem', *OR Spektrum*, Vol. 19, No. 2, pp. 123–129.

Salomon, M.; van der Laan, E.; Dekker, R.; Thierry, M.; and Ridder, A. 1994, 'Product remanufacturing and its effects on production and inventory control', Management Report Series No. 172, Rotterdam School of Management, Erasmus University, Rotterdam, The Netherlands.

Sarkis, J.; Darnall, N.; Nehman, G.; and Priest, J. 1995, 'The role of supply chain management within the industrial ecosystem', *Proceedings of the 1995 IEEE International Symposium on Electronics and the Environment*, Orlando, Florida, pp. 229–234.

Spengler, Th.; Püchert, T.; Penkuln, T.; and Rentz, O. 1997, 'Environmental integrated production and recycling management', *European Journal of Operational Research*, Vol. 97, No. 2, pp. 308–326.

Taleb, K. N.; Gupta, S. M.; and Brennan, L. 1997, 'Disassembly of complex product structures with parts and materials commonality', *Production Planning and Control*, Vol. 8, No. 3, pp. 255–269.

van der Laan, E. 1997, 'The effects of remanufacturing on inventory control', PhD Series in General Management 28, Rotterdam School of Management, Erasmus University, Rotterdam, The Netherlands.

van der Laan, E. and Salomon, M. 1997, 'Production planning and inventory control with remanufacturing and disposal', *European Journal of Operational Research*, Vol. 102, No. 2, pp. 264–278.

van der Laan, E.; Salomon, M.; and Dekker, R. 1995, 'Production planning and inventory control for remanufacturable durable products', Report 9531/A, Erasmus University, Rotterdam, The Netherlands.

van der Laan, E.; Salomon, M.; and Dekker, R. 1996, 'Production remanufacturing and disposal: A numerical comparison of alternative control strategies', *International Journal of Production Economics*, Vol. 45, No. 1–3, pp. 489–498.

Part 4

Issues for SMEs

This part addresses the situation of small and medium enterprises (SMEs) in the context of total product systems that are dominated by large firms, such as lead retailers, with formidable power and financial resources. SMEs are in a precarious position, whether as suppliers to the large players or as their direct competitors. This presents them with a number of challenges – primarily how to survive in competitive market conditions, which include increasing globalization and the relocation of operations to low labour cost countries.

According to Dixon et al. (2002) there are 3.7 million SMEs in the UK employing about 55 per cent of the private sector workforce. These SMEs have an annual turnover in excess of £1 trillion and account for 40 per cent of UK GDP. This pattern of economic significance is similar across the European Union. It is erroneous, however, to assume homogeneity amongst SMEs. Firms vary widely in terms of factors such as size, turnover, maturity, and the nature of their business.

By size, the European Commission identifies three SME categories:

- micro-enterprises – up to 10 employees;
- small enterprises – up to 50 employees;
- medium enterprises – those with up to 250 employees.

The three categories are very different in such respects as their access to capital, their organizational and technological sophistication, and the availability of specialized capabilities in production, training, sales and other business functions. They have many strengths and many weaknesses.

SMEs also display sectoral diversity. For instance, their *direct* role is very limited in sectors such as energy and telecommunications supply – although their *indirect* roles, such as in providing support services for large companies, can be significant. By contrast, small firms – particularly micro-enterprises – generally remain important in retailing, despite the growth of large retail chains.

Variations in the motivations and cultures that drive SMEs are worth noting. Many SMEs are 'growth averse' (Gray, 1995). They have, for example, little interest in initiatives aimed at assisting them in adapting to changing circumstances and improving their operation. Rather, they are 'lifestyle firms' where a primary motivation is to sustain proprietorial lifestyles. Lifestyle firms are juxtaposed with 'growth firms' where innovation and growth are prime motivators.

Since they are not a single category, discussing the role of SMEs in supply system contexts means proceeding through case studies which demonstrate their diversity and potential. This is the approach taken by most of the authors of chapters in this part.

The complex interplay between in-house and external expertise and knowledge is central to the operation of any organization. In a study of a sample of SMEs in three UK regions, Bryson and Daniels (Chapter 4.1) investigate their increasing reliance on outside sources. They explore the management strengths and weaknesses of the SMEs and their consumption of advice from Business Link, a UK network of agencies providing specialist advice for SMEs – an example of 'traded knowledge'. They find that the firms are weakest in the use and management of external expertise; owner-managers are particularly poor at managing the interface with external sources of advice. They also highlight the importance of 'untraded knowledge', transferred informally through the nexus of the local business community, 'the jungle drums in the village'. Understanding the behaviour of SMEs as consumers of external advice is important in the development of regional economic policy and in constructing a meaningful support framework for their economic and commercial activity.

Palpacuer and Parisotto (Chapter 4.2) also write about local networks and development issues, but approach them from a different perspective. They report an International Labour Organization (ILO) research project that identified patterns of interaction between networks – specifically global value chains and local firms in industrial districts – and explored how such interaction affects the conditions of work and employment at a local level in the competitive context of globalized production. Their focus is highly internationalized manufacturing industries – textiles, clothing, electronics and automobiles – and they draw attention to the fact that global networks may be less prominent, and less influential, in other sectors. Two critical issues emerge from the study. The first is the concentration of power and the appropriation of value in lead companies and global first-tier suppliers. The authors suggest that 'These results underline the need for local industries to adopt diversified development strategies', which include new approaches to innovation and markets. Second, they observed inequalities among workers arising from new forms of industrial organization that produce global intensification of labour market com-petition and affect groups of workers in diverse locations differently, some gaining more than others. The authors formulate recommendations for policy-makers, such as the ILO, which suggest that the policy-making institutions themselves should adopt a network form of organization in order to build consensus and to better assist local development.

Cave et al. (Chapter 4.3) note that in the aerospace sector, as well as in others, SME suppliers are, for several reasons, becoming increasingly remote from their OEM buyers. For example, there are often many tiers of the supply hierarchy between them, or they may have been delisted as suppliers. One consequence is that the SMEs are unaware of the needs of their end-customers and, conversely, the OEMs do not have an overview of the particular technical and other capabilities offered by the SMEs. Another is that lower tier companies have their prices continually forced down. The authors explore one possible strategy for addressing such issues: the formation of a technology integrator organization. 'This enables a virtual community of small, technology businesses to come together as an identifiable enterprise to bid for specific packets of work, either to a level 1 supplier or directly to the prime contractor.' The development of one such integrator is discussed, together with the issues that this strategy raises. For example, how does the behaviour of this integrator compare with that of various other virtual supply chain communities established in other sectors and countries? What level of transfer of technology and knowledge can take place in this context?

The chapter by Amesse et al. (Chapter 4.4) concentrates on similar issues in the aeronautical sector, taking a slightly different perspective. The authors consider the quality of technology transfer in subcontracting partnership agreements within the supply chain, looking at how such agreements are managed and emphasizing the need for collaboration, co-operation and sharing. Their conclusions are somewhat sceptical: that the main contractor and its subcontractors do not necessarily develop the same perceptions of their subcontracting agreements; that the technology transfer flows are mainly unidirectional, going from the main contractor to its subcontractors; and that partnering seems to be an idealized condition rather than a reality. Thus the potential for technology transfer is limited, and the authors question 'whether high-quality technology transfer is indeed possible under the conditions of the subcontracting agreements in question'.

Gupta and Brennan (Chapter 4.5) provide a detailed, six-month case study of the successful implementation of JIT methodology in an SME that makes small items for the catering industry. The objective was to introduce a climate of continuous improvement. By managing the project holistically, considerable benefits were achieved, for example in changing to flexible production methods, reducing manufacturing costs and reducing lead times. The authors imply that success in this case should encourage other SMEs to consider a similar route to continuous improvement.

The last two chapters take Scottish SMEs as the subject of their case studies. In the first, Cano et al. (Chapter 4.6) explore benchmarking in the Scottish tourist industry. This sector is a major source of income for the Scottish economy and is extremely diverse, and competition is fierce in the area of service standards. Benchmarking had previously been applied within the large players, but had not been reported in SMEs.

The authors devised and carried out a five-stage benchmarking exercise on the core competencies of three small businesses, a rural hotel (customer loyalty), a tour operator (attracting new customers) and a new visitor attraction (innovation). The exercise identified transferable good practice between the three organizations, but also had a creative, synergistic effect in that it led to cross-organizational team building. This is aligned with the policy of developing clusters in the Scottish commercial environment and the businesses are now in a strong position to develop new joint ventures. As a pilot project in the adaptation of benchmarking to service

SMEs, this points to the potential for further application of appropriate tools in small, non-manufacturing businesses.

Finally, Wagner et al. (Chapter 4.7) review the significance of electronic commerce and the Internet in supply chain management and examine the role of ICTs in the strategies of a sample of SMEs in central Scotland, through interviews with their senior managers. They explore the adoption of e-business in the companies from many perspectives, for example technical aspects, customer demand, regional networks, communities of practice and support from development agencies. Key factors identified in the process are combined into a conceptual model, which offers a framework for understanding these influences. They find that the level of adoption is very different for different types of SMEs and that much progress remains to be made. This will depend on the provision of appropriate educational help, training and advice from government and business development agencies.

REFERENCES

Dixon, T, Thompson, B & McAllister, P: *The Value of ICTs for SMEs in the UK: A Critical Literature Review*, Report to the Small Business Service, The College of Estate Management, 2002, URN 02/1377

Gray, C: SME success as a function of human capital development, paper presented to the 40th World Conference of the International Council of Small Business, Sydney, June 1995

The Secrets of Industry Are in the Air or on the Jungle Drums in the Village: Traded and Untraded Knowledge and Expertise: Interdependencies between SMEs

J. R. Bryson and P. W. Daniels

We take trade magazines, there are four in our business which are pretty essential and give us a good overview of what is happening in advertising in general. They produce a lot of potential new business leads, and there are other books and reference manuals that are published that we can buy into for information. You've also got electronic information, Reuters' databank. We get all sorts of information on what clients are doing and about personnel changes in advertising. So we've got no problems sourcing information and then there's the jungle drums in the village itself [localised agglomeration]. There are the formal gatherings and then there's the casual bit in the pub. (interview, London advertising company, our emphasis)

We are a member of a local business club. It's just handy to meet these people and get local information which can be useful to the future performance of this business. It is very rare to go to one of these events and not come back with something. Very rare indeed. (interview, West Midlands manufacturing company)

Introduction

During the 1980s and 1990s the United Kingdom experienced a dramatic growth in employment in business service activities – in those companies which supply expertise and knowledge which are considered to add value to the output of their clients (Bryson, 1996; Bryson et al., 1997a). The growth of business service activities is part of a wider process of economic and social restructuring that has occurred since the early 1970s. Business services play an important role in stimulating industrial development and innovations amongst client companies (Bailly et al., 1987; Ley and Hutton, 1987; Bryson, 1997a). Despite a significant recent body of research into the operational dynamics of small business service firms (Keeble et al., 1991; Bryson et al., 1993a; 1993b; Birley and Westhead, 1994; Kirby, 1997; O'Farrell et al., 1998), few studies have been undertaken into client use of external business service expertise (Bryson, 1997a; Bryson and Daniels, 1998c). Business service expertise needs to be understood in relationship to the management strengths and weaknesses of client companies. It is the quality of the relationship between the client and the business service provider, and the way it is managed, which determines the success or failure of a consultancy project. The growing significance of business service expertise for client companies suggests that more research needs to be undertaken into SMEs and their use of external expertise. The relationship between SME owner-managers and external expertise is especially important given the dependence of large companies on SMEs in their supply chain, and the limited management resources of the majority of SME owner-managers.

This paper identifies the management strengths and weaknesses of a sample of SMEs in the United Kingdom, before exploring their consumption of external business service expertise provided through the agency of Business Link, the UK's 'one-stop-shop' advice initiative for SMEs (Bryson, 1997b), or direct from the private sector. The reasons for employing outside expertise and the relationship between the internal and external environment of SMEs are explored. Business service expertise is only one form of knowledge and expertise available to SMEs, and it is a traded form. Business service expertise may not be as important as other forms of untraded knowledge and expertise transfer. Interviews with SMEs highlight the importance of 'the jungle drums in the village' as a valuable source of advice and expertise. 'The village' in this quotation refers to a localised business community, but it also applies to industries with social networks which function nationally and internationally.

Traded and Untraded Interdependencies

The employment of business service expertise by clients is an attempt to remove uncertainty and reduce exposure to risk (Scott, 1988). It does this in two ways. First, it reduces employment overheads by only employing experts when they are required. Client companies are thus able to maintain their competitiveness because some information development costs are externalised to business service firms. They are also able to recruit 'temporary' employees who have been trained in different corporate environments and cultures. The possibility always exists for a client to 'head-hunt' a business service employee, internalising their expertise. This is advantageous for the business service company as their 'inside' professional will generate new business, and continue to promote the reputation of the company.

Secondly, it acquires access to a range and depth of expertise which cannot be created inside a company. Firms become dependent on knowledge and expertise which exist outside their borders. Such external business service expertise acts to reinforce that available from board level interlinkages between companies in the form of non-executive directorships. Boardroom interlinkages operate to gather information about corporate practices, regulatory and political changes, and macroeconomics expectations (Scott, 1979; Useem, 1984; Mizruchi, 1991). Explicit boardroom linkages, and implicit linkages as a result of using the same business service expertise, allow companies to exchange information, to innovate and to retain their competitive position. Such linkages allow the continual benchmarking of organisational performance and behaviour, as well as the transfer of information and expertise. They are also an important form of untraded interdependency (Storper, 1995; 1997).

The transformation of the economy away from employment in manufacturing related activities to service activities has important implications for towns and cities, as well as reflecting alterations in the organisation of economic activities (Bryson, 1997c). Lash and Urry suggest that towns and cities should be increasingly considered as 'centres for the switching of information, knowledge, images and symbols' (1994, p. 220; see also Mulgan, 1991). The concentration of professional activities concerned with the acquisition, transformation and interpretation of knowledge, in post-industrial spaces or service spaces, affects such spaces in terms of the provision of communication infrastructure as well as leisure and culture activities. This growth in the importance of knowledge has resulted in the 'objectification' of human capital (Castells, 1989). The concentration of this human capital in key locations affects both the operations of individual enterprises and the competitiveness of national economies.

Concentration of professional capital in key urban centres has important implications for the range, availability and quality of professional expertise in peripheral locations. Such concentrations may result in differential access to a whole series of strategic business service activities. The concentration of business service companies in service spaces generates new knowledge and expertise which can be consumed by any client, no matter where they are located, as long as the client possesses the capability to identify, access and utilise such service expertise effectively. Such information rich environments also offer opportunities for individuals to create a reputation for a particular type of service expertise which may become of global significance. Service spaces contain information-intensive companies functioning as innovation, information and expertise transfer agents. Effectively they operate as pivotal information nodes in the global economic system (Castells, 1996).

Large companies have both the ability and the resources to search for the right types of external expertise irrespective of the location of the business service supplier (Bryson, 1997a). They are able to maintain contacts with centres of business service excellence, thereby acquiring access to the latest management and technological innovations. In contrast SMEs have limited management time and resources to search for external expertise. They also employ very few external business service firms, and thus have limited opportunities to acquire experience of choosing business service companies, and of managing the relationship with outside suppliers of external expertise.

Part of the transformation in the ways in which organisations are structured reflects differences between the relationship of core and support activities. Firms have been transformed into 'extended' or flexible firms, in which the boundaries between externalised and internalised management expertise have become increasingly blurred. Management and other forms of expertise do not necessarily have to be contained within the confines of an organisation, but can exist in a state of symbiosis. Organisations with blurred boundaries can develop a just-in-time approach to expertise and knowledge, but the management of symbiotic relationships demands both management time and expertise. Much work has been undertaken into the concentration on core activities by large firms, and the impact this has on the externalisation of support and management functions (Perry, 1990; Goe, 1991). Comparatively little work, however, has explored the blurring of the SME management boundary (Hitchens et al., 1994; Hitchens, 1997).

The most effective way to obtain, interpret and implement new information and knowledge is by co-present interaction (Boden and Molotch, 1994). Such interaction is much more complex than face-to-face interaction as it includes the advantages that may accrue to a company from a location surrounded by similar companies or business service firms. Untraded interdependencies may develop which produce innovations as a consequence of tacit knowledge and expertise transfer (Marshall, 1909; Storper, 1995). Co-present interaction thus includes 'inadvertent' meetings that 'occur when people of the same ilk frequent the same spaces' (Boden and Molotch, 1994). It also is assisted by the location of the headquarters of professional organisations in global cities. The presence of these institutions offers possibilities for co-present interaction leading to the acquisition of new clients, the formation of new companies, and the development of innovations – and, of course, for untraded interdependent interaction. Such interaction creates trust, and results in the transfer of embedded knowledge (Granovetter, 1985). The co-presence of business service firms with some of their clients 'shapes the possibilities of trust between them' (Friedland and Boden, 1994; see also Friedland and Palmer, 1994). It also determines the extent to which client firms develop strategies and structures to cope with market uncertainty (Beck, 1992).

Notions of untraded interdependencies and co-presence raise serious questions concerning the role of business service expertise in relation to other sources of advice, knowledge and information (Bryson and Daniels, 1998b). Capitalist production is controlled by the articulation of information into knowledge. Knowledge is required to identify suitable sources of capital and raw materials, manage the labour force, and manipulate the transformation of the finished commodity into capital. The overemphasis in producer service research on one type of knowledge and expertise obscures the numerous different types of information and knowledge which flow

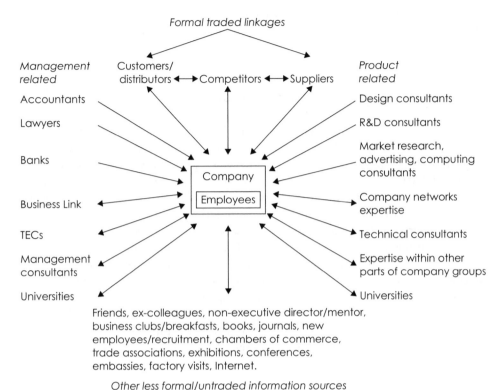

Figure 1 Traded and untraded information and knowledge flows into SMEs

into client organisations via other sources and routes (Figure 1). There are at least ten ways in which an organisation acquires new types of knowledge: a new managing director; boardroom linkages; the recruitment of a new manager; publications and other forms of media; scrutiny of competitors' products; external training; interim management; takeover activity; movement of knowledge down the supply chain; and various forms of untraded interdependency, such as membership of a trade association, discussions in pubs and golf clubs, and other forms of social interaction. We want to return to the ideas of the Cambridge economist Alfred Marshall. Writing in 1909 about agglomeration economies he noted that:

> The mysteries of [a] trade become no mysteries; but are as it were in the air, and children learn many of them unconsciously. Good work is rightly appreciated; inventions and improvements in machinery, in processes and the general organization of the business, have their merits promptly discussed; if one man starts a new idea it is taken up by others and combined with suggestions of their own, and thus becomes the source of further ideas. (pp. 152–3)

Thus, the secrets of industry are in the air and not necessarily in the hands of the nearest management consultant or business adviser. Companies acquire information about new management practices, machines and potential employees from forms of untraded interaction which are driven by social relationships structured around co-present interaction.

Methodology

The findings presented in this paper are derived from an ESRC funded project exploring the relationships between SMEs and their use of externally provided knowledge and expertise. Part of this project involved a postal survey of a representative sample of SMEs in England distributed during the summer of 1996. The survey covered independent manufacturing, business, professional and technical service enterprises, exploring their characteristics, strengths and weaknesses and their use of a whole series of both public and private sector external advisers. Choice of these sectors is justified by their importance as key income-generating components of both the national and the regional economic base. Companies in the sample are independently owned, employing between 10 and 250 employees. A pilot survey of 118 firms was undertaken which achieved a response rate of 8%. The questionnaire was subsequently shortened and simplified. The survey, based on a stratified random sample in the chosen sectors from the Dun and Bradstreet national register, achieved a response rate of 10%, with 156 responses (Table 1). It includes slightly larger

Table 1   Characteristics of the respondents to the postal survey

	No.	%
Employment size		
1–10	15	10
11–20	39	25
21–40	38	24
41–80	28	18
81–150	15	10
>150	17	11
Missing cases	4	3
Sector		
Manufacturing	72	47
Transport, storage and communications	15	10
Renting of equipment	9	6
Computer and related activities	6	4
Research and development	4	3
Other business services	46	30
Total	152	100
Missing cases	4	

numbers of service (84 firms) than manufacturing (72 firms) enterprises. The regional pattern of respondents closely replicates that of the total population of VAT-registered businesses in these sectors. The majority of the companies operated from a single site (59%), but 10% operated from more than five sites. Respondents to the survey had a median employment size in 1996 of 32 full-time. Over the period 1992–96, companies had generally increased in size by nine full-time employees.

The response rate is low in comparison to other SME surveys (Keeble and Bryson, 1996). Follow-up telephone calls identified three factors which contributed to this response rate. First, the survey dealt with 'issues relating to the management of firms', and a proportion of SMEs considered that this topic was not relevant to their activities. Secondly, the surveys concentrated on sources of external information and advice. Some SMEs not using either private or public sector external advisers decided not to complete the questionnaire. Thirdly, the recent dramatic increase in research into SMEs has resulted in some companies being inundated with unsolicited postal questionnaires. This problem is intensified by the use of a commercial database which can be purchased by anyone.

Detailed face-to-face interviews were undertaken with a sample of 60 SMEs (34 manufacturing and 26 service companies) equally divided between London, the West Midlands and Cumbria. These interviews provide an understanding of the ways in which different types of SME utilise external information in different operating environments. This stage also involved face-to-face interviews with private sector consultants and representatives of Business Link consulted by each of the SMEs in the interview survey.

The Management Strengths and Weaknesses of SMEs

One of the most interesting findings of this research is the identification of the management weaknesses and strengths of SMEs (Table 2). This list, which is in rank order from the weakest to the strongest elements of management, can be considered in three groups.

First, SMEs are weakest in management areas involving liaison with external organisations and individuals. The weakest element is the use and management of external expertise. To avoid wasting money, a company employing an outside expert has to invest a considerable amount of internal management time in the formulation of the project brief, and the management of the relationship with the external adviser. Without this internal expertise, SME owner-managers may be sold packages which are inappropriate, or implement ideas which are not suitable for the culture and organisation of their company. Consultancy projects will have a higher risk of failure as the owner-manager will not possess the skills required to manage the external provider of expertise. In one of our case studies a consultant had taken over the running of the company from the managing director rather than acting as an adviser. In another case, the consultant had become a permanent addition to the management team, being engaged for the past three years, for one day a week, for general advice rather than for a specific project. This weakness has a geography

Table 2 Strengths and weaknesses in particular management areas (scale of 1 to 5 with 1 as weakest)

		Mean
1	Use of external advisers	2.89
2	Use of advertising and promotional methods	2.89
3	Innovation and R&D	3.14
4	Recruitment	3.22
5	Identifying and fulfilling the training needs of staff	3.25
6	Use of management concepts and techniques	3.34
7	Use of business information	3.37
8	Personnel management	3.39
9	Development of a company culture	3.55
10	Business planning	3.62
11	Experience in management	3.75
12	Financial management	3.91
13	Relationships with creditors and suppliers	4.09
14	Other (practical knowledge, customer relations, creativity, sales)	4.27

Table 3 Strengths and weaknesses in the use of external advisers by location of SMEs (scale of 1 to 5 with 1 as weakest)

Location of SMEs	Mean
London	3.1
South East	3.2
East Anglia	2.0
South West	3.1
West Midlands	3.0
East Midlands	3.0
Yorkshire and Humberside	3.1
North West	2.3
North	2.4

which is related to the South East and the availability of external expertise (Table 3). Companies located in the North West and the North are weaker in the management of external advisers than those in London and the South East. Companies located in East Anglia are weakest in this skill, maybe because East Anglia is too close to London to develop its own business service community, or maybe because of the dispersed location of business activity in this region.

This finding has important policy implications. Internal and external diseconomies may result from SMEs' inability to manage the relationship with outside suppliers of expertise. The implementation of policies designed to improve and/or subsidise

SME access to external business service expertise (for example the Business Link initiative in the United Kingdom: see Bryson, 1997b; Bryson et al., 1997b; Bryson and Daniels, 1998a) will be undermined unless resources are directed to overcoming this management deficiency.

Secondly, elements 4, 5, 8 and 9 (Table 2) are weaknesses based around personnel management. Inability to engage in successful employee management and development will have important implications for the future prosperity of an SME. These weaknesses suggest that organisations like Business Link need to explore ways in which SME owner-managers can develop their recruitment and personnel management skills. This is especially important in a service driven environment in which the success of a client–customer relationship is increasingly dependent on the service or employee component of the interaction (Hochschild, 1983).

Thirdly, the strongest management areas are those which are experienced daily or are routine business practices. Thus, relationships with customers, creditors and suppliers are regular occurrences providing opportunities for SME management to develop a good working relationship based around trust. Business planning and financial management have become accepted features of SME management, as banks will not lend without evidence of a company's future profitability and of the existence of acceptable financial management controls.

SMEs and Traded Interdependencies

One of the arguments for the establishment of the Business Link's network of one-stop advice shops was that SMEs would benefit from access to sources of external expertise and advice. A major problem facing SMEs and Business Link is the limited time SME managers have to consider their management weaknesses. They are just too involved in the day-to-day running of their company (Ram, 1994). Using external advisers is one way to overcome, but not necessarily solve, a management weakness. A total of 84% of respondents to the postal questionnaire had employed either public or private sector advisers. One-third (51) of firms had employed only private sector advisers, and 29 firms had not used external advisers. Nearly one-third (31%) of private sector consultants employed by SMEs were SMEs, 24% were sole practitioners, 17% were specialist computer consultancies and 11% were large multifunctional consultancy companies. Those companies which had not employed advisers had done so because it was considered to be not required or not justified, or to be too expensive. Some companies noted that they did not employ external expertise as they had no knowledge of what was available.

The most utilised public sector advice agencies were the Training and Enterprise Councils (TECs) (37%), followed by Business Link (33%) (Table 4). SMEs consulted public sector advice agencies predominantly because of the availability of grants, subsidised consultancy and value for money (37%) and because they were good sources of general information and advice (33%) (Table 5). Fifteen per cent stated that the services were good value for money, or just inexpensive. Private sector consultants were most frequently employed for their specialist knowledge and

Table 4   Use of public sector advice services

	No.	%
Business Link	38	33
Enterprise Initiative	29	25
Local Council Economic Development Services	6	5
Training and Enterprise Councils	42	37
Total	115	

Table 5   Reasons for using or not using public sector advice agencies

Reasons for use	No.	%	Reasons for non use	No.	%
For information and advice	31	33	Not required	27	57
Grants and finance for consultancy available	21	22	No confidence in them/people/services	11	23
Free, cheap, value for money	14	15	Unaware of what is available	6	13
Training courses	9	10	Requires specialist expertise	3	6
Company appraisal/quality systems	9	10	Total	47	
Other	10	11			
Total	94				

skill (37%) and for an independent impartial analysis of a problem (Bryson and Daniels, 1998a, p. 271). External advisers are able to examine the operation of an SME without the constraints imposed by day-to-day management responsibilities. Just under one-fifth (18%) of SMEs employed an external adviser because they required intensive help for a short period of time, and 12% because there was insufficient time to develop the required skills or expertise internally.

Consultants provided specialist technical advice to clients (25%), or undertook elements of a specific project (13%) (Table 6). Sometimes they offered basic management advice in the areas of human resource management (7%) and market research (7%). In comparison to large companies, the SME client/consultant relationship is unbalanced, with the majority of consultants not working in partnership with internal staff. A survey of the use of consultants by large companies found that 43% (Bryson, 1997a) worked closely with internal staff. This type of interaction only occurred in 13% of SMEs and is another indication of a serious SME problem with the management of the relationship with external advisers. In 12% off cases the consultant provided a 'blueprint for change', with clients expecting their in-house

Table 6 Tasks undertaken by consultant

	No. of mentions	%
Provided specialist technical advice	60	25
Undertook elements of a specific project	31	13
Worked in partnership with internal staff	30	13
Provided a blueprint for change	28	12
Training role	24	10
Implementation of change	19	8
Human resource advice	17	7
Market research advice	16	7
Other	13	5
Total	238	

Table 7 How the last private sector adviser employed was identified?

	No.	%
Networking	40	38
Previous use	18	17
Via DTI, TEC, Chambers of Commerce, Business Link	15	14
Mailshot/cold call	13	12
Sought specialist skills	8	8
Via accountant, bank, solicitor	6	6
Via Business Link	5	5
Total	105	

staff to implement the proposal. Such a strategy will only work if the internal staff have been actively involved in the construction of the 'blueprint'.

Of those companies not using public sector advice agencies, 57% stated that it was because such advice was not required, and surprisingly, given the marketing of the Business Link initiative, 13% were not aware of public sector advice agencies. Twenty-three per cent considered that public sector advice agencies were too idealistic or not practical and that they had no confidence in them, their services or their employees. There appears to be a significant problem over the ways in which a small proportion of SMEs are interpreting the types of advice available via government funded agencies (Table 5).

Overall, the choice of consultants depended heavily on three related characteristics (Table 7). The first was the perception of the reputation of a consultancy company and the individual consultant held by business friends and acquaintances. The decision to employ a particular consultancy company is thus strongly influenced by untraded

Table 8   Proportion of SMEs using private sector external advisers for particular types of advice

	%
Information technology and computerised systems	35
Marketing (advertising and public relations)	29
Legal issues	28
Personnel management/recruitment	28
Finance and administrative systems	28
Business planning	27
Market research and intelligence	24
Organisational change and development	19
Financial management	16
Environmental issues	9

interdependencies, or in other words 'the jungle drums in the village'. The second was previous client experience of working with the consultancy. In most cases this will reflect experience of working with a particular consultant rather than a company. The third was recommendation from a public agency, for example a TEC or a Business Link. The SME search strategy for a consultant is locationally restricted, and this is explained by the notions of co-presence and embeddedness explored above (Bryson and Daniels, 1998a, pp. 272–3).

Surveyed firms were asked about their use of private sector external firms and expertise in ten areas, ranging from information technology to environmental issues (Table 8). Within this, by far the highest reported use of external experts was for information technology and computerised systems (35%). This is not surprising given the growth in specialised software packages targeted at the SME sector. Not surprisingly, marketing is the next most highly used group of external advisers. It is significant that advertising and promotional methods have already been identified as a key SME management weakness. The significance of and need for marketing consultancy advice are a recurrent theme in most surveys of SME performance (see Small Business Research Centre, 1992). Well over one-quarter of firms had employed outside legal advisers, but this represents expertise which cannot be developed and retained inside a company.

The consideration of a firm's future growth objectives and business strategy is an important area in which a proportion of SMEs are seeking external advice. Thus, 27% of firms had employed independent business planning advisers, almost certainly management consultants. Just under a quarter of companies had also sought external market research advice, which would support either a marketing initiative, or techno-logical innovation. Overall then, it is in the areas of information technology, marketing, legal issues, personnel management, finance and business planning in which SMEs seek help most frequently.

The least frequent use of external advice was in the areas of 'environmental issues' (9%) and financial management (16%). Many SMEs are too small, or too concerned with everyday management issues, to give much attention to environmental issues. SMEs, however, can no longer ignore environmental legislation. Uncertainty over this legislation is one of the most difficult problems facing the SME manufacturing company. SMEs generally have poorly developed systems for keeping up-to-date with environmental legislation. Most SMEs learn about new regulations from technical journals, trade associations and the Health and Safety Executive. Some of the banks have also begun to attempt to raise public awareness of environmental issues. For example, NatWest provides information concerning environmental issues to its business customers, and the Co-operative Bank has recently established the Centre for Business Ecology in Manchester. This centre is separate from the bank, and operates to introduce companies to academic specialists from the four Manchester universities. The Co-operative Bank's involvement with this centre derives from the belief that pollution implies waste, and that waste costs money. The argument is, thus, based around profitability, rather than the protection of environment. Similarly, the University of Birmingham has established the Centre for Environmental Research and Training (CERT) to provide environmental advice to SMEs.

One of the most surprising aspects of Table 8 is the low proportion of SMEs consulting external experts for advice over financial management. This is a difficult finding to interpret. Most SMEs will consult an accountant who will also provide them with advice over aspects of financial management. Perhaps small firms consider that they are unable to afford this type of expertise, or that they are able to obtain this advice from the public sector.

Untraded Interdependencies: Jungle Drums in the Village?

The concentration of research on management consultancy and business support agencies has encouraged both academics and policy-makers to ignore the role of untraded interdependencies or formal and informal linkages which exist between companies and individuals. It is commonly assumed that SME owner-managers are too preoccupied with the day-to-day running of their companies to search for information or knowledge which may impact on company performance (Bryson and Daniels, 1998a; Ram, 1994). However, the economy consists of organisations which are linked together by common types of knowledge, machines and modes of organisation. Knowledge flows tacitly and explicitly between companies as soon as people interact or a rival's product is purchased for examination. SMEs are engaged in a continuous process of interactive learning which is not just related to the employment of a management consultant or a visit by a Business Link personal business adviser (Bryson, 1997b). SMEs learn from their own internal experiences, but also from a variety of external sources: competitors, suppliers, customers, universities and many other types of individual and organisation (Figure 1). Firms learn from their competitors through both informal and formal linkages (Foray, 1991; von Hippel, 1987).

Informal linkages or untraded interdependencies may consist of the recruitment of staff trained by a competitor, the employment of the same business service firms and equipment suppliers, or the transfer of knowledge through friendships and acquaint-ances. The intensification of competition in the chocolate industry in the 1970s led to increased secrecy between competing manufacturers in the United Kingdom. Visits of Cadbury's managers to Rowntree Mackintosh plant, for example, were things of the past. Thus, Cadbury's now had to rely on the recruitment of staff from competitors and on technology transfer and knowledge from equipment suppliers (Bryson et al., 1996). According to Kleinknecht and Reijnen, internal research and development (R&D) departments are conducive to the generation of internal know-ledge, but also serve 'as an observatory that enhances a firm's capability to exploit external sources of knowledge' (1992, p. 357; see also Cohen and Levinthal, 1989). Such exploitation relates to untraded interdependencies between companies in the same sector as well as to the operation of social networks between members of R&D departments.

Some of the most important untraded interdependencies are the result of the creation of relations of trust based on personal reputation. The importance of trust in binding individuals together is well known in traditional economic theory. Marshall, writing as early as 1890, commented that the chief difficulty in obtaining suitable employment is to 'convince a sufficient number of those around that [they possess] these rare qualities . . . firstly a high order of business ability and probity, and secondly, the "personal capital" of a great reputation'. Successful traded exchanges may establish the necessary conditions to produce trust based on reputation which will lead to the establishment of untraded interactions between individuals. In this case the argument is that the ties that bind industry together are based on the establishment of trust between individuals, and that this trust is articulated through social networks. The important point is that an individual will treat knowledge obtained from a relationship of trust as superior to that obtained from an unknown, unproven, untrusted source. This explains the failure of many attempts to persuade SMEs to use information or consultancy services provided by government. A reputation takes a long time to establish and is easily destroyed. The owner of a small West Midlands subcon-tracting engineering company noted that a Business Link manufacturing consultant 'had wonderful theories in this room [MD's office] but when we went out on the shopfloor he couldn't cope with the environment' (interview). The apparent inability of the consultant to deal with a real situation has turned this company away from using the services of Business Link. Organisations attempting to provide SMEs with advice need to be extremely careful in the way in which they establish and maintain their contact with the management team.

Consultants and Business Link are a comparatively minor mechanism employed by SMEs to acquire information. They have an important impact as they are con-sulted at irregular intervals and outsiders are frequently considered to have superior expertise to in-house staff. In many cases, however, the advice of consultants is ignored as being inappropriate or too expensive or impossible to implement. The face-to-face interviews identified that the most important source of information used by 65% of SMEs was information obtained from customers (Figure 2). This can take

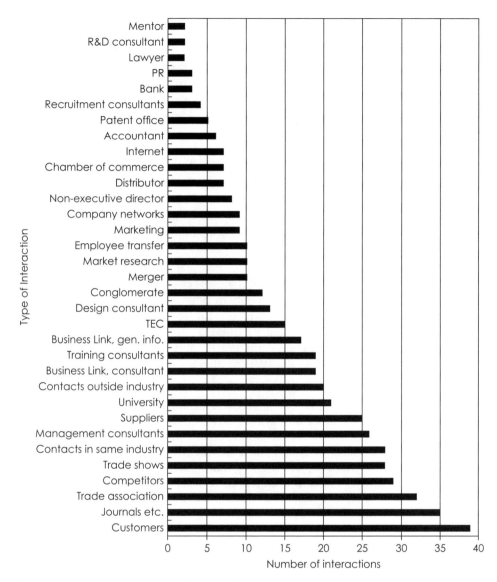

Figure 2 Sources of external information and expertise consulted by the 60 case study SMEs

the form of learning about export procedures, new production methodologies, or machines. One company noted that: 'you can do so much on the phone, so much by fax, but there is nothing like visiting clients, you pick up a lot more just by talking to individuals than you would ever do by talking on the phone' (interview). A good example of client related information flows is the relationship which exists between a large company and its supply chain. Knowledge and information flows are informal and valued as they are founded upon a long-term established reputation.

Journals and magazines were consulted by 58% of companies, with owners noting that they were the best way to keep up with current management fashions. Books may be an initial source of ideas, but 'if it is not on the shelf . . . I will just pick up the phone and ask someone' (interview). Books, however, can be dangerous in that ideas which are more suited to a different business sector or size of company may be discovered and implemented. One of the partners of a London advertising company reads business and management books avidly. According to the managing director of this company: 'he would have been better off going down the pub and listening to people. There are some useful ideas in them and some extremely good tips and hints, but they don't provide a model for running a business. Business is about 90% expediency and 10% business theory, because you are dealing with people' (interview). The partner worried the managing director about the lack of management method in the company and forced the company to employ KPMG to undertake a review of the business. KPMG's response was that the company was: 'chaos, it's total chaos, but it's a chaos that works, we don't know why it works, but all we know is that you shouldn't change it' (interview).

Trade associations were consulted by 53% of companies. Trade associations frequently convert densely written government and European Union documents into easy to read guides, as well providing a forum for the discussion of common problems (Bennett, 1998). The social networking aspect of trade associations as well as breakfast and luncheon clubs must not be underestimated. A director of a manufacturing company based in the West Midlands notes that:

> Yesterday, I went to a meeting of the British Sports and Allied Industries Federation on exports to Denmark, which is a small but important market of ours, and there I met somebody who exports cloth, and someone who exports chocolate bars, and somebody who exports fishing equipment. None of these are remotely related to our industry, but all have a tale to tell: 'Which shipping line do you use? How do you fly there? Where do you get the best priced air fares? Is it better to have distributors in X and Copenhagen or just in Copenhagen?' They are not consultants with their own agenda, but people who are earning at the sharp end, and their experience is very practical and is formed by the most important question of all: how do you make money out of this market? You form allies, you develop business contacts and acquaintances, and most people are very helpful, and staggeringly open, especially once they know you are not a competitor.

Forty-eight per cent of companies noted that competitors are a valuable source of information. For example, both quarry owners in Cumbria and Savile Row tailors in London talk to competitors in an attempt to promote their respective industries. The managing director of an engineering company based in Coventry noted that one of the partners 'was very well plugged into the engineering mafia' (interview). Companies visit trade exhibitions in the UK and Europe predominantly to learn about rival products, but also to provide an opportunity to talk to competitors. In one case, a manufacturer of hotel towel rails attended a German exhibition because the company wanted to develop a bathroom range for the general public. They identified a design which they have altered and are now selling in the UK. Informal information exchange may occur between SMEs located in different countries. Thus, a Cumbria based training provider shares information with a company based in Portugal and another in Germany.

The diversity of information flows into and between SMEs is highlighted in Figure 1. The most effective flows of advice are those which are obtained from a relationship of trust or from an apparently successful competitor. It is impossible to determine the importance of these 'secrets of industry which are in the air' in relationship to traded sources of advice. One of the best ways, however, to alter SME business behaviour is by the dissemination of advice through an informal network of social contacts rather than via management consultants and Business Link companies. The formal mechanisms have their place, but they may be much less important than other sources of expertise.

Conclusion

The operation of both large and small private and public sector organisations consists of a complex interplay between in-house and external expertise and knowledge. Increasing business environment complexity, competition, internationalisation, and technological change, as well as the operation of government policies designed to encourage SMEs to consult outside advisers, have all contributed to a recent growth in demand from SMEs for outside expertise and knowledge. The relationship between an SME and outside flows of knowledge and expertise is much more complex than just flows of knowledge from private sector consultants and organisations like Business Link. Most studies highlight the role of accountants, bank managers, trade associations and friends and acquaintances (Bryson and Daniels, 1998a; Wheelock, 1992), but very few explore the complex web of information, knowledge and advice in which SMEs are situated. Management consultants and other forms of business adviser may be of limited significance in relation to customers, competitors and the business media. The problem is how to devise measures for determining the significance of different forms of information and expertise flows into and between SMEs. Without this type of measure, policy-makers will discount the importance of these types of expertise flow. Any attempt to measure their impact will fail given the complexity and heterogeneity of the client/consultant relationship. The important point is that all companies are embedded into a regional economy, and more specifically into a web of dynamic social relationships.

The success of SME business support policies would be substantially improved and access to these services widened if organisations like Business Link were able to access informal support networks. The problem is, however, that this type of activity will not contribute directly to the earning stream of a Business Link company, or be suitable for evaluation in any formal manner. The 'jungle drums in the village' will always be one of the most successful means for obtaining and disseminating information, as the social relationships in such a 'village community' will be founded on established reputations and social relationships. Evaluating the impact of business advice may, however, be detrimental to the medium- and long-term performance of

SMEs. Impact studies force consultants to undertake projects which have obvious short-term financial impacts on company performance. Such short-termism will fail to capture the frequently intangible impact of formal external advice. The impact on business performance and/or culture may occur over a period of years, rather than in a single financial year, and be impossible to relate to a single client/consultancy interaction.

There is another way of interpreting the impact of business service firms on client behaviour. Increasing competitiveness as a consequence of global competition has resulted in a transition away from the relatively stable firm, with few alterations in management and operational structure, to the dynamic firm, with an emphasis on change and constant improvement. Expertise and advice that exist within an organisation will be concerned with maintaining the status quo. The employment of an external professional not situated within the power structure of the organisation will disturb the status quo. The organisation may reject the external expert's recommendations, but the very process of rejection will have forced the company to consider its current practices. Thus, an inexpert external professional may be equally as effective in encouraging a client to consider current practices as the most experienced external professional. This may be the paradox of the relationship between external expertise and a client organisation. Any external independent analysis will be of benefit if it forces management to step back from everyday business issues and consider the wider picture. Anything that forces the SME owner-manager to reconsider their activities must be good for the continuing success and performance of the small and medium sector of the British economy.

REFERENCES

Bailly, A.S., Maillat, D. and Coffey, W.J. (1987) 'Service Activities and Regional Development: Some European Examples', *Environment and Planning A*, 19, pp. 653–668.

Beck, U. (1992) *Risk Society*, Sage, London.

Bennett, R.J. (1998) 'Business Associations and Their Potential to Contribute to Economic Development: Reexploring an Interface between the State and Market', *Environment and Planning A*, 30, pp. 1367–1387.

Birley, S. and Westhead, P. (1994) 'New Producer Service Businesses: Are They Any Different from the New Manufacturing Ventures?', *Services Industries Journal*, 14, pp. 455–481.

Boden, D. and Molotch, H.L. (1994) 'The Compulsion of Proximity', in Friedland, R. and Boden, D. (eds) *Space, Time and Modernity*, University of California Press, Berkeley, pp. 257–286.

Bryson, J.R. (1996) 'Small Business Service Firms and the 1990s Recession in the United Kingdom: Implications for Local Economic Development', *Local Economy Journal*, 11, pp. 221–236.

Bryson, J.R. (1997a) 'Business Service Firms, Service Space and the Management of Change', *Entrepreneurship and Regional Development*, 9, pp. 93–111.

Bryson, J.R. (1997b) 'Small and Medium-Sized Enterprises, Business Link and the New Knowledge Workers', *Policy Studies*, 18, 1, pp. 67–80.

Bryson, J.R. (1997c) 'Obsolescence and the Process of Creative Reconstruction', *Urban Studies*, 34, 9, pp. 1439–1458.

Bryson, J.R. and Daniels, P.W. (1998a) 'Business Link, Strong Ties and the Walls of Silence', *Environment and Planning C: Government and Policy*, 16, pp. 265–280.

Bryson, J.R. and Daniels, P.W. (1998b) 'Recipe Knowledge and the Four Myths of Knowledge-Intensive Producer Service Research: The Knowledge Which Producer Service Professionals Bring to Their Clients', *Working Papers on Services, Space, Society*, no. 3, Service Sector Research Unit, University of Birmingham and the University of Bristol.

Bryson, J.R. and Daniels, P.W. (1998c) 'Small Firms, Business Link and the Management of Change and Innovation', *Working Papers on Services, Space, Society*, no. 5, Services Sector Research Unit, University of Birmingham and the University of Bristol.

Bryson, J.R., Keeble, D. and Wood, P.A. (1993a) 'The Creation, Location and Growth of Small Business Service Firms in the United Kingdom', *Service Industries Journal*, 13, 2, pp. 118–131.

Bryson, J.R., Keeble, D. and Wood, P.A. (1993b) 'Business Networks, Small Firm Flexibility and Regional Development in UK Business Services', *Entrepreneurship and Regional Development*, 5, pp. 265–277.

Bryson, J.R., Daniels, P.W. and Henry, N. (1996) 'From Widgets to Where? A Region in Economic Transition', in Gerrard, A.J. and Slater, T.R. (eds) *Managing a Conurbation: Birmingham and Its Region*, Brewin Books, Birmingham, pp. 156–168.

Bryson, J.R., Keeble, D. and Wood, P.A. (1997a) 'The Creation and Growth of Small Business Service Firms in Post-Industrial Britain', *Small Business Economics*, 9, 4, pp. 345–360.

Bryson, J.R., Churchward, S. and Daniels, P.W. (1997b) 'From Complexity to Simplicity? Business Link and the Evolution of a Network of One-Stop-Advice Shops: A Response to Hutchinson, Foley and Oztel', *Regional Studies*, 31, 7, pp. 720–723.

Castells, M. (1989) *The Informational City*, Blackwell, Oxford.

Castells, M. (1996) *The Rise of the Network Society*, Blackwell, Oxford.

Cohen, W. and Levinthal, D. (1989) 'Innovation and Learning: The Two Faces of R&D', *Economic Journal*, 99, pp. 569–596.

Foray, D. (1991) 'The Secrets of Industry Are in the Air: Industrial Cooperation and the Organizational Dynamics of the Innovative Firm', *Research Policy*, 20, pp. 393–405.

Friedland, R. and Boden, D. (1994) 'Now Here: An Introduction to Space, Time and Modernity', in Friedland, R. and Boden, D. (eds) *Space, Time and Modernity*, University of California Press, Berkeley, pp. 1–60.

Friedland, R. and Palmer, D. (1994) 'Space, Corporation, and Class: Towards a Grounded Theory', in Friedland, R. and Boden, D. (eds) *Space, Time and Modernity*, University of California Press, Berkeley, pp. 287–334.

Goe, W.R. (1991) 'The Growth of Producer Service Industries: Sorting Through the Externalisation Debate', *Growth and Change*, 22, 4, pp. 118–141.

Granovetter, M. (1985) 'Economic Action and Social Structures: The Problems of Embeddedness', *American Journal of Sociology*, 91, 3, pp. 481–510.

Hitchens, D.M.W.N. (1997) 'The Adequacy of the Supply of Professional Advisory Services to Manufacturing Firms in Rural Mid-Wales', *The Service Industries Journal*, 17, 4, pp. 669–690.

Hitchens, D.M.W.N., O'Farrell, P.N. and Conway, C. (1994) 'Business Service Use by Manufacturing Firms in Mid Wales', *Environment and Planning A*, 26, pp. 95–106.

Hochschild, A.R. (1983) *The Managed Heart. Commercialization of Human Feeling*, University of California Press, Berkeley.

Keeble, D. and Bryson, J.R. (1996) 'Small Firm Creation and Growth: Regional Development and the North–South Divide in Britain', *Environment and Planning A*, 28, pp. 909–934.

Keeble, D., Bryson, J. and Wood, P. (1991) 'Small Firms, Business Services Growth and Regional Development in the United Kingdom: Some Empirical Findings', *Regional Studies*, 25, 5, pp. 439–457.

Kirby, D.A. (1997) 'Small Technology-Based Professional Consultancy Services in the United Kingdom', *The Service Industries Journal*, 17, 1, pp. 155–172.

Kleinknecht, A. and Reijnen, J.O.N. (1992) 'Why Do Firms Cooperate on R&D? An Empirical Study', *Research Policy*, 21, pp. 347–360.

Lash, S. and Urry, J. (1994) *Economies of Signs and Spaces*, Sage, London.

Ley, D. and Hutton, T. (1987) 'Vancouver's Corporate Complex and Producer Services Sector: Linkages and Divergence within a Provincial Staple Economy', *Regional Studies*, 21, pp. 413–424.

Marshall, A. (1890) *Principles of Economics*, London.

Marshall, A. (1909) *Elements of Economics of Industry: Being the First Volume of Elements of Economics*, Macmillan, London.

Mizruchi, M.S. (1991) 'Market Relations, Interlocks, and Corporate Political Behaviour', *Research in Political Sociology*, 5, pp. 167–208.

Mulgan, G. (1991) *Communications and Control: Networks and the New Economics of Communication*, Polity Press, Cambridge.

O'Farrell, P.N., Wood, P.A. and Zheng, J. (1998) 'Regional Influences on Foreign Market Development by Business Service Companies: Elements of a Strategic Context Explanation', *Regional Studies*, 32, 1, pp. 31–48.

Perry, M. (1990) 'Business Service Specialisation and Regional Economic Change', *Regional Studies*, 24, pp. 1331–1347.

Ram, M. (1994) *Managing to Survive: Working Lives in Small Firms*, Blackwell, Oxford.

Scott, A.J. (1988) *Metropolis: From the Division of Labor to Urban Form*, University of California Press, Berkeley.

Scott, J. (1979) *Corporations, Classes and Capitalism*, Hutchinson, London.

Small Business Research Centre (1992) *The State of British Enterprise: Growth, Innovation and Competitive Advantage in Small and Medium-Sized Firms*, University of Cambridge.

Storey, D.J. (1994) *Understanding the Small Business Sector*, Routledge, London.

Storper, M. (1995) 'The Resurgence of Regional Economies, Ten Years Later: The Region as a Nexus of Untraded Interdependencies', *European Urban and Regional Studies*, 2, 3, pp. 191–221.

Storper, M. (1997) *The Regional World: Territorial Development in a Global Economy*, Guilford Press, New York.

Useem, M. (1984) *The Inner Circle: Large Corporations and the Rise of Business Political Activity in the US and UK*, Oxford University Press.

von Hippel, E. (1987) 'Cooperation between Rivals: Informal Know-How Trading', *Research Policy*, 16, 5, pp. 291–302.

Wheelock, J. (1992) 'The Flexibility of Small Business Family Work Strategies', in Caley, K. et al. (eds) *Small Enterprise Development: Policy and Practice in Action*, Paul Chapman, pp. 151–165.

Global Production and Local Jobs: Can Global Enterprise Networks Be Used as Levers for Local Development?

Florence Palpacuer and Aurelio Parisotto

To create and retain good jobs is a central objective of employment and industrial policies at the local, national and international levels. As a result of globalization, the context in which such a goal is to be achieved has undergone important changes, generating new challenges for policy-makers. One main challenge is to use globalization as a lever for local development, by helping local firms and workers take advantage of the opportunities opened up by the global economy. This derives from an awareness that the development of transnational networks of economic activities generates unprecedented possibilities for accessing new markets and resources, acquiring new skills and capabilities, and developing international competitive advantage. Another key challenge is to contain the social and economic imbalances resulting from global integration, by spreading its benefits and costs throughout local industries and communities. This responds to the growing concern that global connections may provide an unstable basis for local growth and development, and disrupt and divide local industries and communities, marginalizing those actors that fail to develop strong global linkages. Meeting such challenges calls for significant changes in policy-making. It requires the identification of the driving forces that shape the development of global networks of economic activities, the assessment of the opportunities and constraints that these networks create for local firms, workers and institutions, and the design of innovative responses in promoting local development.

To address these broad issues, in 1998 the International Institute for Labour Studies of the International Labour Organization (ILO) launched a research project on 'Global Production and Local Jobs'. The project mobilized a variety of conceptual approaches and case study material, stimulating innovative debates among scholars of diverse academic background, international experts and policy-makers. In line with major ILO policy orientations, it identified patterns of interaction between global and local forces that significantly shape conditions for the emergence or preservation of decent work within the context of global competition (ILO 1999). It is useful to recall that 'Decent Work', the primary policy goal of the ILO today, is defined as a multidimensional concept that implies access to employment as well as the recognition of fundamental rights at work, basic social protection for workers and their families, and the exercise of voice and participation directly and indirectly through self-chosen organizations (ILO 1999; Parisotto 2001).

Research under the project on 'Global Production and Local Jobs' uncovered complex articulations between global and local dynamics in contemporary forms of industrial organization. Global pressures arising from products and financial markets exert significant influence on the behaviour of firms and workers in the world economy, yet both groups of actors remain embedded in social and institutional contexts that present distinct logics at the local level. A key insight of the programme has been the recognition that complementary analytical frameworks should be combined in novel forms to analyse the interplay between global and local forces and, ultimately, devise new orientations for employment and development policies.

This article draws on the results of the project. It combines insights from the business strategy, global value chain and industrial district literatures to highlight salient features of global production networks. On that basis, it identifies major issues arising for local firms and workers in the context of globalization, and suggests new perspectives for political responses at the local level. The first section will set the scene by uncovering the organizational processes underlying globalization in a variety of industries including textiles and clothing, electronics and automobiles. It will analyse the emergence of network forms of organization by which lead firms respond to changes in their competitive environment, and explore how global and local dynamics interact in these networks. Focusing on highly internationalized manufacturing industries will serve to identify key dimensions of globalization, keeping in mind that global networks might be less prominent in, or present distinctive shapes in, other industries. The second section will draw attention to three questions of central concern to local development strategies: how local firms can not only enter global networks but, more importantly, build up network positions that allow them to achieve and maintain competitive advantage; how the quantity and quality of local jobs are affected in that process; and how local policy-makers can provide effective support to the sustainable integration of local firms and workers within global networks. Some conclusions are presented in the third section.

New Patterns of Production within Global Networks

During the decades following the Second World War, industrialized countries enjoyed a period of exceptional economic growth and social peace, while developing countries made historically unprecedented economic and industrial progress (Singh 1994). Despite strong expansion of world trade, such developments essentially took place within the context of domestically organized industries. The 1970s and following decades witnessed a number of structural transformations in the organization of industrial activities. On the international scene, transactions increased tremendously: world trade grew at a much higher rate than world output, and since the 1980s the growth of foreign direct investment has far exceeded the expansion of trade (ILO 1996; 1998). Such increase has been accompanied by substantial changes in the nature of international operations through a growing functional integration of productive activities, or the emergence of 'global production networks' in which complementary activities performed in various locations are closely coordinated through a diverse array of intra-firm and inter-firm arrangements (Dicken 1998; Ernst 1997; UNCTAD 1993; 1995).

This section will examine the rationale underlying the development of enterprise networks before drawing on the global value chain (GVC) framework to analyse the main structural dimensions of global forms of production. We will argue that it should be combined with other 'territorially based' approaches – such as the business system, systemic competitiveness and industrial district perspectives – in order to better grasp the social and institutional context in which global networks operate at the local level, and how this context influences network dynamics.

The development of network forms of organization

Enterprise networks are transforming the organization of industries from both a domestic and an international perspective, increasingly blurring the line between the two. As Reich (1991) wondered, what is a 'British' car, or an 'American' computer, when a large number of their components have been made in different countries? Networks are also obscuring the traditional distinction between market and hierarchy, as they are based on a mix of intra-firm and inter-firm arrangements that do not strictly belong to either one of these categories. Some observers elaborate on this idea by considering that the shift to network forms of organization introduces elements of market governance within the firm while infusing elements of hierarchy within market exchanges (Zenger and Hesterly 1997).

Inside the firm, the shift to network forms of organization involves a decentraliz-ation of decision-making and greater reliance on horizontal coordination across functions and units. These principles apply to the coordination of activities between affiliates of multinational corporations (Ghoshal and Bartlett 1990); between different business functions such as R&D, design, production and marketing (Ernst 1997); as well as within individual units or functions, as indicated by the growing use of teamwork in manufacturing (Fröhlich and Pekruhl 1996). Outside the firm, relations become more closely integrated as the principle of horizontal coordination is extended to complementary activities performed by suppliers and customers. These new external links might rely on formal arrangements such as long-term contracts, but students of network dynamics emphasize that their essence is defined by informal inter-firm cooperation based on trust, stability and continuous learning (Badaracco 1991; Helper et al. 2000; Powell 1990). Such collaborative relations become of growing importance in the context of vertical disintegration strategies by which firms increasingly focus on a distinct set of activities or core competencies, and farm out complementary activities to their network partners (Harrison 1994).

As emphasized by management researchers, the development of network forms of organization constitutes an efficient response to changes in the nature of competition and the sources of competitive advantage (Miles and Snow 1986; Starr 1991). Faced with growing complexity, uncertainty and cost pressures in their competitive environment, large firms are moving away from hierarchically organized, vertically integrated structures in order to increase their capacity to innovate, react more quickly to external changes, improve product quality and cut down operating costs. Enhanced pressures also stem from financial markets, where corporations must exhibit higher financial performance in order to boost share prices and gain support from institutional investors (Chew 1997; Lazonic and O'Sullivan 2000; Useem 1996). In response to such pressures, firms can increase their return on invested capital by focusing on highly remunerative activities such as brand-building and product development, while externalizing standard manufacturing activities within global networks. Firms' rationale for developing network forms of organization is therefore firmly anchored in competitive dynamics that operate simultaneously on product and financial markets (Gibbon 2003; Perez and Palpacuer 2002).

The structure and dynamics of global production networks

Firms' strategies to develop network forms of organization have led to a reconfiguration of industries along a variety of dimensions including size and specialization, inter-firm relations, and the spatial distribution of activities. The GVC perspective provides a basic framework to analyse the resulting organization of activities within highly internationalized manufacturing industries (Gereffi and Kaplinsky 2001). Global value chains, or 'global commodity chains' in their more classic appellation, have been defined as 'sets of inter-organizational networks clustered around one commodity or product, linking households, enterprises and states to one another in the world economy' (Gereffi et al. 1994: 2). They can be considered as forming the specific industrial, geographical, social and institutional environment within which firm-level production networks operate.

The analytical distinction between firm-level networks and their GVC context is in line with recent theoretical contributions to the study of globalization and economic development. For instance, Sturgeon (2001) proposes differentiating between a 'value chain', or sequence of complementary activities, and a 'production network', defined as a set of inter-firm relationships, in order to highlight the strategies by which network members develop competitive positions and organize interrelationships along a chain of productive activities. From a broader perspective, Dicken et al. (2001) suggest that globalization can best be understood by combining structural approaches to the global economy, such as the GVC framework, with a focus on social relations between actors involved within networks, as adopted in actor-network theory (ANT). Henderson et al. (2002) similarly distinguish between agents – including firms – and structures – including sectoral characteristics – in their characterization of global production networks. Although we do not go down to the level of actors as individuals, as done in the ANT approach, our perspective seeks to articulate the GVC framework with a dynamic, firm-level analysis of network relations.

Our starting point is that the four main dimensions of GVCs can be used as an organizing scheme to highlight key characteristics of global production networks. They include (Gereffi 1994):

- an input–output structure, or sequence of interrelated value-adding activities, including product design and engineering, manufacturing, logistics, marketing and sales;
- a governance structure, namely power relations arising from asymmetries in market base, resources and capabilities that determine how economic surplus is distributed within the chain and how activities are coordinated within and across firms;
- a geographical configuration, referring to the spatial dispersion or concentration of activities within and across locations;
- a social and institutional context, formed by the norms, values and regulatory frameworks of the various communities within which firms operate.

Competitive dynamics within the value chain

The input–output structure of global production networks encompasses a broad range of activities requiring a variety of competencies and capabilities, and forming a 'value chain' in Porter's (1985) terminology. Adopting a value chain perspective is essential to understand the new forms and logic of competition in global industries. In complex and dynamic environments, competitiveness depends less on the possession of extensive material assets, and more on firms' ability to master the organizational processes by which customer demands for specificity, quality and timeliness can be met. Some authors refer to this transformation by pointing to the importance of organizational competencies and capabilities as primary sources of competitive advantage (Teece et al. 1997). Others emphasize the new role of services, or intangible activities, as superior sources of value creation (Dicken 1994; Rabach and Kim 1994; Reich 1991). All underline that those stages of the value chain that predominantly involve intangible activities, such as product design and development, marketing and brand-building, are gaining strategic importance compared with manufacturing activities that are primarily associated with the material transformation of inputs into outputs. The capacity to coordinate complementary activities across complex global value chains is also becoming in itself a major source of competitive advantage. Firms that maintain direct control over these intangible, service-intensive functions are thus in a position to appropriate a substantial share of the value created within global networks (Kaplinsky 2000; Palpacuer 2000a). These functions require hard-to-imitate, complex competencies and skills that are scarce and can therefore command significant returns. Because they lend themselves to scale economies, they are also protected by strong entry barriers.

Governance through value appropriation and inter-firm coordination

The governance structure plays a key role not only in the creation and distribution of value, but also in the coordination of global production networks, and as such it has attracted particular attention from scholars involved in GVC analysis. Coordination applies, first, to complementary activities that must be matched from the perspective of output volume and product characteristics and, second, to relations between network members that must be defined on the basis of shared interests in order to allow for cooperation to develop. From a strategic perspective, the coordination of global production networks requires some degree of centralization in order to ensure an efficient use of resources, rapid decision-making and the emergence of a global vision driving the network. For these reasons, management researchers stress the role of the lead firm, continuously engaged in attracting and selecting members, in sustaining network relationships by managing conflict and learning, in positioning the network in the market, and in building the structure and culture of the network (Sydow 1992: 114; also see Jarillo 1988; 1993).

Recent theoretical developments on network governance identify a variety of ways in which lead firms might exercise this coordinating role. Palpacuer (2000a) argues that lead firms make simultaneous use of cooperation, market and hierarchy in managing internal and external competencies, thus highlighting the diversity and complementarity of coordinating mechanisms within global production networks. Such diversity can also be found in the typology of network forms developed by Gereffi et al. (2002). Networks are here considered to lean towards either greater cooperation and social embeddedness, as typified by industrial districts, or greater hierarchical control through direct monitoring, as increasingly exercised by head-quarters on their foreign subsidiaries, or greater market-based coordination, as shown in Sturgeon's (1998; 2002) study of network dynamics in the American electronics industry.

GVC analysis emphasizes that the governance structure of global production networks takes a variety of forms depending on the nature of activities performed within the chain. Gereffi's (1994; 1999) typology highlights the existence of two different network configurations in global industries: producer-driven chains (PDCs) developed by large multinationals maintaining equity ties with their affiliates across the globe, and buyer-driven chains (BDCs) formed by large retailers or branded marketers that arrange for the manufacture of their products through global out-sourcing. The former are typical of capital- and technology-intensive industries such as automobiles or computers, while the latter have emerged in labour-intensive industries such as footwear and apparel. Lead producers and lead buyers share a common characteristic, however: they retain direct control over strategic, intangible activities such as product design and development, marketing and logistics, while farming out a growing part of manufacturing activities to other network members. Accordingly, it is control over intangible activities that allows lead firms to 'govern' global networks, namely, to exercise power in terms of value appropriation, even when they do not directly coordinate inter-firm productive relations throughout the whole production chain. For instance, American lead firms such as Polo Ralph Lauren directly control branding and product design activities, but outsource to Hong Kong service providers the task of coordinating a substantial part of their global production activities.

A 'multiple-scale' geographical configuration

The geographical shape of global production networks results from a combination of local, regional and trans-regional dynamics, or 'a complex intermingling of different geographical scales' in the words of Dicken et al. (2001: 95). To clarify these articulations, the global and the local can be seen as stylized ends of a continuum along which regional, national and other intermediary levels of analysis can be distinguished. These various levels of network dynamics are well documented in the apparel, electronics and automobiles industries. At the global level, examples include linkages developed between American and East Asian producers, which involve independent firms, joint ventures and multinationals' affiliates (Dicken 1998; Henderson 1997). At the macro-regional level, Bair and Gereffi (2002) highlight the recent growth of North American networks in the apparel chain, under the influence of the North American Free Trade Agreement (NAFTA). Macro-regional networks in Europe, North America and Asia are also an important feature of the auto and electronics industries (Dicken 1998; Gereffi 1996; Henderson 1997). Their growth has been analysed by some observers as a shift away from inter-regional networks (see for instance Bair and Gereffi 2002), while others emphasize that strong complementarities persist between global and regional linkages in the new geography of global production (Gibbon 2003). The latter view suggests that lead firms combine the specific skills and competitive advantages of various regions and countries in building and maintaining global networks. In other words, locations are not entirely substitutable for one another within the world economy.

Finally, specialized productive activities tend to be clustered in particular places within countries that participate in global production networks. Economic geographers such as Scott (1996) and Sassen (1991) have argued that the very processes of globalization contribute to a polarization of resources, capabilities and economic growth at the sub-national level. According to this view, global industries are locally anchored within agglomerated production complexes, as illustrated by the poles of Silicon Valley, Hsinchu, Penang and Bangalore in electronics, or Los Angeles and Hong Kong in garments, to name just a few. Conversely, students of industrial districts are pointing to a growing penetration of global forces within the most dynamic local clusters (Cossentino et al. 1996; Palpacuer 1997; 2002; Schmitz 1995). To conceptualize the links between global networks and local industrial transformation, it is thus useful to think of local industrial clusters as forming particular nodes in global production networks. The key dimensions of activity, governance, and social and institutional conditions are combined into specific configurations within each node.

The social and institutional dimensions of global production networks

Although it recognizes that networks comprised in global value chains are 'socially constructed and locally integrated' (Gereffi et al. 1994: 2), GVC analysis tends to remain underdeveloped with regard to the fourth dimension of global chains, namely their social and institutional context (Henderson 1996). By contrast, more traditional frameworks to analyse industrial development fail to capture the global dynamics of production, but they fully highlight the role of social and institutional forces in explaining the structure and performance of geographically circumscribed economies. In fact, it can be argued that the social and institutional dimensions of production activities are more location-specific than chain-specific. For instance, Katz and Darbishire (2000) have shown that country-specific labour market structures and institutions play a critical role in shaping employment relations systems, although they are affected by the spreading of new practices in highly globalized sectors. Czaban and Henderson (2003) show that the unfolding of global production networks in Hungary has been conditioned by the institutional and business legacy of a central command economy. In order to understand how the global governance of production networks interacts with different institutional and social forces at the local or national level, it is thus necessary to combine GVCs with 'locally oriented' analytical approaches. Three of these – the business system, systemic competitiveness and industrial district perspectives – are discussed below. Each puts emphasis on particular aspects of interactions between social, institutional and economic forces at the local level.

The *business system* approach draws attention to the influence of social and institutional factors in shaping the organization of production activities in a given country. Business systems are defined as 'distinctive ways of coordinating and controlling economic activities which developed interdependently with key institutions that constitute particular kinds of political, financial, labour and cultural systems' (Whitley 1996; 1999). They include key characteristics of: firms, such as their growth patterns, ownership and risk management; inter-firm relations, such as the extent of cooperation; and internal systems of coordination and control, such as the division of labour, the nature of authority relations and the nature of employment relations within the firm. This framework has been primarily applied at the national and regional levels to highlight differences between business systems found in Europe, East Asia and North America. Combined with a global perspective, it can be used to investigate how firms embedded in distinct business systems participate in GVCs, and how the specific role and behaviour of these firms in turn influence the development of global value chains (Czaban and Henderson 2003). For instance, American firms have been found to exercise greater formal control, set more stringent product and service expectations, and make greater investment in supplier training than their European counterparts (Gibbon 2001; 2002). Such differences in lead firms' sourcing patterns can usefully be explained with reference to the broader business systems within which American and European firms are embedded.

Ranging from the national to the local, the *systemic competitiveness* framework highlights complementarities between various levels of political and economic action in promoting successful industrial development (Esser et al. 1996). Key conditions to achieve such a goal include: at the 'meta' level, the existence of shared cultural values, a basic consensus among social actors and an ability to formulate jointly a development strategy; at the 'macro' level, national policies providing a stable economic environment; at the 'meso' level, policies targeted to specific regions and industries, involving government and non-government actors such as business and labour organizations; and at the 'micro' level, dynamic networks of firms oriented towards continuous improvement and learning. This framework has been used to analyse how local industrial communities have responded to changing competitive conditions in the context of globalization, and how policy initiatives at the national, local and sectoral levels supported or hampered their capacity to adapt (Meyer-Stamer, 1998).

The *industrial district* perspective also stresses the role of local institutions in supporting economic development, while putting special emphasis on the need to promote trust and social cohesion in local communities. As emphasized by Zeitlin (1992), the geographically concentrated networks that make up industrial districts are characterized by the existence of recurring tensions between specialized firms – such as merchants, manufacturers and subcontractors – between employers and employees, and between skilled and unskilled workers. In this context, trust and social cohesion do not result from a pre-existing cultural consensus. They are produced by the deliberate actions of institutions that provide collective services, such as training and marketing support, as well as institutions for collective wage setting and dispute resolution (Cossentino 1996). Both types of institutions encourage firms to compete on the basis of continuous innovation and upgrading, rather than through squeezing labour costs and jeopardizing product quality (Piore and Sabel 1984). Such a perspective is of particular relevance to explore the role of tripartism, collective bargaining and other platforms for social dialogue within the context of globalization.

It is thus from a local perspective that the implications of global production networks for industrial development, employment and policy-making can best be assessed. Whether global integration stimulates local development, and the kind of jobs and activities created in that process, will depend on interactions between the global strategies of lead firms driving transnational networks, and the ways in which local firms, workers and institutions respond to the opportunities and constraints generated by this global environment.

Implications for Industrial Upgrading, Employment and Local Development Policy

Global production networks constitute new forms of organization that are presumably more open and mobile than traditional forms based on domestic vertically integrated production. As such, they offer new opportunities for local firms and industries to participate in, and perhaps benefit from, the global economy. To assess this potential requires a closer look at the internal organization of global networks and at factors shaping that organization at the global and the local levels. A similar perspective is needed to assess the impact of global networks on the quantity and quality of local jobs. Finally, networks might provide a new organizational model not only for enterprises but also for institutions and actors involved in local development policies. These three themes are explored below.

Global networks and local industrial upgrading

To what extent can global production networks provide a vehicle for local industrial development? How easily can local producers enter these networks, move up and achieve sustainable competitive advantage? These questions raise issues relating to the degree of openness of global production networks and to the learning dynamics by which new network members can increase the value content of their activity and strengthen their position within a network.

Open, closed and 'permeable' networks

The openness of a production network can be defined as the ease of entry for both new firms and new locations. Ideally, a totally closed network would comprise a limited set of linkages developed by a lead firm in a few sites, whereas a totally open network would be characterized by continuous change in the partners involved and their locations. The degree of network openness varies according to industry-specific characteristics and the features of the business systems within which network firms are embedded. Buyer-driven networks in garments and footwear tend to be more open than producer-driven networks in, say, automobiles, mainly as a result of lower entry barriers in the low-skilled, labour-intensive production activities of BDCs. As mentioned earlier, lead firms in the same industry might exhibit different networking behaviours depending on the idiosyncrasies of their national environments. For instance, Japanese electronics companies have been slower than their American counterparts to diversify their supply base and extend the geographical scope of their production networks in East Asia (Ernst 1997). Japanese networks also tend to be more socially embedded and less market-oriented than American networks (Smitka 1991; Sturgeon 2002).

The most successful production networks, however, are neither closed nor open but 'permeable' (Richter and Wakuta 1993). They are characterized by an evolving tiered structure in which a first tier of selected, stable partners is surrounded by a more mobile row of second-tier suppliers. The existence of such a structure has been documented at the local level, for example in Japanese automobiles and electronics networks (Nishiguchi 1994; Smitka 1991) and in American garment networks (Palpacuer 1997), and at the global level, for example in the networking behaviour of lead firms such as Nike (Donaghu and Barff 1990), Benetton (Harrison 1994), and other large American retailers (Gereffi 1994). Second-tier positions typically involve low-skilled, low-value activities that are relatively easy to enter, such as contract manufacturing based on manual assembly, but provide a weak basis for learning and growth. Second-tier suppliers compete mainly on costs and lack the organizational capabilities needed to meet lead firms' standards in terms of volume, quality, flexibility and reliability. As a result, they fail to create and retain enough value to propel cumulative investment. It is important to emphasize that beyond the simplified distinction between first-tier and second-tier positions, the number of tiers or subcontracting layers can be quite large, particularly for the manufacture of simple products that might be carried out in the informal sector, at times extending global networks into the home of individual production workers.

Learning and upgrading within global networks

The challenge for a local firm, then, is not so much to enter global networks, which might be done relatively easily on the basis of low costs, but to reach more profitable positions within these networks. Such strategies are made possible by the dynamic nature of global production networks: positions within networks are not fixed but are constantly challenged by competition, so that firms might move up or down the tiered structure depending on their performance. Upgrading a supplier's position implies an improvement in the value content of local industries and the broadening of the range of activities performed at the local level. Gereffi (1995) conceptualizes such evolution as an ideal sequence of export roles that local producers might perform within GVCs, ranging from export-processing assembly to original equip-ment manufacturing (OEM) and original brand-name manufacturing (OBM). East Asian producers have followed such a trajectory in industries such as garments and electronics, where they have developed sustainable competitive advantage, further consolidating their competitive positions by diversifying their client base and market segments. Accordingly, industrial upgrading can be defined as encompassing improvements in production processes, product quality, the range of functions performed by suppliers and, finally, the range of clients served on global markets (Palpacuer 2000b).

Of central importance to the upgrading process are the learning dynamics by which local producers can develop their competencies and capabilities within global chains. As shown by case studies in the automobile, electronics and garment industries, learning typically requires a mutual commitment of lead firms and their suppliers.

The former provide engineering assistance and training, as well as financial resources when relationships are based on equity ties. The latter invest in equipment and specialization. Through continuous information exchange and joint problem solving, suppliers can learn to meet lead firms' standards and reach a first-tier position within their production networks. The capabilities developed through such learning dynamics can then be leveraged to acquire new know-how, develop new products and enter new networks, thus opening a new growth perspective for local firms. Lee and Chen (2002) found such a learning trajectory in the industrial upgrading strategies of Taiwanese electronic producers. In this case, as in others, the particularities of the business system within which local firms are embedded plays a significant role in determining firms' willingness and ability to engage in a learning process. Both the local entrepreneurial culture and active state support to local development, for instance, have been instrumental in helping East Asian producers to achieve sustainable positions in global industries (Gereffi 1995).

Obstacles to industrial upgrading

Successful cases of learning and industrial upgrading can be found in global production networks, but the difficulties involved in replicating these strategies should not be ignored. Obstacles relate to the nature of activities performed within global networks, the nature of relationships between lead firms and their suppliers, and the geographical distribution of activities within global networks.

First, local firms are likely to face substantial entry barriers into the most profitable activities of value chains, nowadays increasingly associated with strategic services such as marketing and R&D. As global networks evolve towards greater functional integration, entry barriers also rise in network positions that previously provided a port of entry into more profitable activities, such as first-tier supplying. Humphrey (2003) uncovers such evolution in the auto component sector, showing that large automakers increasingly rely on selected first-tier suppliers on a global scale. Similarly, Sturgeon (1998; 2001) documents the rise of 'turnkey' production in electronics, where bundles of integrated services are offered by leading global suppliers. In apparel, some East Asian suppliers have also transformed themselves into global service providers that coordinate garment production worldwide on behalf of large US clients (Gereffi 1995; Gibbon 2001). These strategies produce a trend towards concentration and rising size of firms in first-tier supplying, thus reducing local firms' prospects of entering this segment of global production.

Second, local supply firms face the difficulty of overcoming transactional dependency *vis-à-vis* lead firms. As shown in Japanese electronics and auto networks (Nishiguchi 1994), and in US-based garment networks (Palpacuer 1997; 2002), the learning process by which suppliers can evolve towards more complex and remunerative activities involves a phase of high concentration in which lead firms might account for as much as 80 per cent of suppliers' revenues. Serving one major customer facilitates the development of trust and the acquisition of specific competencies (Sako 1992), but also increases suppliers' vulnerability. The next step for suppliers is thus to diversify their clientele, a phase that requires some degree of standardization of products and production. Such a step has been successfully taken by global contract manufacturers in electronics, thanks to the emergence of generic, codified manufacturing technology allowing for scale economies and a broadening of contract manufacturers' market base (Sturgeon 1998). These findings suggest that the acquisition of competencies via close inter-firm linkages might be easier at specific phases of industrial change, when new competencies and forms of work organization emerge within an industry. Once competitors have mastered new competencies and competitive positions are consolidated, economies of scale recreate entry barriers for newcomers into the most profitable segments of global chains. Additional rounds of technological and organizational innovation will be needed for newcomers to rise up to more profitable positions.

Finally, the advantages provided by geographical proximity in strengthening network relations might impede industrial upgrading in distant locations. Scott (1996) argues that transactions based on trust and specific competencies can be carried out most effectively within local networks, whereas standardized transactions can be easily performed with remote partners. The diffusion of just-in-time production techniques has also been considered to favour local production (Abernathy et al. 1999). Global transactions might thus remain limited to standard arm's-length exchanges involving few interdependencies between lead firms and their remote suppliers. Such a conclusion, however, risks overlooking other forms of complementarities between local, regional and global networks. In electronics, for instance, American lead firms have transferred a large range of support functions to East Asian locations (Ernst 1997). This strengthening of global linkages has happened concurrently with a deepening of regional networks within East Asia (Henderson 1997). Consequently, remoteness from lead firms' core locations is not an insurmountable obstacle to local industrial upgrading. This, as pointed out by Dicken (1994), does not imply that every local industry can hope to participate and upgrade within global production networks, because first-tier positions remain few in number and unevenly distributed geographically. The rise of global first-tier suppliers accentuates this phenomenon by promoting a centralization of component design and other key support activities in these suppliers' core locations, so that higher-value service activities have actually been found to decline in other locations (Humphrey 2003).

Global networks and local jobs

Entry at the bottom end of global production networks is a commonly considered strategy for job creation in developing countries, as illustrated by the substantial increase in the number of Export Processing Zones (EPZs) observed during the last decades (ILO 1996). However, the majority of developing countries that have adopted such a strategy have only registered limited success. Even when a zone has taken off in terms of job creation, local production activities have been typically restricted to the simple, low-skilled assembly of imported inputs. The prevalence of labour-intensive activities has generated powerful pressures to compete by 'sweating' labour. Such pressures were reinforced, rather than mitigated, by labour market conditions at the local level, because these zones are usually characterized by a weak enforcement of labour standards, hostility to trade unions and the subordination of young female workers. As emphasized by the ILO (1998), such forms of integration within global networks are highly unstable and can hardly provide a lever for sustainable local development. It is only by increasing the value content of local activities that more sustainable forms of integration within global networks can be achieved. Changes in the social and institutional context of local activities are concurrently needed in order to promote a durable and widespread improvement of local employment conditions.

Improving job quality through upgrading

In the 1990s, a new model for competitiveness and human resource management became prominent in academic and policy circles. To achieve a sustainable competitive advantage and preserve or improve workplace standards, it recommends that firms follow the 'high road', namely compete on product quality and customer service rather than costs, and develop the skills, involvement and motivation of the workforce instead of squeezing labour costs. Within the developed world, this model refers to the best practices of leading firms in the United States, Japan and Europe (Appelbaum and Batt 1994; Boyer 1991). Similar patterns have emerged in the competitive strategies and employment practices of dynamic firms in fast-growing East Asian economies (Kuruvilla 1996; Verma 1997). Based on case studies of Singapore, Malaysia, the Philippines and India, Kuruvilla (1996) shows how countries that moved from low-cost to higher-value-added export-oriented strategies experienced a shift in the focus of their industrial relations and human resource policies, from cost containment to skills development and workforce flexibility. Similar shifts towards workers' skills improvement through training and education have been identified in the upgrading clusters of Torreón (Mexico) in the garment industry (Bair and Gereffi 2003), Singapore and Scotland in electronics (Sturgeon 1998), as well as India and Brazil in the auto component sector (Humphrey 2003).

Verma (1997) highlights the rationale underlying this strategic shift: foreign investment and contract manufacturing are initially attracted on the basis of low wages and low unionization, but as production expands, capital inflows generate a transformation of labour market conditions in the form of rising wages, growing labour shortages and mounting demands for unionization and collective bargaining. At this stage, two options are available to local policy-makers. One is to recreate initial labour market conditions through wage control and union repression. The other is to adapt by following a 'high-road' strategy, namely upgrading workers' skills through training and education, and linking wages to productivity. In a virtuous cycle, higher-skilled and more motivated workers bring more value to production activities, thus making firms more profitable and allowing them to pay higher wages. Two different sets of global pressures might be at work in fostering such a trajectory: one coming from global buyers' growing requirements for speed, responsiveness and quality; the other stemming from the entry of lower-cost competitors with large reserves of cheap labour.

Beyond improving production workers' skills, industrial upgrading can contribute to the creation of higher-skilled jobs at the local level through the development of support services such as component purchasing, logistics management, or component design. This has actually been the case in locations such as Singapore, Scotland, or Mexico (Bair and Gereffi 2003; Sturgeon 1998). In locations where service functions are not centralized, however, job diversity might actually decline as local firms focus on manufacturing in order to maintain their competitiveness within global networks (Humphrey 2003). Upgrading should also boost local wages in return for greater worker contribution to local value creation, although such an evolution is not readily observable in upgrading clusters, as will be discussed below.

Obstacles to a sustainable improvement of employment conditions

The upgrading path described above raises a number of issues concerning the extent and sustainability of improvements in employment conditions at the local level. First, the gains derived from industrial upgrading may be unequally spread among different groups of workers. Vulnerable groups include 'guest workers' imported in response to local labour shortages, as well as workers employed by smaller suppliers and subcontractors that perform lower-value-added activities within global networks. Humphrey (2003) found that in the Brazilian and Indian auto industries, improvements in employment conditions remained largely restricted to lead firms and first-tier suppliers while conditions rapidly deteriorated down the production chain. Drawing from a broad range of case studies in developing countries, Nadvi and Schmitz (1994) also found that upgrading patterns in industrial clusters were internally uneven. As some local producers improved their position within global networks, others continued to perform low-skilled activities less conducive to improvements in employment conditions. Accordingly, upgrading *per se* does not correct the inequalities in employment conditions that are inherent in outsourcing practices. On the contrary, such practices might contribute towards explaining the rising wage inequalities observed in developed and developing countries over the last decades (Palpacuer 1998).

Second, the value created through industrial upgrading does not seem to be shared with workers in the form of higher wages. Case studies in the Mexican centre of Torreón, a major producer of jeans for the US market (Bair and Gereffi 2001), in the Mexican auto component centre of Ciudad Juárez (Carrillo 1998), and in the auto and electronics industry of Hungary (Czaban and Henderson 2003), suggest that local labour market conditions in terms of labour shortage and labour regulation play a greater role than firm-level upgrading strategies in promoting wage increases. In other words, higher wage levels appear to depend more on tight local labour market conditions and/or demanding collective agreements and labour laws than on individual firms' upgrading strategies. These results underline the role of local institutions in improving employment conditions, in the face of global downward pressures on production workers' wages. In the context of global competition, upskilling, more participative forms of management, and better health and safety conditions can indeed enhance workers' commitment to meet a firm's industrial upgrading objectives without the lure of higher wages. Similarly, lead firms and first-tier suppliers might invest in training and education, work reform, and a cleaner and safer work environment, all of which directly improve productivity of local plants, while maintaining a tight control on wages in line with performance requirements set by major buyers and shareholders. This indicates that the sharing of the gains derived from industrial upgrading cannot be left to market forces if upgrading is to contribute to local development.

Third, industrial upgrading typically involves some form of worker displacement, either directly through declining numbers of production workers, or indirectly through the emergence of new job profiles that make workers' skills obsolete or less valuable in the local labour market. Direct displacement derives from productivity gains allowing firms to reduce the number of workers employed for a given level of output, while indirect displacement has been observed in relation to shifts in the gender composition of local employment. According to Sturgeon (1998: 24), the transition from manual to automated circuit-board assembly has meant a 'whole-sale de-feminisation' of electronic manufacturing, or substantial job losses for women making up the bulk of hand assembly workers in this sector. Likewise, Carrillo (1998) observed that the proportion of women employed in *maquiladoras* was diminishing as these local industries evolved from simple assembly to higher-quality production and engineering activities. These cases highlight the need to focus explicitly on the gender dimension of global value chains and devise appropriate policies (Barrientos 2001).

Finally, in a number of countries such as the Republic of Korea, Singapore and Malaysia, the 'high road' has been combined with elements of a 'low road' including union repression and/or restrictive labour laws (Kuruvilla 1996; Verma 1997). Overall, the mixed results concerning the employment outcome of upgrading strategies raise a number of questions. Can local industries develop a sustainable competitive advantage on the basis of uneven improvements in employment conditions? It might be argued that long-term growth and development require greater participation at the workplace as well as a diffusion of growth dividends within the various social groups making up a local community. If a durable and widespread improvement of employment conditions is a necessary foundation for local development, what role should local institutions play in achieving this goal? Available evidence suggests that competitive forces alone are not likely to produce such a social outcome, so that firm-based upgrading strategies need to be complemented by a consistent set of supportive policies.

Network models and local development policy

The extent to which local industries can take advantage of globalization to engage in a process of learning, upgrading and improvement in employment conditions depends

on the social and institutional context of local economic activities. The highly publicized cases of Third Italy and Silicon Valley show that industrial clusters that
succeed in the global economy have built a culture of learning and innovation
supported by a local institutional infrastructure including governments, local banks,
research and training institutes, employers' and workers' associations and other civil
society organizations. These institutions have developed a web of formal and informal relations between local firms, workers and policy-makers that sustains a dynamic
of continuous improvement and reinforces social ties within the local industrial
community (Pyke et al. 1990; Saxenian 1994).

The development of global production networks is now placing new demands on
these local institutions, which need to redefine their role in relation to changes in
the forms and logic of competition. Just as enterprises are transforming their modes
of operation, both internally and in their relations to other firms, in order to build
a sustainable competitive advantage, forward-looking institutions are striving to find
new, flexible ways of interacting between themselves and with businesses in order to
support industrial competitiveness and social cohesion. The sustainable integration
of local firms within global production networks requires enhanced networking
strategies by local development agencies and institutions. As emphasized by Morgan
(1996), such a 'networking model of development' is based on a pragmatic perspective that moves beyond the traditional opposition between neo-liberal and statist
views that respectively give prominence to the market or to the state as a primary
vehicle for economic development. Operating as policy networks can help local
institutions simultaneously to support the acquisition of new knowledge and competencies in the industrial community, and to ensure greater equity in the distribution
of gains among local social groups.

Support the development of local competencies

Local policy networks might contribute to support skills building and upgrading in
a variety of ways. First, innovative local industrial strategies should be articulated
within a global perspective. A better understanding of how global production
networks are structured and how particular sets of firms operate within them could
provide a basis for developing a vision of what the local industry could become as
globalization proceeds. A global perspective could help firms, SMEs in particular, to
identify and assess opportunities and threats, and to establish connections to foreign
markets and critical outside competencies. According to Saxenian (1997), local
government agencies have followed such an approach in promoting the development of the Taiwanese semiconductor industry. Local agencies have defined their
industrial policies by consulting intensively and continuously with overseas Taiwanese
engineers working in Silicon Valley, and have encouraged the transfer of knowledge
from these engineers back to their home country. By so doing, they have contributed
to the development of close social linkages between Taiwan and Silicon Valley that
proved instrumental in allowing Taiwanese firms to upgrade their position in the
global electronics industry.

Second, networks can provide an organizing principle for implementing development policy in a decentralized, flexible and responsive manner. Inside state agencies this involves locating decision-making at the level most closely associated with policy implementation, thus increasing responsibilities at the local or regional level as opposed to the national level. Between local actors, networking calls for a greater reliance on the complementary roles of intermediary organizations such as employers' and workers' associations, as well as other forms of civil society organizations. The tacit knowledge and political credibility acquired by these institutions can decisively help in implementing development policies (Morgan 1996; Sabel 1994). Between institutions and enterprises, a network-based policy puts emphasis on continuous interaction in the provision of support services. For instance, the effectiveness of training and consultancy services would be greatly improved if their design, implementation and appraisal were performed on the basis of close communication between providers and recipients. The Garment Industry Development Corporation (GIDC) operating in the New York garment industry provides a successful example of networking strategies. Jointly established by the City of New York, employers' and workers' associations, GIDC receives funding from the federal and local states and relies on a set of complementary competencies to help local suppliers build new capabilities and upgrade their position in the global garment industry. It contributes at the same time to alleviating the problems of insertion faced by ethnic minorities that make up the bulk of entrepreneurs and workers in the local garment industry. Support services are focused on skills development, organizational improvement and the building of close inter-firm linkages between suppliers and lead firms, underlining the importance of intangible assets as a source of local competitiveness. They also include childcare for the immigrant women who predominantly perform sewing activities in the local industry (Herman 1998).

Support consensus-building among local actors

Cooperation between various types of local actors necessarily generates conflicts and tensions within an industrial community. As emphasized by the industrial district perspective, such conflicts should not be seen as obstacles to the building of trust and social cohesion. On the contrary, the expression of divergent interests through debates and social dialogue is a necessary step towards achieving consensus among various actors involved in collective action. According to Zeitlin (1992: 287), 'trust relations in industrial districts seem more a consequence than a precondition of practical cooperation among local actors, and social consensus less an antithesis of conflict than an outcome of its successful resolution'. The challenge facing policy-makers is to provide a platform for dialogue among local actors in order to allow for the expression of local divergences, and to channel conflicts into a constructive search for solutions. Such a role encourages local actors to develop a shared vision of their future as a community, an important condition for achieving sustainable growth and development.

As shown by the history of Italian industrial districts, institutions that succeed in governing this process of conflict resolution become the embodiment of trust and social consensus among local actors. They gain the legitimacy needed to implement successful development strategies, namely strategies that are adhered to by those primarily concerned. In that perspective, tripartite mechanisms that regulate relationships between governments, employers and workers can play an important role in sustaining social cohesion. They can prevent firms from engaging in a type of cost-based competition detrimental to employment conditions, and provide for an equitable sharing of growth dividends among local firms and workers. However, traditional tripartite systems might find it difficult to sustain their role within the context of globalization. As local industries become part of global networks, industrial relations within these industries might be disrupted, and the underlying norms and values supporting them might be transformed. In that process, local institutions including governments, employers' and workers' associations can be challenged in their ability to unify and aggregate interests in the industrial community. Cossentino (1996) witnessed such evolution in the Italian district of Emilia-Romagna. As the district became embedded into global production networks, new lines of division emerged among local firms and workers that unevenly benefited from global integration. Such evolution has weakened social consensus and hampered the definition of a concerted development strategy at the local level. At this stage, the cluster faces the need to rebuild social cohesion through a new process of conflict resolution. A similar pattern is observable in the recent evolution of the New York garment industry under the impact of globalization (Palpacuer 1997).

The above examples suggest that in a global and dynamic environment, local interests have to be constantly realigned in order to maintain the social consensus needed to support growth and development within industrial clusters. In this regard, the role of policy networks becomes of particular importance in promoting a continuous dialogue among local actors. The open, flexible nature of such networks should allow for new lines of interest to be expressed and integrated into the process of consensus-building. Alongside traditional tripartite actors, new forms of organizations arising from civil society may play an important role in that process, helping to integrate broader social concerns within the traditional industrial development agenda, as observed in Ireland, New Zealand and South Africa (Baccaro 2002; O'Donovan et al. 2000). Within the context of globalization, the process of consensus-building should also span local, regional and international institutions. Local initiatives need to be supported by complementary actions at the national and global level, as illustrated by recent attempts to promote ethical sourcing and more socially responsible behaviour within global production networks.

Concluding Remarks

The project on 'Global Production and Local Jobs' has highlighted interactions between global and local dynamics in contemporary forms of industrial organization by combining complementary analytical frameworks such as the global value chain and industrial district models. Two central issues stand out of our analysis. First, current changes in the organization of global production networks point to a growing concentration of power and value appropriation in the hands of two groups of firms: lead firms controlling strategic knowledge-intensive activities and, to a lesser extent, first-tier suppliers offering integrated manufacturing services on a global scale. Entry barriers are thus rising into the most profitable segments of value chains, making it difficult for newcomers to replicate the upgrading strategies earlier adopted by global suppliers. These results underline the need for local industries to adopt diversified development strategies, including the search for innovation to overcome barriers set by market leaders in GVCs, the search for market access outside lead firms' networks, and a diversification of targeted end-markets. Such strategies do not rule out participation in global production networks, but involve a critical assessment of upgrading opportunities offered by global chains, aimed at minimizing the risk for local suppliers to remain 'sandwiched' between unattainable positions at the top of GVCs and unsustainable positions at the bottom end of global value chains.

Second, the new forms of industrial organization produce an intensification of labour market competition at the global level so that the gains derived from industrial upgrading are often shared unequally among local workers, and not necessarily in the form of higher wages. Policy-makers should address issues of rising inequalities, worker displacement and wage pressures if industrial upgrading is to contribute to local development. We believe that doing so involves going beyond traditional policy approaches and reshaping operational modes of policy-making institutions along the lines of a network model. Such a form of organization will be needed for policy-makers to stimulate innovation in local industries and to promote social dialogue, consensus-building and a sharing of growth dividends at the local level. These policy considerations implicitly refer to local clusters in industrialized countries, however, and as such avoid a difficult question. What is to be done when local actors and institutions that are assumed to play an essential role in governing industrial development are weakly organized, or lack independence, or are repressed and left with no voice, or simply do not exist? This question goes far beyond the scope of this article. Three propositions, however, are worth submitting. First, greater social dialogue and democratic participation in decision-making, in addition to being fundamental goals *per se*, ultimately provide the necessary foundation for any location to achieve sustainable industrial development and social progress. Second, initiatives to foster dialogue and participation should be taken not only at the local but also at the international level. Third, the ILO, with its principles, its international standards and its technical expertise, has a role to play in assisting individual countries and in mobilizing the international community. Its mission to promote sustainable development through 'Decent Work' takes on a renewed importance within the context of global production.

REFERENCES

Abernathy, F., J. Dunlop, J. Hammond and D. Weill (1999) *A stitch in time: lean retailing and the transformation of manufacturing*, New York: Oxford University Press.

Appelbaum, E. and R. Batt (1994) *The new American workplace*, Ithaca, NY: ILR Press.

Baccaro, L. (2002) 'Civil society meets the state: a model of associational democracy', International Institute for Labour Studies Discussion paper no. 138.

Badaracco, J. L. (1991) *The knowledge link*, Boston: Harvard Business School Press.

Bair, J. and G. Gereffi (2001) 'Local clusters in global chains: the causes and consequences of export dynamism in Torreón's blue jeans industry', *World Development*, 9, 1885–1903.

Bair, J. and G. Gereffi (2002) 'NAFTA and the apparel commodity chain: corporate strategies, inter-firm networks, and industrial upgrading', in G. Gereffi, D. Spener and J. Bair (eds) *Free trade and uneven development: the North American apparel industry after NAFTA*, Philadelphia, PA: Temple University Press, 23–50.

Bair, J. and G. Gereffi (2003) 'Industrial upgrading, networks and employment in the apparel commodity chain', *Global Networks*, 3, 143–69.

Barrientos, S. (2001) 'Gender, flexibility and global value chains', *IDS Bulletin*, 32, 3, 83–93.

Boyer, R. (1991) 'New directions in management principles and work organization: general principles and national trajectories', paper presented at the OECD Conference on 'Technical change as a social process: society, enterprises and individual', Helsinki, 11–13 December 1989, CEPREMAP, CNRS, EHESS.

Carrillo, J. (1998) 'Industrial upgrading in Mexico: the case of General Motors', paper presented at the international workshop on 'Global production and local jobs: new perspectives on enterprise networks, employment and local development policy', International Institute for Labour Studies, Geneva, 9–10 May.

Chew, D. (1997) *Studies in international corporate finance and governance systems*, New York: Oxford University Press.

Cossentino, F. (1996) 'The need for a new regulatory and institutional order', in F. Cossentino, F. Pyke and W. Sengenberger (eds) *Local and regional response to global pressure: the case of Italy and its industrial districts*, Research Series 103, Geneva: International Institute for Labour Studies, 99–110.

Cossentino, F., F. Pyke and W. Sengenberger (1996) *Local and regional response to global pressure: the case of Italy and its industrial districts*, Research Series 103, Geneva: International Institute for Labour Studies.

Czaban, L. and J. Henderson (2003) 'Commodity chains, foreign investment and labour issues in Eastern Europe', *Global Networks*, 3, 171–97.

Dicken, P. (1994) 'Global–local tensions: firms and states in the global space-economy', *Economic Geography*, 70, 101–28.

Dicken, P. (1998) *Global shift: transforming the world economy*, New York: Guilford Press.

Dicken, P., P. F. Kelly, K. Olds and H. Wai-Chung Yeung (2001) 'Chains and networks, territories and scales: towards a relational framework for analysing the global economy', *Global Networks*, 1, 89–112.

Donaghu, M. T. and R. Barff (1990) 'Nike just did it: international subcontracting and flexibility in athletic footwear production', *Regional Studies*, 24, 537–52.

Ernst, D. (1997) 'From partial to systemic globalization: international production networks in the electronics industry', Berkeley Roundtable on the International Economy (BRIE) Working Paper 98.

Esser, K., W. Hillebrand, D. Messner and J. Meyer-Stamer (1996) 'Systemic competitiveness: a new challenge for firms and government', *CEPAL Review*, August, 39–53.

Fröhlich, D. and U. Pekruhl (1996) 'Direct participation and organizational change', *European Foundation for the Improvement of Living and Working Conditions*, Dublin, Ireland: Loughlinstown Co.

Gereffi, G. (1994) 'The organization of buyer-driven global commodity chains: how US retailers shape overseas production networks', in G. Gereffi and M. Korzeniewicz (eds) *Commodity chains and global capitalism*, Westport, CT: Greenwood Press, 95–123.

Gereffi, G. (1995) 'Global production systems and third world development', in B. Stallings (ed.) *Global change, regional responses*, Cambridge: Cambridge University Press, 100–42.

Gereffi, G. (1996) 'Commodity chains and regional divisions of labour in East Asia', *Journal of Asian Business*, 12, 75–112.

Gereffi, G. (1999) 'International trade and industrial upgrading in the apparel commodity chain', *Journal of International Economics*, 48, 37–70.

Gereffi, G. and R. Kaplinsky (eds) (2001) 'The value of value chains: spreading the gains from globalization', *IDS Bulletin*, special issue, 32, 3.

Gereffi, G., J. Humphrey and T. Sturgeon (2002) 'Developing a theory of global value chains: a framework document', paper presented at the Global Value Chain Conference, Rockefeller Foundation and Institute for Development Studies, Rockport, MA, 25–28 April. http://www.ids.ac.uk/ids/global/rockport.html.

Gereffi, G., M. Korzeniewicz and R. Korzeniewicz (1994) 'Introduction: global commodity chains', in G. Gereffi and M. Korzeniewicz (eds) *Commodity chains and global capitalism*, Westport, CT.: Greenwood Press, 1–14.

Ghoshal, S. and C. Bartlett (1990) 'The multinational corporation as an interorganizational network', *Academy of Management Review*, 15, 603–25.

Gibbon, P. (2001) *Segmentation, governance and upgrading in global clothing chains: a Mauritian case study*, Copenhagen: Centre for Development Research.

Gibbon, P. (2002) *South Africa and the global commodity chain for clothing: export perform-ance and constraints*, Copenhagen: Centre for Development Research.

Gibbon, P. (2003) 'At the cutting edge? Financialisation and UK clothing retailers' global sourcing patterns and practices', *Competition and Change*, forthcoming.

Harrison, B. (1994) *Lean and mean: the changing landscape of corporate power in the age of flexibility*, New York: Basic Books.

Helper, S., J. MacDuffie and C. Sabel (2000) 'Pragmatic collaboration: advancing knowledge while controlling opportunism', *Industrial and Corporate Change*, 9, 443–87.

Henderson, J. (1996) 'Globalization and forms of capitalism: conceptualisations and the search for synergies', *Competition and Change*, 1, 403–10.

Henderson, J. (1997) 'The changing international division of labour in the electronics indus-try', in D. Campbell, A. Parisotto, A. Verma and A. Lateef (eds) *Regionalization and labour market interdependence in East and Southeast Asia*, Geneva: International Institute for Labour Studies, 92–127.

Henderson, J., P. Dicken, M. Hess, N. Coe and H. Wai-Chung Yeung (2002) 'Global production networks and the analysis of economic development', *Review of International Political Economy*, 9, 436–65.

Herman, B. (1998) 'Keeping New York in fashion: the Garment Industry Development Corporation', paper presented at the international workshop on 'Global production and local jobs: new perspectives on enterprise networks, employment and local development policy', International Institute for Labour Studies, Geneva, 9–10 May.

Humphrey, John (2003) 'Globalization and supply chain networks in the auto industry: Brazil and India', *Global Networks*, 3, 121–41.

ILO: International Labour Office (1996) *World labour report 1995–96*, International Labour Organization, Geneva.

ILO: International Labour Office (1998) *World labour report 1997–98*, International Labour Organization, Geneva.

ILO: International Labour Office (1999) *Decent work*, Report of the Director-General, International Labour Conference, 87th Session 1999, Geneva.

Jarillo, C. J. (1988) 'On strategic networks', *Strategic Management Journal*, 9, 31–41.

Jarillo, C. J. (1993) *Strategic networks: creating the borderless organization*, Oxford: Butterworth-Heinemann.

Kaplinsky, R. (2000) 'Globalization and unequalization: what can be learned from value chain analysis?', *Journal of Development Studies*, 37, 117–46.

Katz, H. and O. Darbishire (2000) *Converging divergences: worldwide changes in employment systems*, Ithaca, NY: Cornell University Press.

Kuruvilla, S. (1996) 'Linkages between industrialization strategies and industrial relations/human resource policies: Singapore, Malaysia, The Philippines, and India', *Industrial and Labour Relations Review*, 49, 635–56.

Lazonic, W. and M. O'Sullivan (2000) 'Maximizing shareholder value: a new ideology for corporate governance', *Economy and Society*, 29, 13–35.

Lee, J.-R. and J.-S. Chen (2002) 'Dynamic synergy creation with multiple business activities: towards a competence-based growth model for contract manufacturers', in R. Sanchez and A. Heene (eds) *Theory development for competence-based management: advances in applied business strategy*, Stanford, CT: JAI Press, 209–28.

Meyer-Stamer, J. (1998) 'Clustering, systemic competitiveness and commodity chains: how firms, business associations and governments in Santa Catarina (Brazil) respond to globalization', paper presented at the international workshop on 'Global production and local jobs', International Institute for Labour Studies, Geneva, 9–10 May.

Miles, R. E. and C. C. Snow (1986) 'Organizations: new concepts for new forms,' *California Management Review*, 28, 62–73.

Morgan, K. (1996) 'Learning-by-interacting: inter-firm networks and enterprise support', in *Networks of enterprises and local development*, Paris: Organization for Economic Cooperation and Development, 53–66.

Nadvi, K. and H. Schmitz (1994) 'Industrial clusters in less developed countries: review of experiences and research agenda', Discussion paper 339, Institute of Development Studies, University of Sussex, England.

Nishiguchi, T. (1994) *Strategic industrial sourcing: the Japanese advantage*, New York: Oxford University Press.

O'Donovan, P., S. Marshall and K. Mbongo (2000) 'The role of civil society in promoting decent work: lessons from innovative partnerships in Ireland, New Zealand and South Africa', International Institute for Labour Studies, Geneva, Discussion Paper 124.

Palpacuer, F. (1997) 'Development of core–periphery forms of organizations: some lessons from the New York garment industry', International Institute for Labour Studies, Geneva, Discussion Paper 95. www.ilo.org/public/english/bureau/inst/papers/1997/dp95//index.htm.

Palpacuer, F. (1998) 'Competitiveness, organizational change and employment: a review of current trends and perspectives', report prepared for the Task Force on the Country Studies on the Social Dimensions of Globalization, International Labour Organization, Geneva, Switzerland.

Palpacuer, F. (2000a) 'Competence-based strategies and global production networks: a discussion of current changes and their implications for employment', *Competition and Change*, 4, 353–400.

Palpacuer, F. (2000b) 'Global production networks, industrial upgrading, and local jobs', paper presented at the meeting on 'Industrial upgrading', SSRC Working Group on Industrial Upgrading, Social Sciences Research Council, San José, Costa Rica, 11–15 October.

Palpacuer, F. (2002) 'Subcontracting networks in the New York garment industry: changing characteristics in a global era', in G. Gereffi, D. Spener and J. Bair (eds) *Free trade and uneven development: the North American apparel industry after NAFTA*, Philadelphia, PA: Temple University Press, 53–73.

Parisotto, A. (2001) 'Economic globalization and the demand for decent work', in R. Blanpain and C. Engels (eds) *The ILO and the social challenges of the 21st century*, The Hague: Kluwer.

Perez, R. and F. Palpacuer (eds) (2002) 'Changing modes of governance, competitiveness and strategic choice: a case study of food multinationals in Europe', *ERFI*, University of Montpellier, report prepared for the French Government, Commissariat Général au Plan, Service des Etudes et de la Recherche, France.

Piore, M. J. and C. F. Sabel (1984) *The second industrial divide*, New York: Basic Books.

Porter, M. (1985) *Competitive advantage: creating and sustaining superior performance*, New York: The Free Press.

Powell, W. (1990) 'Neither market nor hierarchy: network forms of organization', in B. M. Straw and L. L. Cummings (eds) *Research in organizational behaviour 12*, Greenwich, CT: JAI Press, 295–336.

Pyke, F., G. Becattini and W. Sengenberger (1990) *Industrial districts and inter-firm co-operation in Italy*, International Institute for Labour Studies, International Labour Office, Geneva.

Rabach, E. and E. M. Kim (1994) 'Where is the chain in commodity chains? The service sector nexus', in G. Gereffi and M. Korzeniewiez (eds) *Commodity chains and global capitalism*, Westport, CT: Greenwood Press, 123–42.

Reich, R. (1991) *The work of nations*, New York: Vintage Books.

Richter, F.-J. and Y. Wakuta (1993) 'Permeable networks: a future option for the European and Japanese car industries', *European Journal of Management*, 11, 262–7.

Sabel, C. F. (1994) 'Learning-by-monitoring: the institutions of economic development', in N. J. Smelser and R. Swedberg (eds) *The handbook of economic sociology*, Princeton, NJ: Princeton University Press, 137–65.

Sako, M. (1992) *Price, quality and trust: inter-firm relations in Britain and Japan*, Cambridge: Cambridge University Press.

Sassen, S. (1991) *The global city: New York, London, Tokyo*, Princeton, NJ: Princeton University Press.

Saxenian, A. (1994) *Regional advantage: culture and competition in Silicon Valley and Route 128*, Cambridge, MA: Harvard University Press.

Saxenian, A. (1997) 'Notes on industrial upgrading', prepared for the SSRC CRN on 'Globalization, local institutions and development', 20 September.

Schmitz, H. (1995) 'Small shoemakers and Fordist giants: tale of a supercluster', *World Development*, 23, 9–28.

Scott, A. (1996) 'Regional motors of the global economy', *Futures*, 28, 391–411.

Singh, A. (1994) 'Global economic changes, skills and international competitiveness', *International Labour Review*, 133, 167–84.

Smitka, M. (1991) *Competitive ties: subcontracting in the Japanese automotive industry*, New York: Columbia University Press.

Starr, M. K. (1991) *Global corporate alliances and the competitive edge*, New York: Quorum Books.

Sturgeon, T. (1998) 'Network-led development and the rise of turn-key production networks: technological change and the outsourcing of electronics manufacturing', paper prepared for the International Institute for Labour Studies, International Labour Organization, Geneva.

Sturgeon, T. (2001) 'How do we define value chains and production networks?', *IDS Bulletin*, 32, 3, 9–18.

Sturgeon, T. (2002) 'Modular production networks: an American model of industrial organization', *Industrial and Corporate Change*, 11, 451–96.

Sydow, J. (1992) 'On the management of strategic networks', in H. Ernste and V. Meier (eds) *Regional development and contemporary industrial response: extending flexible specialization*, London: Belhaven Press, 113–29.

Teece, D. J., G. Pisano and A. Shuen (1997) 'Dynamic capabilities and strategic management', *Strategic Management Journal*, 18, 509–33.

UNCTAD: United Nations Conference on Trade and Development (1993) *World investment report*, New York: United Nations.

UNCTAD: United Nations Conference on Trade and Development (1995) *World investment report*, New York: United Nations.

Useem, M. (1996) *Investor capitalism*, New York: Basic Books.

Verma, A. (1997) 'Labour, labour markets and the economic integration of nations', in D. Campbell, A. Parisotto, A. Verma and A. Lateef (eds) *Regionalization and labour market interdependence in East and Southeast Asia*, Geneva: International Institute for Labour Studies, 260–78.

Whitley, R. (1996) 'Business systems and global commodity chains: competing or complementary forms of economic organizations?', *Competition and Change*, 1, 411–25.

Whitley, R. (1999) *Divergent capitalisms: the social structuring and change of business systems*, New York: Oxford University Press.

Zeitlin, J. (1992) 'Industrial districts and local economic regeneration: overview and comments', in F. Pyke and W. Sengenberger (eds) *Industrial districts and local economic regeneration*, Geneva: International Institute for Labour Studies, 279–94.

Zenger, T. and W. S. Hesterly (1997) 'The disaggregation of corporations: selective intervention, high-powered incentives, and molecular units', *Organization Science*, 8, 209–22.

4.3

The Role of an Integrator Organisation in a Virtual Supply Chain

Frank Cave, Chris West and Alan Matthews

Introduction

The rationalisation of the aerospace supply chain has dramatically reduced the number of suppliers interfacing directly with the prime contractors. This has meant that thousands of SMEs have not only been cut off from contact with the prime but, because of their individual economic insignificance, have also been judged ineligible to bid for work from the next level of suppliers. The barrier thus created has disadvantages for both sides. The SMEs are denied a view of the technological needs of the prime, which is denied a view of the specialist skills, innovations and technologies available in the SMEs.

Since the 1950s the UK and European aerospace industry has demonstrated three major characteristics: consolidation, collaboration, and reorganisation or rationalisation. In 1955 there were more than 20 OEM/prime manufacturers in the UK. By 1985 this was reduced to three. From the 1980s the industry has reorganised from expansion, back to core business, to outsourcing and, by the late 1990s, was moving out of the lower tiers of manufacturing altogether.

In their attempts at rationalisation, OEMs are:

- moving up the supply chain;
- becoming prime contractors or system integrators;
- performing less manufacturing themselves, so pushing more work into the supply chain;
- reducing the number of suppliers with whom they deal directly;
- releasing many senior, experienced and knowledgeable managers.

There are two key consequences for the SMEs. First, there is an even greater remoteness from the OEMs and thus even less awareness of long term strategies and requirements. This leads to uncertainty regarding their own strategy and an unwillingness to invest. The OEMs then complain about the lack of long term vision and investment by the SMEs and feel justified in placing work in low labour cost areas overseas. Second, as OEMs reduce the number of suppliers they deal with, the number of layers tends to increase, though there is some consolidation. At the very least, the cost from a lower tier company to the OEM should rise due to extra handling/transaction costs. In practice the opposite happens: the lower tier company has its price forced down. SMEs face the choice of competing on cost whilst maintaining standards of quality, innovation and service or looking for work outside the aerospace sector.

One approach to address these two issues is the formation of a technology integrator organisation. This enables a virtual community of small, technology businesses to come together as an identifiable enterprise to bid for specific packets of work, either to a level 1 supplier or directly to the prime contractor. The paper describes the background and progress of such an integrator, the Advanced Aerospace Technology Guild (AATG) Limited, and discusses some of the practical and theoretical issues encountered.

Method of Study

Study of the integrator approach is ongoing. As mentioned above, the aerospace industry is dynamic. Prime contractors continuously adapt or change in many respects, in particular in their purchasing strategies and in supply chain management. There have been acquisitions and consolidation, the effects of which are not yet complete. In addition there have been significant upheavals in the external economic environment, not least the events of 11 September 2001.

Under these conditions, the selected study method was action research. As well as participating in events, meetings and the decision-making of the group, we conducted a series of extended, face-to-face interviews with members of the AATG management team and with SME members of the organisation. A key focus for the study is action learning.

The Integrator Organisation

AATG represents a group of over 60 companies, collectively committed to a flexible reorganisation of the middle and lower tier supply chain to meet the needs of OEM and higher tier customers. It was set up to meet the need for a single interface supply of multi-discipline/multi-company products and services. It started in February 2000 and from its first formation was registered as a private limited company. Interest in the concept was sufficient for it to have an official launch event in November 2000.

AATG membership consists of two groups, associates and companies, which are supported by a core management team of four people. The associate group consists of almost 80 individuals, most of whom are former senior managers with OEM or prime contractors. The large majority of associates are semi-retired and about 20 can be described as 'active'. This group contains significant high level experience in project, programme, operational and technical management.

The second group contains approximately 60 associated companies; these are almost exclusively SMEs. Though they all have significant business in the aerospace sector, they frequently operate in other industrial sectors as well, e.g. automotive. A significant feature of the operation of the organisation is that no money is involved. There is no membership subscription and no payment for contributions to the functioning of the organisation. The core management team does not receive any payment. AATG has no significant tangible assets.

Activities

AATG has three main activities. The first is jobshopping or supply of the services of experienced managers on a contract or project basis. Clearly, with the pool of associates, this is achievable. Though it has never been considered a real income generator, it has proved useful in establishing credibility and a method of working with prime contractors and others.

The second activity has been described as 'thinking'. This is primarily supported by three or four associates who are interested in integrated development activity to support the aerospace sector. Outcomes of this activity include a research project on the aerospace knowledge base for the UK Department of Trade and Industry (DTI), a project bid under EU Framework 5 and an expression of interest (EOI) for a Framework 6 project. They are also involved in establishing the Aerospace Innovation Centre, a £20m technology transfer and brokerage initiative in the North of England.

The third activity, the trading group, came from an early idea for a partnership or consortium amongst the SMEs. Appropriate members of the associate population would provide the 'glue' for the effective management of a virtual or extended enterprise (or possibly of a real company). The model is shown diagrammatically in Figure 1. It consists of a core with three rings or levels of activity: a commercial ring, a product ring and a support ring. Trading with OEMs would be performed at the level of the commercial ring, whilst the product ring provides manufacturing capability at the bill of materials level. The support ring provides expertise such as legal, contractual and financial. AATG acts as the core or integrating organisation for the three levels of activity.

Initially three communities with the potential to form trading groups were identified amongst the members: a 'systems' community, an 'electronics' community, and what is best described as an 'aerostructures' community. This last group is the subject of the present study.

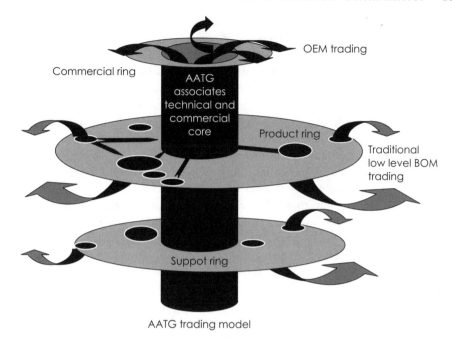

Figure 1   The AATG aerostructures trading model

Basis for Founding a Trading Group

The organisation itself has put forward the following arguments as the basis for its operation: an enhanced potential for technology transfer in the supply chain; the potential to reduce costs; and other perceived benefits to both SMEs and primes/OEMs.

The aerospace supply chain is characterised by poor information flow. A common complaint from SMEs is that the primes/OEMs do not share their strategic or technology plans with them. Order giving and visibility is short term, even on occasion postdated! One result of poor information flow is that there is very little transfer of design or manufacturing technology down the supply chain. What is not often appreciated is that there is very little transfer up the chain either.

SMEs are frequently the holders of leading edge process knowledge and understanding, which could lead to better product design and more efficient production. The best SMEs may have better expertise than companies higher up the chain, especially since many manufacturing skills are no longer retained in-house by the primes. Improved information flow by the closer working implied in the model could lead to more added value work for the SMEs, e.g. involvement in design. However it is the view of AATG that taking layers out of the supply chain is not sufficient to achieve the benefits. There is a need to change the mindsets, skills and knowledge of the various parties.

As mentioned before, pressure to reduce costs is a key driver in the industry. One prime is currently asking all suppliers for 5% year-on-year cost reduction on existing orders. Because of their intimate process knowledge, SMEs frequently know how to drive costs out of particular components. Faced with uncertainty over the level and timing of future orders, it is often not in their interest to do so and, with long chains of communication, they may not be given the opportunity to influence cost at the design stage. Other cost savings envisaged in the model come from reduced transaction costs through working together rather than in a chain. It is also expected that using flexible management resources will reduce overhead costs. It has been proposed that because of more direct and immediate information, the model will lead to a reduction in risk, especially regarding timescales.

Clearly the key benefit to the SMEs is that by presenting themselves to the primes/OEMs as an extended enterprise, they can bid collectively for work of a scope that individually they would not otherwise have been able to consider. The increased need for project management skills and resources can be met by using the management expertise released by the OEMs, i.e. the associates. The model will bring them closer to other SMEs and to the primes. It requires them to collaborate more closely with other SMEs who are not primarily competitors, rather partners. This has potential for cross-fertilisation of ideas and access to new markets via their partners. By being closer to the primes they improve access to knowledge of the drivers and strategy of the end market.

The benefits to OEMs of accepting this innovative approach are that, because they are using SME skills more directly, they will become more aware of the SME's capabilities, skills and knowledge and have the opportunity to adjust their designs accordingly. Yet they also achieve their objective of limiting the number of direct suppliers.

The Hurdles

Of the three identified communities, only the aerostructures one has formed a trading group. Both the 'systems' and 'electronics' communities present such a breadth of activities that they have so far proved difficult to structure. The aerostructures function has a simpler set of activities, enabling it to focus more easily. At present the trading group has 12 active companies and a number of related associates. Apart from a series of meetings to determine its function and strategy, it has undertaken considerable external networking activity. This includes numerous meetings and presentations of the community concept and trading model to government (DTI), regional development agencies and business support groups and sections of academia, as well as to primes, OEMs and individual SMEs.

Whilst the concept has been modified and developed over this period, the overall response has been one of approval and encouragement. In particular the view of senior managers in the primes is that they would like to see this kind of development in the supply chain. However, to date the group has not yet received a work order or been asked to bid for a work package.

Research among the members has produced little evidence of current technology transfer links between SMEs and primes. The general view is that this rarely happens. Evidence of changing mindsets is also disappointing. It is estimated by AATG that, of the approximately 600 SMEs in North West England who consider themselves to be part of the aerospace supply chain, only 20 or 30 show any interest in trying new ways of working, though many more see the need for some change in existing arrangements. Conversations with middle managers in the primes also indicate great pessimism. They report that in a highly dynamic and uncertain environment, attitudes to suppliers will not change at the operational level.

Positive Developments

Nonetheless there have been some positive outcomes. The first of AATG's activities, 'jobshopping', has demonstrated extra value. The placing of associates as temporary executives or consultants with a prime has helped to establish both AATG's credibility and the agency concept as an acceptable form of contracting for the prime. This is a step nearer the integrator concept.

Other significant learning has taken place which is best shown in an example. One of the member companies, dealing directly with a first tier company, arranged for AATG to make a presentation to its client. During the visit, a chance opportunity arose to show how the trading group could achieve both technology transfer and cost savings in one of the client's products. The client is now negotiating how these might be implemented. This incident taught AATG the value of a visible demonstration in obtaining commitment from an order giver. It also highlighted the need for detail and rigour in the contractual and confidentiality agreements between the members themselves. The involvement of a committed AATG member company who already has a relationship with a higher tier organisation, as in this instance, is being actively pursued as a way forward in winning work for the group.

Recognising its need for further rapid learning and the value of practical demonstrations, the group has embarked on a new initiative, the 'dummy bid'. In this project the co-operation of a prime contractor is being sought who will offer the group the opportunity to prepare a paper bid against a work package which has in fact already been allocated. The group will not have prior knowledge of the details of the successful bid. This project has two objectives. The first is to demonstrate whether or not the virtual organisation can produce an acceptable bid and whether reduced cost and risk can be shown. The second objective is to use it as an action learning exercise in which the organisational systems developed and the management processes used can be studied and assessed against the outcome. A careful watch will be kept for any instances of possible technology transfer. This initiative has been discussed with the members, and a group of companies and associates willing to take part has been identified. Support of business development agencies and research support from Lancaster University Management School has been secured. An approach to a selected prime contractor received a warm response and a formal proposal has recently been submitted. The initiative is ongoing.

Practical and Theoretical Issues Arising

As a private company, AATG has received small amounts of income from consultancy, research projects and from commission on placing associates. All other costs have been met from the resources of the individuals or companies. This raises a number of issues yet to be resolved. The various activities require funding now, and there is the possibility of future returns. To whom should these returns belong? Should the virtual trading group be formalised? If so, should it be a not-for-profit organisation, a non-distributing organisation or a standard business venture? Who should be its stakeholders/shareholders?

The role of public funds poses another issue. To date, AATG and the trading group activity have not received any funding from public sources, either government or development agencies. Yet the group is aware of several initiatives in the aerospace supply chain and in virtual enterprise, both in the UK and elsewhere in the EU, which do receive public funds, in some cases considerable amounts. For example, the Aerospace Innovation Centre previously mentioned will receive £20m from public sources. Is this lack of financial support to the trading group because there other more important priorities for public money, or is it part of the north/south divide in the UK? It has been observed that most associate members are in the north of the UK, and most companies in the south. This may possibly reflect the 'rationalisation' behaviour of the prime contractors. Further, would acceptance of public money restrict the planned activities of AATG?

Issues pertaining to virtual enterprises in general have arisen, such as appropriate governance mechanisms, their suitability and the management of the trading group. One area of keen concern to the SMEs is the sharing of information. As time goes on, the perceived benefits also need to become more tangible; after all, the objective of the group is to win more work collectively. Can the benefits be clearly demonstrated to other potential members?

A specific issues for this model is that of external project management by the associates. Is there any evidence that this mode of management works, or will work? The suitability of the associates for the core role is worth examining further. Can they carry out the task required of them? They are being asked to adopt, and even excel, at a new and innovative way of working. As semi-retired people, are their skills and expertise ageing or indeed as relevant as is believed, for the virtual environment and challenge? As former 'large company' people, can they relate effectively with their SME partners?

A key issue for all sides is that of credibility. The virtual trading group is a relatively new operating model, certainly in the eyes of the primes. It also has the liability of newness, i.e. a perception of increased risk. Its virtual nature has given rise to a key question raised by all levels within the primes, namely: 'Who are we contracting with?' Within the trading group this does not yet have an answer; indeed it is not yet determined how they will contract with each other. The first proposal was that the order placer would contract with whichever company was most appropriate, i.e. had responsibility for final delivery, or had the largest part of the order. The group would then contract with one another. However it was soon determined that the SME members were uneasy about contracting individually with the order giver; they saw the benefit of the trading group as it being led by a single entity all the time. They preferred AATG to provide this function and act as a figurehead.

Whilst the AATG management team were prepared to accept this position, they were then faced with the issue of how to share the risk throughout the group. To date this has been covered in a 'teaming agreement' which all the group have signed up to, but the general belief is that the practicalities will determine the solution to be adopted.

How the primes view contracting with a virtual integrator or agency organisation depends on who within the prime is asked. The primes themselves are in a state of flux and, while staff at the strategic purchasing level are very positive and encouraging, the practical procurement personnel are clearly very uncomfortable about this and there have even been signs of positive resistance. It has been suggested that it might be more acceptable with lower tier order givers.

The lack of perceptible technology transfer in the supply chain emphasises a commonly held view that it is a 'body contact sport'. Talking about technology at a distance is not effective. This encourages us to think that closer working between the group and the primes, and between the members themselves, will produce identifiable evidence of increased activity in this area.

A very practical issue arising was the very low percentage of SMEs showing interest in supply chain innovation, even though they acknowledge serious risk in the present situation.

Discussion

A key area for consideration is the current position of the AATG concept and trading group model in the wider environment relative to other initiatives. AATG is aware of several other supply chain and virtual enterprise projects at regional, national and EU level. The COBRAT initiative in Brindisi and the work of the VIVE project are two with particular relevance. At the international level, the Australian HunterNet project has close similarities. The AATG members are naturally cautious about 'reinventing the wheel' and are looking to these other projects for guidance and the opportunity to learn from their experiences. The assimilation and dissemination of such knowledge is a typical role for the second or 'thinking' activity of AATG. However, the resource of this group is quite limited and it may be that this function might be appropriate for an academic partner.

A number of models of the application of virtual organisations of SMEs in technical areas have been reported both in R&D and in product development. Weisenfield et al. (2000; 2001) identify a number of problem areas, namely commitment, interface management, marketing and information management. The extent of this last problem depends on the size of the network. Whilst each of these is an issue for AATG, there are also a number of contrasts with their biotechnology group,

BioRegioN. Whereas the group they studied had extensive regional support, AATG does not. In BioRegioN the core is based in an extensive physical headquarters from which the paid staff merely 'manage' the network. This contrasts markedly with AATG which, as previously mentioned, is constituted as a private company, has no assets, has no paid staff and actively participates in the network. However, one of the striking similarities is the low proportion of the sector companies which take an active part in the network.

A second area for consideration is the scope for academic inputs and outputs. Since AATG is primarily a bottom-up initiative of the SME members, it demonstrates the strengths of expert knowledge of the industry and the weaknesses of a lack of intellectual frameworks. It is believed that academic management theory may have some value to add to the exercise which, at the same, time offers a unique opportunity for action research.

Examination of theory may help in addressing some of the issues identified in earlier sections. There is a wide and growing literature on industrial networks, supply chain management and virtual enterprises. Classification of the network from the variety of network models available (Araujo and Easton, 1996) might be a first step. Lamming and colleagues (2000) identify fundamental differences in types of supply networks. They suggest that the appropriate form of a supply network can be determined by three aspects of the product or service offered: innovativeness, uniqueness and complexity. The issue of information sharing in the AATG trading group and the level of innovativeness of its 'product' may pose a problem for this model. Cravens et al. (1996) suggest that, by closer examination of the characteristics of the group, it would be possible to determine in which network form it should be built and developed: value-added, hollow, virtual or flexible. Guidance is also available into how it might best be turned into a value-creating network which enhances customer value (Campbell and Wilson, 1996).

A final feature worth commenting on at this stage is that as the group activity extends, sharing of knowledge with other members and external sources is taking place. There is evident action learning in the group. For many SMEs this is a preferred style of learning (Lordan et al., 2000a; 2000b). There is a belief that the project is at a stage where the demand from the participants for new, external knowledge is expanding rapidly. This need may even be restraining development. This will require the kind of mindset changes AATG have already identified and is seen as a challenge for the academic partners (Hensman et al., 1999). The learning and the ability to reapply it is important for the future of the group. The ability to share and learn the embedded, tacit knowledge of the partners is considered a key to sustaining the future competitive advantage of the network (Campbell and Wilson, 1996).

An issue on which it is not yet possible to comment is the extent to which the establishment of an integrator organisation and virtual supply chain has achieved its objectives: an increase in technology transfer; a reduction in the distance between the SMEs and the primes; and a reduction in the cost/risk of supply. It is hoped that, should the 'dummy bid' exercise be approved, then this may soon be possible.

REFERENCES

Araujo, L. and Easton, G. (1996), 'Networks in socio-economic systems', in Iacobucci, D. (Ed.), *Networks in Marketing*, Sage, London

Campbell, A.J. and Wilson, D. (1996), 'Managed networks: creating strategic advantage', in Iacobucci, D. (Ed.), *Networks in Marketing*, Sage, London

Cravens, D.W., Piercy, N.F. and Shipp, S.H. (1996), 'New organisational forms for competing in highly dynamic environments: the network paradigm', *British Journal of Management*, 7, 203–218

Hensman, N., Duckett, L., Cave, F., Lordan, M. and Ashcroft, G. (1999), 'Culture and process modification as the key to learning in innovation by SMEs', *Proceedings of 3rd Enterprise and Learning Conference, Paisley*, pp. 113–125

Lamming, R., Johnsen, T., Zheng, J. and Harland, C. (2000), 'An initial classification of supply networks', *International Journal of Operations and Production Management*, 20, 6, 675–691

Lordan, M., Hensman, N., Wright, M. and Cave, F. (2000a), 'The growth and development of small firms as a result of participation in knowledge networks', *Proceedings of 23rd ISBA National Small Firms Policy and Research Conference, Aberdeen*, pp. 681–697

Lordan, M., Hensman, N., Wright, M. and Cave, F. (2000b), 'Business network formation: the impact on knowledge transfer and economic development of SMEs', *Presented at the TII Annual Conference, Funchal, Madeira*

Weisenfield, U., Fisscher, O. and Pearson, A. (2000), 'The virtual organisation – a case study of benefits for small firms', *Proceedings of 23rd ISBA National Small Firms Policy and Research Conference, Aberdeen*, pp. 1305–1317

Weisenfield, U., Fisscher, O., Pearson, A. and Brockhoff, K. (2001), 'Managing technology as a virtual enterprise', *R&D Management*, 31, 3, 323–334

Issues on Partnering: Evidence from Subcontracting in Aeronautics

*Fernand Amesse, Liliana Dragoste,
Jean Nollet and Silvia Ponce*

Introduction

The transfer of technology has been studied and analysed extensively in terms of flows between the North and the South. More recently, an important concern has been the transfer of technology within the boundaries of the firm, that is, between the R&D function and production, between R&D and marketing, or among individuals (see, for example, Gupta et al., 1985; Souder and Padmanabhan, 1989; Leonard-Barton, 1995). However, in the most recent work, it is the inter-organizational transfer of technology that is capturing interest: alliances, joint ventures or buyer–seller relationships among highly sophisticated firms have become an important topic of study. With regard to aeronautics, the transfer of technology has been assessed mainly for related firms belonging to other industrial sectors (Lambert, 1993). We are interested, however, in the transfer of technology that takes place between closely related firms. Thus, our work focuses on the technology transfer among subcontracting firms within the aeronautical industry. In this setting, we expect a high potential for such transfers because of the high complexity of the technologies required for the products and processes. Lambert (1993, p. 56) points out that a homothetical link exists between the level of complexity of the technology and the potential for a transfer: a higher degree of complexity is associated with greater potential for transfer. However, we are also interested in exploring the interconnectedness of firms and the possible effects their relationships might have on the quality of the technology transfer.

The purpose of this article is to present the main findings of our exploratory research, which looks at the technology transfer that occurs in subcontracting relationships between six subcontractors and one main contractor in aeronautics. Quebec's aeronautical industry has been selected as the focus of our study. In this research, our objectives are:

1 to identify the types of subcontracting agreement in the aeronautical industry and to propose a theoretical typology of subcontracting for practical application to the aeronautical sector;
2 to explore the possible impact of each type of subcontracting agreement and the way the relationship is managed with respect to the quality of the transfer of technology;
3 to provide some empirical evidence to main contractors so that they can become aware of the potential of their subcontractors as a source of technical information and capitalize on the opportunities for developing knowledge and innovation through a combination of their know-how.

. . .

Quebec's Aeronautical Industry

Highly concentrated in Montreal and surroundings, Quebec's aeronautical industry represents 57% of the Canadian aerospace industry (see, for example, Les Affaires 500, 1997). It has a strong position in international markets (e.g. Bell Helicopter Textron has almost 60% of the world market for civilian helicopters; CAE Electronics has 70% of the world market for flight simulators; and Pratt and Whitney has 40% of the world market for turbo-propulsion engines). The industry is 'naturally' organized as a three-level pyramid in the same pattern as the international aeronautical industry (Lambert, 1989) (see Figure 1). In the first two tiers, there are 12 main contractors: the final aircraft assemblers (such as Canadair and Bell Helicopter Textron), and manufacturers of highly sophisticated equipment (such as simulators by CAE Electronics) and major subsystems (such as Pratt and Whitney and Rolls Royce). In the third tier, there are about 140 subcontracting firms (Lefebvre et al., 1993). This hierarchy results in highly interconnected firms because subcontracting takes place horizontally as well as vertically. For example, Pratt and Whitney deals with more than 70 of the 140 subcontractors in the sector and some of its subcontractors, medium firms, are subcontractors of other main contractors (for example, Canadair and Rolls Royce), but at the same time they can also be main contractors for many other small and medium businesses. Therefore, it is no surprise to see the development of networks, partnerships and manufacturing consortia within which streams of technical information flow following different patterns that are not strictly hierarchical.

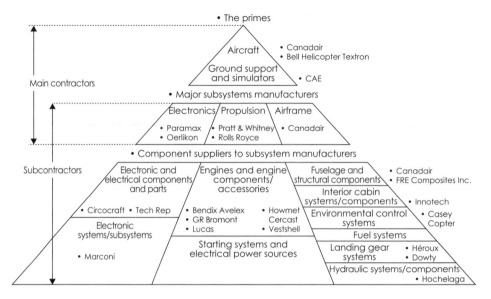

Figure 1   Structure of Quebec's aeronautical industry (adapted from Lambert, 1989 and Senik, 1992)

The main features of this industrial sector are the degree of precision required in the manufacture and assembly of products and the complexity and variety of technologies that demand an ever-increasing specialization and segmentation of the manufacturing processes. The primes, the first tier, work on final product design, assembly and marketing, while the second tier of subcontractors provides them with engines, propulsion systems, undercarriage systems, fuselages and main sub-assemblies. These major subsystems manufacturers, the second tier, hold the intellectual property of the goods they provide to the primes. These specialized suppliers own their know-how, holding patents and supplying brand-name products. Their products are customized or at least adapted to the specifications dictated by the primes in terms of quality, flexibility and delivery.

In the third tier of the pyramid are the more 'traditional' subcontractors and suppliers of special products. These subcontractors offer a large spectrum of services in the fields of mechanics, thermal and surface treatments, electronics, computers and transformation of composite materials. The specialized suppliers' fields are cutting tools, screwing, melting and other areas. The main contractors delegate this type of service and activity, but the subcontractors are subordinated to technical guidelines, blueprints and schedules.

Thus, Quebec's aeronautical industry carries on a highly heterogeneous and wide range of interrelated subcontracting activities, from the manufacture of simple and highly standardized parts to highly sophisticated, customized sub-assemblies. We find in this high-tech environment a rich context for the study of such issues as flows of technological information, technology transfer and innovation. It should be noted that some firms in this sector spend up to 16% of sales on R&D (Senik, 1992; Grammond, 1997).

The aeronautical sector faces most of the issues that characterize the business environment nowadays, that is, increasing competition, globalization, turbulent and changing markets, rapid technological change, and the growing need for a knowledgeable workforce (Lefebvre and Lefebvre, 1999). In short, it is an industrial sector highly committed to innovation strategies, emphasizing supply chain management and subcontracting partnering (Fitzgerald, 1997; Grammond, 1997).

Because the aim of our exploratory study is to contribute to determining and enhancing the potential for the transfer of technology embedded in subcontracting relationships in this high-tech environment, in the next section we review the conceptual grounds of subcontracting to establish its links with the technology transfer dimension, bearing in mind that the managerial components of subcontracting must also be integrated into the framework.

Revisiting Subcontracting

Subcontracting has been generally considered as a practice driven by cost reduction or as an option to cope with manufacturing capacity fluctuations. Nevertheless, it has been identified as a strategic component and as a factor of change since the 1970s (see, for example, Byle-Ottenheim et al., 1973). More recently, some changing trends have been observed, inspired by the Japanese business model of supplier relationships and driven mainly by the adoption of such management programs as total quality management and just-in-time, whether as a result of efforts to become a world-class organization or simply as a consequence of obtaining ISO 9000 certification, where the development of criteria for supplier selection is required. Still, the growing complexity of technologies makes it increasingly difficult for a single company to master all the knowledge and know-how required for the manufacture of its products, a situation that contributes to the ever-increasing number of subcontracting agreements, partnerships and strategic technological alliances. At the same time, a reduction in the number of subcontractors accompanied by the disappearance of small, non-innovative firms has taken place. Some have been replaced by subcontracting firms that no longer perform a passive role of simply producing what they are asked to do. Consequently, firms are becoming more involved at the early stages of product design, development and manufacturing. Firms largely recognize that supplier relationships are important technically, economically and managerially, as well as strategically, if they are to maintain and improve their competitiveness regardless of their size or the industry sector to which they belong. But apart from the reduction in the supplier base (Pratt and Whitney, for example, reduced its supplier base from 800 in 1986 to 330 in 1992), and a rethinking of the type of relationship (partnering, alliance or other form), the determinants of subcontracting relationship still need to be explored to provide an understanding of its full potential and to identify the role it could play in the current business environment.

By looking for the operationalization of this business concept called subcontracting in order to determine the types of subcontracting emerging in the aeronautical industry, we find in the literature that the term itself is multi-faceted and potentially heterogeneous. We observe that many efforts have been reported to define

Table 1 Approaches for defining subcontracting

Subcontracting is defined:	Author(s)
• in terms of technical, economic and legal characteristics	Valentin (1979)
• as a form of internationalization (a new form of foreign investment for developed countries, an industrialization driver for developing countries)	Zampetti (1973), Watanabe (1978) and Berthomieu and Hanaut (1980)
• as a subset of upstream inter-industrial relations of a firm	Manzagol and Saintonge (1990)
• as one category of outsourcing	Barreyre (1968), Chaillou (1977) and Patry (1994)
• as the simplest form of collaboration	Tidd et al. (1997)
• in terms of substitution and subordination	Martin (1992)
• as a work order for manufacturing (parts, components, sub-assemblies or assemblies) and/or execution of operations	UNIDO (1975)

subcontracting as a business concept. Because it involves neither buying nor outsourcing, but rather some combination of the two, this ambiguity has not helped disentangle its complexity. In Table 1, we present some definitions to illustrate the diversity of meanings and the plurality of perspectives. Some authors consider subcontracting in a very general way (Valentin, 1979), others as a form of internationalization (Zampetti, 1973), as a part of outsourcing (Barreyre, 1968; Chaillou, 1977; Patry, 1994) or as a simple form of collaboration (Tidd et al., 1997). Although the characteristics of the subcontracting relationship are studied by some authors, they generally do not circumscribe all its dimensions (see, for example, Martin, 1992; Manzagol and Saintonge, 1990; UNIDO, 1975).

By considering the commonalities, we can only state that subcontracting is a relationship whereby a firm, named the main contractor (or the prime contractor), places an order with another firm, named the subcontractor, for the manufacture, transformation, assembly and/or finishing of a component incorporated into a good to be sold by the main contractor. However, many questions remain unanswered. Does subcontracting have some specific properties that could be enhanced to get more than a cost reduction, a better quality of products and services or a good relationship? What is needed to manage a subcontracting relationship? How should the technological dimensions of subcontracting be approached? And, finally, how should a subcontracting agreement be characterized in a practical manner?

The literature review does make it possible to distinguish between two broader perceptions of subcontracting, just like two opposite streams: the one stemming mainly from the marketing and purchasing domains, emphasizing the potential of subcontracting partnering with dynamic actors involved in innovation and technology (see, for example, Axelsson, 1987); and the other arising mainly from the technology transfer literature, where subcontracting remains an asymmetric relationship

Table 2 Identified criteria for subcontracting characterization

Criteria	Proposed subcontracting classifications	Author(s)
Complexity of the industrial sector	Commercial subcontracting (e.g. textiles and clothing industry) and industrial subcontracting (e.g. automobile, aeronautic industries)	Berthomieu et al. (1983)
Duration	Permanent and occasional subcontracting	
Nature of the job to execute	Subcontracting of capacity, subcontracting of specialty and subcontracting of supply	Chaillou (1977)
Frequency and scope of the relation		
Autonomy of subcontractors	Subcontracting of specialty, subcontracting of economy and intermittent or complementary subcontracting	UNIDO (1975)
Manufacturing capabilities of main contractors		

under the guidance of sophisticated and established firms in developed countries teaching very small firms (usually in less developed countries) the basics of the industrial discipline, such as production efficiency or quality. These two streams suggest a fundamental question about subcontracting, that is, what are the conditions that lead to one perception – or reality of subcontracting – or the other?

The typologies developed do not provide an answer because they are inevitably determined by the nature and complexities of subcontracting definitions and perspectives. In fact, we find a wide range of criteria reported leading to different types of subcontracting agreements (see Table 2).

It should be noted that no classification takes into account the technological dimension. In fact, subcontracting as an environment for technology transfer and knowledge creation by the combination of know-how between a main contractor and its subcontractor has not been sufficiently analysed. It is surprising that the technical dimension has not been considered in the typologies because some previous works have revealed the important role of the technology contribution in subcontracting agreements. For instance, Amesse et al. (1989) found that in the performance of contracts, unexpected technological results such as the 'commercialization of new products and services' by the subcontractor, followed by improvements in 'organization and methods', are the most significant byproducts of the development of technologies in the subcontracted activities of the European Space Agency for the Canadian space industry. The same results have been reported early on for the

European aerospace industry (BETA 1980; 1988) and later for software development in the service industries (Garcia et al., 1996).

Therefore, to capture the technological elements contained in subcontracting, we adopt the general typology developed by Garcia et al. (1996), which takes into account suppliers' innovation and technology transfer capabilities. By combining this typology with the most relevant criteria identified in the typologies presented in Table 2, we propose three types of subcontracting likely to occur in the aeronautical industry. In ascending order of technological component, they are defined as:

- *Subcontracting of economy (small suppliers)*   Simple, customized work (finishing, assembly, drilling, etc.) not requiring product innovation; mainly cost-reduction-driven activities; highly limited autonomy even in the choices of production methods. The subcontractor is highly dependent on the main contractor, which is sometimes its sole customer.
- *Subcontracting of specialization (up-and-coming suppliers)*   Performance of work by a subcontractor that has better facilities – tools, equipment and personnel – than the main contractor; the subcontractor has developed special techniques with or without the assistance of the main firm; the subcontractor has the skills required to improve the technical drawings and quotations provided by the main contractor; and the subcontractor occasionally performs new product development and/or processes and improves them continuously. The main contractor and its subcontractor's technical structures (information and competencies) are complementary.
- *Subcontracting of supply (competitive technology suppliers)*   The subcontractor owns the rights or property of goods delivered to the main contractor; the subcontractor performs the design, chooses the means of production, constantly develops new products/processes; and the subcontractor carries out procurement and technology transfer at international levels. This relationship is characterized by a better equilibrium in the power of negotiation with the main contractor.

Because the purpose of our research is to explore the role of subcontracting, and more specifically the possible impact of the type of subcontracting agreement on the quality of the technology transfer that takes place between a main contractor and its subcontractors, we also take into account the managerial issues involved. We might expect that different types of subcontracting agreement should have a different impact on the quality of the technology transfer, depending on the way the relationship is managed. Thus a subcontracting agreement could lead to different forms of technology transfer depending, for example, on the strategic choices performed by the managers and/or the way they are implemented. However, technology transfer happens at different levels: product design and adaptation, manufacturing processes, organization and management. It can also take different forms: licensing on the basis of patents and know-how, equipment sales, technical assistance, quality control and conformity to the specifications and standards, training, access to technological information and so on. It follows that we need to integrate the many variables and characteristics involved. This is discussed in the following section.

An Integrated Framework for Assessing Technology Transfer in Subcontracting

To ensure integration of the managerial dimension into the technology transfer dimension of the typology derived, we propose four key criteria for assessing any type of subcontracting agreement:

1 the main contractor's strategic objectives (why the main contractor subcontracts, i.e. the main contractor's decision);
2 the subcontractor's capabilities and overall competencies (what the subcontractor can do, and the subcontractor's core capabilities as well as its limitations, as defined by Prahalad, 1993 and Javidan, 1998);
3 innovation and technological transfer capabilities (how the technology transfer takes place, i.e. the technological content of the subcontracting relationship);
4 the characteristics of the management style (how the subcontracting agreement is managed, i.e. the relationship and the interactions).

The proposed integrated framework is presented in detail in Table 3. It describes the elements of the four criteria, allowing for meaningful characterization of subcontracting while distinguishing among the three types of subcontracting proposed in the previous section. So we define:

*   *subcontracting of economy*, as the relationship that exhibits the lowest quality of technology transfer and the highest level of dependency responding to a cost-driven strategy on the part of the main contractor;
*   *subcontracting of specialization*, as the relationship that involves a more relevant quality of technology transfer and a medium level of dependency where labour division is the main contractor's goal;
*   *subcontracting of supply*, as the relationship involving the highest quality for the transfer of technology and a low level of dependency fulfilling the technological leadership strategy followed by the main contractor.

This framework constitutes the conceptual basis of our exploratory research, as well as a preliminary proposition for practical purposes to the aeronautical sector to be adapted or refined by individual firms.

Quality level of technology transfer

We have postulated that the quality of the technology transfer is implicit in the type of subcontracting. However, at the same time, we are looking for the impact the type of subcontracting agreement could have on the quality of the transfer. Thus, to approach the relationship between the type of subcontracting agreement and the technology transfer, we start by considering that the technology transfer, as well as

Table 3 Integrated framework for assessing technology transfer in subcontracting

Type of subcontracting	Capabilities and overall competencies[a]					Innovation and technology transfer capabilities		Management style characteristics		
	Strategic objectives: Main contractor's goal	Subcontracting object	Nature of work	Production capabilities	Organizational structure	Innovation capabilities	Type of possible technology transfer	Nature/scope of the relationship	Contract nature	Dependency level
Subcontracting of economy (small suppliers)	Cost advantage	Goods with a low technical component	Manufacturing, assembly, and finishing of components	Complementary/competitive	Deficiencies in organization, planning and marketing structures	None (products/processes) Work to order	One-way (source: the main contractor by contagion)	Intermittent to permanent/structural	Well defined; complex; explicit and limited duration	High (the main contractor is the only customer or almost the only one)
Subcontracting of specialization (up-and-coming technology suppliers)	Specialization (labour division)	Relatively complex goods; the main contractor knows the specifications in detail	Process design, manufacturing, assembly and finishing[b]	Complementary	Sufficiently developed	Occasional (processes)	One-way at the organization level; two-way in products/processes by contagion	Permanent/structural	Relatively defined; long duration	Medium (the main contractor is the most important customer)
Subcontracting of supply (competitive technology suppliers)	High level of specialization of the subcontractor and its technological leadership	Individualized and complex goods that satisfy a specific need of the main contractor; the industrial property belongs to the subcontractor[c]	Product and process design, manufacturing, assembly and finishing[d]	Complementary/collaborative	Well developed	Constant (products/processes)	Two-way, interactive (products and process design and development)	Permanent/structural	Broad terms; hard to negotiate; long-term duration	Low (the main contractor is only one of the firm's many customers)

Classification criteria

[a] According to the concepts defined by Prahalad (1993) and Javidan (1998).
[b] The subcontractor may suggest some improvements to the technical quotations; some possibilities of participation in product design.
[c] The subcontractor of supply owns the technical quotations and sometimes the licences; its manufactured products are brand-named.
[d] Commercialization is possible.

subcontracting, is both a process (link, connection, learning process, exchange) and a contract. Our hypothesis is that subcontracting could channel the transfer of technology. In addition, beyond the fact that it could facilitate the dissemination of knowledge or its adaptation to the specific conditions of a subcontractor, we also assume it as a contributing factor to technical and scientific knowledge and to the innovation process of the firms involved. Accordingly, the *quality level* of the techno-logy transfer should be determined by the following: the *content of the transfer*, that is, more or less basic know-how versus highly specific know-how transferred, or basic technologies versus key technologies transferred; the *dynamic extent of the transfer*, that is, unidirectional (one-way transfer only), bidirectional (a two-way transfer, an exchange), or multidirectional (a set of relationships involved in exchanges, a network formed at least by the main contractor and its subcontractors); and the *scope of the transfer*, that is, the implicit knowledge shared (innovation capabilities developed, strategic exchanges) accompanying the explicit knowledge specified by the terms of the contract. Consequently, our hypothesis is that the type of sub-contracting contract and the way it is managed should have a direct influence on the quality of the transfer.

When technology transfer is conceptualized as a process, the assessment of its quality should involve both the *type of subcontracting agreement* and the way the *relationship* is managed. So, we could assess the *quality level* through the absorptive capacity of the subcontractor, the content, the dynamic extent and the scope of flows of technological information, that is, through the *management style* character-izing each type of subcontracting agreement. Yet, a subcontracting agreement could lead to different forms of technology transfer, but it could also interfere with and inhibit this transfer depending on the way it is managed. It follows that a low quality of technology transfer will likely occur when technology is mastered only at con-trol levels characterized by unidirectional flows of information, occasional contact frequency, discrete contacts and exchanges limited to the contract. A higher quality of technology transfer should occur when technology is mastered at levels where innovation takes place partly because bidirectional and multidirectional flows of information are developed, systematic and continuous contacts among participants take place, and exchanges are a result of shared strategic orientations rather than dictated by contract clauses. Firms involved in this type of subcontracting agreement should be empowered to deploy their innovative capabilities, management skills, and communication and collaborative abilities so as to reach ever higher quality levels.

These are the main arguments supporting our goal to determine the extent to which a given type of subcontracting could induce technology transfer, the type of transfer possible and the conditions favouring or impeding the technology transfer. They are all essential elements for driving us to propose the framework.

Our Study and Findings

To meet the objectives of our exploratory research, we structured the study through the formulation of the following four propositions, subsequently confirmed by the results:

P1   In the aeronautical industry, subcontracting leads to different types of agreement and contracts.

P2   The quality of the technology transfer between a main contractor and its subcontractor is influenced by the type of subcontracting agreement.

P3   The quality of the technology transfer between a main contractor and its subcontractor depends on the way the relationship is perceived and managed.

P4   Subcontracting has the potential to contribute to the process of knowledge creation and dissemination through bidirectional and multidirectional interactions.

Methodology

Nine in-depth, structured interviews were performed, three of them with managers highly involved in the strategic decision-making process of awarding subcontracting agreements for a main contractor, a firm that has an excellent reputation in Quebec's aeronautical industry and is internationally recognized. These managers each identified two subcontracting agreements where, *according to their judgement, technology transfer took place* (the subcontracting agreements concern complex accessories, tooling parts, spare parts and raw materials, none considered critical). At the same time, they enabled us to interview the six subcontractors involved in the identified agreements. Although this is a 'convenience sample' and not a random one – since the agreements were selected by the respondents – the research is in fact a combination of two data-collection methods: the information, ideas and perceptions of those who have practical experience (nine people directly involved in the six subcontracting agreements) and case analysis. It should also be noted that we collect dyadic data from both the main contractor and the subcontractor for each subcontracting agreement, so as to assess their relationship.

As a support for the interviews we used a questionnaire that covered the aspects summarized in the integrated framework presented in the previous section and asked for general information, technology transfer and management of the relationship (see Dragoste, 1997).

It should be noted that this research is exploratory (Maxwell, 1996). It is our purpose not to test the framework proposed, but rather to use this framework to provide some evidence of the dynamics of the technology transfer processes occurring in subcontracting relations. So, the application of the proposed framework to the six subcontracting agreements allows us to explore some issues which are summarized in the next section.

Findings on the type of subcontracting

The data collected allowed us to classify the six subcontracting agreements. Effectively, we found different types of subcontracting agreement in our sample. By applying our framework, we identified three agreements as subcontracting of economy; one agreement as a hybrid of subcontracting of economy and subcontracting of specialization, indicating that a sharp classification is not always possible; one agreement as subcontracting of specialization; and one agreement as subcontracting of supply.

Surprisingly, we also observed in our sample that *economy* prevails in the subcontracting agreements and blurs all the other objectives. In fact, the group of respondents disagree with regard to the perceptions developed concerning their agreements. The respondents give different responses regarding the type of subcontracting agreement and the main contractor's strategic goal. Subcontractors systematically perceive their subcontracting agreements (all six agreements) as the result of the main contractor's cost-driven strategy, whereas the main contractor respondents recognize this strategy in only half of the agreements (the three agreements classified as subcontracting of economy). What we observed in our sample is that the main contractor looks after the technology transfer, but its actions do not support its objectives, particularly when assessed by the terms of the contracts and the management of the relationship. Thus, its subcontractors always perceive a cost-driven strategy, and this perception blurs any other objective. These facts suggest that subcontracting is always both a subcontracting of economy and a subcontracting of supply or specialization, thus joining the results observed by Dyer et al. (1998) for a larger sample in US automakers' partnering. These authors reported 'an intriguing finding' when they studied US automakers and suppliers, arguing that 'partnering does not differ significantly from the arm's-length relationships' because cost-driven behaviour prevails. Nevertheless, our observations further suggest that a subcontracting of economy also seems to foster subcontracting of specialization or of supply.

Findings on the nature of the technology transfer

We observed in our sample that technology transfer effectively takes place but is mainly unidirectional, going from the main contractor to the subcontractors. The exception is for subcontracting of supply, where a bidirectional transfer of technology is revealed, suggesting that the type of subcontracting could have a major impact on the dynamic extent of the transfer. Multidimensional transfer is not exhibited by any type of subcontracting in our sample.

We also observed that partnering is not the rule. Even when these subcontracting relationships take place in a very dynamic high-tech industrial sector, 'traditional' subcontracting practices still dominate (high dependency, one-way technology transfer, absence of innovative capabilities in the technology transferred). It suggests that cost reduction, increasing productivity, flexibility and competitiveness – all being essential elements required to succeed in a context of globalization and rapid technological change – constitute a complex environment that does not yet allow for sharing collaborative and interactive strategies, regardless of the type of subcontracting agreement involved and the long-term duration that characterizes all the agreements analysed.

Concerning the mode of the technology transfer, our sample shows that the most common mode is quality control and conformity to standards set by the main contractor. This mode of transfer is always present regardless of the type of subcontracting agreement, as should be expected because of the precision requirements for products in this industrial sector. More or less the same is observed for access to technological information, while training is limited only to subcontracting of specialization. Technical assistance indicated by the main contractor as a mode of technology transfer for the agreement, classified as subcontracting of supply, is not recognized by the subcontractor, highlighting once again the differences in their perceptions.

Concerning the content of the transfer, we observed that product design and development, manufacturing processes as well as organizational and managerial transfers are more frequent in subcontracting agreements of specialization and supply. Subcontracting of economy is strongly limited to organizational and managerial transfers and occasionally to transfer in manufacturing processes. No product design or product development transfers were reported.

In addition, the absorptive capacity of subcontractors is observed only in terms of control and maintenance of the technology transferred for most of the agreements. Capabilities for modifying the transferred technology are limited to subcontracting of supply and specialization, while capabilities for innovating on the basis of the transferred technology are completely absent in all the agreements.

Innovation capabilities as core competencies related to products are constantly deployed only in the context of subcontracting of supply. Process innovation was reported as occasional and in only one of the subcontracting agreements of economy.

Findings on management of the subcontracting relationship

In analysing the type of subcontracting agreement and management of the relationship, we observed in our sample that the frequency of communication between the main contractor and its subcontractor is systematic only for subcontracting of specialization and supply. For subcontracting of economy, it is individualized with formal and well-identified channels of communication. Moreover, formal and standardized documents exist for all types of agreement. Formal meetings and informal exchanges were also reported, and the scope of communication is said to be on contract and strategic matters. Paradoxically, all respondents agree on these two aspects though, at the same time, they reported a strong dependency or at least a medium dependency in all the agreements. It must be taken into account that under one of the agreements, subcontracting of specialization, 90% of the subcontractor's sales are to the main contractor.

While our sampling does not allow for generalization, we observed a higher quality level of technology transfer confirmed for subcontracting of supply (in the subcontractor's absorptive capacity as well as in content, dynamic extent and scope of the transfer, though with room for improvements). A lower quality level was observed for subcontracting of economy.

It should also be noted that, with regard to the main contractor's requirements concerning the transfer of management technologies for continuous improvement, a subcontractor expressed misgivings, saying that, in addition to the insecurity created by the clauses of their contract, they were now asked to disclose confidential information concerning costs and manufacturing processes. He also added that because of the nature of the knowledge transfer involved, they were forced to disclose their technical competencies. These observations illustrate the negative perceptions that a subcontractor develops and their impact on the technology transfer: instead of favouring the transfer, the subcontractor resists it because he feels deprived of its unique source of power, the minimum control over the uncertainty faced by its main contractor.

Apparently our observations are in opposition to the findings of Kamath and Liker (1990), particularly because their work reveals that dependence promotes supplier innovation and investment. Instead, we observe that dependence inhibits and limits the transfer of technology. In fact, we rather think that our observations stress the importance of the managerial dimension of the dyadic relationship, which is not considered by the contingency approach of Kamath and Liker. Indeed, our observations agree with the 'inconsistency' dimension identified by Ford et al. (1986). Inconsistency, that is 'ambiguity or lack of clarity in interactions', captures the dynamic nature of any relationship. This dimension makes it possible to align dependence behaviour with the two versions (or perceptions) developed in any type of subcontracting agreement, because it induces changes in intentions and interpretations, thus allowing for the opportunities that subcontracting offers and the corresponding managerial actions needed to improve the subcontracting relationships.

Implications for Managerial Actions

As a growing number of companies 'are emphasizing supply chain management' in aeronautics and seeking to form partnerships with their subcontractors (see, for example, Fitzgerald, 1997), this study suggests for them some practical as well as conceptual aspects, as follows.

Learning process   The learning process should become a key issue for taking advantage of the potential of subcontracting relationships. Our research suggests that there is room for change in terms of management practices regarding agreement and contract clauses and new product development capabilities. Managers are asked to create synergies between tangibles – material resources, equipment – and intangibles – knowledge, relationships, perceptions – to ensure the performance of their firms. The business conditions in the aeronautical industry demand from managers that they know how to collaborate with their suppliers and customers. The integrated framework for assessing subcontracting provides a practical guide for identifying improvement aspects. It also constitutes a preliminary structured tool to be tested, adapted and refined by individual firms. It could also be useful for aligning the type of agreement to be developed and the aspects that a firm – a main contractor or a subcontractor – should consider to trigger its action and make a match possible between its technological needs, managerial actions, relationships and objectives.

The logic underlying suppliers' management is that not all subcontractors need to develop the same type of subcontracting; some kind of segmentation is required. However, this does not imply that partnering is convenient exclusively in one type of subcontracting. In fact, different aspects of any subcontracting relationship could be enhanced by different types of partnering and emphasis on developing a 'dyadic relationship', rather than promotion of individual interests and interpretations. The more managers are involved in developing partnering, the easier it will be for them to identify the appropriate aspects and required actions to succeed in building subsequent subcontracting partnerships, thus elaborating further on the framework proposed.

Nature of subcontracting contracts   Trust is a critical component of the development and maintenance of a client–supplier relationship when a long-term partnership to the advantage of both is envisioned (see, for example, Smaltzer, 1997). We observed in our sample that subcontracting agreements and contracts are usually complex and, more often than not, take the form of an open contract rather than a long-term contract, leaving the subcontractor in a fragile situation involving constant insecurity. In the cases we studied, the subcontracting agreements have a contractual nature described by length and continuity. There is a formalized period associated with the contract but no end date. In practice, because of this kind of clause, the main contractor seems to exercise control over subcontractors (in terms of cost, quality and delivery). We argue that, in such cases, the main contractor misses an opportunity to build up a more profitable relationship. Under these conditions, it is no surprise that subcontractors resist sharing useful information and restrain their technological exchanges or any form of collaboration. The combination of know-how does not take place, technology transfer is inhibited and no knowledge creation or innovation really occurs. Development and implementation of coherent policies and practices stimulating and promoting an environment that facilitates and intensifies the exchanges, such as guarantees for the partnership and defined incoming business for a period of time, could significantly improve the working conditions and reinforce the relationships. These practices should, ultimately, result in the sharing of strategic orientations with carefully chosen subcontractors having common interests. When the relationship reaches that level, it becomes a powerful competitive advantage for main contractor and subcontractor alike. It then becomes possible to obtain much more than cost and quality-control benefits from a subcontracting agreement: innovative collaboration, knowledge creation and technological developments should also normally be fostered.

Autonomy and dependence   Our observations suggest that by regarding technology transfer and innovation opportunities not as byproducts but as strategic components, main contractors could develop a specific capacity for building up and
improving their subcontracting relationships. We observed that some subcontractors
attribute a negative value to the information provided because they interpret the
transfer as an interference by the main contractor in the management of their
business. Firms want to keep their autonomy and be independent. Therefore, an
adapted style of management that takes into account the subcontractors should
provide for autonomy as well as for a 'convenient dependability' established between
the parties allowing for space for individual and collaborative growth. Moreover,
it can be recognized that, because of strong dependencies, main contractors cut
themselves off from any benefit and learning experience stemming from subcontractor networks through other types of relationships. Establishing complementarity
between a main contractor and its subcontractor should then be essential for fruitful
collaboration.

Different perceptions   Our study suggests that if technology transfer is perceived
as a control instrument, it will not be favoured by a subcontractor. However, if the
main contractor does not facilitate exchanges by inhibiting the technology transfer,
the subcontractor will not share its technological resources. As long as a subcontractor
perceives technological transfer as a 'threat' that increases its dependence and improves
the main contractor's ability to control the relationship, the technological potential
of subcontracting relationships is misused and undermined. Consequently, a learning
process that transforms the capabilities of a main contractor and its subcontractors
should be supported by involvement, aligned perceptions and a shared vision for
building on a competitive advantage that will favour a continuous flow of innovation
and technology transfer, allowing for business consolidation of both the main contractor and its subcontractor.

Conclusions

Our study is exploratory and, as such, analyses a limited sample of subcontracting
agreements. Still, it allows us to observe a recurrent concern and an old question
that confronts management practitioners and academics alike: the gap between
formulated strategies and actions. Our observations suggest that *perceptions* play a
key role in the assessment of this gap in addition to being a strong indicator of the
inner contradictions in the actions performed:

1   We observed in our sample that perceptions of the subcontracting relationship
    limit the potential for high-quality technology transfer. Even when the main
    contractor is concerned with technology transfer, cost-driven actions blur the
    technological objectives of any type of subcontracting agreement.
2   Even though the six subcontractors were aware of a technology transfer, they
    were unwilling to accept it, suggesting that it is perceived as a threat that will

increase their dependency. A transfer does occur, but it remains unidirectional and limited.

3   It has also been observed that some managerial conditions of contracts are not conducive to a better quality of technology transfer: open contracts, formal communication and a limited amount of informal communication do not create opportunities for implicit knowledge exchanges.

4   The many contradictions arising from the analysis of subcontracting relationships should lead us to ask whether high-quality technology transfer is indeed possible under the conditions of the subcontracting agreements in question.

We have argued that the essence of high-quality technology transfer is partnership, sound collaboration, cooperation and sharing. A strategy that calls for 'learning to collaborate', knowing the partner, and discovering complementarities, as well as 'double loop learning' as defined by Argyris (1991), should be required for the two-way technology transfer that is the basis for multidimensional exchanges. The subcontracting relationship could become a 'quasi-firm' but our study suggests the necessity of additional efforts, and a commitment by management if the benefits of the investments in subcontracting are to be achieved. The framework proposed here could well constitute a basis to perform future research on a larger sample of main contractors and their subcontracting relationships.

REFERENCES

Amesse, F., Bach, L., Divry, C., Lambert, G., Prémont, B., Spiero, F., Tahmi, E., 1989. Les effets économiques indirects des contrats de l'ASE sur l'économie canadienne. BETA, CETAI, Université Louis Pasteur, Strasbourg, HEC, Montréal.

Argyris, C., 1991. Teaching smart people how to learn. Harvard Business Review May–June, 99–109.

Axelsson, B., 1987. Supplier management and technological development. In: Håkansson, H. (Ed.), Industrial Technological Development. A Network Approach. Croom Helm, New Hampshire, pp. 128–176.

Barreyre, P.Y., 1968. L'impartition, politique de la firme pour une entreprise compétitive. Hachette, Paris.

Berthomieu, C., Hanaut, A., 1980. La sous-traitance internationale peut-être un facteur d'industrialization? Revue Internationale du Travail 119 (3), 341–353.

Berthomieu, C., Chanel-Reynauld, G., Guichard, J.P., Hanaut, A., Longhi, A., 1983. Structure industrielle et sous-traitance. Presses Universitaires de France et CNRS–Université de Nice.

BETA, 1980. Les effets économiques indirects des contrats de l'ASE. Rapport pour l'Agence spatiale européenne, Strassbourg.

BETA, 1988. Étude sur les effets économiques des dépenses spatiales européennes. Rapports, vols 1 and 2, pour l'Agence spatiale européenne, Strasbourg.

Byle-Ottenheim, J., Le Thomas, A., Sallez, A., 1973. La Sous-traitance. Chotard et Associés, Paris (chs. 4 and 5).

Chaillou, B., 1977. Définition et typologie de la sous-traitance. Révue Économique XXVIII (2), 265–285.

Dragoste, L., 1997. Sous-traitance et transfert technologique dans l'industrie de l'aéronautique au Québec. Unpublished Master's Thesis, École des Hautes Études Commerciales, Montreal, March.

Dyer, J.H., Dong Sung Cho, Wujin Chu, 1998. Strategic supplier segmentation. The next 'best practice' in supply chain management California Management Review 40 (2), 57–77.

Fitzgerald, K.R., 1997. Aerospace purchasers take broad, long-term view. Purchasing, 9 October, 68–69.

Ford, D., Håkansson, H., Johanson, J., 1986. How do companies interact? Industrial Marketing and Purchasing 1 (1), 26–41.

Garcia, A., Amesse, F., Silva, M., 1996. The indirect economic effects of Ecopetrol's contracting strategy for informatics development. Technovation 10 (9), 469–485.

Grammond, S., 1997. La coopération internationale: le passeport vers l'avenir. In: Les Affaires 500, p. 15.

Gupta, A.K., Raj, S.P., Wilemon, D., 1985. The R&D-marketing interface in high-technology firms. Journal of Product Innovation Management 2, 12–24.

Javidan, M., 1998. Core competence: what does it mean in practice? Long Range Planning 31 (1), 60–71.

Kamath, R., Liker, J., 1990. Supplier dependence and innovation: a contingency model of suppliers' innovative activities. The Journal of Engineering and Technology Management 7, 111–127.

Lambert, D., 1989. Analyse de l'industrie aéronautique canadienne et québecoise: perspectives de développement. Working paper no. 89-07, CETAI, École des Hautes Études Commerciales, Montreal, May.

Lambert, G., 1993. Variables clés pour le transfert de technologie et le management de l'innovation. Revue Française de Gestion June–July–August, 49–72.

Lefebvre, E., Lefebvre, L.A., 1999. Global strategic benchmarking, critical capabilities and performance of aerospace subcontractors. Technovation 18 (4), 223–234.

Lefebvre, E., Lefebvre, L.A., Harvey, J., Le Luel, A., 1993. Sous-traitance et compétitivité: le secteur de l'aéronautique et de l'aérospatiale au Québec. Conseil de la Science et de la Technologie, August.

Leonard-Barton, D., 1995. Internal technology transfer in new product and process development: modes of interaction. In: Allouche, Pogorel (Eds.), Technology Management and Corporate Strategies: A Tricontinental Perspective. Elsevier Science BV, The Netherlands, pp. 239–270.

Les Affaires 500, 1997. Quatre fabricants québécois dominent les sommets mondiaux de l'industrie aérospatiale, p. 14.

Manzagol, C., Saintonge, J., 1990. La sous-traitance industrielle: nouveaux chantiers de développement régional. Office de planification et de développement du Québec, Ministère du Conseil Exécutif, Quebec.

Martin, Y., 1992. La sous-traitance au Québec. Working paper no. 92-04, CETAI, École des Hautes Études Commerciales, Montreal, November.

Maxwell, J.A., 1996. Qualitative Research Design. An Interactive Approach. Applied Social Research Method Series, vol. 41. Sage Publications, Thousand Oaks, CA.

Patry, M., 1994. Faire ou faire-faire: la perspective de l'économie des organisations. Cahier Cirano, École des Hautes Études Commerciales, Montreal, August.

Prahalad, C.K., 1993. The role of core competencies in the corporation. Research-Technology Management Nov–Dec, 40–47.

Senik, D.P., 1992. Aeronautics. Sectorial study prepared for Comité du bilan de l'activité scientifique et technologique de la région de Montréal, Conseil de la Science et de la Technologie, May, p. 75.

Smaltzer, L.R., 1997. The meaning and origin of trust in buyer–supplier relationships. International Journal of Purchasing and Material Management Winter, 40–47.

Souder, W.E., Padmanabhan, V., 1989. Transferring new technologies from R&D to manufacturing. Research Technology Management Sept–Oct, 38–43.

Tidd, J., Bessant, J., Pavitt, K., 1997. Managing Innovation. Integrating Technological, Market and Organizational Change. John Wiley & Sons, Chichester (p. 204).

UNIDO, 1975. La sous-traitance et la modernisation de l'économie. United Nations, New York.

Valentin, G., 1979. Les contrats de sous-traitance. Librairies Techniques, Paris (pp. 8–19).

Watanabe, S., 1978. International sub-contracting: a tool of technology transfer. Asian Productivity Organisation, Tokyo (cited in Watanabe, S., 1980. La sous-traitance internationale et l'intégration économique régionale des pays membres de l'ANSEA: le rôle des multinationales. In: La Sous-traitance Internationale. Une Nouvelle Forme D'investissement. Études du centre de développement, OECD, Paris, pp. 251–273).

Zampetti, S., 1973. La sous-traitance industrielle internationale et les pays en voie de développement. Reflets et perspectives de la vie économique. Problèmes Économiques, No. 1331, 18–26.

4.5

Implementation of Just-in-Time Methodology in a Small Company

Surendra M. Gupta and Louis Brennan

Introduction

For a company to compete successfully in today's environment, cost, quality and responsiveness play a vital role. Thus a company needs continuous progress in improving quality and decreasing manufacturing costs and lead times. Just-in-time (JIT) offers a means of continuous improvement.

The objective of JIT is the production or provision of defect-free goods in the required amount at the right time. The JIT philosophy evolved from a number of principles such as the elimination of waste, reduction of production cost, total quality control and recognition of employees' abilities.

Several elements have often been cited as necessary requirements for the successful implementation of JIT systems (Finch and Cox 1986), namely stable, uniform workload, focused factory, reduced setup times, group technology, total preventive maintenance, cross-trained employees, just-in-time delivery of purchased parts and *kanban*.

Mehra and Inman (1992), on the basis of a survey of JIT implementation, concluded that JIT production strategy and JIT vendor strategy were significant elements of JIT implementation. Success in JIT implementation was assessed based on downtime, inventory and workspace reductions, increased quality, labour and equipment utilization and inventory turnovers. The elements of JIT production strategy were: setup time reduction, in-house lot sizes, group technology, cross-training and preventive maintenance. The elements of JIT vendor strategy were: vendor lot sizes, sole sourcing, vendor lead times and quality certification of suppliers. Thus, it can be seen that there is substantial agreement on the elements that influence successful JIT implementation.

In the context of JIT implementation, there are a number of ways in which small manufacturing firms may differ from larger ones (Finch 1986), namely lack of clout with suppliers to effect changes in delivery schedules; limited resources to make the required operational changes; because of size, the entire operation may need to be phased into JIT without the benefit of using a particular area as a testing ground; and lack of exposure on the part of top management to JIT.

Consequently, the implementation related elements cited above have been divided into two groups (Finch and Cox 1986): (1) those that are independent of the firm size (focused factory, reduced setup times, group technology, total preventive maintenance, cross-trained employees and *kanban*); and (2) those that relate to the firm size and may be more difficult for the small manufacturing firm to satisfy (stable, uniform workload and just-in-time delivery of purchased parts). This means that small companies implementing JIT may have to concentrate on a smaller set of the elements, without a guarantee of eventual full-scale implementation. For example, in a survey of 32 small manufacturing firms, Golhar et al. (1990) have reported that the surveyed firms have focused on employee involvement to improve quality, inventory reduction and increasing employee participation.

This paper describes the experience of a small manufacturing company in implementing JIT. The motivation for the company's JIT initiative is presented, followed by a discussion and analysis of the actions undertaken and the associated accomplishments.

The Company

The company in question has been in operation since the 1940s and produces small durable articles for the catering industry. The company has a workforce of about 150 employees. Because of space constraints, space utilization became a major consideration within the company. This, in turn, highlighted the work in process (WIP) and inventory levels. Motivated by the desire to reduce its inventory, the company decided to implement JIT in its facility. Whereas the company produces a variety of products, the focus of the implementation revolved around three product lines (for reference purposes, these products will be referred to simply as products A, B and C).

The Flow Process

The overall flow process of the company is depicted in Figure 1. The raw material is delivered into the receiving area and is stored there. There are four main processes located on the production floor; shearing, press operations, fabrication and assembly. Each process function has a supervisor and the overall production flow is directed by a production manager. Based on job orders received, the production manager makes a weekly production schedule and gives it to the appropriate supervisor. The operations performed within the different process areas are described as follows:

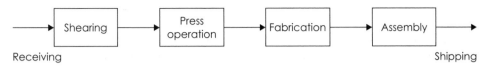

Figure 1 The flow process

1 *Shearing department* In this area the raw material is sheared according to the required dimensions. Depending on the product line, the number of shearing operations required varies from four to six. The sheared material is then transferred to the press room.
2 *Press room* Here, the sheared material is punched and notched in one step. The material from the press room is transferred to the fabrication department.
3 *Fabrication department* Here the material is moulded and bent to the required shape. This may require as many as seven steps. The material from the fabrication department is transferred to the assembly department.
4 *Assembly department* In this area all the fabricated material is assembled into a final product. An assembly can require up to 15 distinct steps. For example, to assemble an item from product line A, 13 steps are required. Among others, these steps include spot welding, drilling, riveting, cleaning and final assembly.

Deficiencies in the Old System

The following observations were made on the conditions that prevailed prior to the beginning of the implementation process:

1 The supervisor of the assembly department spent a lot of time in the other areas of manufacturing (shearing, press operations and fabrication) pursuing the material needed for assembly. Since there was no coordinated schedule followed, the parts were not delivered to the assembly department on time unless there was a constant push from the assembly department supervisor. Consequently, the supervisor concentrated on bringing the parts to his area. As a result, manufacturing problems in the assembly department often went unsolved for prolonged periods.
2 There were large accumulations of WIP at each process. Furthermore, no count was maintained on the number of parts. The supervisors always got more material fabricated than they needed. The accumulated WIP made the determination of cycle time difficult and made the processing areas appear untidy. During the assembly process, if an employee found a defective part or made a mistake in the process, he scrapped the part and started off with a new part instead of rectifying the problem. This led to waste and substandard work.
3 There was no systematic approach to assembling the products. Since each individual assembled the product in whatever way she herself decided, neither were

the most efficient methods followed nor was there any defined sequence of operations provided to the employees. As a result, the production capacities varied drastically when different employees assembled the same product.

4 Some employees used workbenches to assemble the product while others used the floor. Since there was no workbench concept among the employees, this led to a lack of uniformity in the assembly process. The area did not look very professional. As a result, customers visiting the plant left with a poor impression of the company.

5 There was no flexibility among employees, i.e. an employee was assigned to only one product type. The employees were not cross-trained to work on different products. When an employee was absent, the other employees did not know how to work on that product because of the absence of multi-functional training.

6 There were no standards on the throughput time of a product. Thus, the performance of the production area could not be evaluated. Due to limited information on production capacities, the marketing department could not make credible commitments to customers.

7 There was a lot of traversing between different activities associated with the assembly process because of poor layout and lack of coordination. It was estimated that traversing consumed up to 25% of the assembly time resulting in increased product cycle times.

8 The company manufactured to customer orders. However, due to the above mentioned problems, the manufacturing lead time in responding to customer orders tended to be highly erratic. Even though the typical quotation given to customers ranged from 4 to 6 weeks, the actual delivery times varied from 4 to 8 weeks.

The problems described in this section are indicative of a disorganized and inefficient manufacturing system which contributes to waste in many forms and to a loss of customer confidence. Thus, a programme based on continuous elimination of waste and consistent improvement in productivity was required. JIT is such an approach.

The Objective

Prompted by the preceding observations and analysis, the company committed itself to a programme of continuous improvement based on JIT. The company's choice was largely influenced by reported successes of JIT for other manufacturers. Thus, the main objective of the company became the implementation of a JIT system from receipt of raw material to product shipping and the establishment of a flexible manufacturing assembly line for the three products. This paper reports the progress and outcome of JIT implementation over a 6-month period.

Implementation Methodology

Work Design

To gauge the status of the then existing production process, a series of time studies were carried out. This resulted in estimates of the production capacities for each of the three product lines. The estimated capacities were 50 units/week, 73 units/week and 75 units/week for products A, B, and C respectively. Based on observations made during the time studies, the following steps were taken in order to improve the working environment:

1   An operation sequence was generated for each product, so that the same sequence could be followed by all employees. The sequence of operations, together with the details of the methods and tools to be used for every operation, was listed on a manufacturing process sheet and the employees were trained to follow these sequences.

2   In order to assemble a product, the fabricated material had to traverse between the spot welding booth, grinding machine, acid cleaning and assembly operator workstation. Because all the spot welding work was not done in a single pass, there was a lot of traversing between the spot welding machine and assembly operator workstations. To minimize the traversing time, the layout of the assembly area was altered to that the assembly operator workstations were adjacent to the spot welding booth. The flow sequence was also altered to obviate the need for traversing between the assembly area and the grinding machine. The traversing between the assembly operator workstation and the acid cleaning centre was eliminated by providing an acid cleaning machine on a table at the workstations.

3   Workbenches were set up for each assembly operator. These workbenches were furnished with plastic bins and tool boxes. A baseplate was set up on the workbench so that during the process of assembly, the assembler could use the baseplate to hammer parts. The employees were trained to use the workbenches for assembling the parts. The implementation of the workbench concept reduced space requirements and resulted in a clean working environment.

Inventory reduction

To begin the process of inventory reduction, an upper limit of one week's inventory, for each product line at the various processes, was established. A colour coded *kanban* was designed to indicate the material description, quantity, flow sequence, etc. The *kanban* was laminated and was attached to an appropriate trolley, as explained in the following.

A trolley was designed to hold enough material for 30 pieces of a product. A trolley was set up in each process area for each product type. In order to set up a trolley, the floor was laid out with yellow paint outlining the cart dimensions. The designation of the marked areas for the different departments is as follows:

1   In the shearing department, an area close to the shearing machine was laid out for three trolleys. Each trolley was designated for a specific product type. The three trolleys were placed in designated locations with a *kanban* on each trolley. These trolleys traverse between the shearing department and the press room. When any trolley is found to be empty at the designated location, the material is sheared according to the *kanban* specification and placed on the trolley.

2   There are two sets of three trolleys near the pressing operation. One set traverses between the shearing department and the pressing operation. The other set traverses between the pressing operation and the fabrication department. The *kanbans* are colour coded to give them unique identifications depending on the areas in which the trolleys traverse. When a trolley that traverses between the pressing operation and the shearing department is found to be empty, the supervisor of the pressing operation rolls an empty trolley to the allocated location in the shearing department. He exchanges the empty trolley for a loaded one and rolls it back to the designated location near the pressing operation. When a trolley that traverses between the pressing operation and the fabrication department is empty, the sheared material from the trolley that traverses between the shearing department and the pressing operation is worked on by punching and notching the material. The punched and notched material is placed on the empty trolley that traverses between the pressing operation and the fabrication department.

3   At the fabrication department, there are two sets of three trolleys. One set traverses between the pressing operation and the fabrication department, while the other set traverses between the fabrication and the assembly departments. When a trolley for punched and notched material is empty, the supervisor of the fabrication department takes the empty trolley to an assigned location in the pressing operation and exchanges it with a filled trolley which is rolled back to the allocated location at the fabrication department. When the trolley that traverses between the fabrication department and the assembly department is found to be empty, the material pulled from the pressing operation is worked on and placed on the empty trolley.

4   In the assembly department, there is one set of three trolleys representing a single trolley for each product type. When a trolley is empty, the assembly department supervisor brings the trolley to its assigned location at the fabrication process and exchanges it with a filled trolley. This filled trolley is then rolled back to the assembly department and placed at the assigned location. The parts are assembled according to the weekly schedule.

Employee training and involvement

The employees were cross-trained to work on any of the three products. This resulted in a consolidated flexible assembly line.

The employees and the supervisors had hour-long meetings every week. During that hour there was a lecture on some aspect of JIT and its advantages. Updated pictures of the areas prior to the changes and after the changes were shown to the employees as a means of illustrating the improvements and progress made up to that point in time. This process of continuous education and involvement made the employees aware of the importance of change and played a significant role in improving employees' morale and gaining their cooperation.

Achievements

Increase in production capacities

To evaluate the impact of the changes described above, a series of time studies were carried out on each of the three products and their production capacities were determined. There was a dramatic increase in the capacities for the three products. On the average the capacities increased by 44%. This constituted a major achievement. Specifically, the capacities for products A, B and C became 81 units/week, 93 units/week and 108 units/week, respectively (representing a 62%, 27% and 44% increase, respectively). Based on these capacities, the cost of each product diminished, thus making the products significantly more competitive in the market. As a result, it was possible for the company to capitalize on the already existing market.

Material handling reduction and space savings

Material handling was reduced by more than 50% in the assembly area, resulting in a 40% reduction in production cycle time. Reduction in WIP resulted in space savings. This provided ample space for accommodating the trolleys. Furthermore, the elimination of the clutter improved the appearance of the plant.

Stabilization and reduction of lead time

An important benefit of JIT implementation was the impact on the lead time in responding to customer orders. Not only did the changes allow the company to meet the delivery times quoted to customers, but it also enabled the company to quote shorter lead times (2–3 weeks). The stabilization in the lead time halted the erosion of confidence among the existing customer base while the reduction in lead time made the company more competitive.

Observations

1   The focus of this endeavour was on internal aspects of the company (JIT production strategy) such as the movement of parts from receiving to the manufacturing

area and then on to shipping. However, JIT vendor strategy remains undeveloped. In part, this stems from the management's desire to initially gain experience with JIT techniques and their workings within the company. In addition, they felt that because of their size, they lacked sufficient clout with their vendors.

2   The changes implemented so far constitute a starting point for the implementation of the JIT philosophy. The employees and the management are still adjusting to this new idea and the learning curve has still not reached a plateau.

3   Initially, the employees and the supervisors showed resistance to change and the idea of JIT. This lack of cooperation could be attributed to the natural reluctance on the part of employees, who had been involved in producing the products for up to 20 years, to embrace such a major change. They felt intimidated by JIT and felt that they might fail to meet the challenges of JIT. This obstacle to JIT implementation was overcome by educating the employees in the importance of JIT and the necessity for change given the company's role in the global market. Thus, in implementing JIT in a small company dominated by long-serving employees, one can expect a lot of resistance from them. Patience is required, since even the simplest of detail must be communicated to the employees, if the goal of the JIT implementation is to be achieved.

4   JIT is a holistic concept which requires the participation of everybody within the organization. Meeting this requirement demanded organizational commitment and company-wide effort. The employees were given roles sufficient to ensure their full participation and develop a sense of responsibility. This is consistent with the experience reported by Cheng and Musaphir (1993) for a medium manufacturing company.

5   Implementation of JIT reduced productivity in the short term since priority attention was given to the unearthing of the root causes of manufacturing problems. However, productivity increased rapidly once the problems were identified and corrected.

6   The operation of JIT required constant monitoring. Otherwise, JIT might have failed because of the tendency of employees to revert to old practices.

7   In order for the momentum of the implementation process to be maintained, a continuous effort is being made to sustain employee involvement and motivation. For example, quality circles involving people from different departments have been formed as a means of facilitating employees' input and participation in the process.

Conclusions

This paper has described an implementation of JIT in a small manufacturing company. A summary of the process-based problems and the JIT implementation steps and benefits is given in Table 1.

In implementing JIT, the company focused on internal elements. Even so, the results obtained were impressive. Basic work design changes were instrumental in enhancing the material flow and reducing the level of material handling. The introduction of a *kanban* system led to a substantial reduction in inventory levels.

Table 1 Process-based problems, JIT implementation steps and benefits

Process area	Function	Problems observed	Implementation	Benefits
Shearing department	Shearing	No proper schedule	Trolley setup Pull system	Easy flow of material Reduction of lead time from 1 week to 1 day
Press room	Punching and notching	No proper schedule No proper identification of incoming and outgoing material	Pull system Proper identification of goods with *kanban*	Easy flow of material
Fabrication department	Bending	No proper schedule No proper identification of incoming and outgoing material	Pull system Proper identification of goods with *kanban*	Easy flow of material
Assembly department	Assembling	Excess WIP Untidy work centre No proper process flow No cross-functional training No workbench concept	Pull system Move workcentre Set up a sequence of operations Training workers	Reduced lead time Reduced work area Reduced travel Tidy workcentre Higher capacity Higher productivity

Employee development played a major role in the success of the implementation process. Cross-training of the employees led to a flexible assembly line while various employee involvement exercises maintained their interest and motivation.

REFERENCES

Cheng, T. C. E., and Musaphir, H., 1993, Some implementation experiences with just-in-time manufacturing. *Production Planning and Control*, 4, 181–192.

Finch, B., 1986, Japanese management techniques in small manufacturing companies: a strategy for implementation. *Production and Inventory Management Journal*, 27, 30–38.

Finch, B. J., and Cox, J. F., 1986, An examination of just-in-time management for the small manufacturer: with an illustration. *International Journal of Production Research*, 24, 329–342.

Golhar, D. Y., Stamm, C. L., and Smith, W. P., 1990, JIT implementation in small manufacturing firms. *Production and Inventory Management Journal*, 31, 44–48.

Mehra, S., and Inman, R. A., 1992, Determining the critical elements of just-in-time implementation. *Decision Sciences*, 23, 160–174.

Learning from Others: Benchmarking in Diverse Tourism Enterprises

Michele Cano, Siobhan Drummond, Chris Miller and Steven Barclay

Introduction

Scotland has the vision to be a world-class tourist destination. It has many distinctive assets, including majestic scenery, natural environment, cultural and historical attractions, sporting events and vibrant cities. Although the country is already an important tourist destination, it has yet to realize this vision.

The provision of a quality of service to complement the features above is one way to ensure sustainable long-term growth. Learning from others can help to improve quality of service and develop a competitive advantage, benefiting individual organizations and the Scottish tourism industry as a whole.

The aims of the research were to formulate a method for facilitating benchmarking among diverse organizations and to determine the extent to which these diverse organizations could learn from each other.

Benchmarking is a quality tool that can help in this process and it can be used in a variety of industries, both services and manufacturing (Emulti and Kathawala, 1997). However, for small companies benchmarking may be too time-consuming or too expensive (Micklewright, 1993) and the tourism industry contains many small businesses that would not consider benchmarking for these reasons. The method presented here will show that small companies can partake in benchmarking without the fear of escalating costs or indeed the fear of sharing information with perceived competitors.

Benchmarking methods fall into four main categories: internal, competitive, functional and generic (Camp, 1989; Zairi and Leonard, 1994). These can be defined as follows:

- competitive benchmarking: a comparison with a direct competitor;
- internal benchmarking: the search for best practices internally;
- functional benchmarking, which looks at specific functions with similar functions that are 'best in class' (usually non-competitor);
- generic benchmarking, which considers processes that extend across functional barriers and organization sectors.

For the case studies in the research, generic benchmarking was considered to be the most appropriate. Existing methods considered were the Xerox model (Camp, 1989) and the Vaziri method (Zairi and Leonard, 1994). The method used in this research study is based on the six-step model for tourism businesses of Cano and Drummond (2000) which is as follows:

1 decide what to benchmark;
2 understand internal processes;
3 decide on best in class;
4 collect data;
5 analyse results;
6 implement actions.

Tourism in Scotland

Tourism in Scotland has grown substantially over the last 30 years, and currently accounts for over £2.5 billion expenditure each year (Scottish Executive, 2000). The industry mainly comprises small, independent businesses in the diverse sectors of accommodation, attractions and events, travel and transport.

The nature, size and location of these organizations often lead to poor communication among the sectors. The opportunity for developing the communication system and encouraging the process of 'learning from others' is further hampered by the structure of the public sector tourism organizations charged with strategic development and marketing of the tourism industry.

Tourism performance in Scotland has been poor over the last few years when compared with other European and competing destinations. This situation was exacerbated by the strength of the currency and the outbreak of foot and mouth disease.

The research in this study reflects the needs of the tourism sector at large. It was undertaken with the intention of providing a platform for learning from others and sharing best practices.

Profile of Participating Businesses and Their Core Competencies

Business A is an hotel which, like many rural businesses in the Scottish hospitality sector, is not sufficiently close to a large centre of population to attract great numbers of people. The business has adopted a strategy of developing a high product and service quality that people are prepared to travel for – not just on one occasion but repeatedly. In addition, attention to identifying customer needs through staff training and the high level of customer satisfaction has resulted in very high customer loyalty.

Business B is a Scottish-based tour operator selling package holidays direct to the public, rather than through the conventional route of the travel agent. It offers departures from 19 airports throughout the UK and Ireland and carries over half a million passengers to the most popular resorts. The business is one of Europe's fastest growing holiday companies and it leads the way in attracting new business.

Business C is a new visitor attraction. The visitor attraction design is very modern, and every detail is original with a view to entertain, to educate and to inspire. The 'hands-on', interactive nature of the organization makes it an excellent example of best practice in innovation, and the organization considers that the adoption of innovation as a core competency is essential given the nature of the attraction, and the need to ensure future growth.

The perceived core competencies of the three businesses are customer loyalty, attracting new customers and innovation, respectively. According to Watson (1993), a company should concentrate its resources on monitoring those benchmarks that indicate performance in core competencies.

Customer loyalty gives improved opportunities for identifying customers and provides a means of closing the service gap by improving communication between service provider and consumer.

It is important to distinguish between customer satisfaction and customer loyalty. Customer satisfaction is a prerequisite for loyalty. The customers' expectations must be met or exceeded in order to build loyalty. To develop loyal customers, managers must have *extremely* satisfied customers. Research by Reichheld and Aspinall (1993/94) found that 90% of customers who change suppliers were satisfied with their previous supplier. In addition, Heskitt et al. (1997) found that on a five-point scale, with 5 being very satisfied and 4 being satisfied, less than 40% of those rating the service a 4 intended to return while 90% who rated the service a 5 intended to return. This implies that managers should not be satisfied with a 4; if they want to get loyal customers they must get 5s. Furthermore, according to the research carried out by Reichheld and Sasser (1990), by reducing customer defections organizations can improve profits from 25% to 85%.

Attracting new business is crucial to remaining competitive in the tourism industry. The cost of attracting new business can be high, but if it is built into the business strategy then it can be offset by the success in retaining customers and innovation. Some businesses excel at this activity by removing barriers, improving access and using technology to shorten the distribution channel.

Innovation is critical in the tourism industry because all products eventually decline and consumers become increasingly sophisticated and seek new products. However, the risk of failure is high and a process to manage and develop innovation should be introduced. Innovation can be achieved in a number of ways but the process generally involves idea generation, screening, development and testing, test marketing and commercialization (Kotler and Armstrong, 1997). Innovation can come from internal sources, by building relationships and partnerships with customers and suppliers and by seeking inspiration from competitors.

Method

It is essential that a framework be devised for the benchmarking exercise to provide a focus for the benchmarking effort, to drive the process forward to the production of useful results and to provide a base from which future improvements to the method can be derived.

The diversity of tourist operations, both in size and in the nature of their operations, makes it difficult to apply the well-documented benchmarking approaches. In particular:

- It must be possible to derive worthwhile results with the modest resources available to the smallest organizations.
- It may not be possible to benchmark directly comparable operations. Hence quantitative performance measures and targets are unlikely to be appropriate.
- The availability of benchmarking partners may be limited. The key question is, 'What can we learn from this organization?', rather than, as in classic benchmarking studies, 'What are our key processes, who are the leading exponents, and what can we learn from them?'

The method adopted for the benchmarking study is illustrated in Figure 1.

The starting point was a SWOT analysis of the partner organizations. This confirmed that each organization possessed strengths which included retaining customer loyalty, attracting new customers and innovation.

A focus group was used to identify indicators of these broad competencies by asking the question, 'What would be the characteristics of organizations which had such a strength?' The indicators were derived from both individual practical experience and group discussion. For example, in the case of customer loyalty, the focus group findings echoed the findings of Heskitt et al. (1997) in that loyalty is determined by excellent customer service. The dimensions of service quality in the Servqual model (Parasuraman et al., 1991) of customer service, with which the focus group were familiar, informed much of the group's thinking. By contrast, the group identified an indicator for attracting new customers which related to the formation of business partnerships. This was derived from the practice, within business C, of attracting customers through sponsorship of exhibits.

The final sets of indicators were as follows:

Customer loyalty
- Tangible aspects of service delivery meet or exceed customer expectations.
- Services are delivered dependably and accurately.
- Staff are helpful and provide a prompt service.

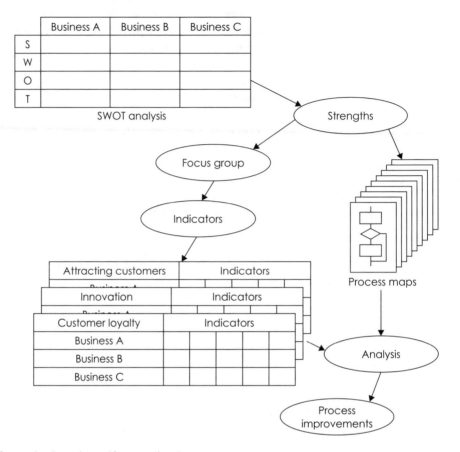

Figure 1   Benchmarking method

- Staff are knowledgeable and courteous, and convey trust and confidence.
- Customers are provided with caring, individualized attention.
- Links with the customer are maintained between acts of service delivery.

Attracting new custom:
- Business partnerships are formed.
- The organization knows its customers.
- Marketing media are appropriate to the customer.

Innovation
- Employees are from diverse backgrounds.
- Social relations are maintained with other organizations.
- Ideas from a member of staff are followed through.
- The organization is prepared to take a risk.

In parallel with the focus group, processes relating to each of the competencies were mapped for each of the organizations, giving a total of nine process maps. These were:

- *Customer loyalty*   Customer experience in a basic service operation.
- *Attracting new customers*   The process of advertising the product or service.
- *Innovation*   The process by which new ideas for promotion are derived.

Finally, matrices were drawn up which allow processes to be analysed by asking two questions of each process:

1   Can the process be strengthened by modifications related to the indicators identified by the focus group?
2   Can elements of the process used by the organization possessing particular strengths in this area be adapted for use by the other organizations?

Consider, for example, innovation. The first indicator suggested that, in an organization where innovation is a strength, employees are from diverse backgrounds. The process map for business B showed that innovation is driven primarily by customer complaints. The first question would therefore be, 'Is there any part of this process which could be strengthened by ensuring that those taking part in the process come from more diverse backgrounds?' This gave rise to the following possible questions:

- Is it possible to rotate staff in the customer service department to include customer service representatives?
- Are all staff given an opportunity to comment on the preventative measures adopted?
- Is it possible to diversify the staff involved in assessing the feasibility of the innovations suggested?
- Is it possible to include staff from support departments, or from outside the organization, in the continuous improvement and innovation process?

The fourth indicator of innovation was identified as: 'The organization is prepared to take a risk'. The leader in terms of innovation was business C. The second question to be asked is: 'Can elements of the process by which business C demonstrates its willingness to take risks in innovation be adopted by other organization?' The process map for business C shows that innovations are subject to a formal feasibility study. Possible improvements include the use of formal feasibility study techniques by the other businesses, which include formal assessment of risk.

Discussion

The method outlined above was carried out on research basis and constitutes a pilot study. The authors propose that, to realize the benefits of the method, the following five-stage procedure should be adopted:

1   A workshop to carry out SWOT analysis of the participants; to identify indicators for the strengths identified; and to identify business processes relating to these strengths.

2   Process mapping of the identified key processes (carried out at each individual site). The emphasis here is on the businesses taking ownership of this activity with facilitation by experts as required.

3   A workshop to analyse the maps in terms of transferable best practices using the matrices identified in the method.

4   Individual businesses will then implement the findings with the help of the other businesses as well as the external experts.

5   Evaluation and feedback. It was felt that a review meeting was useful not only in disseminating the results and evaluating the success criteria, but also in terms of starting new projects for the parties involved.

The research has sown the seeds for improvements in the areas of customer loyalty, innovation and attracting new customers, and the anticipated benefits are now being realized.

It was found that it was not just the formal approach outlined above which yielded results. The method used has much in common with the creativity techniques of brainstorming and morphology and this gave rise to ideas on best practices on businesses other than those of the participants. Furthermore, the synergistic approach has resulted in the development of informal partnerships, enabling the potential for future collaborative ventures. Currently, there is an initiative to develop further clusters in various sectors of the Scottish economy, one of these being the tourism industry. The approach described resulted in the potential for a cluster development.

Conclusions

The research presented has shown that it is possible for organizations to learn from each other using an effective but low-cost structured approach. The method adopted provides:

- A formal structured approach, which achieved useful results in the transfer of core competencies among the three organizations. The core competencies were associated with customer loyalty, attracting new customers and innovation.
- A successful combination of benchmarking and creativity techniques.
- A focus for cross-organizational team building which is closely aligned with the current policy of cluster development in the Scottish commercial environment. This has enabled the three businesses to develop a relationship facilitating future ventures.

REFERENCES

Camp, R.C. (1989) *Benchmarking: The Search for Industry Best Practices that Leads to Superior Performance* (Milwaukee, ASQC Quality Press).

Cano, M. & Drummond, S. (2000) Benchmarking in the Scottish tourism industry, *Proceedings of the 3rd International Conference on Building People and Organisational Excellence*, Aarhus, Denmark, 20–22 August.

Emulti, D. & Kathawala, Y. (1997) An overview of benchmarking process: a tool for continuous improvement and competitive advantage, *Benchmarking for Quality Management and Technology*, 4, pp. 229–244.

Heskitt, J.L., Sasser, E.W., Jr & Schlesinger, L.A. (1997) *The Service Profit Chain* (New York, Free Press).

Kotler, P. & Armstrong, G. (1997) *Marketing: An Introduction*, 4th Edn (Englewood Cliffs, NJ, Prentice Hall).

Micklewright, M.J. (1993) Competitive benchmarking: large gains for small companies, *Quality Progress*, June, pp. 67–68.

Parasuraman, A., Berry, L.L. & Zeithaml, V.A. (1991) Refinement and reassessment of the SERVQUAL scale, *Journal of Retailing*, 67, pp. 420–450.

Reichheld, F.F. & Aspinall, K. (1993/94) Building high-loyalty business systems, *Journal of Retail Banking*, Winter, pp. 21–29.

Reichheld, F.F. & Sasser, E. (1990) Zero defections: quality comes to services, *Harvard Business Review*, 68, Sept./Oct., pp. 105–111.

Scottish Executive (2000) http://www.scotland.gov.uk/library2/doc02/stbcd-00.htm.

Watson, G.H. (1993) How process benchmarking supports corporate strategy, *Planning Review*, 21, No. 1.

Zairi, M. & Leonard, P. (1994) *Practical Benchmarking: The Complete Guide* (Oxford, Chapman & Hall), pp. 12–15.

4.7

E-Business and E-Supply Strategy in Small and Medium Sized Businesses (SMEs)

B. A. Wagner, Ian Fillis and U. Johansson

Introduction

Electronic commerce is one of the most important forces shaping business today (Watson et al., 2000, p. 43). Although few would argue with the proposition that it presents a huge opportunity for creating economic value, nevertheless doing business digitally brings with it significant risks (Adshead, 2001). In circumstances where there are no tried and tested models, developing an e-business strategy involves forays into uncharted waters for most managers. Recent research has shown that, despite technology facilitating improved business practice in terms of developing electronic markets, electronic data interchange and Internet commerce (Whiteley, 2000), a number of SMEs have not taken advantage of this new mode of carrying out business (Smyth and Ibbotson, 2001; Cox et al., 2001; Quayle, 2002; Peer et al., 2002).

Given the foregoing, this paper offers some insights into the degree of e-business implementation and e-supply strategies in Scottish small and medium enterprises (SMEs). Throughout the paper, the term 'e-business' and other related phrases are used interchangeably to mean companies which utilise e-technology in their business operations. The following section will briefly review the concept and philosophy of supply chain management, and how information technologies are forcing managers to rethink and reshape their business strategies, their use of technologies and their relations with suppliers and customers.

Literature review

Supply chain management captures the notion of organisation and coordination of activities from procurement of raw materials to the final customer. That is, each individual activity services another by focusing on operations across firms' boundaries as opposed to seeking to only optimise internal firm efficiencies (McIvor and McHugh, 2000; Hickins, 2000). In so doing, economic benefits such as reduced time to market and lower costs may be achieved, as well as reduced operating expenses, increased revenue growth, and improved customer service levels (Graham and Hardaker, 2000). The crucial integrating mechanism is via dynamic information exchange which requires cooperation between firms. Analysts' studies have shown that large companies that have completed supply chain projects typically enjoy improvements in individual supply chain functions ranging from 10 to 80 per cent. Overall supply chain cost improvement is usually 10–50 per cent (Cross, 2000).

The Internet is being promoted as a means to facilitate collaboration between enterprises in the supply chain to bring about massive cost-saving efficiencies (Tucker and Jones, 2000; Adshead, 2001). It provides advantage through the power of information networks, while redefining, and at times eliminating, activities in the network (Cross, 2000). Although the supply chain accounts for about 60–70 per cent of the transactions in any company (with the remaining 30 per cent being with the end user), and a similar share of the company's ability to add value, the e-concept remains 'off the radar' for many senior managers and executives (Bovel and Martha, 2000).

The challenge of cooperation between firms has always been in achieving the necessary changes in business culture, that is behaviour change and the management of conflict arising from, but not limited to, diverse goals of the parties involved, and unequal risk and rewards (Boddy et al., 1998). Although the arguments appear compelling, the evidence is that industry is not rushing headlong into the arms of super-efficient e-business (Cox et al., 2001; Peet et al., 2002). Attitudes tend to be reactive (Adshead, 2001), with too many companies taking a non-strategic perspective, thereby limiting opportunities to reshape business (Bovel and Martha, 2000). As well as this, there is a misalignment between what the Internet delivers today and the traditional IT infrastructure that supports difficult to change in-house applications (Ricknell, 1998).

Ricknell (1998) notes that Internet users struggle to integrate their intranets with legacy systems, and so restrict their options in delivering appropriate solutions. Also SMEs do not have the skill or time to implement all the intranet applications being requested by the business (Bridge et al., 1998; Stokes, 2000; Smyth and Ibbotson, 2001).

The literature indicates that an important influencing factor in the adoption of e-business was concern with losing any competitive position, with either powerful customers spurring firms into action, or a fear of the consequences of being left behind (Cross, 2000; Adshead, 2001). At this early stage it is not clear if organisations slower to implement e-business are adversely affected or competitively disadvantaged.

. . .

Retailers can be viewed from a more advanced perspective and many retail businesses would now recognise and embrace the concept of supply chain management. Retailer activity has become more global in its extent and activities, and consequently they are better at managing and operating supply chains (Loughlin, 1999; Reynolds, 2000). Most supermarkets are aware that input from suppliers can be helpful to them (Doherty et al., 1999). Implementation of concepts such as quick response (QR) and efficient consumer response (ECR), involving years of investment in systems, have seen many of them achieve the near impossible – cutting costs to the bone, while introducing processes that ensure shelves are always full (Holmes and Srivastava, 1999; Field, 2000). The complexity involved in meeting this demand is bewildering, involving major organisational change (Kotzab, 1999; Fraser et al., 2000). It requires accurate sales forecasting, increased integration with shipping hubs, real-time integration with back-end systems and call centres, real-time tracking and scheduling, invoice reconciliation and performance management (Adshead, 2000). Retailers are pushing the boundaries of Internet technology and capability by developing retail exchanges. Proponents of exchanges see them as having considerable power to improve the supply chain and thus the end product for the consumer. Supporters of these exchanges emphasise their competitive and integrating value; however, this may not be the case in reality (Sparks and Wagner, 2003).

Larger companies with resources and technical budgets are in a stronger position to implement e-supply strategies, SMEs will continue to find this a challenge. Smyth and Ibbotson's (2001) survey found that the micro enterprise exhibited much lower rates of e-business activity than the larger firm, although greater adoption rates were, not unexpectedly, identified in the smaller, high-technology firm. They also identified a number of barriers, some being grounded in a competency/skills gap framework. Development of appropriate skills, investment in staff training and poor knowledge of the Internet start-up process were viewed as central barriers to e-business implementation and growth.

Similarly, the Internet in the UK is not being used to its maximum potential in managing supply and demand effectively. Indeed, claims made for the Internet to transform all aspects of supply chain management appear to be excessive, with only 23 per cent of the organisations surveyed currently using the Internet to improve aspects of their supply management activities (Cox er al., 2001, pp. 247–50). According to Cox et al. (2001), use of the Internet for procurement and logistics is still at an emergent stage, but larger organisations appear likely to be the first to demonstrate the costs and benefits from early adoption. For the most part, the majority of e-business strategies are only in the developmental stage and not sufficiently robust, which may mean that companies are developing and implementing inappropriate e-business solutions. These findings have also been supported by Quayle (2002), Daniel et al. (2002), Rowley (2002) and Peet et al. (2002).

Internet competencies have been examined by Durkin and McGowan (2001a; 2001b). They support the view that the Internet can facilitate relationships through its ability to transfer information between actors in a network. By gaining Internet-based competencies, a firm can bypass traditional business barriers such as physical distance between markets, allowing improved interaction between members of a network. A broad range of skills are central to enabling these procedures to occur, and include: knowledge of the medium; the vision to predict its usefulness in future business strategies; the ability to translate the vision into proactive business practice; having some technological awareness of how the Internet operates; and being able to control future business growth using existing technologies.

It seems clear that the first step in a successful e-business strategy is having the company's own systems in order (Feller, 2000). Companies may also need to help their business partners by defining their hardware, software and Internet service provider configuration, thus emphasising the importance of close relationships between supply chain partners as a prerequisite to adopting e-business (Brorson, 1998). As has been found in ECR implementation (Angeles, 2000), it is essential to build B2B relationships through communication first and transaction processing second, after both partners develop a real appreciation of the power of the Internet. Researchers and practitioners need to see the Internet for what it is: an enabling technology and a set of tools that can be used in almost any industry and as part of almost any strategy. Only by integrating the Internet into overall strategy will this powerful new technology become an equally powerful force for competitive advantage. The main problem to date is that this has not been done to any meaningful extent.

Development of the Conceptual Model

Globalisation, technology, e-business barriers and competency-based issues have been shown to interact in the development of e-business in the smaller firm. These have been assembled in a working conceptual framework (Figure 1) in order to understand the process of e-business development in the smaller firm, as well as endeavouring to explain why some firms lack the commitment to developing this orientation. (For a fuller explanation of the conceptual development, refer to Fillis et al., 2003.) Macro-level factors are the drivers behind technological change. Globalisation effects, and the subsequent removal of a range of geographical and physical barriers, offer new opportunities for the smaller firm in domestic and international markets. Instead of presenting an all-embracing framework, it is believed that specific industry and sectoral factors will influence the SME in its demand for e-business; for example, the needs of the hi-tech computer software company differ greatly from the craft micro-enterprise. However, both benefit in different ways from the adoption of new technology (Fillis, 2000). For example, the former can trade their products virtually while the latter can save time searching for export-related information, using the time freed up to develop new products. Attitudes will vary depending on a range of firm and managerial level factors. The micro-enterprise has different needs from the multinational corporation; business to business organisations will use the web to interface differently from business to consumer companies. It is expected that a range of positive and negative attitudes will be found among firms of all sizes, but particularly strong differences are expected within the smaller firm. On identifying these differences, it is also predicted that quite separate sets of business, marketing, entrepreneurial and Internet competencies will be identified. In addition, fostering

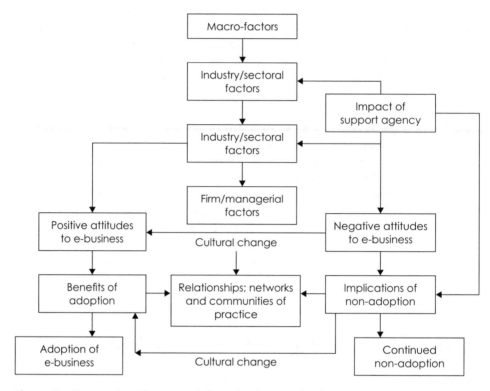

Figure 1   Conceptual framework for e-business adoption

cultural and philosophical change may be required to increase active participation in e-business usage among those firms which initially show low levels of interest. Targeting appropriate programmes of business support from government and other agencies can enable this cultural change. There will, of course, be other companies expressing no interest whatsoever in adopting an e-business orientation.

Research Context and Aims

The DTI, in association with Scottish Enterprise, has proactively encouraged company participation in e-business. In support of this development, local enterprise councils (LECs) have provided low-cost education and training workshops to raise awareness of the benefits of e-commerce to small businesses in the areas. Despite considerable publicity, the take-up for e-business introductory courses was disappointing. In addition, although some SMEs had constructed basic websites, many of these firms have yet to integrate the technology throughout the business. Many set up a website and wait for 'something to happen', instead of running the website alongside other marketing and supply activities.

The foregoing context is the background for this project. The aim was to investigate reasons why local companies appeared not to be interested in utilising e-commerce as a business and supply chain tool. This would involve ascertaining the current state of connectivity within local companies and investigating the socially complex behaviour associated with implementation and utilisation of e-commerce strategies. The literature pointed to the importance of nurturing supply chain partners in the successful implementation of e-supply strategies, and with such a behavioural emphasis the researchers felt it would be difficult to capture this using a quantitative survey technique. In order to yield deeper insight into the local and current situation, issues were explored by adopting a more exploratory and qualitative approach to data collection (Strauss and Corbin, 1998).

. . .

Research Findings

Macro-factors

Macro-factors were drawn from the literature and have been voiced by respondents as motivating e-business adoption. The main concern with the notion of rapid expansion was the speed at which small companies would be required to change, in terms of production, skills and logistical infrastructure. In addition, the tension experienced by some entrepreneurs and owner/managers was identified as another factor, in terms of the impact of growth on their chosen lifestyle and degree of control and influence over the product and company culture. The macro-factors influencing e-business adoption also included a recognition of technology as a driver for growth and removal of geographical barriers.

Industry and sector factors

According to the data, the propensity to develop e-business activities varies by sector. E-business adoption in a B2B environment has been found to be mainly customer driven. In the sample (distribution shown in Table 1), suppliers involved with powerful customers had little choice but to implement e-business strategies in order to maintain that business. In most cases the customer and supplier worked quite closely so that the customer's needs were accommodated. However, there was no evidence that the customer assisted the supplier company in the investment of equipment.

Traditional, longer-running businesses such as the foundry were found to be less likely to conduct business in a virtual environment. Although the foundry managers were proactive in developing internal e-mail links and also designing a website, there was little attempt to extend this into a wider business context. The foundry customers, mainly bulk raw material suppliers, were reluctant to conduct business over the Internet, such as order processing and payment. Reasons given were that the marketplace was quite small and all players had developed long-standing relationships, with systems and procedures perceived as efficient. This reluctance on the part of the

Table 1   Industry sector of participating firms

Industry sector	No. of companies
Engineering	5
Information technology	6
Manufacturing	4
Service	5
Total	20

main customers to see potential or recognise the need to change resulted in minimal, if any, investment in Internet technology.

As would be expected, SMEs in high-technology industries exhibited greater e-business participation rates than firms from a lower technology base. In some cases it was fundamental, and they had been conducting business in this manner from the outset. Industry specific technology drivers ensured that these companies were early adopters and e-business was now a way of life.

Firm/managerial factors

Managers were keen to exploit the potential of the Internet and those firms with high degrees of entrepreneurial orientation exhibited high e-business adoption rates. Some did voice concerns regarding the impact on their lifestyle if the company were to grow too large.

An important factor influencing degree of connectivity was the level of skills and competencies within the firm. Although most respondents stated that there was a range of technical competencies within the firms, there was a dearth of specifically related e-business competencies. It was in those firms where managers possessed superior e-business skills that we saw evidence of implementation beyond that of an inactive website. Paradoxically, these firms and managers were held back because they had to spend time training and educating staff in technology skills and behaviour change, and in some cases educating their customers as well. For the most part, managers recognised the potential growth benefits to the business, but factors such as time to train staff and lack of internal competencies resulted in sub-optimising the technology available.

Positive attitudes to e-business

Positive attitudes were demonstrated in small companies that were subsidiaries to substantial larger companies, driven by the parent organisation and also supported in terms of technology competencies and resource commitment.

E-mail and websites were standard with all participants, but implementation rarely went further than that, with the exception of high-technology SMEs. Business was still conducted using traditional communication media, although two companies did have EDI as a means of transferring real-time data from the customer to the supplier.

As has been stated already, e-business was driven by the customer, and only by a supplier in a niche market situation. For example, this applied to the gas generator company which, at the time of interviewing, was using the Internet to extend the company marketplace and had gained new business in Japan and other parts of the world as a result of the website. The company was currently making further technological investments to extend the scope of the website, including online procurement and logistical capabilities. However, the company had limited internal competencies and was dependent on external consultant support to provide ongoing training and maintenance. Although the manager recognised this, he had some misgivings as to the duration of assistance given by the LEC, as this would be a long-term project and of considerable economic importance to the area. This company had grown from start-up to in excess of £4 million profit in three years.

Negative attitudes to e-business

Customer influence over the direction and strategy of the supplier was considerable, and in some instances it was a one-way street, with the supplier gaining little from the supposed improved communication. Indeed, the customer expected more information from the supplier, but did not recognise that sharing real-time information, demand data, as well as forecasting and scheduling planning, would enhance both companies' business potential. As with all technology purported to improve supply chain relationships, the reality is often different from the rhetoric.

Some negative attitudes and cultures within firms towards e-business were also evident. Managerial time to be invested in change management is something that SMEs are not geared up to. Also, anxiety about the ability to handle increased business reinforced negative attitudes as well as skills issues. Funding was seen as a major problem for SMEs in general and not specifically related to technology. It was the experience of a number of the respondents that government and, in particular, lending institutions, had an adverse attitude to supporting SMEs. Other negative attitudes include a concern for security and fraud.

Benefits of adoption

Improved customer services was one of the most important benefits cited by most of the interviewees in terms of improved communication, increased speed and efficiency from supplier to customer. Overall, the reasons cited as benefits for adoption were fairly standard. However, most of the firms in the sample were in the early stages of adoption. Therefore, although they had certain expectations, the data indicate that few sustainable or real benefits were clear at this time.

Factors that influenced this finding included cost of implementation, behavioural change and training of internal staff, supplier or customer development, and a dearth of technological skills within the organisations. Managers who possessed such competencies tended to be further forward in the implementation of sophisticated supply strategies, such as order processing and payment online. But still the problem remained of educating customers or suppliers in their use.

Implications of non-adoption

The data suggest that few real performance benefits are evident in the early stages of adoption, and that the expectation of potential benefits motivates early adopters. It may be better to be prepared, for the danger of losing valued customers is also a powerful driver. Non-adoption may be a competitive disadvantage as the players in the network take up and implement e-supply strategies, but it is not clear whether adoption is a competitive advantage due to the inertia shown by many.

Relationship/network/communities of practice

The B2B business environment encourages closer customer and supplier relationships, and the study provides evidence of some long-standing, close business relations. As with other solutions such as ECR in retailing or JIT in manufacturing, success must be based on a strong and supportive working relationship between the customer and supplier. In other words, e-business is a means of improving business potential but is not an end in itself. The Internet was not seen as a substitute for improving working relations between customers. Network relationships remain very important to SMEs, and the smaller companies already operate within communities of practice which are more influenced by personal affiliations than e-business.

The nature of the business clearly drove the ability to work online with supply chain members. But even in those circumstances, companies were inhibited because of weak links in the supply chain, either downstream with customers, or upstream with suppliers. In order for the e-supply strategy to be effective, all members have to develop at the same time. As a consequence, companies whose corporate strategy involved e-business forced suppliers to adapt and change with them, creating a ripple effect throughout that particular supply chain: communication, information acquisition and aspects of relationship management improve. Early adopters can force the strategic direction of their supply chains; however, we do not have evidence that e-supply strategies have been fully implemented in any business in our sample. Above all, if the customer does not see the potential or recognise the need to change, very little will happen.

Local enterprise agencies

Although many firms in the sample took advantage of funding and assistance from the LEC, this was still seen as insufficient for the full integration into the business. Overall, the LEC was seen as appropriate for general support but lacked an understanding of the smaller firm's e-business needs. That is, they gave assistance to set up a website, but this did not go beyond an initial start-up phase. Thereafter, the SME was left on its own, with the choice of involving a consultant on a longer-term basis. In general the feeling was that the companies could not fault the LEC for the help they got up to a point, but that they were left to deal with the more complex implementation, both internally with employees and externally with customers and suppliers. The problem of limited e-business skills and competencies surfaced once more, both within the LEC and also within the firms.

Discussion of Findings

Some of the literature advocates that adoption of e-business and e-supply strategies will have a dramatic and positive effect on both the customer and supplier business in terms of transforming the business strategy, redefining business relationships and providing first-movers with competitive advantage (Keogh et al., 1998). The research does not support this, and is more in line with Whiteley (2000), Smyth and Ibbotson (2001) and Quayle (2002), who suggest that, despite the technology, many SMEs are not taking advantage of Internet commerce.

The hi-tech companies in our sample had used the Internet as an integral part of their business strategy before it became a popular buzzword. In other cases, first-mover advantage has been inhibited because it could not be translated widely in the supply chain. Traditional buying rather than progressive practices were emphasised. Little was to be gained from being more advanced than customers whose lack of strategic vision affected themselves and others in the supply chain (see also Bovel and Martha, 2000). Uncertainty regarding the impact of e-business on marketing and supply strategies was also inhibiting.

This, coupled with a dearth of e-business skills and competencies, may be a factor influencing the apparent reluctance to adopt e-business in a serious manner. Also, an SME has little time or resources to detract from daily business activities. Ricknell (1998) suggests that many SMEs do not have the time or skill to implement all applications necessary to conduct e-business. Employees, customers and suppliers all have to be educated and trained. This takes time and money, and many small businesses do not have either time or financial capabilities.

All companies in the sample possessed a high level of awareness of the reported potential of e-business. Although most were in the very early stages of implementation, for example developing a website profile, one small company had entered the global marketplace very quickly (Christopher, 1992; Cross, 2000).

Efficiency gains and cost savings seem to be very small in companies that deal with few large customers and handle very little information or invoices, but it is difficult to understand why the larger customers do not realise advantages and potential savings.

In some cases the promise of e-business to increase the market and give access to new customers was seen as a threat rather than an opportunity, with increased e-business increasing price pressure. SMEs might perceive their positions and margins being undermined, as buyers become more powerful and demanding. This is already happening in the retail industry: retailers have finely tuned the management and operation of their supply chains and have achieved reduced costs while improving processes (Doherty et al., 1999; Holmes and Srivastava, 1999).

A sudden increase in business may also be seen as a threat to the SME that cannot fulfil its commitment to new customer demand. The importance of the potential impact of e-business and its consequences for business structure and internal processes need to be fully understood. Field (2000) emphasises that implementation is complex and bewildering and involves major organisational change.

Internet adoption has so far not demonstrated benefits in terms of reduced transaction costs or improved supply chain efficiency. This corroborates other studies (Cox et al., 2001) that the Internet is mostly being used to gather information and communicate with suppliers.

Face-to-face contact between customers and suppliers is still seen as the most appropriate means to conduct supply strategy and is therefore a barrier to adoption. Considerable importance was attached to the quality of business relations, the amount of information sharing and openness, and the level of trust between trading partners.

The evidence suggests that early adopters are hi-tech companies and are more compelled to use Internet technologies, whereas there is a 'wait and see' mood in the older industries, especially if there is no pressure by customers. These findings are similar to those of Cross (2000), Adshead (2000) and Cox et al. (2001).

The literature emphasises the need for integrated supply chain management, but there is no evidence in our study that this is happening. Indeed there is virtually no internal integration of e-supply strategies, never mind extension into the wider supply chain.

Major barriers were funding and expertise beyond the initial website design. Even companies which claimed to be early adopters were only able to develop so far, and were then inhibited by constraints beyond their control. Government support in terms of grants and consultants were offered up to this point. Thereafter it was up to the SME to retain the consultant to further implement the internal strategy within the organisation and oversee supply chain integration. This would involve long-term change management within the business, requiring extensive funding and management time. There appears to be a short-term outlook on the part of the government agencies as well as a dearth of e-business competencies within the agencies themselves. SMEs can be supported up to a point, after which they are on their own. Fundamentally, if the government wishes to succeed in its targets for e-business implementation it may be advised to radically rethink its strategy to support these companies.

Figure 2 presents our revised conceptual framework from the findings of this exploratory study. It is important to bear in mind that the sample used was very small and that the research was conducted in a limited geographic area. Nevertheless,

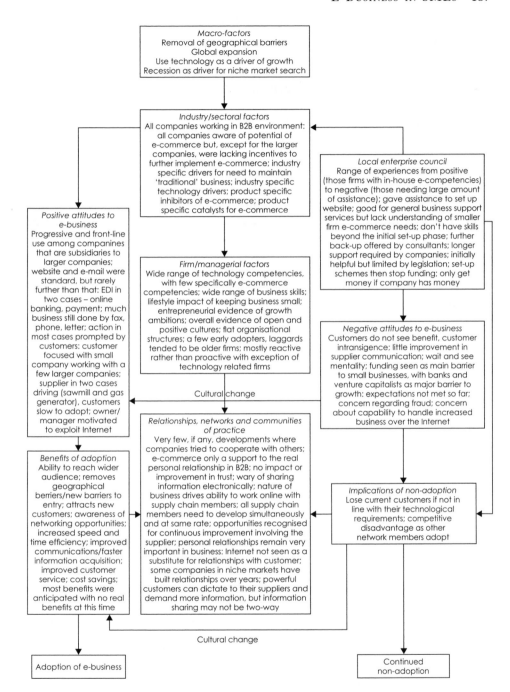

Figure 2   Revised conceptual framework for e-business adoption

this study does seem to follow patterns identified by much larger surveys (Cox et al., 2001; Quayle, 2002; Peet et al., 2002).

Conclusions

The study sought to explore the level of e-business and e-supply implementation in SME firms in the Scottish central belt. This was an exploratory study using a small sample with possible geographic biases. The creation of an e-business strategy is seen as prerequisite to implementation and integration. Firms in this study were at different stages of implementation, those with limited e-business experience being less advanced than small, high-technology firms. Those in the latter category had more in-house skills to support Internet adoption. Others relied heavily on assistance from outside agencies such as Scottish Enterprise and independent consultants. The role of government agencies and support services is clearly critical. SMEs do not have the means to conduct detailed analysis, nor do they have time or resources to divert from day-to-day business. It may be that some of the SMEs in our sample did not understand the full implications of e-business in terms of long-term growth and profit.

REFERENCES

Adshead, A. (2000), 'The e-supply chain is only as strong as its weakest link', *Computer Weekly*, 2 November, pp. 42–6.

Adshead, A. (2001), 'E-supply chain savings are more than just dotcom hype', *Computer Weekly*, 3 May, pp. 20–4.

Angeles, R. (2000), 'Revisiting the role of Internet – EDI in the current electronic scene', *Logistics Information Management*, Vol. 13 No. 1, pp. 45–57.

Boddy, D., Cahill, C., Charles, M., Fraser-Kraus, H. and Macbeth, D.K. (1998), 'Success and failure in implementing supply chain partnering: an empirical study', *European Journal of Purchasing and Supply Management*, Vol. 4, pp. 143–51.

Bovel, D. and Martha, J. (2000), 'From supply chain to value net', *Journal of Business Strategy*, Vol. 21 No. 3, July, pp. 25–36.

Bridge, S., O'Neill, K. and Cromie, S. (1998), *Understanding Enterprise, Entrepreneurship and Small Business*, Macmillan, London.

Brorson, B. (1998), 'From the trenches', *PC Week*, pp. 103–7.

Christopher, M. (1992), *Logistics and Supply Chain Management: Strategies for Reducing Costs and Improving Services*, Pitman Publishing, London.

Cox, A., Chicksand, L. and Ireland, P. (2001), *The E-business Report. CIPS, ILT, IOM*, Earlsgate Press, Boston, MA.

Cross, G.J. (2000), 'How e-business is transforming supply chain management', *Journal of Business Strategy*, Vol. 21 No. 2, March, pp. 36–43.

Daniel, E., Wilson, H. and Myers, A. (2002), 'Adoption of e-business by SMEs in the UK: towards a stage model', *International Journal of Small Business*, Vol. 20 No. 3, pp. 253–69.

Doherty, N.F., Ellis-Chadwick, F. and Hart, C.A. (1999), 'Cyber retailing in the UK: the potential of the Internet as a retail channel', *International Journal of Retailing & Distribution Management*, Vol. 27 No. 1, pp. 22–36.

Durkin, M. and McGowan, P. (2001a), '"Net effect" – views from the periphery: exploring the role and importance of the Internet on marketing activity in entrepreneurial firms', *Irish Marketing Review*, special issue, Spring.

Durkin, M. and McGowan, P. (2001b), 'Exploring a more complete competency spectrum in entrepreneurial small firm Internet marketing', paper presented at the Marketing and Entrepreneurial Track at the AMA Summer Educators Conference, Washington, DC.

Feller, A. (2000), 'E-business strategy and the integrated supply chain', *Transportation and Distribution*, Vol. 41 No. 5, May, pp. 127–30.

Field, C. (2000), 'Handing over the goods', *Computer Weekly*, 18 May, pp. 48–56.

Fillis, I. (2000), 'An examination of the internationalisation process of the smaller craft firm in the UK and the Republic of Ireland', unpublished doctoral thesis, University of Stirling, Stirling.

Fillis, I., Johansson, U. and Wagner, B. (2003), 'A conceptualization of the opportunities and barriers to e-business development in the smaller firm', *Journal of Small Business and Enterprise Development*, Vol. 10 No. 3.

Fraser, J., Fraser, N. and McDonald, F. (2000), 'Insight from industry: the strategic challenge of electronic commerce', *Supply Chain Management: An International Journal*, Vol. 5 No. 1, pp. 7–14.

Graham, G. and Hardaker, G. (2000), 'Supply-chain management across the Internet', *International Journal of Physical Distribution & Logistics Management*, Vol. 30 No. 34, pp. 286–96.

Hickins, M. (2000), 'Allies', *Marketing Review*, January. pp. 54–61.

Holmes, T.L. and Srivastava, R. (1999), 'Effects of relationalism and readiness on EDI collaboration and outcomes', *Journal of Business and Industrial Marketing*, Vol. 14 No. 5–6. pp. 390–402.

Keogh, W., Jack, S.L., Bower, J. and Crabtree, E. (1998), 'Small, technology-based firms in the UK oil and gas industry: innovation and internationalisation strategies', *International Small Business Journal*, Vol. 17 No. 1, October, pp. 57–68.

Kotzab, H. (1999), 'Improving supply chain performance by efficient consumer response: a critical comparison of existing ECR approaches', *Journal of Business and Industrial Marketing*, Vol. 14 No. 5–6, pp. 364–77.

Loughlin, P. (1999), 'Viewpoint e-business strengthens supplier's position', *International Journal of Retail & Distribution Management*, Vol. 27 No. 2, pp. 69–71.

McIvor, R. and McHugh, M. (2000), 'Partnership sourcing: an organisational change management perspective', *Journal of Supply Chain Management*, Vol. 36 No. 3, Summer, pp. 12–31.

Peet, S., Brindley, C. and Ritchie, B. (2002), 'The European Commission and SME support mechanisms for e-business', *European Business Review*, Vol. 14 No. 5, pp. 335–41.

Quayle, M. (2002), 'E-business: the challenge for UK SMEs in the twenty-first century', *International Journal of Operations & Production Management*, Vol. 22 No. 10, pp. 1148–61.

Reynolds, J. (2000), 'E-business: a critical review', *International Journal of Retail Distribution Management*, Vol. 28 No. 10, pp. 417–44.

Ricknell, D. (1998), 'Strengthening links in the supply chain', *Computer Weekly*, June 18, pp. 10–34.

Rowley, J. (2002), 'Strategy and synergy in e-business', *Marketing Intelligence & Planning*, Vol. 20 No. 4, pp. 215–22.

Smyth, M. and Ibbotson, P. (2001), 'Internet connectivity in Ireland, a joint report by the Bank of Ireland and the University of Ulster', available at: www.bbankofireland/whats_new/item.php?whatsnew_id=8.

Sparks, L. and Wagner, B.A. (2003), 'Retail exchanges: a research agenda', *Journal of Supply Chain Management: An International Journal*, Vol. 8.

Stokes, D. (2000), 'Marketing and the small firm', in Carter, S. and Jones Eves, D. (Eds), *Enterprise and Small Business: Principles, Practice and Policy*, Pearson Education Ltd, London.

Strauss, A. and Corbin, J. (1998), *Basics of Qualitative Research: Techniques and Procedures for Developing Grounded Theory*, 2nd ed., Sage, Thousand Oaks, CA.

Tucker, D. and Jones, L. (2000), 'Leveraging the power of the Internet for optimal supplier sourcing', *International Journal of Physical Distribution Management*, Vol. 30 No. 3–4, pp. 255–67.

Watson, R.T., Berthon, P., Pitt, L.F. and Zinnkhan, G.M. (2000), *Electronic Commerce: The Strategic Perspective*, The Dryden Press, Orlando, FL.

Whiteley, D. (2000), *E-business: Strategy, Technologies and Applications*, McGraw-Hill, London.

Index